P.L. Patrick Rau (Ed.)

T0216674

# Cross-Cultural Design

## Methods, Practice, and Case Studies

5th International Conference, CCD 2013
Held as Part of HCI International 2013
Las Vegas, NV, USA, July 21-26, 2013
Proceedings, Part I

Springer

Volume Editor

P.L. Patrick Rau
Tsinghua University
Institute of Human Factors and Ergonomics
Department of Industrial Engineering
Beijing, China
E-mail: rpl@mail.tsinghua.edu.cn

ISSN 0302-9743      e-ISSN 1611-3349
ISBN 978-3-642-39142-2      e-ISBN 978-3-642-39143-9
DOI 10.1007/978-3-642-39143-9
Springer Heidelberg Dordrecht London New York

Library of Congress Control Number: 2013941216

CR Subject Classification (1998): H.5, K.3, H.3, H.4

LNCS Sublibrary: SL 3 – Information Systems and Application, incl. Internet/Web and HCI

© Springer-Verlag Berlin Heidelberg 2013

This work is subject to copyright. All rights are reserved by the Publisher, whether the whole or part of the material is concerned, specifically the rights of translation, reprinting, reuse of illustrations, recitation, broadcasting, reproduction on microfilms or in any other physical way, and transmission or information storage and retrieval, electronic adaptation, computer software, or by similar or dissimilar methodology now known or hereafter developed. Exempted from this legal reservation are brief excerpts in connection with reviews or scholarly analysis or material supplied specifically for the purpose of being entered and executed on a computer system, for exclusive use by the purchaser of the work. Duplication of this publication or parts thereof is permitted only under the provisions of the Copyright Law of the Publisher's location, in its current version, and permission for use must always be obtained from Springer. Permissions for use may be obtained through RightsLink at the Copyright Clearance Center. Violations are liable to prosecution under the respective Copyright Law.
The use of general descriptive names, registered names, trademarks, service marks, etc. in this publication does not imply, even in the absence of a specific statement, that such names are exempt from the relevant protective laws and regulations and therefore free for general use.
While the advice and information in this book are believed to be true and accurate at the date of publication, neither the authors nor the editors nor the publisher can accept any legal responsibility for any errors or omissions that may be made. The publisher makes no warranty, express or implied, with respect to the material contained herein.

*Typesetting:* Camera-ready by author, data conversion by Scientific Publishing Services, Chennai, India

Printed on acid-free paper

Springer is part of Springer Science+Business Media (www.springer.com)

# Foreword

The 15th International Conference on Human–Computer Interaction, HCI International 2013, was held in Las Vegas, Nevada, USA, 21–26 July 2013, incorporating 12 conferences / thematic areas:

Thematic areas:

- Human–Computer Interaction
- Human Interface and the Management of Information

Affiliated conferences:

- 10th International Conference on Engineering Psychology and Cognitive Ergonomics
- 7th International Conference on Universal Access in Human–Computer Interaction
- 5th International Conference on Virtual, Augmented and Mixed Reality
- 5th International Conference on Cross-Cultural Design
- 5th International Conference on Online Communities and Social Computing
- 7th International Conference on Augmented Cognition
- 4th International Conference on Digital Human Modeling and Applications in Health, Safety, Ergonomics and Risk Management
- 2nd International Conference on Design, User Experience and Usability
- 1st International Conference on Distributed, Ambient and Pervasive Interactions
- 1st International Conference on Human Aspects of Information Security, Privacy and Trust

A total of 5210 individuals from academia, research institutes, industry and governmental agencies from 70 countries submitted contributions, and 1666 papers and 303 posters were included in the program. These papers address the latest research and development efforts and highlight the human aspects of design and use of computing systems. The papers accepted for presentation thoroughly cover the entire field of Human–Computer Interaction, addressing major advances in knowledge and effective use of computers in a variety of application areas.

This volume, edited by P.L. Patrick Rau, contains papers focusing on the thematic area of Cross-Cultural Design, and addressing the following major topics:

- Cross-Cultural Product Design
- Cross-Cultural Design Methods and Techniques
- International Usability Evaluation
- Case Studies in Cross-Cultural Design

The remaining volumes of the HCI International 2013 proceedings are:

- Volume 1, LNCS 8004, Human–Computer Interaction: Human-Centred Design Approaches, Methods, Tools and Environments (Part I), edited by Masaaki Kurosu
- Volume 2, LNCS 8005, Human–Computer Interaction: Applications and Services (Part II), edited by Masaaki Kurosu
- Volume 3, LNCS 8006, Human–Computer Interaction: Users and Contexts of Use (Part III), edited by Masaaki Kurosu
- Volume 4, LNCS 8007, Human–Computer Interaction: Interaction Modalities and Techniques (Part IV), edited by Masaaki Kurosu
- Volume 5, LNCS 8008, Human–Computer Interaction: Towards Intelligent and Implicit Interaction (Part V), edited by Masaaki Kurosu
- Volume 6, LNCS 8009, Universal Access in Human–Computer Interaction: Design Methods, Tools and Interaction Techniques for eInclusion (Part I), edited by Constantine Stephanidis and Margherita Antona
- Volume 7, LNCS 8010, Universal Access in Human–Computer Interaction: User and Context Diversity (Part II), edited by Constantine Stephanidis and Margherita Antona
- Volume 8, LNCS 8011, Universal Access in Human–Computer Interaction: Applications and Services for Quality of Life (Part III), edited by Constantine Stephanidis and Margherita Antona
- Volume 9, LNCS 8012, Design, User Experience, and Usability: Design Philosophy, Methods and Tools (Part I), edited by Aaron Marcus
- Volume 10, LNCS 8013, Design, User Experience, and Usability: Health, Learning, Playing, Cultural, and Cross-Cultural User Experience (Part II), edited by Aaron Marcus
- Volume 11, LNCS 8014, Design, User Experience, and Usability: User Experience in Novel Technological Environments (Part III), edited by Aaron Marcus
- Volume 12, LNCS 8015, Design, User Experience, and Usability: Web, Mobile and Product Design (Part IV), edited by Aaron Marcus
- Volume 13, LNCS 8016, Human Interface and the Management of Information: Information and Interaction Design (Part I), edited by Sakae Yamamoto
- Volume 14, LNCS 8017, Human Interface and the Management of Information: Information and Interaction for Health, Safety, Mobility and Complex Environments (Part II), edited by Sakae Yamamoto
- Volume 15, LNCS 8018, Human Interface and the Management of Information: Information and Interaction for Learning, Culture, Collaboration and Business (Part III), edited by Sakae Yamamoto
- Volume 16, LNAI 8019, Engineering Psychology and Cognitive Ergonomics: Understanding Human Cognition (Part I), edited by Don Harris
- Volume 17, LNAI 8020, Engineering Psychology and Cognitive Ergonomics: Applications and Services (Part II), edited by Don Harris
- Volume 18, LNCS 8021, Virtual, Augmented and Mixed Reality: Designing and Developing Augmented and Virtual Environments (Part I), edited by Randall Shumaker

- Volume 19, LNCS 8022, Virtual, Augmented and Mixed Reality: Systems and Applications (Part II), edited by Randall Shumaker
- Volume 21, LNCS 8024, Cross-Cultural Design: Cultural Differences in Everyday Life (Part II), edited by P.L. Patrick Rau
- Volume 22, LNCS 8025, Digital Human Modeling and Applications in Health, Safety, Ergonomics and Risk Management: Healthcare and Safety of the Environment and Transport (Part I), edited by Vincent G. Duffy
- Volume 23, LNCS 8026, Digital Human Modeling and Applications in Health, Safety, Ergonomics and Risk Management: Human Body Modeling and Ergonomics (Part II), edited by Vincent G. Duffy
- Volume 24, LNAI 8027, Foundations of Augmented Cognition, edited by Dylan D. Schmorrow and Cali M. Fidopiastis
- Volume 25, LNCS 8028, Distributed, Ambient and Pervasive Interactions, edited by Norbert Streitz and Constantine Stephanidis
- Volume 26, LNCS 8029, Online Communities and Social Computing, edited by A. Ant Ozok and Panayiotis Zaphiris
- Volume 27, LNCS 8030, Human Aspects of Information Security, Privacy and Trust, edited by Louis Marinos and Ioannis Askoxylakis
- Volume 28, CCIS 373, HCI International 2013 Posters Proceedings (Part I), edited by Constantine Stephanidis
- Volume 29, CCIS 374, HCI International 2013 Posters Proceedings (Part II), edited by Constantine Stephanidis

I would like to thank the Program Chairs and the members of the Program Boards of all affiliated conferences and thematic areas, listed below, for their contribution to the highest scientific quality and the overall success of the HCI International 2013 conference.

This conference could not have been possible without the continuous support and advice of the Founding Chair and Conference Scientific Advisor, Prof. Gavriel Salvendy, as well as the dedicated work and outstanding efforts of the Communications Chair and Editor of HCI International News, Abbas Moallem.

I would also like to thank for their contribution towards the smooth organization of the HCI International 2013 Conference the members of the Human–Computer Interaction Laboratory of ICS-FORTH, and in particular George Paparoulis, Maria Pitsoulaki, Stavroula Ntoa, Maria Bouhli and George Kapnas.

May 2013                                        Constantine Stephanidis
                                    General Chair, HCI International 2013

# Organization

## Human–Computer Interaction

## Program Chair: Masaaki Kurosu, Japan

Jose Abdelnour-Nocera, UK
Sebastiano Bagnara, Italy
Simone Barbosa, Brazil
Tomas Berns, Sweden
Nigel Bevan, UK
Simone Borsci, UK
Apala Lahiri Chavan, India
Sherry Chen, Taiwan
Kevin Clark, USA
Torkil Clemmensen, Denmark
Xiaowen Fang, USA
Shin'ichi Fukuzumi, Japan
Vicki Hanson, UK
Ayako Hashizume, Japan
Anzai Hiroyuki, Italy
Sheue-Ling Hwang, Taiwan
Wonil Hwang, South Korea
Minna Isomursu, Finland
Yong Gu Ji, South Korea
Esther Jun, USA
Mitsuhiko Karashima, Japan

Kyungdoh Kim, South Korea
Heidi Krömker, Germany
Chen Ling, USA
Yan Liu, USA
Zhengjie Liu, P.R. China
Loïc Martínez Normand, Spain
Chang S. Nam, USA
Naoko Okuizumi, Japan
Noriko Osaka, Japan
Philippe Palanque, France
Hans Persson, Sweden
Ling Rothrock, USA
Naoki Sakakibara, Japan
Dominique Scapin, France
Guangfeng Song, USA
Sanjay Tripathi, India
Chui Yin Wong, Malaysia
Toshiki Yamaoka, Japan
Kazuhiko Yamazaki, Japan
Ryoji Yoshitake, Japan
Silvia Zimmermann, Switzerland

## Human Interface and the Management of Information

## Program Chair: Sakae Yamamoto, Japan

Hans-Jorg Bullinger, Germany
Alan Chan, Hong Kong
Gilsoo Cho, South Korea
Jon R. Gunderson, USA
Shin'ichi Fukuzumi, Japan
Michitaka Hirose, Japan
Jhilmil Jain, USA
Yasufumi Kume, Japan

Mark Lehto, USA
Hiroyuki Miki, Japan
Hirohiko Mori, Japan
Fiona Fui-Hoon Nah, USA
Shogo Nishida, Japan
Robert Proctor, USA
Youngho Rhee, South Korea
Katsunori Shimohara, Japan

Michale Smith, USA
Tsutomu Tabe, Japan
Hiroshi Tsuji, Japan

Kim-Phuong Vu, USA
Tomio Watanabe, Japan
Hidekazu Yoshikawa, Japan

## Engineering Psychology and Cognitive Ergonomics

## Program Chair: Don Harris, UK

Guy Andre Boy, USA
Joakim Dahlman, Sweden
Trevor Dobbins, UK
Mike Feary, USA
Shan Fu, P.R. China
Michaela Heese, Austria
Hung-Sying Jing, Taiwan
Wen-Chin Li, Taiwan
Mark A. Neerincx, The Netherlands
Jan M. Noyes, UK
Taezoon Park, Singapore

Paul Salmon, Australia
Axel Schulte, Germany
Siraj Shaikh, UK
Sarah C. Sharples, UK
Anthony Smoker, UK
Neville A. Stanton, UK
Alex Stedmon, UK
Xianghong Sun, P.R. China
Andrew Thatcher, South Africa
Matthew J.W. Thomas, Australia
Rolf Zon, The Netherlands

## Universal Access in Human–Computer Interaction

## Program Chairs: Constantine Stephanidis, Greece, and Margherita Antona, Greece

Julio Abascal, Spain
Ray Adams, UK
Gisela Susanne Bahr, USA
Margit Betke, USA
Christian Bühler, Germany
Stefan Carmien, Spain
Jerzy Charytonowicz, Poland
Carlos Duarte, Portugal
Pier Luigi Emiliani, Italy
Qin Gao, P.R. China
Andrina Granić, Croatia
Andreas Holzinger, Austria
Josette Jones, USA
Simeon Keates, UK

Georgios Kouroupetroglou, Greece
Patrick Langdon, UK
Seongil Lee, Korea
Ana Isabel B.B. Paraguay, Brazil
Helen Petrie, UK
Michael Pieper, Germany
Enrico Pontelli, USA
Jaime Sanchez, Chile
Anthony Savidis, Greece
Christian Stary, Austria
Hirotada Ueda, Japan
Gerhard Weber, Germany
Harald Weber, Germany

# Virtual, Augmented and Mixed Reality

## Program Chair: Randall Shumaker, USA

Waymon Armstrong, USA
Juan Cendan, USA
Rudy Darken, USA
Cali M. Fidopiastis, USA
Charles Hughes, USA
David Kaber, USA
Hirokazu Kato, Japan
Denis Laurendeau, Canada
Fotis Liarokapis, UK

Mark Livingston, USA
Michael Macedonia, USA
Gordon Mair, UK
Jose San Martin, Spain
Jacquelyn Morie, USA
Albert "Skip" Rizzo, USA
Kay Stanney, USA
Christopher Stapleton, USA
Gregory Welch, USA

# Cross-Cultural Design

## Program Chair: P.L. Patrick Rau, P.R. China

Pilsung Choe, P.R. China
Henry Been-Lirn Duh, Singapore
Vanessa Evers, The Netherlands
Paul Fu, USA
Zhiyong Fu, P.R. China
Fu Guo, P.R. China
Sung H. Han, Korea
Toshikazu Kato, Japan
Dyi-Yih Michael Lin, Taiwan
Rungtai Lin, Taiwan

Sheau-Farn Max Liang, Taiwan
Liang Ma, P.R. China
Alexander Mädche, Germany
Katsuhiko Ogawa, Japan
Tom Plocher, USA
Kerstin Röse, Germany
Supriya Singh, Australia
Hsiu-Ping Yueh, Taiwan
Liang (Leon) Zeng, USA
Chen Zhao, USA

# Online Communities and Social Computing

## Program Chairs: A. Ant Ozok, USA, and Panayiotis Zaphiris, Cyprus

Areej Al-Wabil, Saudi Arabia
Leonelo Almeida, Brazil
Bjørn Andersen, Norway
Chee Siang Ang, UK
Aneesha Bakharia, Australia
Ania Bobrowicz, UK
Paul Cairns, UK
Farzin Deravi, UK
Andri Ioannou, Cyprus
Slava Kisilevich, Germany

Niki Lambropoulos, Greece
Effie Law, Switzerland
Soo Ling Lim, UK
Fernando Loizides, Cyprus
Gabriele Meiselwitz, USA
Anthony Norcio, USA
Elaine Raybourn, USA
Panote Siriaraya, UK
David Stuart, UK
June Wei, USA

## Augmented Cognition

## Program Chairs: Dylan D. Schmorrow, USA, and Cali M. Fidopiastis, USA

Robert Arrabito, Canada
Richard Backs, USA
Chris Berka, USA
Joseph Cohn, USA
Martha E. Crosby, USA
Julie Drexler, USA
Ivy Estabrooke, USA
Chris Forsythe, USA
Wai Tat Fu, USA
Rodolphe Gentili, USA
Marc Grootjen, The Netherlands
Jefferson Grubb, USA
Ming Hou, Canada

Santosh Mathan, USA
Rob Matthews, Australia
Dennis McBride, USA
Jeff Morrison, USA
Mark A. Neerincx, The Netherlands
Denise Nicholson, USA
Banu Onaral, USA
Lee Sciarini, USA
Kay Stanney, USA
Roy Stripling, USA
Rob Taylor, UK
Karl van Orden, USA

## Digital Human Modeling and Applications in Health, Safety, Ergonomics and Risk Management

## Program Chair: Vincent G. Duffy, USA and Russia

Karim Abdel-Malek, USA
Giuseppe Andreoni, Italy
Daniel Carruth, USA
Eliza Yingzi Du, USA
Enda Fallon, Ireland
Afzal Godil, USA
Ravindra Goonetilleke, Hong Kong
Bo Hoege, Germany
Waldemar Karwowski, USA
Zhizhong Li, P.R. China

Kang Li, USA
Tim Marler, USA
Michelle Robertson, USA
Matthias Rötting, Germany
Peter Vink, The Netherlands
Mao-Jiun Wang, Taiwan
Xuguang Wang, France
Jingzhou (James) Yang, USA
Xiugan Yuan, P.R. China
Gülcin Yücel Hoge, Germany

## Design, User Experience, and Usability

## Program Chair: Aaron Marcus, USA

Sisira Adikari, Australia
Ronald Baecker, Canada
Arne Berger, Germany
Jamie Blustein, Canada

Ana Boa-Ventura, USA
Jan Brejcha, Czech Republic
Lorenzo Cantoni, Switzerland
Maximilian Eibl, Germany

Anthony Faiola, USA
Emilie Gould, USA
Zelda Harrison, USA
Rüdiger Heimgärtner, Germany
Brigitte Herrmann, Germany
Steffen Hess, Germany
Kaleem Khan, Canada

Jennifer McGinn, USA
Francisco Rebelo, Portugal
Michael Renner, Switzerland
Kerem Rızvanoğlu, Turkey
Marcelo Soares, Brazil
Christian Sturm, Germany
Michele Visciola, Italy

## Distributed, Ambient and Pervasive Interactions

## Program Chairs: Norbert Streitz, Germany, and Constantine Stephanidis, Greece

Emile Aarts, The Netherlands
Adnan Abu-Dayya, Qatar
Juan Carlos Augusto, UK
Boris de Ruyter, The Netherlands
Anind Dey, USA
Dimitris Grammenos, Greece
Nuno M. Guimaraes, Portugal
Shin'ichi Konomi, Japan
Carsten Magerkurth, Switzerland

Christian Müller-Tomfelde, Australia
Fabio Paternó, Italy
Gilles Privat, France
Harald Reiterer, Germany
Carsten Röcker, Germany
Reiner Wichert, Germany
Woontack Woo, South Korea
Xenophon Zabulis, Greece

## Human Aspects of Information Security, Privacy and Trust

## Program Chairs: Louis Marinos, ENISA EU, and Ioannis Askoxylakis, Greece

Claudio Agostino Ardagna, Italy
Zinaida Benenson, Germany
Daniele Catteddu, Italy
Raoul Chiesa, Italy
Bryan Cline, USA
Sadie Creese, UK
Jorge Cuellar, Germany
Marc Dacier, USA
Dieter Gollmann, Germany
Kirstie Hawkey, Canada
Jaap-Henk Hoepman, The Netherlands
Cagatay Karabat, Turkey
Angelos Keromytis, USA
Ayako Komatsu, Japan

Ronald Leenes, The Netherlands
Javier Lopez, Spain
Steve Marsh, Canada
Gregorio Martinez, Spain
Emilio Mordini, Italy
Yuko Murayama, Japan
Masakatsu Nishigaki, Japan
Aljosa Pasic, Spain
Milan Petković, The Netherlands
Joachim Posegga, Germany
Jean-Jacques Quisquater, Belgium
Damien Sauveron, France
George Spanoudakis, UK
Kerry-Lynn Thomson, South Africa

Julien Touzeau, France
Theo Tryfonas, UK
João Vilela, Portugal

Claire Vishik, UK
Melanie Volkamer, Germany

## External Reviewers

Maysoon Abulkhair, Saudi Arabia
Ilia Adami, Greece
Vishal Barot, UK
Stephan Böhm, Germany
Vassilis Charissis, UK
Francisco Cipolla-Ficarra, Spain
Maria De Marsico, Italy
Marc Fabri, UK
David Fonseca, Spain
Linda Harley, USA
Yasushi Ikei, Japan
Wei Ji, USA
Nouf Khashman, Canada
John Killilea, USA
Iosif Klironomos, Greece
Ute Klotz, Switzerland
Maria Korozi, Greece
Kentaro Kotani, Japan

Vassilis Kouroumalis, Greece
Stephanie Lackey, USA
Janelle LaMarche, USA
Asterios Leonidis, Greece
Nickolas Macchiarella, USA
George Margetis, Greece
Matthew Marraffino, USA
Joseph Mercado, USA
Claudia Mont'Alvão, Brazil
Yoichi Motomura, Japan
Karsten Nebe, Germany
Stavroula Ntoa, Greece
Martin Osen, Austria
Stephen Prior, UK
Farid Shirazi, Canada
Jan Stelovsky, USA
Sarah Swierenga, USA

# HCI International 2014

The 16th International Conference on Human–Computer Interaction, HCI International 2014, will be held jointly with the affiliated conferences in the summer of 2014. It will cover a broad spectrum of themes related to Human–Computer Interaction, including theoretical issues, methods, tools, processes and case studies in HCI design, as well as novel interaction techniques, interfaces and applications. The proceedings will be published by Springer. More information about the topics, as well as the venue and dates of the conference, will be announced through the HCI International Conference series website: http://www.hci-international.org/

General Chair
Professor Constantine Stephanidis
University of Crete and ICS-FORTH
Heraklion, Crete, Greece
Email: cs@ics.forth.gr

# Table of Contents – Part I

## Cross-Cultural Product Design

## Cross-Cultural Design Methods and Techniques

## International Usability Evaluation

## Case Studies in Cross-Cultural Design

# Table of Contents – Part II

## Cultural Issues in Business and Industry

## Culture, Health and Quality of Life

# Cross-Cultural and Intercultural Collaboration

# Culture and the Smart City

## Cultural Differences on the Web

# Part I

# Cross-Cultural Product Design

# Re-engaging with Cultural Engagement: Innovative Product Design of Cultural Field Experience

Tsen-Yao Chang[1,*] and Fang-Wu Tung[2]

[1] Department of Creative Design, National Yunlin University of Science and Technology,
Yunlin County, Taiwan
changty8908@gmail.com
[2] Department of Industrial and Commercial Design,
National Taiwan University of Science and Technology, Taipei, Taiwan
fwtung@mail.ntust.edu.tw

**Abstract.** This study aims to construct the components of effective analysis of cultural products to develop a design process that is appropriate for the cultural field. The research concept is based on an integrated experience of design experiments. Targeting the actual demands of the cultural field, the cases analyzed provide pragmatic solutions. This study contributes a systematic and timely process of design in the cultural field with the use of a complex scenario, as well as the application of such a process to produce concrete results in design service. Results can aid in future planning and implementation of solutions.

**Keywords:** cultural field experience, cultural product, product design, experience design.

## 1    Introduction

Cultural assets are the key element of creating local sustainable experiences. When globalization carries on more actively, it wipes local cultures out more easily. But, when the world becomes more internationalized, local traditions appear more important. Cultures are associated with extensive economic benefits. These cultural activities, be it a festival, service experience or engagement enlivened,   all are associated with the development of related products, with derivative benefits that often carry weight in respect to the propagation and preservation of a culture. What cultural product design is capable of is being the media conveying cultures and exhibiting lifestyle. When a culture spreads in the form of products, not only does it transform, employ and communicate the contents of local culture but also highlights recognition of local culture and the image that symbolizes the local place.   For designers of product development, when facing the complexity of cultural field, it is necessary to effectively assess the questions and design demands to set out efficient design processes. The contribution of this study is an attempt to develop a systematic and flexible process to identify and implement a design. Results can provide designers

---

* Corresponding author.

P.L.P. Rau (Ed.): CCD/HCII 2013, Part I, LNCS 8023, pp. 3–9, 2013.
© Springer-Verlag Berlin Heidelberg 2013

with guidelines on re-examining and re-promoting cultures and giving new economy and heritage to cultures. These cultures should embrace international views and strike a balance between local demands and those of a globalized business.

## 2    Literature Review

The emotion and narratives in cultures are a key boost to promoting marketing locality. Where nations, cities as well as regions begin to give serious thought to the preservation and development of their own cultures, "cultures" become crucial opportunities of adding value to each region and create separation and distinctiveness of markets. Globalization, causing homogenization though, is not all negatively influential; it does create different opportunities. The emotion and narrative contents in cultures are capable of evoking resonance, which matches the contemporary consumption culture well, allowing  consumers to look for unique emotional experiences and touch of stories whereby to get psychologically satisfied. That encourages local industries to reconsider the features of local cultures, based on which they develop local cultural product, whereby to assist in the development and preservation of local culture and creation of global business opportunities. As experience economy becomes a fashion, sensible elements like emotion and culture are taken into account for every operation of industry, with focus placed on the increase of total feeling of service in consumers.   The abundant creativity locally in Taiwan has been treated by diverse cultures; together with the diverse and unique sense and looks of Taiwan cultures, it is the energy for adding value to cultures that can be employed to industrial development, field development, brand development and product development.

### 2.1    Developing Creative Tourism in Cultural Experience Field

Living today requires more than the satisfaction with materials as in the past; it needs updating emotional experiences now. What is needed first is recreational life, in which people begin to pursue creative experience in space of travel. A main form of recreation is cultural experience. Different cultural contexts and lifestyles are understood through knowing regional scene and sight, of geography and of human. Richards and Raymond define 'creative tourism' as *'tourism which offers tourists the opportunity to develop their creative potential through active participation in courses and learning experiences which are the characteristic of the destination where they are undertaken'* (2000:18). In the perspective of travelers, they are allowed more time, space and resources to interact with local places, even to learn different lifestyle. From the angle of local economic development, travel of cultural experience is a means to allow local assets, both tangible and intangible, to possibly become elements of product that can be experienced and marketed. Thus, cultural experiences can become ways of providing enjoyment, excitement and expression of emotion. Richards (2011:1237) emphasizes, the common components of creative tourism are 'participative, authentic experiences that allow tourists to develop their creative potential and skills through contact with local people and their culture' (Richards, 2011:1237). Therefore, the research intends to develop an adoptable design process that helps consumers go deep into the field and creates for them profound, unique cultural impression.

## 2.2    Cultural Awareness and Product Development

Consumers are no longer interested in standardized product produced in mass production (Delaney et al. 2002:46); cultural differences that exist between nations, cities, fields and groups become important elements of identification used in experiences and consumption. In the cultural tour to a country, shopping is probably a simplest form of cultural experience (Hsieh & Chang, 2006). Memorabilia can inspire tourists to use them to compare with their daily life they are used to, and to widen their view of world, realizing the differences between their own culture and others, further to experience cultural life more really (Littrell, 1990). By consumption of cultural product, tourists expect to ensure unique experiences that is impossible in their home countries (Lee, Kim, Seock & Cho, 2009). Hence, in the condition of tourism development, how to effectively transform the local resources feature into product with benefit of added economic value is what the designer should contemplate when accessing to the field and presenting the design.

When designing, however, designers are also subject to their own cultures (Press and Cooper, 2003); the presence of cultural differences will force them to self-adapt based on different cultures and divide their own product (Van Raaij, 2005). Different comprehension of cultures thus becomes a distinct condition for designers when making design. They use their own feeling and perspective for the cultures, combine their practice of design, based on regional humane features for designing, employing local cultural features as design contents, to create uniqueness and differentiation in the competitive global market and increase competitiveness and identification of product (Lin, R. T., 2007). To convey cultural messages and present cultural values via product; to enhance the appeal and emotional bond of cultures through beautification by design.

## 3    Research Method

Based on the above context and on the product design process, this study constructed a process that suits the development of the cultural field. The aim is to provide designers with elements of effective analysis of the structure of cultural products. A case study that divided the process of design and analysis into three stages was used, as shown in Fig. 1.

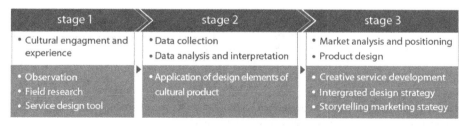

**Fig. 1.** Stages of the product design process to promote the cultural field

Stage 1: Selecting a specific cultural field, which was Longshan Temple in Taipei City. For this field, data were gathered, observation made and cultural context explored, gaining insights into the gaps and opportunities of the field, to propose possible concepts of creative products. Field survey was used to introduce the perspective of service design; service design tools were used to uncover field problems.    With customer journey map used as design and observation tools, contemplation and search were made as to the stages of: "How does a customer become aware of the service?", "How does a customer join the service?", "What are the different ways a customer might use the service?", and "How does a customer grow with the service?" to understand the gaps arising in the steps from acquiring information to entering the field and exiting it, and to present designer's insights. The gaps identified at this stage were 1. Entering field: the tourists are not familiar with the place, do not know the course of visiting nor the meaning of the equipment used in the temple;    2. In the field: they have no ideas about the gods or the rules of visiting; 3. Exiting the field: unfamiliar with other scenic sites around the field, or about selection and sending memorabilia. Having identified these questions, the designer began to analyze existed products, whereby to understand the property of similar products in market.

Stage 2: Gathering data. This step included obtaining information on the designs of related products in the market, analyzing their design concepts and elements, and from the comparison of these elements, constructing    the narrative elements that suit the development of the field culture. These elements will serve as the basis for future design ideas.

Stage 3: Working on product    proposals with the use of the design elements obtained in cultural product analysis at the previous stage, with center placed at cultural emotion and idea which can be translated into stories as marketing strategies, and by developing in the directions of product functions, pattern styling, manufacturing techniques and material applications ( as shown    Fig. 2),    respectively, or by recombining them, with expert opinions expressed in interviews taken into consideration as well as reflecting to the marketing and mass production for merchandising the relevant items. Such design process can serve as an innovated one for constructing cultural fields.

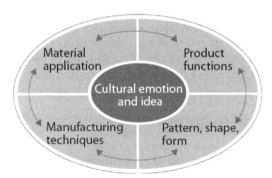

**Fig. 2.** Design elements of cultural products, with cultural emotion and idea as the core values from which development can be pursued in each of the directions of product functions, pattern styling, manufacturing techniques, and material application.

The design overall is about the creative product stressing on visualized information for the purpose of making the creative items that help tourists understanding the ritual culture of Longshan Temple, so that believers and travelers visiting the Temple can have recognition by way of the designed cultural product. The series of items, which was created by linking the observed gaps and the five elements under study, combines the properties of function, guide and memory. It dawns on visitors to Longshan Temple about the sequence of pilgrimage and what each deity blesses. It also includes amulets of which visitors can take one piece with them after the visit hoping for peace. The tour guide texts further include the introduction to a tour to the business areas around the Temple and marketing the history of Manga area of Taipei, where the Temple sits. All this history and experience will bear the value of reference and memory for one who has paid the visit.

## 4 Results and Discussions

Basically, this study focused on the search for design gaps and building of a model for commercial design. Regarding the process of service design into which cultural creative product is introduced, it was found that in the model as Fig. 1 shows, design creativity can help preserve cultural values and present distinct looks and impressions. Fig. 3 shows Case 1, a guide booklet designed for the field overall to solve the trouble for first-time visitors in knowing the sequence of pilgrimage. The booklet has contents including information on the stores around the field. The information presented renders peripheral clustering effect to this cultural field, which draws crowds and makes feedback. Case 2 represents a set of postcards that describe the processes and tools used in the design process. The concept is to communicate the beauty of crafts in Taiwan through postcards sent to people in other countries. Case 3 is a graphical representation of lottery poems. The idea was to connect tradition and modern graphics by creating new characters for each poem on the basis of the image of a "dragon," a representative symbol of prosperity in Chinese culture. Rendering dragons with a symbolic image creates a character that represents novelty. These are only a few examples alongside many other items yet to develop.

**Fig. 3.** Three design cases that introduce innovative cultural products in which the design elements of cultural product are applied

## 5    Conclusion and Recommendations

The whole design process begins by field observation, which, with the assistance of service design tools, allows the designer to uncover and catalogue more systematically the gaps existing in the field, whereby to effective shorten the time of early-stage design and observation without wild-goose chase-like exploration. That is followed by steps of design process, which reorganizes elements employable in product design through field analysis. This is literally building the design database for cultural field to become basic data for extended application in future design. In establishing the design items, the observational results in Stage 1 are considered. The identified gaps are solved by designing, and relevant design factors are comprehensively compared. The directions of emotions and ideas, product functions, pattern styling, manufacturing techniques, and material application are also considered to produce the final design products at the final stage. These steps comprise the process of product design and development for the cultural field of Longshan Temple ( as shown Fig. 4).

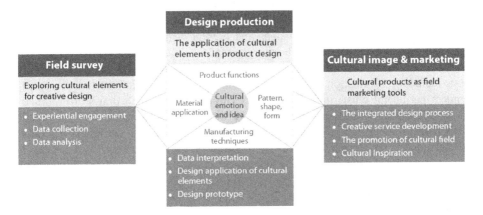

**Fig. 4.** Constructs in the process of product design and development for the cultural field of Longshan Temple

The purpose of design processes is to minimize a black box process and thus make all design steps transparent. Unquestionably, the creativity and ingenuity of a design ultimately rely on the designer's cumulative experiences and distinctive insights. However, we will still attempt to clarify the process steps of design in the hope of shortening the trial period involved.   In addition, we will be able to allow systematic assessments and analysis of the resources involved in local features during future planning on field tourism by local regions. This aim can be achieved through related tools and the design directions reorganized in this study, so that maximum benefits can be achieved.

**Acknowledgments.** The authors gratefully acknowledge the financial support for this research provided by the National Science Council of Taiwan under Grants No. NSC-101-2410-H-224-041.

# References

1. Delaney, M., McFarland, J., Yoon, G.H., Hardy, T.: Global Localization. Innovation – Global Design and Cultural Identity, 46–49 (Summer 2002)
2. Hsieh, A., Chang, J.: Shopping and tourist night markets in Taiwan. Tourism Management 27(1), 138–145 (2006)
3. Lee, Y., Kim, S., Seock, Y.-K., Cho, Y.: Tourists' attitudes towards textiles and apparel related cultural products: A cross-cultural marketing study. Tourism Management 30(5), 724–732 (2009)
4. Lin, R.T.: Transforming Taiwan Aboriginal Cultural Features into Modern Product Design: A Case study of a cross-cultural Product Design Model. International Journal of Design 1(2), 44–53 (2007)
5. Littrell, M.A.: Symbolic significance of textiles crafts for tourists. Annals of Tourism Research 17, 228–245 (1990)
6. Press, M., Cooper, R.: The design experience: the role of design and designers in the twenty-first century. Ashgate, Aldershot (2003)
7. Richards, G., Raymond, C.: Creative tourism. ATLAS News 23, 16–20 (2000)
8. Richards, G.: Creativity and tourism: The state of the art. Annals of Tourism Research 38(4), 1225–1253 (2011)
9. Van Raaij, F.W.: Applied consumer behaviour. Longman, London (2005)

# An Exploration on Tactile Styles of Products

Yung-Ting Chen and Ming-Chuen Chuang

National Chiao Tung University
No.1001, Daxue Rd., East Dist., Hsinchu City 300, Taiwan
triplemomo@msn.com, cming0212@gmail.com

**Abstract.** As an exploratory phase of the continuous study regarding tactile style of products, this paper employed semi-structured focus interview as the method to investigate and summarize whether people had more feelings towards products with vivid and obvious style for future reference. Therefore, this study intended to 1. identify the design styles that provoked strong feelings for the reference of tactile style in the future; 2. file the representative products and major form features of the design styles; 3. construct a set of vocabulary for the further images evaluation on design and tactile style in the future. In this research, 11 design experts were interviewed. All of them had long-term experience in design and profound understanding of design style. All of the interviews were videotaped and edited for a comprehensive analysis to yield results as follows: 1. In accordance with the frequency mentioned by the experts, 7 design styles for products that stimulate strong feelings were identified; 2. Summarizing the contents and forms of design styles, it was discovered that evolution of design style progressed incessantly like following a spiral path; 3. The representative products and their form features (shapes, materials, and colors) of each design style were classified; 4. The representative feeling images of each of the design style were obtained and summarized to derive a set of 28 paired image words for further image evaluation.

**Keywords:** design style, tactile style, product feature, image, semi-structured interview.

## 1 Introduction

Current researches regarding the issue of tactility are mostly focused either on the study of the relations between tactility and the materials, or on exploration of the image and cognition of the materials and textures, in terms of tactility, vision, combination of tactile and vision [5,6,10,11]. There are a few researches examine the discrimination of materials and textures from the perspectives of tactility only, or vision and tactility together [1,7,13]. However, there are limited and insufficient studies exploring the integrated feeling of tactile style. Therefore, how to effectively and explicitly probe into the relationship between tactile, styles, and their corresponding images becomes important issue. This topic has also been the researcher's long-term engagement. Regards as the exploratory phase of the long-term research, this study investigated and summarized the design styles of products that communicate strong

P.L.P. Rau (Ed.): CCD/HCII 2013, Part I, LNCS 8023, pp. 10–20, 2013.
© Springer-Verlag Berlin Heidelberg 2013

and salient feelings in relation to the forms, styles, and images of the corresponding products.

Generally speaking, people acquire environmental information with five senses, which operate both independently and interactively. Moreover, each of these senses influences the operation of the other senses [12]. These feelings are regarded as synesthesia, i.e. the stimuli of one particular sensory response may lead to other sensory responses [3]. Vision and tactility are interrelated regarding the evaluation of product image, i.e. synesthesia exists in the evaluation. The identification of the form of an object often depends on the information acquired through both vision and tactility. Therefore, this research aims to investigate products with explicit and vivid design (visual) styles for the reference of the study of tactile style of products in the future.

In general, most studies investigate design style through two approaches. For example, multidimensional scaling (MDS) is employed to construct people's perceptual space of the stimuli, based on the data of differences among stimuli. With reference to the groupings pattern among stimuli in this space, perceptual (design) styles can be identified [4,9]. Second, it emphasizes the analysis of stimuli' images to examine the similarities and differences of the feelings stimulated by the stimuli; stimuli with similar feeling are classified into same style. This approach focuses on the construction of a set of adjectives to evaluate the style images. With these adjectives, the images of the stimuli can be evaluated with semantic differential (SD) survey. Likewise, it is possible to group stimuli, according to their closeness of locations in this image space, into the same style [2,7].

From above, one is able to understand that if we intend to investigate styles and their corresponding feelings, we need to identify the appropriate styles for evaluation, to construct a set of image vocabulary as evaluation scale, and screen out proper the stimuli as the representatives for each style. Therefore, in order to start a complete investigation on tactile style and image, the goals of this study include the following: 1. Identify the design styles that provoke strong feelings as reference for the study of tactile style in the future; 2. Categorize the representative products for each design styles and conduct morphological analysis to these products; and 3. Construct a set of image vocabulary for the further SD evaluation. These research findings will be applied to the study of tactile style and image of products in the future.

## 2    Method

In order to collect and summarize the salient design styles of products that stimulate strong feelings for studying tactile style in the future, this study conducts interview on 11 design experts who have a master or doctoral degree, and more than 5 years of design teaching or practical design experience. During the interview, the design experts are required to list the product design styles resulting in deep and clear perception as many as possible, and also to describe the features, such as the sensory perception, image and association of each style. At the meantime, the experts are also asked to list the shape, type and common material of the representative products for each style. The interview lasts for 1~2 hours or so. The entire interview process is recorded in video, and the interview content is sorted in script after the expert interview. Moreover, the interview content is integrated and summarized based on the question items.

## 3      Results

### 3.1      Identification of Salient Design Styles

First, the items of style proposed by the expert interviewees were counted and compared to facilitate choosing salient design styles for future analysis. Summarizing the design styles proposed by the 11 expert interviewees, 22 design styles were derived, as shown in Table 1.

**Table 1.** Design styles proposed by the experts

| Scandinavian modern (4) | Trans High Tech (5) | Modernism (4) | Minimalism (7) | Archetyp e (5) | Memphis (5) | High Tech (8) |
|---|---|---|---|---|---|---|
| Ready-made(5) | Green design (6) | | | | | |
| Japanese Zen (3) | Thai design (3) | Streamline (2) | Bio mimicry (3) | Bauhaus (2) | Pop art (2) | Retro (1) |
| Art Nouveau-Glasgow (1) | International style (2) | Art Nouveau design (2) | Postmodern ism (3) | Design humor (1) | Alchimia (1) | |

* No particular reference for the style; ( ) the frequency of the item mentioned

This table shows that the styles that were mentioned four times or more (mentioned by at least 4 experts) included: Trans High Tech, Scandinavian modern, High Tech, Archetype, Memphis, Modernism, Minimalism, Ready-made, and Green design. These 9 items are design styles that people are highly familiar with and well-known. After further examination of these 9 design styles, it was discovered that the contents and expressive means of Ready-made and Green design did not fit the purpose of this study. Therefore, these 2 design styles were excluded from this research. Finally, only 7 of the 9 styles listed in the upper row of Table 1 were explored in this study.

### 3.2      Connotations of the Design Styles

This research summarized the connotations of the 7 design styles in accordance with the contents of descriptions about the styles provided by the experts. For example, four experts have mentioned the characteristic and special features about the style of Modernism. Therefore, the described contents of Modernism style by these experts were adopted for analysis with the KJ method. First, the keywords of the contents were extracted and written on index cards. Then, these cards were further classified in accordance with their similarity of meanings. The same process was applied to the analyses of the remaining styles until all 7 styles were analyzed and summarized.

As can be noticed from the resulted affinity diagrams, the major constituting factors of each style consisted of: 1. The contents and context of the style; i.e. the experts' insight of the particular styles which explicates the spirit and thinking of the style; 2. Design core to indicate the concepts and features of the styles; 3. Constituting features; i.e. the performance and application of forms, colors, and materials referred to manifest the styles,; and 4. Perceptual image; including images with physical (feelings provoked through tactility and vision) and psychological (preferences, emotions, and applications brought to users through styles) dimensions. In Table 2, the overall concepts of each style are summarized briefly.

**Table 2.** Framework and concepts of the design styles

| Design styles | Constituting items | Contents |
|---|---|---|
| Modernism | Contents & context | "Long-lasting", "Sustainable and inherited spirit", "Thinking of traditional industrial design ", "Utopian thinking" |
| | Design core | "Simple and concise (the lesser the better) ", "Practicality", "Purposeful design" |
| | Constituting features | "Geometric and primitive form ", "Simple and plain color ", "Emphasis on the proper use of material and texture" |
| | Perceptual image | "Psychological feeling (such as clean, boring, and more) ", "Visual feeling (such as form, features, and more) ", "Tactile feeling ", "Physicality (such as usages, and more) ", "Sociability " |
| Scandinavian modern | Content & Context | "Heritage of modernistic style ", "Timeless", "Balance among technological, naturalistic, and humanistic concern" |
| | Design core | "Interaction between human and products", "Correspondence of demand and function" |
| | Constituting factor | "Application of both organic curves and clear-cut line", "Utilization of local materials", "Vivid and bright colors" |
| | Perceptual image | "Psychological feeling (affinity to people, practical, and more) ", "Visual feeling (such as form and color) ","Tactile feeling (such as cold, practical, or physical) " |
| High Tech | Content & context | "Similar to Modernism", "Pro technological thinking", "Conveying the thinking of the times" |
| | Design core | "Mass production for industrial purpose", "Creation with technology" |
| | Constituting features | "Geometrical and modular configuration", "Fine processing ", "Limited but vivid and bright colors", "Use of industrial materials" |
| | Perceptual image | "Psychological feeling (positive feeling and perspective) ", "Visual feeling (such as special form feature) ", "Tactile feeling (such as practicality and physicality) " |
| Minimalism | Content & context | "Complies with Modernism", "Anti-Post Modernism (Memphis) " |
| | Design core | "Insists on simple forms", "Depends on technological presentation ", "Ultra-simple and keep on basic functions (but thoughtful functions) ", "No excess thinking", "Emphasis on visual representation (form and constitutive style) ", "Less design" |
| | Constituting features | "Geometrical and simple forms", "Use of hue-less color (black, white and grey) ", "Use of industrial materials", "Expression of the materials' texture" |
| | Perceptual feeling | "Psychological feeling (indifference, practicality, Zen, and more) ", "Visual feeling (such as features of materials and forms) ", "Tactile feeling (such as physicality and practicality) ", "Other (sociability) " |

**Table 2.** (*Continued*)

| | | |
|---|---|---|
| **Archetype** | Content & context | "Anti- Post Modernism", "Similar to Minimalism ", "Recalls the ideas of Oswald Mathias Ungers ", "The ideas of Aldo Rossi", "The ideas of Philippe Starck" |
| | Design core | "Collage of geometrical forms", "Use of meaningful form", "Use objects' primitive shapes" |
| | Constitutive features | "Simple form", "Mild colors, the materials' original colors", "No particular restriction on using materials" |
| | Perceptual image | "Psychological feeling (such as familiarity) ", "Visual feeling (such as features of forms) ", "Tactile feeling (such as physicality) " |
| **Trans High Tech** | Content & context | "Anti High Tech's style", "Presents the thinking of the time this style developed (pessimistic, anti-war) ", "Expresses distrust towards technology" |
| | Design core | "Emphasis on designer's sentiments and purpose", "Non-mass production ", "Symbolic" |
| | Constituting features | "Incomplete and irregular forms", "Dull colors", "The use of multiple materials" |
| | Perceptual image | "Psychological feeling (negative viewpoint and feeling) ", "Visual feeling (such as form and materiality) ", "Tactile feeling (materiality) " |
| **Memphis** | Content & context | "Anti-Modernism", "Retro style", "Challenge to conventional thinking", |
| | Design core | "Expression of conflict", "Feature of contrast ", "Characteristics of Hippies " |
| | Constituting features | "Diverse forms", "Emphasis on decoration", "Rich in using colors", "Combination of various textures" |
| | Perceptual image | "Psychological feeling (funny) ", "Visual feeling (such as decorative, colorful, and more)" |

In Table 2 shows that each style has its own thinking, ideas, meanings, and considerations in design; therefore, they are different in form and constitution. In addition, it was discovered from the experts' descriptions in the interviews that there was certain developing pattern between these styles. From their interrelationship, it was clear that the changes and development in styles moved along a continuous line. They were repetitive and fluctuating. In other words, the transformation in design styles likes a continuous spiral. Indeed, styles progressed in endless cycles (from complexity to simplicity and vice versa). With the progression in time, styles demonstrates their unique features; sometimes they may display similar contents but without overlapping. As a result, design styles are becoming more diverse and interesting.

### 3.3 Representative Products of the Mentioned Styles and Their Design Features

The research then continues to analyze the contents of the "constituting features" of the mentioned styles and their corresponding designs from the description collected in the interviews. The KJ method was employed again for this analysis; the concluded constituting features and contents of each style is summarize in Table 3.

From Table 3, we can observe the slight differences in form constitution among some styles, such as Modernism, Scandinavian modern, High Tech, Minimalism, and

Archetype. Although all these styles inherited simplicity and plainness in form, forms of Modernism were developed in accordance with the rule of "Form follows function," whereas the simple and concise forms of Scandinavian modernism were accompanied by organic forms. Regarding High Tech, it employed the features of production aided by technology, which was manifested through the exposition of structures to display the beauty of structure and production with technology. In addition, its geometric form was the reflection of the features of the modular structure. In an opposite manner, the salient feature of Minimalism was completely decoration free, trying to conceal all sorts of structure. It also demanded less in terms of form, color, and materials. Finally, Archetype, manifesting as another kind of ultra-simplistic form, was a response to people's longing for genre and meaningful forms with simple geometric forms. For Trans High Tech, it worked contrary to the features of High Tech. It demonstrated features of non-mass production, such as irregular, unsmooth, unsteady, and imperfect feature in form and texture. Memphis emphasized visual effects. It focused on decorative features, diverse colors, and more, demonstrating form with strong visual effects.

**Table 3.** Constituting features and contents of the design styles

| Design styles | Constituting features | Contents |
|---|---|---|
| Modernism | Geometric and primitive form | "Simple forms and simple lines", "No excess decorations, Form follows function", "Simple structure design", "Configured by circle, square, or lines" |
| | Simple colors | "Simple colors", "Frequent use of black, grey and white", "Metallic color (materials' original colors)" |
| | Emphasis on the choice of material and texture | "No limitation in adopting materials", "Mainly use new and mass produced materials", Use mainly metal, such as steel, stainless steel, steel pipes, curved pipes, with leather" |
| Scandinavian modern | Organic curves and clear-cut lines | "Transformation and extract from natural and bionic forms", "Use both organic curves and clear-cut lines", "Simple and primitive surface finishing " |
| | The use of local materials | "Local feel; use local materials", "Use natural materials (wood) ","No limitation in adopting materials" |
| | Vivid and bright colors | "Use bright and vivid colors to cheer up the mood casted by cold climate", "No limitation on using color scheme", "Use materials' original colors" |
| High Tech | Constituted by geometric forms and modules | "Mainly geometric lines", "Exposed structures (displayed through glasses) "Modular assemblage", "Geometric configurations (circles and squares) " |
| | Processing | "Emphasized on forms made with technology (by bending, fretwork, perforation, stamping) ", "Accurately calculated with the computer " |
| | Few but strong colors | "Use materials' original colors(metallic color) ", "Simple colors", "Bright colors |
| | The use of industrial materials | "Industrial materials for mass production (plastic, fill-seal board, cement, inflated sandbag, alloy, steel parts, stainless steel, steel plates, aluminum) " |

**Table 3.** (*Continued*)

| | | |
|---|---|---|
| **Minimalism** | Geometric forms, simple forms | "Regular and systematic formation ", "Hidden design", "Geometric forms, simple, concise", "Shrinking of form volums, simple structures", "Application of primitive forms", "Design-free, decoration-free" |
| | Use no color | "Very simple color", "Use cold colors, such as black, white, and grey", "Retain materials' original colors", "Avoid using warm colors" |
| | Application of industrial materials | "Application of industrial materials (with little limitation) ", "Few materials, simple texture", "Use very few composite materials ", |
| | Representation of materials' quality | "Smooth or matted surface", "Mainly represent the materials' features" |
| **Archetype** | Simple forms and compositions | "No decoration, simple forms", "Application of meaningful forms", "Assembled with very basic geometric forms", "Use the very genre form of the objects" |
| | Mild color, display the materials' colors | "Use of mild colors", "Use pale colors ", "Display materials' original colors", "No color coating, or electroplating" |
| | No limitation in adopting materials | "No limitation in adopting materials", "Use of specials materials" |
| **Trans High Tech** | Incomplete and irregular forms | "Irregular forms", "Organic curves", "Irregular surfaces", "Symbolic form" |
| | Dark and dull color | "Use of dark and dull colors", "Rusty brown ", "Massive use of vivid red as the key color", |
| | Use of multiple materials | "Use of industrial materials (similar to High Tech) ", "Natural materials (such a cement, rotten wood, leather) " |
| **Memphis** | Diverse forms | "Bionic form (animals) ", "Organic forms", "Classical forms", "Irregular forms" |
| | Emphasis on decoration | "Use special patterns", "Diverse patterns", "Imitation of different materials' textures (imitation of plastic) ", "Diverse, conflict, exaggerated and excessive visual decorations" |
| | Rich colors | "Rather strong in color scheme (contrast colors) ", "Rather bright in color", "Diversified color scheme (with many colors) " |
| | Little variations in using materials | "Infrequently using of special materials", "Frequently using of Melamine sheets " |

Considering the adoption of materials, some styles had preference for particular kinds of materials. Modernism, for example, preferred using metal or curved pipes of stainless steel. Scandinavian modern tended to use wood, and Memphis, decorative melamine sheets. Overall, for practical purposes, industrial materials were mainly adopted. Although there were certain degrees of overlapping in their choices of materials among some styles, it was still possible for us to distinguish the design styles into two major categories: ones with emphasis on materials' original properties (Modernism, Scandinavian modern, High Tech, Minimalism, and Archetype) and the ones without emphasis on materials' original properties (Trans High Tech and Memphis).

The representative designs corresponding to each design style identified by the expert interviewees then were summarized in this stage. Experts raised many examples of buildings as representative designs. Since this study aimed to investigate the design

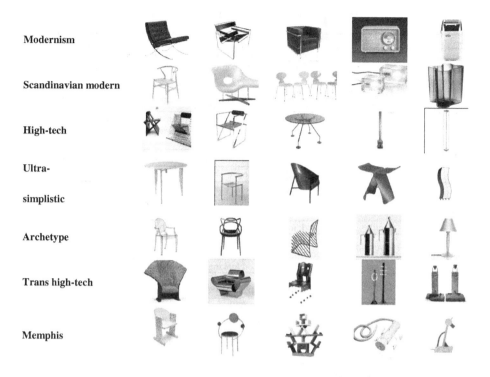

**Fig. 1.** Representative products of the design styles

styles of products, therefore, examples regarding architecture were not discussed in this paper. As for the descriptions and information of the products, products' names, forms, styles, and brand names mentioned by the experts were recorded and summarized. The representative products, the most frequently mentioned and clearly described products, of each style were summarized in Figure 1.

## 3.4    Perceptual Image

Finally, the perceptual feelings of each design style raised by the experts were summarized. The vocabularies of the feelings (in physical and psychological dimensions) proposed by the experts for each style were identified and integrated in accordance with the similarities of meaning. Psychological feeling, visual feeling, and tactile feeling are the three major aspects of feeling on design style. They either co-exist or overlap. Thus, these adjectives were then classified into categories of psychological, visual, tactile dimension, or the other, if they don't fit into these categories. Consequentially, the related perceptual feelings and images of each style were derived, as shown in Table 4.

**Table 4.** Perceptual image of the design styles

| Design styles | Feelings | Details of feelings |
|---|---|---|
| **Modernism** | Psychological | Humanistic, clean, dull, technological, monotonous, efficient |
| | Visual | Simple, clear-cut, non-decorative, non-colorful, simple, modest, pure, meek |
| | Tactile | Functional, purposeful, unobvious, smooth, sharp, hard, |
| | Other | Long-lasting, always in-fashion |
| **Scandinavian modern** | Psychological | Home-style, vivid, interesting, pure, transparent, harmonious, simple, clean, low profile, convenient, considerate, tender, warm, closeness, concordant |
| | Visual | Rich in color, bright, not icy, not hard, warm, daring color, organic |
| | Tactile | Soft, tactile oriented, usable |
| **High-tech** | Psychological | Rough, technological, cold, coarse, lofty, inapproachable |
| | Visual | Accurate, transparent, bright, simple lines, meek, module, bright, shiny, loyal, steady, conflict, calm |
| | Tactile | Cold, infrequent interaction, solid, stable |
| **Minimalism** | Psychological | Plain, cold, clean, silent, non-humanistic, monastic, remote from people |
| | Visual | Hard, simple, good looking, not handy, cold tone, cold, plain |
| | Tactile | Limited tactile, not strong, not obvious, low profile, not warm, angular, hard, flat, sharp |
| | Others | Long-lasting, always in fashion |
| **Archetype** | Psychological | Steady, not dangerous, warm, familiar, surprising, stunning, conflict, attractive |
| | Visual | Light colors, mild, no decorations, simple, pastiche, meek |
| | Tactile | Conflicted, rough, not strong |
| **Trans high-tech** | Psychological | Fancy, strong feeling, repressive, ironic, interesting, messy, lively, decadent, scared, dangerous, unstable, conflicted, passive, disgusting |
| | Visual | Incomplete, broken, wrecked, decadent, rusty, weird, paradoxical, deranged, complicated, not safe, cold, dark |
| | Tactile | Not handy, hesitant to use |
| **Memphis** | Psychological | Interesting, hippies, typical, retro style, contrast, strong |
| | Visual | Decorative, bright colors, organic, contrast, conflict, exaggerating, morphing patterns |

It can be found from this table that, indeed, there are particular feelings for different styles. In other words, different styles may stimulate different feelings. However, at the same time, different design styles share some common feelings in visual, tactile, and psychological dimension. In general, form features and colors, mainly appealing to vision, are the major source stimulating the feelings corresponding to styles, first. Psychological and tactile feelings come later. Moreover, the materials' properties will simultaneously affect tactile and visual feelings. Then, they will further stimulate psychological feelings. Some feelings in different dimension overlap and are interrelated; for instance, if an object looked cold, it gave people the feeling of coldness and then, it further made people feel tranquil and cold. Therefore, this research integrated similar feelings in visual, tactile, and psychological dimension. Then similar or opposite words of feeling in different style were further combined and coupled into opposite adjective pairs. Finally, 28 opposite adjective pairs were summarized, as shown in Table 5, for further SD evaluation on styles.

**Table 5.** Vocabulary for feelings

| Ironic-praiseworthy | Long-lasting outdated - | Steady-unstable | Funny-boring | Lively-dull | Hard-soft |
|---|---|---|---|---|---|
| Simple-complicated | Conflict-harmonious | Geometric-organic | Smooth-coarse | Clean-messy | Pure-fancy |
| Decorative-plain | Pessimistic-optimistic | High-class-cheap | Safe-dangerous | Close-alienated | Bright-dark |
| Daring-conservative | Humanistic-non-humanistic | Calm-passionate | vivid-colorless | Rough-delicate | Cold-warm |
| Diverse-monotonous | Low tactile-tactile oriented | Technological-handmade | | Good looking-loathsome | |

# 4    Conclusion

The results of this research are summarized as follows: 1.The experts identified 7 salient design styles which were used frequently in daily life, including Modernism, Scandinavian modern, High Tech, Minimalism, Archetype, Trans High Tech, and Memphis. 2.From the descriptions of the styles, it was discovered that styles had a strong legacy. The changes in the form and content of the styles tended to be a transformation from complicated to simple, and the other way round. Overall, it constituted a progressive spiral. 3.Regarding the styles, there were fixed relations between perceptual images and experiences. There were also obvious differences in expressing tactile feeling and visual feeling.  4.Regarding the descriptions of perceptual experiences, the description of form and color received more attention. Meanwhile, the tactile feeling was derived from the contact with texture of products. However, vocabulary and adjectives were used commonly in both areas. Furthermore, psychological feelings were furthered provoked by vision and tactility.  5.Consequentially, a set of common feeling vocabulary was summarized from the design styles discussed in this research. There are 28 pairs of image vocabulary that could be used in the further SD evaluation on design styles. In conclusion, the findings of this research can be treated as worthy references for academic studies of tactile styles of products. The feeling vocabulary regarding the styles can be used as references by researchers in conducting similar semantic evaluations. For the designers, these adjectives can also be applied in their design of the product form.

# References

1. Chen, W.Z., Chiou, W.K.: A study on tactile interfaces as an aid to home electronic appliance operation for the visually impaired. In: Proceedings of HCI International 1999 (the 8th International Conference on Human-Computer Interaction), pp. 740–744. Lawrence Erlbaum Associates, Mahwah (1999)
2. Chuang, M.-C., Chang, Y.-J., Chen, Y.-T.: A Study on Tactile Image of Products - Using Handleless Cups as a Case Study. In: IASDR the International Association of Societies of Design Research (2011)
3. Cytowic, R.E.: Synesthesia: A Union of the Senses, 2nd edn. MIT Press, Cambridge (2002) ISBN 0-262-03296-1

4. Espe, H.: Symbolic Qualities of Watches. In: Object and Images-Studies in Design and Advertising, pp. 124–131 (1991)
5. Hollins, M., Faldowski, R., Rao, S., Young, F.: Perceptual dimensions of tactile surface texture: A multidimensional scaling analysis. Perception & Psychophysics 54(6), 697–705 (1993)
6. Karlsson, M., Velasco, A.V.: Designing for the tactile sense: Investigating the relation between surface properties, perceptions, and preferences. CoDesign 3(1), 123–133 (2007)
7. Kao, C.-H.: Exploring the Relationship between the Style and Image and the Goggles Feature - From the Style of Prototype. Journal of Design 7(1), 33–46 (2002) (in Chinese)
8. Lin, Z., Han, K.: Discrimination of size by sight and touch in adults. Information on Psychological Science 4, 1–4 (1984)
9. Maurer, C., Overbeeke, C.J., Smets, G.: The Semantics of Street Furniture. In: Object and Images-Studies in Design and Advertising, pp. 86–93 (1991)
10. Picard, D., Dacremont, C., Valentin, D., Giboreau, A.: Perceptual dimensions of tactile textures. Acta Psychologica 114(2), 165–184 (2003)
11. Picard, D.: Partial perceptual equivalence between vision and touch for texture information. Acta Psychologica 121(3), 227–248 (2006)
12. Schultz, L.M., Petersik, J.T.: Visual-haptic relations in a two-dimensional size-matching task. Perceptual and Motor Skills 78, 395–402 (1994)

# The Study of Style for Kogi Pottery Art in Life

Chi-Hsiung Chen[1,2] and Shih-Ching Lin[2]

[1] Department of Product Design, Chungyu Institute of Technology,
No. 40, Yi 7th Rd., Keelung 20103, Taiwan, R.O.C.
chenchs@cit.edu.tw
[2] Graduate School of Creative Design, National Yunlin University of Science and Technology,
No.123, University Rd., Sec. 3, Douliou, Yunlin 64002, Taiwan, R.O.C.
chenchs@yuntech.edu.tw

**Abstract.** There are plentiful and diverse culture assets and local sources in Taiwan, and thus the national soft power has been valued gradually, the traditional craft industries also being focused as well. Koji pottery art has essential place in the architectures of Taiwan tempos, and it was considered as the representation of gods in the local belief which was sacredness in Taiwan. However, the elaborate Kogi pottery art which was applied in tempo architectures is intergrading in people's life at home due to the constructive promotion to cultural creative industries from the government. Therefore, the study collected and discussed the develop status of Kogi pottery crafts via literature analysis extensively, as well as to explore the differences of the traditional implements that introduce to life art and analyze the styles via morphological analysis. The study has three conclusions as follows: 1. New opportunity can be created by introducing cultural creative ideas to Kogi pottery industry which allow it transforming to elaborate craft industry from traditional one. (2) Kogi pottery art work still has the unique style by describing abstract implications through concrete forms. (3) Kogi pottery is trending toward simplification but nonetheless retains its symbolic meaning and achieves its goal of continuing its cultural heritage.

**Keywords:** Kogi, cultural creativity, style.

# 1 Introduction

## 1.1 Background and Motive of This Study

Taiwan is located at the transportation hub of the Pacific Ocean, and has been influenced culturally by countries including Spain, Holland, China, and Japan, which has resulted in its current diverse form of culture and further evolved into Taiwan's own unique culture. Traditional art plays an integral role in the evolution of history and culture, allowing history to pass down through the ages under the interpretation of works of art. Of the many existing traditional craft industries, Kogi pottery art is of the most important in Taiwan's temple architectures. Its colorful opera figures made from glazed plastic pottery along with the included illustrations of landscapes or floral

P.L.P. Rau (Ed.): CCD/HCII 2013, Part I, LNCS 8023, pp. 21–30, 2013.
© Springer-Verlag Berlin Heidelberg 2013

patterns as well as its integration with multicolored stained glass have created rich styles and colors, and resulted in unique temple styles, becoming an integral part of temples in Taiwan (Chuan-Hu Jiang, 2005). Kogi pottery is an art form that uses real imagery to express abstract concepts and thoughts, and expresses traditional Chinese philosophies through history, culture, and legend, serving as a strong means of inner education of the mind and soul.

In the past, Kogi pottery was limited to décor for temple architectures. In folk beliefs, Kogi potteries are tools used by the gods, and therefore give people a holy impression. In recent years, however, cultural creativity has taken the globe by storm, and countries around the world are actively enhancing the cultural strength of their countries promoting their country's cultures. In Taiwan, the government is also actively promoting the cultural creativity industry and emphasizing local characteristics. Therefore, traditional crafts are once again in the spotlight. With its fine craft and artistic aesthetics, traditional crafts are entering people's everyday life, which is creating a whole new opportunity for arts and crafts.

In addition to analyzing the historical background of Kogi pottery, this study also looks into the meaning of Kogi pottery art work in traditional temple architectures and explains the significance of incorporating Kogi pottery art into aesthetic aspects of our daily lives. Furthermore, 50 Kogi pottery art artifacts have been collected from the Internet and various books for this study, and type analyses will be conducted to provide a categorization of their styles, thereby providing a basis to related industry vendors for producing innovative products. Research objectives include: (1)To look into the difference in meaning of Kogi pottery art when used in temples and in day-to-day art.(2)Analyze the style in which Kogi pottery art is incorporated into everyday aesthetics.

## 2    Literature Review

### 2.1    The Origin of Kogi Pottery

Kogi is a form of low-temperature soft pottery that is colored and glazed. Its formation temperature is between 500 and 800 degrees. It is also called "Kogi burns" or "Kogi clay." The coloring style of Kogi pottery has been influenced by the colors produced in Jing-De-Zhen of Shanxi Province, glass art, and western Cloisonné. From early single-color works, to subsequent tri-color and five-color works, Kogi pottery have now evolved to include multiple colors (Chiayi Government Department of Cultural Affairs, 2012). During the Japanese Meiji era, Japanese scholars discovered that the Kogi pottery found on the Indochina Peninsula originated from Canton Pottery, and therefore Canton Pottery was called "Kogi Clay" in the Japanese antiques industry. During this period, it was said that King Yeh was a disciple of a craftsman of Canton Pottery, therefore the Japanese called pottery produced in the Chiayi area Kogi Burns (Chuen-Yue Li, 2005). Kogi pottery in Taiwan is mostly used in temple architecture. Its rich glazed coloring mostly tell stories of folk beliefs, traditional teachings, loyalty and comradely, as well as other historical tales. They not only serve as decorations for the architectures, but also serve to teach people valuable lessons.

Kogi pottery that is produced in low temperatures and formed with glazed colorings has styles and shapes that almost come to life. In addition, cut-and-paste techniques also add additional layers and depth to these high-quality art pieces.

**Kogi Pottery Used in Temple Decoration.** Kogi pottery in Taiwan is mostly used for the decoration of temples. Yi-Zheng Shieh (2009) consolidated the contents of publications from various experts and found that themes include literature and history, folk stories, Buddhism and the worshipping of gods, as well as landscapes and animals, as organized and shown in Table 1.

**Table 1.** Themes used in Kogi Pottery for Temple Decoration in Taiwan (Yi-Cheng Shieh, 2009 and this study)

| Item | Type | Themes |
|------|------|--------|
| Literature and Historical Themes | History | Tales of the Gods, Tales of the Three Kingdoms, Tales from the Tang Dynasty, Tales from the Sui and Tang Dynasties, Tales of the Tang Moon House, and the Soldiers and Generals of the Yang Family |
| | Literature and Legend | Tales of Myths, Literary Stories, Operas and Novels, and Poems and Rhymes |
| Folk anecdotes | Social education | Filial story, Carps Jumping over the Dragon Gate, pursuit of longevity in Mount Nanping. |
| | Good omen | Birth delivered by Kirin, extraordinary wealth, official promotion, auspicious eight treasures, fortune delivered by Guanyin; The fisherman, the woodcutter, the farmer, and the scholar. |
| Fairy Buddhist | Religious worship | The Eight Immortals, Guanyin, the three gods of fortune, prosperity and longevity, the eighteen Arhats, the four spirits, the five spirits, and the dark eight immortals. |
| Landscape with animals and birds | Good harvest | All kinds of grains, fish, shrimp, crap, clam, twelve Chinese zodiac. |

The temple is the center of Chinese folk beliefs, and the topics utilized by Kogi Pottery are closely related to Chinese traditional society and folk beliefs. By recording the abstract myths and historical background in the appearance of the temple through Kogi Pottery, we have not only beautified the temple appearance and made it look solemn, but also achieve the goal of educating the audience based on these themes.

## 2.2    The Definition of Style

The term "style" was applied to the form design since the beginning of 16th century. In mid-19th century the definition of style became the central concept of design and art history. The style includes aesthetics not only from visual appreciation but also involving sensory perception and experience. Therefore the style has been regarded as a kind of methodology and become the central concept of fundamental design and art history from which various different forms of styles have been developed. The discussions by domestic and foreign scholars related to style are as shown in Table 2.

**Table 2.** The definition of style (summarized by this study)

| Year | Scholar | Definition |
|------|---------|------------|
| 1963 | Kroeber | A system with coherent ways or pattern for dealing with certain thing. |
| 1989 | Walker | The styles have been formed and developed by different special social ethnic groups as a method for them to communicate with other social ethnic group and to ensure own identities. |
| 1994 | Ming-Jeng Chuan Jun-Jih Chen | The style refers to the combination of art characteristics within certain specific time frame and region. The presentation of style is the specific demonstration of contemporary culture. |
| 2000 | Jun-Cheng Sheu | The presentation of design style and the use of factors will be different along with the advancement of technology and the media revolution. There will be representative design styles in different time periods. |
| 2001 | Guei-Feng Lee | Style is the upper level structure of relics, while material is the lower level structure of relics. The former is spiritual, while the latter is materiality. |

### 2.3   Artwork of Life

The traditional crafts can include a part of folk relics. The artworks are with folk attributes yet they are not the same as folk relics. The criteria of discussion and evaluation are functionality, aesthetics, pattern, decoration, production technology, and cultural meaning (Shou-Ying Jiang, 2005). In the past, the crafts were often used for temple buildings or housing decoration of local gentry. However, along with the changing times, the Taiwanese traditional culture has been under the impact of Westernization and the emergence of minimalist style such that the traditional crafts have been gradually phase out. Stimulated by the aggressive promotion of cultural creative industries by our government, the traditional industries get to start over with a new look. The artworks developed now are no longer only for the temple buildings. They have also been introduced to daily lives after miniaturization thus leading to the birth of artworks of life. They have become the decorations in our lives leading to creation of new value.

## 3      Research Methods and Process

### 3.1   Research Methods

1. Literature review: the analysis and comparison based on literatures for understanding the cultural context of the art of Kogi Pottery and investigating its value and essence.
2. Sample analysis: it is mainly the detailed analysis based on collected literature sample data which can be photographs, literatures, statistics, or specific objects. All components of sample data should be summarized and arranged systematically.
3. Morphological analysis: the morphological analysis is to classify all independent factors for conducting analysis in accordance with each independent and complete component database system (Norris, 1963). In this study we focus on the detailed analysis on the forms, colors and styles of Kogi Pottery samples in order to understand the product features and meaning, and analyze its style vocabulary.

## 3.2    Research Process

The process of this research can be divided into three phases. In Phase I we will set the research objects and purposes and then proceed with literature review and exploration for establishing the theoretic basis of this research. Phase II is about collection of sample data, and in this research we will widely collect relevant merchandises on the market for classification analysis in order to understand the variety of Kogi Pottery merchandises and to explain the vocabulary difference in the applications for temple buildings and life artworks. In Phase III we will understand the design elements and presentation style of Kogi Pottery at current stage by morphological analysis.

# 4    Results and Discussions

## 4.1    Sampling and Summarizing

Along with the emergence of cultural creativity industry, the commercialization of traditional crafts has also become trendy such that the auspicious vocabulary represented by the Kogi Pottery artworks used for traditional temple decorations has been gradually applied to gifts and collectibles and thus entering the arts of family lives. In this research we have widely collected the Kogi Pottery merchandises on the market, and we have collected a total of 50 pieces of samples from the Internet and magazines.

**Table 3.** Analysis on Kogi Pottery Cultural Product Samples (as revised in the research)

| Category | Item | Photo | Description |
|---|---|---|---|
| Decoration | Figure | | They are mostly designed using gods or historical figures as the main idea. Gods have the meaning of giving bless and peacefulness whereas historical figures have historical stories as background which add attractiveness to the products. |
| | Animal | | Animals are mostly 12 Chinese Zodiac animals, elephants and tigers that have the implication of being auspicious. |
| | Mythical Creature | | Mythical creatures are representative mascots in Chinese myths that also have the function of seeking luck and avoiding calamity. |
| Wall Decoration | Framed Decoration | | As for wall decorations, they are designed using abstract shape with a traditional element such as simple lines. In addition to having the meaning of being auspicious, it gives the value to art collection. |
| Hanging Ornament | Small Accessory | | The hanging ornaments are mostly small or cute mascots to emphasize on the idea that they are portable and have the meaning of giving protection and inviting wealth. |

**Sample Classification.** The aforementioned literatures and collected data will be the reference for the arrangement and classification of samples of this research. In this research we have classified the Kogi Pottery merchandises into three major categories based on the method of use such as figurine, wall decor, and hang décor. The application vocabularies and attributes of these merchandises are summarized in Table 3.

Kogi pottery art mainly focuses on figures, animals and mythical creatures. Figures refer to gods and historical figures, animals refer to 12 Chinese Zodiac animals, elephants, lions and peacocks as well as other auspicious animals and mythical creatures refer to qilin, phoenix and other creatures that represent auspiciousness in Chinese myths.

## 4.2    Morphological Analysis on the Kogi Pottery Art

In the research, the representative kogi pottery products seen in the market are divided into decoration, wall decoration and hanging ornament. Moreover, morphological

**Table 4.** Morphological Analysis on Kogi Pottery Decorations (as revised in the research)

| Item | Content | | | |
|------|---------|--|--|--|
| Picture | | | | |
| **Type** | **Category** | **Shape** | **Color** | **Style** |
| Figure | Figurative Figure | Historical figures are used as the main idea and most of them are figurative figures. | Bright colors are mainly used and colors are used to distinguish the figure's personality. | 1. Realistic style 2. Small, realistic and cute style |
| | Abstract Figure | The figures' abstract images are transformed to figurative figures. | Bright colors are mainly used and colors are used to distinguish the figure's personality. | 1. Realistic style 2. Small, realistic and cute style |
| Mythical Creature | Abstract Type | The abstract mythical creatures are transformed to figurative figures. | Bright colors are used to show mythical creatures' sacred and honorable images. | Realistic style |
| Animal | Figurative Type | The abstract meanings of figurative animals are used to represent gods that give protection to people. | Different bright colors are used with secondary colors being alike colors. | Streamline lines are used to create the realistic mythical style. |

analysis is used to categorize the three design techniques, which are (1) Shape design, (2) Color application and (3) Style formation, in order to understand the differences in the styles of kogi pottery decorations sold in the market. (Table 4)

In terms of the style design of kogi pottery decorations, abstract figures and mythical creatures are transformed into figurative figures. For animals, the existed animals are deified using simple lines for which figurative shapes are used to show the abstract meanings. In terms of colors, similar colors are used to match the bright colors on the decorations to represent the sacred and dignified images. As for style representation, most of the decorations are of realistic style. (Table 5)

In the past, kogi pottery art used to value realistic style. Now, the art is tended to be simplified and emphasizes on the meaning of the product. As for the color, bright colors are used as the main color. Although the overall style has changed, the realistic style is still used to show the meaning of cultural heritage. (Table 6)

**Table 5.** Morphological Analysis on Kogi Pottery Decorations (as revised in the research)

| Item | Content | | |
|------|---------|---|---|
| Picture | | | |
| Type | Shape | Color | Style |
| Description | They are designed using the shapes of auspicious mythical creatures or the shapes that represent the auspicious words. The lines are tended to be simple. | Bright colors are used to conform to the meaning of being auspicious. | With simplified style design and bright colors, realistic style is used to emphasize the meaning of the product. |

**Table 6.** Morphological Analysis on Kogi Pottery Hanging Ornament (as revised in the research)

| Item | Content | | |
|------|---------|---|---|
| Picture | | | |
| Type | Shape | Color | Style |
| Description | The overall element is bionic shape. The lines are simplified to form a new type of kogi pottery art. | The colors are mostly bright to emphasize on the ideas of being auspicious and giving protection. | Realistic style is the overall style. Simple lines are used, which introduces a cute style. |

The colors used in kogi pottery are mostly bright. However, different uses of the kogi pottery art lead to different types of art. In terms of the hanging ornaments, the lines of the sculptures in temples are simplified yet the original images are maintained. With bionic shape, simplified lines and bright colors, the implications of them being auspicious and protective can still be seen while the simple and cute realistic style is created.

**Type of Kogi Pottery Art.** The types of kogi pottery art differ according to the place where it is placed. The style design is used in decoration for which most of them are designed with reference to the sculptures nearby temples. As for the design of the wall decorations, the traditional meaning is maintained which gives a realistic style. In terms of the hanging ornaments, most of them are created using abstract shape and lines yet due to the small size, most of them look cute.

## 4.3    Comparison Analysis on the Meaning of Kogi Pottery Art

In the research, the elements of the application are divided into figure, mythical creature and animal. The representative elements of their uses in temple art and living art are compared and analyzed in terms of their representative meaning. The results are shown in Table 7.

The application elements of kogi pottery art are closely related to the traditional implications. Whether it is the history of the figure, the symbol of the mythical creature or the nature of the animal, all of the symbolic meanings are maintained to let kogi pottery art to be easily accepted by people, which also allow people to believe the function of the art is exactly the meaning represented.

**Table 7.** Comparison analysis on kogi pottery in temple decoration and living art (as revised in the research)

| Element | | Temple Art | Living Art | Comparison Analysis |
|---|---|---|---|---|
| Fig-ure | For-tune, Pros-perity, Lon-gevity | The gods worshipped by the general public, which are taking charges of giving fortune, promoting people to a higher rank and allowing people to live longer. | They have the meaning of lots of fortune, great career promotion and longer life. | With semantic referral, the meanings represented by the elements are the same as the meanings of the words. |
| | Mazu | Worship: with the meaning of having mercy and giving bless. | It has the meaning of giving bless and protection. | While borrowing the image of Mazu having mercy, it is used in daily life and has the implication of giving blessed. |
| | Lord Empe-ror Wen-chang | Worship: with the meaning of intelligence | It has the meaning of praying for good exam results and passing ex-amination. | The meaning of being intelli-gent is applied as to relate to the modern examination system while emphasizing on the meaning of passing examina-tion successfully. |
| Myth ical Crea ture | Dra-gon, Phoe-nix | Ancient mythical creates which have the meaning of providing protection. | Symbols of in-fluential officials | The symbolic meaning of the mythical creatures is used directly for which they represents winners. |
| | Qilin | It has the meaning of auspiciousness and sympa-thy. | It has the meaning of being auspi-cious. | The meaning of the word is the same as the meaning of the word in the ancient times to emphasize on the significance. |

**Table 7.** (*Continued*)

| An-imal | 12 Chi-nese Zodiac ani-mals | In the ancient times, the years were divided into 12 terrestrial branches, for which each of the branch has a representative animal. The nature of the animal is used to give each of them special meanings. | Each animal has its own represent-ative meaning for which all of the animals share the meaning of giving protection. | The representative meaning of the nature of each animal is applied in the design of the art to emphasize on the meaning of giving protection. |
|---|---|---|---|---|
| | Tiger | It has the meaning of giving protection and is also the symbol for dignity and power. | It is the symbol for dignity and power. | The traditional meaning is used directly to add value of collec-tion. |
| | Ele-phant | The word for elephant sounds like auspiciousness in Chinese which gives the meaning of being happy and auspicious. | As elephants drink water with their nose and water is related to good fortune, it gives the meaning of accumulating great fortune. | The meaning of the word comes from the meaning of the word that sounds like elephant and the nature of elephant which give two different mean-ings. |
| | Lion | Most of the lions seen are stone sculptures and sym-bolize power and authority which give protection to the temple. | The images of a lion are used to design sword lion and Fu lion which have the meaning of keeping devils away and bringing good luck. | As the lions are the king of all animals, it has the image of having authority. The meaning of it has transformed from "house guarding" to seeking luck and avoiding calamity. |

## 5     Conclusion

The aim of the research is to discuss the differences between kogi pottery art in tem-ples and kogi pottery art in living art while analyzing the style of kogi pottery art in living art. The information used in the research are collected via international and domestic literature, photo samples shoot by the researcher and photo samples found on the Internet. Through comparison analysis, the differences in the meanings of kogi pottery art in temple and living art are understood. Lastly, with morphological analy-sis, the style of the living art is analyzed and understood. The overall research results can be concluded into three points as follows:

1. New opportunity can be created by introducing cultural creative ideas to the kogi pottery industry, allowing it to transform from a traditional industry to a refined craft industry.
2. Based on the ways of using and the differences in function, there are different types of kogi pottery art, for which the iconic shape is used to illustrate the abstract meaning and create the unique style.
3. The shapes of kogi pottery art are tended to the simplified yet the symbolic mean-ings are maintained to accomplish the goal of cultural heritage.

# References

1. Norris, K.W.: The Morphological Approach to Engineering Design. In: Conference on Design Methods. Pergamon (1963)
2. Kroeber, A.L.: An Anthropologist Looks at History. California a University (1963)
3. Walker, J.A.: Design History and The History of Design, vol. 12. Pluto press, London (1989)
4. Jiang, S.-Y.: Traditional Craft Scope in Taiwan and Research Method. Academic Conference Papers of Theses on Traditional Arts written by Master's and PhD Students Subsidized by National Center for Traditional Arts, p.253 (2005)
5. Jiang, Q.-H.: Diverse Cultures in Taiwan. Wunan Publication, Taipei (2008)
6. Li, Q.-F.: On the Pen Container with Simple Shape Woodcut of Ming and Qing Dynasty. Bulletin of the National Museum of History 2001 40 (2001)
7. Li, C.-Y.: Research on Taiwan Kogi Pottery Art and the Effect on the Development of Local Cultural Industry. Master's Thesis, In-service Master Program of Department of Fine Arts, National Taiwan Normal University (2005)
8. Zhuang, M.-Z., Chen, J.-Z.: Discussion on the Design Style Perception of Eastern and Western Chairs. Industrial Design (87), 35–45 (1994)
9. Hsu, C.-C.: A Study of the Visual Essence and Style in Assessment of Web Design. Master's Thesis, Institute of Applied Arts, National Chiao Tung University, p. 15 (2000)
10. Hsieh, Y.-Z.: The Research of Product Design by Using the Taiwan Kogi Pottery Culture. Unpublished Master's Thesis. Tatung University (2009)
11. Kogi Pottery Exhibition Room, Chiayi City Government (2012)
12. http://www.cabcy.gov.tw/kogi/index.asp

# The Study of Modern Emergency Products under the Direction of New Ergonomics

Jianxin Cheng, Meiyu Zhou, and Junnan Ye

School of Art Design and Media, ECUST
M.BOX 286, NO.130, Meilong Road, Xuhui District, Shanghai 200237, China
cjx.master@gmail.com, zhoutc_2003@163.com,
yejunnan971108@qq.com

**Abstract.** The rapid development of computer and internet technology has led to human beings' society into the era of information, and brought certain influence on the modern design and innovative design. Moreover, product design is now emphasizing on design ideology such as Humanisms, Culture and People-Oriented design. That is products serving for users and all their shapes, function, color, material and structure showing the respect and care for their users, furthermore, they are endeavoring in providing some virtual using experience including Humanities, History, Emotion, Joviality and Security. Recently, natural disasters such like earthquake, snowstorm, fire, typhoon, flood and drought always cost enormous casualties and economic loss. As a result of the government's popularization and promotion of disaster prevention and rising awareness of the meaning of safety, emergency products come up to exist in our daily life. However, emergency indications would send people a sense of fear, which should lower their life quality. New ergonomic, mainly based on researching methods as Physiology, Psychology and Anthropometry etc., and gives prominence to some interdisciplinary subjects, for example, Social Psychology and Economics etc. It is focusing on service system and ergonomic issues. On the topic of disaster emergency design, this paper suggests three researching methods for it: PDCA model, Quantitative Analysis, Semantic Differential. Then how could Emergency Products produce high life quality? The essay records the researching theorization which has been used before. They are based on the people-oriented ideology, through in four phases of the establishment of the design goals (design target selection and judgment), the preliminary design (understanding and analysis of the design goals, design concept engineering), deep design (product detail design) and design confirmation (completion of the design goals) to practice and research.

**Keywords:** Emergency Products, Modern Living Quality, New Ergonomics, Product Service Design.

# 1 Introduction

Thanks to the computer information technology and the rapid development of internet, human beings' society had been led into the era of information, which has also caused great impact on the modern design environment and innovative design ideology. Based on the traditional decor and modern functionalism , product design is

P.L.P. Rau (Ed.): CCD/HCII 2013, Part I, LNCS 8023, pp. 31–40, 2013.
© Springer-Verlag Berlin Heidelberg 2013

emphasizing on design ideology such as Humanism, Culture and People-Oriented design. That is products serving for users and all their shapes, function, color, material and structure showing the respect and care for their users, moreover, they are endeavoring in producing some virtual using experience including Humanities, History, Emotion, Joviality, Safety.

Recently, natural disasters such like earthquake, snowstorm, fire, typhoon, flood and drought always cost enormous casualties and economic losses. As a result of the government's popularization and promotion of disaster-prevention policies and rising awareness toward safety, emergency products come up to exist in our daily life. While, their existing as the emergency indications (Fig. 1) must have sent people a sense of fear, which should affect their life quality.

**Fig. 1.** Emergency Indications

Design comes from life and it should always serve for life. When comes to the design of emergency products, designers need to feel their clients' requirements so as to change the unreasonable elements in design, and make the products reach the rationality of function and structure as well as the harmonious relations of shapes, color and the environment. Thus the real **High Life Quality** experience can be provided to people.

If we describe the industrial age as the **Materialistic Society**, in which value is created from tangible products. Then era of information can be described as **Unmaterialistic Society**, a digital society of information or service where value is created from intangible information. Now we are upon the edge transferring from **Materialistic Society** to **Unmaterialistic Society.** People's emotional requirements are changing from function to behavior and mentality as well. Design's conversion from **Materialistic** to **Unmaterialistic** means after the basic function people are now pursuing **emotion**, an unmaterialistic request. And that is what immaterialized product design exactly is.

# 2     The New Ergonomic Researching Methods of Disaster Emergency Design

Apart from Physiology, Psychology and Anthropometry, the new ergonomic gives prominence to some interdisciplinary subjects, for example, Social Psychology and Economics etc. And it emphasizes   the service system design and ergonomic issues. On the topic of disaster emergency design, here are the main new ergonomic methods I'd like to mention.

## 2.1     PDCA Model

PDCA model was evaluated from the PDCA model improved by American Quality Management Specialist. There are four steps: plan-do-check-act cycle model (Fig. 2). PDCA model is feasible for each emergency product design task. And the P stands for design working Planning, including the confirmation of directions, target and associated activities. The D, means Doing, is the realistic execution of design work and process to realize the design target. The C, indicates design Checking, is to find out the existing issues in design procedure or from the result. Finally A, representing taking action to the design issues, is the judgment to the design check. The successful design experience should be praised and modularization together with standardization that should be popularized. The failure should be summarized to avoid in the next design work. Then, the remaining issues will go to the next PDCA cycle. (Fig. 2)

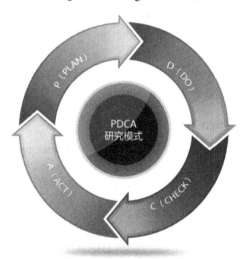

**Fig. 2.** PDCA model

## 2.2     Quantitative Analysis

The innovative activity of design should never leave the analysis towards data and information. Hence quantitative analysis claims its necessity. Associated with Kansei

Engineering, quantitative analysis means using quantified standards to measure things. And that might give people a better knowledge of subjects; therefore people could reveal the nature of things, the development patterns and the relationships between them scientifically. All in all, quantitative analysis focuses on the issues of Quantity, finds out traits and logical relation among all elements and finally computes and analyzes with the mathematical model. Quantitative analysis requires mathematical knowledge. And factor analysis, principal component analysis and cluster analysis are the most common models [5].

### 2.3    Semantic Differential

Semantic differential is one of the most useful means in researching consumers' perception. American Psychologist Charles E. Osgood invents the semantic differential in 1942. The method combines assessment procedure and association to study the psychological image of testers. It was originated from the study towards accompanying sensation. And the accompanying sensation is the feeling of some sense perception while others perception is stimulated. For example, music may transfer us images of mood and color. The SD contains subjects, testers, concepts and measurements. The subjects can be abstract or realistic either. The measurements are pairs of opposite adjectives. And to gain more stable data, it requires at least 30 testers. Osgood raised two adjective-collecting methods, association and documents investigation. The first one is to collect the testers' first impression of the given concept . And the other one is to exact vocabulary concerned about the concept from articles and dictionary. Usually, there come 5 to 7 selecting levels in each evaluation. Then testers are asked to choose, with their perceptual feeling, the level to reflect subjects [5].

## 3      The Design Procedure for Emergency Products under the Instruction of New Ergonomics

### 3.1    Establish the Design Task

The first task of design emergency products always comes up with potential design concept and requirements. At the end of the brain storm, market researching and new ergonomics methods, the final design target and directions would have been determined.

During the period confirming and selecting the design concept and requirements, suitable methods should be used to describe and sum it. To reflect some conceptual questions such as who will be the user of our products? What can they do for people? What issues will be solved? In which way people's life will be changed?

In the first phase in design of emergency products, for instance, we've found by research that many problems occurred in earthquakes hit the city. They vary from the amount and power of earthquakes, the hardship in forecast, the poor prevention, the lack of facilities, the importance of seismic design of building structures, the lack of family-use emergency products such as alarms and emergency kits, the poor connection between emergency products with daily commodities and the fact that girder is stronger than the wall etc. After the refinement stage and brainstorm. A new concept born, it is a concept of self-help shower facility for Earthquake. The target users are family members. When an earthquake occurs, the facility might be capable to provide people with secure space. Thus it solves the dilemma of escape issues and the combination of seismic products with daily commodities. So High living Quality can be achieved.

## 3.2    Preliminary Design

The second phase is to further the design target and direction, using user-oriented ergonomics, in which the design concept and requirements will be translated into design property and standards. And in this period, the perception gap between market, designers and customers are required to be narrowed. Then we can gain some realistic elements by researching users' habits, cognitive characteristics and combining the realistic users' requirements and design concept.

Currently, emergency products design based on ergonomics includes these 3 aspects; 1, Discussing users' feeling and requirements from the view of people's factor and psychology; 2,Finding out the design traits of users' Kansei image in the qualitative and quantitative level; 3, Rebuilding the ergonomic model and man-machine system for emergency products. The specific procedure can be separated into six parts (Fig. 3):

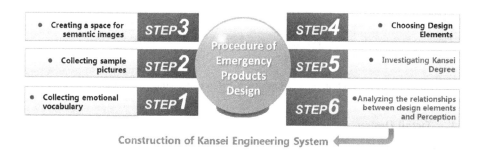

**Fig. 3.** Procedure of Emergency Products Design

Step6, the most time-consuming one, is usually launched in the method like to relative quantitative analysis. At this time, many scholars are using Fuzzy theory, neural network theory and genetic algorithms etc. to do the research.

After the design procedure under Kensai Engineering, design requirements and quantitative result of target can be affirmed, and it is going to be the design traits and standard for the design next phase.

During the qualitative analysis of representative customers, theories such as design consumer psychology, ergonomics, anthropology etc. can be applied to analyze user's requirements and expectations. The researching content mainly includes these points: user groups' features, products functional frame structure, users' task model and psychological model, users' character settings etc. From users' basic status to their potential feelings, all of them can be the study objects.

Fig. 4 illustrates the concept of life guarantee demands different emergency products design requirements in different phase of earthquake.

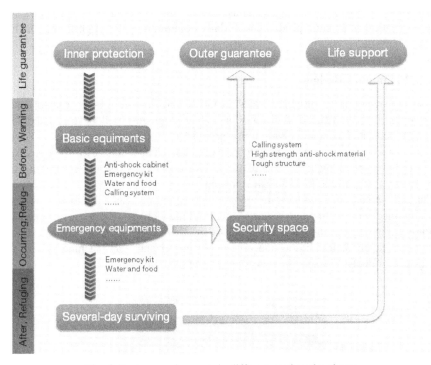

**Fig. 4.** Design requirements in different earthquake phases

### 3.3    Detail Design

The effective design methods and theory above are reliable ways improving design concept into realistic design elements. And designers will make detail design work with specific design elements and definite users' requirements.

In detail design phase, external shapes and function structure comes first. Then modern science  technology is used to analyze and build conceptual models. After the repeated checking scale, ergonomics, manufacturing feasibilities, and material costs, the final scenario will be born. Designers using CAD to render product images and conduct 3D model fabrication. During which the detail, color format, surface process and craft issues will be raised and solved. In the end enormous elaborations and test will be carried out to ensure the final model meets the target visual shapes. (Fig. 5 to 7.)

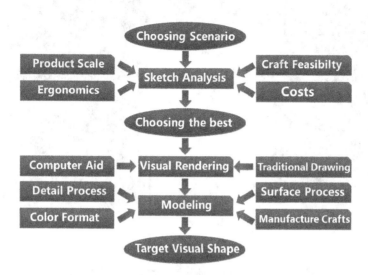

**Fig. 5.** The design procedure for emergency product design under the instruction of new ergonomics

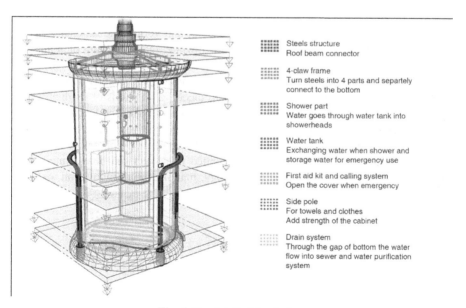

**Fig. 6.** The detail of the design

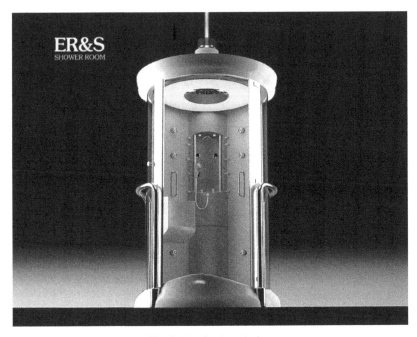

**Fig. 7.** The final rendering

### 3.4    Design Verdict

After the last phase, the models have been tested and edited, which further to perfect the design scenario, manufacture the sample model and verdict the rational relationships between their shapes and functions. Meanwhile, manufacturing plan and initial market strategy have also been made and affirmed.

In this phase consumers' feedback needs to be consulted frequently as well as the detail of shapes are refined elaborately, so as to meet the standards of products property and style. To realize the design target scheduled and make fine feasible working and manufacturing model, detailed instruction and informative manual is necessary, which includes structure, mechanic units, materials selection, color format and crafts concerned. Furthermore, patent should be applied to protect the image intellectual property rights of products function, technology, manufacturing innovation, external shapes and brand image.

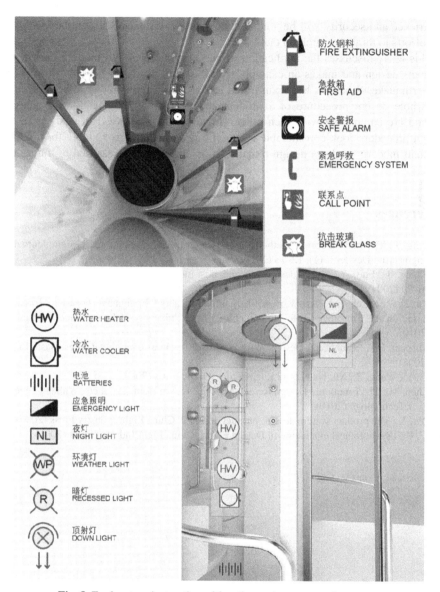

**Fig. 8.** Explanatory instruction of function and power supply system

## 4    Conclusion

With the development of maturity and popularity of modern scientific technology, people's life quality keep rising, so as their requirements in spiritual level of products. The society desires new Kansei forms. Nowadays new ergonomics has become a solid foundation in design development, how to combine the emergency products with daily commodities effectively and finally bring people with High Life Quality experience and security will be a new topic, and our designers and scholars will take any efforts to think, research on that topic.

This essay discusses the application of New Ergonomics into modern emergency products design and makes an example with the concept of self-help shower facility for earthquake. What has been confirmed is that New Ergonomics can be utilized in the whole design procedure of a product and qualitative and quantitative analysis method are compatible with each other. However, the massive data analysis in the design procedure took considerable research time, whether it is suitable for the high efficient modern products design remains to be argued and researched by future designers.

# References

1. Ding, J.: The main theories, methods and research trends of emotional design. Journal of Engineering Design 17(1), 12–18 (2010)
2. Cheng, J., Luo, Y.: Great design era and post-industrial society. Creative Industry (5), 36–39 (2004)
3. Ye, J.: Research and Design of self-help Products about Earthquake Disaster Mitigation Based on the Concept of Life Support. East China University of Science and Technology (2010)
4. Norman, D.A.: Emotional Design: Why We Love (or Hate) Everyday Things. Basic Books (2005)
5. Li, Y., Wang, Z., Xu, N.: Kansei Engineering. Ocean Press (2009)
6. Chen, M.: The Emotional Design Research about Modern Home Products. Wuhan University of Technology (2010)
7. Wu, X.: The product system design: product design 2. China Light Industry Press (2000)
8. Li, B.: Psychological evaluation of Design Effect. China Light Industry Press (2001)

# Designing "Hometown Feeling" Into Products

Chiu-Wei Chien, Si-Jing Chen, and Jun-Liang Chen

Graduate School of Creative Industry Design, National Taiwan University of Arts
Ban Ciao City, Taipei 22058, Taiwan
{chiewei,jing0503,freeimage5361}@gmail.com

**Abstract.** Hometown is always full of childhood memories and energy for life. Hometown, as a subject for cultural and creative products can help novice designers express their feelings. Designers are bound to create unique and attractive cultural and creative products with such outpouring of sentiment of hometown. There are three major categories of design elements that can be developed from hometown as a topic: natural environment, festival and folk arts, and artificial constructions. The study chooses the program which was conducted in the Product Development Course as a case study. This course was scheduled for junior students under the Department of Industrial Design, National United University. This study attempts to discover how the feelings of hometown will impact designers, and how those feelings are embodied in their cultural and creative products. The goal of this study is to provide consumers a type of commodity that combines emotional connections and usefulness in order to present valued cultural and creative products that demonstrate local color and at the same time meet the needs of modern life by way of transforming the meaning and style of cultural elements.

**Keywords:** Feeling of "hometown", cultural and creative product design.

## 1    Introduction

Taiwan has been focused on producing "physical products" (Consumer Electronics for example) in the past when technological techniques were under development. Now we are striving to develop "Cultural Artifacts" in which cultural value is added. As for the future, we should direct our effort to produce "experience products" which promote Taiwanese life styles. [1] Cultural and Creative Industry seemed to be in a blossoming state with government's support/ promotion along with the cooperation of industry, official and academic areas. However, there are enough cultural depth but did not show its rich connotation in current plight of the cultural creativity. It has unlimited creativity in design, but rarely touches people's hearts; it has diversity in product types, but is scarcely accepted by consumers [2]. In academic areas, cultural and creative product design courses have been an important theme within design-related departments. We can detect this phenomenon by the artworks of Young Designers' Exhibition, YODEX. Industrial Design type works have grown in quantity in recent years. (One of factors that judges put emphasis on is cultural quality: works that show the depth of culture, specialty and express the image of Taiwan are highly encouraged.) Based on the data

P.L.P. Rau (Ed.): CCD/HCII 2013, Part I, LNCS 8023, pp. 41–50, 2013.
© Springer-Verlag Berlin Heidelberg 2013

gathered from Young Designers' Exhibition, YODEX website in 2011 and 2012, total registration numbers in 2012 have increased by 29% compared with the number in 2011, 2612 pieces of work in 2011 and 3376 pieces in 2012; among those registration numbers, Product Design genre increased by 4% (1296 pieces increased to 1349), and Industrial Design genre has increased by35% (391 pieces increased to 528 pieces.) From this we can see that craft & art type of cultural creative products is now what students are enthusiastic about. Therefore, determining the theme would be critical when instructing students who are new to the study of cultural creativity product design to accomplish a work that is creative and also arouses a certain degree of feelings within the designer. The theme of "hometown" affects everyone's memory and emotions. In this study, we try to induce strong sensational thoughts in students who lack life experiences and by using diverse design elements we can thus create unique cultural creative products.

## 2    Design Elements of "Hometown"

### 2.1    Affection of Hometown

Take Shiy Der Chin (1934-1981), an important painter in contemporary Taiwan society as an example. When learning Arts at Paris in 1960s, Shiy Der Chin continually found himself in between modern arts and nostalgia. Shiy said: When I was away from my hometown, I was just like a plant rooted in the wrong place. I needed nutrition from my hometown, lived in my own country, felt the lives and emotions of my people. This is from where I created my art sense. Taiwan gives lives and original source to my works that Paris could not [3]. In contemporary culture and literature critics, city is quite an important subject; it is the contrasting idea of the countryside. The former represents the creation of cultivation which implies noise and disturbance, the latter represents the wonderful notion of rural life as simple, natural, and unadulterated[4]. For some artists, the subject of creation is closely tied with their affection for hometown. When Marc Chagall (artist, 1887-1985) was away from his hometown for further development in Paris, he painted his hometown, village, land and animals. Each work demonstrates Chagall's deep memories for his hometown and represents his searching for hometown and memories [5]. Accumulated memory is something that is totally personal and one of a single human's creations that can't be copied or imitated; it is impossible that two people share the same memory. Each structure of memory is utterly individual and also the collection of personal characteristics [6].

Sometimes, the measurement of emotion has something to do with geographic location or environments that indicate some special meanings. By memorizing, recording, writing and daily living activities, people generate subjective notions for the space, and a meaning for a place thus formed and created. It is the accumulation of the interaction between personal life experiences and the environment [7]. Jioufen located in New Taipei City was once a prosperous township of gold mining, and when the gold sources dried up, Jioufen were back to silence. However, Jioufen has its unique geographical landscape. Located within the hills in northeast Taiwan Jioufen village is next to the Mt. Keelung and faces the sea near the coast. The whole little town is located on the hill, so it is famous for its narrow steep stair scene. In 1989, the film "City of Sadness" was released which wakened people's memory of Jioufen. It seems that the prosperous old streets, buildings, mines and the glamorous gold digging days are flashing before our eyes. Jioufen thus became one of the 10 most popular spots in Taiwan. At the same time, Jioufen is also the hometown of the director and playwright of the film "City of Sadness", who has multiple identities as a director, writer and script writer. He is recognized as the greatest storyteller in Taiwan [8]. The geographical landscape of Jioufen surely has greatly influenced people who live there for their rich life experiences. Influence of culture shock of two hometown for immigrants who are usually more than the non-immigrant stronger. Daniel Libeskind (born 1946), an architect of Polish-Jewish descent, was selected to be the master planner for rebuilding the World Trade Center site in New York City. His parents are Holocaust survivors; his family moved to Israel in 1957 and the Libeskinds moved to New York City on one of the last immigrant boats to the United States in 1959. His architectural work is spreading all around the world. In his speech inaugurating the rebuilding of the World Trade Center site, Daniel Libeskind said: "My plan was called 'Memory Foundations': I told them I recalled my memories about our family first arrived here by ship at the Port of New York when I stood in the bottom of the pit, just in the near ocean, at that time I was looking up at the Statue of Liberty, this memory became one of sources of inspiration for my design."Because Daniel Libeskind listens to experiences, his work touches people and arouses wide sympathy, and it demonstrates that there are plenty of feelings within people's heart [9]. that's why he is so   well acknowledged and has won many international competitions. Hometown evokes strong emotions that many people can relate to.

## 2.2    Classification of Hometown Design Elements

The purpose of "hometown" theme applied to cultural and creative products discussed in this study is to promote distinctive features of cities, villages, towns and places in Taiwan. Thus, people can refer to the information on the website of the Tourism Bureau, Republic of China (Taiwan) to see what the features that are worthy of Taiwan promoting are. Features are properly categorized as design material references used for the design project that we discuss in this study. This Feature category provides students with preliminary concepts for cultural and creative product design which also helps them to have a good start. There are 8 subjects on the website of the Tourism Bureau, Republic of China (Taiwan), which are listed as follows: 1. Discover Taiwan: General Information, Climate, Natural Environment, History, Literature and Art, Religion and People 2. Attractions: National Scenic, National Parks, National Forest, Recreation Farms, Hot Spots, Factory Tour and Tourism Towns. 3. Festival: Events Calendar, traditional festivals, Lantern Festival, Religious Activities, Indigenous Ceremonies, Hakka Cultural Activities, Specially industry Activities.4. Tastes of Taiwan: Gourmet Cuisine, Taiwan Snack, Local Product Products.5. Shopping: Metropolitan, Business Circles, Feature Markets, Leading Brands Circles, Souvenir Shops. Others are 6. Travel Suggestions, 7. Accommodations and 8. Getting Around: Transportation Guides. Subjects 6, and 7 are excluded for further analysis as they are pertain only to travel information rather than to physical descriptions of Taiwan. Thus we select subjects 1-5 for analysis as demonstrated in Table 1. In subject 1, general introduction covers 3 perspectives of knowledge including nation history, natural scenery, traditional crafts and festivals. The travel spots listed in Subject 2 introduce natural environmental areas and traditional architectures. Subject 3 includes all of the traditional festivals and a wide varieties of cuisines are listed in Subject 4, food types are divided into nature ingredients like fruits & vegetables and processed foods. As for the Subject 5, it presents metropolitan, modern development and shopping areas that coexist with traditional markets/architecture and foods. Thus we have 3 categories, natural sceneries belongs to 'Natural Environments' with the ecological and environmental concepts,

**Table 1.** The analysis of three design elements of Taiwan features by the Tourism Bureau Taiwan

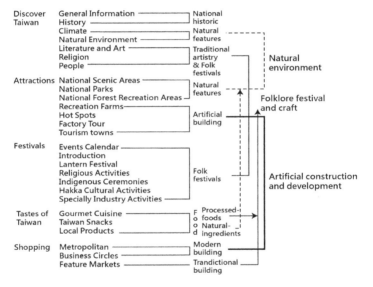

'Traditional Folk Arts & Festivals' and Artificial Construction Development' which refer to modern society construction compare traditional activities and images. Ingredient Foods are under the 'Natural Environments' category since they are products of natural environments, and processed foods thus are under the 'Artistry & Festivals' category. Traditional architecture is protected under modern construction development as historical sites, as a way that we to save traditional culture and therefore it belongs to the 'Artistry & Festivals' category. As demonstrated in Table 1, the design elements of "hometown" are categorized into 3 major types: 1. Natural Environments; 2. Artistry & Festivals and; 3. Artificial Construction Development. These categories are used as the reference for the "hometown" subject design project, in hopes of guiding young designers to create more types of cultural and creative products. We assume that categories: 1. Natural Environments,and 3. Technology permeated and defined modern culture[10], Artificial Construction Development could likely lead to more modern cultural and creative products while 2. Artistry & Festivals should thus bring more traditional elements into the products.

# 3    Case Study

## 3.1    Twelve Design Cases

These twelve cases are from a project called "Cultural and Creative Design," and which used "My Hometown" as the subject matter. The project was conducted as part of a junior-year course named Products Design Development under the Department of Industrial Design, National United University, during 2011. Chosen from 50 works, these cases with total scores are over 80 points were judged superior. According to their different properties, they are divided into three groups. As hometown is the subject matter, the project expects each student to design a product that can present local color, meet with a favorable reception in modern life, and be promoted nationwide or even to the world stage with integration of local landscape, crafts, and culture. As shown in table 2 the works are: group A takes the natural environment as the design element, in table 3 the works are: group B focuses on folk arts, and in table 4 the works are : group C addresses artificial construction.

**Table 2.** The description of Group A. Design elements by the natural environment

|  |  |  |  |
|---|---|---|---|
| A1.Pei-Yu Sung @2011 | A2.Yueh-Hsin Hsu @2011 | A3.Chia-Ju Wan @2011 | A4.Liwun Zeng @2011 |
| Hometown: Keelung Subject: Tofu-rock candlestick | Hometown: Miaoli Subject: Pretty berry | Hometown: Taoyuan Subject: Meet lotus | Hometown: Hsinchu Subject: Chasing wind |
| There is a special tofu rock geology in Keelung Peace Island. The feeling is present in the product between seawater and tofu rock, a kind of interaction between the liquid and solid. The product can be taken home to enjoy the scenery as you can see it on the coast. | The family's source of income is the cultivation of strawberries, so profound feeling with them. The profile and pedicle of a strawberry becomes the product type of shape to create a sweet time for enjoying strawberries. | Lotus is the main economic crop in the agricultural township of Guanyin in Taoyuan county. Tableware links lotus and Guanyin township, and to shows the features of the lotus "out from the mud without being contaminated" | Trumpet-like terrain created Hsinchu wind -a famous city. Designed for LOHAS bicycle lights, the form is trumpet-shaped, the curve of fan blades as the wind, the power of light and music as produced by the wind. |

**Table 3.** The description of Group B. Design elements by folklore festival and craft

| B1.Wen-In Lin @2011 | B2. Shiun-Ling Li@2011 | B3.Ying-Shiou Chen @2011 | B4.Chia-Cheng Liu @2011 |
|---|---|---|---|
| Hometown: Meinong Subject: Meinong's wedding favors | Hometown: Kinmen Subject: Baby Sling of wind-lion-lords | Hometown:Tainan Subject: Gold Lion | Hometown: Chiayi Subject: Lion eye |
| For Hakka people the paper umbrella symbolizes auspicious significance and so the paper umbrella and the wedding accessories combined offer a blessing for happiness for each of the wedding guests. The entire set consists of a spice jar, sauce dish and chopsticks. | There are inner meaning of quell wind and anti-evil and peace within Kinmen Wind-Lion-lords. To design the inner meaning of wind-lion lords into baby sling. When baby has grown up the sling becomes a mother's bag. | There are inner meaning of "festivity and peace" is brought from the lead lion-Gold Lion of song-jiang-troupe of wujhu-lin in Tainan. The letter opener is the object for product design. When we were receiving the letter and the letter was opened, just like to get the message with missing for festivity and peace. | The styling of teapot is according to Koji ceramic of Lion-Eye in Chiayi. The transparent part of teapot is a symbol of Lion-Eye , as well as the hollow eyeball become a tea container. The Lion-Eye can take care the feeling while we are steeping and drinking tea. |

**Table 4.** The description of Group C. Design elements by artificial construction and development

| C1.Wan-Lin Yang@2011 | C2.Yi-Wen Chen@2011 | C3.Yenting Lin @2011 | C4.Mei-Hui Lu@2011 |
|---|---|---|---|
| Hometown: Kaohsiung Subject: Return to harbor | Hometown: Taipei Subject: Happiness of Military Village | Hometown: Kaohsiung Subject: Make your own Kaohsiung memory | Hometown: Taipei Subject: Gathering happiness |
| The starting point is by Kaohsiung. Like a safe haven for the Kaohsiung people, home is a safe haven for everyone. I hope to increase the family close interaction. We go out every day for commuting or going to school as our departure back to port. Putting up the key chain action as we cast off the anchors on dry land. | Sih-Sih South Village is the first military dependents in the capital, Taipei, Taiwan. The stacker of nostalgic picture frame was designed by the image of dwarf room of military dependents, and the material was wood. | The idea of disposable film camera came from container of Kaohsiung harbor, the concept of loading memory was inspired by the appearance of container. Each purchase the disposable film camera is brand new one as the symbol of empty container, after use it just like to load your memory inside. | The design subject is the Taipei Yuanshan children's playground. It is hoped that through this product, based on the elements of the shape and color of playgrounds famous rides that the design - a playable and available memo clip for fun - allows the user to temporarily forget some troubles. |

## 3.2     Classification and Analysis

This part of the study is classified into three main points referring to each designer's hometown and topic:

**1.** There are connections between the type of a designer's urban-rural style and his chosen design elements:

(1) The theme for group A is the natural environment; hence the style of hometown in group A is famous for its regional agricultural products, such as strawberries from Dahu Township in Miaoli County, lotus from Guanyin in Taoyuan County. Counties with special geographical features are also included. For example, the tofu rocks from Keelung (A1), and the wind of Hsinchu county (A4) also belong to this group. (2) The design topic for group B is festival and folk arts. Therefore, the ones chosen in this group are regions which are abundant with traditional and cultural heritages. For instance, Tainan, which has the most first-ranked historical sites (B3), is full of this type of design elements; others like the well-known Winding Lion Gods in Kinmen, traditional oil paper umbrella art in Meinong, Kaohsiung, and lion-eye teapot from Chaiyi, originated from regional festivals. (3) Artificial construction is the subject matter of group C. This group focuses on thriving international metropolises, for example, the two special municipalities, Kaohsiung City (C1, C3) and Taipei City (C2, C4). Obviously, designers who were born and grew up in big cities seem to have more images of and sentiments about modern rather than traditional construction culture.

**2.** Group B, which uses festivals and folk arts as major design element, is the traditional style of cultural and creative products, and is the most popular group among students as well. Beginners who choosing the style of group B have a slight chance to fail, and their design is readily approved. Although the natural environment has existed on this plant earlier than cultures and history, Group B's festival and folk arts is incomparable when it comes to study and application of cultural and creative commodities. Human beings do not treat nature with enough veneration and there is concern for why, to some degree, human care more about things created by themselves than about nature. In group C, designers use artificial construction as the design element, which is also the modern one of the three. To young designers, this group is closer to their lifestyle than the other two groups. Therefore, it turned out to be the type of element least picked by students. Because of two reasons:(1)The existing design cases of group C are less than group A and B, no reference cases are difficult to design to the novice designers.(2)Few students live in metropolis in the National United University. However, many interesting designs emerged in this group because it strikes a chord in the heart of designers the most. This is supposed to be the kind of commodities of culture and creativity with a huge potential market.

**3.** It is the genre of cultural elements of hometown that influences the final style of cultural and creative product design. In this design project, the most emotional cultural elements of hometown are selected and used to design daily necessities that people nowadays would use. So, the two most design elements for this design project that designers all should use are "cultural elements" and "daily necessities", and it is the genre of cultural elements that determine if the final work is in traditional or modern style of commodity. We can say that the selected cultural elements will influence more than the type of daily necessities, which after all are just objects that people would use everyday. Again, the design style determining point is depends on the selected cultural elements of hometown: elements that fit into category 2. 'Artistry & Festivals', elements of category 3. 'Artificial Construction Development," or modern style of design elements that belongs to category 1.'Natural Environments.'

### 3.3      Product Association- Cultural Features Transformed into Product Design Feature Level

Design cases analyzed in 3-2 have mentioned the transformation of cultural images and types. In other words, designers use cultural feature derived elements when creating products. Evaluating what types of products match perfectly with what design element applications is crucial as this also determines if the product is likely to be successful because it influences the final presentation. We might overlook aspects of users' experiences that are important to them[11]. As a consequence, according to Chi-Hsuan Hsu (2004), Rung-Tai Lin, (2005) in the later phase of designing, cultural features transform products in properties and levels and thus provide the criteria for product association. We can refer to 3 cultural levels demonstrated in Fig.1: physical/material, behavioral /social, spiritual/idea. Taking A1 Tofu Rocks Candlestick as the subject, we can analyze the three cultural levels and properties of it in section 3-3. In outer (physical) level, the appearance and texture of Tofu Rocks (blocks of tofu-shaped rocks) belong to the visual level that relates to the shape of the product. For mid (behavior) level, it indicates the function and operation of the product (the crevices between the blocks become the space for candles). This can be viewed as the usability level. For the inner (physiological) level, it tells the story and meaning of the product: the interaction of sea water and tofu rocks, the interaction of liquid and solid material, just like melting liquid wax pouring over the candlestick forms crevices between blocks which resembles the scene of waves lashing Tofu Rocks. This is once again the representation of experiences and memories.

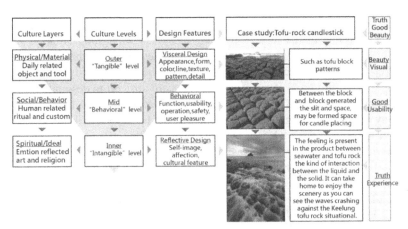

**Fig. 1.** Case study of Tofu-rock candlestick by Attributes of cultural product design (Hsu, 2004; Lin, 2007)

After analyzing the three cultural levels of the cultural elements, how do we decide the most suitable product type to use? Combing cultural materials with design for daily necessities and the physical representation of the product is the final purpose. According to the result that derives from Fig.1, the final phase of this design case analysis is to do "Product Association". As seen in Table5, after determining the cultural layer, cultural level and design features of the product, there comes the "keyword" for the particular level and layer that represent the product best and which most precisely describe the product. We then use this keyword to do further association of that particular product. Brainstorming is a good method for evaluating the three vital levels of cultural products which are: visual beauty, usability good and true representation of experiences/memories. We evaluate all of the criteria of the product to decide if it confirms the beauty, good and trueness principles, and then the most accurate product type would emerge. This also means that the designer has reached the census and design motivation for this certain cultural element and product type.

**Table 5.** Product Association - Cultural characteristics transform into product design features level

| Culture Levels | Culture Layers | Design Features | Key word | Product Association (housewares) | Evaluation | | |
|---|---|---|---|---|---|---|---|
| | | | | | B | G | T |
| Outer "Tangible" level | Such as tofu block patterns | [Beauty] Visual | Massive cutting | Chessboard, puzzles, Collage floors, chocolate, food cutter, palette, makeup plate, jewelry design, tiles | | | |
| | | | Tofu | Quilts, nail files, shelves, racks, modular, racks | | | |
| Mid "Behavioral" level | Between the block and block generated the slit and space, may be formed space for candle placing | [Good] Usability | Pick up Placed Fixed Move | Checkerboard palette, make-up tray, shelves, racks, modular racks | | | |
| Inner "Intangible" level | The feeling is present in the product between seawater and tofu rock the kind of interaction between the liquid and solid. | [Truth] Experience | Interaction between the liquid and solid. | Vases, potted plants, tableware / plate, condiment bottles, cups | | | |
| | | | Liquid→Sold Sold→Liquid | →Ice Box, →Ice cream container | V | V | |
| | | | | →Candlestick | | V | V |
| | | | Liquid→Gas | → Flavor container | V | V | V |
| | | | | | | V | |

# 4    Conclusion

Cultural creative design is facing a new market phase now that consumers are setting higher standards for products, thus exploring for new themes and inspirations would be the solution. In this "hometown" theme cultural and creative product design project we have categorized and analyzed the travel features of Taiwan on the Tourism Bureau, Republic of China (Taiwan) website in order to provide Design major students with diverse references. Then we make designers examine if there are unique cultural properties of their hometown that can touch both them and consumers. In consequence, we can conclude this study with the three points below:

1. Design elements of the natural environment and artificial construction development have higher potentials for further development; it contains fresher and more modern senses, and it might better suit the new generation designers in finding a whole new style of cultural creative product design.
2. Cultural elements should go with practical products and by cultural meaning and types of transformations, consumers are provided with products that have double values; functional products that have emotion connections. This would expand the cultural and creative product markets.
3. Products applied with an inner layer or spiritual type of cultural elements evoke more emotions that designers have towards their hometown, and are easier to present in-depth cultural and creative product design.

# References

1. Lin, R.T., Lin, P.H.: A Study of Integrating Culture and Aesthetics to Promote Cultural and Creative Industries. Journal of National Taiwan College of Arts 5(2), 81–106 (2009)
2. Lin, R.T.: Preface- A Study of Essentiality of Cultural and Creative Industries 16(4) (2011)
3. Shiy, D.J.: The Letters of Shiy Der Chin for Chuang Chia Tsun, version 2. Linking Publishing, Taipei City (1987)
4. Raymond, W.: The country and city. Hogarth Press, London (1993)
5. Lin, L. F.: The Memory of My Hometown Li Fang Lin's Painting Creation, Taipei Municipal University of Education, Graduate Program of Visual Arts, Master's Thesis (2005)
6. Hung, L. (trans.), Rebecca R.: Committed to Memory. Owl Publishing House, Taipei City (2010)
7. Ho, S.H.: Study of Chung Li Han's hometown writings and identity formation process – base on works produced in Chung Li Han's Returning to Hometown Periods. In: 2006 The Conference On Literature for Junior Schalors, 1st edn. National Museum of Taiwan Literature, Taipei city (2007)
8. Wu, N.C.: These People, Those Things. Booklife Publication, Taipei City (2010)
9. Wu, C. H. (trans.), Libeskind, D.: Breaking Ground: Adventures in Life and Architecture. Readingtimes, Taipei City (2006)
10. Thomas, P.H.: Human-Built world. The University of Chicago Press, Chicago (2004)
11. Marc, S.: Human-Centered Design as a Fragile Encounter. Design Issues 28(1), 72–80 (2012)

# Human Factors Design Research with Persona for Kids Furniture in Shanghai Middle-Class Family

Linong Dai[1,2] and Boming Xu[1]

[1] Nanjing Forestry University
No.159 Longpan Rd., Nanjing, P.R. China
[2] Shanghai Jiaotong University,
{Lndai,phdboming}@126.com

**Abstract.** There is a huge market for Chinese kids furniture, which, however, is still designed on the level of traditional Ergonomics. The paper, targeted at Shanghai middle-class family, analyzes the correlation between the needs, purpose, behavior and viewpoints of multi-users, based on the data collected through Ethnography. With many factors such as family structure, environmental factor and educational notion taken into account, it constructs user segmentation of multi-users' kids furniture in terms of persona and accordingly gives suggestions on Human Factors Design of kids furniture.

**Keywords:** Persona, Kids furniture, Middle-class family, User research.

## 1 Introduction

It is reported that there are 300 million children under 16 in China, which accounts for one fourth of the whole population of China. In China the children of 40% families have their own room equipped with kids furniture and 46% families have the desire to buy kids furniture. China's kids furniture trade develops so quickly that it takes only 10 years for its market share to rise from zero to one tenth and so it creates a great opportunity for business and design prospect [1].

Now the human factors design of kids furniture in China is still on the stage of traditional Ergonomics focused on product safety and human body size, and hence cannot show the real complex market in a scientific way. The author of the paper hopes to analyze the research of Human Factors Design of kids furniture and ultimately constructs user segmentation and accordingly gives suggestions on Human Factors Design of China's kids furniture in terms of persona. The data employed for the present research was collected through Ethnography and analyzed through clustering analysis.

Considering such factors as Chinese cultures, purchasing power and the fact that the consumers of brand kids furniture are mainly from big cities, the research takes middle-class families in Shanghai as subjects.

## 2 Methodology and Researching Process

Alan Cooper first formally put forward the method of designing in terms of Persona in 1999. Currently the method is mainly applied in the development field of internet

P.L.P. Rau (Ed.): CCD/HCII 2013, Part I, LNCS 8023, pp. 51–59, 2013.
© Springer-Verlag Berlin Heidelberg 2013

products in China [2]. So far there has been no tentative application of the method in furniture designing field.

This research is divided into three steps: desktop research, ethnographic research and design analysis.

## 2.1 Desktop Research

Now the Human Factors Design of kids furniture in China mainly includes: physical sizes for different ages, safety for children, children's color cognitive ability, furniture decoration, environmental protection and interest, etc. This kind of designing notion results in the serious homogenization of Kids furniture trade. Products are broadly grouped according to different furniture materials, for different ages or genders of children. And this kind of design is just the application of traditional Ergonomics [3].

Many studies, however, have shown that the research into the holistic family environment and the concept of family education of children has been playing a significant role in children's physical and mental development. The psychiatrist K. Menninger (1945) thought: mental health refers to the state in which people can happily adapt to the environment most efficiently and vise versa [4]. The study conducted by Huang Boqing, Hong Junfeng and Xu Qinghong holds that among the environmental factors, home is the main place in which children develop and form their unique character. The crucial few years are spent in the home for the development of children's character and the acquisition of their behavior [5]. And so this generates a need to shift the research into Human Factors Design of kids furniture in China from traditional Ergonomics to the Sociological segmentation of products aimed at different lifestyles and variant educational concepts.

It is reported that the generation structure of Chinese family has changed. 75.2% married grown sons and daughters don't live with their parents in China. Nuclear families (e.g. a family of two generations, that is, father, mother and children) take up the highest proportion while four-generation families merely accounts for 1.9% [6].

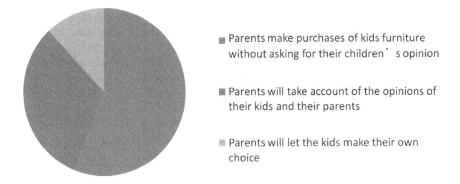

**Fig. 1.** Different families purchase kids furniture in different way

A local survey conducted by the magazine Good Housewives in 2011 reported the findings that more than 46% city middle-class nuclear families have nannies [7]. According to the survey, 56% parents make purchases of kids furniture without asking for their children's opinion and 32% parents will take account of the opinions of their kids and their parents, and 12% parents will let the kids make their own choice in the buying of kids furniture [8].

## 2.2    Ethnographic Research

This research took the eight families as subjects with independent children room, those located in six different districts in Shanghai. The subjects were selected in terms of different ages, careers, and family structures in a comprehensive way. The research required the subjects have a residential space of more than 100 m², in which the independent children's room covers more than 9 m². Meanwhile the yearly income of each family of three people is between 150,000 to 300,000 RMB.

The researcher of the study spent one whole year following up and observing and interviewing the subjects on the spot to learn about their family life. The subjects were invited to take photos of their family life, which should display all the children-related activities and objects in the home, and they were also required to describe the activities in written words. In the meantime, the researcher regularly paid a visit to the families of the subjects, took pictures on the spot, and asked the subjects and their kids to explain the operation process of the written records of their family activities, their attitudes to and opinions about the activities, through which the researcher learned about their way of living and their notions about education.

**Fig. 2.** Photos taken from 8 Shanghai middle-class families

## 2.3    Design Analysis

Through clustering analysis of a multitude of ethnographic research data, the researcher, collecting the advice from designers and furniture market experts, found that such factors as family environment, family members, family relationship, philosophy of life, education concept, who buy the furniture and who will use the furniture are directly correlated with the data of user groups. Based on the desk research data, the researcher extracted four factors which influence the most:

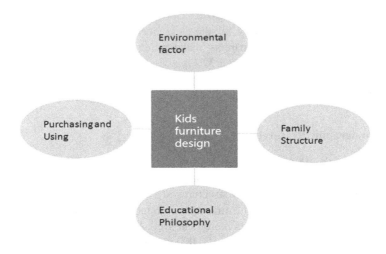

**Fig. 3.** Four factors for kids furniture desgin

**Environmental Factor.** All children, particularly those of low age, widely use the other space of their home with the living room most frequently used while the dining room and the bath room the second. In this sense, the design of kids furniture should be involved in the whole home furnishing design. Family size and which room is picked as the children's room will make the Human Factors Design of kids furniture differently.

**Family Structure.** The number of family members and family relation structure usually determine who will take care of children and how they will educate children. Nuclear families with just father, mother and kids still constitute the main family structure. They can consider living with nannies or grandparents, who will, on their behalf, look after the kids. Even for nuclear families, some families arc taken charge of by both parents, while others by only one of them.

**Educational Philosophy.** More commonly seen are such traditional educational modes as parents hoping their children will have a bright future, a kind mother and a stern father, or grandparents doting. Yet there has been a gradual increase in pursuit of educating in a democratic, more natural and human way.

**Purchasing and Using.** Generally speaking, the proportion of children who are allowed to involve themselves in making a purchase decision is very low. More involvement of children in making a purchase decision, however, will be the future trend as parents get more education and influence from western democratic notions.

# 3    Persona

Real user behavior and opinions were collected through desktop research and ethnographic research. In the stage of design and analysis, the group in charge of creating persona held assimilation meetings at which the research data were processed through clustering analysis. All the data were tagged and categorized in terms of user

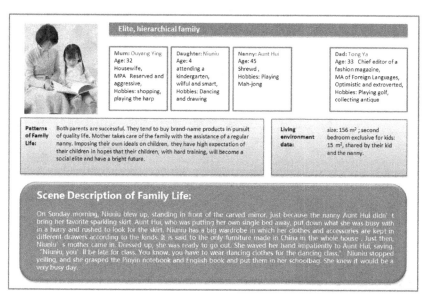

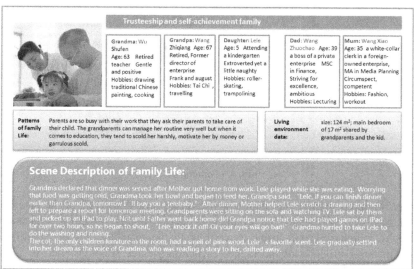

**Fig. 4.** The descriptions of the persona of the four family types

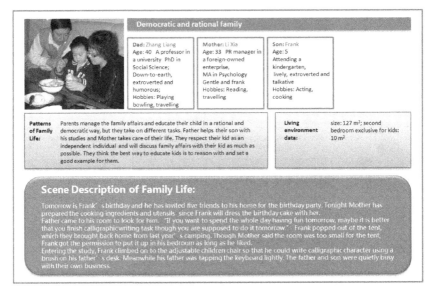

**Democratic and rational family**

**Dad:** Zhang Liang
Age: 40  A professor in a university  PhD in Social Science; Down-to-earth, extroverted and humorous; Hobbies: Playing bowling, travelling

**Mother:** Li Xia
Age: 33  PR manager in a foreign-owned enterprise, MA in Psychology Gentle and frank Hobbies: Reading, travelling

**Son:** Frank
Age: 5
Attending a kindergarten, lively, extroverted and talkative Hobbies: Acting, cooking

**Patterns of Family Life:** Parents manage the family affairs and educate their child in a rational and democratic way, but they take on different tasks. Father helps their son with his studies and Mother takes care of their life. They respect their kid as an independent individual and will discuss family affairs with their kid as much as possible. They think the best way to educate kids is to reason with and set a good example for them.

**Living environment data:** size: 127 m²; second bedroom exclusive for kids: 10 m²

**Scene Description of Family Life:**

Tomorrow is Frank's birthday and he has invited five friends to his home for the birthday party. Tonight Mother has prepared the cooking ingredients and utensils  since Frank will dress the birthday cake with her.
Father came to his room to look for him. "If you want to spend the whole day having fun tomorrow, maybe it is better that you finish calligraphic writing task though you are supposed to do it tomorrow." Frank popped out of the tent, which they brought back home from last year's camping. Though Mother said the room was too small for the tent, Frank got the permission to put it up in his bedroom as long as he liked.
Entering the study, Frank climbed on to the adjustable children chair so that he could write calligraphic character using a brush on his father's desk. Meanwhile his father was tapping the keyboard lightly. The father and son were quietly busy with their own business.

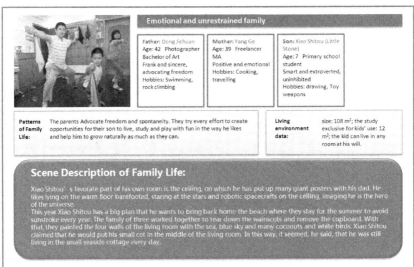

**Emotional and unrestrained family**

**Father:** Dong Jichuan
Age: 42  Photographer Bachelor of Art Frank and sincere, advocating freedom Hobbies: Swimming, rock climbing

**Mother:** Yang Ge
Age: 39  Freelancer MA
Positive and emotional Hobbies: Cooking, travelling

**Son:** Xiao Shitou (Little Stone)
Age: 7  Primary school student Smart and extroverted, uninhibited Hobbies: drawing, Toy weapons

**Patterns of Family Life:** The parents Advocate freedom and spontaneity. They try every effort to create opportunities for their son to live, study and play with fun in the way he likes and help him to grow naturally as much as they can.

**Living environment data:** size: 108 m²; the study exclusive for kids' use: 12 m²; the kid can live in any room at his will.

**Scene Description of Family Life:**

Xiao Shitou's favorite part of his own room is the ceiling, on which he has put up many giant posters with his dad. He likes lying on the warm floor barefooted, staring at the stars and robotic spacecrafts on the ceiling, imaging he is the hero of the universe.
This year Xiao Shitou has a big plan that he wants to bring back home the beach where they stay for the summer to avoid sunstroke every year. The family of three worked together to tear down the wainscots and remove the cupboard. With that, they painted the four walls of the living room with the sea, blue sky and many coconuts and white birds. Xiao Shitou claimed that he would put his small cot in the middle of the living room. In this way, it seemed, he said, that he was still living in the small seaside cottage every day.

**Fig. 4.** (*Continued*)

behavior, opinions, motive and demography. Based on the analysis of the data, four key factors were extracted: environmental factor, family structure, educational philosophy, purchasing and using. According to the matching degree of different factors, the user group with the highest matching degree was classified as a user segmentation with its unique traits retained which are different from those of other user segmentations. The moderation of the persona number considered, four types of family persona were ultimately defined through clustering analysis. Follow-up visits were made and the users were asked to make an evaluation of the defining persona which was then modified accordingly. Persona was established on the above work. There was a need to write stories about the characters in order to create the persona. The writings included the demographic data of each family member, the setting of primary and secondary roles, introduction about accommodation condition, patterns of family life and the outline of values and educational philosophy. The vivid detailed account of the real situations displayed the using of kids furniture and users' attitude towards it. Family persona identified in this way can serve as a mode for user segmentation of sociological and anthropological significance.

The four family personae generated in this research include: elite, hierarchical family, trusteeship and self-achievement family, democratic and rational family, emotional and unrestrained family.

# 4     Design Guidance

In the light of family persona, the Human Factors Design guidance will consider as a whole the factors such as environmental factor, family structure, educational philosophy, purchasing and using, and gives suggestions from the following perspectives: purchasing decision maker of kids furniture, the overall home furnishing features, the essentials of kids furniture designing and provides designing demo pictures.

## 4.1     Kids Furniture Design Guidance for Elite, Hierarchical Family

Children in this kind of family usually have their own room, but the buying and displaying of the furniture are decided on by one of the parents who prefers More classic, vintage and brand-name furniture, highlighting such factors as mental development, hi-tech, health, education and internationalization. The furniture has one function for one piece with a remarkable appearance. The material, with solid wood as the first choice, is selected carefully. Furniture for storage is in a large demand. Kids of low age usually live with a nanny, so the furnishing of children room should include the nanny's furniture.

## 4.2     Kids Furniture Design Guidance for Trusteeship and Self-achievement Family

The grandparents usually live with their grandchildren in the same room. The parents tend to make the choice of furniture for their kids. They pay more attention to function, favoring low-profile style. Adjustable furniture is the most popular, furniture with multi-functions, like solid wood furniture with high cost-effective, are more favored in the market. Adjustable cots are best –selling and second best-selling are adjustable desks. They prefer Simple, rustic and moderate style to hi-tech and new material.

### 4.3    Kids Furniture Design Guidance for Democratic and Rational Family

Parents work together to decide what furniture to buy and they will buy furniture according to their shopping plan, which not only heeds the matching of furniture with the whole family furnishing but also shows respect for the kid's preference. Adult furniture in other rooms is also accessible to kids. The design of this kind of furniture is focused on kids' interests at different age, modular basic function, and the matching of structure and diversifying surface decoration. The decorating style displays eye-catching or fashionable elements for kids, such as hot children TV series or popular children games.

### 4.4    Kids Furniture Design Guidance for Emotional and Unrestrained Family

The family members usually follow their hearts in buying furniture, from adult furniture to kids furniture, which usually do not match each other. Kids in this type of family have the say in buying furniture. The family furnishing displays a blending style without considering the overall uniformity and space functions are unclear. Kids have more freedom to choose where to rest, study or play. So the kids furniture might be moved to anywhere. Remarkable or creative appearances will attract such parents even their functions are similar. As a consequence, kids furniture for this type of family should pay more attention to creativity and imagination, and highlight emotion appeal to kids. And so design for single piece of furniture is more important than for the whole set of furniture. In form design, priority should be given to the elements like representational and interesting image that is liable to catch kids' attention, or abstract with indefinite functions. Solid wood is preferred to other material while structure should be simple, strong and durable yet not delicate.

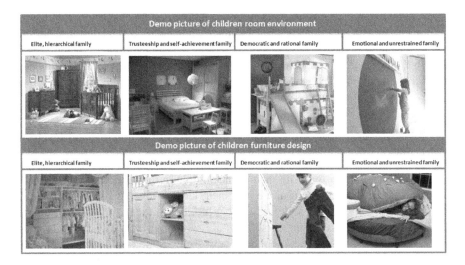

**Fig. 5.** Demo pictures for different Personae

# 5     Conclusion

Traditional Human Factors Design of kids furniture, simply following technological and material change, focuses its main attention on children's physical size and safety. It, as a consequence, gives rise to product homogeneity and fierce market competition. This research, based on ethnographic research, enables designers a full view of the diversity of user groups and the complexity of markets. The user segmentation mode through creating persona allows designers and enterprises to directly perceive users and markets through senses and hence design products with more accuracy. It is also conducive to the strategic positioning of the product purchasing and the way of marketing.

The user data employed for the present research are obtained through ethnography. Though the number of sample cases is limited, more attention has been, in the process of the selection, paid to the integrity and diversity of the data. It makes it possible to obtain quality anthropological and sociological data and hence ensures the building of persona. Meanwhile the research, as a beneficial attempt, will introduce the research methodology of the internet into the traditional business of furniture design and bring new business opportunities for the market competition of kids furniture involved in a price war. With the advent of the information age, further research should be made into users and more cross-field and diversifying studies be done of design to ensure the victory for the enterprise in the future market competition.

# References

1. The Current Market Situation and Development Prospect of Kids furniture (2011), http://www.szfa.com,
   http://wenku.baidu.com/view/dc979b2b915f804d2b16c15c.html
2. Wu, Q., Liu, J.: Persona and Its Application to Design. Design 2, 80–83 (2010)
3. The Survey Report of Kids furniture, Kunming University of Science and Technology (January 13, 2012),
   http://wenku.baidu.com/view/782b3a84d4d8d15abe234e2b.html
4. Mastering the Basics of Physical and Mental Health (August 29, 2012), http://hi.baidu.com/cssxx2008/blog/item/833627fd89b2af40d7887dcb.html
5. Huang, B., Hong, J., Xu, Q.: Temperament Characteristics and Family Environment of Attention Deficit Hyperactivity Disorder Children. Chinese Journal of Clincal Rehabililation (2003)
6. Wang D.: Survey Results Released on the Dynamic Tracking of Chinese Families for 2011, Beijing Daily (2011) (August 6, 2012), http://www.sass.org.cn/familystudy/articleshow.jsp?dinji=634&artid=85939 (August 12, 2012)
7. A Survey Report on the Quality of Chinese Family Life for 2011(2011), http://blog.sina.com.cn/s/blog_49fa3ec30102dvnu.html (October 5, 2011)
8. United Products of Sohu News: A Comprehensive Survey Report on Kids furniture Consumption (2010), http://home.focus.cn/news/2010-09-15/188360.html

# A Study of the Attraction Factors
# of Japanese Pop-Culture by Young People in Taiwan

Chen-hao Fan[1], I-Hsin Fan[2], Huang-Tsun Lu[3], and Su-yao Lee[4]

[1] National Taiwan University of Arts/Taiwan Design Center, Taiwan
[2] National Union University, Taiwan
[3] Taiwan Design Center, Taiwan
{Edward_Fan,harveylu}@tdc.org.tw, magfan@nuu.edu.tw,
suyao@hotmail.com

**Abstract.** "Beauty is the only way to be competitive!" In recent years, due to the energetic efforts that has plunge into the design industry from countries all around the world, the design field in Taiwan is highly valued; through the use of various kinds of designing methods, it is expected that this positive effort of "design" can increase vitality, competition and cultural standard of the Taiwanese life. Therefore, "design" must not only stress the importance of the high quality technology to improve the competitiveness in the design industry, but more important, how to focus on the viewpoint of the industry and the commercial market. Only in this way we can build a true strategy and create strong design energy from the heart. The emotional design of the Japanese goods, compare from consumer goods from all around the world, has always been distinct; furthermore, the same market response also emerged in the Taiwan commercial market. How do the Japanese goods provoke the emotional intention for consumer to purchase? How does it touch our perception neural? How can we truly seize the perceived value of the consumer? Therefore, through the bestseller condition analysis of the Japanese goods, and taking it forward to understand the preference factors of the Taiwan commercial market. Using EGM interviewing sixteen high personal involvements, then employing Quantification theory I to calculate the charm functional of the Japanese goods in Taiwan. The attempt is to seek to reason why Japanese goods became popular in Taiwan. The use of EGM can capture the particular features of the conditions that arouse the two aspects of the purchase intentions: the "top down" abstract value judgment and the "bottom up" concrete condition of the consumer goods, organizing the factors and conditions of the preference and expectations in the Taiwan commercial market. Ultimately to create similar products that extracted the fundamental spirits of the Japanese goods, meanwhile, blending in with the environmental conditions of the Taiwan commercial market; therefore, via the methods of product design to create goods that can conform to the emotional need of the Taiwanese consumer. By this way, we can pursue the success of emotional Taiwanese goods that can deeply touch the heart of the consumers and stimulate the consumption of the product; encouraging consumer to purchase this heart contented good and opening a new business opportunity to companies.

P.L.P. Rau (Ed.): CCD/HCII 2013, Part I, LNCS 8023, pp. 60–69, 2013.
© Springer-Verlag Berlin Heidelberg 2013

This research via the concept of charm engineer, employing the high involvement oral interview data of EGM, furthermore, using KJ Method to convergence categories, understand facts, and complying data. Below are six general aspects which help us know the main charm factors and condition of how Japanese goods attract the Taiwanese consumers: 1. Marketing. 2. Trend: Fashion trend. 3. Profession. 4. Convenience. 5. Comfortable. 6. Abundant.

Therefore, the comprehensive research combined EGM, statistics of Quantification theory I, and charm functional to analyze if user can attain comfort from all aspects or whether if the design is humanized to provide convenience when manipulating; afterwards, based on the theory of consumer cognitive psychology and the six basic conditions of commodities: origin, background, material, technology, craftsman, and quality to sum up this research. Hence, "The most profound emotional value for Taiwanese consumers" concludes to the four conclusions: 1.Feel of Ease and Supreme Quality; 2.Innovation within the Traditional Field and the Spirit of the Craftsman; 3. Leading Technology and Innovation; 4. Social Care

**Keywords:** Japanese Goods , Evaluation Grid Method , KANSEI Engineering.

# 1    Introduction

The research is about how "Japanese products" seize the "heart" of "Taiwanese" consumers. Focus is placed on how Taiwanese consumers recognize Japanese products in general and value them. The research therefore selected interviewees who are potential shoppers with stronger purchase powers, and who are classified as "knowledge-oriented" customers. The interviewees are limited to users highly involved in Japanese products in the Next Generation. For the needs of the interview, the, the samples were required to be tangible "products". There was no restriction about where the products were bought or what kind they were. There was no restriction about the ratio of male and female interviewees either. It was expected by harvesting information extensively and allowing interviewees to talk freely, a critical charm formula can be developed and "heart" values of Japanese products can be identified.

# 2    The Study

Design is not merely place emphasis on the competence to maintain high quality, or enhancing competitiveness, it is also related to the view points of industries and commercial market. This is the only way to strategize powerful "heart" design capacity.

Norman stated in his 2005 thesis "Emotional Design" that consumer are not merely using products, their emotions are profoundly engaged in the activities. As designs receive more and more attention, and the level of demand is higher, it is time for emotional consumption. Consumers do not rely on functional demands only but for their emotional needs as well. Japanese products, i.e. designs carrying unique aesthetic and cultural features, are good examples. As eye-catching and attention demanding as these products are at consumer market, good designs represent quality assurance and satisfaction. Producing a useful "product" is not enough. All details concerning user experience need to be taken into consideration. This is about designing a "product" that creates certain atmosphere, fulfills customer expectation, and provides happiness at different times. Only such designs deserve the dynamics to impress users.

Why are Japanese products so attractive? Why are they so desirable? Why can they produce such sensations? How did their designers perceive values in the mind of customers? What magic is cast on these products? Why do customers feel satisfied and happy through the products in different times? This research attempts to find out the charms of Japanese products and analyze their advantages.

In-depth interviews with highly involved users about their favored elements of their favored Japanese products can provide clues as to popular elements, reasons for popularity, preferred design styles, customer desire, and trends, and these clues can serve as reference to Taiwan's consumer market. Targeting at users highly involved in Japanese products, the research employs more precise and detailed in-depth interviews. It is hoped that from the interviews and subsequent analysis can be inspirational. The design elements that make Japanese product so popular are be integrated into creating new products in Taiwan's consumer market. In the end, it is expected that when products of similar nature are designed, the elements can be applied in fusion with Taiwan's environmental features to create products that fulfill the emotional needs of local consumers and provide happiness. When these designed products are launched, they can be recognized, and desired. Consumers are more willing to purchase these impressive products carrying commercial opportunities.

The research analyzes the reasons for the popularity of Japanese products, and identifies the preferences in Taiwan's consumer market. By applying Evaluation Grid Method, EGM, the research intends to find out why Japanese products are so favored in Taiwan. EGM helps visualize the temptation of these products, so as to provide a clearer understanding of the "metaphysical abstract values and concrete conditions" of each product. By understanding why and how Japanese products attract Taiwanese consumers, the study points out their preferences and expectation. With EGM methodology, the research expects to identify the why Japanese products are attractive to Taiwanese consumers "philosophy-wise" and "function-wise". With the idea of "function prioritizing over philosophy", the intangible "heart" factors of Japanese products in Taiwan are analyzed; abstract charm factors and charm formula were developed into concrete criteria for future application. With the idea of "philosophy prioritizing over function", the research serves as a reference for designers when they are creating new ideas, for importers when they are choosing what to import, for consumers when they are choosing what to purchase.

This research expects to gain an extensive appreciation of the values in the mind of users highly involved with Japanese products. Some restrictions, for instance limited time, financial support and human resources, form challenges to the research. It is expected that future studies may advance the research on the foundation laid by this one. Challenges include:

1. With limited financial and human resources, the researcher only interviewed 16 users highly involved in Japanese products while adopting EGM approach. Other 35 highly involved users take questionnaires. Despite a coherent and reliable conclusion was drawn from quanified calculation, this analysis is based on too small a pool. It is suggested that researchers in the future expand the pool and conduct empirical analysis, which will give their researches more credibility and cogency.

2. The "product" used during in-depth interviews with highly involved users are actual product samples (but some of them could not be easily carried or maintain, for example, an exhibition was held in Odaiba Japan to celebrate the $30^{th}$ anniversary of GUNDAM, a robot. The exhibition could not be brought to the interview so videos and photos were presented to interviewees instead.) Without presenting the products, interviewees may have to rely on their imaginations. With products, there were still some problems because the environmental atmosphere was not completely created for interviewees to perceive. It is suggested that researchers and interviewees return to the site for the atmosphere and the research will be more accurate.

The main purpose of this research is to identify how "Japanese products" seize the "heart" of "Taiwanese" consumers by using EGM, Quantification Theory Type I and theories about emotion engineering. It is expected that more and more researches will be advanced in the future and be based on the charm formula developed in this study.

1. The first phase: literature review and question clarification: Based on literature review, the research clarifies the relations between "heart", "Japanese products" and fashions in Taiwan and Japan; defines the relations between philosophies, functions and cultures; indicates the engineering theories referred to in the research. The engineering theories include "Miryoku Engineering" for understanding recognition and values of consumers, consumer involvement theory, EGM, Quantification Theory Type I, KJ method (affinity diagram). After these information constructed a structure for the research, and a list of in-depth interviewees was confirmed, the research entered the second phase, i.e. evaluation.

2. The second phase: establish hierarchy of values in the mind of consumers: After the phase of clarification, 16 interviewees who are also users highly involved in "Japanese products" are selected for focus group. Based on the original evaluation items from the 32 samples, questions about post-metaphysics (concrete images) and metaphysics (abstract concepts) were asked. Answers were calculated based on EGM, and the points were integrated into key items. KJ method (affinity diagram) was used for classification, and finally Quantification Theory Type I programs were used to develop a charm formula of Japanese products in Taiwan.

3. The third phase: analysis and evaluation based on theories and data: Analysis based on EGM, metaphysical and post-metaphysical factors and Quantification Theory Type I was conducted. Along with the theoretical findings from literature review and engineering theories, research data, a conclusion about the "heart" factors of Japanese product was reached.

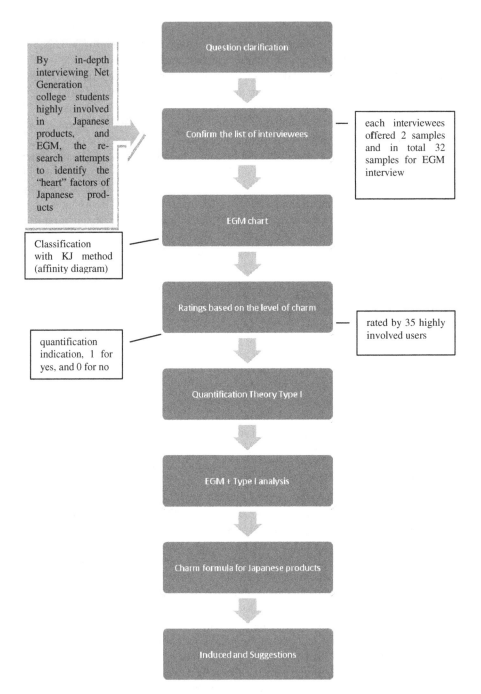

**Fig. 1.** Methodology and Flow Chart

The dissertation surveys the "sensual", "aesthetic", "fashion perceptive" and "emotional" responses to Japanese products of highly involved consumers. Their tangible descriptions are analyzed with EGM, to verify the charm factors of Japanese products to Taiwanese products. At a later stage, the analysis is evaluated and assessed. From user experiences, the "heart" value is derived, and that is the focus of in-depth interviews. The scope of trendy products in the research are based on the definition of fashion as "patterns and styles accepted and embraced by the general public at the time being that are communicative and spreading".

After the questions are clarified, the methodology and framework of the research is built. Among college students, 16 interviewees were selected. Samples provided by these interviewees were analyzed to identify the intangible "heart" factors, for the next phase of spiral in-depth interviews.

The 32 sets of charm factor data collected from 16 interviewees were induced and summarized with KJ method (affinity diagram) and given different ratings according to their charm level to complete an EGM chart. With Quantification Theory Type I, the data was analyzed and used to develop a charm formula for "Japanese products in Taiwan". The formula can be used to assess and rate Japanese products in the future. Based on all quantified data and literature review, conclusions were drawn and suggestions were put forward.

The EGM analysis adopted in the research contributes to clarifying the concrete factors and advantages of "items" and identifying the value and charm. The methodology is often used on researches about Miryoku (Charm) Engineering. "Tangible samples" are used during in-depth interviews and capture key information. Real products and pictures were presented at interviews and visualize the thoughts of interviewees. This approach has be developed and used for over 70 years (Denain, 1989). Scholars and researchers believe that in-depth interviews are more credible than focus group. Several successful cases prove that EGM is an effective and credible research methodology to capture values of products and the perception of consumers. As a critical research methodology for Miryoku (Charm) Engineering, EGM was originated from psychology. It was used to apprehend concepts from individuals, to summarize them into lists, to dig out the profound cognition and perception of consumers, to present the mindset of target consumers more completely and affluently, and to share survey results with other researchers.

The verbal data derived from the concepts of Miryoku (Charm) Engineering and EGM were induced and classified with KJ method (affinity diagram). Information was converged to identify the charm of Japanese products to Taiwanese consumers. They include the following six aspects:

1. Marketing: eye-catching; marketing techniques
2. Fashion: trendy, in vogue
3. Craftmanship: experts, reliability
4. Convenience: handy, user-friendly, and functional
5. Comfort: good for the mind, body and soul
6. Richness: diversified series of products

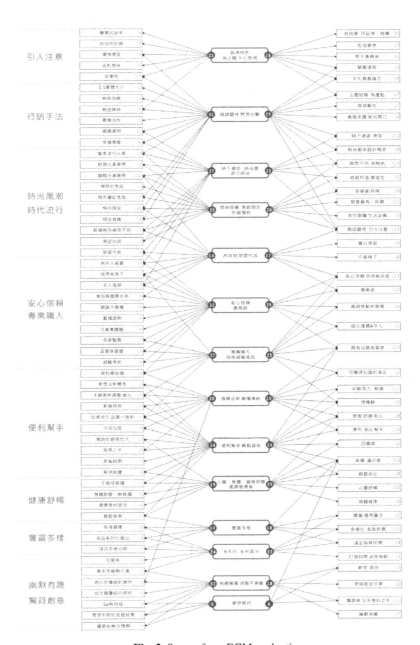

**Fig. 2.** Scores from EGM evaluation

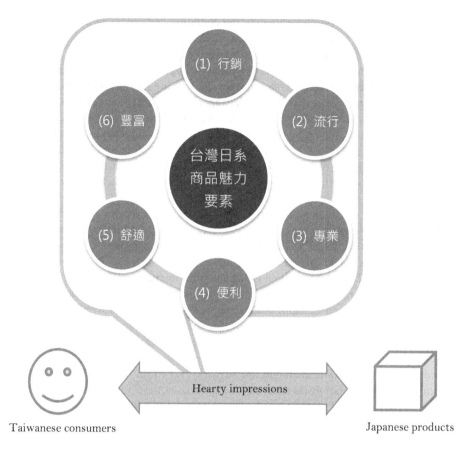

**Fig. 3.** Charm Factors of Japanese products in Taiwan

## 3    Conclusions

Based on the EGM analysis, data derived from Quantification Theory Type I, and information collected from charm formula, and "abstract" philosophical viewpoints and mindsets, in combination with logical and sensible arguments, this Kansei Engineering-oriented research concludes that "the values of Japanese products in Taiwan" are charming for these reasons: (1) feel of ease and supreme quality; (2) innovation within the traditional field and the spirit of the craftsman; (3) leading technology and innovation; (4) social care. These factors are exactly the values, emotions and concerns of consumers.

After this macroscopic research of "heart" values was completed, it is suggested that future research and narrow the scope and deepen discussions. The study offers three suggestions for future researches:

1. The research focused on understanding the cognition and values of consumers for Japanese products in Taiwan by harvesting extensive information from highly involved users and allowing them to talk freely about their "heart" values. This was not limited to one specific Japanese product or category. There was no restriction on the ratio of male and female interviewees. Identifying the "heart" factors of Japanese products in general that attract Taiwanese consumers, the research expects that in the future, more studies can be committed to certain specific Japanese product or subcategories, for example, animation fans, people attracted to Japanese cultures, or people interested in Japanese cuisines. A complete and specific target group for EGM will give subculture studies a clearer focus. In that case, a more profound discussion will lead to a more definite value factor and charm formula for the group.

2. Interviewers and researchers in charge of induction require professional training at a mature level and constant practices. For one: During EGM in-depth interviews, it was observed that not all interviewees have design background, so they have little understanding for EGM, and were somewhat worried. It would be more comforting for researches to brief about EGM and offer instruction. For two: Laddering technique was employed during the interview to capture concepts, concrete post-metaphysical ideas and metaphysical perceptions. This requires repeated practice and exercise as well as a logical mind so that interviewees are less tired after two hours of discussion. This can help maintain the completeness of the information collected.

3. Modern industries and technologies are advanced very fast, so are trendy products from Japan. The same observation can be applied on the "minds" (heart) of consumers. The taste and preference of consumers change with time, new trend and new technologies. The research therefore claims that the consumer cognition for Japanese products in Taiwan, value factors, and charm formula need to adapt at product evaluations based on vogue, trend, presentation techniques at the time being so as to better respond to the values and expectations of consumers.

# References

1. Ahtola, O.T.: Hedonic and Utilitarian Aspects of Consumer Beharivor: An Attitudinal Perspective. Advances in Consumer Research, pp. 7–10 (1985)
2. Brown, A.L., Bransford, J.D., Ferrara, R.A., Campione, J.C.: Learning, remembering, and understanding. In: Flavell, J.H., Markman, E.M. (eds.) Handbook of Child Psychology, 4th edn. Cognitive Development, vol. 3, pp. 77–166. Wiley, New York (1983)
3. Costa, D.L.: Mediating the metacognitive. Educational Leadership 42(3), 57–62 (1984)
4. Dickson, Sawyer: The Price Knowledge and Search of Supermarket Shoppers. Journal of Marketing 42, 42–53 (1990)
5. Norman, D.A.: Emotional Design Why We Love (or Hate) Everyday Things. Perseus Books Group, New York (2005)
6. Drucker, P.F.: The Post-Capitalist World, The Public Interest, p. 89 (1989)
7. Guenter, E.: The historical influences of Creativity and its measurement in American Education: 1950-1985. UMI, Michigan (1985)
8. Guilford, J.P.: Creativity. American Psychologist 5, 444–454 (1950)

9. Hofstede, G.: Culture's Consequences. Sage, Beverly Hills (1980)
10. Howard, E.G.: Art, Mind, and Brain: A Cognitive Approach to Creativity. Basic Books, US (1982)
11. Phau, I., Lo, C.C.: Profiling Fashion Innovators: A Study of Self-Concept, Impulse Buying and Internet Purchase Intent. Journal of Fashion Marketing and Management 8(4), 399–411 (2004)
12. Kaister, P., Tullar, W.: Student Team Projects by Internet. Business Communication Quarterly 63(4), 75–82 (1997)
13. Kotler, P.: Marketing Management, 8th edn. Prentice-Hall International,Inc., New Jersey (1994)
14. Nagamachi, M.: Special Issue-Kansei Engineering:An ergonomic technology for product development. Industrial Ergonomics 15(1) (1995)
15. Rita, D., Folkes, V., Wheat: Consumer's price perception of promoted products. Journal of Retailing 71, 112–115 (1998)
16. Ross, M.: Grand Loyalty-What, Where, How, Much? Harvard Business Review 34 (1974)
17. Kasier, S.B.: The Social Psychology of Clothing-Symbolic Apperances in Context. Macmillan, U.S.A (1989)
18. Sternberg, R.J., et al.: Practical Intelligence in Everyday Life. Cambridge University Press, US (2000)

# Interaction Design Research
# of Home Integrated Ceiling Based on Neo-Ergonomics

Qing Ge[1] and Yin Wang[2]

[1] Hangzhou Vacational & Technical College,
Zhejiang 310018, P.R. China
[2] Zhejiang Sci-Tech University, Zhejiang 310018, P.R. China
{age_qing,bwangyin1973}@126.com

**Abstract.** With the emergence of intelligent home furnishing concept by the Internet and Internet of things, different industry convergence is increasing. As interactive environment products, the furnishing integrated ceiling established on the neo-ergonomics will bring the new psychological experience which make the environmental layout, space function, interpersonal communication, environmental value different from the traditional kitchen plane ceiling. Bandura's "reciprocal determinism" provides theoretical basis for the primary three dimensional interactive design concept in neo-ergonomics. And the environmental factors in interactive innovation will become more and more importance, which make the product innovation work tremendous effect.

**Keywords:** Interaction Design, Neo-ergonomics, Integrated Ceiling.

## 1 Introduction

Integrated ceiling which originated in China is a burgeoning industry. The industry has developed from kitchen top to the whole house top space and wall. At present there are about 800 integrated ceiling production enterprises in China and nearly 1000 brands with the production value of about 20 billion Yuan each year. The Value of integrated ceiling products is to create a comfortable home furnishing environment for users through the overall product module innovation design and terminal home furnishing design. Because of the characteristics of good quality, convenient construction, recyclable use, integrated ceiling products have been included in the "national comfortable housing demonstration project".

With the rapid development and fierce competition of integrated ceiling industry, product innovation design of necessity will change from product styles to the user experience. Interaction is the core of experience. If we has a good interactive products, then it will must bring good user experience. As environmental products, the integrated ceiling must be considered from the whole bedroom environment when we do the interaction design research.

P.L.P. Rau (Ed.): CCD/HCII 2013, Part I, LNCS 8023, pp. 70–75, 2013.
© Springer-Verlag Berlin Heidelberg 2013

## 2     The Theoretical Basis of Neo-Ergonomics — Reciprocal Determinism

American psychologist Bandura has put forward the "reciprocal determinism". He argued " behaviour, human factors, environmental factors were in fact determinants as mutual connection and interaction to generate function ". Bandura criticized behaviourists' environmental determinism, who thought that the behaviour (B) was affected by the environmental stimuli (E) control to the organism and the formula was: B=f (E). He also opposed to humanist personal determinism, who thought that the environment depends on the individual how to produce effect and the formula was: E=f (B). He believed that these were unilateral determinism.

Bandura's theory is unique in the behaviour characteristic, who distinguishes the person's behavior and cognitive factors. Then it pointed out the the role of cognitive factors in determining behaviour. In addition, it considers that the environmental, behavioural, cognitive factors are the mutual decision factors and pays attention to the person's behavior and cognitive factors impacted on the environment to avoid the mechanical environment of behaviourism. [1]

Therefore the interaction design focuses on people. But the main research methods of traditional ergonomics is based on physiology, psychology, anthropometry. Researchers pay more attention to relationships between the interaction of "people - object" in the narrow interaction design study in traditional ergonomics. Because the interaction design study early was in the light of interaction between human and computer, which limited the development of interactive design. And the new ergonomics is different from the traditional and pay more attention to new cross disciplines involved human factors engineering, sociology, anthropology, economics, environmental science and so on, whose concept have new extend and formed new different special research and the corresponding conclusion.

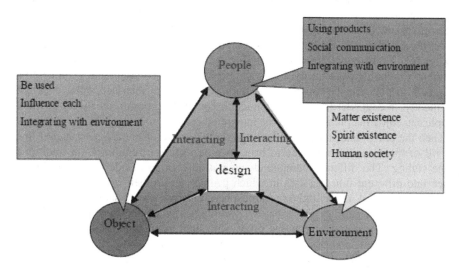

**Fig. 1.** The theory of "Three-in-One", the primary three dimensional interactive design concept

Today much traditional ergonomics research still focuses on digital products between people and network interaction. The study of the environment is only used as an auxiliary element. But the environment's importance can not be ignored as one of the basic elements in the model of "Three-in-One". The three elements human-object-environment constitute the basic design contents and subjects. And the interactive relationship between them and design constitute the theory of "Three-in-One", the primary three dimensional interactive design concept. Thus the object is not just "matter" itself, but also includes the relationship between people and object, between people and people, people and environment, object and object, object and environment, environment and environment as shown in figure 1.

## 3    The Important Basis for Interactive Environment Product Design — Neo-Ergonomics

The relationship between people and environment is the topic never out of date. The neo-ergonomics explores the principles and methods of product interaction through analysing environment psychology. And it researches the relationship between people and the surrounding material and spiritual environment from ecological, culture, language, social, psychological and other aspects in the complex human and environment interactive system. It also follows the principle of interaction research approach; advocates the research principles of real life environment, multiplicity methods selection principle, multiplicity interactive interpretation principles; explores the value of design objects; create new products which make people's psychological needs be reflected in the environment.

Therefore the neo-ergonomics can use some basic theories of psychology methods and concepts to study human activity in the environment and human responses to the environment and feedback to the related product design. It aslo attaches great importance to people's psychological tendency living in the artificial environment and combines environment selection and creation.

As the environment design, the basic focus of integrated ceiling products design always is to make people or families living with them have a good indoor top environment, psychological security, fields and privacy. The neo-ergonomics can help the designers to plan for the top space on purpose, to design interface, color and light pertinently, to engender indoor environment harmony and comfort creatively in which people can enjoy the pleasure from the integrated ceiling products.

Then the compound integration ceilings show a sense of hierarchy, scattered low, get rid of the visually monotone to bring people's sense of emptiness in traditional plane ceiling. The different compound integration ceilings divide the whole indoor space into different function area in which people can do their own things just with the shape, material, color, lighting, atmosphere change. At the same time the compound integration ceilings can created psychologically independent private area to make people gain respect, have free safety with light and function hiding processing so as to create a safe and comfortable indoor environment.

With the emergence of intelligent home furnishing concept in the Internet and Internet of things industry, the integrated ceiling product function will also be affected into the big Internet.

In addition to the basic spatial structure features, the integrated ceiling personalized will must be varied with the development of home furnishing industry integration. And the continuous innovation ,such as more interesting visual experience and boundary functions, will also make the room internal environment becomes more human. So the neo-ergonomics brings us a lot of inspiration in the integrated ceiling product innovation:

**1. The Environment Is an Important Factor to Decide to Design Object**
The environment has a decisive influence to design object. But it can play this role only when the environment and human factors has been combined and activated by appropriate matter". This effect depending on specific analysis is not only before "matter" into the environment, but also after. Designers can find the events' rules surrounding people based on user and environment interaction experience before the "matter" into the environment and foresee the results under some circumstances to adjust the design direction and target. They can gain experience not directly through contacting with "matter" on this ability, but observing through the user's behaviour to adjust their own design and details.

**2. The Interaction between People and Environment Determines the Design Object (Matter)**
People are neither completely passive reaction controlled by environmental; nor completely free entity who can do as one pleases. The Human-object-environment effected the design process and results through the three dimensional interaction process. So it is useful to concern for the environment to the design system construction and self adjustment function and makes the system improve and develop the self reactive capacity when the design object into it.

**3. The Design Direction Is the Interreaction of Three Dimensional Interaction**
The relationships and interactions between environment, human and design object is an interactive decision process. Human factors, object factors and environmental impact generate function by connecting each other's determinants in the design behavior. This process is the interaction between the three's interaction, but not the two or two-way interaction. It is easy to exaggerate the role and ignore other factors and cause conclusion partial barge to discuss alone on one or two elements.

# 4      The Case Analysis of Integrated Ceiling Design

The integrated ceiling innovation based on neo-ergonomics must be as a result of specific design ideas finally. As shown in Figure 2, it is a kind of compound ceiling in the corridor of the bungalow style by innovation design. This design studied the human-object-environment relationship in the corridor based on the neo-ergonomics, so the overall style is simple and generous. The top flower plate embossed forms echoing relationship with the wallpaper patterns and the intermediate strip module can be conveniently replaced by other buckle or appliances. It is easily to mix a variety of home furnishing style by direct and indirect light complementary, dot and surface light combination. The ceiling is very suitable to join at the top near the entrance to solve the smoldering problem by changing shoes or shoe cabinet in a lot of home to keep the indoor air to fresh and lasting.

**Fig. 2.** Compound ceiling in the corridor of the bungalow style

**Fig. 3.** Compound ceiling in the dining room of the new classical style

The restaurant compound ceiling of new classical style shown in figure 3 is a very good work, which thoughtfully considered the human relationship. So the overall effect is neat and elegant, color and buckle design full of tension. The designers well consider the human relations with environment in compound ceiling design of study room in fig 4. The ceiling ,the wall and the ground formed a good corresponding relationship, in which the curly vines pattern with strong artistic atmosphere gave a psychological sense of serenity to users. A large area of dispersed light was used for creating a relaxed atmosphere in which people could read or think very comfortably. And the lamp module design around can play a good role of lighting crafts, antiques and other items.

**Fig. 4.** Compound ceiling in the Study of the bungalow style

## 5    Summary

The living environment is a multilevel large system. As one of the three basic elements (ceiling, ground, wall) in the interior space, the future product competition of integrated ceiling will must be paid attention to the high level of user experience. If we can create living environment to meet people's psychological demand based on the neo-ergonomics in product innovation, the development of products will be more competitive and help enterprises to upgrade the brand to achieve a win-win with customers.

## References

1. Ren, N., Cheng, Y.: Network instruction Interaction Based On Bandura's Interaction Determinism. Modern Educational Technology 1 (2005)
2. Lin, Y., Hu, Z.: Environmental psychology. China Architecture & Building Press, Beijing (2000)
3. Ge, Q., Wang, Y.: The Research on Industrial Design Application in Integrated Ceiling Product Innovation. Advanced Materials Research 421 (2012)

# Some Thoughts on Haptic Aesthetics
# for Design Transmodal Aesthetics

John Kreifeldt

Professor Emeritus of University Tufts University
Medford, MA USA
John.Kreifeldt@tufts.edu

**Abstract.** Designing for total user satisfaction is or should be the goal of human centered product design. However, satisfaction is a complex function of multiple interdependent variables many of which are only recently being explored. Among these are the haptic senses and sensations. Considerable research attention is currently given to them particularly in interface design. However, the existence and role of haptic emotions and aesthetics in product design and their interactions with visual aesthetics and emotions seem to be comparatively overlooked. The proposition is made herein that an object should be so designed that it is as pleasurable to hold and use as it (or its image) is pleasing to look at. Furthermore, it should be so designed that viewing it or its image arouses the appropriate virtual haptic responses. That is, the object should be designed so as to maximize its haptic as well as visual aesthetics and emotions. As an aid to progress in this area, this paper makes the argument for more recognition of the existence of a visual ➔ <u>virtual</u> haptic synesthesia; the evocation of mentally aroused haptic sensations which follow on viewing an object or even its image. Such sensations may lie below the conscious level but still be potent in forming the viewer's total aesthetic and emotional response to an object.

The descriptor "transmodal aesthetic" is used here in postulating a related phenomenon in which a feature or object which affects one sensory aesthetic will influence the aesthetic response of another sense. In the product case for instance, this occurs when an object or feature of it which is pleasing to the haptic senses results in the object (or image of it) being pleasing to the visual sense. This postulates or acknowledges that if the hand finds something pleasant/unpleasant, it will evoke pleasing/displeasing emotions to the eye rather than vice-versa.

Because we are not often consciously aware of the haptic sensations evoked in us by visual stimuli, we must learn to conscientiously attend and respond to them. This will greatly increase our appreciation of art in general and product design in particular.

This paper is a discursive attempt to set out several aspects of fundamental virtual haptics which should be explored in their role of providing haptic pleasure as an important aspect of product design. Several areas for research into haptic aesthetics and their relationship to visual aesthetics particular for products are suggested.

**Keywords:** aesthetics, art, design, haptics, product, sculpture, synesthesia, transaesthetic.

P.L.P. Rau (Ed.): CCD/HCII 2013, Part I, LNCS 8023, pp. 76–85, 2013.
© Springer-Verlag Berlin Heidelberg 2013

# 1    Introduction

"Haptic" is derived from the Greek haptikos, from haptesthai, meaning to touch or grasp. Haptic includes the tactile sensations through skin receptors, kinesthetic and proprioceptive sensations from the muscles and joint receptors. It is the most important sense in that we can live without sight and hearing but without haptic sensations informing our brain of our interior and exterior world and our relation to it, we would perish. We would be unable to do such things as make coordinated movements or feel pain and all that follows from those deficits. Considerable scientific attention is finally being devoted to issues of the haptic senses for interfaces and industrial purposes[1]. However researches into haptic aesthetics for product design appear to be in its infancy. This paper discourses on issues of haptic responses to visual stimuli using as examples, faute de mieux, pictorial stimuli.

We often describe what a product _looks_ like by how we _imagine_ it would _feel_. For example, we commonly describe (at least in English) an object as _looking "heavy"_, or _"hard"_ or _"sharp"_ or _"soft"_ or _"cold"_ or _"sticky"_ or any of a number of fundamental haptic descriptors. But we don't describe how something _feels_ by how it _looks_. We don't say that something _feels_ "red", or "dark", or "high", or such. As will be stated later, it seems that in a general sense, the hand informs the eye rather than vice versa.

Consider this quote discussing a recent textile exhibition: "… finely woven silks in a display so _visually intense_ you could swear you _feel_ the fabrics' _smoothness_ on your _skin_"[2] [italics mine]. The writer is describing her very intense _virtual_ haptic sensation in response solely to visual stimulation.

In fact, there is a powerful urge to touch objects[3]. Gombrich[4] relates that visitors in front of a life-size marble sculpture of a large furry dog generally wanted to stroke it. In fact the custodians had to wash it once a week because so many did. He further says that: "… the stroking gesture may well have been compounded of irony, playfulness, and a secret wish to reassure ourselves that, after all, the dog was only of marble." [This suggests some reasons why people want to touch objects.] Nor are such impulses confined to actual objects. Gombrich further relates the great but controversial art connoisseur and critic Bernard Berenson's account of "ideated sensations" in front of paintings which _stimulated_ his _tactile sense_ and changed the _tonus of his muscles_. [This suggests how an object, in this case a painting, can affect a sensitive observer.] Gombrich also mentions that touching things can serve as a cross-check on hypotheses we may form about an object.

Figure 1 shows a kitten sleeping in a woven basket. In this picture we have the pleasurable though _virtual_ haptic finger sensations as though we were feeling the soft fur of the sleeping kitten as well as running our fingers over the strongly textured basket. Part of the pleasurable sensations, both visual and virtual haptic, lies in the contrast between the wispy, soft, irregular fur of the kitten and the hard, bumpy, regular surface of the basket. These contrasts add to more than the separate virtual sensations. It is not too much to say that we can "feel" the small head and body of the kitten as well.

**Fig. 1.** Kitten in basket

Or consider in Figure 2 the Chinese scroll painting by Dai Jin, the famous the 15<sup>th</sup> century landscape painter. With his art the master artist of such pictorial images can cause the sensitive viewer to experience strong haptic illusions as in the commentary quoted below.

**Fig. 2.** "Returning Home Through the Snow" (c. 1455) by Dai Jin

"In the artist's quick brushstrokes, we *feel* the winter wind whipping his thin robe. As our eye *moves up* to tree branches outlined in snow, to an expanse of empty sky and distant bare mountains, the *chill* of this man's lonely walk engulfs us.  … By contrast, other hanging scrolls feature tiny, anonymous figures that draw us inside the scene. We *climb* the mountain path that stretches before them, *glide* along the twisting river, *brush against* low-hanging branches, *feel* our heart rate slow as we marvel at the scenery."[5] (My Italics to indicate the virtual haptic sensations)

As modern peoples, we have consciously or unconsciously downplayed attention to virtual haptic sensations and the role they play in our aesthetic evaluations of an image or object. *"The aesthetics of non-Western cultures have traditionally been framed within the West in terms of Western categories of visual arts or musicology, with little or no consideration given to the possible aesthetic role of the proximity senses. An instance of this is provided by Navajo sand paintings which have been incorporated into Western museums and aesthetic discourse as objects for the gaze, while for the Navajo their tactile qualities are fundamental*[6].

Nearly blind when old, Edgar Degas (1834 – 1917) commented that "Sculpture is a blind man's art." and relied on his haptic senses of touch to model wax figurines of dancers and horses which were later cast in bronze such as the famous "Little Dancer" in Figure 3.

**Fig. 3.** The Little Dancer (Degas)

The artist Hebborn in deploring the pernicious influence of the rise of photography speaks of "the ancient tactile meaning once attached to line, and understood by our whole anatomy – our physical and subtle bodies – being replaced by a mechanical copying of shape and shadow which speaks only to the eyes."[7]. He also speaks of reproductions of a painting being impossible to convey truly the tactile quality of the handling of a painting depending as it does "on a variety of touch and texture, impasto, scumbling, and glazed transparencies, all of which are painterly qualities."

The phenomenal Taiwanese sculptor/artist Mary Leu[8] can sculpt wood as in Figure 4 so expertly that it not only fools the eye (a 3-D trompe-l'oeil) but it can also give rise to the most powerful virtual haptic sensations as though it were also being felt. Her skill at producing minute texture and the appearance of fabric is astounding. Viewing this picture in Figure 4 of the actual sculpture still produces very strong virtual haptic sensations of the fabric's texture and pliability. Viewing the actual piece in her gallery in Yilan, Taiwan produces not just visual pleasures but also the additional pleasurable virtual haptic sensations of actually lifting and manipulating it.

**Fig. 4.** Carved wood shoe

## 2     Virtual Haptic Synesthesia

Based on the above comments and examples, Figure 5 suggests a *visual* → *(virtual) haptic synesthesia*, i.e., the evocation of virtual haptic sensations triggered by stimulation of the visual sense (but not vice-versa although there may be such cases[9]). The figure illustrates that in viewing the actual object we can consciously attend to otherwise unconscious *virtual* haptic sensations arising from the imagined sensations evoked by the object's textures, hardness, and more which are primary to touch. Other virtual haptic sensations such as size, thickness and thinness can be aligned with the imagined spread of the fingers and finally the virtual haptic sensations of weight, balance and the important but elusive sense of the moment of inertia (MOI) although the latter is unlikely to be accessible virtually in as much as the object's MOI which pertains to the distribution of the mass about some point such as the balance point, center of gravity or point of grasp. MOI is a physical property which like the center of gravity is not visible but is a definite factor in haptic sensations.

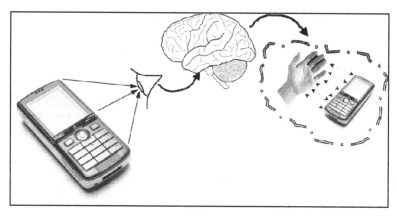

**Fig. 5.** Visual➔Virtual Haptic Synesthesia

However it is possible to imagine actually using familiar objects such as the pieces of tableware in Figure 6[10]. Our long familiarity with such utensils can help assess mentally what they might feel like actually using them. The objects in the set of silverware are visually pleasing to the eye but they are for (and perhaps primarily) functional use as well in which case the haptic sensations arising in use will determine their total pleasing or displeasing aesthetics and user satisfaction. An object may be well designed to please the eye yet still be haptically displeasing in actual use because of poor "feel" in the hand, difficulty in grasp and clumsy manipulation arising from the various shape factors controlling weight, weight distribution, center of gravity and moment of inertia. Whether or not any virtual haptic sensations agree with the <u>actual</u> ones, as well as the degree to which the visual aesthetics are influenced by the virtual and actual haptic sensations are important researchable questions.

**Fig. 6.** Silverware setting

Considerable attention is appropriately paid to the role of texture in design. (This includes two and three dimensional art objects such as in Figures 5.) But designers should be aware that tactile sensitivity as defined by the two point threshold declines fairly severely with increasing age[11]. This however does not likely apply to those virtual haptic sensations, pleasurable or otherwise arising from viewing objects.

Although as illustrated in the examples above we readily form strong virtual haptic sensations from visual images, we are considerably less able to make a mental image of an object from haptic information. This is familiar to those who have played games as children where the objective was to identify an object while blindfolded and so leaving only haptic sensations for that purpose.

Imagine looking at a picture or object. We cannot "take it in" all in one glance. Our field of sharpest vision is a cone about $3^0$ wide. Therefore only that which falls within this cone is imaged sharply on our retina while that which lies outside is less and less sharply imaged as distance from the cone center increases. For example, if we look at an image which is 3 feet away, the spot of sharpest vision is about 2 inches across. So that a painting which is, say, 2' x 3' requires our shifting the 2" diameter vision spot over its surface while our mind builds up an image composed of these many shifted retinal images. For a simple example, look at a word on this page and while staring at it and without shifting your gaze, try to discern what the words are two to the left and right and two lines above and below. At a common reading distance of 18", the sharpest field of view of the $3^0$ cone is about 1" across on the paper.

Similarly, we cannot identify an object by "feel" all at once. We must "feel" it at our fingertips, finger spacing, tactile and thermal properties, etc. Also we assess its static and dynamic properties such as its weight, balance and MOI. Out of this we try to form a mental image as a composition of all this information. However, haptic-to-visual synesthesia is not as direct as visual-to-virtual haptic.

During April, 2012, an illustrative interactive haptic experiment was in place at the Shisanhang Museum in the Bali District of New Taipei City in Taiwan. An object such as the pistol in Figure 7 was hidden from view inside a box into which the hand could be inserted and the object "felt" by moving the fingers over it. Importantly, the object was fixed in place and could not be moved or picked up. For all but the simplest objects I found it very difficult or impossible to identify them. For example, I could not identify a .45 caliber pistol although I have handled handguns many times and this type in particular during my military service and elsewhere. Perhaps the difficulty in identification was because I could not actually pick it up and orient it in my hand, or because the object was fastened in an unfamiliar orientation. This has many interesting aspects. Perhaps if I could have actually picked it up, I would have been able to identify it. Moving my fingers around on it did not help. That is, I could not form a mental image from the partial haptic images although there was no doubt that they were strong. I was able to identify such features as texture on the handle and body, the ring of the trigger guard, sharp projections of hammer and sight, etc., but not the whole. Thus while vision ➔ virtual haptic synesthesia is quite strong, the reverse; haptic ➔ vision seems to be much less strong which is itself an important researchable issue.

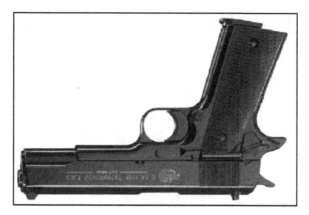

**Fig. 7.** .45 caliber pistol oriented "upside down"

It is a very worthwhile and sensitizing experience to spend some time in a museum in front of sculptures and objects and concentrate on the virtual haptic sensations you receive by mentally running your hands and fingers over their surfaces. (Of course, this can be performed anywhere.) Spend time in front of each object doing this and your enjoyment and appreciation of both the piece and its artist will increase dramatically. You can also do this in front of paintings by "feeling" the rounds and smooths, angles and lines and such and being attuned to the various emotions it evokes.

To the extent our satisfaction with a product depends on how it actually "feels", it is important in design to convey as much as possible its actual feel to the imagination of the viewer. Pleasant virtual haptic sensations as well as pleasing visual appearances could also be very important in a competitive purchase/use environment particularly for objects which cannot be handled prior to purchase.

## 3     Transmodal Aesthetics

I would like to use here the term "transmodal aesthetic" to describe the phenomenon by which one sensory aesthetic may influence the aesthetic response of another sense. I propose that to some extent our aesthetic and emotional response to visual images is based strongly on our actual (or virtual) aesthetic and emotional haptic responses. "The hand tells the eye" means that we learn much of our visual aesthetic/emotional responses from our haptic experiences. And this holds for both virtual and real haptic aesthetic responses. To what extent and under what circumstances this happens is a researchable question.

So, as distinct from <u>visual</u> → <u>(virtual) haptic synesthesia</u> we have <u>haptic aesthetics</u> → <u>visual aesthetics</u>. Instances of the latter are most clearly seen in the cactus-like spiky teapot of Figure 8. Our emotional reaction to this visual image must be based on our virtual haptic sensations which are themselves based on our actual (and usually painful) haptic experiences with sharp points. If we had never encountered sharp points before, it is unlikely that this image would affect our reactions in the disturbing manner it does.

**Fig. 8.** Spiky teapot art object ancoraimparo.org

The image of Meret Oppenheim's "furry cup and spoon" in Figure 9 is a further example of the <u>haptic aesthetics → visual aesthetics</u>.    In looking at this image of an actual object, we receive a strong virtual haptic sensation as though the cup or spoon were actually touching our lips and fingers. To the extent this haptic sensation is unpleasant, so is the visual emotion the image arouses. It is likely that our emotions would be even stronger if viewing the actual object of Figure 9.    If we had never had any haptic experiences with fur, it is again unlikely this image or the object would cause the reactions and emotions they do.

**Fig. 9.** Breakfast in a Fur Teacup. Meret Oppenheim. 1936.

# 4    Research

The preceding discussion mentioned several researchable haptic/vision questions. Others are summarized below in no particular order.

1. How much do the aesthetics of the "look" of an object depend on the <u>mental</u> aesthetics of the "feel" of the object?
2. How much do the aesthetics of the "look" of an object depend on the <u>actual</u> aesthetics of the "feel" of the object?
3. To what extent and under what circumstances is there any relationship between <u>mental</u> and <u>actual</u> aesthetics of feel?
4. To what extent do rankings by visual and haptic aesthetics of <u>similar</u> objects agree?
5. To what extent do rankings by visual and haptic aesthetics of <u>dissimilar</u> objects agree?
6. Are some people more sensitive to haptic aesthetics than others?
7. What are the haptic dimensions of an object?
8. What makes an object "feel good" in the hand?

## 5    Conclusion

Because of the pleasures and displeasures we (can) derive from our haptic senses, both virtual and actual, an object should be designed so as to be as pleasant to hold and use as it is pleasing to look at. Furthermore, it should be so designed that viewing it or its image arouses the appropriate virtual haptic responses. Research into the fundamental essentials of both real and virtual haptic experiences is in its infancy and represents perhaps the last frontier in design.

## References

1. Advances in Haptics (see for example). InTech (April 01, 2010)
2. Wall Street Journal, Leisure and Arts (April 12, 2012)
3. Kreifeldt, J., Lin, R., Chuang, M.-C.: The Importance of "Feel" in Product Design Feel, the Neglected Aesthetic "DO NOT TOUCH". In: Rau, P.L.P. (ed.) Internationalization, Design, HCII 2011. LNCS, vol. 6775, pp. 312–321. Springer, Heidelberg (2011)
4. Gombrich, E.H.: Art and illusion. Princeton University Press (1969)
5. Wall Street Journal, Leisure & Arts. Scroll in the NY Metropolitan Museum of Art (September 17, 2012)
6. Howes, D., Classen, C.: Sounding Sensory Profiles. In: Howes, D. (ed.) The Varieties of Sensory Experience. University of Toronto Press (1991)
7. Hebborn, E.: Drawn to Trouble, p. 80, 45. Random House, NY (1991)
8. Mary Leu Fine Carving Art Gallery, Yilan, Taiwan (2012)
9. Kitahara, I., Nakahara, M., Ohta, Y.: Sensory Properties in Fusion of Visual/Haptic Stimuli Using Mixed Reality. In: Advances in Haptics, April 1. InTech (2010)
10. By kind permission of Prof. Rungtai Lin from his talk: Learning Six Principles of Chinese Characters for Product Design (2006)
11. Stevens, J.C.: Aging and Spatial Acuity of Touch. Journal of Gerontology: Psychological Sciences 47(1), 35–40 (1992)

# RFID-Based Road Guiding Cane System
# for the Visually Impaired

Chen Liao, Pilsung Choe, Tianying Wu, Yue Tong, Chenxu Dai, and Yishuo Liu

Department of Industrial Engineering, Tsinghua University, Beijing, China
mrliao89@gmail.com, pchoe@tsinghua.edu.cn, wty3805@gmail.com,
tongy07@foxmail.com, sun.dai@qq.com, creatovi@gmail.com

**Abstract.** The RFID-based road guiding cane is a navigation system especially designed for the visually impaired. Geographic location, traffic light signals, and business information are saved in a series of RFID labels constructed beneath the sidewalk. With the road guiding cane reading the RFID labels, the visually impaired can locate themselves, be aware of traffic light signals, and find business information near them on the road. After users set the destination, the cane automatically directs the routes for users via voice by specifying the current location and keeping track of previous locations. Compared with the Global Positioning System, the RFID-based road guiding cane system is more reliable, more accurate, cost-saving, and versatile in providing precise location-based services for the visually impaired.

**Keywords:** RFID, visually impaired, road guiding cane, navigation system, Internet of things.

## 1 Introduction

Transportation safety can be a major issue for many people, especially those who are visually challenged. They could find themselves in very dangerous situations once they become lost and fail to receive help. Business information is also of great importance for them. Without knowing the surrounding environment, many people can have trouble finding shops or even a toilet when away from home on the road. Because few location-based services are often provided, the activity of the visually impaired becomes highly restricted.

To reduce these information barriers, an intelligent navigation system has been especially designed for the visually impaired to assist them in road navigation and information acquisition. The RFID application is considered to be very helpful in ensuring transportation safety of the visually impaired as well as helping to enrich their daily lives.

This study first introduces an analysis of interviews we conducted on the visually impaired to learn more about their difficulties in real life. Shortcomings of current sidewalks are summarized with an introduction to RFID technology. Then, the RFID-based road guiding system is presented for the overall system design, the hardware design, and the software design. Discussions and summary conclusions then follow.

P.L.P. Rau (Ed.): CCD/HCII 2013, Part I, LNCS 8023, pp. 86–93, 2013.
© Springer-Verlag Berlin Heidelberg 2013

## 2       Interviews of the Visually Impaired

In December 2011, we conducted interviews with 10 visually-impaired people (8 males, 2 females; ages: 53 to 74) to learn about the transportation difficulties they encounter in real life. Seven were totally blind, and the other three had very low vision. The subjects were interviewed at a social welfare organization called "Hong Dandan" in Beijing China.

In the interview, we investigated the reasons why these individuals want to go outdoors, what they would like to carry with them, places they often went to, behaviors when they walked on the road, vehicles they frequently took, the influence of weather changes, and whether they were always accompanied by other family members. Additional difficulties they encountered in real life were also surveyed.

As identified from the interview, these individuals enjoyed to go to libraries to read Braille books or visit scenic spots to relax. Mobile phones, canes, and drinking cups were evaluated as necessary for them to carry. Besides, all of the subjects preferred to take the bus instead of the subway. They argued that subway transfers as well as the ticket system were too complex for them. Five subjects described their walking on a special sidewalk, while the other five would often walk against the curb of the sidewalk. Weather changes greatly influenced the choices of nine people when going out. Furthermore, only one person regularly ventured out with company. Others reported that they were always without company because they did not want to bother other family members.

Results from the interview shed light on the development of a new cane system. All subjects carried some kind of cane with them and stated it was useful to detect objects and for them to be recognized by other pedestrians. However, they also complained about the poor quality, the expensive price, and the heavy weight of these canes. They expected a cane of higher quality with more functions, and available at an affordable price. Nine subjects expressed their need for a navigation cane, and eight subjects preferred that the cane told them signal changes when they approached traffic lights.

## 3       Improvement of Sidewalks

Globally, the number of people of all ages who are visually impaired is estimated to be 285 million, of whom 39 million are blind [1]. Solving the transportation problems for these visually-impaired people will let them equally participate in social life. Currently, the main measure taken by the government is to build special sidewalks for the blind on the road. With the help of the sidewalk and the cane, the visually impaired can better sense objects in front of them and walk in a straight line or turn at crossroads.

### 3.1    Shortcomings of the Current Sidewalks

The tile of the current sidewalk for the visually impaired has been designed in two patterns - on one, there are four convex strips indicating a straightforward direction; the other tile pattern is 36 convex circles (6×6) to alert the visually impaired to the end of a road, a crossroad, or non-barrier facilities.

However, current sidewalk for the visually impaired has several inherent drawbacks:

- First, it only offers direction-leading and movement-restricting functions, so it cannot provide any location information to users. Thus, the visually impaired often miss their destination even they are on the sidewalk. In addition, visually-impaired people learn nothing about the facilities along the road, such as bus stops, shops, and public restrooms, which keeps them from taking advantage of these essential services;
- Second, the sidewalks can easily have other obstacles that may hurt visually-impaired users without any warnings;
- Finally, the convex part of the tile may trip females who wear high-heeled shoes.

### 3.2    Improvement Using RFID Technology

Radio-frequency identification (RFID) is the use of a wireless non-contact system to transfer data from a tag attached to an object for automatic identification and tracking purposes [2]. Its appearance sheds light on the improvement of the current sidewalk for the visually impaired because it offers several advantages:

- The RFID tag has a globally unique ID that can be used as a marker;
- To discern the RFID tag doesn't require a line of sight like the earlier bar-code technology [3];
- The passive RFID tag doesn't require batteries [4];
- The distance for identification of the tag can be adjusted by modifying the coefficient of the RFID receivers as well as the tag itself [5];
- The RFID tags can be protected by passwords set for content.

Thus, the RFID tag can store unique location information. In addition, as the tag requires little maintenance, it can be constructed beneath the sidewalk and be discerned distantly. As the password can protect it from malicious interpolations, the RFID tag can be both endurable and cost-saving.

In previous studies, the RFID was applied in a robot-assisted indoor navigation system [6, 7]. Kulyukin et al. utilized the RFID in robot-assisted navigation in grocery stores [8]. However, the robot was too big to carry. Apart from these studies, Shiizu et al. developed a white cane system that helped navigate people indoors using a colored navigation line and the RFID tags at turning points [9]. However, if this system was applied outdoors, the stability of the system would be challenged because the colored line could be damaged too easily.

# 4    System Design

## 4.1    System Overview

As shown in Fig. 1, the RFID-based road guiding system has two parts- the RFID tags and the road guiding cane. Location and business information is previously stored in the RFID tags which are later constructed beneath the sidewalk. When a visually-impaired person walks on the special sidewalk, the RFID receiver inside his road guiding cane will identify the RFID tags nearby. After the RFID tags are discerned, that information is transmitted to the embedded system in the cane. According to the type of information recorded, the embedded system will present business information or perform a real-time calculation to give precise direction to the destination. The feedback is given via voice.

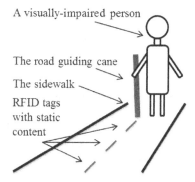

**Fig. 1.** System design under navigation mode

RFID tags with static content are put beneath the sidewalk. RFID tags with dynamic contents are used to indicate the traffic-light signals. As shown in Fig. 2, when the visually impaired person gets close to the traffic lights, the RFID receiver on the cane will identify the RFID tag with dynamic traffic content. The content of this tag is overwritten by an RFID transmitter on the traffic lights with the current signal. Thus, a person can obtain the current light information correctly via his cane.

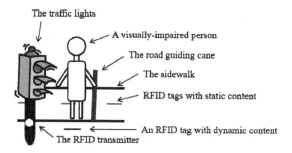

**Fig. 2.** System design under traffic-lights mode

It is often the case that roads are under maintenance and warning signs are placed around the obstacles. However, visually-impaired people cannot see these clearly; thus they are at serious risk. In order to ensure their safety, an RFID tag with obstacle content can be pasted on the warning signs. As shown in Fig.3, when the visually-impaired person approaches a warning sign, the road guiding cane will identify the RFID tag containing the obstacle information. Then, a warning is sent to the person via voice. Because the RFID tag is attached to the warning sign, as soon as the maintenance is over and the sign is removed, there will be no warning tags on the original sidewalk.

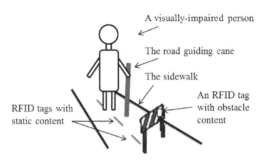

**Fig. 3.** System design under obstacle-detection and business information modes

RFID tags can store not only location, traffic-light signals, and warnings, but also business information. Shops along the route can place their product sales as advertisements into the tag in front of their shops; bus groups can store bus routes inside RFID tags near bus stops; public restrooms can also publish their locations. This extensibility may attract more sponsors to participate in the system construction, either by putting advertisements or other useful information in the RFID tags.

## 4.2    Hardware Design

### RFID Tags

As shown in Fig. 4, each RFID tag contains two data parts. The first part specifies the type of tag- a normal static tag, a dynamic traffic tag, or a warning tag. The second part stores the text used to express the location, business message, or warning information. All content is protected by a password associated with the unique number of the RFID tag. Further, all passwords are kept in a safe database.

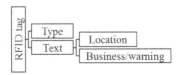

**Fig. 4.** Data storage in the RFID tag

According to users' suggestions in the interview, the distance between two consecutive RFID tags with static content is suggested to be 2 meters. The working frequency of the Ultra-High-Frequency RFID tags would be set at 915MHz to facilitate distant tag reading.

**Road Guiding Cane**

As shown in Fig. 5, the road guiding cane has three parts: Input, computation, and output. Keys were carved with Braille characters on the top of the cane for input. The RFID receiver with an antenna is utilized to identify the RFID tags within a region. All RFID tags form a network in which a single tag is treated as a node. If two nodes are connected to an edge, they become the closest nodes to each other. The map of the network is then stored in the memory. Then, the input is conveyed to the Micro Control Unit (MCU), which identifies the type of tag and calls different treatments. The message is finally outputted by an output trumpet with a power amplifier.

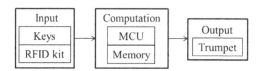

**Fig. 5.** Hardware framework for the road guiding cane

A prototype of the road guiding cane is shown in Fig. 6.

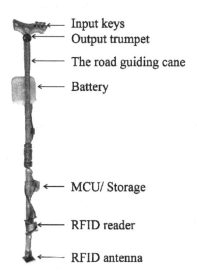

**Fig. 6.** Prototype of the road guiding cane

### 4.3    Software Design

The objective of the algorithm inside the MCU is to treat input information differently based on its type. If traffic-light signals are received, then the output message will be the signals. If warnings of obstacle are detected, then the trumpet outputs a warning message immediately.

As for normal static RFID tags, the aim of the algorithm is to give correct navigation to the destination. After the target is chosen by the user, the algorithm keeps a record of the location discerned. When a new RFID tag is scanned, the shortest path from this node to the final destination is computed using the Dijkstra algorithm [10]. As with previous locations, the current location, and the next optimal location are already determined, it is easy for the system to compute the direction of the next movement. In addition, navigation direction can be determined.

The program has been optimized as a robust design. It is known that when the RFID receiver detects a tag, it will often read it thousands of times in a second. This repetitive reading can be a major interference for the system. To solve this problem, the program reads 20 tags in each round of the algorithm. It then selects the tag with the highest occurrence frequency. We experimented in the process to show very good results in real contexts.

When visually-impaired people walk on the sidewalk, there are three potential circumstances where things can go wrong. The first circumstance is that they walk in the wrong direction and the tag being read is not on the optimal path to the desired destination. In this circumstance, the program will recalculate the optimal path, and navigate correctly with the help of previous locations. The second circumstance is the person misses some tags on the optimal path. In fact, this issue would not disturb the navigation. Hence, the program would not recalculate the optimal path. The third circumstance is when the person walks so slowly that the system reads the same tag multiple times. The system, however, is able to detect repetitive tag reading, so when this happens, repetitive routing will be neglected by the system.

## 5    Discussion and Conclusions

Compared with the Global Positioning System, the RFID-based road guiding cane system is better for the visually impaired in three respects.

First, the system is more accurate at providing location services. As for the GPS, the highest quality signal is reserved for military use, and the signal available for civilian use is intentionally degraded. The precision of civilian GPS is 10 meters (33 ft) [11]. However, the precision of the RFID-based road guiding system could be less than 1 meter (3.3 ft) if the parameters of the RFID receiver and RFID tags are properly set. Moreover, the GPS signal only covers outdoor locations, while the RFID-based system covers both outdoors and indoors if tags are laid at these places.

Second, the RFID-based system has more functions and contains business information that can greatly enhance the life quality of the visually impaired. By applying the RFID-based road guiding system, the visually impaired will not only get needed navigation services, but also acquire business information as well. For example, when a person walks past a shop, he or she will hear it from the cane. Thus, that person is able to "see" the shop just like a person with normal vision. On the other hand, the shop can put advertisements inside the tag and also support the construction of the sidewalk near its shop.

Third, the system costs less and is easy to update. The cost of the UHF RFID tag is less than $0.1 and the road guiding cane is about $100. The system is also easier to update than a GPS is. For the GPS, if new information is added, the whole system must be updated with firmware that might be as large as several gigabytes. However, if new tags are added to the RFID-based system, one only needs to modify the related RFID tags using an RFID writer. The sidewalk also needs no reconstruction since we could modify all tag content instantly via a password.

In this study, we carried out a "user-centered design" for the visually impaired so as to build an RFID-based road guiding system. Location, traffic light signals, and business information are kept in the UHF RFID tags constructed beneath a sidewalk. With a road guiding cane reading these RFID tags, a visually-impaired person can get navigation services, traffic light signals, business information, and warnings for obstacles when walking on that sidewalk. Compared to the use of a GPS, the proposed system has better accuracy and precision, more functions, and a major price advantage. This study should be followed by a field test of the visually impaired using this new system.

## References

1. World Health Organization: New Estimates of Visual Impairment and Blindness (2010), http://www.who.int/blindness/en/
2. Wikipedia: Radio-Frequency Identification (2012), http://en.wikipedia.org/wiki/Rfid
3. Want, R.: An Introduction to RFID Technology. IEEE Pervasive Computing 5(1), 25–33 (2006)
4. Nikitin, P.V., Rao, K.V.S.: Performance Limitations of Passive UHF RFID Systems. In: Proceedings of the IEEE Antennas and Propagation Symposium, pp. 1011–1014 (2006)
5. Dobkin, D.M., Weigand, S.M.: Environmental Effects on RFID Tag Antennas. In: 2005 IEEE MTT-S International Microwave Symposium Digest, pp. 135–138 (2005)
6. Kulyukin, V., Gharpure, C., Nicholson, J., Osborne, G.: Robot-Assisted Wayfinding for the Visually Impaired in Structured Indoor Environments. Autonomous Robots 21(1), 29–41 (2006)
7. Kulyukin, V., Gharpure, C., Nicholson, J., Pavithran, S.: RFID in Robot-Assisted Indoor Navigation for the Visually Impaired. In: Proceedings of Intelligent Robots and Systems 2004, pp. 1979–1984 (2004)
8. Kulyukin, V., Gharpure, C., Nicholson, J.: Robocart: Toward Robot-Assisted Navigation of Grocery Stores by the Visually Impaired. In: Intelligent Robots and Systems 2005, pp. 2845–2850 (2005)
9. Shiizu, Y., Hirahara, Y., Yanashima, K., Magatani, K.: The Development of a White Cane which Navigates the Visually Impaired. In: Engineering in Medicine and Biology Society 2007, pp. 5005–5008 (2007)
10. Dijkstra, E.W.: A Note on Two Problems in Connexion with Graphs. Numerische Mathematik 1(1), 269–271 (1959)
11. Hightower, J., Gaetano, B.: Location Systems for Ubiquitous Computing. Computer 34(8), 57–66 (2001)

# Exploring Local Characteristic Product Analysis from an Emotional Design Perspective

Yu-Ju Lin [1], Wei-Han Chen[1], and Tai-Jui Wang [2]

[1]Graduate School of Creative Industry Design, National Taiwan University of Arts
Ban Ciao City, Taipei 22058, Taiwan
naralin@mail.tcmt.edu.tw, aska199@yahoo.com.tw
[2] Department of Mass Communication, Chinese Culture University
Taipei 11114, Taiwan
tyraywang@gmail.com

**Abstract.** Taiwan's local industries are well-developed; however, over time, various local industries have encountered the problem of transformation. This change has prompted businesses to gradually shift their focus to aesthetics and emotional design when developing new products. Consequently, Taiwan's Ministry of Economic Affairs and small and medium enterprises (SMEs) share the objective of recreating local commercial opportunities to assist in local industry development and promote product innovation regarding Taiwan's local characteristic industries. The following topics are worthy of further investigation: (1) whether products' added cultural value can elicit consumer acknowledgement and generate deep emotional impressions; (2) whether a correlation exists between the emotional perception of these cultural products and cultural elements; and (3) whether new values can be created using an interdisciplinary collaborative model of local characteristic industries and industry optimization transformation. Considering globalized competition, designers should seek the essence of originality from their own culture and establish a unique cultural distinction for local characteristic products to improve the product design value and competitiveness. Based on data analysis and a literature review, this study analyzed the development of an integrated relationship between Taiwan's local characteristics and design industries. Data from relevant analyses indicated the following: (1) Localized life and cultural characteristics and local spirit can sufficiently influence the innovation of local characteristic products; (2) successful local characteristic products must satisfy three levels of emotional design, namely, the visceral, behavioral, and reflective levels; and (3) integration of local characteristic industries and the experience economy concept requires an interdisciplinary exchange platform to stimulate industry innovation and drive emerging industries.

**Keywords:** local characteristic industry, emotional design, cultural product, interdisciplinary.

## 1 Introduction

Driven by globalization and technologization, the twenty-first century features highly competitive markets that have prompted nations throughout the world to shift their

P.L.P. Rau (Ed.): CCD/HCII 2013, Part I, LNCS 8023, pp. 94–103, 2013.
© Springer-Verlag Berlin Heidelberg 2013

economic focus to a culturally centered industry orientation. Subsequently, innovation and creativity have become the foundations of industry development. A country's prosperity is fundamentally determined by whether it possesses superior innovative mechanisms and abilities, and whether it can obtain an advantage in international competition. The primary role of government is to improve the production environment to stimulate business upgrades and innovations [1]. In 2002, the Executive Yuan in Taiwan began promoting the Challenge 2008: Six-Year National Development Plan as the most important current domestic policy. This plan included the Cultural and Creative Industry Development Plan, which incorporates the One Town One Product (OTOP) policy and generated emerging industry concepts, such as tourism and creative living, to form a more substantial and sustainable economy [2]. Local characteristic industries warrant considerable attention because the majority of people employed in local traditional industries are residents of rural villages, particularly in the Asia-Pacific region. Therefore, enhancing the development of local cultural industries is extremely significant for maintaining economic stability and promoting sustainable development. Relevant knowledge and skills must be transferred to manufacturers, and the value and cultural significance of products must be conveyed to potential consumers [3]. The primary topics discussed were as follows: (1) the correlation between local characteristic industries and cultural products; (2) the relevance of cultural products regarding the mode of emotional experience design; and (3) the correlation between local characteristic industries and design in interdisciplinary collaboration.

## 2    Literature Review

### 2.1    Design of Cultural Products with Local Characteristics

Local characteristic industries include industries unique to a region and traditional industries that exhibit individualism and excellent characteristics after repackaging [4]. Cultural product designs target local characteristics to re-examine and reconsider relevant cultural elements, employ creative designs, and emphasize cultural identity to present cultural elements with a new appearance and explore users' psychological satisfaction [5]. Consequently, the relationship between the designer, consumer, and product is further defined on a cultural level, particularly emphasizing the mutual effects of culture and products. Cultural product designs do not only originate from the designers' knowledge and imagination, but also from the designers' understanding of consumer lifestyles and the influence of a product's cultural background. In addition to embodying traditions and symbolism, culture plays an active role through commercialized creativity [6]. With culture as a medium, local characteristic products provide satisfaction to consumers on both functional and psychological levels. Finally, designers project their personal experiential affect onto products by illustrating cultural perceptions that resonate with consumers and satisfy their affective needs (Fig. 1).

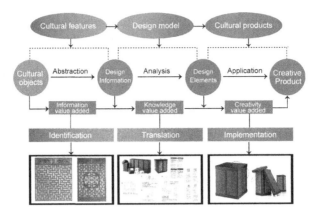

**Fig. 1.** Mode of value added through cultural creativity (Lin, 2007)

## 2.2    Emotional Design of Local Characteristic Products

Considering the development trends and effects of a globalized economy, designs have gradually exhibited a consistent and international style that corresponds to the increasing similarity of lifestyles despite environmental variations. However, without individual characteristics, these designs cannot reflect regional cultural characteristics [7]. Various countries throughout the world have begun developing design styles that accentuate their personal cultural characteristics; this has resulted in design variations that highlight the current globalized design trend of seeking differences within commonality. This trend entails enhanced shaping of characteristics through design localization to address the current challenges of market globalization. Furthermore, greater emphasis is placed on adding value to products through design to transfer key elements, such as brand culture and value [8]. Norman identified another crucial factor for products besides function, that is, emotion. Emotional design comprises the following three levels: visceral (the external appearance and texture of products), behavioral (product function), and reflective (individual feelings and perceptions) levels. Thus, emotional design is crucial for future developments in the design and service industries, which increasingly emphasize customization and interactive design to accommodate the design principles of different levels [9]. According to the above

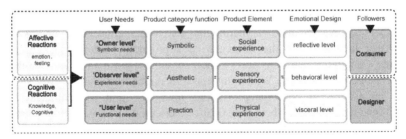

**Fig. 2.** The five dimensions of affective and cognitive reactions (Source: data compiled in this study, 2012)

discourse, which is summarized in Fig. 2, the emotional perception of local characteristic products reflects the mutual effects of the affective and cognitive reactions produced by the designer and consumer through the five dimensions of user needs, product function, product element, emotional design, and followers.

### 2.3    Local Characteristic Industries and Interdisciplinary Design Collaborative Models

Globally, industry development has shifted from the previous unitary manufacturing pattern to comprehensive experience economies. Similarly, Taiwan's economic activities have switched from traditional agriculture to business and services. With rapid industry and community changes, local characteristic industries have adopted diverse and comprehensive development directions [10]. Interdisciplinary resource collaboration for local characteristic industries endeavors to increase the design service capacity and expand the application dimension of design aesthetics. The incorporation and cooperation of different industry disciplines can generate innovative creative elements (Fig. 3). Using interdisciplinary collaboration to resolve financial and aesthetic issues through design requires the participation and cooperation of interdisciplinary qualified design professionals. Thus, innovative local characteristic development can be achieved, stimulating the clustering of design service activities and facilitating the development of local characteristic industries [11].

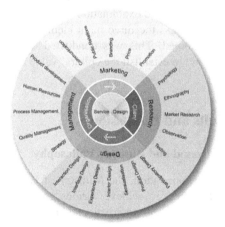

**Fig. 3.** Service design requires an interdisciplinary collaborative team and collaborative creation methods

## 3    Research Methods

This study primarily employed a literature review and content analysis methods to conduct an investigation. The primary topics discussed were as follows: (1) the correlation between local characteristic industries and cultural products; (2) the relevance of cultural products regarding the mode of emotional experience design;

and (3) the connection between local characteristic industries and design in interdisciplinary collaboration. This study was conducted in four phases, which are briefly described below.

- Phase 1: Based on related literature and using the Taiwan OTOP Design Awards as a case study, the business philosophy and development of this project was examined and analyzed. In addition, this phase targeted the background development of the Taiwan OTOP, assessing and tabulating the differences compared to that of other countries.
- Phase 2: In this phase, 26 winning entries in the product packaging design category of the Taiwan OTOP Design Awards from 2007 to 2012 were analyzed. Specifically, the visual design elements of each entry were examined regarding cultural significance, cultural characteristics, and the correlation between brand culture and local industries.
- Phase 3: From the perspectives of design material, function, and connotations, analysis was conducted using the degree of cultural perception regarding the local characteristic products of the case study. The analysis results were then matched to the three levels of emotional design (i.e., visceral, behavioral, and reflective levels).
- Phase 4: The local characteristic industry development model of the Taiwan OTOP project was investigated using the content analysis method. Four design companies were targeted to conduct analysis regarding interdisciplinary collaboration with traditional industries. An integrated examination was performed after the local characteristic products that possess the three main elements of emotional design for each company were combined. This was conducted to identify the essence of Taiwan's local cultures and to establish the cultural value and connotations of local characteristic industries.

## 4    Research Results and Discussion

### 4.1    Case Study Background and Business Philosophy

With local industries as the foundation, the Ministry of Economic Affairs has promoted the Taiwan OTOP project to achieve various goals, such as establishing an innovative economy, encouraging consumerism, and building a lifestyle of health and sustainability (LOHAS). Consequently, the policy objectives of revitalizing and promoting local economies and employment can be accomplished.

**Table 1.** Various global representatives promoting the OTOP/OVOP (One Village One Product) movement each year

| Country | Japan(OVOP) | Taiwan(OTOP) | Malaysia(SDSI) | Thailand(OTOP) | Malawi(OVOP) | Philippines(OTOP) | Indonesia(OVOP) | Peru(OVOP) | Senegal(OVOP) | Kenya(OVOP) |
|---------|-------------|--------------|----------------|----------------|--------------|-------------------|-----------------|------------|---------------|-------------|
| Age | 1979 | 1989 | 1992 | 1997 | 2003 | 2004 | 2004 | 2010 | 2011 | 2011 |
| Logo | | | | | | | | | | |

This global chronology shows that the OTOP movement, which originated in Asia, has spread to most countries throughout the world. This movement has attracted the attention of industries and markets and is the primary development policy of several governments worldwide, thereby achieving globalization. Table 1 shows that Taiwan began considering and promoting local characteristic policies fairly early; however, Taiwan's local cultural industries continue to experience subsistence difficulties. Further investigation of local industry attributes and maturity is required to effectively address the inadequate depth and scope of local characteristic industries and provide assistance accordingly.

### 4.2    Visual Design Elements of Local Characteristic Products

This study sampled and tabulated 26 winning entries in the product packaging design category of the Taiwan OTOP Design Awards for 2007 to 2012. In this study, four commonly examined visual design elements (i.e., text, imagery, structural shapes, and materials) were summarized and analyzed. The results, as presented in Fig. 4, show that the majority of the designers used structural shapes complemented with storytelling to strengthen the link between the cultural characteristics and the product. The second most commonly employed design element was the inclusion of Chinese characters that expressed the essence of the work and demonstrated the integration of a unique local cultural spirit.

**Fig. 4.** Visual design element analysis of the entries winning Taiwan OTOP Design Awards

### 4.3    Analyzing Local Characteristic Products through Emotional Design

This study conducted a three-level emotional design analysis of the 26 winning entries in the product packaging design category of the Taiwan OTOP Design Awards. Visceral design refers to the product's external appearance, form, and texture. The visceral level is users' first impression of the product appearance; thus, functional design has a direct effect on the affect and resonates with the viewer.    Attraction is a visceral-level phenomenon, a reaction to the object's appearance [12]. This study analyzed the texture and material dimensions of local characteristic products, which were defined by the extrinsic cultural attributes of visceral design. The classification of general and local materials shown in Fig. 5 indicates that most (19) of the 26 designers used general materials, and seven used local materials.

**Fig. 5.** Visceral design analysis of local characteristic products

Typically, behavioral design is directly correlated to usage and comprises functionality, comprehensibility, ease of use, and physical sensation. Among these, functionality is considered the most crucial on the behavioral level regarding product experience [13]. The behavioral design of local characteristic products emphasizes functional significance. At this level, designers strive for a supplementary function that enables users to experience Taiwan's unique cultural atmosphere when using the product. This study conducted behavioral design analysis of the functional dimension of local characteristic product packaging designs. As shown in Fig. 6, a classification of single-function and multi-function designs shows that most (22) of the designs were single-function, although four were multi-function.

**Fig. 6.** Behavioral design analysis of local characteristic products

Reflective design focuses on the meaning of the message, culture, and product. Awareness, feelings, emotions, and perceptions exist only on the reflective level, which easily varies according to differences in culture, experience, education, and among people. Design on the reflective level can induce strong and continuous effects in users that typically requires a reaction and time to develop [14]. The reflective design of local characteristic products emphasizes memories and individual perceptions and cognition. At this level, designers endeavor to create a memorable and shareable story for users. A classification of the natural landscape and historical human elements indicates that either of these two elements accounted for 50% of the entries (Fig. 7).

**Fig. 7.** Reflective design analysis of local characteristic products

According to the results of the three-level emotional design analysis of cultural products examining the visceral, behavioral, and reflective levels (Figs. 6 to 8), this study differentiated the variations by quantity and concluded the following: (1) From a visceral design perspective, the number of local characteristic products that used general packaging materials more than doubled the number of products that used local characteristic materials; (2) from a behavioral design perspective, the number of single-function winning entries exceeded the number of multi-function winning entries; and (3) from a reflective design perspective, the difference between the number of culture-themed designs that used the natural landscape and the designs that used historical humanity was minimal.

## 4.4    Interdisciplinary Collaboration Analysis of Local Characteristic Industries

Taiwan OTOP project recommended collaboration by combining differing industries and pathways and using these cooperative relationships to design products with developable value. The results of the survey are summarized as follows: (1) Applying design to create value: transform cultural products, preliminary products, services, and experiences into optimal products or services acceptable to consumers, and promote the value perception of design throughout industries and society to    enhance the overall quality of life and the environment. (2) Using creative ideas for design: revitalize traditional products by combining the creative ideas of local characteristic business owners and design professionals, applying local characteristics, and adopting Taiwan's native local materials. (3) Effectively employing innovative technologies for design: Use the advantage of industry clusters and improve technological innovation to prompt the development of traditional industry values, establish interdisciplinary design exchanges, and enhance domestic design development and competitiveness.

**Table 2.** Case study of interdisciplinary design collaborative models for cultural products

| Name | Design Concept | Design in Interdisciplinary Collaboration | Product |
|---|---|---|---|
| Discover Formosa, Let's Enjoy A Cup of Tea Together! | The concept of displaying professional images on postage stamps is used here to express feelings of love for Taiwan. Illustrations are used to distinguish the four steps that convey the careful manu-facturing of tea: picking the leaves; drying them in the sun; kneading the leaves; and baking the leaves. Three mouth characters (口) put together form the word for product (品), the meaning of which is to view the colors, smell the aroma, taste the flavor and experience the wisdom of this tea product. | Award Winner \| Magic Creative Advertising Cooperative Unit \| Cha-Tei Ltd. | |
| The Xiang Xi Lin Men | The Xiang Xi Lin Men gift box design fuses the festive elements that represent the red double happiness character together with rice cookies to form a 3-D gift box in the shape of the double hap-piness character (囍). pairing every flavor of miniature rice cookies with traditional Taiwanese joyous celebra-tions in a reinterpretation of festival culture. | Award Winner \| Chuan-Li Rice Cookie Food Ltd. Cooperative Unit \| Arty Design | |
| ChaTei-Joyful Series Tea Gift Box | Attentive Attitude of ChaTei, Flavor, Taste and Aroma of Freshly Finished. As the homonym of Taiwanese "Drink tea", "ChaTei" means genial greetings and serving tea that embodies the Tai-wanese locals' passion and sincerity just as teapot keeps tea warm at the perfect temperature. | Award Winner \| Cha-Tei Ltd. Cooperative Unit \| Magic Creative Advertising | |
| Emotion in Every Grain | This gift box contains Camellia oil and vermicelli full of Hakka characteristics, as its box can serve as the tissue box and the opening of the box is the place where the handkerchief was kept in Hakka blue shirt. The way to draw out the tissue is like that to draw out the handkerchief from the blue shirt. | Award Winner \| Chuan-Li Rice Cookie Food Ltd. Cooperative Unit \| 20/20 Creative Co. Ltd. | |

# 5     Conclusion

This study conducted a preliminary investigation of cultural products and the use of emotional design modes by local characteristic industries. This study found that the product packaging designs that use local characteristics are mostly developed from unique local resources to produce differentiable characteristics that can be incorporated into the local image. Overall, interdisciplinary design collaboration enables traditional industries to create works with connotations that convey a mutual understanding. The findings of this study are summarized as follows: (1) Localized life and cultural characteristics and local spirit can sufficiently influence the innovation of local characteristic products. From the perspective of economic development, the emergence of local characteristic industries is based on internal demand. Local characteristic products can be expanded to export sales and, thus, provide a source of survival for local economies. Additionally, industry supply can be increased by cultivating Taiwanese brands, creating product differentiation, and combining products and service; (2) successful local characteristic products must satisfy three levels of emotional design (i.e., the visceral, behavioral, and reflective levels), seek design innovation by overturning traditions, and create a newfound awareness of the local area and an accumulated affect for current generations. Subsequently, the development of local characteristic products in Taiwan can expand and prosper, as well as reinforce intangible values, such as residents' influence, generosity, and skills; (3) the integration of local characteristic industries and the experience economy concept requires a platform for interdisciplinary design exchanges to stimulate industry innovation and drive emerging industries. The aesthetics of traditional industries must be continually enhanced, and the sustainable development of these industries is only possible through the incorporation of design.

## References

1. Tung, H.: Theoretical basis and direction of the transformation of government industrial policy in the context of economic globalization. Academia Bimestris (6), 112–117 (2008)
2. Hsieh, M.J.: Taiwan OTOP Project. The National Policy Foundation (2012)
3. Liao, S.Y., Hsu, C.P.: Policy to promote industries with local characteristics - Japan, Thailand and Taiwan as an example. Local Self-government and Democratic development Seminars. B2-1-1 - B1-12 (2009)
4. ITRI, The local characteristics heritage transformed the local industry. Industrial Development Bureau, MOEA (2003)
5. Chen, C.C., Li, Y.J.: The Application of Kano Model on Exploring the Attractive Attributes of Cultural Product Design. Journal of Design 13(4), 25–41 (2008)
6. Lin, R.T.: Learning Principles of Chinese Character for Product Design. Art Appreciation 1(6), 1–9 (2005)
7. Ho, M.C., Lin, C.H., Liu, Y.C.: Some Speculations on Developing Cultural Commodities. Journal of Design 1(1), 1–15 (1996)
8. Lin, R.T., Lin, P.S.: A Study of Integrating Culture and Aesthetics To Promote Cultural and Creative Industries. Art Appreciation 5(2), 81–106 (2007)
9. Norman, D.A.: Emotional Design. Basic Books, NY (2004)
10. Huang, Y.M.: Labor Transitional Process in Taiwan. Journal of Cyber Culture and Information Society (1), 257–278 (2001)
11. Tang, H.H., Lin, Y.Q.: The Influence and Problems of Scenario Design Approach on Multi-disciplinary Collaboration Design. Journal of Design 16(3), 21–44 (2011)
12. Lee, C.K.: A Study on the Husserl's Concept of Affection. Philosophy Research Papers. National Chengchi University, Taipei (2007)
13. Tsai, Y.J.: Some Phenomena of College Students' Use of. Mobile Phone in terms of 3-Level Emotional Design. Design Management Research Papers. Ming Chuan University, Taoyuan (2010)
14. Chung, Y.S.: Exploring emotional concept for product design issues. Industrial Design Research Papers. National Yunlin University of Science and Technolog, Yunlin (2006)

# The Cognitive Difference
# of Visual and Imaged Tactile Sense of Product Forms

Mei-Ting Lin[1], Jui-Ping Ma[1], and Chih-Long Lin[2]

[1] Graduate School of Creative Industry Design,
National Taiwan University of Art, Taipei, Taiwan
[2] Crafts & Design Department, National Taiwan University of Art, Taipei, Taiwan
gua_gua@mail2000.com.tw, artma2010@gmail.com, CL.Lin@ntua.edu.tw

**Abstract.** Product morphology has affected the diversity of consumers' preference. When consumers obtain the product image through perceptual organs, it is possible for the visual sense to replace other senses and generate synesthesia. This study is intended to explore: 1. whether if the visual sense and imagined tactile sense of product forms are consistent in preference; and 2. whether if the cognition preference of the four products with different figure is consistent when viewing the objects simultaneously and individually. The experiment designed four cups with different forms and separately processed a two-phase test of the visual and imagined tactile senses. The analysis result shows that visual and imagined tactile sense possesses slight consistency with product preference, which both reached significant level. Therefore, the preference results of most test subjects in both visual and imaginary tactile sense achieved consistency. Among the four cups, Cup 2 revealed far lower score in the visual sense than in the tactile sense within the pleasure degree, while Cup 3 shown far greater visual points than tactile. The results of experimenting the four cups with different forms yet with same color and material, did not agree with our hypothesis, the anticipation to see and the anticipation to touch were in inverse proportion. The outcome indicated that creative design products via the consumer's view may emerge cognitive difference. Thus, the results of this study can provide products which are in development a better understanding of consumer perception and a foundation for future studies.

**Keywords:** Product Form, visual, imagined tactile sense, cognitive differences.

## 1 Introduction

The cultural creative industry has rise in recent years, "the necessity of to cultural product development is to improve the quality of life and social and cultural levels, thus, design is no longer the pursuit for technical development and beautiful forms, but to focus more on cultural heritage and maintenance" [4]. A designer incorporates images into products with the employment of one feature and collocating with other kinds of features to produce his/her creations based on the needs, feelings, and ideas of people. However, the perceptual capability to images varies from person to person, therefore, designers is required to have a good interest and idea of how images, forms,

P.L.P. Rau (Ed.): CCD/HCII 2013, Part I, LNCS 8023, pp. 104–112, 2013.
© Springer-Verlag Berlin Heidelberg 2013

and the characteristics of forms are related when the products employed as a media to convey the imagery [7]. Through consumers' concern, products create semantics, the conveyance of the semantics direct response of the products, which includes expression of preference. Semantics is generated through sensory organs, the senses of sight and touch are the cognitive interface of human's primary perception towards products, thus, the Drink Up cup series the from JIA Inc., was selected as test samples to acquire the following two goals: 1. whether if the visual sense and imagined tactile sense of product forms are consistent in preference; and 2. whether if the cognition preference of the four products with different figure is consistent when viewing the objects simultaneously and individually. The Drink Up series consists of four cups with various forms designed for four family members or friends so that each person can recognize his/her cup  without confusion. With such interesting creativity, a test was conducted to find out whether if intention of different forms can really meet the expectations of general consumers.

## 2    Product Image

The visual sense has a dominance trait towards the complex sensory perception of vision and touch and is often a substitute for the tactile sense. From an application level, people in general rely more on the visual sense in perceiving the image of a · product, which explains the possibility that complex sensory perceptions are replaced by the visual sense in the same context [2]. Perception is the main foundation for people to transform the product form into image. In addition to acquiring perceptual experience from the stimulation of sensory physiology functions, it can also be obtained through a person's subjective interpretation of stimulations, which classified as sophisticated psychological activity, a few psychological factors may affect the perceptual experience [6]. The activity of forms starts with conveying the expression of an idea and ends with the perception of understanding, the core of the two activities resides in expression and communication. Creative activities originate from the dialogue between the thoughts of the creator, thus, communication consists of not only the outward conveyance of the creator's ideas and the interaction between thoughts within, but also the internal feelings, transformation, sharing, and propagation of the audience [1].Image is a psychological feature, it consist subjective experience to a certain level and is also the reproduction of perceptual experience – creating associative thinking via characteristics expressed by the conceptual meanings of an object through a series of psychological processes consisting perceptual feelings, perceptions, and cognition [3]. The image cognition of product is correlated with the life experience and cultural background of the user, which is classified as the emphasis of perceptual experience in the psychological process; associative thinking includes "visual," "tactile", and "manipulative" [5].

## 3     Method

There were 81 test subjects selected as valid samples, 23 males and 58 females. Four cups with identical material and color yet different forms (see Fig.1) were processed in a four stage questionnaire.

*In Stage 1,* the test subjects were given 20 seconds to "visually see" the forms of the four cups simultaneously and asked to provide their order of preference in the most intuitive manner.

*In Stage 2,* the test subjects were allowed to visually see the four cups individually and provide their preference ratings on a 10-point scale.

*In Stage 3,* the test subjects were given 20 seconds to "imagined tactile sense" simultaneously and asked to provide their order of preference in the most intuitive manner.

*In Stage 4,* the test subjects were allowed to imaginarily touch the four cups individually and provide their preference ratings on a 10-point scale.

|        Cup 1        |        Cup 2        |        Cup 3        |        Cup 4        |

**Fig. 1.** The four sample items were used in this study. The order from left to right is Cup 1, Cup 2, Cup 3 and Cup 4.

## 4     Data Analysis

The result analysis was conducted in 3 phases with 81 valid questionnaires, analysis information is shown below:

*In Phase 1,* the analysis focused on the 1 to 4 preference ranking of the "visual sense" tests on the four cups at the same time and the 1 to 4 preference ratings on the four cups of the "imagined tactile sense" tests to see if there is any consistency in these two stages.

*In Phase 2,* the analysis paid individual attention to the preference ratings from 1 to 10 points on the four cups in the "visual sense" tests and the preference ratings from 1 to 10 points on the four cups in the "imagined tactile sense" tests to see if there is any consistency in these two stages.

*In Phase 3,* the analysis involves consistency analysis between the simultaneous ranking and individual scores in Stage 1 and 2's "visual sense" tests with the simultaneous ranking and individual scores in Stage 3's "imagined tactile sense" tests. The relation among these 3 phases is shown in Fig. 2.

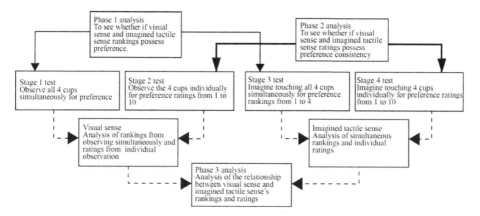

**Fig. 2.** Analysis diagram

## 4.1    Analysis of Preference for Visual and Imagined Tactile Senses

Phase 1 analysis: the results of rankings given in "visual sense" test of Stage 1 and "imagined tactile sense" of Stage 3 were then processed the aggregation of the individual rating frequency to verify the hypothesis of consistency between visual senses and imagined tactile senses. In both stages of the test, the examinees were allowed to view the four cups simultaneously and write down the rankings for each cup based on their preference. Figures 3 are the quantity distribution outcome of the visual sense test preference ranking and imaged tactile sense test rating of the four cups. The result reveals that cups 1 and 4 possess preference consistency between visual and imagined tactile senses; as for cups 2 and 3, the quantity outcome which ranked first place showed difference in the preference distribution of visual and imagined tactile senses. Only 15 test subjects gave first place to cup 2 regarding visual preference, whereas 29 rated first place in imagined tactile sense. For the quantity distribution of  the second to fourth places, consistent decline was found in range of both visual and imagined tactile senses, indicating that the test subjects expected more tactile preference from cup 2 than in visual preference. For cup 3, thirty three test subjects gave first place in visual preference, while only 16 gave tactile preference first place. The consistent decline of the visual and imagined tactile sense preference range indicates that cup 3 provided test subjects with greater visual pleasure than tactile anticipation. One interesting finding is that of the four cups, the form difference between cups 2 and 3 was the smallest, yet the degree of difference after analyzing was actually greater than the other two cups.

Phase 2 analysis: a cross-reference was processed to analyze the individually examined preference results obtained from the "visual sense" test of Stage 2 and "imagined tactile sense" test of stage 4. It was assumed that in Phase 2 analysis that the preference should be consistent no matter if the four cups were observed collectively or individually, therefore, the result should correspond to the outcome of 1 analysis.

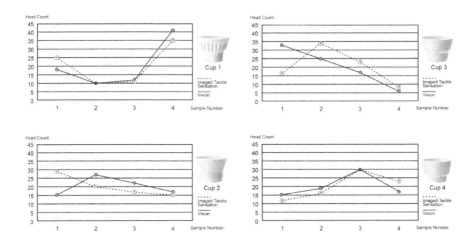

**Fig. 3.** The quantity distribution outcome of the visual sense test preference ranking and imaged tactile sense test rating of the four cup

During the test, the examinees were allowed to see only one cup at a time before rating the preference of the cup on a 1-10 point scale, 1 being the lowest and 10 being the highest. The Stage 2 "visual sense" test and Stage 4 "imagined tactile sense" test were then conducted separately, the ratings for each of the cups obtained from the two stages were added together (see Table 1). After acquiring the aggregation, the total of each cup was analyzed by the One-way ANOVA analysis to determine an F value of 0.0171. The tests were conducted to see whether there is difference between the test subject's visual and imagined tactile senses, outcome indicates preference consistency for all four cups, as shown in Table 2. The visual senses and imagined tactile sense rating for each was then analyzed by a two-tailed test, which obtained the results as followed: .475** for cup 1, .386** for cup 2, .462** for cup 3, and .485** for cup 4 (see Table 3). From the above data, we can realize that the four cups has both achieved significant level in the visual and imagined tactile senses.

The analysis of the 3 phases mentioned above revealed that the assumption where there should be consistency between visual sense and imagined tactile sense and that there should consistency as well as the preferences consistency for observing simultaneously and individually, however, in this case, the result of the four cups being tested together and tested separately did not correspond. The outcome for testing the cups together indicated that the preference of cup 2 was greater in imagined tactile sense than in visual sense; as for cup 3, the preference was greater in visual sense than in imagined tactile sense.

**Table 1.** Visual/tactile sense ratings

|      | Vision | Tactile |
| ---- | ------ | ------- |
| Cup1 | 431    | 442     |
| Cup2 | 479    | 508     |
| Cup3 | 523    | 503     |
| Cup4 | 472    | 438     |

**Table 2.** One-way analysis of variance (ANOVA)

|                   | SS     | df | MS      | F      |
| ----------------- | ------ | -- | ------- | ------ |
| Between Groups    | 24.5   | 1  | 24.5    | **0.0171** |
| Within Group      | 8569.5 | 6  | 1428.25 |        |
| Total             | 8594   | 7  |         |        |

**Table 3.** Correlation derived from two-tailed test

|                                   | cup1   | cup2   | cup3   | cup4 |
| --------------------------------- | ------ | ------ | ------ | ---- |
| visual sense &Imaged tactile sense | .475** | .386** | .462** | .485 |

## 4.2 Consistency Analysis on Preference of Observing Simultaneously and Individually

Phase 3 analysis: the sequence from 1 to 4 obtained in the Stage 1 "visual sense" test when looking at the cups together and the ratings from 1 to 10 obtained from Stage 2 test when looking at the cups individually were processed according to rank and aggregate scores separately to calculate the means and standard deviations. The same process was conducted on the sequence from 1 to 4 obtained in the Stage 3 "imagined tactile sense" test when looking at the cups together and the ratings from 1 to 10 obtained from Stage 4 test when looking at the cups individually. The results were analyzed to find out whether if there is any preference consistency when looking at the cups simultaneously and individually.

Table 4 contains the analysis data which indicates the standard deviations of the four cups in the "visual sense" test. The standard deviations of the selected first place to fourth place gradually increased, indicating that the degree of dispersion increased according to the preference level ranking from first place to fourth place and that, the fourth place given by test subjects showed the greatest rating difference. No patterns were observed in the standard deviations obtained from the "imagined tactile sense" analysis (see Table 5). As for the "visual sense" test, the ranking of preference in observing simultaneously was consistent with the preference ratings in observing individually, yet there were no preference consistency for "imagined tactile" in neither simultaneous nor individual observations. The only consistency observed from both "visual sense" and "imagined tactile sense" tests was the standard deviation for cup 1, which also rank first place, was all smaller than 1, suggesting that cup 1, ranking first place, shows the most consistency when either the cups are observed together or individually in the "visual sense" and "imagined tactile sense" tests. The visual sense standard deviation diagram is shown in Table 4, while the imagined tactile sense standard deviation diagram is shown Table 5; the data acquired from the two tables suggests the ratings if the mean decreased from the first place to fourth place, however, the "imagined tactile sense" revealed greater rating difference than "visual sense."

If we divide the 10-point rating scale into 4 sections with 10~9 points being the highest section, 8~6 being the medium high section, 5~3 points being the medium low section, and 2~1 points being the lowest section, via means analysis, we realize that cups which ranked first place in the "visual sense" test, scored an average of 7.72~8.50, with a high-low rating difference of 0.78, the cups was located in the medium high section and failed to reach the highest section. For cups ranking in second place, the mean ratings were 6.68~6.00 with a high-low rating difference of 0.68, which also located in the medium high section but in the lower half of the section (7 points). For cups ranking third place, the mean ratings were 5.58~5.00 with a high-low rating difference of 0.58, which fell into the medium low section. For cups ranking fourth place, mean ratings were 4.24~3.00 with a high-low rating difference of 1.24, which also fell into the medium low section. As for the "imagined tactile sense" test, the cups ranking first place were given a mean ratings of 8.64~6.88 with a high-low rating difference of 1.76, which was located below the in the medium high section and failed to reach the highest section. For cups ranking second place, the mean ratings were 6.50~6.05 with a high-low rating difference of 0.45, which was located in the medium high section but in the lower half of the section (7 points). For cups ranking third place, the mean ratings were 4.97~6.13 with a high-low rating difference of 1.16, which fell between medium high and low sections. For cups ranking fourth place, the mean ratings were 4.60~2.91 with a high-low rating difference of 1.69, which fell into the medium low section. It is clear that the 4 cups were generally given low ratings in both the "visual sense" and "imagined tactile sense" tests. On a scale of 1 to 10 points, the highest mean rating was less than 9 and all ratings failed to reach the highest section, whereas the means of "imagined tactile sense" test possessed great difference in high-low ratings, suggesting that most of the test subjects were not satisfied in the visual sense test and were not willing to touch them.

**Table 4.** Means and standard deviations for observing simultaneously and individually in the "visual sense" test

|      | Ranking 1 | | Ranking 2 | | Ranking 3 | | Ranking 4 | |
|------|------|------|------|------|------|------|------|------|
|      | mean | SD | mean | SD | mean | SD | mean | SD |
| Cup1 | 8.50 | 0.76 | 6.00 | 1.73 | 5.58 | 1.75 | 3.68 | 1.80 |
| Cup2 | 7.73 | 1.65 | 6.56 | 2.02 | 5.36 | 1.52 | 3.59 | 1.59 |
| Cup3 | 7.79 | 1.65 | 6.36 | 1.79 | 5.24 | 1.80 | 3.00 | 1.83 |
| Cup4 | 8.20 | 1.28 | 6.68 | 1.52 | 5.00 | 1.79 | 4.24 | 1.59 |

**Table 5.** Means and standard deviations for observing simultaneously and individually in the "imagined tactile sense" test

|      | Ranking 1 | | Ranking 2 | | Ranking 3 | | Ranking 4 | |
|------|------|------|------|------|------|------|------|------|
|      | mean | SD | mean | SD | mean | SD | mean | SD |
| Cup1 | 8.64 | 0.84 | 6.40 | 1.11 | 5.45 | 2.02 | 2.91 | 1.08 |
| Cup2 | 8.00 | 1.36 | 6.05 | 1.88 | 5.06 | 1.43 | 4.60 | 2.12 |
| Cup3 | 6.88 | 2.32 | 6.50 | 1.60 | 6.13 | 1.73 | 3.88 | 1.45 |
| Cup4 | 8.25 | 1.53 | 6.13 | 2.39 | 4.97 | 1.89 | 4.00 | 2.06 |

# 5    Conclusion

For a consumer to accept a product, the first stage of preference judgment is to see and touch, yet most products originates from the creativity of designers, products are rarely produced due to the preference of general consumers. A set of cups each with  different forms stands out significantly from other conventional cups in terms of creativity. Thus, the design concept to explore these cups is: "This set consists of four different shaped cups, allowing your friends and family to pick their own favorites!"

Questionnaires were used to analyze visual preference and to investigate whether if the imagined tactile sense analysis exist any difference. After four stages of tests and three phases of analysis, it was found that neither visual nor imagined tactile senses produced the anticipated outcomes. In the data where cups 2 and 3 were selected as first place, the preference of cup 2 was far greater than tactile expectation than visual sense, whereas it was the opposite for cup 3 as the preference to it was far greater in visual sense than imagined tactile sense; others that ranked from second to fourth place showed consistence of gradual decline for both visual and imagined tactile sense. More-over, as to cup 1 and cup 4, the rankings from the first to fourth place consistently de-creased as well. Interestingly, of the four cups, cup 1 had the greatest difference, while the same could not be said for the other three. Difference was observed in cup 2 and cup 3 , yet because the research only employed questionnaires to analyze the preference of visual and imagined tactile senses, hence, the study was unable to be determined the reason of the affect, this interesting finding may support subsequent studies.

As we take the visual and imagined tactile senses ranking data of the four cups, which is ranked from first to fourth place, and each added up the 1 to 10 ratings, result shows decreasing consistency as expected. However, after the calculation of each mean by sequence, the means of rankings 1 through 4 all fell within the medium high section between 8 to 6 points and the medium low section between 5 to 3 points, indi-cating the examinees' satisfaction difference towards the cup set was not significant, the median outcome suggests that none of the test subjects were very satisfied or very unsatisfied with any of the cups. To analyze the 1 to 10 point rating from the standard deviation point of view, the standard deviation of each group was located between 1 and 3 with 0.76 being the smallest and closest value to 1, indicating that the ratings given by the test subjects for the products revealed great difference. This suggested two possible results: 1. there was significant preference difference between observing the cups simultaneously and individually; and 2. there was significant satisfaction difference between the test subjects regarding the cups.  Due to the fact that the ques-tionnaire data could not provide a valid outcome, thus, this study can only provide the questionnaires for future studies to employ and achieve a more comprehensive analy-sis concerning consumers' preference.

Personalized products are the trend of design, a set of products with different shapes is anticipated to create novelty for consumers and to achieve a high level of preference, yet our experiment indicates that the product fails to fulfill its purpose. This issue is still worth investigating regarding product research; the results of this study can provide products which are in development a better understanding of con-sumer perception and a foundation for future studies.

# References

1. Chang, C.H.: Current Psychology. In: Tung Hua Book, Taipei, Taiwan (1995)
2. Chang, C.C.: Perceptual Factors Underlying Users' Image Perception toward Product Form. Doctoral thesis. National Chiao Tung University, Hsinchu, Taiwan (2000)
3. Jan, R.H.: The Corresponding Relationship between Product Image and Form Features. Master's thesis. Ming Chuan University, Taoyuan, Taiwan (2004)
4. Lin, B.L.: A Stardy on the Visual and Tactile Image of Form—Taking the Shape of Plastic Bottles as Examples. Master' s thesis, Ming Chuan University, Taoyuan, Taiwan (2002)
5. Lin, R.T.: Cultural creativity added design value. Art Appreciation 1(7), 26–32 (2005)
6. Tsai, C.Y.: A study on the influence of the form and the texture on product image through visual and tactile perception. Master's thesis, National Yunlin University of Science & Technology, Yunlin, Taiwan(2004)
7. Yang, T.L., Ho, C.M., Luh, D.B.: Gestalt-oriented approach to form creation. Journal of Design 16(4), 19–34 (2011)

# Discovering the Use of a Home Smart Telephone: A Persona Approach

Weijane Lin, Chih-Lo Chen, Chien-Ting Yang, and Hsiu-Ping Yueh

Department of Library and Information Science, National Taiwan University
Department of Bio-Industry Communication and Development, National Taiwan University
No. 1., Sec. 4., Roosevelt Rd., Daan Dist., Taipei 10617, Taiwan, R.O.C.
vjlin@ntu.edu.tw

**Abstract.** This ongoing study examined the users' needs, perceptions, performance and expectations toward a multifunctional home-use smart telephone. Through systematically discovering users' behaviors, this study investigated 317 participants' use of the target product, and profiled the target users of personas within different scenarios. Three major patterns of use were found in this study, and the suggestions were made to improve the interface and marketing strategies with references to the personas concluded in this study.

**Keywords:** Home phone, Smartphone, Persona.

## 1 Introduction

With the common ownership of home-use telephone in households in many developed countries, the use of a domestic telephone involved a variety of everyday living activities that were communicational, informational, recreational and even safety-related. According to a governmental statistics (2012) in Taiwan, although the owning rate was declining accompanied with the growing ownership of mobile phones and broadband networks, averagely every household owned 1.2 home-use telephone in the past decade. The availability of home-use telephone has made it a significant device in national information and communication infrastructure. The functions and the services available by home-use telephones have been rapidly and extensively developed with making alliances with telecommunication, broadcasting, medical and social networks by the assemblages of ICT technologies. However, while more functions were integrated into an originally single-purposed appliance, the users might be overwhelmed by the unfamiliar conceptual models thus hampered their acceptance and performance of using it. Consequently, to understand users' requirements and behaviors in advance would be necessary for such a product to be developed and implemented. In this vein, this study examined the users' needs, perceptions, performance and expectations toward a multifunctional home-use smart telephone to discover their use by the systematically presentation of personas.

While the user-centered design approach gained more and more attention in product development, the difficulties remained in practices when the design teams intended to include the actual users. The needs and goals of users were not always

P.L.P. Rau (Ed.): CCD/HCII 2013, Part I, LNCS 8023, pp. 113–117, 2013.
© Springer-Verlag Berlin Heidelberg 2013

communicated effectively between the designers and the users. Misunderstanding occurred in communications due to various levels of expertise and experiences, and it was not easy to leverage the features of the product between the satisfactory experiences of all users. The idea of persona that coined by Cooper (1999), served as a design target, a communication tool and an instrumental method that widely acknowledged by the industry.

Following the user-centered design principles, personas facilitated designers to construct the detail and image of target users by drawing characters in order to design a product that satisfied the user needs (Pruitt & Adlin, 2006). It referred to the archetypal character that represented a group of users who share common goals, attitudes and behaviors when interacting with a product or service. A persona served as a fictitious user for designers, and facilitated them make difficult decisions from the users' perspectives during the product design and development (Chang, Lim, & Stolterman, 2008). In addition to a general and broad image of the user population, to construct a persona involved qualitative and quantitative collection of data to profile real people in order to discover their own needs, motivations and goals in details (Idoughi, Seffah, & Kolski, 2012). The data was analyzed and integrated by a contextual presentation that incorporated the scenarios, backgrounds, behaviors and emotions of users when interacting with the product (Lester, Converse, Kahler, Barlow, Stone, & Bhogal, 1997).

By adopting the persona-based approach, a practical goal of this study is providing the designers with the genuine life experiences of users to develop products and services that meet their needs. Comparing to the previous design practices and studies, in which designers misunderstood the users' thoughts to be similar to theirs, and the failing pursuit to design a perfect product that satisfied every user, personas authentically reflected different users, whether novice or expert, and revealed the obstacles and problems they had encountered (Lindgren, Chen, Amdahl, & Chaikiat, 2007). Personas suggested not an average model of users, but a context-rich user scenario. Additionally, personas that contained rich information of target users also served experiential reference for designers to evaluate the usability of the products, and provided insightful information to form marketing strategies (Cooper, Reimann, & Cronin, 2012).

This study aimed to discover the use of a home-use smartphone by the persona-based approach. The overall goals of this study are:

1. Investigate the users' perceptions and performances with using the target product of a home phone.
2. Incorporate persona to profile and present the target users of a multifunctional home phone.
3. Explore the implications of the interface and functionality design facing the developing of a multifunctional home phone.

## 2     Methodology

In this study a commercial product of a smart home-use telephone provided by a telecommunications company in Taiwan was subjected as the target product. And the personas that use this target product were developed. For a real project and the commercial product, applying personas that consisted of widely collected user data would help the designers better understand the users' requirements. Additionally, through the thorough investigation of the target users, potential markets and users groups could be found.

Followed the principles of constructing personas, to understand the user experience of the home-use smart telephones and the characteristics of different user groups, both quantitative and qualitative data from multiple sources was collected. These sources included the focus group interview of heavy users, the articles post on the online user community where experiences of using home-use smart telephone were shared. Additionally, literatures and reports regarding specific user groups' life and consumer behaviors were also referred.

This study adopted the purposeful sampling strategy to recruit 317 experienced users in total to participate in this study. According to their frequency and familiarity with the target product, 7 participants were selected for a focus group interview, while 310 of them were interviewed by phone with a structural survey about their use. Based on the analysis of these participants' use behaviors, personas for the target product were developed. These personas detailed different purposes and scenarios of use, and specifically this study took four major steps until the personas were developed.

1. Documents analysis: Qualitative investigation including the collection of opinions regarding the target product in several online user communities and the analysis of the official documents was conducted.
2. Focus group interview with the heavy users of the target product: 7 users were selected as the subjects in this stage by their product use logs. Sample questions of the interview included the reason of purchasing the target product, the benefits and challenges of using the target product, the functions and services of frequent and rare use.
3. User Survey: 310 interviewees were sampled from the existing users of the target product, and interviewed by phone with a structural questionnaire that developed in house by the researcher. The instrument consisted of four major aspects that investigated the users' purposes, frequencies, perceptions and expectations of each function and service provided by the target product.
4. Development of personas: With reference to the findings of the previous steps, personas that described the target users were developed accordingly.

## 3    Preliminary Results

Among the 7 users participated in the focus group interview, 4 were males and 3 were females. Their age ranged from 31 to 70, all have the target product installed at home for more than 1.5 years. The major reason of purchased is for the convenience, novelty and the trust in the branding of the telecommunications company. Most of the users compared the target product with the computers and regarded it as more intuitive to use without complex prerequisites.

The functions that frequently used by the users were largely accessing daily life information including the weather reports, lottery, local maps and hospitals. While the other major functionalities that emphasized by the stakeholders, the surveillance and videoconferencing services, were rarely used by the interviewees. This found gap also revealed that the target consumers of the product were not the major users of the product.

The findings of the survey that targeted the 310 current users suggested that the major user population were the elderly couples, which echoed the results of the focus group interview. Users in nuclear family style, who were young couples with one or two children were the secondly frequent users of the target product. Based on the users' purposes that derived from the preliminary findings, 3 personas were developed to accumulate the large amount of real user data and represent the target users' profiles.

### 3.1    Persona A: Use for Daily Life Information

The first persona represented the user population of housewives whose major purpose of the target product was to access daily life information. Compared to other consumer-electronics, she is more satisfied with the interface of the home-use smart telephone. In order to depict the scenario of requiring daily life information by using the home-use smart telephone, we searched for the empirical studies about the information needs, hobbies, and consumer behaviors of housewives and women who are retired.

The scenario of use suggested that the users could access weather, calendar and security information readily and conveniently at the door when they went out, leisurely check the sales information with the music played on, and made reservations with the transportation services. The information and services the users expected for a home-use smart telephone were often connected with other home appliances and activities such as television, intercoms, newspapers and magazines.

### 3.2    Persona B: Use for Communication

This persona represented the middle-aged who use the target product for contacting family members for caring and greeting purposes. Theoretical and practical references about the family communication and the facilities of elder caring and healthcare were referred to design the scenario for this persona. The users could make video phone calls easily in more casual settings, and with integrative use of the surveillance functions, the users valued the home-use smart telephone more than mobile phones.

The scenario of use also suggested that the interface of the home-use telephone served the functionality of videoconferencing better than television and computer. Telephone was regarded usable for various users including the elders and the children, and therefore served better for communication purposes.

### 3.3    Persona C: Use for Surveillance and Security System

According to the findings of the interviews, the target product was then compared to other products to discover the advantages and weakness of it. And by referring to the consumer studies of security products, the persona C was developed to represent users who seek for affordable solutions of home security. The simplified functionality of surveillance satisfied the users by offering alarming and recording services.

## 4    Discussion and Further Investigation

The current study examined the users' needs, perceptions, performance and expectations toward a home-use smart telephone. Through the preliminary investigations, three personas were developed with references to qualitative and quantitative materials that profiled the users. By adopting the persona approach, it was possible to provide a vivid and accurate representation of the target users, and communicate the users' needs and goals more effectively with the stakeholders.

The preliminary findings of the study supported that the residential home phone represented differently in its nature from smartphones, and suggested different user expectations and experiences. For endeavors that intended to extend the functionality of the appliance, or to enable residential home phone of more integrative services with other home appliances, it was noteworthy to consider the conceptual models discovered in this study. With reference to the personas developed by this current study, effective and efficient user experiments could be conducted continuously under the designated scenario to drive and validate the stakeholders' and users' concerns about the product design.

## References

1. Chang, Y.N., Lim, Y.K., Stolterman, E.: Personas: from theory to practices. In: Proceedings of the 5th Nordic Conference on Human-computer Interaction: Building Bridges, pp. 439–442 (2008)
2. Cooper, A.: The Inmates are Running the Asylum. Macmillan Publishing Company Inc., New York (1999)
3. Cooper, A., Reimann, R., Cronin, D.: About Face 3: The Essentials of Interaction Design. Wiley Publishing, Indianapolis (2012)
4. Lindgren, A., Chen, F., Amdahl, P., Chaikiat, P.: Using personas and scenarios as an interface design tool for advanced driver assistance systems. In: Stephanidis, C. (ed.) UAHCI 2007 (Part II). LNCS, vol. 4555, pp. 460–469. Springer, Heidelberg (2007)
5. Pruitt, J., Adlin, T.: The Persona Lifecycle: Keeping People in Mind throughout Product Design. Morgan Kaufmann Publishers (2006)
6. Lester, J.C., Converse, S.A., Kahler, S.E., Barlow, S.T., Stone, B.A., Bhogal, R.S.: The persona effect: affective impact of animated pedagogical agents. In: Proceedings of the SIGCHI Conference on Human Factors in Computing Systems, pp. 359–366 (1997)
7. Idoughi, D., Seffah, A., Kolski, C.: Adding user experience into the interactive service design loop: a persona-based approach. Behaviour & Information Technology 31(3), 287–303 (2012)

# A Study of Aesthetic Analysis on Modern Crafts

Po-Hsien Lin[1], Mo-Li Yeh[2], and Rungtai Lin[1]

[1] Graduate School of Creative Industry Design, National Taiwan University of Arts
Daguan Rd., Banqiao Dist., New Taipei City 22058, Taiwan
t0131@ntua.edu.tw, rtlin@mail.ntua.edu.tw
[2] Department of Fashion Design, Hsing Wu University
Linkou, New Taipei City 24452, Taiwan
1101moli@gmail.com

**Abstract.** Based on the perspective of academic application and cultural dissemination, this study intends to explore the aesthetic value of Taiwan modern
crafts. Through an approach of style analysis, this study examines the works
selected from Taiwan Crafts Competition Award and Modern Crafts Yii Project.
Both qualitative and quantitative methods are employed to explore the artistic
essence and cultural reference of the creations. The study places the works in
stylistic context to establish a theoretical framework of aesthetic analysis and
criticism of Taiwanese modern crafts. A questionnaire is developed to obtain
information required for style analysis. The data is analyzed using "Multidimensional Scaling" (MDS). The Consensus Assessment Technique (CAT) is
employed in the study. A CAT questionnaire developed by Amabile is used to
examine the performance of the works in three difference dimensions of creativity, technical goodness, and aesthetic appeal. Finally, a statistic technique of
Multiple Regression Analysis will be employed to explore the significance of
these three factors in each style of the works.

**Keywords:** Modern Crafts, Aesthetics, Style Analysis.

## 1 Introduction

Starting from 2001, National Taiwan Craft Research and Development Institute
(NTCRI) have held National Crafts Awards for 6 years, which was the most directional
and representative crafts award in Taiwan. From 2007, National Crafts Awards was
consolidated with Taiwan Craft Design Competition and found Taiwan Crafts Competition. This competition has been divided in two groups, including Traditional Crafts
and Innovative Design; it is not only representing the most recent standard of Taiwan
design industry but also reflecting the cultural significances of the modern time in
Taiwan.

The design project, Yii, was conceived by NTCRI (National Taiwan Craft Research Institute) and TDC (Taiwan Design Center). It aims to combine traditional
craftsmanship techniques and modern design concept, which not only successfully
initiate a new page of craft style but also open up infinitive possibilities of crafts
materials. Up to 2010, the manufacturing orders from the world have exceeded one

P.L.P. Rau (Ed.): CCD/HCII 2013, Part I, LNCS 8023, pp. 118–127, 2013.
© Springer-Verlag Berlin Heidelberg 2013

hundred million dollars. The traditional cognition on 'crafts' with the concept of 'modern' can evolve the diverse and abounding value which becoming the most successful example in the development of Taiwan creative industry.

This study focuses on analyzing the awarded champions in Taiwan Crafts Competition as well as the selected works from the digital exhibition of The Project Yii. Through quantitative analysis from diagnosis observation of experts, the objectives of this research can be achieved as follow:

1. To analyze the form of style to distinguish modern crafts.
2. To promote the aesthetic value of Taiwan modern crafts.
3. To establish a new aesthetic model for the development of Taiwan modern crafts.

## 2    Literature Review

### 2.1    Meaning of Modern Crafts

Shui-Long Yen, also known as the father of crafts in Taiwan, had suggested that crafts making artists should possess the correct understanding of the nation and society and create works which can capture people's will and is able to employ as daily-used products, moreover, use best of the beauty of raw materials and modern life adaptations [10]. From the origin of craft making, human has made use of tools to solve their daily problems. When the basic life requirement is settled, crafts should sublimate into a tool for soul cultivation.

Recent craft has begun the growing emphasis of expressing cultural features and aesthetics performance, more and more consumers favor products that integrates with the beauty of craft. Norman, points out that a successful design must includes the aspects of usability, practicality, and aesthetics. He claims that the emotional side of design may be more critical to a product's success than its practical elements [8]. In the 21st century, emotional design is in huge demands, which can be carried out through the aesthetic value of craft [6].

Based on Article 3 in the Law for the Development of the Cultural and Creative Industries, the "Cultural and Creative Industries" referred to the following industries that originate from creativity or accumulation of culture, which through the formation and application of intellectual properties, possess potential capacities to create wealth and job opportunities, enhancing the citizens' aesthetic attainments and elevating living environment. Hereon, the citizen's aesthetics accomplishment is advertised by the cultural and creative industries as non-economy achievements.. On the other hand, the raise of citizen's aesthetics accomplishment is the fundamental gateway to open up the consumer market of cultural and creative industries.

In the article 'Constructing the Value of Modern Craft', Guo-Zhen Chen proposed the conceptual value of modern craft through the study of various international brands. She suggested many conceptual values of modern crafts: Highly value nature and humanity, respect traditional craftsmanship, integrate with science and technology, delightful living, express the local style, initiate a new fashion trend, and so on [3].

Jeff Dayu Shi claims that modern crafts are "a saleable product that possesses both aesthetics and artistry", he stated that any design which lack aesthetic perception will lose its meaning [5]. This proves that modern crafts have strengthened its commercialization and modernization. Chian-Chi Lin has also pointed out that because modern aesthetic must possess popularization and navigability, modern should own high aesthetic sensitivity, which is the subtle difference that distinguishes itself from traditional crafts [5].

In conclusion, to achieve the targets "to create wealth and job opportunities, to enhance the citizens' aesthetic attainments, and to elevate the citizens' living environment", stated in the Law for the Development of the Cultural and Creative Industries, modern craft takes craftsmanship as a carrier, culture as a connotation, and intergrades with design skills, to not only explore the lifestyle of people, but by sculpting the attraction of branding, creating distinguish and stylish products in the commercialized process as the fruitful results of the creative industry.

## 2.2    The Quantitative Exploration of Craft Aesthetics Analysis

To take account of the characteristics of art research, this paper will be supporting the art work analysis with quantitative research and by taking advantage of "consensus assessment technique" (CAT), we can integrate the observations and feedbacks of academics and experts. CAT was developed by an American psychologist, Teresa M. Amabile, to evaluate creativity through industrial products. For centuries creativity has been regarded as a mental trait of mankind, Amabile suggests defining creativity from a "product" perspective [1]. Hao-Cheng Chiu indicated that the CAT proves to be a useful tool for evaluating various types of works, via the nearly year-long inspection of numerous research series. The evaluation range includes Chinese poetry, storytelling, and art creation, applicable targets are adults and children [4].

Amabile stated that the evaluation process should notice the following key points: First, the evaluator must possess a certain level of knowledge background of the assess work. Second, evaluator must not be influenced by other people during the evaluation process. Third, evaluator should evaluate the various index of one work at a time and not comparing a certain index with numerous works simultaneously. The principle of Amabile will be considered as an important reference during the actual execution of this research [2].

The scale that Amabile developed has experienced multiple corrections and improvements; in 1983, he not only designed 23 items in the scale of art domain, but also provided a descriptive definition for each evaluation item.

Through factor analysis, the 23 items from above can be categorized into three main groups, creativity, technique, and aesthetics, and by eliminating the items with low factor capacity, we remain with 17 factors divided into three attributions:

1. Creativity--creativity, novel use of materials, novel idea, effort evident, variation in shapes, detail, complexity.
2. Technique--technical goodness, organization, neatness, planning evident, representationalism, symmetry, expression.
3. Aesthetics-- liking, aesthetic appeal, display.

# 3     Methodology

## 3.1     Research Instrument

This study focuses on the awarded champions of "Taiwan Crafts Competition" and the current digital exhibition from classical works of "The Project Yii". Via quantitative research to explore the styles of works, we first combine related literature reviews with interview data to draw up a scale for analyzing various craftwork styles. The results would be employed into multidimensional scaling (MDS) for analyzing. MDS is a data analysis for categorizing observation values, furthermore, to analyze the potential structure hidden behind the scenes [9].

Through the five point scale survey composed by 16 groups of polar adjectives chosen by professionals (Table 1), the research develop a modern crafts aesthetic semantic differential scale questionnaire, which was then taken into MDS for further analyzing.

**Table 1.** The 16 Groups of Polar Adjectives of Semantic Differential Scale

| tactile-visual | freehanded-realistic | traditional-modern | material-expressive |
|---|---|---|---|
| novel-ordinary | classical-avant-garde | functional-nonfunctional | conflicting-harmonic |
| natural-artificial | linear-curvilinear | integral-compositional | geometric-organic |
| ethereal-steady | gorgeous-plain | conventional-creative | intuitive-deliberate |

## 3.2     Research Object

As for the work selection process of the research object, the pieces are chosen from two portions, one selected from "Taiwan Craft Design Competition" and the other selected from "The Project Yii". Selection principle for the Taiwan Craft Design Competition are to chose the first prize pieces, one from the Traditional Crafts and one from the Innovation Design, due to the reason which the competition has been enforced for four years since 2010, there will be a total of 8 pieces put into selection process; second prize will be selected when first prize is absent.

In addition, products from "The Project Yii" is chosen according to the introduction of the Yii brand and current product list announced by the National Taiwan Craft Research and Development Institute, which listed 58 series of modern crafts beginning from 2007 to 2009; 37 works are currently displayed on the official website [7]. After consulting and compiling the opinions of experts, this study has chosen 10 representative works from the two events as research objects: Taiwan Craft Design Competition (4 pieces), and The Project Yii (6 pieces).

**Table 2.** Titles and Codes of 10 Representative Works of the Study

| P1 | P2 | P3 | P4 |
|---|---|---|---|
| | | | |
| Hello | Taste of Memory | The Offering of the Blessing Boat | Zen Garden |

| P5 | P6 | P7 | P8 | P9 | P10 |
|---|---|---|---|---|---|
| | | | | | |
| Lace Bowl | Moon Cup | World Cup: Black Lotus | Brick Plate | Cocoon project: Sofa | Bamboo Barstool |

# 4    Data Analysis

The study completed 92 effective questionnaires, covering different gender and three diverse educational backgrounds (craft and industrial design, design-related, non-design), the significant outcomes and discoveries are concluded as below:

## 4.1    MDS Analysis of Work Styles

The study begins with employing the MDS analysis to analyze the 10 selected pieces with the 16 groups of adjectives. According to the results of the two dimensional composition formed by MDS and the factor analysis between the selected pieces and the 16 groups of adjectives, this study has first completed the two dimensional distribution map of the 10 pieces. The map indicated that pieces such as no. 3 *The Offering of the Blessing Boat*, no. 10 *Bamboo Barstool*, no. 4 *Zen Garden*, and no. 5 *Lace Bowl* was distributed on the extreme positions of the X and Y axis (as shown in figure 1).

To explore the cognitive spatial position of each attribute, the research then applies the multiple regression analysis to calculate the included angle of each attribute located on the composition and created a cognitive map of the 16 attributes; we can see from the distribution map that the correlations coefficient between attribute 1 (Free-handed-Realistic) and attribute 14 is only .097, which means the relationship of the two attributes is practically uncorrelated, the included angle of the two attributes is approximately $90°$, hence, is chosen for explaining the representative axis in the two dimensional cognitive space.

As you can see in fig. 3, p9 and p10 has landed in the first quadrant (Functional/Realistic); p2, p4, and p7 landed in the second quadrant (Functional/Realistic); the third quadrant (Nonfunctional/Freehanded) landed p5 and p6; the fourth quadrant (Nonfunctional/Realistic) landed four pieces, including p1, p3, and p8.

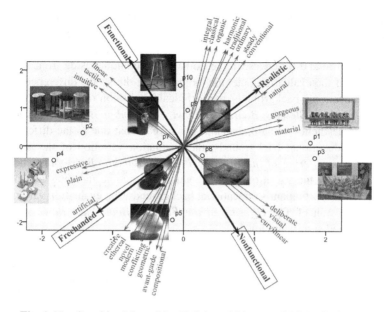

**Fig. 1.** The Cognitive Map of the 10 Selected Pieces and 16 Attributes

## 4.2    The CAT Analysis of the Evaluation of Works

This research analyzes the creativity of the 10 works by employing the CAT scale and evaluating these pieces by creativity, technique, and aesthetics dimensions (As shown in Table 3). The Kendall's coefficient of concordance was employed to verify whether if the 10 selected pieces possess consistency in the sequence of the three dimensions, the calculated outcome W=.736 has achieved significant level (p < .05), the participant's evaluation shows that the works in the dimensions of creativity, technique, and aesthetics all possess a consistent ranking.

**Table 3.** The Ranking of Integral Expression

| Works | | | | | | | | | | |
|---|---|---|---|---|---|---|---|---|---|---|
| Mean | 4.15 | 3.96 | 3.89 | 3.88 | 3.84 | 3.81 | 3.71 | 3.64 | 3.51 | 3.32 |
| Ranking | 1 | 2 | 3 | 4 | 5 | 6 | 7 | 8 | 9 | 10 |

In order to explore how participants opinions were affected by the educational background, An ANOVA test was conducted based on the evaluation data of four works derived from the outcome of MDS analysis. The selected works including *Blessing Boat, Zen Garden, Lace Bowl,* and *Bamboo Barstool* were located on the extreme ends of the X and Y axis of the two dimensional distribution map.

Table 4 is a summary table of ANOVA for products evaluation by educational background. In the domain of creativity, the mean score of *The Offering of the Blessing Boat*, *Lace Bowl*, and *Bamboo Barstool* demonstrates significant variance due to educational background differences. In the domain of technique, aside from *Zen Garden*, the variation of the evaluation outcome indicates that due to the difference of the participant's educational backgrounds, the technical expression of the three other pieces, *The Offering of the Blessing Boat*, *Lace Bowl*, and *Bamboo Barstool*, reached significant level. In aesthetics domain, data analysis reveals that due to the difference of the participants' educational backgrounds, the evaluation variation of the aesthetic expression of *The Offering of the Blessing Boat* and *Bamboo Barstool* reached significant level. Finally, the variation of the evaluation outcome indicates that due to the difference of the participant's educational backgrounds, the evaluation variation of the integral expression of *The Offering of the Blessing Boat*, *Lace Bowl*, and *Bamboo Barstool* reached significant level.

**Table 4.** Analysis of Variance for Products Evaluation by Educational Background

| Variables | Works | F | M | | | Scheffe's post hoc |
|---|---|---|---|---|---|---|
| | | | C&D | DR | ND | |
| Creativity | *Blessing Boat* | 5.91** | 3.88 | 4.25 | 4.39 | 3>1 |
| | *Zen Garden* | 0.14 | 3.34 | 3.31 | 3.31 | 1>2 |
| | *Lace Bowl* | 4.39* | 4.54 | 4.08 | 4.21 | |
| | *Bamboo Barstool* | 6.94** | 4.13 | 3.54 | 3.51 | 1>2, 1>3 |
| Technique | *Blessing Boat* | 5.94** | 3.81 | 3.84 | 4.24 | 3>1, 3>2 |
| | *Zen Garden* | 0.51 | 3.51 | 3.29 | 3.39 | |
| | *Lace Bowl* | 4.87* | 4.22 | 3.71 | 4.11 | 1>2 |
| | *Bamboo Barstool* | 5.5** | 4.11 | 3.75 | 3.54 | 1>3 |
| Aesthetics | *Blessing Boat* | 5.78** | 3.47 | 3.45 | 4.13 | 3>1, 3>2 |
| | *Zen Garden* | 0.08 | 3.21 | 3.31 | 3.21 | |
| | *Lace Bowl* | 2.27 | 4.45 | 3.95 | 4.04 | |
| | *Bamboo Barstool* | 5.87** | 4.14 | 3.54 | 3.28 | 1>3 |
| Integral Evaluation | *Blessing Boat* | 6.76** | 3.72 | 3.85 | 4.25 | 3>1, 3>2 |
| | *Zen Garden* | 0.04 | 3.35 | 3.30 | 3.30 | |
| | *Lace Bowl* | 3.87* | 4.40 | 3.91 | 4.12 | 1>2 |
| | *Bamboo Barstool* | 7.29** | 4.12 | 3.61 | 3.44 | 1>2, 1>3 |

$*p < .05$, $**p < .01$, C&D: Craft and industrial design, DR: Design-related, ND: Non-design

### 4.3 The Multiple Regression Analysis of Work's Preference

To explore how the three creative indexes affect the preference of products, this study took a further step and processed the multiple regression analysis, taking the dimensions of creativity, technique, and aesthetics as independent variables and the participant's preference towards the product as the dependant variable, the following are the results of the four examined products (Table 5).

**Table 5.** Three Indexes to Predict the Preference of the Works

| Works | Predictor variables | B | r | β | t |
|---|---|---|---|---|---|
| Blessing Boat | Creativity | .152 | .577*** | .091 | 0.922 |
| | Technique | .300 | .626*** | .167 | 1.619 |
| | Aesthetics | .637 | .766*** | .601 | 6.634*** |
| | R=.785 | R²=.617 | | F=47.248*** | |
| Zen Garden | Creativity | .133 | .660*** | .096 | 0.905 |
| | Technique | .071 | .670*** | .048 | 0.436 |
| | Aesthetics | .775 | .828*** | .722 | 7.678*** |
| | R=.833 | R²=.694 | | F=66.432*** | |
| Lace Bowl | Creativity | .341 | .716*** | .226 | 2.910** |
| | Technique | .229 | .692*** | .156 | 2.024* |
| | Aesthetics | .588 | .836*** | .587 | 7.931*** |
| | R=.872 | R²=.760 | | F=92.952*** | |
| Bamboo Barstool | Creativity | .129 | .686*** | .090 | 0.878 |
| | Technique | .299 | .679*** | .191 | 2.011* |
| | Aesthetics | .614 | .809*** | .611 | 6.582*** |
| | R=.828 | R²=.686 | | F=64.120*** | |

*p<.05, **p<.01, ***p<.001

By looking at the work of *The Offering of the Blessing Boat*, F value of the integral regression model is 19.872, achieving significant level (p<.001), therefore, the score can be established as the basis for preference prediction. In the regression formula, the outcome shows that the aesthetics dimension reveals the highest significance (β=.601 , p<.001).

Looking at the work, *Zen Garden*, the F value of the integral regression model is 66.432, achieving significant level (p<.001), therefore, the score can be considered as the basis for preference prediction. In the regression formula, the aesthetics dimension reached significant level (β=.722 , p<.001).

The F value of the integral regression model is 92.952 for the work of *Lace Bowl*. The score can be considered as the basis for preference prediction (p<.001). In the regression formula, the outcome shows that the aesthetics dimension reveals the highest significance (β=.587 , p<.001), followed by creativity dimension (β=.226 , p<.01), and finally the technique dimension (β=.156 , p<.05), all three dimensions have all achieved significant level.

The F value of the integral regression model is 64.120 for the work of *Bamboo Barstool*. The score can be considered as the basis for preference prediction (p<.001). In the regression formula, the outcome shows that the aesthetics dimension reveals the highest significance (β=.611 , p<.001), followed by technique dimension (β=.191 , p<.05), and finally the creativity dimension, the first two dimensions have both reached significant level.

# 5    Conclusions and Recommendations

## 5.1    Discussion of Findings

This research focuses on the grand prize winners of "Taiwan Crafts Competition" and classical works from "The Project Yii". Through the induction of research outcome, the conclusions are acquired as below.

**MDS Analysis of Works Style.** The study employs MDS analysis to the champion works of "Taiwan Crafts Competition" and the current digital exhibition from classical works of "The Project Yii", a total of 10 pieces of works process for style analysis, also employing realistic-freehanded and functional-nonfunctional attributes as independent dimensions, establishing four potential structures of work styles:

1. Functional/Realistic orientation: the cognitive images include integral, classical, organic, harmonic, traditional, ordinary, steady, and conventional.
2. Functional/Freehanded orientation: the cognitive images include linear, tactile, focus on expression, plain, and artificial.
3. Nonfunctional/Freehanded orientation: the cognitive images include creative, ethereal, novel, modern, conflicting, geometric, avant-garde, and compositional.
4. Nonfunctional/Realistic orientation: the cognitive images include natural, gorgeous, focus on material, deliberate, visual, and curvilinear.

In accordance with data analysis, the number of works was evenly distributed in the four quadrants; two works were located in the first quadrant (Functional/Realistic), works including *Cocoon project: Sofa* and *Bamboo Barstool*; three works were located in the second quadrant (Functional/Freehanded), works including *Taste of Memory*, *Zen Garden*, and *World Cup: Black Lotus*; two works were located in the third quadrant (Nonfunctional/Freehanded), works which includes *Lace Bowl* and *Moon Cup*; in the fourth quadrant (Nonfunctional/Realistic) includes three pieces, *Hello*, *The Offering of the Blessing Boat*, and *Brick Plate*.

**CAT Analysis of Works' Expression.** The research results indicates the participant's evaluations towards the creativity, technique, and aesthetics dimension of each work, the sequence holds a consistent order. That is, when a work acquires a higher integral evaluation, the average performances in the creativity, technique, and aesthetics dimensions will also show better outcome.

**Multiple Regression Analysis of Works Preference.** Research findings show that the three dimensions and work's preference both holds a positive correlation, the overall regression model all achieved significant level, thus, the three dimensions can be established as the basis for preference prediction, as for the participants, the aesthetics dimension is easier to influence the work's integral preference.

## 5.2    Recommendations

Synthesizing the above results, this study provides suggestions concerning relative modern crafts development issues, the advice are listed as below:

1. To improve the national craft competition and reward system, it is suggested to integrate the evaluation of government, artists, and academics, by discussing and carefully planning the program.
2. Thorough technical training is the foundation of promoting the entire industry, educational institutes should emphasize the importance of craft education development, thus, the institutes should take on a more positive attitude and action towards providing students with competition award opportunities.
3. The aesthetics dimension is the easiest mean to influence a work's integral preference, aside from enhancing the aesthetics training of professionals, how to increase crafts appreciation of average consumer through education is the critical factor for facilitating national craft development.
4. To manage international market and create international brands are the main targets for the development of modern crafts, it is crucial for cultural administrative units and educational institutes to process interdisciplinary collaborations by implementing scholarship programs, providing grants and opportunity for outstanding gifted students to visit and engage in advance study abroad.

**Acknowledgment.** This study was partly sponsored with a grant, NSC100-2410-H-144-008, from the National Science Council, Taiwan.

# References

1. Amabile, T.M.: The social psychology of creativity. Springer, N.Y (1983)
2. Amabile, T.M.: Creativity in context: Update to the social psychology of creativity. Westview Press, Oxford (1996)
3. Chen, G.Z.: Constructing the value of modern craft. Taiwan Craft 35, 12–17 (2009)
4. Chiu, H.C.: Measurement and consensus assessment of creativity (2005)
5. Education Resources and Research, 30, 267-298
6. Lin, C.C.: The future of Taiwan creative industry: exclusive interview with Jeff Dayu Shi, manager of Dragonfly/modern crafts alliance creative director. Taiwan Craft 28, 52–57 (2008)
7. Lin, R.T.: Cultural creative products derived from aboriginal twin cup-the Linnak. Art Appreciation 3(2), 21–28 (2008)
8. National Taiwan Craft Research and Development Institute: Introduction and current product list of Yii brand (2010),
   `http://163.29.89.217/zh-tw/Bulletin/`
   `Content.aspx?Para=343&Control=4&Page=2` (retrieved January 15, 2013)
9. Norman, D.A.: Emotional Design: Why We Love (or Hate) Everyday Things. Basic Books, New York (2004)
10. Wang, P.C.: Multivariate analysis. Higher Education Publishing Co., Taipei (2003)
11. Yen, S.L.: Taiwan craft. Kuang Hua Books, Tainan (1952)

# Research on Symbol Expression for Eye Image in Product Design: The Usage of the Chinese Traditional "Yun Wen"

Chi-Chang Lu[1] and Po-Hsien Lin[2]

[1] Crafts and Design Department, National Taiwan University of Arts
Ban Ciao City, Taipei 22058, Taiwan
[2] Graduate School of Creative Industry Design,
National Taiwan University of ArtsBan Ciao City, Taipei 22058, Taiwan
{t0134,t0131}@ntua.edu.tw

**Abstract.** In visual arts, using the eyes to deliver the message of life and emotion of a living thing has always been emphasized. The expression of the eyes is usually a combination of the eyeballs, pupils, eyelids, and eyelashes, etc. Among these, the pupil is of a crucial character. It completes the image of an eye and shows the direction of the line of sight. In this article, the authors wish to create a new way to show the symbols of eyes based on the Chinese traditional cloud pattern- Yun Wen in the area of the product design. The design will combine the features of both the traditional cultural style and the vogue. It will also present the eastern aesthetics difference between visual similarity and visual dissimilarity.

**Keywords:** Clouds pattern (Yun Wen), Chinese traditional pattern, decoration, eye image, cultural implication, product design.

## 1    Introduction

At a product design event, the first author exhibited a teapot based on the form of the Chinese Prehistoric Pottery Gui-tripod. The Chinese traditional clouds pattern - Yun Wen- was selected for the symbolic decoration of a bird's crest and wing to incorporate extra traditional cultural elements into the design. The softness and the dynamic movement of the curved line successfully express the feature and image of crest and wing. Subsequently, the form of an owl was also added to the design. The form of eyes has become one of the important considerations. The focal point of this article is how the authors extracts the characteristic and image of eyes that can achieve a perfect balance of combining various patterns into one through the new design form of Yun Wen. In visual art, eyes have always been the key to delivering the message of life and emotion of a living thing. An idiom of Chinese- Hua Long Dian Jing - means that to put life into an object in painting by dotting the dragon's eyeballs emphasize that eyes are the key point in life construction. The Chinese philosopher Mengzi also said that watching people's eyes could reveal their thoughts and emotions. The above examples explain the correlation between eyes and inner feeling.

P.L.P. Rau (Ed.): CCD/HCII 2013, Part I, LNCS 8023, pp. 128–137, 2013.
© Springer-Verlag Berlin Heidelberg 2013

Post-modernism Design broke away from Functionalism and brought more interest and feeling in life. Creative Industries have been expanded all over the world and become the key branches of the economy. Creative Industries, based on sense perception and multiculturalism, are interested in localism, distinctive national features, and traditional craftsmanship. Since the Deco revised and animation came to style, the descriptions toward human being as well as animals' entireties or parts becomes the main method to decorate implements.

## 2    Research Purposes

In visual art, the eye is usually presented through the combination of eyeball, pupil, eyelid, and eyelash. Among them, the pupil is a crucial character. Pupils complete the image of eyes and also show the direction of the line of sight. Whether in a realistic or exaggerated expression, drawing the pupil in a closed form as a circle or oval shape with dark color is an almost unaltered method used in painting and sculpture.

Based on the Chinese traditional clouds pattern - Yun Wen - this study seeks to create a brand new form for presenting the eye's image. The research area has been narrowed down to the eyes of birds only. Its purposes are to develop patterns which: a. possess local and traditional cultural styles; b. possess contemporary characteristics with both the style of abstractionism and minimalism; c. can represent the eye's image in certain backgrounds not necessarily realistic; d. can show the direction of the line of sight, and are able to deliver the dynamic features of eyes.

## 3    Literature Review

### 3.1    The Cultural Implications of Chinese Traditional Patterns

In semiology, a traditional pattern is not only a decorative form of beauty, but also a system of symbolisms. The German philosopher E. Cassirer(1874-1945) claimed that man should be defined as an animal symbolicum (a symbol-making or symbolizing animal), and sought to understand human nature by exploring symbolic forms in all aspects of a human being's experience.

In ancient China, related thoughts about semiology are also abundant and can be found in very early literature. *The Tao-te Ching*, "If you can talk about it, it ain't Tao. If it has a name, it's just another thing. Tao doesn't have a name. Names are for ordinary things. Stop wanting stuff; it keeps you from seeing what's real. When you want stuff, all you see are things."It pointed out that all things in the world are distinguished by their name that had been created by man.

*Book of Changes* said,"The sage was able to survey all the complex phenomena under the sky. He then considered in his mind how they could be figured, and (by means of the diagrams) represented their material forms and their character. Hence these (diagrams) are denominated Semblances (or emblematic figures, the Hsiang)."

According to *Book of Changes*, the Eight Trigrams came from observation in the world, and through the figure to symbolize specific or abstract thinking. This condition had been confirmed by archaeological excavation such as the Kuahu Bridge (6000-5000B.C.). There are many Sun Patterns painted or engraved in the pottery to symbolize sun worship. Later, the Hemudu Archaeological Site (5000-4000B.C.) had more decorative patterns including astronomical phenomena, vegetations, and creatures. Above all, the figure combined sun and bird, origin of the myth - Golden Crow Bearing Sun - is the most outstanding pattern. This discovery confirms that ancient patterns always bore some cultural thought at that time. In other archaeological sites of the Yangshao Culture, equal in age to Hemudu Culture, more painted pottery described the social life and the world of ideas with concrete or abstract figures.

The pattern of the Eight Trigrams is an extremely abstract geometric figure which is better than a figurative form to deliver the concept of an intelligible world. The same phenomenon is also reflected in Chinese prehistoric pottery. Abstract figures are far more common than specific descriptions. It noted that there is more the idea of the level of thinking, is a cultural symbol. Pattern in the form of visible, belongs to the level of expression, semiology call it Signifier. The referential concept of thinking is called Signified, on behalf of the connotation level. From the perspective of semiology, a Chinese traditional pattern as a means of awareness and understanding of the objective world is indeed a meaningful word in the form of language.

Prehistoric patterns were more for exploring and understanding the objective world. Later, historical period patterns gradually turned to Auspicious Patterns for seeking happiness and luck. Especially in the Ming and Qing Dynasties of China (A.D.1368-1911), auspicious patterns flooded every corner of human life. In Ancient China, Mainland Cultural character and the traditional agrarian social model brought their people an idea of self-sufficiency in material life. Advocating the practical also became a custom of the arts and was represented in traditional auspicious patterns.

### 3.2    Different Eye Designs Shown on the Chinese Traditional Utensils

The appearance of the animal eye is mainly constituted by the eyeball and the dark pupil. The eyeball is covered by the upper and lower eyelids, and so only partially exposed through the almond-shaped Palpebral Fissure. The shape of Palpebral Fissure is often different in animal species due to individual characteristics. In addition, behavior and emotion may also effect partially or entirely. The shape of Palpebral Fissure, the position of the eyeball, as well as the size of the pupil, can cause eyes to assume many different expressions. The Eye is the Window to the Soul, this adage illustrates the eye's diversity in expression, and the correlation with inner feelings.

The pupil is another focus in drawing eyes. It gives the dynamic sense and shows the direction of gaze, and other emotional characteristics. But whether realistic or hyperbolic method, the eyeball is always painted as the closed form of circle or oval with a dark color.

**Eyes Image of the Prehistoric Era in China.** Animal image artifacts appeared in about the Middle Neolithic period in China such as the birds and pigs in the Hemudu Culture, the fish, deer, frogs, and Seaman patterns and so on in the Yangshao Culture. At that time, some of the eyes of animals were depicted using only a single dot or circle, others might add the outer concentric circle to symbolize the palpebral fissure and pupil. But in some painted pottery of the Yangshao Culture, we usually can see clever arrangements for pupil position to empathize different expressions. Another example is the Fish Pattern with Human Face (Fig. 1), the depiction of the human eyes are much more than the animals. For example, almond-shaped eyelids, or sleep state line eye, which shows the variety performance for the eyes' imagines of the original residents . In northern China and years about Yangshao late period, the Hongshan culture (4000-3000B.C.) attracted much attention for its exquisite jade craft. The jade of the Hongshan culture has more specific animal images than Hemudu and Yangshao, which shows the significant cultural meaning of this pattern for the culture. These animal-shaped jades include some realistic birds, cicadas, fish, turtles, pigs, etc., but the focus is still the dragon - fantasy gods. The Jade Dragon of Hongshan culture including the Slotted-shaped Dragon (sculpture in the round), Y-shaped Artifact (front plane-like) and Circulators [1], had a common prominent feature: two large round eyes almost occupying the entire head. Between the eyes, the two upper and lower arcs are connected like a bridge. As a whole, it is very similar to the Animal mask patterns on ancient Chinese bronze ware. Following the Hongshan Culture, the pattern - God with Animal's Face (Fig. 2) was well known in the Liangzhu Culture (3300-2200B.C.). This pattern with a relief animal mask at the bottom has a pair of prominent eyes is as the main character. The center of the eyes is double ring of concentric circles to symbolize the eyeball and pupil and is surrounded by egg-shaped eyelids that are covered with thin sculptured wire. The two eyes are connected with a short bridge, very similar to the Hongshan Jade Dragon. The man of God is like riding on the animal with a sitting posture and its eyes also consist of double concentric circles. The difference is that the outer ring has two short lines or triangular tip at both sides to denote the Canthal angle of the eye. The same comparison also appears on many jade cong for their Simplification of God with Animal's Face to explain the distinction between man and animal.

**Fig. 1.** Fish Pattern with Human Face     **Fig. 2.** God with Animal's Face     **Fig. 3.** Chen Wording Type Eyes

**Eye Images of the Bronze Age in China.** The main decoration in Chinese Bronze Age is the animal, especially the Animal Mask Pattern. There are three bronze plates decorated **with** the Animal Mask and inlay turquoise found at the Erlitou Culture site (2080-1580B.C.).  It has the two kinds of eyes; round and almond-shaped. Most of the Animal Mask Patterns in Chinese Bronze ware belongs to the Shang and early Western Zhou dynasties(1562-771B.C.), and the stylized Chen Wording Type Eyes (Fig. 3) is its characteristic. This is an impressionistic approach to express the eyelid and the pupil image, and named by its shape similar to the Chinese word "minister" in seal script. Chen Wording Type Eyes were also used in jade and became a significant characteristic of that time. After the mid-Western Zhou dynasty, the specific animal prints were instead by Variant zoomorphic patterns, such as Chieh-chu Wen(竊曲紋)、Chung-huan Wen(重環紋)、Po-chu Wen(波曲紋)、Lin Wen(鱗紋). These patterns were evolved from the Animal Mask, dragon, phoenix, etc., but had already been simplified or deformed. [2]. The Chieh-chu Wen also known as the animal eye cross-linked pattern is descriptive of two animals connected to each other by one eye [3]. Part of the eye image followed the previous form and also had the Chen Wording Type Eye.

### 3.3    Eye Designs Displayed in Comics

Comics are a visual art form that describes things by special drawing techniques. Its characteristics are as follows:

a. A painting with a concise form, but always paying attention to its significance.
b. A painting with a strong sense of irony or humor.
c. Exaggerate features containing more than ironic significance.
d. A painting with some concise techniques which directly reveal the essence of features and items.

Because the demand for a strong narrative, the techniques of exaggeration, metaphor, symbol, etc., become important method,. Eyes, our so-called window to the soul, naturally become a performance focus in comics. The internet furnished more than 150 kinds of comic eyes, which shows that the function of the eye in comics is very important. For comics, eyes in addition to being exaggerated also give meaning or moral in special situations through metaphor or a symbol. For example, a vortex eye pattern represents dizziness. (Fig. 4)

**Fig. 4.** "Dizzy" eye pattern in comics    **Fig. 5.** Vortex pattern in prehistoric painted pottery    **Fig. 6.** Flower-like cloud pattern

### 3.4    The Traditional Pattern in the Long Historical Stream – Yun Wen

For Yangshao Culture painted pottery, the Banpo types of pottery uses straight lines as the main graphic elements. Alternatively, Miao Digou type is almost wholly composed of arcs, forming a significant difference. Later, Chinese traditional decoration gradually evolved to organic lines with more curvature. It is unique in using straight and curve line alternately. The straight line is strong, clear, simple, stubborn, and direct, with a male character. The curved line is relatively elegant, soft, noble, indirect, slender, and soft with female characteristics. The original purpose of this study is to design a bird's eye form. Birds have more supple and smooth characteristics compared to wild beasts, so traditional patterns always used a circular motif for the eyes. Based on this principle, the design choice of the arc complex form - Yun Wen for displaying the traditional cultural style is appropriate. Yun Wen is composed of spiral, S-shaped, and C-shaped patterns, presenting the surrounding, extending, undulating and convoluting art forms, showing rich dynamic changes and mysterious atmosphere.

**The Tradition of Yun Wen.** Yun Wen - the cloud pattern - is one of the Chinese traditional decorative patterns and can be traced back to prehistoric painted pottery decoration- vortex pattern.(Fig. 5). And the Yunlei Wen for Shang and Zhou dynasties(1562-221B.C.), the cloud scroll patterns for Warring States period(475-221B.C.). However, the skill of representing the cloud patterns can be sure to be started from the southern state of Chu during the Warring States Period. The traditional Chinese ideologies think that the cloud and Qi(氣) are the same and   signify the heavens, the mysteries of the universe. The clouds pattern - Yun Wen -matures further in the Han Dynasty(206B.C.-A.D.220), have been widely used on palace, clothing, utensils and more with other combination, such as dragons, beasts, birds to convey the feeling of flow and speed. Due to the influence of Buddhist culture in the Wei, Jin and Southern and Northern Dynasties(A.D.220-581), the Streamers cloud pattern in decorative painting often set off as a bodhisattva, dragon, or phoenix. The Flower-like cloud pattern(Fig. 6) in the Sui and Tang dynasties(A.D.581-907) is realistic, plump, beautiful, and very decorative and also makes the picture lively, reflecting a rich and satisfying public aesthetic taste. During the Song and Yuan Dynasties(A.D.960-1368), the Ruyi-cloud pattern was combined with Ruyi and Ganoderma patterns, and can be used alone or with other patterns to give new meanings. During the Ming Dynasty(A.D.1368-1644), the most unique pattern was the Group-cloud pattern; complex, strong sense of order and symmetry, with delicate double hook processing into a highly patterned situation. The Qing Dynasty(A.D.1644-1911) launched a lavish, complicated decoration - The Stack-cloud pattern - Uniform fine curve of twists and turns, through freely changeable, endless combinations to form its own characteristics [4].

**The Cultural Connotation of Yun Wen.** The endless cloud pattern are highly associate with **Chinese** ancestors' understanding to the natural phenomenon of the cloud. The cultural connotation of the cloud pattern can be roughly summarized by the following three points [5]:

1. The relationship between the cloud and Qi. Qi(氣) is one of the objects of pre-Qin and later philosophers concerned about. They thought that Yuan Qi is the origin of the heavens and the earth and all things are generated from the interaction between Yin(陰) and Yang(陽). Qi is a pictograph resembling rising steam; the original meaning is just the clouds. The ancient Chinese believed that the cloud is Qi and Qi is the cloud. Therefore the Qi and the cloud are the same.
2. The relationship of Yun Wen and Immortal Thoughts. The natural cloud is unpredictable. It comes and goes without a trace of mystery. People since ancient times had already linked the cloud and gods, mythical beasts, ghosts and goblins. The gods as well as monsters in ancient Chinese legends usually take cloud as there rides. Immortal Thoughts flourished in the Han Dynasty, so the cloud pattern become very popular. Yun Wen not only has rich and vivid images but also possesses more Chinese pattern Unique Artistic Beauty related to the immortality concept.
3. The auspicious significance of Yun Wen. The cloud makes rain to moisten all things so it can bring good luck to the people. In addition, the Cloud and Fortune are homonyms in Chinese pronunciation and connote the meaning of luck and fate. Therefore, the Yun Wen is also a Chinese traditional auspicious pattern. Related to Chinese traditional patterns and auspicious significance, Lucky cloud pattern, Ruyi-cloud pattern, etc., were essential decorations in folk painting, embroidery and engraving.

### 3.5    Styles – The Modern Style and the Eastern Myth

**Abstract, Minimalist – Modern Fashion Style.** The perfect combination of technology and art in a handicraft era had created a brilliant traditional craft. The Industrial Revolution brought new technologies, new materials, and new methods of production, but didn't bring any new art for reference to design. Therefore, the mass production by the machine brought a sharp downfall in the artistic quality of the product, and the decrease of the artistic tastes of consumers. In order to solve this problem, the Arts and Crafts Movement, Art Nouveau and Art Deco Movement arose. But these movements were not the most effective way to solve the problem because they chose to escape or fight against industrial technology contrary to the trend of the times. Compared to manual techniques, industrial production technology is indeed a step forward. The key point is that it is necessary to find a new art form to adapt to the new production technology and so create quality products that belong to the machine age. Abstract trend of Modern Art provided an excellent solution to resolve this contradiction.

Abstract trend of Modern Art began with Cezanne and developed into cubism and abstract art. They followed rationalism and used geometric shapes and minimalist color to extract the performance of objects. These features were just in tune with the requirements of mass production and considered to be the best choice for machine production. Modernism design is born on this basis and became the most stable, most influential style in the First half of the 20th century. Although Modernism design had been criticized by Post-modernism and leaving the design style to become more diverse. However, the trend that the shape and decoration of abstract and simplify is already taking shape, not possible to go back to the old ways of the traditional complicated fine decorative.

**Between Similarity and Dissimilarity – Eastern Myth.** Emphasis on the abstract, minimalism and vogue seems to have lost the charm of the Oriental tradition – the hazy mood of the subtle and impressionistic. How to pursue such flavor? The late Ming painter Shi Tao advocated painting to be "Unlike what the like is really like", thank thought that painting must to pursue the rhyme of the image of the outside rather than stick to the original shape. Likewise, the recent painter Qi Baishi summarized the ancestors' paintings experience, advocated "Wonder from the Similarity and Dissimilarity".

# 4    Practice of the Works

### 4.1    Consideration of the Work Form

Yun Wen is one of the most representative of traditional Chinese ornamentation; the composition of arc curves and the sense of movement were required for these design activities. It not only can achieve the basic shape of the eyes, but also convey the flow characteristics of the eye. The clouds patterns and forms are various and complicated, they can be the extremely simple Vortex pattern, or other combination such as Group-cloud pattern or Stack-cloud pattern. We initially selected Vortex pattern to present a simple, abstract, and minimalist style features of the eyes. Vortex-shaped line as a base to the Vortex pattern is an open curve line, with some qualities of dynamic, rotary, etc., full of uncertainty characteristics [6]. As a result, the comic uses of the vortex pattern instead of eyes to indicate that dizzy feeling. Therefore, this study hopes to utilize the vortex pattern as the image of the eye. To rule out the uncertainty evoked by the lines is the main concern. After much thought and effort to get ideal results, characterized as follows:

a. The Vortex pattern is started from the center to the semicircular morphology to symbolize the "eyes" image, and then extended out and back gradually closing the circle to constitute the appearance of the eye contour.
b. In order to avoid the endless extending feeling that volute lines brings, we interchange hierarchy in the end part of the "eyes" and the outer ring. In addition, both ends of the pack to the ground floor produced the Vortex pattern convergence sense.
c. We use the curved surface, especially render eyes with a greater curvature.

## 4.2    Examination of the Work Form

Examine the complete Cloud-vortex Eye, we preliminarily consider that the affections as following:

a. With the inner and outer rings' interchange of a hierarchy at the end of the pupil part, we not only create the effect of segmentation around eyeballs and eyes, but also generate the alternative   light and shadow to produce the impression of three-dimension.
b. Although, there is no actual closed circular form, but through the guide lines of opening end, and the circular arc surface. We can feel the presence of the pupil from the psychological level. This is just the Law of Closure advocated by Gestalt psychology, which not only can complete the image of the pupil effect, can also raise the attention of the viewer by its ambiguity.
c. Through the unilateral opening form of the pupil, a directive visual line was created from the closed side to the open side, this design also brought out the emotion filled with of vitality .
d. Different from the traditional direct simulation, Cloud-vortex Eye presents the image of the eye and Life by an impressionistic abstract form to complete the oriental flavor that "Wonder from the Similarity and Dissimilarity".

## 4.3    Case Study

**The Owl Image Teapot.** The owl's most significant feature that distinguishes it from other birds is the "face plate" organization; it is also the most important part of showing owl images. The teapot design case considered rendering the owl's face plate with parabolic concave, not only to comply with the actual form of the owl's face plate, but also to strengthen the changes and contrast effect by means of light and shadow. Relative to the parabolic concave, owl eyes are placed with a relatively protruding independent segmentation in the appropriate position in the face plate. Finally, the eyes were joined together with the spout in the upper middle of both sides of the plate to symbolize the bird beak and complete the characterization of the owl's head image. Although the beak position and the actual shape do not match, the overall expression of the owl image is successful. (Fig. 7)

**The Owl Image Tea Cup.** The face plate originally considered was similar to the former case teapot but it was found that the effect was not ideal using the digital 3D stereoscopic construct. First, the outside of the cup seemed to be rather flat and mono-tone and second, the inside had a reverse convex form detrimental to its integrity. In addition, considering that the structure of face plate with eye separation would raise the concreteness, and not only increase the complexity, but also affect the abstract that author tried to present. Therefore, we tried to combine the face plate and eye with an approximate egg-shaped arc extending out through the vortex pattern. Moreover, during the process of making the eyes to the "face plate", the original outer arc surface is also gradually changed into the plane or intrados. Finally, the molded nose and beak image at the lower position between two "face plates", get produced very good recognition results. (Fig. 8)

**The Bird Image Teapot.** Unlike the aforementioned owl teapot, this case did not specifically refer to specific bird. Because it is not an owl, the characteristic of the face plate was removed and the Cloud-vortex Eye directly attached to an appropriate position in on the pot body. But because the closed circular feature is considerable separated from the pot body, the effect was not ideal. We tried adjusting the outer ring of the Cloud-vortex Eye to form an open state which gradually disappeared into the pot body. The results not only achieved a more coordinated overall symbolic eye form but also the effect remained evident. (Fig. 9)

**Fig. 7.** The owl image teapot    **Fig. 8.** The owl image tea cup    **Fig. 9.** The bird image teapot

## 5    Discussion and Conclusion

**Reflection of the Design Cases.** After completion of the aforementioned three design cases, the effect of the Cloud-vortex Eye applied to the eyes of the birds can be considered successful:

a. Yun Wen is a very traditional Chinese characteristics with rich auspicious mean-ings. The effect of changes in its liquidity is also suitable for modern design. Yun Wen as a foundation element to render the image of the eye allows the product to show a specific style of traditional culture.
b. The Cloud-vortex Eye, which looks like a stretched tail of unilateral Tai Chi, advo-cates traditional cultural thinking with perfect integration and dynamic beauty.
c. The Cloud-vortex Eye has the qualities of concise and rich layering and also an abstract, minimalist style of contemporary fashion.
d. The Cloud-vortex Eye does not have the absolute image of the eye, but we inter-change the inner and outer ring's of hierarchy, and the guide lines of the opening end of the circular arc surface. We can feel the presence of the pupil from the

psychological level. Especially in context with beak characteristics, the symbolic expression of the eye is very obvious.

e. Through the disparity of both sides pupils, particularly convey the visual directivity. The flow characteristics of the vortex pattern also create the eye a sense of vivid life.

f. Distinguished from the traditional direct simulation of two-round, Cloud-vortex Eyes, the impressionistic abstract form, showing the oriental flavor - Wonder from the Similarity and Dissimilarity is better reached.

**Key to the Design of "Swirly Cloud Eyes".** From the evolution of three actual cases, the Cloud-vortex Eye is not necessarily confined to the initial circular contour. It may be able to extend endlessly, or gradually disappear integrated into the main body. The only constant is the interchange of **hierarchies** the end of the pupil and the outer arc of the eye surface form. This mode can be regarded as the design key of the Cloud-vortex Eye.

**Possible Development in the Future.** In this study, the designs of the Cloud-vortex Eye used in a bird's eye **symbolic** expression are successful. Might they be applicable to eyes of the other animals, or might it help develop more emotional characteristics? These questions are worthy of further exploration.

**Acknowledgment.** This study was partly sponsored with a grant, NSC99-2622-H-144-002 -CC3, from the National Science Council, Taiwan.

# References

1. Jiang, M.Y.: Preliminary study of the Chinese Neolithic Yulong. General Education and Trandisciplinary Research, 6 (2009)
2. Yeh-liu, T.Z.: History of Chinese decorative arts. SMC Publishing, Taipei (2002)
3. Ma, C.Y.: Chinese bronzes. SMC Publishing, Taipei (1991)
4. Yang, M.: Application of Yun Wen in modern design and teaching. Literary Studies, 3 (2009)
5. Yang, W.N.: The significance and modern values of Chinese traditional Yun Wen. Big Stage, 4 (2008)
6. Yang, C.T.: Introduction to shapes principle. Yifeng Tong Press, Taipei (1996)

# An Empirical Research on Experience Evaluation and Image Promotion of Wuxi Fruit Brand: The Case of the Brand Package of Yangshan Shuimi Peaches

Wei Xiong[1], Liang Yin[1], Xinli Lin[1], and Shengli Lu[2]

[1] School of Design, Jiangnan University, Wuxi 214122, China
[2] Wuxi PeachWell IOT Technology Co. Ltd., Wuxi 214122, China
xiongw03@163.com, {yl401402,kathy_lin1990}@hotmail.com,
lu_sunny@139.com

**Abstract.** This research takes the theory of brand experience as the guidance, uses the brand experience evaluation as its method and aims the service design as its target. And the research is to search for the new theory and model of promoting brand image. We have designed creatively the semantic analysis scale of experience evaluation of Wuxi fruit brand *Yangshan Shuimi Peaches*. Psychologically, we evaluated 3 types of the packages of *PeachWell* Brand: A (the original package), B (new package) and C (new package). After that, we collected the CSI (Customer Satisfaction Index) data, which showed the difference: B>C>A. Demographic samples divided by different means all had their own different requires of brand packages. These CSI data showed us that the new package B and C made more contributions to upgrading the brand. According to the result analyses of the empirical research on brand experience, we bring up the detailed service design plans and positive advices of promoting the brand image.

**Keywords:** Brand experience, Experience evaluation, Brand image promotion, Empirical research.

## 1   Research Theories and Application Value

In this topic, we studies the experience evaluation of the hang package of *PeachWell* Brand *Yangshan Shuimi Peaches* (the original Package A). To enhance its brand image, we designs new packages (the new Package B and C) to facilitate our empirical research. And we did association analysis on the data and factors got from the psychological evaluation of user experience by designing experience evaluation chart (*Yangshan Shuimi Peaches* semantic analysis chart). In view of the above, the empirical research is conducted in order to improve Wuxi local fruit brand.

P.L.P. Rau (Ed.): CCD/HCII 2013, Part I, LNCS 8023, pp. 138–147, 2013.
© Springer-Verlag Berlin Heidelberg 2013

A (Original)                    B (New)                    C (New)

**Fig. 1.** Package Design Proposals for *Yangshan Shuimi Peaches* Brand

# 2    Chinese Peach Brand Market and the Feature of *Yangshan Shuimi Peaches*

## 2.1    Features of *Yangshan Shuimi Peaches* Brand Experience

Feature of *Yangshan Shuimi Peaches* Brand Scene Experience: Compared to peaches from other production places in China, *Yangshan Shuimi Peaches* of Wuxi is famous for its large size, beautiful color, thin skin, thick flesh, juicy and sweet taste with rich fragrance.

Feature of *Yangshan Shuimi Peaches* Brand Emotion Experience: *Yangshan Shuimi Peaches* are the special local products of Wuxi. As a kind of healthy and nutritious local special fruit, *Yangshan Shuimi Peaches* are among the top choices in the concept of "to send health as a gift".

Feature of *Yangshan Shuimi Peaches* Brand Action Experience: Due to its high price, *Yangshan Shuimi Peaches* which is beneficial to all ages only have the main customer group of mid-age customers with some teenagers and the elders.

Feature of *Yangshan Shuimi Peaches* Brand Thingking Experience: In Chinese cultural, peach is the symbol of auspiciousness, longevity and youthfulness while the peach flowers represents spring and talisman. So there formed unique "Peach Culture" in Chinese profound history with thousand years.

# 3    Brand Experience Theory Oriented Research on *Yangshan Shuimi Peaches* Package Design

## 3.1    Summary about the Theory of Brand Experience

In recent decades, the theory of brand experience has greatly developed through researches done by numbers of scholars both at home and abroad, such as Holbrook & Hirschman, Rooley, Padgett & Allen, Pine & Glimoref, Petromilli & Michalczyk, Ellwood, Pinkerf, Dube & Le Bel and Schmitt. Based on the four-pattern brand experience theory of Brakus, Schmitt and Zarantonello in 2009, the topic describes brand experience in aspects of Scene Experience, Emotion Experience, Thingking Experience and Action Experience.

### 3.2    Analysis of *Yangshan Shuimi Peaches* Brand Package Experience

In this article, we suggested 20 pairs of adjectives to evaluate user experience about *Yangshan Shuimi Peaches* package:

— Scene Experience: good-looking, warm-colored, bright-colored, simple, vivid, with-details, useful, spiritual;
— Emotion Experience: unique, high-class, prestigious;
— Action Experience: intuitive, collectable, protective, anti-counterfeiting, fresh-reflective, good-quality;
— Thinking Experience: traditional, meaningful, local-featured.

By collecting cognition adjectives about brand experience of Wuxi *Yangshan Shuimi Peaches* Package above, we made evaluation tool about brand experience of *Yangshan Shuimi Peaches* package in scientific empirical way. After experience evaluation, we got quantization layer about packages of the same brand and made evaluation index. To lay foundation for further brand shaping and promotion, we also output parameter to quantatively differentiate various brands which will provide effective design position and design strategy for Wuxi fruit brand system service design.

## 4    The Empirical Research about Evaluation of *Yangshan Shuimi Peaches* Brand Package Experience

### 4.1    Introduction of Empirical Design

In this topic, we chose the hand package with anti-counterfeiting trace technology of *PeachWell* as our target of *Yangshan Shuimi Peaches* brand package experience evaluation, which is Package A for short. And based on brand experience theory, our research group of the design school designed Package B & C for *PeachWell* Brand to compare psychological evaluation of the original Package and the new designs.

The semantic analysis scale of Yangshan Shuimi Peaches package design, our evaluation tool, consists of 20 adjectives (Test Variables). Our evaluation object are original Package A (referred as Package A below), redesigned Package B (referred as Package B below), and redesigned Package C (referred as Package C below). And we get the result from Customer Satisfaction Index, referred as CSI below. We mainly discuss the common point, different point, maximum and minimum value of CSI of three packages, In appliance with Schmitt's brand experience theory, we collect adjectives about Scene Experience, Emotion Experience, Action Experience, Thinking Experience of Yangshan Shuimi Peaches package experience. After pre-experiment, finally we made the testing questionnaire. In our questionnaire interview, we mainly collect various people's CSI about Yangshan Shuimi Peaches package experience and do association analysis and factor analysis between customer feature and their CSI. We hope that the result analysis of our empirical research will lead the improvement of Yangshan Shuimi Peaches package service design.

## 4.2     The Empirical Research Design (Semantic Analysis Scale Design)

*Initial Questionnaire Design:* Brain Storm: We list over 100 adjectives about *Yangshan Shuimi Peaches* and its package, including Scene Experience, Emotion Experience, Action Experience and Thingking Experience.

Choose Variables: Categorize the adjectives in different types of experience, make them into question frame and rank the questions. Combining Likert scales and Osgood semantic analysis scales, the initial questionnaire consists of 42 variables with five attitude scores.

*Pre-experiment of Questionnaire:* 20 questions were issued in *De Fier's* way, and the response rate was 100% and all the 20 questionnaires were available.

Test the discrimination of all the 20 available questionnaires. Choose 20 variables with maximum average deviation out of the 42 variables to form experimental questionnaire. The 20 variables comprehensively four aspects of brand experience theory: Scene Experience, Emotion Experience, Thinking Experience and Action Experience.

*Empirical Research Implementation*: Testing: Part of the questionnaires were distributed in urban and rural areas of Wuxi. And they were all finished on-site.  In addition, to get evaluation of consumers from other places, questionnaires were not only send peer-to-peer through *QQ* software, E-mails, but also they were distributed nationwide by online professional survey platform *Questionnaire Star* (http://www.sojump.com/jq/2116939.aspx).

Tested: In formal research, there are 241 questionnaires issued, with 241 response and 201 questionnaires available. Among the tested customers, there are 99 males and 102 females. Not only design students from technical school, undergraduate school and graduate school but consumers in different career are also included in the test.

*ERP Data Processing:* Questionnaires that are not finished seriously are regarded as invalid questionnaires. In appliance with software of SPSS 17.0 and Excel, questionnaire data were input, calculated to conduct association analysis and factor analysis.

## 4.3     Empirical Research Association Analysis and Result Discussion

**Original and New Package Design Evaluation Experience Analysis for Yangshan Shuimi Peaches Brand PeachWell**

According to Figure 2: CSI of Package A ranges from 2.42 to 3.63. The element with the highest consumer evaluation is "protective" of behavior experience with CSI (3.63), while collectable element gets the lowest CSI evaluation with 2.42. Package B gets CSI score from 3.31 to 4.15 with consumer's positive evaluation in all aspects, among which, the lowest CSI appears in collectable of intellectual with 3.31 score. And Package B's unique and prestigious elements of Emotion Experience get the highest average CSI of 4.15. Package C achieves CSI of 3.23 to 4.02. Its highest CSI score is 4.02 of warm-colored element of Scene Experience, while the lowest CSI score is 3.23 of collectable element of Thinking Experience.

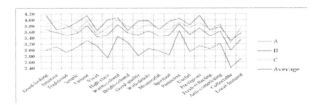

**Fig. 2.** Experience Analysis of Brand Package A, B and C

From average CSI curves, we can tell that the CSI arranges from 2.99 to 3.87. The highest score exists in the "protective" element of Action Experience with CSI score 3.87 for the reason that the three packages uses patented suspension technology of hang package. User's collectable evaluation of Thinking Experience has the highest average CSI of 2.99, suggesting that as a high-class gift package, all the three packages of Yangshan Shuimi Peaches need improvement in Thinking Experience.

Comparing the curves of Package A, B and C, CSI of Package A in lower than Package B & C in every evaluation aspect. In 13 aspects out of 20, Package B achieves higher CSI than Package C. So users experiences best about Package B. So the overall experience rank is B better than C, and better than A (B>C>A).

In summary, the suspension design of Package A, B, C enhances consumer experience in protection. To Package A, consumers accept its simple red- white appearance in Scene Experience. However it still has improvement space for users' affective and Thinking Experience. The peach flower element of Package B & C positively enhance consumers' brand experience. But as high-class package, Package B & C have to bring customers better Thinking Experience, especially in collectable. Comparing simplicity and details, consumers prefer simplicity rather than too many details.

**Brand Scene Experience Analysis of Yangshan Shuimi Peaches Package Design**
According to Figure 3, there are associate differences between customer's region and their Scene Experience. The curves representing CSI of consumers from the midwest countryside and s&m midwest cities is relatively higher than that of other regions. The lowest CSI belongs to consumers from coastal cities and midwest cities.

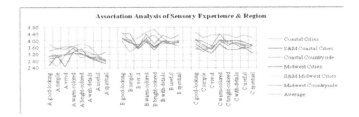

**Fig. 3.** Association Analysis of Scene Experience & Region Chart

1. Package A get the lowest CSI range from 2.47 to 3.83 in Scene Experience. Customers' evaluation differs most greatly in aspects of good-looking, simple and vivid.
2. Customers from different region evaluate Scene Experience of Package B with highest CSI from 3.33 to 4.67. While CSI of simple and bright-colored differs greatly. Moreover, in aspects of vivid, bright-colored, warm-colored and with details, CSI of midwest countryside are higher than that of other regions.
3. CSI of different regions for Package C ranges between 3.2 and 4.5 in the Scene Experience. Package C may gain more favorite by midwest countryside customers in Scene Experience.

**Brand Emotion Experience Analysis of Yangshan Shuimi Peaches Package Design**
The CSI curve distribution of Figure 4 shows that customers with secondary and tertiary education have higher CSI than other education level consumers, while undergraduate and graduate consumers give lower evaluation than consumers with other education background. That means, to some extent, consumers' Emotion Experience evaluation is inversely proportional to their education level.

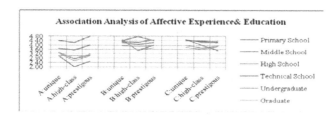

**Fig. 4.** Association Analysis of Emotion Experience & Education Chart

Analyzing Package A, its Emotion Experience CSI ranges from 2.0 to 4.8. Consumers CSI are relatively higher in aspect of unique and prestigious than high-class.

To Package B, CSI of different education level consumers ranges from 3.5 to 4.8 point. Among the three aspects, unique has the minimum difference with 3.95 to 4.50, which indicates that all consumers hope packages to be distinctive. On contrary, high-class has maximum difference between 3.40 to 4.80, suggesting that consumers' opinion about high class varies greatly. That is our solid facts of our differentiated brand package design.

To Package C, Emotion Experience CSI ranges from 3.50 to 4.47. But consumers of middle school, high school and technical school have concentrated CSI around 4.40, apparently higher than 3.8 CSI of consumers with college education. So the package is controversy in Emotion Experience and need to be redesigned through further discussion into user experience to explore the reason.

**Brand Action Experience Analysis of Yangshan Shuimi Peaches Package Design**
From curve distribution in Figure 5, we can find that consumers from CSI of midwest cities and coastal countryside are relatively low, especially for Package A. CSI of coastal cities and s&m coastal cities show little difference in the three packages. That means consumers from coastal cities, mostly with better economic condition and

open-mind, care little about Action Experience. Contrarily, coastal countryside and midwestern consumers consider more about Action Experience in their decision.

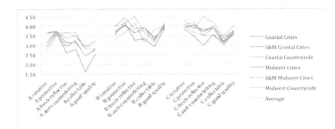

**Fig. 5.** Association Analysis of Action Experience & Region Chart

1. Analyzing Package A, its Action Experience CSI of consumers from various areas is the lowest, from 1.60 to 3.66. Consumers show greatly different attitude toward anti-counterfeiting and collectable, indicating that package design strategy need further investigation on market segmentation.
2. Package B CSI are between 2.93 to 4.50. Among that, both midwest and coastal rural consumers' CSI differs greatly to consumers from other regions. Especially in aspect of fresh-reflection, rural consumers' CSI is much higher than that of other regions. So to rural consumers, they have more expectation to the fresh-reflection of package.
3. To Package C, CSI of different regions ranges from 3.0 to 4.5.  Midwest rural consumer's CSI differs greatly from other region, which apparently appears in fresh-reflective aspect with higher CSI of 4.5 scores. Because they are relatively unfamiliar with *Yangshan Shuimi Peaches* and far away from urban lifestyle. .

**Brand Thinking Experience Analysis of Yangshan Shuimi Peaches Package Design**
In Figure 6, there is obvious stratification in variously educated consumers' CSI about Yangshan Shuimi Peaches packages, indicating that consumers with different education level have independent Thinking Experiences. So designers should take it into consideration in package design. Generally speaking, primary and secondary education consumers' CSI are relatively higher, while bachelor degree or above consumers' CSI are lower, which suggests that consumers with higher education expect more on Thinking Experience.

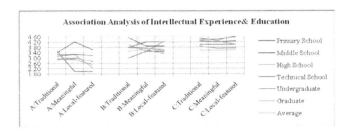

**Fig. 6.** Association Analysis of Thingking Experience & Education Chart

Analyzing Package A, consumers' Thinking Experience evaluation is the lowest among 2.0 to 4.2 score ranges. Consumers share similar attitude on its tradition factor with CSI around 3.2. But their attitudes toward packages meaning and local feature differentiates greatly.

For Package B, variously educated consumers' CSI ranges from 3.77 to 4.53. Technical students' CSI of 3.77 varies greatly with graduate students' CSI of 4.53. As both the tested technical school students and graduate students are major in design, it shows that consumers have different experience about tradition according to their education levels.

Consumers' CSI about Package C's Thinking Experience range from 3.58 to 4.60. We can tell from its plain and uniformly distributed curves that, to some extent, the three aspects of consumers' Thinking Experiences influence each other.

### 4.4    Factor Analysis and Result Discussion of the Empirical Research

**Premise Inspection of Factor Analysis.** The premise of factor analysis is the relatively strong correlation between original variables, from which we can consolidate several common factors that reflect common characteristics of the original variables with *Bartlett Sphericity* Test and *Kaiser-Meyer-Olkin* Test. *Kaiser* gave frequently-used KMO metrics: above 0.9-very suitable; 0.8-suitable; 0.7-general; 0.6-less suitable; less than 0.5- unsuitable. In this research, its *Bartlett Sphericity* Test value of Package Adjective scale is 2772.889 with 0.949 KMO value. Its Sig value is close to 0, indicating that they are very suitable to be factor molecules.

**a. Common Factor Extraction** *(Chart can not be displayed due to limited space)*

Through factor extraction and rotation of 41 website experience variables in 179 available samples, we extracted three common factors with characteristic root above 1 in PCA (Principle Component Analysis), see details in Chart 1. The three extracted common factors explained 65.719% total variance of original variables. Variances of factors' explanatively original variables are redistributed after factor rotation. And factor variances are changed to make factors easier for explanation.

In the gravel diagram, the abscissa represents the number of common factor, while the ordinate *Eigen* value. The first factor with high *Eigen* value makes the biggest contribution to original variables explanation. From the second factor, *Eigen* values decrease gradually. After the third factor, *Eigen* values of the factors are small and ignorable break stones at the foot of the mountains, making little contribution to original variables explanation. So it is appropriate to extract the first three common factors with *Eigen* values above 1.

**b. Factor Matrix Rotation** *(Chart can not be displayed due to limited space)*

Through orthogonal rotation, this subject successes in making most of the variables with great differences in load coefficient in every common factor after the convergence of eight times rotate iterations. In Chart 2, there are eight adjectives with higher load in the first factor. The first factor mainly interprets 8 variables: Q9 and Q16 have higher load in the second factor; Q17 and Q20 have higher load on the third factor.

**Factor Nomination Interpretations and Brand Package Design Inspiration.**
According to rotation ingredient matrix and result analysis of arranged rotation ingredient matrix (Chart 2), it is easy to see the relationship between every main component and its high load content, and nominate the three factors.

a. **Vivid and Prestigious Factors,** including 8 adjective variables: vivid (Q6), unique (Q5), high-class (Q7), prestigious (Q16), useful (Q15), spiritual (Q13), protective (Q14), bright-colored (Q9). Vivid and prestigious factors maintain more Emotion Experience variables: vivid (Q6), unique (Q5), high-class (Q7), prestigious (Q16) and some Scene Experience such as spiritual (Q13) and bright-colored (Q9), consisting eight elements of composite related experience. Among experience evaluation of three brand packages, Package B Emotion Experience evaluation CSI is 4.15, indicating that vivid and prestigious factor makes the main contribution. That inspires us that the package designers should pay attention to design elements of vivid and prestigious factors (as eight variables mentioned above). Thus, designers can combine those design elements creatively and form different style brand package design of *Yangshan Shuimi Peaches*, creating product series service design with brand personality and characteristics.

b. **Culture and Detail Factors,** maintaining 8 adjective variables as well: collectable (Q19), local-featured (Q20), anti-counterfeiting (Q18), meaningful (Q12), traditional (Q11), good quality (Q10), warm-colored (Q8). We can take culture and detail factors into consideration, which includes composite related experience combing Thingking Experience and Action Experience. In the empirical research, Package C experience effect tends to the style with culture and detail factors, which have important reference value in improving local-featured brand design.

c. **Intuitive and Simple Factors,** with 4 adjective variables: intuitive (Q2), simple (Q4), good-looking (Q1), fresh-reflective (Q17). Intuitive and simple factors mainly consists of Scene Experience factors, including intuitive (Q2), simple (Q4), good-looking(Q1) and fresh-reflective (Q17). In the empirical research, Package A belongs to this style and achieves high market acceptance.

# 5    Conclusions of the Empirical Research

Oriented by the theory of brand experience, we expect to make innovative contribution to the expansion of the brand theory. *Bernd H. Schmitt* (1999) proposed five-element theory model of brand experience: Scene Experience, Emotion Experience, Thingking Experience, Action Experience and related experience. This article focuses on the five dimensions to explain the specific approach of how brand experience influences brand loyalty.

We make association analysis between package design for *Yangshan Shuimi Peaches* of Wuxi fruit brand and the consumer experience evaluation of fruit brand to theoretically explore the universal law of matching brand design with user experience.

We originally design semantic analysis scale of experience evaluation for *Yangshan Shuimi Peaches* of Wuxi fruit brand. Through psychological evaluation of Package A, B, C for the *PeachWell* brand, we collect consumer satisfaction CSI (Customer Satisfaction Index) and get the differentiated results: B> C> A. Different populations claim for distinctive brand package. And their CSI parameters indicate that the new Package B & C make greater contributions to brand promotion.

According to *Schmitt's* five-dimensional brand experience factors, we choose 20 adjectives to describe the experience of *Yangshan Shuimi Peaches* Package Based on multiple consumer evolution samples: Scene Experience: warm-colored, good-looking, bright-colored, spiritual, good-quality, simple, vivid, with-details; Emotion Experience: unique, prestigious, high-class; Action Experience: collectable, protective, anti-counterfeiting, intuitive, fresh-reflective; Thinking Experience (cultural experience): local-featured, traditional, meaningful.

After factor analysis, we name three main factors: 1. Vivid and prestigious factor; 2. Culture and detail factor; 3. Iintuitive and simple factor. Finally, we get the notice from empirical operation of *Yangshan Shuimi Peaches* experience evaluation: To improve Wuxi fruit brand experience and image, the three main factors make various contribution. Accordingly, it is of great reference value that packages of different styles can be designed to help form a series of brand packaging design.

# References

1. Holbrook, M.B.: The millennial consumer in the texts of our times: experience and entertainment. Journal of Macro Marketing (20), 180 (2000)
2. Holbrook, M.B., Hirschman, E.C.: The experiential aspects of consumption: consumer fantasies feelings and fun. Journal of Consumer Research (5), 132–140 (1982)
3. Pine II, J.B., Gilmore, J.H.: Welcome to the Experience Economy. Harvard Business Review 76, 97–105 (1998)
4. Schimitt, B.H.: Experiential Marketing: How to get customers sense feel think act relate to your company and brand, p. 271. The Free Press, New York (1999)
5. Homburg, C., et al.: Do satisfied customers really pay more? A study of the relationship between customer satisfaction and willingness to pay. Journal of Marketing 69(2), 84–96 (2005)
6. Guo, G., et al.: The Empirical Study on Brand experience's Driving Effects on Brand Loyalty: An Example for Brands with Different Product Involvement. Review of Economy and Management (2), 58–66 (2012)
7. Gao, Y., et al.: How Brand Experience Impacts on Brand Loyalty-The Mediation Effect of Product Involvement. Soft Science 25(7), 126–130 (2011)
8. Qi, Y.: The Theoretical Retrospection and Prospection of Brand Experience Research. Commercial Times (16), 21 (2011)

# A Study of Applying Qualia
# to Business Model of Creative Industries

Hui-Yun Yen[1,3], Christopher Lin[2], and Rungtai Lin[3]

[1] Department of Advertising, Chinese Culture University
11114 Taipei, Taiwan
[2] JIA Inc. Limited
11158 Taipei, Taiwan
[3] Graduate School of Creative Industry Design, National Taiwan University of Arts
22058 Ban Ciao City, Taipei, Taiwan
pccu.yhy@gmail.com, chris.lin@jia-inc.com.hk,
rtlin@mail.ntua.edu.tw

**Abstract.** The experiential economy has entered our life affecting many products with cultural connotations and changing people's lifestyles. It also displays cultural and creative industries that would be outstanding in the world. Chinese culture is the basis for the superior cultural and creative industries in Taiwan. Do the products evoke the sensation and emotion of consumers which designed in culture of value-added? Does the factor correlation between culture style and cultural-products? Are the business models of cultural and creative Industries and cultural-products of Qualia closely related? All of these questions are worthy of further exploration. Based on information analysis and literature review this study presented a framework applicable to any kind of Qualia products and culture and creative industries. The findings are as followed: (1) Cultural style is really enough to affect the design of cultural-products; (2) Successful products should conform to the five factors of Qualia: Attractiveness, Beauty, Creativity, Delicacy and Engineering; successful culture and creative industries should conform to the aesthetic economy business model. Taiwan has the advantage that value-added from Qualia to business model of cultural and creative industry is a presentation of the cultural connotation. Flourishing cultural and creative industries need a start in Taiwan. Marketing and brand building need to be extended by aesthetic from the economy business model to be outstanding in the global marketing in the future. This study includes the relation between cultural-products and consumers, Qualia products and business model exchange platform, international marketing operations and national support and counseling policies for a follow-up study issue.

**Keywords:** Cultural and Creative Industries, Qualia Products, Business Model, Design Value Added.

# 1    Introduction

Global information flows rapidly in recent years. Culture-products of each country are visualized more easily everywhere on the globe. These show that the era of aesthetic

P.L.P. Rau (Ed.): CCD/HCII 2013, Part I, LNCS 8023, pp. 148–156, 2013.
© Springer-Verlag Berlin Heidelberg 2013

economics is coming. People are no longer satisfied with just satisfying their material needs; spiritual needs are more important than material needs. Consumers favor those daily living goods that have some distinguishing feature in addition to their practical function. Furthermore, the country have rich cultural heritage which can support the culture connotation of products, and these products have cultural connotation, personal style and attitude to life that can touch people's hearts. From 2003 to 2008, Taiwan had 651 awards in worldwide design contests, but 75% of the awards were for high-tech products which don't touch people's hearts [1]. Consumers need products which have depth of beauty. Fortunately–Taiwan gradually extended design works to other areas from the high-tech products domain after 2008. Cultural and creative industries corporate philosophy with cultural connotation seem to be different for general industries from their products, and it is worth to explore the correlation between the touched factors of cultural characteristics and creative products.

"Cultural and Creative Industry Development Plan" is one of the Executive Yuan's of Taiwan Government "Challenge 2008 -National Development Plan" which emphasizes that the Cultural and creative design industries are to be the"4Cs"industries. The "4Cs" are "Cultural", "Collective", "Cheerful" and "Creative". Therefore, flourishing cultural and creative industries should be start from Taiwan's local industries and need the support of national policy and the support of the populace. Based on the above reasons, this study explore cultural-products' appearance, their cultural connotation of value-added and related industries. The authors investigate and discuss two issues in this paper. The first is the correlation between cultural style and cultural-products. The second is the correlation between Qualia products and the aesthetic economy business model.

## 2    Literature Review

### 2.1    Qualia Connotation of Culture-Products

Culture is the essence of creativity while creativity takes on the core of the industries; that is, only when craftworks come with cultural significance will they be alive [2]. Designing "Feeling" into products to present the emotional communication of user experiences becomes a design trend in the 21st century. As a result, "design for feeling" becomes the key factor for innovative products [3]. Bermond [4] stated that emotional Qualia are then the phenomenological representations of the end products of the appraisal processes. Therefore, a good product is a craft which exercises a discourse with people through its sensation evoking image and brings inspiration to them. As American design expert Norman stated, affective/emotional factors are the ultimate determiner of the success or failure of product design [2]. Lin [5] also stated that Qualia products are an expression of "Humane" and "Story" while general industrial products are an expression of "Functional" and "Rationality". For these reasons, the good sense of the quality product usually has a moving story.

The Ministry of Economic Affairs in Taiwan promotes the Qualia plan of Small and Medium Enterprises which integration product characteristics of cultural and creative. "Qualia" includes five elements; Attractiveness, Beauty, Creativity, Delicacy and Engineering. The plan proposes that enterprises make the value-addition to the product from Qualia in order to make the consumer experience the products' value [6].The appearance attributes together provide the consumer with an overall impression of the product. Further, they are more actionable and informative than physical properties for designers to use in briefings or product evaluation studies which can be used to assess if consumers do actually perceive the meanings that the designer intended to convey using appearance attributes [7].

## 2.2    The Business Model of Cultural and Creative Industries

In recent years, the rise of the Chinese-speaking world and consumption capacity can support the outputs of the cultural and creative industries. Therefore, it is the biggest advantage of the traditional craft industry to establish market differentiation through cultural.

Lin [5] said designing "culture" into modern products will be a design trend in the global market. The aesthetic experience achieved by connecting design and culture can be a new business model. He proposed the new model is called the "ABCDE Plan" which shows that to turn "Art" into "Business", we need "Creativity" and "Design", which allows the creative products to be transformed into "E-business" [8]. The aesthetic economics business model of Qualia product of this study is based on the "ABCDE Plan" from Lin [8]   et al., and this business model means through the "Culture" to fine "Art ", "Creative" to support "Design" and "Industry" to create "Brand" (shown in Fig. 1).

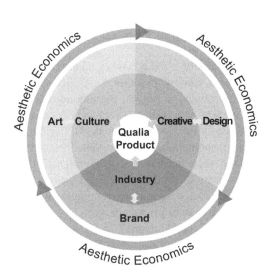

**Fig. 1.** The aesthetic economics business model of Qualia product

# 3    Research Method

This study employed a comprehensive literature analysis and information analysis of cultural and creative industries and cultural-products. The primary objective of this explorative study was to investigate value-added from Qualia to business model of cultural and creative industries. The authors investigate and discuss two issues in this paper. The first is the correlation between cultural style and cultural-products. The second is the correlation between Qualia products and the aesthetic economy business model.

This study is divided into the following four phases.

**The First Phase:** A study of the companies which produce cultural- products in order to analyze their information with research literature, books, magazines, newspapers and web content so as to review the cases of the development of the whole story and corporate philosophy, and list the chronology of these companies' founding dates based on the above.

**The Second Phase:** Five representative cultural-products were selected from each company with editing analysis to research their cultural identity, element of style and correlation between the brands of cultural and creative industries.

**The Third Phase:** Analyze the Qualia sense of the degree of the cultural-products' outward appearances using the method of semantic differential to research their five elements (Attractiveness, Beauty, Creativity, Delicacy and Engineering) of Qualia.

**The Fourth Phase:** Analyze the business model of cultural and creative industry with editing analysis to research the "Culture and Art", "Creative and Design" and "Industry and Brand".

# 4    Results and Discussion

The findings are as followed: (1) Cultural style is really enough to affect the design of cultural-products; (2) To be successful, products should conform to the five elements of Qualia: Attractiveness, Beauty, Creativity, Delicacy and Engineering; (3) The successful culture and creative industries should conform to the aesthetic economy business model.

## 4.1    Case Study with the Brand Spirit

The Executive Yuan "Challenge 2008 -National Development Plan" of Taiwan Government is the dividing line for case studies of craft industries which are well-know. Those companies produce tableware having cultural commodity characteristics. From the companies' establish times, it was found that about every two years a company was established (shown in Fig. 2). It appears that cultural and creative products get attention gradually in the market, and the corporate philosophy of those companies is to pursue a spiritual level lifestyle and cultural style.

2002
"Cultural and Creative Industry Development Plan" is
one of the Executive Yuan's
"Challenge 2008 - National Development Plan" in Taiwan.

**Fig. 2.** The established chronology of craft industries in Taiwan

## 4.2    The Style of Cultural-Product

The main characteristic of the works after 2002 are the use of a single material and minimal style, and cultural connotation and value-added are the important roles for recent works. More and more works of local Taiwan after 2009, because the company has increased, and it has more cultural connotation of mature technology and related policies. It also appears that industries and consumers have a common perception of culture connotation (shown in Fig. 3).

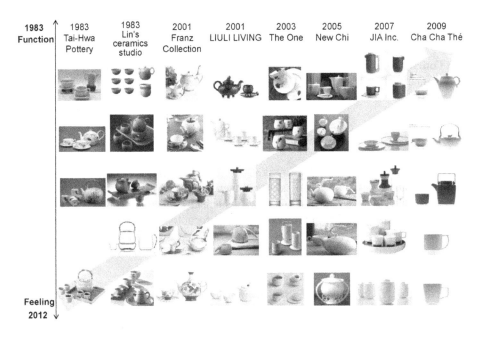

**Fig. 3.** Representative works of craft industries in Taiwan

## 4.3     Analysis of Cultural-Products through Five Elements of Qualia

Qualia products perform of "Human Nature" and demand of the "Emotional" which focuses on the "Story" to embellish our lives [9]. The authors choose thirty two cultural-products of porcelain made after 2002 and analyzed them through based on the five elements of Qualia. Attractiveness and Creativity of Qualia which define the special implications are: Narrative, Cultural and emotional connectivity. The authors use these special implications to analyze the senses of Chinese culture nostalgia in popular views of quality products. The first findings is that the cultural-products' appearance presented cultural connotation are more than cultural-products' ideology presented cultural connotation from analysis of the cultural-products of cultural connotations through Attractiveness and Creativity of Qualia (shown in Fig. 4).

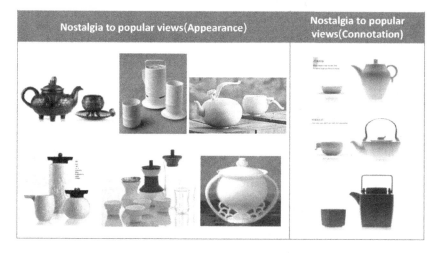

**Fig. 4.** Analysis of the cultural-products of cultural connotations through Attractiveness and Creativity of Qualia

Product aesthetics may stimulate positive and pleasant sensory responses, arouse emotional feelings/expression and create symbolic meanings [10]. The authors choose thirty two cultural-products of porcelain made after 2002 and analyzed them based on the five elements of Qualia. Beauty of Qualia defines the special implications of color, texture, shape, lines, surface ornamentation, details of the handling and component composition. The authors use these special implications to analyze the senses of Beauty of quality products. The second finding based on the analysis of the cultural-products of material and style through Beauty of Qualia showed that the quantity of a single material is about twice the quantity of composite materials, and the quantity of minimal style is about twice the quantity of sophisticated style (shown in Fig. 5and Fig. 6). The quantitative analysis of Qualia of cultural-products is shown in Table 1 and it is also shown the appearance of Qualia products are more than the connotation of Qualia products.

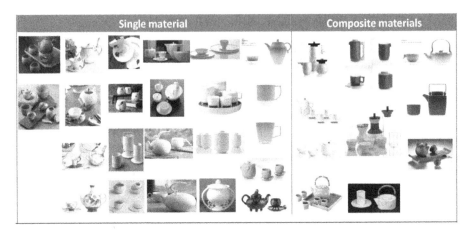

**Fig. 5.** Analysis of the cultural-products of material through Beauty of Qualia

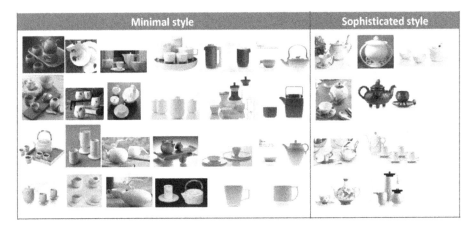

**Fig. 6.** Analysis of the cultural-products of style through Beauty of Qualia

**Table 1.** Quantitative analysis of Qualia of cultural-products

| Attractiveness and Creativity | Nostalgia to popular views (Appearance) | Nostalgia to popular views (Connotation) |
|---|---|---|
| Quantity | 6 | 3 |
| Beauty | Single material | Composite materials |
| Quantity | 22 | 10 |
| Beauty | Minimal style | Sophisticated style |
| Quantity | 23 | 9 |
| Total | 61 | 22 |

### 4.4    Business Model Analysis of Cultural and Creative Industries

The authors choose three companies (Franz Collection Inc., Newchi Company Ltd., and JIA Inc.) and analyzed them based on the aesthetic economy business model. The findings are as follows: 1. Cultural and Arts: promoting an attitude and style of living based on Chinese culture are the corporate philosophies of those companies. 2. Creative Design: Franz Collection Inc. and JIA Inc. have won the cultural creative award in Taiwan as well as the awards in many international competitions; Newchi Company Ltd. and Franz Collection Inc. had been invited to exhibit in internationally renowned museums. It is a great affirmation of Creative Design based on above reasons. 3. Corporate brand: the operational headquarters of these companies are all in Taiwan and their sale networks are domestic and abroad. They are usually exposure by exhibitions and subject operations. Furthermore, Franz Collection Inc. is the casework counseling in the brand Taiwan development plan of the Qualia SMEs (small and medium enterprise) promotion program. Therefore, these companies attach great importance to care corporate brand.

## 5    Conclusion

To conclude, the present study presents preliminary research on cultural-products and the business model of cultural and creative industries. Successful products from the aesthetic economics business model of Qualia product of this study (the "Culture" to fine "Art ", "Creative" to support "Design" and "Industry" to create "Brand"), and successful products with "Qualia" five elements (Attractiveness, Beauty, Creativity, Delicacy and Engineering). Therefore, the result of this research finds that the actual operation in cultural and creative industries and aesthetic economy business model are related to each other, and it appears that the value-added from Qualia to the business model of cultural and creative industries is different from other industries. Taiwan has the advantage that value-added from Qualia to business model of the cultural connotation of cultural and creative industries. Therefore, Taiwan needs flourishing cultural and creative industries, and needs extending to include marketing and building brand by the aesthetic economy business model. So, will it be possible to be well-known in the global marketing in the future. Follow-up studies should include the relationships between cultural-products and consumers, Qualia products and business model exchange platform, international marketing operations and national support and counseling policies.

## References

1. Yang, Z.-N.: Final Report of Roundtable Forum of Cultural and creative industries. ROC National Cultural Association, Office of the President (2009)
2. Yeh, M.-L., Lin, P.-H.: Applying Local Culture FeaturesintoCreative Craft Products Design. In: Rau, P.L.P. (ed.) IDGD 2011. LNCS, vol. 6775, pp. 114–122. Springer, Heidelberg (2011)

3. Ko, Y.-Y., Lin, P.-H., Lin, R.: A Study of Service Innovation Design in Cultural and Creative Industry. In: Aykin, N. (ed.) IDGD 2009. LNCS, vol. 5623, pp. 376–385. Springer, Heidelberg (2009)

4. Bermondb, B.: The emotional feeling as a combination of two qualia: A neurophilosophical-based emotion theory. Cognition and Emotion 22(5), 897–930 (2008)

5. Lin, R.: The servicescapes and Qualia products of creative life industries-A case study of The One Retreat. National Taiwan University of Arts Department of Crafts & Design, NSC Project, NO.NSC-98-2410-H-144-009&010 (2010)

6. Lin, D.-G.: Emotional value innovationtouching products. The Center of Corporate Synergy Development, Zhongwei report, 2012No.1 (2012)

7. Blijlevens, J., Creusen, M.E.H., Schoormans, J.P.L.: How Consumers Perceive Product Appearance: The Identification of Three Product Appearance Attributes. International Journal of Design 3(3) (2009)

8. Lin, R., Lin, C.-L.: From Digital Archives to E-Business-ACase Study on Turning "Art" into "Business". In: 2010 International Conference on e-Business (ICE-B), Athens, Greece (2010)

9. Lin, R., Liu, B.-C., Lee, Y.-J., Su, J.-H., Chang, S.-H.: The servicescapes and Qualia products of creative life industries-A case study of The One Retreat. In: 2010 Conference of TIK (Taiwan Institute of Kansei) (2010)

10. Rahman, O.: The Influence of Visual and Tactile Inputs on Denim Jeans Evaluation. International Journal of Design 6(1) (2012)

11. Official Website of TAI HWA POTTERY CO., LTD.,
    http://www.thp.com.tw/max/ezcatfiles/thp/img/img/653/pan5.swf/

12. Official Website of Lin's Ceramics Studio, http://www.aurlia.com.tw/

13. Official Website of Franz Collection, http://www.franzcollection.com/

14. Official Website of LIULILIVING, http://www.liuliliving.com/

15. Official Website of The One Retreat, http://www.theonestyle.com/

16. Official Website of NewChi, http://www.new-chi.com/

17. Official Website of JIA Inc., http://www.jia-inc.com/

18. Official Website of Cha ChaThé, http://www.chachathe.com/

# Analysis of Cognition Difference of Visual and Imagined Haptic Inputs on Product Texture

Hui-Yun Yen[1,3], Christopher Lin[2], and Rungtai Lin[3]

[1] Department of Advertising, Chinese Culture University
11114 Taipei, Taiwan
[2] JIA INC. LIMITED,
11158 Taipei, Taiwan
[3] Graduate School of Creative Industry Design, National Taiwan University of Arts
22058 Ban Ciao City, Taipei, Taiwan
pccu.yhy@gmail.com, chris.lin@jia-inc.com.hk,
rtlin@mail.ntua.edu.tw

**Abstract.** The rise of aesthetic economics is remarkable over the past few years and it is also displays the culture and creative industry which would be outstanding in the world. The useful feature of the product is not the only reason to buy the product of the consumer. The interface of product aesthetics gives people a sense of beauty and impression; it also promotes people to consume and collect. However many products while similar in visual appearance, differ in their haptic characteristics affect people's willingness to buy. Based on the above reasons, the trend of product design is consumer-oriented. This study analyzes the cognition difference of visual and imagined haptic inputs based on product texture. We choose tea cups with different textures be the stimulus samples in this experiment to investigate the participants' psychological feelings. The purpose of this study is to discover the correspondence between product textures with consumers' feel and generate specific guidelines for design in the future. There are four findings suggested by this paper. The first one is that a product with an attractive visual appearance is not necessarily pleasing to the touch. The second one is people view the products through visual and describe the product bias in emotional thinking. The third one is antonym adjectives of the popular products are less which conform of people with normal mental state. The fourth one is most of visual and haptic adjectives have commonality. Hopefully, industries and multi-cultural style of products will continue to support the future development and growth of aesthetic economics.

**Keywords:** Texture, Visual, Imagined Haptic, Cognition.

## 1 Introduction

The experiential economy era has come to our life affecting many products with culture connotations and changing people's lifestyle. It also displays a culture and creative industry outstanding in the world. A product's useful features are not the only

P.L.P. Rau (Ed.): CCD/HCII 2013, Part I, LNCS 8023, pp. 157–164, 2013.
© Springer-Verlag Berlin Heidelberg 2013

reason for a consumer to buy it. Does the nice looking product also have a good touch? Are a product's visual and haptic sensations consistent? How do people describe visual and haptic sensations?

The purpose of this study was to analyze any cognition differences between visual and imagined haptic inputs on product texture with the goal of designing visually attractive as well as haptically appealing products so as to solidify the culture and creative industry. The significance of the results is manifested on the three specific aspects of industry, designer and consumer. In addition to providing guidance for designers here in Taiwan and, hopefully, industries and multi-cultural style of products, it is also hoped that they continue to support the development and growth of aesthetic economics in the future.

We choose tea cups with different textures as the stimulus samples in this experiment to investigate the participants' psychological feelings with the goal of determining the correspondence between product textures and consumers' feelings so as to generate specific guidelines for future design.

## 2    Literature Review

### 2.1    Product Aesthetics and Perception

Human senses play an important role in people's understanding and experience of products. We see, hear, smell, and touch the artifacts around us in order to learn more about them, but also to experience the sensations per se [1]. In general, the sense of touch can only perceive one input at a time, whereas some other senses such as vision can simultaneously perceive a wide array of information [2]. The degree to which a perceptual system manages to detect structure, order, or coherence and assess a product's novelty/familiarity typically determines the affect that is generated [3]. Dagman, Karlsson, and Wikström [1] proposed that vision has often been described as the most important, dominant sense, but recent studies indicate that the other senses are as important in the way we experience products, or even more important. In addition attractiveness of the product is based on preferences of a person's feelings.

Aesthetic response can be defined as an experience (i.e., visual, emotional) that occurs in reaction to a specific stimulus [4]. At the aesthetic level, we consider a product's capacity to delight one or more of our sensory modalities [3]. The interface of product aesthetics gives people the sense of beauty. It also promotes people to consume and collection. However many products similar in visual appearance but differing in their haptic characteristics can affect people's willingness to buy. Base on the above reasons, the trend of product design is from consumer-oriented. This study analyzes cognition differences of visual and imagined haptic inputs on product texture.

### 2.2    Product Texture

Texture discrimination clearly relies on the detection of differences between adjoining regions, so in some sense elements must be compared with neighboring elements [5].

For example, the honeycomb is composed of a group of lattice modeling, and the lattice modeling must be orderly arrangement. Product texture is an explicit aesthetic property of product aesthetic attributes [6]. Product texture is one of the three factors of visual composition together with modeling and color. It can enrich the surface of the product and it also can be viewed and touched. Actually, texture is fundamentally tactile. People's visual experience of it is based on prior tactile experiences in feeling different texture previously [7].

### 2.3    Semantic Cognition of Product

Cognitive processing is based on people receiving messages by sensory stimulation, and making them into the experiences of knowledge and memory [8]. Sensory stimulation can encourage viewers to imagine how a product looks or feels when in use [4]. Most coders (designer) and decoders (user) have different humanistic backgrounds, education backgrounds and folk customs, and they have different results from the code (product). Therefore, the product's meaning from the designer is the potential factor affecting the user's cognition [9]. Semantic cognition of a product is from communication and combining cognitive engineering. It lets the user cognize products through "Design" and builds the interface between product and user [10]. As Norman [11] proposed, that what the product does for the user helps the user can understand the situation of the product.

## 3    Research Method

Does a visually appealing product have a haptically appealing touch? Are visual and haptic sensations consistent for the same products? How do people describe visual and haptic sensations? Based on a literature review, the trend of product design is consumer-oriented. This study analyzed cognition differences of product texture based on visual and imagined haptic inputs. The authors determined consumer preferences and emotional reactions through a product instance survey. The study tried to explore the aesthetic interface from a product's form in order to help industry produce products which touch the consumers' heart more strongly. In this paper, a combined Kansei engineering method with a survey of images and data analysis was used to analyze the cognition difference of visual and imagined haptic inputs on product texture.

The overall aim of this explorative study was a preliminary investigation of users' product experiences of visual and imagined haptic sensations and how they are verbalized. The participants were 81 college students, and they evaluated the same products at two different points in mode. There were two phases (i.e., visual and imagined haptic) in the questionnaire survey. We investigate and discuss two issues in this paper. The process of this questionnaire survey is shown on Fig. 1.

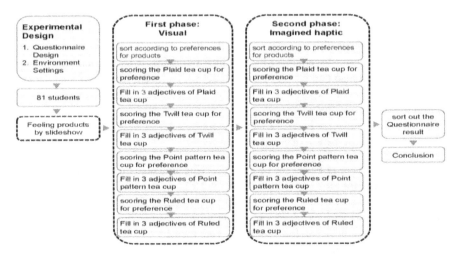

**Fig. 1.** The questionnaire survey process of visual and imagined haptic tests

The stimuli for the questionnaire are four porcelain cups of JIA Inc [11]. The cups colors were white and with the same form but differed in texture. These stimuli are described in table 1.

**Table 1.** The description of the stimuli

| Image | | | | |
|---|---|---|---|---|
| Name | JIA Inc. Persona tea cups | | | |
| Designer | Office for Product Design | | | |
| Background Story | A family of simple teacups which initially seem identical but soon show their own subtle personality. The basic silhouette of 'Persona' is a contemporary reinterpretation of the traditional Chinese tea cup with lid. Closer inspection reveals a series of individual texture like patterns which are almost more haptic than visual. The true qualities of these cups are only fully appreciated once held in the hand or up against the light, when the translucency of the delicate porcelain accentuates the patterns. | | | |
| Texture | | | | |
| Material | Porcelain | Porcelain | Porcelain | Porcelain |
| Size | Ø7.2x9.5cm (180ml) | Ø7.2x9.5cm (180ml) | Ø7.2x9.5cm (180ml) | Ø7.2x9.5cm (180ml) |
| Code of this Research | Plaid | Twill | Point pattern | Ruled |

## 4     Results and Discussion

There were four major results of this questionnaire study. First: the smooth senses of textures (i.e., Twill and Ruled) are more popular than the rougher senses of textures (i.e., Point pattern and Plaid) of visual and imagined haptic. Second: (1) there were many emotional adjectives in the first phase (i.e., visual) (Fig. 2); (2) there were many appearance adjectives and emotional adjectives in the second phase (i.e., imagined haptic) (Fig. 3). Third: the haptic adjectives have positive and negative feelings (e.g., smooth with rough, good touch with bad touch). Fourth: positive adjectives of products decrease with a decline in the product's preference (Fig. 4 and Table 3). There were two types of product adjectives: emotional (e.g., unlovely, comfortable or pretty), and appearance (e.g., smooth, streaked, lumpy or plaid) (Table 3). So the results show that people usually use emotional adjectives to describe products, and they do not use the negative adjective to describe the product which they prefer.

**Table 2.** The code of each feeling

|             | Visual | Haptic | Visual and Haptic | Other |
|-------------|--------|--------|-------------------|-------|
| Appearance  | 1      | 4      | 7                 | 10    |
| Interactive | 2      | 5      | 8                 |       |
| Emotional   | 3      | 6      | 9                 |       |

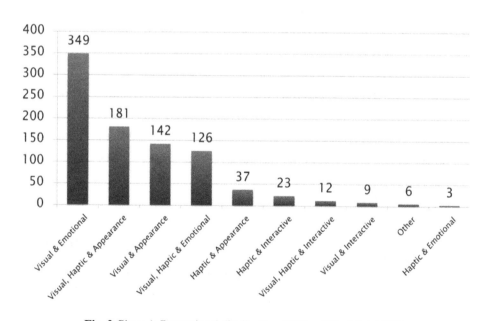

**Fig. 2.** Phase 1: Proportional distribution of "Visual" test (total 888)

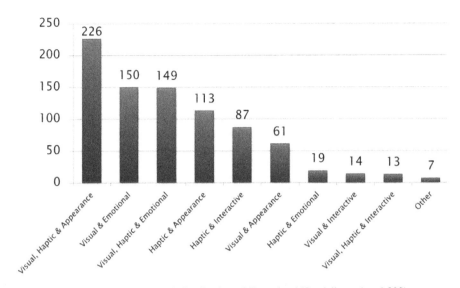

**Fig. 3.** Phase 2: Proportional distribution of "Imagined Haptic" test (total 839)

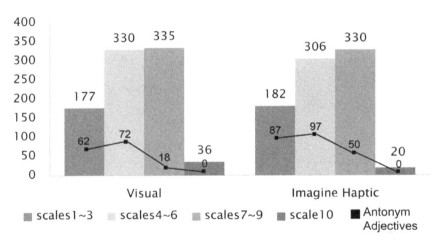

**Fig. 4.** Numbers of different preference of adjectives and numbers of opposite adjectives (black line)

**Table 3.** Sort rankings of stimuli and the three top adjectives (The list is to take single adjectives' quantity more than ten)

| Rank 1. Twill | | | | | | |
|---|---|---|---|---|---|---|
| **Visual and Imagined Haptic** | **Smooth** | **33** | **Comfortable** | **27** | **Slippery** | **26** |
| Visual | Pretty | 20 | *Smooth* | *13* | Tilted | 11 |
| | *Comfortable* | *10* | | | | |
| Imagined Haptic | *Slippery* | *26* | *Smooth* | *20* | Lovely | 18 |
| | *Comfortable* | *17* | Easy to take | 10 | | |

**Table 3.** *(Continued)*

| Rank 2. Ruled | | | | | | |
|---|---|---|---|---|---|---|
| Visual and Imagined Haptic | Common | 33 | Streaked | 30 | Slippery | 24 |
| Visual | *Common* | *16* | Neat | 13 | *Streaked* | *13* |
| | Simple | 11 | Lovely | 10 | | |
| Imagined Haptic | *Slippery* | *24* | Smooth | 21 | *Streaked* | *17* |
| | *Common* | *17* | Comfortable | 14 | | |
| **Rank 3. Point pattern** | | | | | | |
| Visual and Imagined Haptic | Lumpy | 35 | Unlovely | 30 | Common | 26 |
| Visual | Pretty | 19 | *Lumpy* | *15* | *Common* | *13* |
| | *Unlovely* | *13* | Ugly | 12 | | |
| Imagined Haptic | *Lumpy* | *20* | Granulous | 17 | *Unlovely* | *17* |
| | *Common* | *13* | Comfortable | 13 | | |
| **Rank 4. Plaid** | | | | | | |
| Visual and Imagined Haptic | Lumpy | 33 | Plaid | 26 | Granulous | 19 |
| Visual | Neat | 16 | *Plaid* | *14* | Common | 13 |
| | Ugly | 12 | Upright and Foursquare | 11 | | |
| Imagined Haptic | *Lumpy* | *33* | *Granulous* | *19* | Crude | 13 |
| | *Plaid* | *12* | | | | |

# 5    Conclusion

In this paper, the authors attempted to understand people's different sense of product texture in a preliminary way and as a basis for the future implementation of follow-up study. It could help the future study that research about the Haptic of touch entity products, and provide recommendations for follow-up research. The results could help industries and designers understand the meanings and feelings of product texture so that they can consider such factors in future design, and also help in product design and marketing in the future.

There are four findings suggested by this paper. First: a visually attractive product does not necessarily have a pleasant to the touch. Visual and imagined haptic sensation of product texture do not have an absolute relationship but these senses of products and people's past experience have an absolute relationship. People like that products have a smooth sense and the same directional line, and the directional line can be expected both of visual and imagined haptic. Second: people view the products through visual and describe the product bias in emotional thinking. In addition, peopled view the products through imagined haptic sensations and described the product bias based on their thinking about the product modeling and the sense of touch. Third: the popular products have less opposite adjectives (i.e., unlovely, ugly) that conform of people with normal mental state. People described the product with adjectives which having both positive and negative feelings description. For example, rough corresponding slippery and good touch corresponding bad touch. Fourth: most of the visual and haptic adjectives have a commonality. There are two types of product adjectives, one type is emotional (e.g., unlovely, comfortable or pretty), and the other one is appearance (e.g., smooth, streaked, lumpy or plaid). Further research is needed to provide more theoretical underpinnings and cases. Hopefully, industries and multi-cultural style of products will continue to support the development and growth of aesthetic economics in the future.

# References

1. Dagman, J., Karlsson, M.A.K., Wikström, L.: Investigating the haptic aspects of verbalised product experiences. International Journal of Design 4(3), 15–27 (2010)
2. Peck, J.: Does touch matter? Insights from haptic research in marketing. In: Krishna, A. (ed.) Sensory Marketing: Research on the Sensuality of Products, pp. 17–31. Routledge, New York (2010)
3. Desmet, P., Hekkert, P.: Framework of Product Experience. International Journal of Design 1(1) (2007)
4. Rahman, O.: The Influence of Visual and Tactile Inputs on Denim Jeans Evaluation. International Journal of Design 6(1) (2012)
5. Pashler, H.: Cross-dimensional interaction and texture segregation. Perception cl Psychophysics 43(4), 307–318 (1988)
6. Chang, F.-W.: The Influence of Product Aesthetic Attributes on Customer"s Willingness to Buy — An Example of Perfume for Men Unpublished master's thesis, Tamkang University, Taipei, Taiwan (2008)
7. Ke, C.-M.: A Study on the Visual and Tactile Image of Materials. Unpublished master's thesis, National Yunlin University of Science and Technology, Yunlin, Taiwan (1997)
8. Chen, T.-C.: A Study of Textural Image of Material Surface Treatment — A Case of Notebook Computer. Unpublished master's thesis, National Taiwan University of Science and Technology, Taipei, Taiwan (2009)
9. Lin, T.-L., Yu, C.-F.: Research on the Effects of Symbolic Images on Product Form-The Case of Italian Design Style. Journal of Humanities and Social Sciences 1(1), 19–27 (2005)
10. Lin, R., Song, Y.-R.: Total Design the assessment model Human Factors. In: The 9th Annual Meeting of the Ergonomics Society of Taiwan, pp. 247–252 (2002)
11. Norman, D.A.: Living With Complexity, pp. 32–61. Mit Pr., Cambridge (2010)
12. JIA Inc., http://www.jia-inc.com/home/?lang=en

# An Empirical Research on Designing and Promoting the Brand Logo of Yangshan Shuimi Peaches Based on the Theory of Brand Experience

Liang Yin, Junmiao Wang, Ying Shan, Yi Jin,
Zilin Sun, Weifeng Huang, and Binbin Li

School of Design, Jiangnan University, Wuxi 214122, P.R. China
ylxyq074@qq.com, wjmoceandesign@hotmail.com,
{shanyingbetty31,jinyicat}@163.com, sunzilin123@126.com,
all_right@live.cn, lbb1949@yahoo.com.cn

**Abstract.** This research takes the theory of brand experience as the guidance, and is based on *Bernd H. Schmitt's* theory of five-element-pattern brand experience. His theory is basis of brand experience evaluation, and is the starting point and the ending point of brand promotion for us. We have creatively designed the semantic analysis tool of experience evaluation of the logo design of Wuxi fruit brand *Yangshan Shuimi Peaches*. And we evaluated 3 logo designs of *Yangshan Shuimi Peaches* of *PeachWell* brand as an empirical operation of brand experience evaluation. Through the operation of experience evaluation and stratified sampling, we got the index of experience CSI, we learned the layered quantization distinction of the 3 logos A, B and C of the same brand *PeachWell*. This research can provide positive positioning of design for promotion the fruit brand in Wuxi, and can provide effective and scientific design parameters for brand building.

**Keywords:** Brand experience, Brand evaluation, Logo design, Empirical research.

## 1 The Design of Empirical Research Guided by Brand Experience Theory

### 1.1 The Choosing of the Objects of *Yangshan Shuimi Peaches* Brand Logos for Empirical Research

In order to raise the effects on the experience for Yangshan Shuimi Peaches brand logos, we creatively designed four new brand logos. After an evaluation of the user experience in natural experimental conditions, we picked up the best three ones as stimulus variables between the new and old logos: Logo A from the old, the better one Logo B from the new, and Logo C as the stimulus variables for our formal substantial research. By reading the CSI of the 3 logos, we did this research.

P.L.P. Rau (Ed.): CCD/HCII 2013, Part I, LNCS 8023, pp. 165–174, 2013.
© Springer-Verlag Berlin Heidelberg 2013

Logo A                    Logo B                    Logo C

**Fig. 1.** The final stimulus variables of the empirical research

## 1.2    The Guidance of Brand Experience Theories and the Designing of Evaluating Methods for *Yangshan Shuimi Peaches*

This research is exploratory basic research. In the designing phase of this empirical research, we have creatively finished the semantic analysis tool of the experience evaluation of the logo design of Wuxi fruit brand-*Yangshan Shuimi Peaches*. We use *Bernd H. Schmitt's* theory (1999), the five experience patterns for experience: Sense experience, emotion experience, thinking experience, action experience and relative experience. We used the classical consumer experience five-element model of *Schmitt*, and we conducted empirical operation on the experience evaluation of the three *Yangshan Shuimi Peaches* brand logos (A, B and C). Through stratified sampling, we got the experience parameters (Customer Satisfaction Index, CSI), and established the brand logo semantic evaluation database about primary cognitive appraisal adjectives (perceptive, advertent, memorial and understandable, etc.) and advanced cognitive appraisal adjectives (favorable, expectant, interesting and valuable, etc.). By the natural experiment, we developed out of the 20 pairs of adjectives about *Yangshan Shuimi Peaches* brand logo experience evaluation tools. (see Table 1)

**Table 1.** The five-element model of *Yangshan Shuimi Peaches* brand logo experience evaluation

| | |
|---|---|
| Sense experience | juicy-juiceless, plump-edgy, honest-smart, soft -hard, cute-mature |
| Emotion experience | auspicious-inauspicious, joyful-woeful, elegant-tacky |
| Thinking experience | simple-complex, easy to understand-difficult to understand, impressive-unimpressive, superstitious-scientific |
| Action experience | high grade-low grade, positive-negative |
| Relative experience | unique-stereotyped, vivid-dim, folk style-stylish, Wuxi featured-Wuxi featureless, charity-inclined-commerce-inclined, modern-traditional |

# 2    A Qualitative Empirical Research on the Logo Design of Brand Experience for *Yangshan Shuimi Peaches*

## 2.1    The Process of Empirical Research on Brand Experience of *Yangshan Shuimi Peaches* Logo Designs

**Questionnaire Design.** (A) Brainstorming: We collected a large number of adjectives of *Yangshan Shuimi Peaches* brand Logo Based on user experience theories-oriented to form semantic variable database of questionnaire as the primitive accumulation for the design of the questionnaire. (B) Semantic variable library of questionnaire: We design topics based on the *Osgood* semantic differential inventory and *Likert* scale to lay the foundation for the semantic analysis tool of experience evaluation of the logo design of Wuxi fruit brand *Yangshan Shuimi Peaches*. (C) Questionnaire quasi-experimental: We distributed 20 questionnaires about the semantic analysis tool of experience evaluation of the logo design of Wuxi fruit brand *Yangshan Shuimi Peaches*, which consists of the user experience adjective. After two screening and earning the test results of CSI discrimination, we finally retained 20 groups of adjectives items to complete the formal questionnaire design of the empirical research.

**Implementation of the Questionnaire.** (A) Questionnaires and recycling: The formal questionnaire was distributed by 3 ways. 261 questionnaires were distributed, and all of them were returned, the rate of recovery is 100%. And there were 200 valid questionnaires, the effective rate is 77%. Among the valid samples, there were 93 males and 107 females. (B) Data processing: We considered the quality of questionnaires. Then we used SPSS17.0 software to input the data of valid questionnaires to establish a database of the semantic analysis tool of experience evaluation of the logo design of Wuxi fruit brand *Yangshan Shuimi Peaches*, which lay foundation for the further empirical research analyses and results discussion.

**Demographic Characteristics of the Questionnaire.** (A). The gender composition of sample: Female accounted for 53.5% and male accounted for 46.5% of the 200 valid questionnaires. The male-female ratio is approaching to 1:1. So, the results of the comparative are representative and convincing. (B) The age composition of sample: The sample is divided into six age groups. There are 27 people under 18 ages, and 56 people are between18 and 22 years old, 67 people are from 23 to 35, 19 are between 36 and 45, 20 are ranged from 46 to 60, what's more, 11 people are over 60. (C). The education background composition of sample: The sample is divided into six education degrees. 102 people have the undergraduate education or above, these two levels are distributed in 1:1.

**The Statistical Analysis of the Empirical Research.** This empirical research is a report of phased results. We analyzed these data in software SPSS 17.0 and Office Excel 2007. And we will discuss the results from three aspects.

## 3    Quantitative Empirical Researches of *Yangshan Shuimi Peaches* Logo Designs Based on Brand Experience

This research takes the theory of brand experience as the guidance, and is based on Bernd H. Schmitt's theory of five-element-patterns brand experience. His theory is a basis of brand experience evaluation, and is the starting point and ending point of brand promotion for us.

### 3.1    The CSI Analyses of the Population Means of Three *Yangshan Shuimi Peaches* Brand Logos

The evaluation objects of the psychological evaluation tool of *Yangshan Shuimi Peaches* logo design are as follow: Logo A, is an existing logo of *Yangshan Shuimi Peaches* brand named *PeachWell*; Logo B and Logo C are redesigned logos with Wuxi local features. Logo B is inspired by the shape of purple-sand teapot with health function, and Logo C is designed according to the pleasant Wuxi Opera mask. By comparing and analyzing the consumers attitude index CSI of the 3 logos, we get the following 3 results: Firstly, the advantage and disadvantage of the 3 logos in the field of brand experience evaluation CSI; Secondly, the difference of the contribution degrees of the 3 logos to promoting the brand image; Thirdly, the CSI of the redesigned logos combined with local culture elements whether reaching the expected results or not. These analyses mainly include longitudinal analyses and horizontal analyses results.

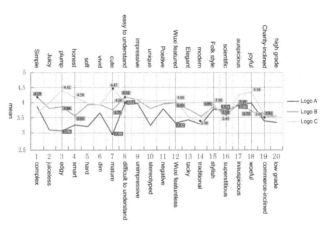

**Fig. 2.** The analyses chart of CSI population means of the 3 brand logos

1. The results of CSI longitudinal analyses among *Yangshan Shuimi Peaches* brand Logo A, B and C.  As Fig. 2 (the analyses chart of CSI population mean of the 3 brand logos) shows: the general attitude index for CSI of Yangshan Shuimi Peaches logos are: Logo A-13764, Logo B-15091, Logo C-15620. The higher score means the more satisfaction consumers have. It can be known that Logo B and Logo C are

more popular than Logo A. What's more, Logo C has the highest popularity. In the attitude index of Logo C, the 7th item (cute-mature) scores the highest 4.47, this shows Logo C gives participants the most direct sensory experience. Besides, in the 14th item (modern -traditional) scores lower for 3.38, this indicates that Logo C have the stronger traditional brand feature but not modern. In conclusion, Logo C can highlight peach characteristics and has traditional features.

2. The results of CSI horizontal analyses among *Yangshan Shuimi Peaches* brand Logo A, B and C (The Comparison of attitude index between the original Logo and redesigned logos).

    A. The comparison of attitude index between Logo A and B. Comparing the attitude index between Logo A and B, the 17th item (auspicious-inauspicious, 3.9 and 3.97) has the minimum difference degree 0.07, which shows that both the 2 logos can form emotional chord of auspiciousness feeling and the emotion experience effects well. The reason is that Logo A mainly expresses the auspiciousness information with the color China Red of China Seal, and Logo B mainly shows the meaning with the round shape of purple-sand teapot. Conversely, the 3rd item (plump-edgy, 3.06 and 3.88) has the maximum difference degree up to 0.82, the seal element of Logo A is lack of round feeling of peaches. Moreover, the difference degree of attitude index in the 12th item (Wuxi featured-Wuxi featureless, 3.32 and 4) is 0.68, which means compared with Logo A, the purple-sand teapot image of Logo B has stronger Wuxi characteristics, and the *Yangshan Shuimi Peaches* brand characteristics has been expressed relatively proper by Logo B.

    B. The comparison of attitude index between Logo A and C. Comparing the attitude index between Logo A and Logo C, the 8th item (easy to understand-difficult to understand, 4.02 and 4.00) has the minimum difference degree 0.02, which shows that the two logos can be easy to cognitive, popular and easy to understand. As a result, they reached thinking experience very well. Conversely, the 3rd item (plump-edgy, 3.06 and 4.41) has the maximum difference degree up to 2.06. Logo A is too tough to make participants associate the logo with their own experience of tasting peach. Obviously, it is not ideal to leave good first impression on participants. Besides, the difference degree of attitude index in the 12th item (Wuxi featured-Wuxi featureless, 3.32 and 4) is 0.77, compared with Logo A, Logo C reflects the Wuxi characteristics better by its image of Wuxi Opera mask, and can more accurately express brand characteristics of the brand, and shows the related experience very well.

3. The comparison of attitude index between redesigned Logo B and C. Comparing the attitude index between Logo B and C, the 12th item (Wuxi featured-Wuxi featureless, 4.00 and 4.09), the 15th item (folk style-stylish,3.85 and 3.96) and the 19th item (charity-inclined-commerce-inclined,3.51 and 3.60) have the minimum difference degrees, which means the 2 logos combined with *Yangshan Shuimi peaches* successfully. The 7th item (cute-mature, 3.75 and 4.47) has the maximum difference degree 0.72, this shows that compared with Logo B, Logo C does better in expressing the loveliness feature. So it is important for Logo B to strengthen the color and shape factors to show the features of peaches.

4. The summary.   According to the results above, Logo A is easier to recognize and to understand, the color and the shape is too simple. So the most important thing is to promote the form so that can stimulate participants' curiosity and desire to purchase. As the redesigned Logo B and C, they use the Wuxi geographical culture featured element better, and basically reach the expected effects of design. Logo B needs to improve in reflecting peaches loveliness feature to make it more affinity. In addition, being more rational on modeling fluency and specification of using color is a good way to enhance the sense of brand products, the sense of quality and credibility. In conclusion, we can come up with such inspiration that it is important for the brand promotion to build the brand round experience. To meet the needs of demanding consumers, it is necessary to establish brand image for farm products with local characteristics, not only to resolve visual stimuli for consumer brands, but also to permeate the brand cultural experience in consumer brand satisfaction. Accordingly, these efforts create long-term brand satisfaction and brand loyalty is improved naturally.

### 3.2    The Results of the Relative Analyses between 3 *Yangshan Shuimi Peaches* Logos and Population Region Distribution

The participants are consist of 8 regions: coastal cities, coastal small and medium sized cities, coastal rural areas, central China metropolitans, small and medium sized cities of midwest, midwest rural areas, northeast cities and northeast rural areas. We analyze the CSI of two sorts of participants come from urban and non-urban. (see Fig. 3). Our evaluating tool includes 20 pairs of adjectives (items), and they constitute the semantic analysis tool of experience evaluation of the logo design of Wuxi fruit brand *Yangshan Shuimi Peaches.* By comparing the association analyses of the CSI between 3 *Yangshan Shuimi Peaches* logos and population region distribution, we make the further discussion of 4 aspects about their common points, different points, maximum and minimum.

1. The relative analysis of CSI of Logo. A between two regions. According to the CSI of Logo A evaluation variables, we can see that the 12th item (Wuxi featured-Wuxi Featureless, normal, difference: 0.01) get the minimum difference degree from urban and non-urban areas. The highly stimulated information can left a deep impression on the customers, and that's the reason why Logo A with its simple but striking color and words is impressive. The minimum mean is in the 7th item (cute-mature: 2.41) which indicates Logo A is lack of loveliness image.
2. The relative analysis of CSI of Logo B between two regions. According to the CSI of Logo B evaluation variables, the minimum difference degree is in the 9th item (impressive-weak, 0.3). This shows that the urban and non-urban participants reach a consensus on thinking experience . Non-urban participants think this logo is simple on sense experience which can tell from the maximum difference degree in the 1st item (simple-complex) In conclusion, Logo B is a simple and an elegant logo which can reflect Wuxi culture and especially attract the group who enjoy high-quality lives.

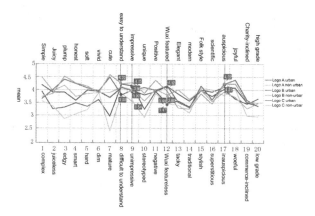

**Fig. 3.** The relative analyses of the CSI between 3 *Yangshan Shuimi Peaches* logos and population region distribution

3. The relative analysis of CSI of Logo C between two regions. According to the CSI evaluation variables of Logo C, the 17th item (auspicious-inauspicious, urban: 4.22, non-urban: 4.21) has the minimum difference degree with high means, which indicates that both of the participants of two areas can have the sense of auspiciousness from Logo C. Conversely, the maximum difference degree is in the 8th item is 0.42, which the non-urban group think it is easier to understand and this is because Wuxi Opera with strong folk style developed from rural, so that it can call the resonance with the non-urban people. Therefore, Logo C has a strong sense of auspiciousness and is full of Wuxi feature. In result, Logo C shows the relative experience very well and is a good choice to be used as the logo of *Yangshan Shuimi Peaches* brand and products for its regional culture features.

4. The relative analyses of CSI of 3 *Yangshan Shuimi Peaches* logos between two regions. According to the relative analyses of CSI between three logos and two regions, we can find that from every aspect of the evaluations, *esp.* on the sense experience, Logo A is too weak to match the shape or color of *Yangshan Shuimi Peaches*. And it is insufficient to promote the regional brand because its shortage of cultural connotation. So it is very necessary to strengthen the regional culture design elements related to sense experience and emotion experience to enhance the brand image. Besides, Logo B does well in the "simple item" (urban: 4.18, non-urban: 3.46) and the "elegant item" (urban: 3.83, non-urban: 4.00), but the class is not very clear in the "high grade" (urban: 3.64, non-urban: 3.46). It still needs to improve in order to differ it into different classes-high grade, mid grade and low grade. Logo C does the best among the three logos on the evaluation of sense experience and emotion experience.

### 3.3    The Relative Analyses between Three *Yangshan Shuimi Peaches* Logos and People's Education Differences

The results of the association analyses between three *Yangshan Shuimi Peaches* logos and people's education qualification differences are based on the CSI acquisition which discriminate the highly educated from the low educated. The higher academic qualified people (including the Bachelor degree, the Master degree or above, a total of 102 people) and the lower academic qualified (including the middle school or the below, the middle school of the same, college for professional training, a total of 98 people), the ratio between them is about 1:1. This is good for us to conclude the results. The relative analyses for CSI of the Logo A, B and C are shown in Fig. 4. The purpose of this study is to learn the brand experience differences among the 3 logos, and to establish the value orientation of the evaluation of brand experience and communication associated with academic qualification, so that we can bring up the strategies and suggestions of promoting the brand image from the education level associated logo design, by reaching the CSI of the people with different education backgrounds.

1. Associated CSI analysis of Logo A between higher and lower academic qualifications. In Fig. 4: As to the Logo A, the two groups CSI association analyses are shown by the "low educated of Logo A" and "highly educated of Logo A" lines (the red and the pink line). In items 2, 3, 4, 5 and 10, the difference degree of attitude index is above 0.5. From the differences of these five items CSI, we can find out the differences between brand recognitions are too large and this is not good for the unified brand effects. These results suggest that the people with different education backgrounds have different user experience for brand logo design, we should make the distinction among the varied brands, to increase the image of the same production brand. The differences of the indexes of the four items 6, 8, 12 and 19 are below 0.1, that indicates Logo A CSI differences are low, brand recognition is high. It also means that this logo can provide the users more unified image, and good for conveying the brand concepts. According to the five-element correspondence of the *Schmitt's* consumers experience and twenty-adjectives model, from the brand experience of Logo A in different education background population, the sense experience has great difference, it is bad for the communication of the overall brand image but it is good for the relative experience. However, for the agricultural products, a more intuitive feeling is in need. At the same time, in the brand experience appeal of *Yangshan Shuimi Peaches*, the sense experience requirements are relatively high, so we need to do better on it. Although Logo A has a good recognition in the relative experience, it is not the first appeal for the agricultural products. Therefore, Logo A can be evaluated as "strong relative and weak sense experience" logo.

2. Associated CSI analysis of Logo B between higher and lower academic qualifications. In Fig. 4, the two groups of people's CSI association analysis of Logo B is shown by "low educated of the Logo B" and "highly educated of the Logo B" two lines (the dark green line and the light green line). Evaluation variable item 9 (impressive-weak) the low educators' CSI is 4.17and the highly educated is 3.68. The brand recognition difference is too large, and it is not good for the unified brand effect. In the evaluations variable item 4, 5, 11, 14, 15 and 16, the difference in attitude index is below 0.1. From these 6 items, user experience of the Logo B is in accord. It have a good effect for conveying the concepts of brand.

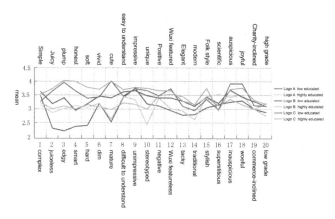

**Fig. 4.** The relative analyses of the CSI between 3 *Yangshan Shuimi Peaches* Logos and education background differences

From the brand experience of Logo B, users' thinking experience has differences, but in the six brand logo design elements index, the sense experience, action experience and relative experience are consistent to the CSI index. Therefore, Logo B can be evaluated as a logo "strong related and weak thinking experience".

3. Associated CSI analysis of Logo C between higher and lower academic qualifications. In Fig. 4, as to the Logo C, the 2 groups' CSI association analyses are shown by "low educated of Logo C" and "highly educated of Logo C" two lines (the C blue line and the C light blue line). In all the above items, there are no indexes above 0.5. From the evaluation variable item 2.3.7.9.10.12.16.20, the difference in this attitude index is below 0.1. From these seven items, the CSI user experience of Logo C won't be affected by the education qualification. This can give the user a unified brand image, and have a good effect on conveying the concepts of brand. From the brand experience of Logo C, sense experience is very impressive. Its CSI index is unified. The brand image experience is strong, and it is also accepted by the customers from different education backgrounds. At the same time, because sense experience of the farm product is very important, Logo C is the best among the 3 logos. The relative experience is also very impressive. This means it is easy to form a fixed consumer groups, and can help improve the consumers' brand loyalty, promote the brand cultural identity. In the thinking experience, it has a good effect on the brand experience communication. Its action experience is also very outstanding, so the Logo C can be regarded as "strong sense and related experience" logo.

# 4    The Conclusion of Empirical Research

This research takes the theory of brand experience as the guidance, and is based on *Bernd H. Schmitt's* theory of five-element-pattern brand experience. *Schmitt's* theory divied consumers' experience to sense experience, emotion experience, the thinking experience, action experience and relative experience, according to the processes of consumers' psychological cognition. His theory is basis of brand experience evaluation, and is the starting point and the ending point of brand promotion for us.

We have creatively designed the semantic analysis tool of experience evaluation of the logo design of Wuxi fruit brand *Yangshan Shuimi Peaches*. And we evaluated 3 logo designs of *Yangshan Shuimi Peaches* of *PeachWell* brand as an empirical operation of brand experience evaluation. Through stratified sampling, we got the index of experience CSI, and established the database of semantic evaluation of *Yangshan Shuimi* Peaches brand logos, with the adjectives refer to recognition evaluation on elementary level (perspective, watchful, of memory, and of understanding) and advanced level (of preference, expecting, interesting and valuable). By the method of natural experiment, we designed the tool to evaluate the experience of *Yangshan Shuimi Peaches* brand logo with 20 pairs of adjectives. Through the operation of experience evaluation, we learned the layered quantization distinction of the 3 logos A, B and C of the same brand *PeachWell*. This research can provide positive positioning of design for promotion the fruit brand in Wuxi, and can provide effective and scientific design parameters for brand building.

## References

1. Schmitt, B.H.: Experiential Marketing: How to get customers to sense, feel, think act and relate to your company and brands. Free Press, New York (1999)
2. Brakus, J.J., et al.: Brand experience: What is it? How is it measured? Does it affect loyalty? Journal of Marketing 73(3), 52–68 (2009)
3. Sakici, Ç., Ayan, E.: The steps of logo design at Kastamonu University, Forestry Faculty. Procedia-Social and Behavioral Sciences (51), 41–644 (2012)
4. Yang, D.-F., et al.: Brand experience, self-presentation and brand love: building brand love through perfect experience. Business Economics and Administration 228(10), 69–77 (2010)
5. Gao, Y., et al.: How brand experience impacts on brand loyalty-with product involvement as moderator. Soft Science 25(7), 126–130 (2011)

# Service Design Research about Redesign Sedentary Office Guided by New Ergonomics Theory

Yingxue Zhao, Craig Vogel, Gerald Michaud, and Steven Doehler

University of Cincinnati
College of Design, Architecture, Art, and Planning
5470 Aronoff Center, Cincinnati OH 45221-0016, USA
anneweihai@gmail.com, {vogelcg,doehlesj}@ucmail.uc.edu,
gerry.michaud@uc.edu

**Abstract.** Current office design is sedentary because it encourages users to work in one good posture as long as possible. Such sedentary office is lethal and inefficient. It needs redesign. To solve this problem, tendonitis experts came up with the new ergonomics theory. It encourages office workers to switch working postures periodically. This working status is defined as dynamic in the paper.

More and more well-known furniture manufacturers sensed this dynamic trend and applied the new ergonomic theory to their product. However, few of their products achieved big success. In order to better apply the new ergonomics theory in office design, a synthesis of context interviews, survey, and observation shadowing was carried out. A triangulation method was used to analyze the research results to get reliable apparent truth.

From the research, it was concluded that a successful new ergonomics office needed nicely designed multi-posture physical environment, proper posture-change stimulation system, and pleasant posture –change experience. This needs industrial design, interaction design, and user experience design to collaborate seamlessly, which actually is a typical service design process. So, only through service design, can a great new ergonomics office be created to encourage users leading a new life style.

This paper offered a brand new direction for office design.

## 1 Why Current Office Is Sedentary and Needs Redesign

Current Office environment originated from Industrial Revolution. "The booming of mass production technology and international trade created a huge need for information processing. Desks and chairs, which used to be luxury decorations, are changed into a daily necessity. "In a short period of time we've been sentenced to the chair." (Katzmarzyk, 2010) With rapidly increasing data processing needs, modern office workers seldom have a chance to move, even compared to 20 years ago. Modern office became very sedentary.

Since the 1960's, the public has come to realize the negative health conditions caused by sedentary office work. It is reported by New York Time on 2010 that such

P.L.P. Rau (Ed.): CCD/HCII 2013, Part I, LNCS 8023, pp. 175–183, 2013.
© Springer-Verlag Berlin Heidelberg 2013

sedentary office life is lethal and exercise is not a perfect antidote for sedentary office life. (Vlahos, 2011) And now, an increasing number of company, such as Google, want to invest on healthier office environment. As a result, most of the famous furniture companies like Herman Miller and Knoll has started develop new products to encourage users move more. The need for redesigning office is emerging.

## 2    Redesign Should Be Guided by New Ergonomics Theory

For quite a long time, people tried to rely on classic ergonomics to update their sedentary office. The definition of classic ergonomics in The *American Heritage Dictionary* is: "Design factors, as for the workplace, intended to maximize productivity by minimizing operator fatigue and discomfort." Which actually is 'How to work (or play) long hours, performing repetitive motions, while using proper body mechanics to minimize the development of tendonitis and other repetitive motion Injury'. Classic ergonomics tried to help users using proper body mechanics by suggesting best working postures.

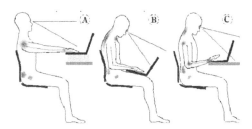

**Fig. 1.** Sit pressure analysis

First, sit was recommended as the best working posture. Ergonomic chairs were developed by the chair industry to address widespread complaints of back pain from workers. Lumbar support is deeply embedded in people's mind as a prime solution (Charis, 2010). However, as time goes by, back pain is still the most costly work related disability, although almost all offices in America are equipped with ergonomic chairs. (UHA, 2011) More recently people became aware of the fact that sitting can cause many issue. It forced the S shape spine into a C shape and put more pressure on the pelvis and spine. (Clark, 2002). (Fig. 1. Sit pressure analysis)

**Fig. 2.** Different Standing Stations

Then some experts suggested stand as an alternative for sit as work posture. Correspondingly a bevy of expensive standing stations showed up. (Fig. 2. Different Standing Stations). However, swelling legs and feet, which may result in the development of varicose veins, were among the problems caused by long time standing in addition to neck and shoulder stiffness.

**Fig. 3.** Perch Posture

Recently, NASA experts recommended a neutral body posture, which is called perching. (Fig. 3. Perch Posture) Perching is a status half way between sitting and standing. It balances our musculature between front and back. (Cranz, 2010). However long time working in this posture still can result in chronic disease such as varicose veins.

It is said by the New York Time, the reason why sedentary office was lethal was not because sit was a bad posture. It was because the users remained one posture for too long a time. (Charis, 2010) "The body shapes itself to the forces placed upon it." (Tucker, 2010). What classic ergonomics dedicated to only can slow that distortion procedure.

Up till recently, researchers realized that a new method for designing office environments was needed. A new theory "new ergonomics" was come up. Tendonitis experts defined new ergonomics as: A way of safely performing ongoing, repetitive motion activities. Understanding how the body interacts with strain and making ongoing adaptations to avoid the creation of a pain causing dynamic. In other words, the new ergonomics focused on ensuring people do repetitive motion in a new way, a new position, every day (Tucker, 2010). The key feature of new ergonomics is encouraging users to change working postures periodically. The state of periodically changing working posture is defined as dynamic working habit in the paper. Working dynamically can help users avoid harms caused by doing repetitive motion.

Redesign office according to new ergonomics theory is good for increasing work efficiency as well. The time adults can focus on a specific task with 100% focus is only 20 minutes. In order to get refocused, rest is needed. (Wikipedia, 2012) During prolonged work periods, workers tend to spontaneously fidget in order to entertain themselves, such as rotating a pen or shaking legs. Dr. Roland Rotz explained this in his co-authored book that fidgeting is a rhythmic sensory stimulation in our body's natural way of activating our under stimulated brain to facilitate focus which allows us comfort and rest (Roland Rotz, 2005). However, the sedentary office environment usually discourages office workers from taking any rest. As a result, many office workers have to pretend to be working hard while they cannot focus and feel exhausted. The new ergonomics theory can turn the office into a more dynamic environment and improve users' work efficiency.

For all the reasons above, it's necessary to update our old sedentary office into dynamic new ergonomics office.

## 3    New Ergonomics Offices Needs Both Mental and Physical Support

The new ergonomics theory has already been successfully applied to classroom furniture design AlphaBetter Desk or "stand up desk" (Fig. 4. AlphaBetter Desk). The desk, which was originated by Abby Brown, is an outstanding alternative for children, teens and adults. AplhaBetter Desk is higher than normal desk and it is paired with a high stool. Such a design enable the users easily switch between good study postures, sit, stand and perch. Another feature of the desk is it has a swinging footrest. The users can fidget with the swing to consume their surplus energy. This design used to be tested in Minnesota and Wisconsin primary schools and became a fad. The kids felt energetic all day and want to have one at home. The teachers commented, "I've never seen students with their heads down, ever." "I can stand at their level to help them." (SAULNY, 2009)This new ergonomics furniture empowered the users both mentally and physically. It naturally encouraged the users to change working postures and develop a new dynamic study style. It fit perfectly into the classroom environment.

However, office environment is quite different from classroom. Although, many famous furniture manufactures, such as Herman miller and Knoll, try to develop more dynamic product, none of them come up with similar breakthrough solutions for office.

**Fig. 4.** AlphaBetter Desk

From all the analysis above, it can be inferred that a successful dynamic office should meet the following rules:

- Should properly stimulate posture change.
- User experience of posture switch should be simple and pleasant.

In order to confirm the hypothesis, a research was carried out. This research focused on administrative assistants. It was because there were a lot of administrative assistants and they lead typical sedentary office life. "According to the Bureau of Labor Statistics, in 2006, secretaries and administrative assistants held about 4.2 million jobs, ranking among the largest occupations in the U.S. economy. About half of them suffer from musculoskeletal disorders. (health, 2010) Americans spend more than $126 billion a year to receive Medicare for back pain (UHA, 2011).

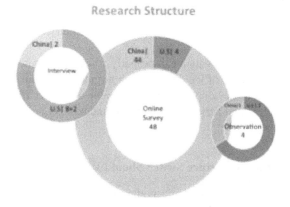

**Fig. 5.** Research Structure

The research was a synthesis of context interviews, a survey, and an observation shadowing. (Fig. 5. Research Structure.) Interview used similar structure of the survey of the questionnaire. The questionnaire had 17 questions in total. There were pre-screen questions, life style questions and questions about users experience. Full version of the questionnaire can be found at http://www.surveypie.com/survey101132. In total, 10 American and 2 Chinese subjects participated in the interview research. Forty-four Chinese and four Americans participated in the survey. Three American offices and one Chinese office were observed.

The research results were analyzed by using triangulation technique. Triangulation is the process of combining several different research methods to illuminate one area of study- in other words- using several research tools to examine the same thing. (Jennifer Visocky O'Grady, 2009) And the research results confirmed the hypothesized design guidelines.

## 3.1    Should Properly Stimulate Posture Switch

Several research data showed that few of the subjects realized that they needed to stay dynamic. More than 50% of respondents had never seen others avoid sitting for a long time or breaking up during the pro-longed sitting. Less than 50% of respondents personally tried to avoid sitting for a long time or breaking up the time spent sitting. Only 30% of the respondents thought activities designed to prevent pro-longed sitting was a good idea. During the observation research, 0% office worker was observed intentionally stretching or attempting to be active. This confirms that reminders stimulating users to switch posture is necessary in redesigning a dynamic office.

Respondents' answers for these questions were interpreted and analyzed. The research result showed that many subjects thought exercising and living a more dynamic office lifestyle was unnecessary and forbidden in current office culture. One of the subjects said, "The office is always so quiet that you dare not to say a word loudly. Let alone do other stuff. Sometimes I really feel depressed." Current offices discourage employers from being dynamic. Stay quite and sedentary in office is deeply embedded in office workers' mind.

As a conclusion, reminders, which can properly stimulate posture change is crucial for introducing new dynamic office design. Such a reminder system can both educate customers and help them develop new working habit. A proper reminder should be able to fit into the silent and serious office environment. Also it must be pleasant for users to follow.

## 3.2    User Experience of Posture Switch Should Be Simple and Pleasant

By asking subjects about their aesthetic preference for healthier office furniture design and office exercise, it can be tell that subjects prefer to choose the options which are low-key, simplicity but versatile. (Fig. 6. Customers' aesthetic preference for office hi-tech, Fig. 7. Appropriate office exercises) So in order to encourage administrative assistants to adopt new dynamic working style, the user experience of posture switch should be simple and pleasant.

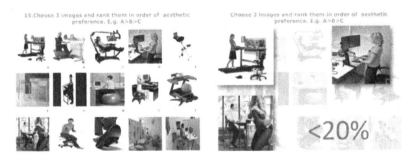

**Fig. 6.** Customers' aesthetic preference for office hi-tech

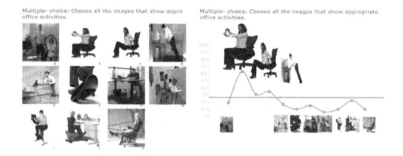

**Fig. 7.** Appropriate office exercises

# 4 New Ergonomics Offices Design Is Service Design

New Ergonomics Offices Design is Service Design. It is because new ergonomics office not only makes users' life more convenient but also tries to encourage users develop a new life style. There are three things needed when design a new ergonomics office. They are scientific multi-postures, proper stimulation and pleasant posture change experience.   In order to meet the requirements, nicely product design, interaction design and user experience design must collaborate seamless. This actually is a service design process.

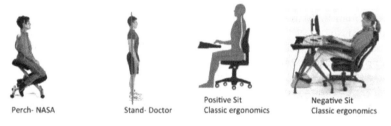

**Fig. 8.** Four Scientific Work Posture

They are perch, stand, positive sit and negative sit. (Fig. 8. Four Scientific Work Posture) The more work postures the office can offer, the more dynamic the new ergonomics office can be.

First, according to the research, four scientific multi-postures were recommended. Second, since the new ergonomics theory meets the needs of human body, it was found during the research that there were times and ways to sent proper stimulation in office environment already. When asked, "Once you sit down, how long will you remain sated?" 88% of respondents confirmed that they needed to stand up and walk around every one or two hour. This is because after one or two hours of work, they naturally felt tired and bored. They needed a break to help themselves refocus.   And these are natural pauses happen in work time. These pauses can be the proper time to send out reminders without interrupting users' normal work and create pleasant user experience.

And many of the subjects decorate their office with their family members' or friends' photos. This indicates that users' memory with their friends and relatives are pleasant experience for the users in the office. So customized reminders by users' relatives and friends may work better than normal reminder.

Third, the reminders must be sent during the natural pauses, through proper way. So, physical furniture needs to be able to monitor the users' working status. At the same time, it must offer at least two of the four scientific postures.

All in all, a new ergonomics office must have physical environment, which enable the users to easily switch between different working postures. This needs industrial design support. Also it should have a nice service system to offer appropriate reminders. Such as a system enable the users or their friends to customize pleasant reminders. This needs interaction design. Last but not the least, the product system and the service system need to collaborate to sent out the reminders properly. Only through such a service design process, can a great new ergonomics office be created to persuade the users to develop a new working life style.

## References

1. Charis: Your Office Chair is Killing You - Meet Public enemy No.1 in today's workplace (April 26, 2010), from Business Week: `http://www.viaseating.com/Newsletters/YourChairIsKillingYou-20BusinessWeek.pdf` (retrieved November 1, 2011)
2. Clark, P.: What's wrong with the Chair- Sitting and the new ergonomics (November 11, 2002), from Body friendly furniture: `http://www.zafu.net/whatswrong.html` (retrieved November 11, 2011)
3. Cranz, G.: Is all that sitting really killing Us? (April 23, 2010), from The New York Times: `http://roomfordebate.blogs.nytimes.com/2010/04/23/is-all-that-sitting-really-killing-us/?scp=1&sq=jack%20dennerlein&st=cse%23jack#galen` (retrieved November 1, 2011)
4. health, C. o. Administrative Professional Health Safety Tips (July 19, 2010), from Centers for Disease Control and Prevention: `http://www.cdc.gov/family/admin/` (retrieved November 1, 2011)
5. Jennifer Visocky O'Grady, K. O.: A Designer's Research Manual: Succeed in Design by Knowing Your Clients and What They Really Need. Rockport Publishers (2009)
6. Katzmarzyk, P. T.: Is All that Sitting Really killing Us? - Sit All Day, Die Early (April 23, 2010), `http://roomfordebate.blogs.nytimes.com/2010/04/23/is-all-that-sitting-really-killing-us/?scp=1&sq=jack%20dennerlein&st=cse%23jack` (retrieved November 3, 2011)
7. Minnesota, U.: Research Voice record (2010), from VoiceThread: `http://voicethread.com/?#q.b440097.i2336645` (retrieved November 2, 2011)
8. Roland Rotz, S.D.: Fidget to Focus: Outwit Your Boredom: Sensory Strategies for living with ADD. IuNIVERSE, iNC.(2005)

9.  Saulny, S.: Students Stand When Called Upon, and When Not (Feburary 24, 2009), from New York Time:
    http://www.nytimes.com/2009/02/25/us/
    25desks.html?_r=1&ref=todayspaper (retrieved )
10. Tucker, J.: New Ergonomics Definition Page (2010), from TendonitisExpert:
    http://www.tendonitisexpert.com/
    ergonomics-definition.html#ixzz1djQd4AAj (retrieved November 1, 2011)
11. UHA. Resource (October 1, 2011) from United Health Association:
    http://www.unitedhealthcareassociation.org/resources.html
    (retrieved November 1, 2011)
12. Vlahos, J.: Is Sitting a Lethal Activity (April 14, 2011),
    http://www.nytimes.com/2011/04/17/magazine/
    mag-17sitting-t.html?_r=4 (retrieved August 1, 2011)
13. Wikipedia. Attention Span (March 9, 2012) from Wikipedia:
    http://en.wikipedia.org/wiki/Attention_span (retrieved November 1, 2011)

# Part II

# Cross-Cultural Design Methods and Techniques

# A Policy or a Silent Revolution: Experience Sharing on Aligning UX Process with Product Development Process

Sean Chiu[1] and Chen-Shuang Wei[2]

[1] Acer Incorporated, New Taipei City, Taiwan, R.O.C.
Sean.chiu@acer.com
[2] Primax Electronics Ltd. Taipei, Taiwan, R.O.C.
carol.wei@primax.com.tw

**Abstract.** User experience has become more emphasized in the consumer electronics industry. In many companies, user-centered design process is being implemented to facilitate the development of user-friendly products. Unfortunately, not all practices ended up with success. In this paper, we pointed out the status quo of dilemma, shared the experience of our process rollout practice, and concluded the steps and strategies we adopted to align the user-centered design policy with traditional product development process. Our goals are to acquire more impacts on the product development in an early phase and to become indispensable to the company. At this current stage, we are delighted with the outcome which gone beyond our expectation and have confidence in the future success.

**Keywords:** user experience, UX process, UX management, UX policy.

## 1 Introduction

Taiwan is a home for most world-class computer, mobile device and consumer electronics industries, which produce and manufacture large proportion of 3C products on the market. Although previous years most of production lines has shifted to China for more competitive labor cost, but head quarters in Taiwan still holds the heart of design and research development. Regardless of the brand companies or original equipment/design manufacturing (OEM/ODM), User-Centered Design (UCD) Process is often discussed as a determination that could guarantee product teams to deliver exceptional user-friendly products when it is successfully executed. In spite of UCD related concepts and topics have been discussed for almost a decade, many User Experience (UX) teams have still struggled to integrate UX culture into corporate because it lacks of process alignment between UX and other teams. Furthermore, there is no clear measurement for UX practice to turn their credibility from deliverables to financial proof in which business stakeholders will trust.

Primax Electronics Ltd. UX team has faced the same issues when running UCD framework inside the company. Last year, we reevaluated the situation and took a different approach to introduce a new UX policy that increases strategic influence for

P.L.P. Rau (Ed.): CCD/HCII 2013, Part I, LNCS 8023, pp. 187–196, 2013.
© Springer-Verlag Berlin Heidelberg 2013

the UX team. The purpose of this paper is to share the experience in how we deploy the new policy by explaining background, methods, actions, and the outcome.

## 2    Background

Undoubtedly, with many years of promotion from Human Computer Interaction communities, UX or usability organizations were broadly established in computer and consumer electronics industry in recent years. Unfortunately, most of stakeholders in the industry only superficially acknowledge that a well-designed and user-friendly product could increase sale and profits and design team should be responsible for all UCD matters.

Besides, UX practice continues facing the challenge that stakeholders still have doubts about that UCD could really benefit them in terms of immediate financial returns. They often hesitate to make investment in early user studies or large group of usability tests because of no metric showing clear relationship between UCD practice and returned benefit from it. The other challenge is that a company lacks for a policy or regulation to well integrate UX practice and product development process, thus it is not conventional for UX team to participate in key activities such as customer/sales product requirement discussion, product design, engineering design, quality assurance and even regular project meetings. Unlike quality assurance or engineer teams, UX team is not considered a standard task force when running a project. It is often treated as an external labor-intensive resource which only provides design material against product requirements from customers or product managers. Not to mention, UX team usually has no opportunity to drive product specification to meet user requirements at early product conceptual stage. Without solving these two challenges, UX team would be considered to be non-vital importance not only for deciding company product strategy but also for efficiently delivering promising products to users hands in spite of the eligibility of UX team.

Primax Electronics Ltd. as one of the leading OEM/ODM companies for computer peripheral is the minority that has a solid UX team and a well-equipped usability lab in this industry. As an early usability practice adopter with practice on various product types, we have done many usability tests and accumulated lots of knowledge, methods and tools since the establishment. However, without full UCD process, most of usability tests were conducted at the late stage of product development. Reports have been often too late for design changes and only stored in database for future reference when similar usability issues were found in other project. Like most of UX groups, to gain influence on other domains and business insight in company, we urged ourselves to implant UCD process by adopting formalized human centered process standard (ISO 13407) (Fig. 1) [1] and hopefully we could reach UX maturity model higher level [2] and have ability to involve users in earlier product development phase. Regrettably, over the past few years, we have tried to deploy more complete UCD workflow but failed many times because of a few reasons. First, standard UCD process doesn't really align with our manufacturing process and can't keep tapping along with development life cycle. Under heavy pressure on delivery schedule, product development stakeholders often complain UCD is the bottleneck for project control. As a result, they will simply skip this type of activities to avoid trouble. Another reason is that there is no good method exists to measure what value that UX services can bring to corporate particularly for fiscal return. Contrary to UX, a successful sale contains many possibilities such as timing to market, channels, promotions, pricing, and more. In addition, without any regulation or process, the usability service has been only like ad-hoc task force supporting business and R&D units as a debugging and concept verification tool let alone involving user in early product design phase. The value of UX service cannot be sustained. After many years of trying, what we learned was we could never expect to change engineers and project managers' mindset or to break up their existing workflow and regulation overnight. Therefore, we realized that an adaptive alignment of UX process and product development and a corporate wide UX policy rollout are more reasonable to deploy UCD process smoothly.

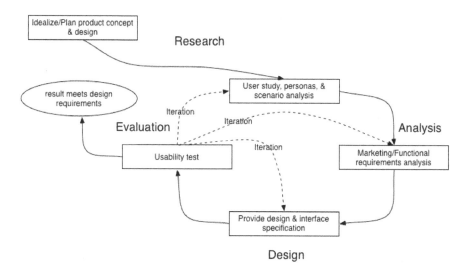

**Fig. 1.** Primax UCD process based on ISO 13407 framework

## 3     The Goal and Actions

From past experience, we knew that by requesting business stakeholders and product development team to follow standard UCD framework designed by us is easier said than done so our main goal was to adaptively set up a corporate level UX regulation that can strongly bind UCD lifecycle to product development process together and this integration must be seamless to reduce the impact on organization and shorten the emerging process. There were three steps we took to complete the new policy roll-out.

### 3.1     Analyze the Situation for Rollout Plan

To come up with a suitable UX policy strategy plan, from political and business management perspective, we started to analyze UX team's position and influence to corporate with SWOT analysis (Fig. 2). We recognized that we had strong usability service credits from some key business units, which could be our pilot run candidates to get valuable feedback from when rolling out the new process. In addition, the team held mature usability service framework toolkit that could be quickly used as new regulation templates with minor transformation. For the weakness of the team, without routine activity with business entities, we often had no initiative of UCD service for products. In order to have access to project information from product teams and plan UCD service for them, we needed to wait for their service requests. After being more aware of our position to corporate, we set out two objectives in the plan to deploy new UX policy smoother. First was to identify existing corporate regulation with formalized process that we can implant UX framework into. Second was to re-structure UX organization to a new form which can be more appropriate to serve stakeholders spontaneously.

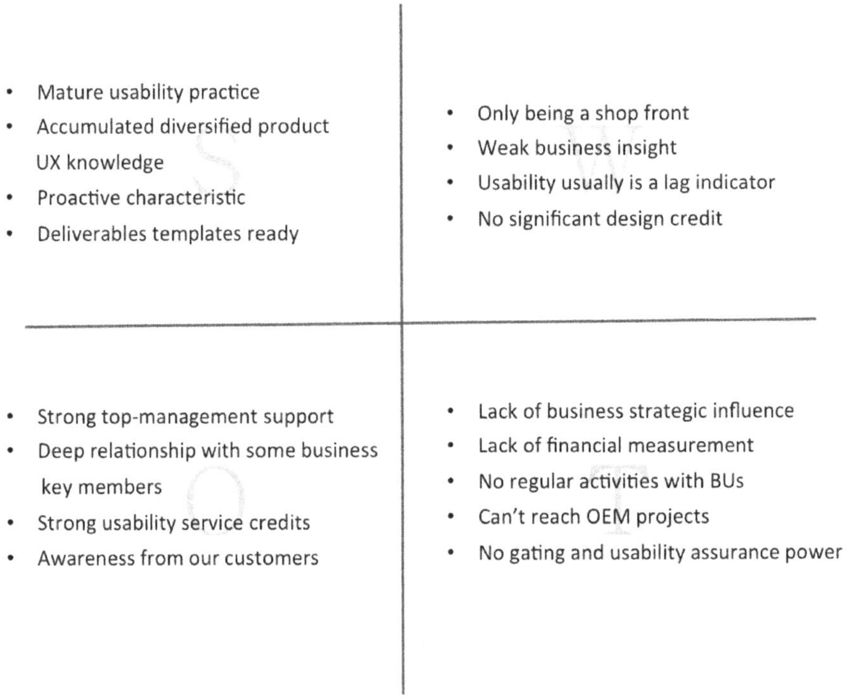

| | |
|---|---|
| • Mature usability practice<br>• Accumulated diversified product UX knowledge<br>• Proactive characteristic<br>• Deliverables templates ready | • Only being a shop front<br>• Weak business insight<br>• Usability usually is a lag indicator<br>• No significant design credit |
| • Strong top-management support<br>• Deep relationship with some business key members<br>• Strong usability service credits<br>• Awareness from our customers | • Lack of business strategic influence<br>• Lack of financial measurement<br>• No regular activities with BUs<br>• Can't reach OEM projects<br>• No gating and usability assurance power |

**Fig. 2.** SWOT analysis of Primax UX team

## 3.2    Process Alignment

To align with product development process seamlessly without hostility, we didn't create a brand new framework to force stakeholders to adopt.  Instead, we decided to modify an existing one. We spoke with Corporate Policy and Engineering Design Center (PEDC), who is in charge of defining, controlling and maintaining corporate level SOP and Quality Assurance Regulation. We evaluated current generic project control system called Manufacturing Process Management System (MPMS) (Fig. 3), which is commonly used for product development project control and material supplies management through all business units. Because it is corporate wide standard operation procedure with strong gating control and it's a regulation driven process, we realized it is our ideal target and took following steps to modify workflow in MPMS to merge UX process in.

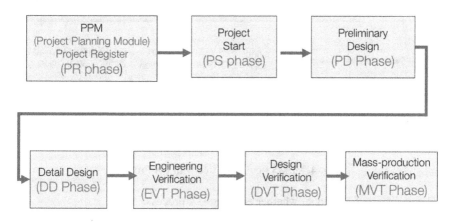

**Fig. 3.** Primax MPMS flow

1. Identify gating point, timing and gating documents format.

In MPMS, gating documents which are major materials need to be reviewed and each phase is signed off by technical leader, product leader and development quality assurance controller to release the project to the next phase. We asked PEDC to add user interface design specifications, UX service plans and usability reports onto the list of gating documents and add UX leader to assess the project detail before project registered and decide whether UX service is needed. When UX services are needed, UX team will perform tasks on MPMS process along with development process and deliver plans, reports or other UX related documents in every phase for development quality assurance controller to review at the gating point.

2. Reform current UCD framework and creating necessary documents, which are suitable and can be managed on MPMS.

We also slightly changed our original UCD framework to cope with every MPMS phase (Fig. 4) and assign standard tasks and deliverables for each phase. Because the deliverables will become gating documents, we reformatted them to meet MPMS standard.

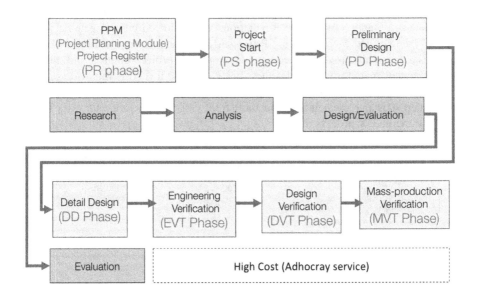

**Fig. 4.** MPMS flow facilitated with UX Process

3. Create criteria for product whether entering UX process.

To increase new policy acceptance and avoid our resource shortage, we couldn't review all projects on MPMS.

We needed to create criteria for UX review (Fig. 5) and it would help project team to understand why some projects need UX services and some do not. The criteria were made based on product types and other index such as maturity of market, new concept of design, customer requirement, and new interface application. There are four product types defined in Primax:

• Type A product: Brand new design of ID, EE, ME, software and etc.
• Type B product: Major components changes
• Type C product: partially changes of EE, ME design with existing housing
• Type D product: changes of color, prints, accessories, and documents.

At the beginning of policy deployment, we decided to exclude type D product.

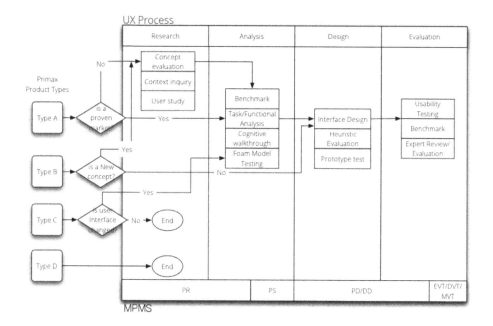

**Fig. 5.** UX service criteria on MPMS

4. Re-implement MPMS and prepare UX management templates.

After redesigning MPMS, PEDC system engineer started to reprogram entire system for the new process flow when we announced the UX regulation effective date for every business entities. Since most of project managers did not know what to provide to us for evaluation of whether UX service is needed, we designed templates that project managers can fill up product information for us to quickly collect their product insight without back-and-forth questions.

5. Set up both regularly and occasionally communication platforms and educational training sessions.

Before new MPMS began being deployed to different business entities, we held several communication meetings for related parties to explain what the new UX regulation and management are and how their current project control styles are not going to be changed dramatically by the new MPMS process. Moreover, we arranged numbers of training sessions to guide them through the new UX standard operation procedure (Fig. 6) on MPMS and clarify project members and UX members' jobs and responsibilities on new system.

Besides, due to the fact that UX activity is becoming mandatory, we took the advantage to convince project coordinators to let UX team member to sit in their regular project meetings thus we can assist them to cooperate with UX activities efficiently and prevent extra cost and time.

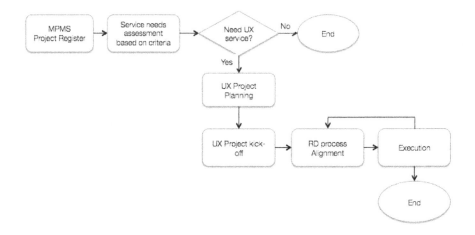

**Fig. 6.** UX Standard Operation Procedure on MPMS

### 3.3    UX Organization Re-structure

Setting up a company policy for UCD is not an easy path. It requires lots of support either from top-down, or bottom-up. Once organization from top-down forced the regulation adaptation, we immediately faced the hostility toward to us from many working fields because the time and cost will be raised as we start to implement UX tasks into development life cycle.

In addition, the old way of running UX practice would not help us buy a ticket to the strategy decision chair since we only participated in project level activities. We needed an organization that could gain us influence on product strategy decision at early UCD stage. We determined that UX team has to be more spontaneous and aggressive than ever so we re-structured team by adopting strategies below:

1. Re-define UX member role and responsibility.

Traditional UX team usually only consists of professionals from usability, human computer interaction, psychology, and design background. When we recruit UX professionals, we usually simply ask if the candidates are qualified in these fields practice and expect their contribution only from such disciplines mostly. As a matter of fact, that's the reason other staffs in organization supposed UX team functions as design entity or verification unit rather than strategy advisory institution and misused us as design material generation or quality assurance resource. But since the communication is relatively important to win us a seat in regular product strategy meeting and being influential, we found that we need to reassign our team member new roles and responsibilities to coordinate all UX activities with project teams closely. The UX project coordinator responsibility includes:

• To proactively communicate with key business stakeholders to gain access to product development status and maintain steady relationship with them

- To coordinate the UX projects on MPMS
- UX standard operation procedure control
- To hold educational training sessions regarding UX regulation and support to grow user experience design knowledge in organization
- To identify and join necessary business units' product strategy meetings and concept brainstorming activities.

2. Identify senior members to act as UX project coordinator.

In order to carry such important role, we needed to identify qualified team members who can be trusted by stakeholders with credibility and high recognition from their previous works.

These senior members have learned to speak a common language as product development team does and understood the engineer's culture and working style. They can demonstrate the leadership and assist project members in partnering with UX people better.

3. Set up regular communication channels with key decision maker in business organization.

After assigning UX project coordinator roles to a few senior members, they were sent out to communicate with key persons and sell our new regulation as well as organizing communication channels to regularly involve in product development activities in different departments.

4. Conduct user research on strategy-related products proactively and deliver the quality reports to business personnel.

For the first of a few months, with the intention of rolling out new UX regulation successfully, we particularly aimed for big time projects to conduct UX tasks on MPMS process and made sure deliverables were extraordinary to earn recognition and appreciation. We expected this approach would bring confidence to strategy table in new UX regulation and hopefully continuously get strong support from top-management until full acceptance of the new UX policy.

# 4    Result

As a result of new the UX process deployment on MPMS, the awareness of user experience team and UX practice was tremendously raised. Although the process roll-out has produced conflict between mid-level employees due to the functional departmentalism, we are able to convince them and smooth out the situation through our project coordinator role. Now, most of projects are plugging-in usability evaluation and test report documents in the system, and on some projects, they are reviewed at manufacturing gating meeting. UX contribution and opinion become significant for projects before going to production. More and more project managers include UX person in the project team at kick-off charter and allow us to affirm products whether they meet user needs before entering implementation phase. Moreover, because UX team members have been increasingly invited to join the regular project review meetings or product requirement discussion with our customers, we are able to conduct user studies and give design suggestions at early stage rather than testing products after working samples ready. This finally empowers UX team to take back the true product UX ownership and the organization looks forward to gradually escalating the maturity level of UX.

## References

1. ISO13407. Human-centred design processes for interactive systems. International Standard, The International Organization for Standardization (1999)
2. Holland, J.: http://johnnyholland.org/2010/04/planning-your-ux-strategy/

# From Global Terminology to Local Terminology:
# A Review on Cross-Cultural Interface Design Solutions

Elke Duncker, Javed Anjum Sheikh, and Bob Fields

Interaction Design Centre,
School of Engineering & Information Sciences,
Middlesex University, London, UK,
{e.duncker,j.anjum,b.fields}@mdx.ac.uk

**Abstract.** This paper provides a brief overview of cross-cultural interface design solutions combining cross-language information retrieval and cross-cultural designing. Language is a part of culture in a sense, but most of researchers deal with these two issues separately because they have many different issues and solutions in nature. The diversity of sources and perspectives taken into account for the review including practitioners'(software localization) and technical (e.g. semantic web, ontologies) solutions, design processes (e.g. cultural finger print), design elements (e.g. cultural markers), and philosophically informed discussions (e.g. semiotics).

**Keywords:** Software localization, semantic web, ontologies, design processes, cultural finger print, design elements, cultural markers, semiotics, human–computer interaction, globalisation, localisation, cultural inclusion.

## 1    Introduction

The potential of the internet as a global access tool for knowledge, goods and services is undisputed. However, this potential cannot be fully realised, as long as the information and services of one culture are less accessible for those who from other cultural groups. This does not only arise from obvious matters such as language translation, currency, formats of numbers and dates, but also from deeply rooted cultural differences that can cause misunderstanding and misinterpretation of information. For example, if the user searches for "Lamb", the relevant information could be found as meat, red meat, Halal meat, kosher, or a non-vegetarian item. So the main problems are what the user is actually searching for, how relevant information can be retrieved and how the user can use a global interface as a culturally aware interface. What can be seen here is that the explosion of knowledge has forced researchers to devise new mechanisms to accommodate cultural classification. It is difficult to provide consistent information in such diverse environments. The user resists accepting non-familiar terminology which is a barrier to the effective and efficient use of global interactive design. This research was carried out to bridge the cultural differences gap.

P.L.P. Rau (Ed.): CCD/HCII 2013, Part I, LNCS 8023, pp. 197–207, 2013.
© Springer-Verlag Berlin Heidelberg 2013

## 2     The Available Solutions

The cultural differences raise research issues ranging from usability to methodological and evaluation studies in relation to product design and process involvement in development [61]. In this context, the following sections discuss available solutions regarding the problems discussed in the above sections.

Researchers and designers always look at the ways to improve usability access to users. They proposed different solutions to improve global interface design. A few of them are discussed here. There are various technical and cultural issues which need to be considered to design products as culturally neutral as possible. Byrne [9] explains a process called by GILT framework which consists of Globalization, Internationalization, Localization and Translation.

### 2.1     Globalisation, Internalisation, Localisation and Translation

Designers need to consider whether to develop a global, cultural-free interfaces or localised versions. In this context, Day [16 cited by 62] describes three stages of specialisation:

- Globalisation: Less culturally standards use across different cultures,
- Internationalisation: Early stage of local customisation,
- Localisation:  interfaces for specific local markets.

Globalisation mainly deals with the necessary technical, financial, managerial, and staffing software to sell in a global market with minimal revision. The globalisation process has concentrated primarily on translating objective aspect of cultural, ignores subjective cultural aspects which are a necessary parts of cultural interfaces [20].

**Internationalisation** is a technical level of localisation and does not require remedial engineering or redesign. It has easily adopted design for international users after the engineering phase [41]. Internationalisation provides a common understanding to use design universally [51][44]. Therefore we need to design architecture which does not need further modification for every local market. Maroto and Bortoli [45] suggested that appropriate measures in the early design phase enhance the effectiveness of internationalisation. Marcus [45] advised that simplification of contents improve the internationalisation. Russo and Boor [58] define internalisation is to identify the culturally specific elements of the product whereas localisation to substitutes it with local content.

**Localisation:** The use of a global website is not convenient due to cultural perceptions and expectations of diverse users. The process of localisation makes websites suitable for target audiences. It generally addresses non-textual components of product and services [41] to cater to the need of local market. According to [25 cited in 13] localisation is a combination of language and technology to produce a cross cultural product. This definition only considers a "product" whereas the Localisation Industry Standards Association [41] extends the reach of localisation by including "services". LISA [41] describes it as "the process of modifying products or services to account for differences in distinct markets". According to LISA [41] localisation needs to analyses linguistic issues, physical issues, technical issues, business and cultural issues to make a decision not to localise or to localise.

Localisation as a "high-tech translation" [41] is a complex process and requires linguistic, technical, cultural, commercial and legal expertise [9]. The key languages technologies Terminology Management Systems, Translation Memory (TM), Machine Translation (MT), Localization Workbenches, and Global Content Management Systems (GCMS) are no the substitution for a human translator [41]. Localisation of design means to enhance its effectiveness for a particular culture [45][52][44]. The possible options for localisation are language, time zones, currency, colour, navigation, etc., [15][49] divided this into the following groups:-

- Linguistic: This process involves translating dates, time, currency, etc.
- Cultural: This process includes cultural aspects of the target audience i.e., images, terminologies, metaphors, colours etc.
- Technical: This comprises the above-mentioned aspects by redesigning the current website to make it more culturally acceptable.

In this context, there is a need for a website to cater for the local context of one culture or a cross-cultural website.

Translation is the replacement of text from one language to another language. A culturally localised interface is more than translation of text. Other important challenges are tangible factors, such as language and infrastructure. However, most studies are related only to language translation [56][17].

Choong, Plocher and Rau [11] grouped cultural dimensions into cognitive (internationalisation and localisation of display elements, information architecture and user interaction, organising and searching information, time), affective (colours and graphics), perceptual (use of metaphors), and functional (uncertainty avoidance). These processes need an analysis of both objective and subjective cultural issues [20][62]. Internalisation and localisation are widely used perspectives in HCI [19][28][44][27][7][3]. Sun [65][66] defined two levels i.e. surface level which covers translation, punctuation, dates, weights, measurements, addresses, currency, etc. issues. Whereas the cultural level deals with images, colours, logic, functionality and communication patterns.

## 2.2    Cultural Marker

Barber and Bader [4] identified localised elements "cultural markers" by usability inspection of several hundred websites belong to different countries and languages. They proposed that incorporation of cultural markers improve the usability for local users. Sheppard and Scholtz [58] proved their research by two mock websites (North American version and Middle Eastern version) as they found the positive effects of cultural markers on user's performance.

The studies on cultural markers effect on website usability by [66][38] found that users prefer websites with cultural markers from their own cultures. Both studies did not produce any statistically significant results. Sun's study [66] found cultural makers play an effective role as culture is constantly changing therefore designers need practical observation from users. Mushtaha and De Troyer [49] emphasised the importance of cultural markers and divided cross-cultural markers for designing cultural based website and localization into five levels; context-dependent, settled, broad, variable and vista. Designer can choose a cultural marker among five cultural markers according to their cultural adaption needs.

## 2.3    Semiotics

The studies by [10][71][33][31] found that the designers use their own cultural specific icons and standards to represent culturally specific things. Different cultures prefer different signs or symbols according to their culture [29]. Semiotics, are 'science of signs' deals with the meaning of signs and symbols through an understanding of the acts of signification. The signs and symbols are assigned to conceptual categories to represent important aspects and ideas. As an infinite process influences user perceptions and give meanings to 'signs' through acts of semiotics (unless otherwise stated most of the work is cited from [30][33].

Concept of Semiotics is an act of interpretation [2][18] cited by [64]. The semiotic modelling is based on "the space of interactions", and "the significance of the user-organisation relationship". Semiotic theories help to find the deep explanations of user attitudes and behaviours and how the dialogue between user and system establish and maintain elements of the user-organisation relationship. They are described as the deconstruction of the interface to detect 'acts of signification'. They emphasise the need of actual meanings of as they can refer to different properties of the interface. Previous studies [53][57][5] cited by [62] did not get success to differentiate between a sign and its meaning. However, [30] applied semiotic principles to the user interface design.

Krippendorff [39], cited in Myers, 1997) defines semiotics as "content analysis". In his context, it is a research technique to find structure and pattern to make inferences from data. Wynn [72], cited in [50] takes semiotics as "conversation analysis." He defines that context of exchange is an important factor to shape the meanings. Therefore researchers need to immerse themselves to understand the context. Discourse analysis [50] is a combination of content analysis and conversation analysis.

## 2.4    Ontology

One of the ways to solve cultural and design issues is that users a raise query in their own language against a foreign language and the result comes in their own language [22]. In ontology, the semantics of terms is defined in terms of axioms and is interpreted in hierarchical relations between terms. However, ontologies do not translate textual input from a source language into a target language [13]. Ontology is an expression based on a specification of concepts, relationships among concepts. The following sections are adopted from [35] unless otherwise stated. Ontology localisation defines as an adoption of ontology of particular language or culture [36] cited in [13]. The advantage of ontology localisation is to reduce the cost as compared to build a new ontology. Ontology localisation is based on software localisation [25] thesauri translation and machine translation.

**Ontology Localisation**

It is a process that takes ontology as input and produces a new ontology extended with labels in addition to the languages [24][13].

**Lexical layer:** It affects the surface level as it just conceptualisation itself and does not consider functionality and behaviour of the software. This layer is language-specific and provides a 1:1 translation for each label, dependent on the localised purpose. It also comprises documentation and online help related to a particular culture.

**Conceptualisation Layer:** In this layer, software functionality and behaviour needs conceptualisation according to the processes and rules related to particular culture. Apart from translation of labels, conceptualisation is also important element of ontology localisation. It is driven by the inexistence of conceptual equivalents in the target culture.

**Thesauri Translation:** Thesauri translation is reuse of existing thesauri or a reasonable translation system that can provide support across the languages. As compared to ontology localisation, it does not need conceptualization. During Thesauri translation contents lose their structure as compared to ontology therefore the relevancy of meaning is always questioned.

**Machine Translation:** Translation of sentences and documents etc., with the whole context from source language to target language is called machine translation. It is difficult to find the most appropriate translation of a target language according to the ontology context. Therefore translations obtained from multilingual lexical resources compare ontological contexts with the original label. A plug-in Label Translator [24] is an ontology editor supporting a semi-automatic functional translator for English, Spanish and German languages. A number of linguistic resources are available to obtain automatic translation such as multilingual lexica (EuroWordNet), multilingual terminologies (IATE10, a multilingual term base of the EU), and translation services (Babelfish, GoogleTranslate) [25] cited in [35]. LabelTranslator has been developed to translate terminology and reuse them in multilingual or cultural ontology (for more details [23][24].

**Ontology Mappings**

Conceptual level: Ontologies describe and construct in different languages by either taxonomical relations (i.e., owl: equivalent Class, owl: sameAs, rdfs: subclass Of, etc.) or domain dependent relations (i.e., ontology properties coming from other ontologies). The Conceptual cross-lingual mappings establish a correspondence between or among concepts including in different ontologies or languages [35].

**Instance Level:** The instance cross-lingual mappings are about individual links instead of associated concepts and are represented by owl: sameAs [35].

**Linguistic Level:** The linguistic cross-lingual mappings establish concepts between their associated linguistic information. This mapping is used where conceptual and linguistic information is a major requirement. There are no semantic relations between the concepts as mappings established between the linguistic descriptions of their concepts are not necessarily exact culturally equivalents but may be the closest correspondences between culture-specific concepts. Cross-lingual ontology mappings are a sub-case of ontology mappings [35].

Vocabulary elements can be captured rdfs: label property but is not sufficient for syntactic variation across languages. The, multilingual lexical information models e.g., LexInfo [8][14][12] or LIR [48][54] cited in Gracia et al., 2012) are complex and need lexicon models for ontologies like the lemon model by [46] cited in [35]. Some models with the combination of first generation ontology localization for translation support to ontology are available. They use multilingual lexical (EuroWordNet), terminological resources and extant translation services for mappings. Multilingual lexical information integrates with ontology localisation tools to support queries in any language and is available via Semantic search engines.

Deeper multilingual lexical knowledge requires supporting cross-lingual natural language processing. However, users interact in different ways such as keyword-based queries. In this context, it is still a research question that how a natural language query can transform into a formal query [40][42][68][6]. Therefore localised semantic information can play a vital role to the serve user. The main problem is how to represent cross-lingual mappings as there are not many approaches to identify mappings between different languages [26]. Semantic Web languages and ontology matching both support cross-lingual ontology mappings.

The main objective of cultural ontology is to create explicit mutual and different perspectives to share understanding [55] cited in [1] i.e., researches [47][37][21] show promising results. However there is a need to develop a more detailed theoretical and empirical research in this area to support multiple languages by integrating machine translation systems [69][34][63] and measures of semantic similarity [35]. Further, it is not always possible to reuse in different linguistic and cultural scenarios as they are domain specific. Ontology localisation needs more research to increase the accuracy of current approaches. Further research also needs to look at how cost can be reduced and how the design could be more users friendly.

## 2.5    Cultural Attractors

Smith [62] describe cultural markers as cultural attractors. These are element of website design that reflect the signs and their meanings of a local culture for interface design. The studies by [32][62] presented the "cultural attractors" after auditing the e-finance websites of India and Taiwan. They developed a generic catalogue of cultural attractors and embedded in to E-commerce sites to help the local audience of India and Taiwan. The cultural attractors are combination of colours, cultural specific symbols, linguistic cues and religious iconography and local oriented identities. These cultural attractors can help the designers and usability evaluators to design cultural specific Web sites for specific cultures or countries. The proposed attractors match the expectations of the users for that particular culture.

## 2.6    Cultural Fingerprint

Smith [62] developed "cultural fingerprint" to compare cultural profile with target cultures. Their user study in cultural usability is influenced by Taguchi's work in Total Quality Management [67] cited by [62]. This bases the concepts of optimisation through the design of experiments. Taguchi is a cost effective method for researchers in cultural diversity [59][60].

The term "culturability" (combination of culture and usability) deals with language, social context, time, currency, units of measure, cultural values, body positions, symbols and aesthetics [4][28]. A study that supports culturability found that visual elements have a direct impact on the user's culture [70].

The studies discussed in this section have attributed differences to various cultural styles, including searching style, cognitive style, language use, perceptions of search systems and information sharing. The main problem in this area is the global acceptance of cultural factors for User Interface (UI). The researchers have a consensus that interface elements affected by culture need to be adjusted and designed according to locale-specific users.

# 3    Conclusion

The above mentioned observations indicate that the research relating to culture and technology with respect to classification needs more attention. Human-Computer Interaction (HCI) experts face the challenges to understand the target culture and its influence. The major problem is how a huge amount of information can be organised effectively. To achieve this, getting an effective access to information is needed. As there is no particular arrangement for the dissemination of knowledge to every culture while widening the access requires resource classified in a cultural context, it becomes the major potential barrier for designers. Consequently, it is time to study how information can be organised for different cultures.

# References

1. Abou-Zeid, E.S.: Towards a Cultural Ontology for Inter-organisational Knowledge Processes. In: Proc. of 36th Hawaii International Conference on System Sciences HICSS-36, Big Island HI, January 6-9, pp. 4–9. IEEE Computer Society (2003)
2. Anderson, J.R.: The adaptive nature of human categorization. Psychological Re'w 98(3), 409–429 (1991)
3. Aykin, N. (ed.): Usability and Internationalization of Information Technology, p. 392. Lawrence Erlbaum, New York (2005)
4. Barber, W., Badre, A.: Culturability: The merging of culture and usability. In: Proceedings of the Fourth Conference on Human Factors and the Web. AT and T Labs, Basking Ridge (1998), http://zing.ncsl.nist.gov/hfweb/att4/proceedings/barber/index.html (accessed November 11, 2004)
5. Blankenberger, S., Hahn, K.: Effects of icon design on human-computer interaction. International Journal of Man-machine Studies 35, 363–377 (1991)

6. Bobed, C., Trillo, R., Mena, E., Bernad, J.: Semantic Discovery of the User Intended Query in a Selectable Target Query Language. In: Proc. of 7th International Conference on Web Intelligence (WI), Sydney, pp. 579–582. IEEE Computer Society Press (2008)
7. Borgman, C.L.: From Gutenberg to the global information infrastructure access to information in the networked world. MIT Press, Cambridge (2000)
8. Buitelaar, P., Cimiano, P., Haase, P., Sintek, M.: Towards Linguistically Grounded Ontologies. In: Aroyo, L., Traverso, P., Ciravegna, F., Cimiano, P., Heath, T., Hyvönen, E., Mizoguchi, R., Oren, E., Sabou, M., Simperl, E. (eds.) ESWC 2009. LNCS, vol. 5554, pp. 111–125. Springer, Heidelberg (2009)
9. Byrne, J.: Localisation: When Language, Culture & Technology Join Forces. Language at Work No. 5 (2009) ISSN: 1904-030X
10. Callahan, E.: Cultural differences in the design of human computer interfaces: A multinational study of university websites. Published thesis, Indiana University (2007)
11. Choong, Y.Y., Plocher, T., Rau, P.L.: Cross-Cultural Web Design. In: Proctor, R.W., Vu, K.-P.L. (eds.) Handbook of Human Factors in Web Design. Lawrence Erlbaum Associates, Publishers (2005)
12. Cimiano, P., Haase, P., Herold, M., Mantel, M., Buitelaar, P.: Lexonto: A model for ontology lexicons for ontology-based nlp. In: Proceedings of OntoLex 2007, Busan, South Korea (2007)
13. Cimiano, P., Montiel-Ponsoda, E., Buitelaar, P., Espinoza, M., Gomez-Perez, A.: A Note on Ontology Localization. Journal of Applied Ontology 5(2) (2010)
14. Cimiano, P., Buitelaar, P., McCrae, J., Sintek, M.: LexInfo: A declarative model for the lexicon-ontology interface. J. Web Sem. 9(1), 29–51 (2011)
15. Cyr, D., Trever-Smith, H.: Localisation Of Web Design: An Empirical Comparison Of German, Japanese, And U.S. Website Characteristics. Journal of the American Society for Information Science and Technology 55(13), 1–10 (2004)
16. Day, D.: Cultural bases of interface acceptance: foundations. In: Sasse, M.A., Cunningham, J., Winder, R.L. (eds.) People and Computers XI, Proc.' of HCI 1996, pp. 35–47. Springer, London (1996)
17. De Angeli, A., Athavankar, U., Joshi, A., Coventry, L., Johnson, G.I.: Introducing ATMs in India: a contextual inquiry. Interacting with Computers 16(1), 29–44 (2004)
18. De Souza, C.: The semiotic engineering of the Human Computer Interface. MIT Press (2005)
19. Del Galdo, E., Nielsen, J.: International User Interfaces. Wiley Publishing, New York (1996)
20. Dunckley, L., Smith, A.: Cultural Factors and user interface design. In: Proceedings of the IEA 2000/HFES 2000 Congress (2000)
21. Eger, S., Sejane, I.: Computing Semantic Similarity from Bilingual Dictionaries. In: Proceedings of the 10th International Conference on the Statistical Analysis of Textual Data, Rome, Italy, pp. 1217–1225 (2010)
22. Embley, D.W., Liddle, S.W., Lonsdale, D.W., Tijerino, Y.: Multilingual Ontologies for Cross-Language Information Extraction and Semantic Search. In: Jeusfeld, M., Delcambre, L., Ling, T.-W. (eds.) ER 2011. LNCS, vol. 6998, pp. 147–160. Springer, Heidelberg (2011)
23. Espinoza, M., Gómez-Pérez, A., Mena, E.: Enriching an ontology with multilingual information. In: Bechhofer, S., Hauswirth, M., Hoffmann, J., Koubarakis, M. (eds.) ESWC 2008. LNCS, vol. 5021, pp. 333–347. Springer, Heidelberg (2008)

24. Espinoza, M., Gómez-Pérez, A., Montiel-Ponsoda, E.: Multilingual and localization support for ontologies. In: Aroyo, L., Traverso, P., Ciravegna, F., Cimiano, P., Heath, T., Hyvönen, E., Mizoguchi, R., Oren, E., Sabou, M., Simperl, E. (eds.) ESWC 2009. LNCS, vol. 5554, pp. 821–825. Springer, Heidelberg (2009)
25. Esselink, B.: A Practical Guide to Localization. John Benjamins, Amsterdam (2003)
26. Euzenat, J., Shvaiko, P.: Ontology matching. Springer, Heidelberg (2007)
27. Evers, V.: Cultural Aspects of User Interface Understanding: An Empirical Evaluation of an E-Learning website by International User Groups. Doctoral Thesis, the Open University (2001)
28. Fernandes, T.: Global interface design: A guide to designing international user interfaces. Academic Press Professional, Inc., San Diego (1995)
29. Fitzgerald, W.: Models for Cross-Cultural Communications for Cross-Cultural Website Design, National Research Council Canada, Institute for Information Technology (2004)
30. French, T.: What kinds of interpretation can semiotics offer to e-commerce site users and designers? In: Proceedings of the First International Workshop Interpretative Approaches to Information Systems Research, Brunel University, UK, July 26–27, pp. 1–6 (2002) ISBN 1-902316-27-4
31. French, T., Conrad, M.: Culture and e-Culture through a semiotic lens: E-banking localization. In: International Conference on Information Society (i-Society), pp. 514–518 (2012)
32. French, T., Minocha, S., Smith, A.: eFinance Localisation: an informal analysis of specific eCulture attractors in selected Indian and Taiwanese sites. In: Coronado, J., Day, D., Hall, B. (eds.) Designing for Global Markets, Proceedings of IWIPS 2002. Products and Systems International, vol. 4, pp. 9–21 (2002)
33. French, T., Smith, A.: Semiotically enhanced Web Interfaces for Shared Meanings: Can Semiotics Help Us Meet the Challenge of Cross-Cultural HCI Design? In: IWIPS 2000, Baltimore, US (2000)
34. Fu, B., Brennan, R., O'Sullivan, D.: Cross-lingual ontology mapping - an investigation of the impact of machine translation. In: Gómez-Pérez, A., Yu, Y., Ding, Y. (eds.) ASWC 2009. LNCS, vol. 5926, pp. 1–15. Springer, Heidelberg (2009)
35. Gracia, J., Montiel-Ponsoda, E., Cimiano, P., Gómez-Pérez, A., Buitelaar, P., McCrae, J.: Challenges for the multilingual Web of Data. International Journal on Web Semantic Web 11(2), 63–71 (2012)
36. Gruber, T.R.: Toward principles for the design of ontologies used for knowledge sharing. International Journal of Human-Computer Studies 43(5-6) (1995)
37. Hassan, S., Mihalcea, R.: Cross-lingual Semantic Relatedness Using Encyclopedic Knowledge. In: Proceedings of the Conference on Empirical Methods in Natural Language Processing, Singapore (2009)
38. Juric, R., Kim, I., Kuljis, J.: Cross cultural web design: An experience (sic) of developing UK and Korean cultural markers. In: 25th International Conference on Information Technology Interfaces (2003)
39. Krippendorff, K.: Content analysis: An introduction to its methodology. Sage Pub., Beverly Hills (1980)
40. Lei, Y., Uren, V., Motta, E.: SemSearch: A Search Engine for the Semantic Web. In: Staab, S., Svátek, V. (eds.) EKAW 2006. LNCS (LNAI), vol. 4248, pp. 238–245. Springer, Heidelberg (2006)
41. LISA, Localization (2008), http://www.lisa.org/Localization.61.0.html (accessed June 04, 2012)

42. Lopez, V., Sabou, M., Motta, E.: PowerMap: Mapping the Real Semantic Web on the Fly. In: Cruz, I., Decker, S., Allemang, D., Preist, C., Schwabe, D., Mika, P., Uschold, M., Aroyo, L.M. (eds.) ISWC 2006. LNCS, vol. 4273, pp. 414–427. Springer, Heidelberg (2006)

43. Marcus, A.: International and intercultural user interfaces. In: Stephanidis, C. (ed.) User Interfaces for All: Concepts, Methods, and Tools, pp. 47–63. Lawrence Erlbaum, Mahwah (2001)

44. Marcus, A.G.: Global/Intercultural User Interface Design. In: Sears, A., Jacko, J.A. (eds.) The Human-Computer Interaction Handbook: Fundamentals, Evolving Technologies and Emerging Applications, 2nd edn. Lawrence Erlbaum Associates (2008)

45. Maroto, J., Bortoli, M.D.: Web Site Localization. In: European Languages and the Implementation of Communication and Information Technologies (Elicit) Conference (2001)

46. McCrae, J., Aguado-de-Cea, G., Buitelaar, P., Cimiano, P., Declerck, T., Gómez-Pérez, A., Gracia, J., Hollink, L., Montiel-Ponsoda, E., Spohr, D., Wunner, T.: Interchanging Lexical Resources in the Semantic Web. Language Resources and Evaluation (2011)

47. Mohammad, S., Gurevych, I., Hirst, G., Zesch, T.: Cross-Lingual Distributional Profiles of Concepts for Measuring Semantic Distance. In: Proc. of the 2007 Joint Conference on Empirical Methods in Natural Language Processing and Computational Natural Language Learning, pp. 571–580. ACL (June 2007)

48. Montiel-Ponsoda, E., Aguado de Cea, G., Gómez-Pérez, A., Peters, W.: Modelling multilinguality in ontologies. In: Coling 2008: Companion volume - Posters and Demonstrations, UK, pp. 67–70 (2008)

49. Mushtaha, A., De Troyer, O.: Cross-culture and website design: cultural movements and settled cultural variables. In: Aykin, N. (ed.) IDGD 2009. LNCS, vol. 5623, pp. 69–78. Springer, Heidelberg (2009) ISBN 978-3-642-02766-6

50. Myers, M.D.: Qualitative Research in Information Systems. MIS Quarterly 21(2), 241–242 (1997), MISQ Discovery, archival version (June 1997), http://www.misq.org/supplements/ MISQ Discovery (updated version last modified: May 21, 2012), http://www.qual.auckland.ac.nz (accessed, June 03, 2012)

51. Nielsen, J.: Why you only need to test with 5 users. Alertbox (2000)

52. Nielsen, J.: Usability 101: Introduction to usability. Alertbox (2003), http://www.useit.com/alertbox/20030825.html (accessed July 15, 2006)

53. Peirce, C.: Collected papers of Charles Sanders Peirce. Belnap Press, USA (1953)

54. Peters, W., Montiel-Ponsoda, E., Aguado de Cea, G.: Localizing Ontologies in OWL. In: Proceedings of OntoLex 2007, Busan, South Corea (2007)

55. Qureshi, S., Hlupic, V., Vereede, G.J., Briggs, R., Nunamaker: Harnessing Intellectual Resources in a Collaborative Context to Create Value, ERS-2002-28-LIS, Erasmus Research Institute Of Management (2002)

56. Russo, P., Boor, S.: How fluent is your interface?: designing for international users. In: Proceedings of the INTERACT 1993 and CHI 1993 Conference on Human Factors in Computing Systems (CHI 1993), pp. 342–347. ACM, New York (1993)

57. Saussure, F.: Course in General Linguistics. Collins Press, London (1974)

58. Sheppard, C., Scholtz, J.: The effects of cultural markers on web site use. In: Fifth Conference on Human Factors and the Web, Gaithersburg, Maryland (1999)

59. Smith, A., Dunckley, L.: Towards a Quality Interface - the application of TQM techniques to Interface design. People and Computers X1. HCI 1996 (1996) ISBN 3-540-760690-51996

60. Smith, A., Dunckley, L.: Using the LUCID method to optimize the acceptability of shared interfaces. Interacting with Computers 9(3), 335–344 (1998)

61. Smith, A., French, T.: The Role of Cultural Theories within International Usability. In: Rauterberg, M., Menozzi, M., Wesson, J. (eds.) INTERACT. IOS Press (2003)
62. Smith, A., Dunckley, L., French, T., Minocha, S., Chang, Y.: A process model for developing usable cross-cultural websites. Interacting with Computers 16(1), 63–91 (2004)
63. Spohr, D., Hollink, L., Cimiano, P.: A machine learning approach to multilingual and cross-lingual ontology matching. In: Aroyo, L., Welty, C., Alani, H., Taylor, J., Bernstein, A., Kagal, L., Noy, N., Blomqvist, E. (eds.) ISWC 2011, Part I. LNCS, vol. 7031, pp. 665–680. Springer, Heidelberg (2011)
64. Springett, M., French, T.: User Experience and its Relationship to Usability: The Case of e-Commerce Web-site Design. In: Workshop: Towards a User Experience Manifesto, Lancaster Uni., pp. 43–48 (2007)
65. Sun, H.: Expanding the scope of localization: A cultural usability perspective on mobile text messaging use in American and Chinese contexts. Doctoral dissertation, Rensselaer Polytechnic Institute, NY (2004)
66. Sun, H.: Designing for a dialogic view of interpretation in cross-cultural IT design. In: Aykin, N. (ed.) IDGD 2009. LNCS, vol. 5623, pp. 108–116. Springer, Heidelberg (2009)
67. Taguchi, G.: Introduction To Quality Engineering. American Supplier Institute, Dearborn (1986)
68. Tran, T., Cimiano, P., Rudolph, S., Studer, R.: Ontology-Based Interpretation of Keywords for Semantic Search. In: Aberer, K., Choi, K.-S., Noy, N., Allemang, D., Lee, K.-I., Nixon, L.J.B., Golbeck, J., Mika, P., Maynard, D., Mizoguchi, R., Schreiber, G., Cudré-Mauroux, P. (eds.) ASWC 2007 and ISWC 2007. LNCS, vol. 4825, pp. 523–536. Springer, Heidelberg (2007)
69. Trojahn, C., Quaresma, P., Vieira, R.: A framework for multilingual ontology mapping. In: Proceedings of the Sixth International Language Resources and Evaluation (LREC 2008). European Language Resources Association, Marrakech (2008)
70. Tsai, I.-C., Kim, B., Liu, P.-J., Goggins, S.P., Kumalasari, C., Laffey, J.M.: Building a Model Explaining the Social Nature of Online Learning. Journal of Educational Tech., and Society 11(3), 198–215 (2008)
71. Vatrapu, R.: Culture and International Usability Testing: The Effects of Culture in Interviews. Virginia Polytechnic Institute and State University (2002)
72. Wynn, E.: Office conversation as an Information Medium. University of California, Berkeley (1979)

# Integration of Characteristics of Culture into Product Design: A Perspective from Symbolic Interactions

Yu-Hsiu Hung[1,*], Wei-Ting Li[1], and Yi Sheng Goh[2]

[1] Department of Industrial Design, National Cheng Kung University, Tainan, Taiwan
{idhfhung,p36011139}@mail.ncku.edu.tw
[2] Institute of Creative Industries Design, National Cheng Kung University, Tainan, Taiwan
ysgoh@mail.ncku.edu.tw

**Abstract.** Cultural insight has become essential for improving designs for global and regional markets. However, little work is done on how to dissect culture and incorporate culture characteristics into design activities to create emotional engagements between products and users. This study, therefore, developed a cultural design model to address this problem. The cultural design model was built based on the notion that meaning evolves from social interactions with objects/symbols in the environment and with people. In the model, the theoretical components of Symbolic Interactions and O'Brien's and Toms' user engagement attributes were adopted and were used to analyze culture and transform cultural characteristics into product design features, as well as to "enable user experience." The effectiveness of the cultural design model was verified through a case study with two groups of Industrial Design students on designing tea cups for Taiwanese tea culture. Results of the study provided evidence of the proposed cultural design model in assisting with cultural design activities.

**Keywords:** Culture, Symbolic Interactions, Design.

## 1 Introduction

Design changes culture and at the same time, is shaped by culture [1]. The interest in designing for culture is growing in industry and academia. Cultural insight has become essential for improving designs and product sales in both the regional and global markets. Observing the design of artifacts produced and consumed in our society often reveals cultural situations, people's lives, and how people communicate [2]. It is culture that gives product meaning, as well as provides the rituals and values where artifacts are used [3].

Studies on products and interfaces have indicated that interfaces showing characteristics relevant to culture increase product usability and performance. For instance, Smith and Chang [4] incorporated cultural fingerprints as a diagrammatic means in improving the acceptability of website design. Smith, Dunckley, French, Minocha, and Chang [5] presented a process model for developing usable cross-cultural websites. They

---

\* Corresponding author.

P.L.P. Rau (Ed.): CCD/HCII 2013, Part I, LNCS 8023, pp. 208–217, 2013.
© Springer-Verlag Berlin Heidelberg 2013

introduced the concept of cultural attractors (e.g., color combinations, trust signs, use of metaphor, etc.) to define the interface design elements of a website that reflect the signs and their meanings to match the expectations of a local culture. Moreover, Moalosi, Popovic, and Hickling-Hudson [2] integrated socio-cultural factors (including social practice factors, material factors, emotional factors, and technology/design factors) into the conceptual design phase to generate culturally oriented products.

The above studies demonstrated the potential for using cultural dimensions/attributes/characteristics for designing innovative products and interfaces. However, most of them did not investigate how to create "emotional engagements" between products and intended users. This study, therefore, was based on the notion that understanding what and how cultural norms and values can be integrated into product design [2] is not sufficient to successful cultural product design. Rather, cultural product design should take an additional consideration, i.e., engaging user experiences. In this study, we describe the development of a cultural design model from the theoretical components of Symbolic Interactions [6] and O'Brien's and Toms' user engagement attributes [7], with the intention to not only help designers transform culture characteristics into product design features, but also engage users in product use. This study also conducted a case study (consisting of tea cup design) to demonstrate the effectiveness of the model. The aim of this paper is to look at cultural product design from symbolic interactions and take cultural product design to the level of enabling user engagement.

## 2 Literature Review

### 2.1 Basis/Philosophy for the Development of Models of Culture

Culture is viewed and defined differently by researchers. It is associated with people, and its content involves a wide range of phenomena, such as norms, values, shared meanings and patterned ways of behaving [8]. Simply put, "culture is communication, and communication is culture" [9]. It "includes race and ethnicity as well as other variables and is manifested in customary behaviors, assumptions and values, patterns of thinking and communication style" [10]. More specifically, culture is the socially transmitted knowledge and behavior shared by some group of people [8]. In the literature, models of culture were proposed to understand culture [9, 11-13]. They are typically developed based on a level of culture and/or philosophies of metamodel(s) of culture.

- **Levels of culture** correspond to layers of mental programming carried by each individual [14]. For example, a national level corresponds to one's country; a social class level corresponds to a person's educational training and income; a level on cognitive style corresponds to an individual's ethnicity, etc. Therefore, cultural differences exist according to nation, region, religion, gender, generation, and social class, etc.
- **The metamodels of culture** [14] define different layers of culture and provide perspectives to look at culture. For example: the Onion Model is made of three

layers (i.e., symbol, hero, and ritual) around a core (i.e., value). All three layers can be trained and learned through practices except for the core. The Pyramid Model is composed of three layers (from top to bottom: personality, culture, and human nature). The model states that culture should be distinguished from human nature on one side, and from an individual's personality on the other. The Iceberg Model is consisted of two layers, the layers above/below the waterline. The layer above the waterline is 10 percent of the iceberg, representing observational behavior of a culture (e.g., actions, thoughts, and words). The layer below the waterline is the major and invisible part of the iceberg, representing beliefs, values, and assumptions of a culture. The Objective and Subjective Model identifies two layers of culture, subjective and objective culture. Subjective culture (e.g., similarities and differences in power and authority) is difficult to measure as it operates outside of conscious awareness. Objective culture (represented with arts, crafts, literature, social customs, and political structure, etc.) is what is real and concrete and is an externalization of subjective culture.

One of the most-used models of culture is Hofstede's cultural model [11]. It conceptualized culture as programming of the mind. The model, examining culture at the level of country, states that people react differently based on the different cultural values they hold. All of the dimensions in Hofstede's model fall under the scope of subjective culture (including power distance, masculinity and femininity, individualism and collectivism, uncertainty avoidance, and time orientation).

## 2.2 Interpretation of Culture with Symbolic Interactionism: A Communication Perspective

Symbolic Interactionism, originated in sociology, refers to the way we (learn to) interpret and give meaning to the world though our interactions with other people [6]. In Symbolic Interactionism, reality is composed of objects (or symbols), each of which carries a meaning. Meaning evolves from social interactions with objects/symbols in the environment and with people. In other words, people interact by interpreting another's act based on the meanings produced by their interpretations.

Blumer, one of the pioneers of Symbolic Interactionism, proposed that symbolic interaction is a communicative process involving five elements: the self, the act, social interaction, objects, and joint action. These interrelated elements constitutes a system that explains the idea of culture [16], as culture is constructed, learned, interpreted, and transmitted among a group of people where meanings are given/shared in supporting social interactions.

Blumer explained the five elements of symbolic interaction as follows: the self (the way that one person acts in relation to the attitudes of others) can become an object/symbol of self-indication ("*a moving communicative process in which the individual note things, assesses them, gives them a meaning, and decides to act on the basis of that meaning*") [16]; individual action is yielded from the process of self-indication; joint action (e.g., rites and norms) consists of aligning individual actions through a process of interpretation of others' actions; social interaction means people interact by interpreting another's act based on the meanings produced by their interpretation.

# 3    Development of a Cultural Design Model

The cultural design model explained in the following includes a three-stage design process (Figure 1) to designing for culture.

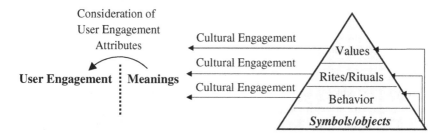

**Fig. 1.** The cultural design model

## 3.1    Analysis, Translation, and Engagement

In this study, culture is viewed through the lens of social communication and symbolic Interactions. Culture, at the same time, can be explained by layers in metamodels of culture. Thus, the theoretical components of Symbolic Interactionism and the philosophies of metamodels of culture were used to form the basis for analyzing culture. The decomposition/analysis of culture can be achieved by identifying the following four levels (from bottom to top) of cultural characteristics:

- **Level 1- Symbols/objects** represent tangibles that carry meanings agreed among individuals in a culture. They reflect objective culture and "the self" and "objects" in Symbolic Interactionism.
- **Level 2 - Behavior** is the actions of an individual in responding to stimuli or others. It reflects objective culture and "act" in Symbolic Interactionism.
- **Level 3 - Ritual/Rite** is a set of actions/behaviors performed by individuals to express the symbolic values. It represents a planned set of activities that combines various form of cultural expressions and that often has both practical and expressive consequences [17]. According to Hartley [15], rites allow for social interactions in different levels, and have multiple consequences; rites can serve as an entry point for new comers. Rituals/rites reflect objective culture and "act", "joint action," and "social interaction" in Symbolic Interactionism.
- **Level 4 - Values** are a synthesis of shared meanings, assumptions, and ideals among people that reflects traditions and are worth striving for [18]. They reflect subjective culture.

Design can be linked to culture through the incorporation of cultural values in products [2]. With respect to designing for culture, therefore, addressing cultural values becomes important. Moreover, meanings are conveyed and adjusted among people based on what they have been informed in the social context [19]. This suggests that symbols and objects in a culture may not necessarily yield meanings by themselves. It is through social behavior and interactions where meanings would take place. Thus, in our proposed cultural design model, addressing cultural symbols/objects in product design is not sufficient. To enable user engagement so that cultural meanings are yielded during user-product interactions, as demonstrated in Figure 1, transforming cultural characteristics in other cultural levels as well becomes essential.

### 3.2     Catalyst to Enable User Engagement

Bannon [20] noted that the emphasis of product design is not effectiveness and efficiency, but how well a product is able to provide users with good experiences. To be able to enable user engagement with products, our proposed cultural design model adopts O'Brien' and Toms' model of user engagement (Figure 1). It includes the following five elements that should be also integrated into product attributes in the design process:

- **Focused attention** refers to users' perceptions of time passing and their degree of awareness about what was taking place outside of their interaction with the product.
- **Perceived usability** pertained to the emotions experienced by users during their interactions with the product.
- **Aesthetics** refers to users' overall aesthetic impressions of the product's attractiveness and sensory appeal pertaining to specific product features.
- **Endurability** refers to users' likelihood to perceive experiences of product usage as "successful," "rewarding," "worthwhile," and working out as planned.
- **Involvement** refers to users feeling of being drawn into and involved in the use of the product.

## 4     Case Study

To verify the effectiveness of the model, we conducted a between-subject comparative case study on the tea cup design.

### 4.1     Participant

Nineteen college students majoring in Industrial Design (sophomore year, mean age=19) were recruited to perform idea-sketching on the topic—Designing tea cups for Taiwanese tea culture. Nine students (three males and six females) participated in the control group. Ten students (five males and five females) participated in the experimental group.

### 4.2     Procedure

Participants in the experimental group were given the cultural design model to support idea-sketching. Participants in the control group were not given any assistance in their idea-sketching activities. Every participant was allowed to use the Internet to collect any information needed for his/her designs. In this study, all participants were given drawing tools and instructed to use one and half hour to perform idea-sketching on the design topic.

After the idea-sketching, participants were instructed to select two of their best ideas. Interviews were conducted with the participants (by two researchers in separate groups) to understand participants' thoughts, ideas, tea culture characteristics, and user engagement elements of their selected sketches. Interviews were audio-recorded and notes were taken for later data analysis.

In the study, the demonstrated Taiwanese tea culture characteristics were developed by former semi-structured interviews with six subject matter experts (two females and four males) who have more than 30 years of tea-drinking experiences. The abstracted tea culture characteristics are as follows:

- **Values** — share, interaction, nature, health, art, tradition, value-added, elaboration, passing down, and experience, etc.
- **Ritual/rite** — behave politely and gently when receiving the tea cup and savoring tea, respect seniors around the tea table, savoring tea with gentle movement, and appreciate the tea with both hands holding the tea cup, etc.
- **Behavior** —review the dried tea leaf to determine the right amount of tea to be measured and the right water temperature to be applied, smell the aroma seeping from under the tea cup, sip the tea to appreciate it's aroma, flavor, taste, and fine finish, warm the pot/cups to ensure the water temperature and tea quality, and savoring the aftertaste of the tea in the mouth and throat, etc.
- **Symbol** — appreciation, respect, calm, not being inclination to either side, and warm-heartedness, etc.
- **Object** — tea boat, tea scoop, tea pitcher, tea towel, brewing teapot, pouring teapot, aroma cups, drinking cups, saucer, preparation tray, pewter tea container, tea packaging, and tea table, etc.

## 5    Results and Discussions

The ideas selected by the participants are shown in Table 1 and Table 2. From the interview with the student participants, we understand that, among the selected/preferred tea cup ideas, participants in the control group overall integrated higher numbers of objects and symbols (Figure 2), whereas participants in the experimental group integrated higher numbers of behavior, rites, rituals, and even values (Figure 2).

Table 3 shows the average numbers of tea culture characteristics integrated in each selected idea. In average, participants in the experimental group incorporated more cultural characteristics (especially cultural values and behavior) into one idea than their counterparts. On the other hand, participants in the control group emphasized less on culture behavior, rites/rituals, and values, but more on cultural symbols/objects on tea cup design. These results suggested that our proposed design model is effective in helping designers perform cultural product design. This is because, from the perspective of Symbolic Interactions, simply transforming cultural symbols and objects into product design features may not necessarily engage users into the cultural meanings that are typically yielded in the context of social interactions and communications in a culture.

In addition, with respect to user engagement, among the selected/preferred tea cup ideas, participants in the experimental group tended to incorporate more user engagement attributes in their product design features than their counterparts (Figure 3). Table 3 shows similar results with Figure 3. From Table 3, we know that, in average, participants in the experimental group integrated higher numbers of user engagement attributes (especially aesthetics, perceived usability, and involvement) into one idea than their counterparts. These results demonstrate the effectiveness of our proposed cultural design model in helping designers engage intended users through product design features.

**Table 1.** Eighteen ideas selected by participants in the control groups

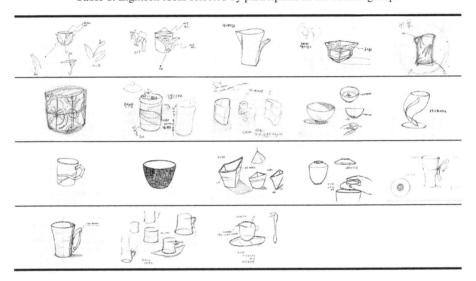

**Table 2.** Twenty ideas selected by participants in the experimental groups

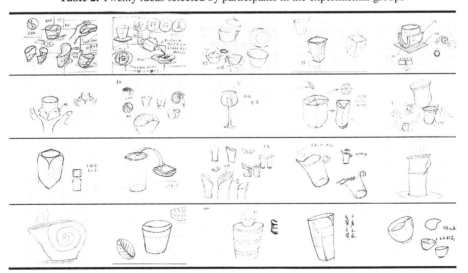

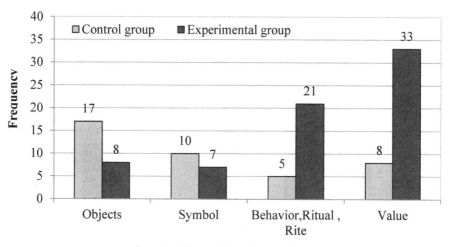

**Levels of tea cultural characteristics**

**Fig. 2.** Frequency distribution for levels of tea cultural characteristics addressed in participants' selected sketches

**Table 3.** The average numbers of tea culture characteristics/user engagement attributes integrated in one selected idea

| Level in the Culture Model | Average Number of Culture Characteristics in One Idea | | User Engagement Attribute | Average Number of User Engagement Attributes in One Idea | |
|---|---|---|---|---|---|
| | Control Group | Experimental Group | | Control Group | Experimental Group |
| Symbol/Object | 1.5 | 0.75 | Focused Attention | 0.28 | 0.55 |
| Behavior | 0.17 | 0.78 | Perceived Usability | 0.28 | 0.85 |
| Rite/Ritual | 0.06 | 0.39 | Aesthetics | 0.11 | 1 |
| Value | 0.44 | 1.65 | Endurability | 0.06 | 0.56 |
| | | | Involvement | 0.28 | 0.78 |

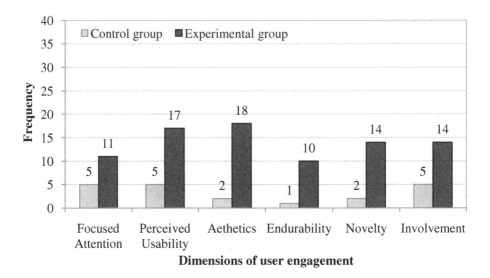

**Fig. 3.** Frequency distribution for the dimensions of user engagement addressed in participants' selected sketches

## 6    Conclusions

The purpose of this study was to develop a cultural model from the perspective of Symbolic Interactions. To engage users into an intended culture and product usage, our model suggested designers integrating user engagement attributes, as well as culture characteristics located at the level of "Symbols/objects" and those at other levels into product design. This study conducted a case study on tea cup design to demonstrate the effectiveness of the model. Results of the study showed that participants who were presented with the cultural design model addressed higher number of tea culture characteristics in their design, especially from the levels associated with cultural behavior, rites, rituals, and values. Participants who did not receive the cultural design model seemed to generate ideas from symbols and objects used in the tea culture, with less emphasis on tea cultural characteristics located in other levels. Results of the study also showed that our cultural design model inspired participants to integrate user engagement attributes in their product design features and usage.

In this study, we do not contend that a design idea has to address all cultural characteristics identified in the cultural design model, meaning that the number of cultural characteristics used in a design cannot be used to determine the quality of a design. However, we did find that, when selecting ideas, participants preferred ideas addressing a larger number of tea culture characteristics. The outcome of the study is limited with the amount of time given to participants to understand the tea culture and to perform design activities in demonstrating the efficacy of the cultural design model. Future studies are needed to address the limitations. It is our hope that through this study, the methods and tools for designing for culture can be advanced.

# References

1. Röse, K.: The Development of Culture-orientated Human Machine System: Specification, Analysis and Integration of Relevant Intercultural Variables. In: Kaplan, M. (ed.) Cultural Ergonomics. Elsevier (2004)
2. Moalosi, R., Popovic, V., Hickling-Hudson, A.: Culture-orientated product design. International Journal of Technology and Design Education 20(2), 175–190 (2010)
3. Press, M., Cooper, R.: The design experience: the role of design and designers in the twenty-first century. Ashgate, Burlington (2003)
4. Smith, A., Chang, Y.: Quantifying Hofstede and Developing Cultural Fingerprints for Website Acceptability. In: Evers, V., et al. (eds.) Proceedings of the IWIPS 2003 Conference, University of Kaiserslautern, Berlin, Germany (2003)
5. Smith, A., et al.: A process model for developing usable cross-cultural websites. Interacting with Computers 16(1), 63–91 (2004)
6. Blumer, H.: Social Problems as Collective Behavior. Social Problems 18, 298–306 (1971)
7. O'Brien, H.L., Toms, E.G.: The development and evaluation of a survey to measure user engagement. Journal of the American Society for Information Science and Technology 61(1), 50–69 (2009)
8. Bailey, G., Peoples, J.: Introduction to Cultural Anthropology. Wadsworth Publishing (1998)
9. Hall, E.: The Silent Language, Doubleday (1959)
10. Borgman, C.L.: The User's Mental Model of an Information Retrieval System: an Experiment on a Prototype Online Catalog. International Journal of Man-Machine Studies 24, 47–64 (1986)
11. Hofstede, G.: Culture's consequences. Sage Publications (2001)
12. Victor, D.: International Business Communications. Harper Collins (1992)
13. Trompenaars, F.: Riding the Waves of Culture. Nicholas Brealey Publishing, London (1993)
14. Hoft, N.: Developing a Cultural Model. In: Del Galdo, E., Nielson, J. (eds.) International User Interfaces. John Wiley and Sons, New York (1996)
15. Hartley, K.C.: Socialization by Way of Symbolic Interactionism and Culture Theory: A Communication Perspective. In: The Annual Meeting of the Speech Communication Association, Chicago, IL (1992)
16. Blumer, H.: Symbolic Interactionism: Perspective and Method. Prentice-Hall, Englewood Cliffs (1969)
17. Harrison, M.T., Beyer, J.M.: Studying Organizational Cultures through Rites and Ceremonials. The Academy of Management Review 9(4), 653–669 (1984)
18. Sathe, V.: Culture and related corporate realities. Irwin, R.D, Homewood (1985)
19. Mead, G.H.: Mind, Self, and Society: From the standpoint of a social behaviorist. In: Morris, C.W. (ed.), The University of Chicago Press, Chicago (1934)
20. Bannon, L.: A human-centred perspective on interaction design. In: Pirhonen, H.I.A., Roast, C., Saariluoma, P. (eds.) Future Interaction Design, pp. 9–30. Springer, Berlin (2005)

# Modality-Independent Interaction Framework for Cross-Disability Accessibility

J. Bern Jordan and Gregg C. Vanderheiden

University of Wisconsin–Madison, Madison, Wisconsin, United States
{jordan,gv}@trace.wisc.edu

**Abstract.** People with disabilities often have difficulty using ICT and similar technologies because of a mismatch between their needs and the requirements of the user interface. The wide range of both user abilities and accessibility guidelines makes it difficult for interface designers who need a simpler accessibility framework that still works across disabilities. A modality-independent interaction framework is proposed to address this problem. We define modality-independent input as non-time-dependent encoded input (such as that from a keyboard) and modality-independent output as electronic text. These formats can be translated to provide a wide range input and output forms as well as support for assistive technologies. We identify three interfaces styles that support modality-independent input/output: command line, single-keystroke command, and linear navigation interfaces. Tasks that depend on time, complex-path, simultaneity, or experience are identified as providing barriers to full cross-disability accessibility. The framework is posited as a simpler approach to wide cross-disability accessibility.

**Keywords:** Cross-cultural product and service design, disability, accessibility, framework, input, output, interaction, user interface, modality independence.

## 1 Introduction

Information and communication technologies (ICT), and other devices and systems with ICT-like interfaces, are widely used for work, education, entertainment, and daily living. However, many people with disabilities find it difficult or impossible to use these systems for a variety of reasons [1]. This difficulty is frequently a result of a mismatch between the user and the task or between the user and the interface. For many ICT systems, the interface is the only barrier to completing a task for a user with a disability. If the user instead had an interface that fit his or her needs, the same task could be completed successfully.

Designing accessible interfaces can be challenging because many factors must be considered. First, the specific needs, characteristics, and abilities of people with disabilities are very diverse [2]. A second factor is that not all accessibility strategies can be used in all design contexts. For example, accessibility may be provided in some software by using established accessibility application programming interfaces (APIs), which work with a user's assistive technology (AT). However, other systems

P.L.P. Rau (Ed.): CCD/HCII 2013, Part I, LNCS 8023, pp. 218–227, 2013.
© Springer-Verlag Berlin Heidelberg 2013

have *closed functionality*, where particular functionality can only be accessed through the built-in user interface. With closed functionality APIs cannot be utilized, so these systems must provide a built-in, directly accessible interface to the user.

A third factor is the many accessibility standards, regulation, guidelines, and published lists of strategies for ICT [3–5]. Two key accessibility regulations in the United States that a designer needs to understand are the Accessibility Standards of the Americans with Disabilities Act and Section 508 of the Rehabilitation Act of 1973. Many other countries have similar types of accessibility legislation in place or under development. The International Organization for Standardization has a number of standards that relate to accessibility, including ISO 9241-20:2008 (ICT accessibility guidelines), and ISO 9241-171:2008 (software accessibility). The Web Content Accessibility Guidelines (WCAG) 2.0 are accessibility guidelines for web content and applications, but also are being cited as guidance for non-web software and content [6]. In addition to the standards and regulations, there are a number of books, chapters, and articles available on accessibility.

The documents and accessibility standards listed above, and others like them, provide accessibility guidance or regulations, but are complex with many detailed provisions that require time and study to understand. The volume and complexity of the information can be overwhelming to new designers or designers new to accessibility. It is difficult for these designers to prioritize accessibility so that the most important features are addressed first [2] and to identify strategies that can address multiple requirements simultaneously.

To facilitate the incorporation of accessibility into the design process, designers need a simpler accessibility framework. In this paper, we describe a framework of basic modality-independent interaction that can be used to more simply understand and address the needs of people with physical and sensory disabilities ranging from mild to severe for many contexts. In this framework we define modality-independent input and output channels and suitable interface styles. With modality-independent interaction, a user can interact with an interface using any input or output modality that fits his or her needs. The input, output, and interaction may be provided by the system itself or through a user's AT. The model is not meant to replace comprehensive accessibility guidelines, but to provide a simpler way to address basic access.

Modality-independent input and output channels have been considered before and are the basis for many of the current accessibility guidelines. On the output side, the information must be available to AT in modality-independent form or in a form that can be easily converted to a modality-independent form in order to allow AT to present information in different modalities to fit the user [7] (this concept is also reflected in WCAG 2.0 Guideline 1.1 [8]).

On the input side, modality-independent input (or an input method that can easily be translated across modalities) is also required. Guideline 2.1 from WCAG 2.0 [8] requires keyboard input to address this need for web content. In this paper we extend these input and output concepts to more types of systems.

## 2     Modality-Independent Interaction Framework

In developing the framework of modality-independent interaction, we considered the needs of users without disabilities and the needs of users with sensory or physical disabilities ranging from mild to severe. The most severe sensory disabilities considered were people who are completely unable to see, unable to hear, and unable to both see and hear. The most severe physical disability we considered was where people have control over only a single customized switch.

In order to be accessible, a system must have accessible input, output, and interaction. These can be transformed into a wide range of forms to fit many users' needs.

### 2.1     System Input

In order to operate an interface, the user must provide input to the system. However, people with physical disabilities may be precluded from using various input devices. To be controllable by a wide range of users, systems must accept modality-independent input, which can be provided by a wide variety of input devices.

We define *modality-independent input* as **non-time-dependent encoded input**. The type of input depends on the capabilities of the system, but must be in a standard format that can be emulated by AT over a standard connection. For computer and mobile-device operating systems, encoded input is keyboard entry using the standard human interface device drivers over USB or Bluetooth. Other examples of encoded input include DTMF tones used by touchtone interactive menu systems and Baudot tones used with text telephones (TTYs). Depending on the interface style, the encoded input might be a subset of that which is accepted by the system. For an interface that requires text input, the encoded input is all of the characters available in that language. For a more limited interface, all interaction may be available using just a few keys (e.g., Shift, Tab, and Enter).

Modality-independent input can be generated through many methods including physical keyboards, Morse code using switches or sip-and-puff [9], chordic keyboards (including Braille keyboards), speech recognition, handwriting recognition, gestures, brain-control interfaces [10], eye or other body movements, or any type of pointing or scanning in combination with a real or virtual keyboard/keyset.

It is important that input not depend on time for several reasons. Some people have difficulty generating specific movements within a particular time span while others need additional time to plan their movements in advance. Generating input with a limited number of switches can take a significant amount of time. Single-switch scanning methods are all time-dependent and customized to the users' abilities. Scanning methods cannot generate input at any arbitrary rate for time-dependent interfaces.

### 2.2     System Output

In order to perceive the output and feedback from a system, the output needs to be available in a modality that each person can use. Modality-independent output can be transformed or translated into forms that fit the user's needs and abilities.

We define *modality-independent output* as **electronic text**. To be completely accessible, the electronic text output must convey all of the information necessary for full interaction. To work with AT, the system must transmit the text over a standard connection in a standard format. The exact connection and format depends on the system capabilities and content language. Simple ASCII character encoding is sufficient for English text, but other encodings may need to be used for other languages.

Electronic text output can be transformed into a wide range of accessible output in different modalities. Text can be transformed into speech, provided on a braille display, or rendered in a user's preferred font size, color, and typeface. Electronic text can also be translated with varying degrees of success into other languages, including sign language presented by computer-generated avatars [11].

The presentation of system output could be improved by adding semantic or modality-specific markup to the text. Semantic markup describes the underlying meaning of content, which could potentially be provided in different ways for different users. Modality-specific markup defines the presentation of content, for example, the exact pronunciation of a name or the font of text. While additional markup may improve the user experience, plain electronic text is the minimum required for modality-independent accessibility.

### 2.3    Interface Styles

Accessibility relies not only on accessible input and output channels, but also on a suitable interface style. There are a wide variety of interface styles including direct manipulation, immersive environments, menu selection, form fill-in, command line, and natural language interfaces [12]. However, some interface styles do not translate well into other modalities. For example, in a visual direct manipulation interface the relationships and commands represented through spatial arrangement or pointing gestures are difficult for many people who are blind.

We have identified three general categories of interface styles that are well-suited to modality-independent interaction: command line, single-keystroke command, and linear navigation interfaces. As much as possible, interfaces should be designed so modality-independent input or output can be used independently or together. For example, a person might like to see the interface on a kiosk's full screen (modality-*dependent* output), but interact with modality-independent input using a set of customized switches on his or her wheelchair.

**Command Line Interface.** With a command line interface, the user submits a string of characters or text to issue commands. Such commands might range from the highly structured format of a command language to natural language input. The acceptable text input depends on the interaction context. The text could be entered using input hardware on the system or through the modality-independent encoded input channel.

**Single-Keystroke Command Interface.** With a single-keystroke command interface, commands are issued in direct response to a keystroke or combination keystroke. Users do not have to submit the text or command as they do with a command line interface. Many common computer keyboard shortcuts are examples of single-keystroke command interaction (such as pressing Ctrl/Cmd+C to copy). To be accessible, the user must also be able to execute combination keystrokes in a serial manner, such as through Sticky Keys.

**Linear Navigation Interface.** With a linear navigation interface, users linearly navigate the elements of a screen by moving a highlight or focus cursor. Once on a desired element, they activate or otherwise interact with it. By default, the focus should be navigable to all elements and wrap with notification at screen boundaries.

At a minimum, the encoded input channel must accept two commands that can be provided with a single switch: *Next-element* and *Action* (which on a keyboard might be the Tab and Enter keys, respectively). A third command, *Previous-element*, is strongly recommended because many users can then step back to an element rather than having to wrap. As much as possible, elements should be fully operable with only the *Next-element* and *Action* commands. This allows a switch user to interact with elements without changing to full keyboard mode. Elements with more complex interaction (e.g., text entry) should accept more input from the encoded input channel.

To simultaneously meet the needs of people with different disabilities, there are some navigation compromises. Linear navigation must be provided by default because it allows a person to traverse all elements along a single dimension, like moving down a list. This makes it easier to search non-visually for an element and to navigate with limited switch input. Another compromise is the level of navigation. People need to perceive all elements, so navigation should move to every element (both interactive and non-interactive) by default. This may be an inconvenience for people with physical disabilities (who may want to navigate only to interactive elements) or for more advanced users (who may want to navigate at different hierarchical levels; e.g., navigating by heading and then switching to element-by-element navigation). To enhance the interface, different modes of navigation might be supported, but for modality-independent interaction the requirement is for linear navigation to all elements.

# 3    Discussion

In the proposed modality-independent interaction framework we outline a simpler and more holistic approach to providing basic accessibility across disabilities than by trying to follow a myriad of accessibility provisions in regulations and guidelines. Designers only need to focus on providing quality modality-independent input, output, and interaction (through appropriate interface styles).

In this section, we discuss the trade-offs associated with different interface styles regarding usability. Additionally, the proposed framework has limitations related to tasks that are inherently inaccessible and the current state of technology. We conclude this section with a discussion of the benefits and uses of the framework.

## 3.1    Interface Style Considerations

Different interface styles may be suitable for different types of devices, tasks, and contexts of use. To determine the most suitable interface style, a designer must balance an interface's efficiency with the cognitive and memory demands imposed on the user. Designers should consider providing multiple interface styles in parallel so that users can pick that which fits them best. For example, an interface could allow for touch screen use, navigation, and provide direct keyboard shortcuts for efficiency.

**Interface Efficiency.** An efficient interface can reduce frustration and increase productivity. Efficiency is a function of the interface, the user's abilities, the method of input, and the output provided by the interface.

*Input.* Input that is most efficient varies widely between users and tasks. While direct single key entry can be very efficient, a large number of choices may be out of the range of motion for a user. Command line input can be efficient for large sets of choices or functions if the user can generate text fairly rapidly, but can be extremely slow if text entry is slow. Navigation might be faster for people who have slow text entry but slower for someone who can enter text quickly. Input efficiency is only one aspect of overall interface efficiency. Users must also receive output from the system, which may be more or less verbose.

*Output.* Interfaces with more electronic text output are less efficient to use because users must take more time to read or listen to the output. The amount and type of output to be provided depends on both the anticipated users and the interface style.

With both command line and single-keystroke command interfaces, text output may range from menus of commands to a simple prompt. A prompt may be efficient for an expert user who has memorized many commands or for systems that process natural language input. However, many users of such interfaces require more than prompts. They may need an explicit menu of the available options (for example, "To make a payment, press 1. For your balance, press 2....") or a method to get help, documentation, and instructions at any time.

For a linear navigation interface, the output is a text representation of the element that is in focus, giving its purpose in the interface. Such text should include important information necessary for operation; for example, the element's type or role, its current status, how it relates to other elements in proximity, etc. Since one is only receiving system output for a single element at a time (for example, "Payment, button" or "Balance, button"), this can be more efficient than systems that present menus from which a user must choose.

**Cognitive and Memory Demands.** Interfaces place cognitive and memory demands on users, some of which may make a particular interface style unsuitable. For example, interfaces that require significant memorization of commands or keystrokes are unsuitable for novice users and for public kiosk implementations.

Linear navigation places relatively low memory demands on users because users navigate lists of options. When on an element, the user only needs to decide yes or no and then activate it or move to another one. However, navigating and then selecting may be more cognitively difficult than directly selecting a desired element [13].

Command line and single-keystroke command interfaces allow a user to directly select a choice, but people must know the desired command(s). This involves memorizing commands, reviewing help documentation, or carefully listening to or reading a menu of options and associated commands. Single-keystroke commands that seem to be arbitrarily assigned may be more difficult to remember than command line input that uses familiar words or phrases. Natural language interfaces may be easier to use because they do not require as much learning and memory as other more structured command formats.

## 3.2    Task-Related Limitations

There are limitations to the proposed framework that are inherent to tasks. In these cases, changing the interface would be insufficient for accessibility; the task itself would need to be fundamentally changed to make it accessible across disabilities.

It is important to note that tasks with such limitations are not automatically inaccessible to all people with disabilities. Instead, such aspects represent barriers to universal accessibility for some people who have physical or sensory disabilities.

**Time-Dependent.** Tasks that depend on time can be difficult or impossible for people who interact with or perceive information from systems slowly. It might take the person extra time to move, manipulate, or control an interface. Some people may take more time to navigate and find the option they want. Getting information in some modalities is inherently slower than looking at a screen and reading text.

Examples of time-dependent tasks are real-time events such as participating in an auction or operating a motor vehicle. Other tasks may have prescribed time limits, such as taking a standardized test. Multimedia is inherently time-dependent. Finally, many tasks are implicitly time-dependent because people must meet some level of productivity and complete tasks in an efficient, timely manner.

**Complex Path-Dependent.** It can be difficult for people with sensory and physical disabilities to create, trace, or follow a path. A path often takes place in spatial dimensions but may have other dimensions as well (e.g., continuous pressure). While it might be technically possible for a person to define a set of points along a path, such input is inefficient and may be inaccessible for practical reasons, especially with long, complex paths. Some people have difficulty with path input because they cannot see the path they are creating or other paths that may already be displayed.

Some tasks require complex path input, such as using a drawing application. Many tasks that require manipulation of a device or interface are path-dependent, for example aiming a camera to scan a barcode requires manipulation in three dimensions. Some path-dependent tasks can be fundamentally changed so they do not require path input. For example, the act of driving a vehicle is a time- and path-dependent task, whereas entering a destination into an autonomous vehicle is a text entry task.

**Simultaneity-Dependent.** Tasks that depend on simultaneous perception and/or operation can be difficult for some people with disabilities. People who must use a single body part or implement to activate all controls would have difficulty with any simultaneous input. Because of limits to attention, simultaneous output can be difficult for everyone to monitor, follow, or track. People with sensory disabilities may have additional problems because of limitations of the output modality they need to use.

Some tasks require a person to be able to perform simultaneous actions. Playing a piano involves pressing keys simultaneously to play chords. Other tasks require a person to perceive simultaneous streams of information. For example, it is difficult to listen simultaneously to a teleconference and a screen reader reading a related document. Reading subtitles or captions might be difficult if the text is replaced quickly and one is also trying to follow fast action or visually displayed information.

**Experience-Dependent.** An input or output experience may be so much a part of a task that changing the experience would be a fundamental change to the task. Users who cannot perform the particular input required, or perceive the output, will be precluded from the experience and the task. There may be ways of providing equivalent functionality and access, but that is not the same as providing the same experience.

Some tasks require a person to be able to perform specific actions. For example, games may have gesture-based controls where making the gesture is part of the gaming experience. Changing the input would fundamentally change the game. Biometric security devices require a person to scan a body part that he or she might not have or might not be able to present to the scanner.

Additionally, some tasks require a person to be able to perceive information in a particular modality. For example the full experience of viewing artwork, watching a movie, or listening to music cannot be simply replicated in a different modality or in text. There are many types of statistical graphics and data visualizations that require visual pattern recognition in order to quickly see trends or patterns that might not be apparent from the raw data. While the meaning or interpretation of some simple data visualizations can be presented through text, there is not always a clear way to provide more complex data visualizations in other modalities. If the modality of the information presented is important to its meaning, then the information is experience dependent.

## 3.3    Current State of Technology

In the current state of technology, there is not yet a good, single protocol for AT interconnection. Current input hardware AT typically uses standard human interface device drivers on serial or USB ports. Output to hardware AT relies on specific device drivers and standard system connections. If AT supported a standard electronic text format, device drivers would not be necessary. In order to have cross-disability access to people who can bring their own AT, standards would need to be adopted or developed. Even without a universal AT connection standard, the modality-independent interaction framework is still useful today.

## 3.4    Benefits and Uses of the Framework

The modality-independent interaction framework can be used for a number of purposes. Those developing new accessibility APIs or accessible systems can use it to ensure that people with severe disabilities have sufficient interaction (for example, cross-disability navigation interfaces need a concept of element focus). The framework is particularly useful for designers who need to provide built-in accessibility. Those designing devices that are traditionally closed to AT could potentially make systems fully accessible to people with sensory and physical disabilities through only a simple connection. Even on completely closed devices where AT connections are not allowed, the framework could help designers focus on the important characteristics of the interface, such as what output text is important and what limited interaction must be supported. For example, the important text output could be provided in speech output for people who are blind, and navigation could use a simple button set that could be used by many people with physical disabilities.

With the framework, designers only need to design one cross-disability accessible user interface for a very wide range of disabilities. It is true that such cross-disability access is not optimized for any particular user or disability category, but providing a set of disability-optimized interfaces would take significant resources for development and maintenance. Some of the compromises inherent in a cross-disability interface could be eliminated through user profiles or settings. Moreover, considerations about efficiency or optimization may not be as important for simple public devices, like a check-in kiosk.

# 4    Conclusion

In the future, a person might come up to a kiosk in a wheelchair with his AT software running on a tablet. Using near field communication, he could establish a wireless connection to the kiosk. After connecting, he could then look at the kiosk's screen and use the joystick on his wheelchair to navigate the screens and make selections. Another user, who is blind, could go up to the same kiosk and pair her smart phone with the kiosk. She might use swiping gestures on her smart phone to navigate the kiosk's modality-independent interface. For each item on the screen, the kiosk would transmit text to her smart phone, which would speak to her privately through headphones.

For tasks that do not have inherent barriers to accessibility, the proposed framework simplifies accessible interface design and facilitates a wide range of accessibility. Additionally, the framework helps designers avoid having to create many separate modality-specific interfaces to meet diverse user needs.

**Acknowledgement.** The contents of this paper are based on work carried out with funding from the National Institute on Disability and Rehabilitation Research, U.S. Department of Education, grant number H133E080022 (RERC on Universal Interface and Information Technology Access). However, the contents do not necessarily represent the policy nor imply endorsement by the funding agencies.

# References

1. Vanderheiden, G.C., Jordan, J.B.: Design for people with functional limitations. In: Salvendy, G. (ed.) Handbook of Human Factors, 4th edn., pp. 1409–1441. John Wiley & Sons, Hoboken (2012)
2. Vanderheiden, G.C.: Accessible and Usable Design of Information and Communication Technologies. In: Stephanidis, C. (ed.) The Universal Access Handbook, pp. 3-1–3-26. CRC Press, Boca Raton (2009)
3. Hodgkinson, R.: 10th Report on International ICT Accessibility Standards: Proposed, Being Developed and Recently Published (2009),
   `http://tiresias.org/research/standards/report_10.htm`
4. International Organization for Standardization/International Electrochemical Commission (ISO/IEC): ISO/IEC TR 29138-2:2009: Information Technology—Accessibility Considerations for People with Disabilities—Part 2: Standards Inventory. ISO, Geneva (2009)
5. Vanderheiden, G. C.: Standards and Guidelines. In Stephanidis, C. (ed.) The Universal Access Handbook, pp. 54-1– 54-21. CRC Press, Boca Raton (2009)
6. Architectural and Transportation Barriers Compliance Board: Telecommunications Act Accessibility Guidelines; Electronic and Information Technology Accessibility Standards. Federal Register 76(236) pp. 76640–76646 (December 8, 2011)
7. Vanderheiden, G.C., Henry, S.L.: Everyone Interfaces. In: Stephanidis, C. (ed.) User Interfaces for All, pp. 115–133. Lawrence Erlbaum, Mahwah (2001)
8. World Wide Web Consortium (W3C): Web Content Accessibility Guidelines (WCAG) 2.0. W3C Recommendation (2008), `http://www.w3.org/TR/WCAG20/`
9. Fleming, B., Lin, A., Philips, B., Caves, K., Cotts, M.: Morse code demystified: A powerful alternative for access to AAC and computers. Paper Presented at CSUN 2003 (2003), `http://www.csun.edu/cod/conf/2003/proceedings/71.htm`
10. Wolpaw, J.R., Birbaumer, N., McFarland, D.J., Pfurtscheller, G., Vaughan, T.M.: Brain–computer interfaces for communication and control. Clin. Neurophysiol. 113, 767–791 (2002)
11. Huenerfauth, M., Hanson, V.L.: Sign Language in the Interface: Access for Deaf Signers. In: Stephanidis, C. (ed.) The Universal Access Handbook, pp. 38-1 – 38-18. CRC Press, Boca Raton (2009)
12. Shneiderman, B., Plaisant, C.: Designing the User Interface: Strategies for Effective Human-Computer Interaction, 5th edn. Addison-Wesley, Boston (2010)
13. Dowden, P., Cook, A.M.: Choosing effective selection techniques for beginning communicators. In: Reichle, J., Beukelman, D.R., Light, J.C. (eds.) Exemplary Practices for Beginning Communicators, pp. 395–429. Brookes, Baltimore (2002)

# "I Know U" – A Proposed VUI Design for Improving User Experience in HRI

Chen Liu[1], Aik Joon Sharyl Quek[1], Shi Jie Alicia Sim[1], and Swee Lan See[2]

[1] River Valley High School, Singapore
{liuchenqd,alicia_simsj}@hotmail.com, sharylquek@gmail.com
[2] Institute for Infocomm Research (I²R), A*STAR, Singapore
slsee@ieee.org

**Abstract.** A new aspect of the VUI design for improving user experience in human-robot interaction is proposed. By leveraging on behavioral analysis, we attempt to identify user's ethnic group from his speech. A preliminary study on Chinese nationals, Singaporean, and Japanese showed that different ethnic group display different speech pattern. However, across ethnic groups, the spoken style of users with same personality does not differ much. Within each ethnic group, speech pattern of users with different personality can be different. We affirmed that personality influences speech and it can be determined in spoken communication.

**Keywords:** Voice User Interface, VUI, Human-Robot Interaction, HRI, behavioral analysis, personality, speech, multi-cultural communications, MySQL, PHP.

## 1 Introduction

Many people envisage that a robot can undertake challenging, or unpleasant tasks for them. However, the development in social robotics has not been able to deliver up to that expectation yet. According to Kirkpatrick and Fisher [1], the development of the robotics market closely resembles that of the personal computers market. The challenge still lies in the area of artificial intelligence and human-robot communications that would allow robots to be easily used by people.

In this paper we propose a new aspect of the Voice User Interface (VUI) design, which can be considered for improving the user experience during human robot interaction, namely to design a robot that can identify a user's ethnic group from the user's speech, and communicate with the user by leveraging on behavioral analysis. We present a preliminary study to discover the speech pattern of three ethnic groups, namely Chinese nationals, Singaporean, and Japanese, and study them with respect to their personality.

Multi-cultural communication is a challenging issue [2]. Programming a robot to recognize speech pattern of people of different ethnic group and personality would allow the robot to recognize and respond to the user more accurately, hence improving the efficiency and quality of human-robot communication. The claim can

P.L.P. Rau (Ed.): CCD/HCII 2013, Part I, LNCS 8023, pp. 228–234, 2013.
© Springer-Verlag Berlin Heidelberg 2013

be tested to develop voice animated virtual robot or personal robot for entertainment, education or even healthcare. The personal robot market in these areas has been forecasted to be a growing market of good ROI potential [1]. If the proposed design option could enhance user experience, it should improve user acceptance of social robots, and thus a significant achievement of the research project.

## 2       Method and Materials

### 2.1       Human Subjects

We invited students of age between 12 and 18 years old in Singapore to participate in this study. We managed to contact and engage 65 students as our human subjects. They comprises:

— 25 Japanese (7 introverts, 18 extroverts)
— 22 Chinese nationals (14 introverts, 8 extroverts)
— 8 Singaporean (11 introverts, 7 extroverts)

The participants were selected based upon their cultural backgrounds needed for this study. The Chinese nationals and Japanese participants must not have stayed in Singapore for more than 2 years, so as to ensure that they were still having their strong cultural essence from their own countries and have not been influenced by the Singaporean culture. By setting this criterion, we hope to ensure that the final result can be accurate and there was no cross cultural effects and bias.

We have both male and female human subjects, and they are identified by their cultural background and personality in this study. Their personality was determined using the DISC psychometric tool to perform human behavioral analysis. Prior to conducting the experimentation with the human subjects, approval was obtained from an institutional review board. Consent forms were given to the participants and approvals were sought from their parents/guardians.

### 2.2       Information Management

To ease data collection, data astorage and data analysis, an information system was designed and developed using PHP scripting and MySQL (see Figs. 1 and 2). The system has an administrator user interface. This controlled access to the sensitive information collected from the human subjects that are being stored in the database of this system for this study.

**Fig. 1.** HTML form (User interface)

Server: localhost ▸ Database: smp_12RV04_database ▸ Table: Human_Subjects

Browse | Structure | SQL | Search | Insert | Export | Import | Operations | Empty | Drop

Database

smp_12RV04_database (2)

smp_12RV04_database (2)

Human Subjects
Human_Subjects

| Field | Type | Collation | Attributes | Null | Default | Extra | Action |
|---|---|---|---|---|---|---|---|
| online_chat_set | int(11) | | | No | None | | |
| face_to_face_set | int(11) | | | No | None | | |
| First_Name | varchar(255) | latin1_swedish_ci | | No | None | | |
| Middle_Name | varchar(255) | latin1_swedish_ci | | No | None | | |
| Last_Name | varchar(255) | latin1_swedish_ci | | No | None | | |
| Age_Group | int(11) | | | No | None | | |
| Email_Address | varchar(255) | latin1_swedish_ci | | No | None | | |
| Contact_Number | varchar(255) | latin1_swedish_ci | | No | None | | |
| Gender | varchar(11) | latin1_swedish_ci | | No | None | | |
| Nationality | varchar(11) | latin1_swedish_ci | | No | None | | |
| School | varchar(255) | latin1_swedish_ci | | No | None | | |
| Personality_Type | varchar(11) | latin1_swedish_ci | | No | None | | |
| Hands_folded | varchar(255) | latin1_swedish_ci | | No | None | | |
| Hands_by_the_side | varchar(255) | latin1_swedish_ci | | No | None | | |
| Others | varchar(255) | latin1_swedish_ci | | No | None | | |
| continuous_eye_contact | int(100) | | | No | None | | |
| broken_eye_contact | int(100) | | | No | None | | |
| Fillers (type/no.) | varchar(255) | latin1_swedish_ci | | No | None | | |
| Interview set: Speaking/s | int(11) | | | No | None | | |
| Interview set: Pause/s | int(11) | | | No | None | | |
| Interview set: Total length/s | int(11) | | | No | None | | |
| Online set: Total length/ words | int(11) | | | No | None | | |

↑ Check All / Uncheck All  With selected:

**Fig. 2.** Database Structure (using PHP MyAdmin and MySQL Workbench)

## 2.3    Procedure

A field study was carried out in the form of an interview with the 65 human subjects in their schools. An invitation letter was sent to the school administrator to obtain their support to participate in this study. Upon obtaining the school's approval, arrangement was made with the respective school teachers to conduct the experiments with the students.

Before the experimentation started, the students registered themselves through the information system created, and they were explained on the objectives and details of this research project.

In order to know the human subjects' personality types, we performed the DISC behavioral analysis on them. The DISC assessment codes were sent to the Chinese nationals and Singaporeans via email and their assessments were done online. For the Japanese participants, as reading English was a challenge for them, we translated the personality assessment into Japanese language to ease their reading and understanding. We assume there is no effect for the different cultural group to use different type of the assessment, since it was a standard psychometric tool that they were using. From this exercise, we could therefore classified the human subjects into Extrovert and Introvert users.

During the experiment, the following questions were posted to the 65 participants:

1. What do you like to do in your free time?
2. What subjects do you like? Feel free to explain why.
3. How long do you spend on the computer in a week?
4. What genre of books do you read?
5. What is your opinion on the popularity of K-pop?
6. Do you have any complaints regarding your school system?
7. Would you please describe your country's culture?
8. How do you manage you schoolwork and other commitments?
9. What do you think of school students attending school with cosmetics/make-up on?
10. If money is not an issue, what would you like to buy or do?

By answering these questions, we recorded and observed the spoken styles of each individual with respect to his or her personality and cultural background to do further analysis.

## 3    Data Analysis

The interviews were recorded using video cameras and audio phones. The following speech patterns were guide for us to perform the data analysis:

1. Length of speech and pauses
2. Length of responses
3. The common fillers used and frequency of usage

Tables 1 and 2 below present the results after analysis.

**Table 1.** Speech patterns results of the introverts and extroverts of Chinese nationals, Singaporeans and Japanese participants

|  | Chinese nationals | | Singaporeans | | Japanese | |
|---|---|---|---|---|---|---|
|  | I | E | I | E | I | E |
| Length of response/s | 102 | 87 | 75 | 71 | 29 | 29 |
| Length of pause/s | 35 | 26 | 34 | 18 | 22 | 22 |
| Length of speech/s | 67 | 61 | 41 | 53 | 7 | 7 |
| Percentage of time spent on speech/ % | 66 | 70 | 55 | 75 | 59 | 59 |
| No. of fillers used | 8 | 12 | 8 | 8 | 1 | 2 |
| *I: Introvert ; E: Extroverts* | | | | | | |

**Table 2.** Analysis on fillers from the experiment

| Speech Pattern | | Chinese nationals | Singaporean | Japanese |
|---|---|---|---|---|
| Length of answer/s | | long | medium | short |
| Top 3 fillers used | 1 | 'Like' | 'err...' | 'eetto' |
|  | 2 | 'yeah' | 'oh' | 'ma' |
|  | 3 | 'ah' | 'like' | 'ssii' |

## 4     Results and Discussion

It was found that different human subjects exhibit different speech patterns. Participants of the same cultural group tend to display similar speech patterns despite personality difference.

For Chinese nationals, if the length of response, length of pause and length of speech is generally long, yet if the number of fillers used is generally few, s/he may be a Chinese introvert. To further confirm the personality, Chinese introvert should have more discontinuous eye contact than continuous eye contact. We also found that the Chinese can be identified as an introvert if s/he has fewer tendencies to fold hands, wave and touch hair. However, if the length of response, length of pause and length of speech is generally short, yet if the number of fillers used is generally more, he or she may be a Chinese extrovert. To further confirm the personality, Chinese extrovert should have more continuous eye contact than discontinuous eye contact. We can also further identify the Chinese as an extrovert if he or she has a greater tendency to fold hands, wave and touch hair.

For Singaporeans, if the length of response and length of pause is generally long, but the length of speech is moderate, he or she may be a Singaporean introvert. To further confirm the personality, Singaporean introvert should have more discontinuous eye contact than continuous eye contact during the speech. We can also further identify the Singaporean as an introvert if he or she has fewer tendencies to fold hands, wave but a greater tendency to clench hands together. However, if the length of response and length of pause is short, but the length of speech is long, he or she is potentially a Singaporean extrovert. To further confirm the personality, Singaporean extrovert should have more continuous eye contact than discontinuous eye contact during the speech.. We can also further identify the Singaporean as an extrovert if he or she has a greater tendency to fold hands, wave but fewer tendencies to clench hands together.

Within each ethnic group, we have also observed that the speech pattern (i.e. speech and pauses) of the introverts and extroverts can be different. However, across ethnic groups, there is little difference in terms of the speech patterns of the speakers of same personality type. We therefore affirmed that personality influences speech [3] and can be determined in spoken communication [4]. Language is a vehicle of personality and effective speech goes hand in hand [5].

We would therefore like to propose a VUI design that makes a robot appear to be a smart pal to consumers. The underlying principle is that the robot knows the user (see Fig. 3), and the user can establish a close and trust-worthy relationship with the robot. The robot is able to identify speaker's ethnic group and personality, and the robot could be more competent and efficient in communicating with the user, allowing the user to have a better user experience through the interaction.

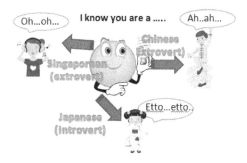

**Fig. 3.** Proposed "I Know U" VUI Design to Improve User Experience in HRI

## 5    Future Directions

A new aspect of the VUI design for improving user experience in human-robot interaction has been proposed in Fig. 3 above. In conclusion, people of different culture and personality displayed different speech patterns and behaviors, such as body movements and eye contact, when communicating. We hope to continue this study by investigating into more aspects of human communication through interviews. We could also research more deeply into the language and communication aspects in different Asian cultures and interview more participants from different Asian cultures. Further studies can be carried out to investigate the other factors affecting speech patterns besides personality and culture, such as gender, age, etc. and we could use more elaborated analytical methods. Last but not least, we hope the proposed VUI could be put into place, and more insights can be captured from the human-robot interaction to increase the productivity and user-friendliness of the personal robot market.

# References

1. Kirkpatrick, K., Fisher, L.: Personal Robotics: Task, Security and Surveillance/Telepresence, Entertainment and Education Robots, and Robotic Components Markets Through 2017. ABI Research (2010)
2. Markel, P.: Cultural Differences Impact Workplace Communication (2009),
   http://www.alliancetac.com/?PAGE_ID=2560
3. Polzehl, T., Möller, S., Metze, F.: Automatically Assessing Personality from Speech. In: IEEE Fourth International Conference on Semantic Computing, pp. 134–140 (September 2010)
4. Friedrich, P., Redfield, J.: Speech as a Personality Symbol: The Case of Achilles, Linguistic Society of America, University of Chicago (1978)
5. Metallinou, A., Lee, C.C., Kazemzadeh, A., Busso, C., Lee, S., Narayanan, S.: Interpreting ambiguous emotional expressions (September 2009)

# Defining Cross-Culture Theoretical Framework of User Interface

Ping Liu[1] and Chun Keung[2]

[1] Department of Media Creative Design, Communication University of China
No.1 Ding fu zhuang East Street, Chaoyang District, Beijing, 100024, P.R. China
pingshui2001@hotmail.com
[2] Department of Chinese Language and Literature, Kookmin University
861-1, Jeongneung-dong, Seongbuk-gu, Seoul, 136-702, Korea
chinalaoshi@hotmail.com

**Abstract.** In an increasing global market place, UI designers are faced with the challenges of offering usable products and services to an enormous variety of users in different cultures. So far, the researchers involved are mostly from anthropology, sociology and computer science. They try to develop or evaluate the usability of products in different cultural contexts. However, their researches concentrate on the technical and evaluative level. The field lacks a systematic theory or principle: how can we convert these research results directly to certain tool or framework which can be used by designers directly. In this paper, we summarized previous researches on culture models and cultural markers, conducted an expert review to organize cultural design issues, and proposed a cross-cultural design element framework which can be directly referred and used by designers when designing products for a certain culture.

**Keywords:** Cultural Factor, Internationalization and Localization, UI Design Elements.

## 1    Introduction

Culture is and always has been a very abstract and complicated concept. It has various meanings to various people with various backgrounds. There are many different perspectives of culture in the literature, but there is no agreement on a specific, common definition of culture. Some examples of such definitions are: Culture is conceptualized as a 'system of meaning that underlies routine and behavior in everyday working life [1]. Culture includes race and ethnicity as well as other variables and is manifested in customary behaviors, assumptions and values, patterns of thinking and communication style [2]. Culture is 'the collective programming of the mind that distinguishes the members of one group or category of people from another, where the mind stands for thinking, feeling and acting, with consequences for beliefs, attitudes and skills [3]. Different cultural models can be derived from different perspectives. These cultural models serve as a starting point as described by, for example, Hofstede (1996) Edward Hall (1989), Trompenaars (1993),Victor (1992) .

P.L.P. Rau (Ed.): CCD/HCII 2013, Part I, LNCS 8023, pp. 235–242, 2013.
© Springer-Verlag Berlin Heidelberg 2013

However, although many researches, such as semiotics research in HCI (Bourges-Waldegg and Scrivener 1998 [4]) has been used to understand how cultural backgrounds influence people's interpretation of UI elements, the results of such researches on culture or cultural models cannot be directly used by designers and UX experts to produces usable products in a certain culture. One reason of this gap between cultural research and production is that designers consider concrete details while cultural researches usually generate abstract descriptions. For example " in some Asian sites the icon representing home is a pair of shoes, instead of a little house" by Fernandez (2000) [5]. Ico-ns and symbols may also have culturally different meanings. In studies by Brugger (1990) [6], only 13 percent of Japanese recognized a first-aid symbol based on the Red Cross, and most did not associate the symbol letter 'I' as referring to information services. These concrete details are seldom addressed by related cultural theories.

In order to successfully build the bridge between these two worlds, user interface designers must increase their knowledge and awareness of cross-cultural differences. In this paper, we first summarize the results of existing mainstream cultural researches, and derive UI design elements based on culture markers through an expert review, and finally propose a design framework for cross-cultural UI design.

## 2     Background – Cultural Models

In order to give detailed views of the abstractness of culture, a number of cultural dimensions have to be identified and emphasized. Different combinations of cultural dimensions form different mental models of culture, which then form the basis for the development of different cultural theories. Hoft [7] describes four models of culture, developed by Hall [9], Trompenaars [10], Hofstede [3],  and Victor [8], which are summarized in Table 1.

**Table 1.** Cultural models and their dimensions

| Author | Focus of Culture | Variables identified |
|---|---|---|
| Geert Hofstede [3] | *Determining the patterns of thinking, feeling, and acting that form a culture's mental programming* | ·Power Distance<br>·Masculinity     vs. Femininity<br>·Individualism     vs. Collectivism<br>·Uncertainty Avoidance<br>·Time Orientation |

**Table 1.** (*Continued*)

| David A. Victor [8] | *Determining the aspects of culture most likely to affect communication specifically in a business setting* | •Language<br>•Environment and Technology<br>•Social Organisation<br>•Contexting<br>•Authority Conception<br>•Nonverbal Behaviour<br>•Temporal Conception |
|---|---|---|
| Edward T. Hall [9] | *Determining what releases the right response rather than what sends the right message* | ·Speed of Messages<br>·Context<br>·Space<br>·Time<br>·Information Flow<br>·Action Chains |
| Fons Trompenaars [10] | *Determining the way in which a group of people solves problems* | •Universalism vs. Particularism<br>•Neutral or emotional<br>•Individualism vs. Collectivism<br>•Specific vs. Diffuse<br>•Achievement vs.Ascription<br>•Time<br>•Environment |

## 3    Cultural Markers and Localization

The term 'Cultural markers' was grist coined by Wendy Barber and Albert Badre to refer to 'Cultural markers are interface design elements and features that are prevalent, and possibly preferred, within a particular cultural group.' it is used to define "the interface design elements of the product that reflect the signs and the meanings to match the expectations of the local culture. The culture attractors typically comprise of colors , color combinations, banners, the use of metaphor ,language clues, navigation controls and similar visual elements that together create a 'look and feel' to match the cultural expectations of the users for a particular domain" (Barber and Badre,1998)[11].

However, when we consider the cultural markers of a certain culture, the size of the population within that culture, and the functional boundary of the culture should all be considered. In a general sense, there are 3 important levels of culture, namely, Globalization, Internationalization and Localization. Culture Markers may refer to different elements when discussing about these 3 levels separately.

Much of the research in HCI regarding culture and Usability has surrounded the internationalization and localization process (Bourges-Walderg & Scrivener1996)[4].

Internationalization "seeks to eliminate culture" (Young 2008)[12] by eliminating cultural symbols, religious references, and so on, while localization caters to the needs of the local target group and is intended to incorporate local content and functionality (Shannon 2000) [13] as well as local, context and culture (McLoughlin & Oliver 1999) [14]. Thus, in this paper, we focus on the level which has the most variety: Localization as the purpose of cross-culture design is to fit the product in a certain culture of a certain area.

From a cross-cultural usability perspective, localization refers to the adaptation of a product, application or document content to meet the language, cultural and other requirements of a specific target market [15] . A well localized design should look like it's been produced in a certain local culture. In order to do this, a product should adapt to a specific language, culture, and expected local "look & Feel". For example, when localizing a website interface, possible options include the change of language, time zones, currency, local color sensitivities, product or service names, gender roles, and geographic examples (Cyr & Trevor-Smith 2004) [16]. Similarly, these issues are very important when localizing the UI of any product. Here we summarized cultural makers related to Localization mentioned by different researchers in history, as shown in Table 2.

**Table 2.** Cultural markers and Localization

| Scholars | Cultural Markers |
|---|---|
| Brugger 1990 | Icons considered international are not necessarily understood globally |
| Russo & Boor 1993 | Care should also be given to the presentation of pictures.Some cultures are very sensitive to how human featuresare represented . |
| Amara &Portaneri 1996 | Design to fit the local writing style. e.g. languages such as Arabic are written right-to-left . |
| Dray, 1996 | Translation of the menus, boxes, and icon text can also be problematic because the length of words varies between languages. |
| Barber & Badre 1998 | Use of color in web design can impact on the user's expectations about navigation, content, and links, as well as overall satisfaction. |
| Callahan 2005 | New technical words in other countries have to be created by adapting English words or creating new ones based on native concepts. |
| Choong & Salvendy 1998 | Using icons versus text for navigation can affect error rates and task completion times depending on culture. |
| Barber & Badre1998 | Specific orientations and page placement vary by culture |
| Duncker 2002 | Icons based on metaphors such as the mailbox, trashcans may be interpreted differently. |
| Callahan 2005; del Galdo1990 | Cultures vary in how they present numbers, time, and dates. |
| Dong & Lee 2008 | The way holistically versus analytically minded people scan a web page is different. Ordering and arrangement of information needs to be considered. |

# 4    Cross-Culture UI Design Framework

## 4.1    Culture Markers and UI Design Elements

Culture Markers listed in Table 2 are still abstract and not well organized to be used directly by designers. In order to convert these issues into something that is meaningful to UI/GUI/Product designers. We have conducted an Expert Review to summarize necessary UI design elements for Cross-Culture products.

First, we use the widely applied 3 levels of design, namely Function, Interaction and Surface, as 3 categories to organize UI design elements. Function is about individual level, settings Input method, Tools and etc. Interaction is about Navigation, Feedback and etc. Surface is about typographic issues, color properties, visual information and so on.

Second, we selected 17 UI/UX experts to conduct Focus Group Interview to generate valuable UI design elements for Cross-Culture products. Since different experts may have different views toward valuable UI design elements in Cross-Culture design based on their knowledge and experience, we selected experts with various experience to try to combine their perspectives. Selected experts are shown in Table 3.

**Table 3.** Selected experts for FGI

| Age | Experts | Experience |
|-----|---------|------------|
| 40+ | 1 people | 20 years |
| 30~40 | 5 people | > 5 years |
| 20~30 | 11 people | < 5 years |

During the FGI, selected experts were asked to assign design elements listed in Table 2 to 3 levels of design (Function, Interaction and Surface), and propose new design elements if necessary. The result of expert interview is shown in Table 4.

**Table 4.** Cross-Cultural Design Elements

| Category | Elements | Definition |
|----------|----------|------------|
| Function | Main/Sub Function | The basic and supplementary features a product or service can provide. |
|  | Function Sequence | Process or steps to use a certain function |
|  | Module | UI components arranged by its functions |
| Interaction | Input Interaction Style | Methods of inputting information or function |
|  | Feedback(Feed forward) | System's response when receiving user's input |
|  | Information Architecture | Information structure of a product or service |

**Table 4.** (*Continued*)

| | Label | The name of an information unit |
|---|---|---|
| | Status Indication | The information indicating the status of a product or service |
| Surface | Color | Main/Sub color used by a product or service |
| | Shape | The form factor of a product |
| | Icon | Text/Graphic to execute a certain function |
| | Material | The texture used by a product or service |
| | Font | The size and form of text used by a product or service |
| | Layout | Arrangement of existing objects in a product or service |
| | Sound | Audio elements provided by a product or service |

## 4.2    Cross-Culture UI Design Framework

With the Cross-Culture UI design elements we derived from expert interview, Hofstede's culture dimension theory can be applied in a meaningful way to product design and evaluation, as shown in Table 5. By referring to this framework, designers can focus on necessary UI elements of cultural aspects when designing a product or service.

**Table 5.** Cross-Culture UI Design Framework

| Category | Elements | PDI | IDV | MAS | UAI | LTO |
|---|---|---|---|---|---|---|
| Function | Main/Sub Function | | | | | |
| | Function Sequence | | | | | |
| | Module | | | | | |
| Interaction | Input Interaction Style | | | | | |
| | Feedback(Feed forward) | | | | | |
| | Information Architecture | | | | | |
| | Label | | | | | |
| | Status Indication | | | | | |
| Surface | Color | | | | | |
| | Shape | | | | | |
| | Icon | | | | | |
| | Material | | | | | |
| | Font | | | | | |
| | Layout | | | | | |
| | Sound | | | | | |

# 5    Conclusion

Designing for a certain culture has long been a challenge in design industry. The abstractness of culture seems to contradict the concreteness of design details. Very often the cultural difference will reveal when we make a mistake. In this paper, we proposed a Cross-Culture UI design framework by selecting the widely-used Hofstede's culture model and deriving valuable UI design elements through an expert interview. In this way, designers can consider and evaluate their design or ideas to judge that if it is suitable for a certain culture or not.

Future studies should focus on evaluating and testing this framework by using it in different cultures, such as Korea, China and US, to get designers' feedback and comments. As a result, a certain design guideline can also be derived from collected data.

# References

1. Bodker, K., Pederson, J.: Workplace cultures: Looking at artifacts, symbols, and practices. In: Greenbaum, J., Kyng, M. (eds.) Design at Work: Cooperative Design of Computer Systems. Lawrence Erlbaum, Hillsdale (1991)
2. Borgman, C.L.: The User's Mental Model of an Information Retrieval System: an Experiment on a Prototype Online Catalog. International Journal of Man-Machine Studies 24 (1986)
3. Hofstede, G.: Culture's consequences, 2nd edn. Sage Publications (2001)
4. Bourges Waldegg, P., Scrivener, S.A.R.: Meaning, the central issue in cross cultural HCI design. Interacting with Computers 9(3) (1998)
5. Fernandez, N.C.: Web Site Localisation and Internationalisation: a Case Study, City University (2000)
6. Brugger, C.: Advances in the international standardization of public information symbols. Information Design Journal (6) (1990)
7. Hoft, N.: Developing a Cultural Model. In: Del Galdo, E., Nielson, J. (eds.) International User Interfaces. John Wiley and Sons, New York (1996)
8. Victor, D.: International Business Communications. Harper Collins (1992)
9. Hall, E.: The Silent Language. Doubleday (1959)
10. Trompenaars, F.: Riding the Waves of Culture. Nicholas Brealey Publishing, London (1993)
11. Barber, W., Badre, A.: Culturability, the merging of culture and usability. In: Proceedings of the 4th Conference on Human Factors and the Web. Basking Ridge, NJ (1998)
12. Young, P.A.: Integrating Culture in the Design of ICTs. British Journal of Educational Technology 39(1) (2008)
13. Shannon, P.: Including language in your global strategy for B2B e-commerce. World Trade 13(9) (2000)
14. McLoughlin, C.: Culturally responsive technology use: Developing an online community of learners. British Journal of Educational Technology 30(3) (1999)
15. Localization vs. Internationalization,
http://www.w3.org/International/questions/qa-i18n.en
16. Cyr, D., Trevor-Smith, H.: Localization of web design: an empirical comparison of German, Japanese, and US website characteristics. Journal of the American Society for Information Science and Technology 55(13) (2004)

17. Brugger, C.: Advances in the international standardization of public information symbols. Information Design Journal (6) (1990)
18. Russo, P., Boor, S.: How fluent is your interface? Designing for international users. In: Proceedings of the INTERACT 1993 and CHI 1993 Conference on Human Factors in Computing Systems. ACM, Amsterdam (1993)
19. Amara, F., Portaneri, F.: Arabization of graphical user interfaces. In: dG E., N J (eds), International User Interfaces. Wiley, New York (1996)
20. Dray, S.: Designing for the rest of the world: A consultant's observations. Interactions 3 (1996)
21. Callahan, E.: Interface Design and Culture, Blaise Cronin. Annual Review Of Information Science And Technology 39 (2005)
22. Choong, Y.Y., Salvendy., G.: Design of icons for use by Chinese in mainland China. Interacting with Computers 9 (1998)
23. Duncker, E.: Cross-cultural usability of the library metaphor. In: Proceedings of the Second ACMIIEEE-CS Joint Conference on Digital Libraries. ACM, Portland (2002)
24. Dong, Y., Lee, K.: A cross-cultural comparative study of users' perceptions of a webpage: With a focus on the cognitive styles of Chinese. Koreans and Americans, International Journal of Design 2 (2008)
25. Callahan, E.: Interface Design and Culture, Blaise Cronin. Annual Review Of Information Science And Technology 39 (2005)

# Integrating Internationalization
# in the User-Centered Software Development Process

José A. Macías

Escuela Politécnica Superior, Universidad Autónoma de Madrid
Tomás y Valiente 11, Madrid 28049, Spain
`j.macias@uam.es`

**Abstract.** Internationalization is a common practice today in software development. In the most basic sense, internationalization is carried out by applying localization design guidelines to face language translation, icon representation, character sets and so on. However, this practice is mostly intended for design purposes, which results insufficient when applying internationalization in huge projects and, specifically, through a concrete development process. In this paper, a broader framework is provided in order to ensure internationalization through a software development process. To this end, a set of activities and sub-activities will be presented involving not only design but pre-development, analysis, implementation and evaluation issues that need to be considered for a right internationalization assurance in international software development. The idea behind is to bridge the gap between simple and usual localization activities and the user-centered software development process as internationalization assurance also helps increase the quality and usability of the software overall.

**Keywords:** Internationalization, Localization, User-Centered Development, Usability, Software Engineering, Software Process.

## 1 Introduction

In a broad sense, software internationalization is garnering increasing attention from both industry and academy. A great variety of approaches have been proposed during the last years to deal with international software development aiming at the localization of software for use in more than one country. In general, existing proposals are mainly based on recommendations and design guidelines that take into consideration different aspects such as language translation, icon representation, character sets, numbers and currency, time and measurement units, and so on [1-3]. However, international software development also requires other activities that should be conveniently considered and planned in order to systematically create international software with an acceptable level of quality. In fact, internationalization is not only related to the user interface of the application. Instead, producing international software involves different technical and non-technical activities in addition to those intended to design the user interface. This way, internationalization issues should be addressed not only in the design and implementation stages of the development, but also in

P.L.P. Rau (Ed.): CCD/HCII 2013, Part I, LNCS 8023, pp. 243–252, 2013.
© Springer-Verlag Berlin Heidelberg 2013

pre-development, analysis and evaluation stages, applying concrete activities to increase the quality of the resulting software through a user-centered development
process. Among others, the mentioned activities should address issues concerning a
suitable internationalization plan, multidisciplinary team building and user-centered
analysis activities based on user, task and context study in order to conveniently separate functional and non-functional requirements to produce successful internationalization goals.

This paper proposes an explicit integration of several internationalization activities
through a development process intended to produce usable software. To this end,
specific stages and a set of add-on activities and sub-activities, in addition to the ones
existing in conventional development processes for usable software, will be provided.
Proposed sub-activities are intended for pre-development –before software construction, analysis –to categorize functional and non-functional internationalization requirements, design, implementation, and also evaluation.

The paper is structured as follow. Section 2 provides related work. Section 3 reports on the main contribution of this paper, that is, the add-on activities and sub-
activities for the internationalization assurance through the proposed development
process. Section 3 presents conclusions and future work.

## 2    Related Work

Development of international software often requires more than just dealing with
language-related issues. In fact, it involves special needs of other countries and cultures that have to be taken into account in the context of a software development
model and not in isolation, as it usually happens. In general, most of the existing approaches only provide internationalization techniques to be applied when developing
the user interface [1-3], or explicit relationships between cultural layers and design
features in general product development [4]. However, little or no approaches have
been proposed to integrate common internationalization user-centered activities with a
software engineering process, which is the main strength of this paper.

Some existing works can be considered of interest to facilitate such integration. For
instance, one interesting approach to obtain contextual information and requirements
in early development stages is cultural models [5], [6]. A cultural model compares the
similarities and difference of two or more cultures by using international variables to
organize cultural data involving national cultures, corporate cultures, the cultural
diversity of groups of users, international markets, etc. Cultural information is useful
to obtain the context of use necessary for early cross-cultural development activities
[7]. In fact, knowledge about patterns of usage [8] and typical user goals may differ
radically from country to country, and this information needs to be capture in advance
to drive the development and design effective usability tests [9].

Concerning design, there is a larger number of existing guidelines involving international concerns. Those facilitate detailed design and implementation of localized
software and user interface prototyping. To cite a few, Microsoft specifies internationalization as a combination of world-readiness and localization [10]. World-readiness

is a developer task, which enables a product to be used with multiple scripts and cultures (globalization) and separating user interface resources in a localizable format. On the other hand, the W3C Internationalization (I18n) Activity [3] includes a working group on addressing different languages, scripts, and cultures, and providing guidelines and specifications to ensure the internationalization of software. Other interesting works report on the icon and symbol design issues [11], the general impact of culture on the design of the user interface, specific Asian and Arabic concerns and the management and production of multilingual documents [1].

As for evaluation, some existing approaches can be considered useful to be integrated in a user-centered development process, such as the international inspection method [12] that involves having people from multiples countries inspecting the international software and analyzing whether it would cause any problems in their countries of origin. Similarly, the international usability testing [1], [2] involves real international users testing the software, or doing it remotely [13] to reduce costs. All in all, cultural difference affects user research processes, and thus cultural effects should be taken into consideration in user testing [14]

As for development processes, there are no specific approaches concerning internationalization. However, this paper proposes a development process model based on the usability engineering lifecycle ISO 9241-210 [15], which replaces the ISO 13407 [16]. In contrast to the ISO13407, the new ISO 9241-210 proposes requirements (not recommendations, as in the previous version) for human-centered design activities. Such requirements imply to understand and specify the context of use (including users, tasks and environments), specify the user requirements in sufficient detail to drive the design, produce design solutions meeting the requirements, conduct user-centered evaluations of these design solutions and modify the design taking account of the results. Additionally, the new standard is based on the user experience. This way, the process is iterative, the design addresses the whole user experience and the development team includes multidisciplinary skills and perspectives, which is well suited for international software development involving international stakeholders.

# 3    A Process Model for Internationalization

In order to tackle the development of international applications, the process model depicted in Fig. 1 has been proposed. It includes four main activity groups:

- Pre-development, addressing initial activities of the software project such as project planning, management and team building.
- Development, where development activities take place. This is based on the ISO 9241-210 iterative process, where the design solution is continuously evaluated and validated by the user after implementing the final system.
- Post-development, including activates related to installation, operation and support, and maintenance until software retirement.
- Integral, mainly related to general quality assurance and documentation activities that take place during the whole project.

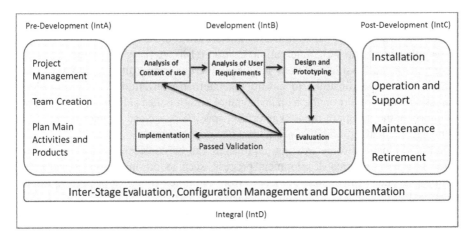

**Fig. 1.** Proposed process model as a framework for internationalization assurance

### 3.1    General Process Model Activities

Some of the activities outlined in the presented process model correspond to those usually specified in standards such as IEEE 1074-1997 [17], where activities are conceived in a development-centered paradigm mostly intended for software engineering. Such common activities are shown in Fig. 1 grouped in project management, including specific sub-activities such as project initialization, planning, monitoring and control. Similarly integral activities, mostly concerned with quality assurance, typically include software configuration management, documentation, and inter-stage evaluation. Also, post-development activities involve different usual sub-activities that can be considered in any project affecting software installation, operation and support, maintenance for correcting and producing new releases and, finally, the software retirement. Even though these mentioned activities and sub-activities are not specifically related to international software development, they have to be taken into account in the process model as international software development also involves different tasks needed to plan, control, install and maintain software.

### 3.2    Specific Activities Proposed for the Internationalization Assurance

Add-on activities proposed to ensure internationalization in the software development process are presented. To this end, proposed activities and sub-activities are given a clause, starting with IntA, IntB, IntC and IntD, to indicate pre-development, development, post-development and integral activities, respectively (see Fig. 1), and thus enumerate each activity correctly in the software process. As commented before, such add-on activities complement others concerning software development that should be also taken into consideration for a complete software development. This paper only highlights the principal activities mainly related to international concerns to carry through internationalization and usability assurance.

**Pre-Development Activities (IntA).** Table 1 depicts the activity grouping proposed for international software pre-development activities and sub-activities. Before software development, various initial concerns need to be considered. First, the use of quality standards should be stated according to suitable normative such as ISO 9241-210 to ensure usability and consider an iterative lifecycle with highly user participation (sub-activity IntA.1.1). Also, there must be specific procedures to manage the different international stakeholders involved in the project (sub-activity IntA.1.2) and communicate with them successfully. Besides, development team members should be selected according to specific internationalization requirements (sub-activity IntA.2.1) and assigned specific roles (sub-activity IntA.2.2). For instance, the development team needs someone who understands foreign languages and cultures and has a technical background. On the other hand, it is important to take advantage of the international nature of the development team [18] to carry out international inspection when necessary. Finally, an internationalization plan should be also defined at the beginning of the project for both usability and internationalization concerns (sub-activity IntA.3.1), including specific activities through a convenient project scheduling as well as intermediate products and evaluations (sub-activity IntA.3.2).

**Table 1.** Pre-Development Activity Grouping for International Software Development

| Main Activities | Sub-Activities |
|---|---|
| IntA.1. Project Management | IntA.1.1. Use of software quality standard for usability ISO 9126 and iterative lifecycle ISO 9241-210 |
| | IntA.1.2. Stakeholder management according to international requirements |
| IntA.2. Team Building | IntA.2.1. Members selection according to international concerns related to the project |
| | IntA.2.2. Assign specific roles to project team members |
| IntA.3. Plan Main Activities and Products | IntA.3.1. Plan internationalization user-centered activities |
| | IntA.3.2. Concrete internationalization user-centered intermediate products and evaluations |

**Development Activities (IntB).** Table 2 depicts the activity grouping proposed for international software development activities and sub-activities. First, a suitable user-centered development process should be considered in order to integrate internationalization activities with a software process that enables the development of usable international software. To this end, the ISO 9241-210 has been considered as a suitable framework to carry through the development of usable and international interactive software under a user-centered paradigm. The process model should be conceived as an iterative process, including highly user involvement in all development activities in order to ensure usability and internationalization at large. The proposed internationalization sub-activities include the analysis of context of use to obtain cultural variables and identify global information (sub-activity IntB.1.1), as well as the way the user works (sub-activity IntB.1.2), which can be achieved remotely (sub-activity IntB1.3). Also, contrasting information between team members and users is necessary under a user-centered approach (sub-activity IntB.1.4). In addition, analyzing specific international scenarios of use can report valuable information in the analysis stage (sub-activity IntB.1.5). Additionally, user requirements elicitation is necessary in order to find out and categorize functional and non-functional requirements. This way, the use of human-computer interaction techniques such as Personas [19], [20] to create specific international profiles (sub-activity IntB.2.1) can be useful. Most of the existing bibliography encourages interaction design guidelines including cross-cultural issues, but even through these design guidelines are used, specific software requirements should be elicited, those involving functional and non-functional internationalization requirements (sub-activity IntB.2.2). For instance, a calculation based on specific currency affects not only to non-functional aspects of the application (presentation), but also to functional ones concerning operations that must be carried out using a certain currency format. In addition, the use of visual techniques to represent and validate requirements is necessary as an input for the design stage (sub-activity IntB.2.3).

Concerning design activities, there have been a great variety of design guidelines and techniques that can be applied in this stage (sub-activity IntB.3.2), mostly related to language translation, icon representation, character sets, numbers and currency, time and measurement units and so on. However, it is necessary to specify some user-centered activities integrated with the process model, such as the evolutionary prototyping (sub-activity IntB.3.1) and the linking to other usability activities that can be related to internationalization ones (sub-activity IntB.3.3) .

With respect to evaluation activities, those should be also considered in order to provide quality and feedback to the iterative development process. To this end, the use of the cultural model previously selected can be useful to evaluate the effectiveness of the international user interface (sub-activity IntB.4.1). On the other hand, the international inspection (sub-activity IntB.4.2) and the international usability testing (sub-activity IntB.4.3) are suitable methods to have a real perception of the internationalization degree of the software. This can be achieved using remote usability testing with users living in their respective countries, which reduces testing costs. Also, intermediate products should be verified in order to ensure the resulting quality (sub-activity IntB.4.4). This happens at all levels, for instance, the translation of all literal strings – i.e., translation verification testing, normally conducted by a person who knows the target language very well. Finally, the validation by international users (sub-activity IntB.4.5) in all products should be considered prior to the implementation stage.

As for implementation activities, aspects concerning the programming language (sub-activity IntB.5.1) should be considered to optimize the code and meet the localization requirements. For instance, fonts and font sizes should be appropriate in the target language. Also, string size is important for the translation into the target language. Same concerns should be considered for writing bi-directional text, display images with localized text, check environment variables such as date, time zone, currency, etc. In general terms, verified internationalization libraries should be used in the implementation stage (sub-activity IntB.5.2) whenever possible to facilitate programming and increase the quality overall. Finally, a suitable international user documentation of the final product must be written and made it easy to understand according to the target audience (sub-activity IntB.5.3).

**Table 2.** Development Activity Grouping for International Software Development

| Main Activities | Sub-Activities |
|---|---|
| IntB.1. Analysis of Context of Use | IntB.1.1. Select a suitable cultural model to identify global information, cultural bias, metaphors and the degree of localization necessary |
| | IntB.1.2. Use of contextual inquiry to understand the user's work style and process |
| | IntB.1.3. Use of remote techniques to capture the user's interaction style by monitoring his/her behavior |
| | IntB.1.4. Check interpretations between international development team and the user |
| | IntB.1.5. Specify international scenarios of use |
| IntB.2. Analysis of User Requirements | IntB.2.1. Use of human-computer interaction techniques, such as Personas, to create specific international user profiles |
| | IntB.2.2. Splitting of functional and non-functional requirements according to international issues |
| | IntB.2.3. Use of visual techniques to represent and validate requirements with international users and team members |
| IntB.3. Design and Prototyping | IntB.3.1. Evolutionary prototyping focusing on localization issues |
| | IntB.3.2. Use of international design guidelines and existing international user interface design standards |
| | IntB.3.3. Linking usability and internationalization design activities |
| IntB.4. Evaluation | IntB.4.1. Use of the selected cultural model to evaluate the effectiveness of the international user interface |
| | IntB.4.2. International inspection evaluation method |
| | IntB.4.3. International usability testing |
| | IntB.4.4. Assessment of intermediate products |
| | IntB.4.5. International user validation |

**Table 2.** (Continued)

| IntB.5. Implementation | IntB.5.1. Use of character encoding and environment variables suitable for localizing the final product |
| --- | --- |
| | IntB.5.2. Use of internationalization programming libraries whenever possible |
| | IntB.5.3. Produce suitable multilingual documentation describing the use of the final product |

**Post-Development Activities (IntC).** There are not concrete add-ons involving internationalization sub-activities for this group of activities. As it mostly depends on the type of software, it would be convenient, however, to facilitate the software installation and distribution to foreign countries, provide international users with the right formation to operate the software and carry out the similar aforementioned sub-activities in the maintenance stage when a change occurs or when a new software release is planned.

**Integral Activities (IntD).** Also in this case, there are not concrete add-ons involving internationalization concerns. It is worth pointing out, however, the importance of inter-stage evaluation to ensure a right process model sequence, as well as the inspections and revisions needed to check the process model's inputs and outputs and the documentation of the project in order to improve its testability and maintainability.

# 4    Conclusions

Software internationalization is an important necessity today. In fact, applications should be developed paying attention to international aspects to be broadly used around the world and avoid the digital divide. This greatly improves the usability of the software overall. On the other hand, a great number of international sales depend on the international usability of products. Companies often have a very large proportion of their sales outside their own country. This is the reason why specific activities and a concrete process model should be provided, in order to ensure the quality of the international software development. This research is concerned with the idea of developing international interactive software, but also with providing a usability and *internationality* assurance at the same time. To do so, this paper presents a framework to integrate specific internationalization activities in a user-centered development process, which is the main strength of this research. Specifically, this research suggests concrete activities and sub-activities to plan and develop international applications, including pre-development activities before software construction, analysis activities to study the context and categorize functional and non-functional requirements involving internationalization, design and implementation issues, and also evaluation concerns that should be considered to ensure and provide feedback in the development model proposed based on a iterative usability engineering process ISO 9241-210.

As future work, the next steps to follow will consist in refining some sub-activities and incorporate others. In fact, it is planned to specify, for each internationalization sub-activity, concrete tasks, techniques, products and supporting tools in order to fully prescribe the process model. Another milestone is formally defining the *internationality* quality attribute by specific metrics to be measured throughout the whole software process and thus systematically control the internationalization assurance.

**Acknowledgements.** This work has been supported by the founded projects TIN2011-24139, S2009/TIC-1650 and TIN2011-15009-E.

# References

1. del Galdo, E., Nielsen, J.: International User Interfaces. John Wiley & Sons, NY (1996)
2. Nielsen, J.: Usability Engineering. Morgan Kaufmann, San Francisco (1993)
3. W3C Internationalization (I18n) Activity web page,
   http://www.w3.org/International/
4. Hsu, C., Lin, C., Lin, R.: A Study of Framework and Process Development for Cultural Product Design. In: Rau, P.L.P. (ed.) Internationalization, Design, HCII 2011,. LNCS, vol. 6775, pp. 55–64. Springer, Heidelberg (2011)
5. Hofstede, G.: Culture and Organizations: Software of the Mind. McGraw-Hill, NY (1991)
6. Hoft, N.: International Technical Communication: How to Export Information about High Technology. John Wiley & Sons (1995)
7. Sun, H.: An Activity Approach to Cross-Cultural Design. In: Aykin, N. (ed.) HCII 2007, Part I. LNCS, vol. 4559, pp. 196–205. Springer, Heidelberg (2007)
8. Schadewitz, N., Jachna, T.: Introducing New Methodologies for Identifying Design Patterns for Internationalization and Localization. In: Aykin, N. (ed.) HCII 2007. LNCS, vol. 4560, pp. 228–237. Springer, Heidelberg (2007)
9. Siegel, D., Dray, S.: Contextual User Research for International Software Design. In: Aykin, N. (ed.) HCII 2007, Part II. LNCS, vol. 4560, pp. 266–273. Springer, Heidelberg (2007)
10. Microsoft Internationalization for Windows Applications,
    http://msdn.microsoft.com/library/dd318661
11. Marcus, A.: Graphic Design for Electronic Documents and User Interfaces. Addison-Wesley, Reading (1992)
12. Nielsen, J., Mack, R.: Usability Inspection Methods. John Wiley & Sons, NY (1994)
13. Nieminen, M., Mannonen, P., Viitanen, J.: International Remote Usability Evaluation: The Bliss of Not Being There. In: Aykin, N. (ed.) HCII 2007. LNCS, vol. 4559, pp. 388–397. Springer, Heidelberg (2007)
14. Lee, J., Tran, T.-T., Lee, K.-P.: Cultural Difference and Its Effects on User Research Methodologies. In: Aykin, N. (ed.) Usability and Internationalization, Part I, HCII 2007. LNCS, vol. 4559, pp. 122–129. Springer, Heidelberg (2007)
15. ISO 9241-210: Ergonomics of Human-System Interaction. Part 210: Human-Centered Design for Interactive Systems. International Standards Organization (2010)

16. ISO 13407. Human-Centered Design for Interactive Systems. International Standards Organization (1995)
17. IEEE Standard for Developing Software Life Cycle Processes, IEEE Std 1074-1997. IEEE Press, New York (1997)
18. Nielsen, S.: Top Management Team Internationalization and Firm Performance. Management International Review 50(2), 185–206 (2010)
19. Cooper, A., Reimann, R., Cronin, D.: About Face 3.0: The Essentials of Interaction Design. Wiley Publishing, Indianapolis (2007)
20. Guo, F.Y., Shamdasani, S., Randall, B.: Creating Effective Personas for Product Design: Insights from a Case Study. In: Rau, P.L.P. (ed.) Internationalization, Design, HCII 2011,. LNCS, vol. 6775, pp. 37–46. Springer, Heidelberg (2011)

# Lessons Learned during a HCI Design Process in Intercultural Context

Alkesh Solanki[1] and Rüdiger Heimgärtner[2]

[1] Continental AG
Regensburg, Germany
alkesh.solanki@continental-corporation.com
[2] Intercultural User Interface Consulting (IUIC)
Lindenstraße 9, 93152 Undorf, Germany
ruediger.heimgaertner@iuic.de

**Abstract.** HCI design incorporates usability engineering. However, "usability" is often misunderstood as just "ease-of-use" or "user friendliness". Whereas it should be viewed as software quality with respect to the context of use, which is a fundamental element in usability studies (cf. [1] and [2]). However, there are cases where usability professionals and software engineers do not share the same culture and the same perceptive (cf. [3]). Therefore, it becomes mandatory to improve the collaboration between HCI (usability) engineering and software engineering. This paper looks into the fallacies of product development process in practice and draws lessons learned.

**Keywords:** HCI, Human-Computer Interaction Design, User Experience, HCI Engineering, Usability Engineering, Software Engineering, Product Development, Automotive, Lessons Learned.

## 1 Human-Computer Interaction Design and Development Process

Within overall product design phase of the product development life cycle, human-computer interaction (HCI) design plays a very crucial role. User interface and user experience have gained the status of one of the main source of differentiation and competitive advantage. As key success factors they also contribute in building the great brands, e.g. iOS, Android, and so on.

In a global industry like Automotive, the user interface design and development is distributed over various locations inclusive of locations in emerging economies. Designing a universal user interface which could give same level of user experience and satisfaction to different user groups has always been a real challenge. In user interface design specification, it has become essential to take consideration of intercultural issues and human factors into account (cf. [4]). Additionally, it does almost become necessary to consider the intercultural issues and human aspects during each phase of the HCI design process (cf. [5]) as well as of the software (SW)

P.L.P. Rau (Ed.): CCD/HCII 2013, Part I, LNCS 8023, pp. 253–260, 2013.
© Springer-Verlag Berlin Heidelberg 2013

development process. Especially when the user interface design is specified in one region and the product is sold in different parts of the world with users having different cultural and technical background (cf. [6]). The implementation, nowadays, is mostly done completely or at least for major parts in best cost locations (in emerging markets) by people with completely different cultural background.

It is not only necessary to use the empathic design approach ([7]) to identify the latent needs of end users; but also necessary to consider the distributed participatory (cooperative) design approach involving all the stakeholders (e.g. employees, partners, customers, citizens, etc.) inclusive end users ([8]) to make sure the product designed meets user needs and is usable. It is also mandatory under current context together with having empathic design of the product also to design empathic development process. One possibility to reduce the problems and to exploit the synergy effects is to establish an integrated product development process.

The whole product development process *could* be an integrated process with HCI (usability) orientation with collaborating life cycle processes of HCI (usability) engineering and software engineering within it.

## 2    Need for an Integrated Product Development Process

Curtis and Hefley (of the Software Engineering Institute) identify three requirements for integrating user interface engineering into product engineering ([9], p. 30):

- "[..] a process needs to be defined for specifying, designing, building, testing, and evaluating a user interface. [..]",
- "[..] this defined process needs to be integrated with the defined process used for developing the remainder of the product (hardware, software, etc.). [..]",
- "[..] The organization must have an established project management discipline, so that it can manage a well-defined process and avoid making commitments that even a sound engineering process could not satisfy. [..]".

Deborah Mayhew has detailed suggestions on appropriate activities for a development process that integrates usability tasks into the software development ([10], [11]).

In sequential product development (cf. Figure 1), the software development process shall follow the HCI design process (like in waterfall model, cf. [12]).

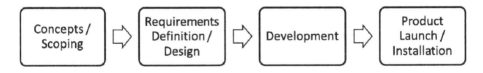

**Fig. 1.** Traditional Product Development Life Cycle (based on [10])

Due to very high market dynamics and market demands for shorter and shorter time-to-market cycles, the product development has been forced to adapt more and more concurrent product development life cycle processes. And, in practice the development process contains multiple loops of incremental and iterative development phases. In such a concurrent and iterative product development both, the HCI design process and the software (SW) engineering process, do run more or less as two parallel life cycle processes and there are feedbacks between the phases of both processes (cf. [13] and Figure 2).

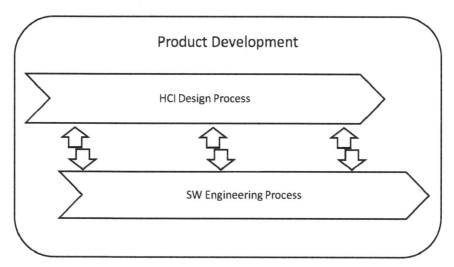

**Fig. 2.** Integrated Product Development Process

In the whole product development there are many stakeholders involved (cf. [14]). All these stakeholders like human-factors specialists (ergonomists), interaction designers, graphics / sound / haptic designers, software developers and R&D engineers, who are all supposed to be HCI specialists, shall work closely with the end-user and at the same time also with the customer (product engineering and product marketing) (cf. [15]). The whole product development and especially user interface development is highly people intensive. People involved do have different levels of motivation, creativity and HCI design (usability) orientation (cf. [16]). This is even truer of people involved in the distributed development process spanned over industrialized and emerging markets. The distributed development process makes it mandatory that all the stakeholders must have the same level of HCI design (usability) awareness and the whole product development process must have achieved higher stage (i.e. at least greater than 3) of usability maturity ([17]).

## 3    A Case Study

It was requested to analyze the current status of a commercial product's development process in a very advanced stage of development (actually just before the commercial launch). There were lots of product usability issues, software stability problems and ever increasing customer reported errors (some of them not fixed for one and a half years). Major shortcomings of overall product development process from product usability point of view were result of lack of understanding of usability and erroneous planning.

### 3.1    Missing Common Understanding of "Usability"

The standard definition of usability is given in section 3.1 of ISO 9241-11:1998(E) as: "The extent to which a product can be used by specified users to achieve specified goals with effectiveness, efficiency and satisfaction in a specified context of use." ([18]).

Unfortunately when the product development process is not usability aware, all the stakeholders involved in product development have different or wrong understanding of product usability.

### 3.2    Usability Engineering Activities Not Planned Properly

Due to budgeting issues, involvement of usability engineering (UE) specialists could not be planned (Indian vs. German argumentation style, cf. [19]): Involvement of UE specialists could not be planned due to budgeting issues. The minimalistic UE process followed was decoupled from SW engineering process.

The user interface specification was prepared by the function/system-specialists, developed for the very first time within the SW development process and finalized in the advanced phases of SW development. The user interface specification was developed without proper consideration of statutory requirements of various markets as well as of expectations of users from various markets and with varying personality, culture and technical background.

The user interface was not designed with usability (in its true sense) in mind. The user interface was developed / implemented *without* human (user) orientation as well as *without* activity (task/usage) orientation.

Usability tests, if at all, were performed with main focus being on functionality and only in Germany. The end user was not involved at all or if involved only during certain phases and not throughout the development process as well as not in the initial phases (neither in HCI analysis phase nor in HCI design phase).

### 3.3    Software Engineering Process Issues

Apart from above mentioned usability engineering issues there were also other specific issues of SW development process.

In the distributed SW development, the SW development process of best cost locations was not at all integrated with the development process of high cost (often strategy driving) locations. Specifics are detailed in the following chapter.

## 4    Lessons Learned

Due to the aspects presented above, the inconsistencies of product design from usability point of view as well as inconsistencies of the chaotic product development process had to be eliminated. Therefore, the following project and process specific urgent activities had to be carried out in retrospect. This led to additionally more efforts and costs which could have been save if the recommendations and lessons learned presented in the following would have been known and considered in advance. This resulted in delayed product launch and reduced return on investment. Only through the merciless mission of the task force constituted of highly esteemed but very expensive experts, the image of the company could finally be saved.

## 4.1   Project Specific

A structural refactoring of HCI design style guide followed by the SW architecture restructuring was taken up. HCI design style guide was updated for interaction concept, feedback strategy and overall consistency.

Application restructuring was done with goals of improving code quality (e.g. commenting, coding guidelines, and naming conventions), architectural quality (e.g. modularity, maintainability, extensibility, and testability) and performance quality (application task schedulability, application task execution time, system/HMI response time, input/key handling algorithm). The application documentation e.g. architecture and design documents, were also prepared. Preliminary  usability  tests were performed during design update phase with surrogate users and after implementation with end users.

For system architectural issues/optimizations it was suggested to do system performance measurements and analysis. Then, depending on the impact analysis it was decided which modifications/improvements must be implemented. At this later stage of development it was possible to implement only the low impact architectural improvements. Additionally, some graphics resource optimization (e.g. graphics layer, icons, fonts, texts, languages, etc.) and graphics performance optimization (e.g. graphics rendering, screen transitions, animations, etc.) were also done. Unfortunately the amount of improvements carried out had to be restricted to minimum in order not to over-escalate budget and timeframe.

## 4.2   Process Specific

It was observed that there is an urgent need of:

a) integrated product development process with HCI (usability) orientation (awareness/maturity) facilitating an effortless collaboration between usability engineering (UE) and software engineering (SE),
b) all stakeholders having to acquire awareness and knowledge about end-users and their usage context,
c) SW engineers having to understand and master HCI design methods and tools,
d) deploying of better SW architecture/module design methods and tools for seamless process integration,
e) usability (HCI) engineering professionals having to start thinking and working like engineers and additionally being able to understand how the technology under use and its limitations affect the product's usability,

f) management not seeing usability engineering activities as unessential and therefore supporting the usability testing,

g) setting up correct product usability goals using proper (or to be developed) usability testing methods and tools.

Additionally following usability life cycle processes of product development should also be strengthened (cf. ISO 9241-210/220).

Proper project infrastructure is mandatory for enabling better information flow between multi-location teams. It also assists in achieving higher levels of integration for a multi-location development process (cf. [20]).

Project management (multi-location / multi-project): as recommended by Curtis and Hefley ([9]), an organization must have acquired a high level of capability in key process area of international project management (cf. [14]).

Localization management: it is very important to manage region specific issues during the product development. E.g. a specific market's legal requirement of having to display a disclaimer was added just before launch.

Personalization management: as a mandatory requirement of internationalization it is almost compulsory for each product to have personalization feature (e.g. user specific settings). These issues have also to be managed properly during product development. E.g. units' selection options were extended just before launch.

Test management was one of the most underestimated activities in the product development planning. Usability tests must be planned by project management throughout the whole product development process.

### 4.3     Product Development Process Review and Process Improvement

It was a good decision from management to appoint a person who had good experience of SW platform as well as of HCI development, who also knew the SW development process, methods and tools very well and has the same cultural background as the development team at the offshore location.

As an external consultant to the project that is in advance stage of development life cycle, one

- has to gather a quick overview of current status of the project;
- must also understand in very short time the SW system – system platform as well as the application;
- has also to analyze the overall development process and especially the HCI development process (incl. methods and tools) as well as the SW development process.

To support the project's development team it was necessary to provide onsite coaching and consulting in areas such as project management, problem resolution management, SW testing, SW construction, SW integration, SW release, etc. as well as to provide coaching and consulting of the SW development team for usability engineering techniques.

# 5    Conclusions

The whole product development process *must* be an integrated process with HCI (usability) orientation with collaborating life cycle processes of HCI (usability) engineering and software engineering within it. All stakeholders of a product development must *inculcate* awareness and acquire knowledge about usability, user experience and HCI design as well as about SW engineering. In other words, the top management and the project management must support global HCI engineering and SW development teams from the beginning through committing and enabling them to use the most appropriate know-how, processes, methods and tools.

# References

1. Bevan, N.: Quality in Use: Meeting User Needs for Quality. Journal of System and Software (Serco Usability Services) 49, 89–96 (1999)
2. Maguire, M.: Context of use within usability activities. Int. J. Hum.-Comput. Stud. 55, 453–483 (2001)
3. Seffah, A.G., Jan, D.M.C.: Human-Centered Software Engineering — Integrating Usability in the Software Development Lifecycle. Springer, Heidelberg (2005)
4. Abdelnour-Nocera, J., Kurosu, M., Clemmensen, T., Bidwell, N., Vatrapu, R., Winschiers-Theophilus, H., Evers, V., Heimgärtner, R., Yeo, A.: Re-framing HCI through Local and Indigenous Perspectives. In: Campos, P., Graham, N., Jorge, J., Nunes, N., Palanque, P., Winckler, M. (eds.) INTERACT 2011, Part IV. LNCS, vol. 6949, pp. 738–739. Springer, Heidelberg (2011)
5. Heimgärtner, R.: Cultural Differences in Human-Computer Interaction. Oldenbourg Verlag (2012)
6. Honold, P.: Culture and Context: An Empirical Study for the Development of a Framework for the Elicitation of Cultural Influence in Product Usage. International Journal of Human-Computer Interaction 12, 327–345 (2000)
7. Crossley, L.: Building Emotions in Design. The Design Journal 6, 35–45 (2003)
8. Beck, E.E.: On Participatory Design in Scandinavian Computing Research (2001)
9. Curtis, B., Hefley, B.: A wimp no more: the maturing of user interface engineering. Interactions 1, 22–34 (1994)
10. Mayhew, D.J.: Managing the design of the user interface. In: CHI 1997 Extended Abstracts on Human Factors in Computing Systems, pp. 178–179. ACM, Atlanta (1997)
11. Mayhew, D.J.: Principles and guidelines in software user interface design. Prentice-Hall, Inc. (1992)
12. Pressman, R.S.: Software Engineering: A Practitioner's Approach. McGraw-Hill, New York (1992)
13. Ressin, M., Abdelnour-Nocera, J., Smith, A.: Lost in agility? approaching software localization in agile software development. In: Sillitti, A., Hazzan, O., Bache, E., Albaladejo, X. (eds.) XP 2011. LNBIP, vol. 77, pp. 320–321. Springer, Heidelberg (2011)
14. Hoffmann, H.-E., Schoper, Y.-G., Fitzsimons, C.-J.: Internationales Projektmanagement: Interkulturelle Zusammenarbeit in der Praxis. Dt. Taschenbuch-Verl, München (2004)
15. Heimgärtner, R., Tiede, L.-W., Windl, H.: Empathy as Key Factor for Successful Intercultural HCI Design. In: Marcus, A. (ed.) HCII 2011 and DUXU 2011, Part II. LNCS, vol. 6770, pp. 557–566. Springer, Heidelberg (2011)

16. Heimgärtner, R., Windl, H., Solanki, A.: The Necessity of Personal Freedom to Increase HCI Design Quality

17. Heimgärtner, R., Windl, H., Solanki, A.: The Necessity of Personal Freedom to Increase HCI Design Quality. In: Marcus, A. (ed.) HCII 2011 and DUXU 2011, Part I. LNCS, vol. 6769, pp. 62–68. Springer, Heidelberg (2011)

18. Nielsen, J.: Usability engineering. Kaufmann, Amsterdam (2006)

19. Carmel, E.: Global software teams: collaborating across borders and time zones. Prentice Hall PTR (1999)

20. Wierzbicka, A.: Cross cultural pragmatics: The semantics of human interaction. Mouton de Gruyter, Berlin (1991)

21. Ramasubbu, N., Cataldo, M., Balan, R.K., Herbsleb, J.D.: Configuring global software teams: a multi-company analysis of project productivity, quality, and profits. In: Proceedings of the 33rd International Conference on Software Engineering, pp. 261–270. ACM Press, Waikiki (2011)

# Conception Pyramid Method
# for Cultural Product Form Development

Tsai-Lin Yang and Ming-Chyuan Ho

Graduate School of Design
National Yunlin University of Science and Technology, Taiwan
philina@stu.edu.tw, homc@yuntech.edu.tw

**Abstract.** Existing methods are found incapable of meeting the needs in form designs of cultural product development and representation, particularly in the aspects of cultural identity and spiritual implication. Focusing on cultural products and with an emphasis on decorative forms, this study proposed the "Gestalt Layer Construct", based on the concepts of text, context and gestalt, among others. Accordingly, a "Conception Pyramid Method for Cultural Product Form Development" is introduced, which consists of six elements, namely Determining subject and collecting creative content, Selecting and allocating idea components, Developing gestalt concept and building gestalt layers, Identifying the best gestalt context, Defining storylines and interpreting gestalt concept, and Implementing and integrating form components. Through a series of metalwork design practices, the proposed procedures were validated and found that it features with innovativeness, usefulness, transferability and effectiveness.

**Keywords:** Cultural Product, Form Development, Design Method, Gestalt Layer, Metalwork Practice.

# 1 Introduction

Designing cultural products is different from designing the traditional, functional, and/or high-tech products, as it requires more emphasis on spiritual content, experiences and emotions. In this case, "Form Follows Functions" or function-oriented design methods are no longer applicable. Form workers have been influenced by the so called "creative industries trends" and unconsciously continued passing on the culture through traditional moral messages (for example, bats represent wealth and bottles imply safety in Chinese cultural context) to create contemporary art. As for cultural product design, a design method that can directly fully interpret cultural allusions or descriptions needs to be developed. Generally, product form is divided into functional and decorative forms (Luh, 1996). The functional form emphasizes functions and rational perceptions that relate to a system and logic of the science and technology, while the decorative form places an emphasis up on culture and emotions in affective and spiritual contexts in terms of human thoughts and knowledge related to philosophy. Cultural entrepreneurs focus on stories for marketing strategies; in the meantime, design trends have evolved from function-driven to user-oriented, which

P.L.P. Rau (Ed.): CCD/HCII 2013, Part I, LNCS 8023, pp. 261–268, 2013.
© Springer-Verlag Berlin Heidelberg 2013

have gradually become a user experience-oriented or user interpretative approach. The importance of rational product functions has gradually declined, while the focus on affective approach applied on cultural perceptions has significantly increased. The main purpose of this study is to propose a conceptual decorative form design method for developing cultural products that not only represent but also reinvent cultural contents.

## 2     Gestalt Layer Construct

This research applies text as the main body, metaphor, and Gestalt contexts based on free creative interpretation from the designers/artists and users/audiences in order to propose a method called the "Gestalt Layer Construct" (Figure 1) for developing form design within certain creative contexts. There are three main components in this approach, namely the idea component, the idea sequence, and the Gestalt layer. The idea component is located at the bottom (e.g., A, B, C, etc.). The contents of which can be derived from the text, such as fictions, poetries, stories, or even images, colors, apparel, photography, music, architecture, and so on. The selection methods include various rational and analytical design research approaches and can also be based on the designer's emotions and intuitions. This research focuses on the emotional and intuitional method through which designers can freely choose all particular contents from the text that touch them the most and can create resonance within the audience as their main idea components.

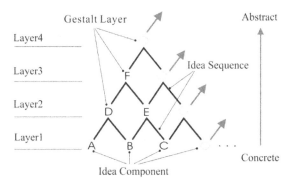

**Fig. 1.** The Gestalt Layer Construct

With attribute-oriented associations of the idea components, Gestalt of form is hierarchically built by creative elements from the bottom to the upper layers (e.g., D is above A and B, and for instance, "the first love" is above "orange" and "lemon" for their attributes in taste – sweet and sour). Due to its relativity, the lower layer can be regarded as the idea components of the higher Gestalt layer (e.g., D and E under F). The link between idea components is called the idea sequence, which functions to associate ideas of different layers for rich conception. The path shows the common attributes or associated meanings shared by each idea component. Each Gestalt layer can be equally regarded as creative concepts generated through the idea sequence.

Spatial concepts therefore exist in idea components, idea sequences and Gestalt layers, while designers' imaginations, creativity, and knowledge about the text and audiences' insights will determine the height of and the amount of branches on the Gestalt Layer Construct (GLC). GLC can explicitly and systematically display how designers or artists develop their train of thought. In this way, it is possible to reveal the mystery of emotional artistic process and present it in a rational system to lead artists to higher levels of creativity and to produce various creative concepts from different perspectives and contents. Based on the aforementioned GLC framework and by expanding it into 3 dimensions, as it can be interpreted from various aspects, a Conception Pyrimid method for cultural product form development is proposed, which has six components, namely: (1) Determining subject and collecting creative content, (2) Selecting and allocating idea components, (3) Developing gestalt concept and building gestalt layers, (4) Identifying the best gestalt context, (5) Defining storylines and interpreting gestalt concept, and (6) Implementing and integrating form components.

## 3    Method Demonstration

The proposed design method will be explained based on a metalwork series entitled "Dream Weaver in the Red Chamber", a series of metal artwork by Yang (2003) based on a Chinese literature classic entitled *The Dream of the Red Chamber*. The full series of metal artwork is a set of accessories symbolizing the twelve maidens mentioned in the story. The artwork chosen in this study is called "Tears of Pearls," which is inspired by the fictitious character Dai-Yue Lin and based on the following reasons: (1) *The Dream of the Red Chamber* is passed from generation to generation and well known to almost every Chinese; (2) Each character in this fiction had distinct personalities and features; (3) Dai-Yue's personality was unique and most well known, therefore the artwork would be easily understood without redundant explanation; (4) the accessories' designs mainly focus on decorative form therefore they will not be affected by any functional issues; (5) the final results of the metal artwork will provide the most realistic interpretation of the idea components. Based on this design case and the design method proposed in this research, the measures taken to create the "Tears of Pearl" are as follows:

1. Determining subject and collecting creative content: Theoretically, all concerned citations are needed for detailed descriptions of the original appearance, personality, talents, and characteristics of Dai-Yue Lin, the main female protagonist. Due to limited length, only a partial excerpt is shown as follows:

   *In Chapter 3: "... She had a pair of eyes, which possessed both cheerful and sad expression, overflowing with sentiment. Her face showed some sorrow stamped on her two dimpled cheeks. She was beautiful, but her whole frame was the prey of a hereditary disease. The tears in her eyes glistened like small specks. Her balmy breath was so gentle. She was as demure as a lovely flower reflected in the water. Her gait resembled a frail willow, agitated by the wind...."*

2. Selecting and allocating idea components: Based on the excerpts, key ideas or phrases are selected as idea components (Table 1). The number of attributes can be modified as long as it can fully express the main theme of the creative subject.

**Table 1.** The idea components of Dai-Yue Lin

| Attributes | Creative component |
|---|---|
| *Name* | Jade girdle hanging in the forest. |
| *Talent* | People would merely feel sorrow about the talent. |
| *Appearance* | Her movement was agitated by the breeze. |
| | Demure as a lovely flower reflected in the water. |
| | Her beauty exceeded Hsi-Tzu's even though she possessed ailment. |
| *Prediction* | Crimson Pearl Grass beside the San-Sheng Stone. |
| | Returned the tears of whole life. |
| *Personality* | The glistening tears. |
| | Her heart had one more aperture than Pi-Kan's. |

3. Developing gestalt concept and building gestalt layers: Through the semantic relationship among idea components and the artist's imaginative skill, the Gestalt layers are stacked and built into an idea tree or conception pyramid (Figure 2).

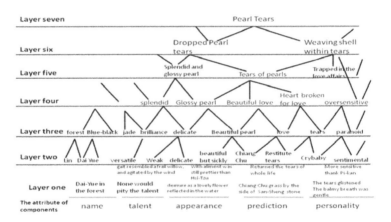

**Fig. 2.** The construction of an idea tree or conception pyramid

4. Identifying the best gestalt context: Gestalt-oriented concepts should be liberated from standard thinking and include lower layers of idea components (Figure 3). The best Gestalt-oriented layer is chosen from top to bottom, and it has the following qualities: coverage of most attractive attributes, easy interpretation in Gestalt title (for instance, "pearl" is easier than "beauty" for association by artists and users), and depth in layers (the deeper the better, for more attractive story and text implications).

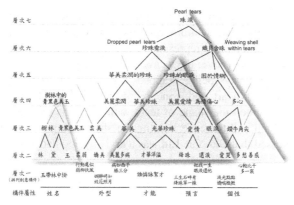

**Fig. 3.** Selection of a Gestalt-Oriented Concept and its Conception Pyramid

5. Defining storylines and interpreting gestalt concept: Based on the best Gestalt-oriented concept of 'tears of pearls' and exclusion of minor components, it is possible to define the form element of each component. The contents and forms covered by the Gestalt-oriented concept can be concretely expressed in images, such as 'pearls', 'love', 'tears', 'paranoid' (in Chinese, it literally means ox horn), etc. Based on the concrete form of each component, the artist should choose one or several idea sequences through which to define the main story line. (Figure 4) The artist then searches for forms of each component derived from the three main story lines that possess strong imagery. Through various comparisons, the shell shapes derived from 'weaving shell within tears' possessed stronger visual representations that could be selected as the main elements of the visual design. On the other hand, tears of pearls, cones, web of love, and heart shapes can also be used as complementary elements. Other elements such as flower petals representing 'delicate', which are not closely related to the story line, were eliminated because they conflicted with the shell shape.

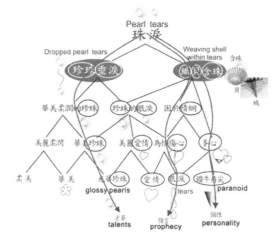

**Fig. 4.** Concretization of form components and definition of the story line

6. Implementing and integrating form components: Based on the visual elements derived from 'weaving shell within tears', the glossy pearl is in the middle of the shell-shaped woven metal and represents Dai-Yue's talent, while the metal weaving symbolizes the web of love; the weaving technique was implemented to interpret how Dai-Yue is always being 'trapped in the web of love'. Furthermore, the shape combination of heart and cone represents the 'paranoid' characteristics. 'Tears of pearls' applied the shape of tears with pearls as the tears. Based on the pearl inside the shell and the cone holding the shell facing downwards like tears, this design expressed that Dai-Yue Lin was a crybaby and had a paranoid personality. (Figure 5)

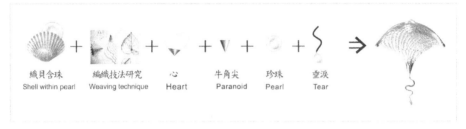

**Fig. 5.** Main visual elements of one of the final designs

The series of jewelry design generated by the implementation of the form creation method proposed in this research consist of five components—a necklace, a hairpin, a brooch, and a pair of earrings. The design was modified to fit the functional requirements and the final work was entitled "Tears of Pearls" (Figure 6).

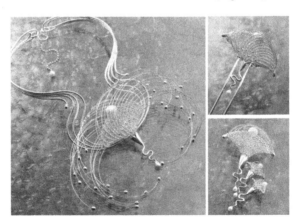

**Fig. 6.** A series of artworks that interpret Dai-Yue Lin's characteristics

## 4    Verification

The proposed process was implemented on the "Dream Weaver of the Red Chamber," and generated 12 series of jewelry design concepts that successfully interpret each role's primary Gestalt-oriented context and develop original and innovative (or significantly differing from general thinking) jewelry designs for females. The suggested method possessed the feasibility and practicability to be implemented in the real design process to develop a new metal weaving technique. These 12 series of metal artworks (each consists of five to eight components) were shown to an expert on *The Dream of the Red Chamber*, who has been the former dean of the College of Liberal Arts at the National Cheng Kung University, Taiwan. He was asked to name each character based on these jewelry series. Amongst the twelve series of metal artworks, except for Pao-Chai Hsue's controversial characteristics, he successfully identified five main characters. The other works were also recognized after hints were provided. Based on verification by the expert, this method was proven valid.

Afterwards, a one-month public exhibition was held for these twelve series of metal artworks. Based on the feedback provided by the audiences, people who had certain knowledge about the twelve maidens in *The Dream of the Red Chamber* would stay longer to appreciate the artwork and were able to guess the main characters without any hints. "Tears of Pearls" was also submitted to the 55th Taiwan Province Art Exhibition and was awarded the First Prize (there were 112 pieces of metalwork submitted in total and 33 pieces were selected for the final round). Another six of the twelve series of metal artwork were submitted to various national level design competitions and successfully won a total of six awards. Based on the performance of the final design works, the validity of this design method was proven. For professional artists in the same field, especially those who participate in national competitions, it is known that the discernment of technical skills is low. Therefore, the main consideration of the judges is creative expressions in terms of main themes and form creations. From this viewpoint, the design method proposed in this research contributed references for this particular subject matter. Furthermore, this method was also taught in a formal teaching curriculum to guide students in the conduction of design activities in order to understand the transferability of the design method proposed in this research. The student design projects conducted based on this design method have successfully achieved various design awards, for examples: Silver Prizes of the 2008 and of the 2010 Young Designers' Exhibition, First Prize of the 2011 Creative Uniform Design Competition, and First Place Award of the 2012 Swarovski Jewelry Design Competition. Based on students' responses and performances, it is assured that this design method possesses transferability and learnability.

## 5    Conclusion

This research introduced the Conception Pyramid Method for cultural product form development. Through a series of metalwork design practices, the suggested procedures were validated and found that it features with innovativeness, usefulness, transferability and effectiveness. The new approach has five characteristics:

1. The process of selecting idea components is based on an existing text, therefore the cultural elements extracted from the text relatively would be more objective and the selection and construction of idea components would also be more holistic and

unbiased. On the other hand, as the admirers possess certain knowledge on the text, they can also observe the design results with more objective and holistic views.

2. The development of the Gestalt-oriented concept depends on personal experience, cultural contents, education, customers, and many other factors. For the same text, it is possible to generate different kinds of Gestalt-oriented concepts and structures that will create diverse representations and lead to various possible art directions.

3. Through different combinations of idea sequences, artists can be lead to develop original ideas with rich creative contents. At the same time, it is possible for artists to keep their creative thinking on track and transform it into a rationally comprehensive and systematical framework.

4. In creative art, it is possible to project personal emotions. In the same series of artwork, the artist can generate different artwork based on his/her personal experience at different times and keep developing new ideas.

5. It is possible to conduct form creation or design in a team. Based on different cultural backgrounds and life experiences, the artists can work together and generate a richer creative capacity.

In the field of creative design and art, researchers need to further explore the rationale of design processes that lead to final design results. The results of design and art creations often have the characteristics of a Gestalt-oriented concept and are difficult to be separated into pieces for verification. Apart from the text, other symbols such as graphics, images, movement, sound, and numbers that can facilitate artists to communicate and apply their ideas can also be researched further.

**Acknowledgments.** This work was partially supported by the National Science Council (NSC101-2622-E-366-001-CC3) of Taiwan.

# References

1. Cao, X., Shih, H.: The Story of the Stone. The first bookstore, Tainan (1983) (verified)
2. Luh, D.B.: Influential Factors and Forces Analysis on Stylability Development. Journal of Design 1(1), 33–50 (1996)
3. Yang, T.L.: Weaving Dream of the Stone history – Reinventing Ornaments in Classic Chinese Literature through Semantic Approach. Unpublished Master's Thesis. National Tainan University of Arts, Tainan (2003)

# Employing Poetry Culture
# for Creative Design with a Polyphonic Pattern

Mo-Li Yeh[1], Po-Hsien Lin[2], and Ming-Sian Wang[3]

[1] Design College, Hsing Wu University
Linkou, Taipei 24452, Taiwan
1101moli@gmail.com
[2] Crafts and Design Department, National Taiwan University of Art
Ban Ciao City, Taipei 22058, Taiwan
[3] Digital and Design Department, Mingdao University
Peetow, Changhua 52345, Taiwan

**Abstract.** With the global village approaching a new era of aesthetic economy powered by culture creative, every country is actively seeking inspirational resources for culturally creative product design. Chinese traditional poetry, full of expression created with poets' fascinating words and still highly appreciated today, carries not only our predecessors' wisdom but also principles which correspond to those for modern creative design. This study starts with the distinctive features of our classical poetry, lays its foundation on traditional theory of Chinese poetry, consults literature regarding the feasibility of employing poetry for cultural creative design, and furthers the trend for such application through investigating current case studies. Further, by integrating related theories of the western Ingarden Phenomenology from *Cognition of the Literary Work of Art* and Chinese construction from *The Literary Mind and the Carving of Dragons*, this study adopts the organic formation of 'level of word', 'level of phrase' and 'level of sentence' for analyses and conversion, employs the concept of 'polyphonic pattern' as a guideline, and develops a step by step concrete process for exploring how the internal meaning and external form in traditional poetry could be transferred and integrated into modern design. With further illustration of actual implemented cases, a model framework for employing poetry culture for creative design is thus completed. In addition to its being a significant and feasible reference for culture creative design, we would like to see this model cause our traditional poetry to shine with a new glamour as well.

**Keywords:** poetry, polyphonic pattern, culture creative, creative design.

# 1 Introduction

In recent years, countries from all over the world have been attempting to employ their "Culture" as features in increasing the value of "Creative Design" for developing an aesthetic economy. Lin [11] indicated that "culture" is a life style, "design" is a life taste, "creative" is a sympathy from a moving experience, while 'industry' is the medium, methods or means for realizing creative cultural design. Therefore, the key to

P.L.P. Rau (Ed.): CCD/HCII 2013, Part I, LNCS 8023, pp. 269–278, 2013.
© Springer-Verlag Berlin Heidelberg 2013

achieving culture creativity in the design industry is the innovative performance deli-vered following the design concept of "initialized with culture, expressed in product and used in life". The essence of culture creative design is extracting culture elements and converting culture symbols so as to endow new aesthetic significance into the design. Most existing Taiwanese culture creative design was inspired by observable culture resources such as natural scenery and life artifacts. Few designs originated from invisible culture resources. This study therefore, takes inspiration from our traditional culture by applying 'poetry' culture and projecting its external forms and internal meanings into creative design. The purpose of this study is to integrate Western and Chinese theories of poetry, develop a model which manifests the process for extracting invisible cultural elements from poetry, converting them into design, and illustrating the actual implementation steps. Through exploring how modern creative application of poetry culture could be achieved, this study would not only serve as an essential reference for multiplying the breadth and depth of culture creative design but also help with the conservation of our culture.

## 2    The Distinctive Features of Chinese Poetry Culture

Hegel [5] claimed, "Poetry is the highest expression in art". Li [10] believed that the definition of culture is: "The results of the mutual activities created by man, this in-cludes tools, social law regulations, art creations and the mental activities of the creating process". Inheriting five thousand years of Chinese history, the culture of "Poetry" is doubtless the most significant part of our cultural heritage. The American philosopher Langer's [9] concept, "Art is the creation of forms symbolic of human feeling", has created a profound impact on modern aesthetic theory. "Poetry" culture itself is the artistic performance of how poets express their feelings through concrete language symbols. The German philosopher Worringer [14] indicated in the book *Abstract and Empathy* that humans can acquire happiness from art, mainly because man can seize the constant changing possibilities from individual events of the outer world and then transform them into eternity with abstract forms. "Poetry", just as Chu [1] claimed, originates from bitterness caused by one's dissatisfaction of the "limita-tions" in life and is produced with imagination as a pursuit for "infinity". He also stated, "Poems possess interior and exterior meanings. You will find reasoning from the interior meaning and discover phenomenon from the exterior meanings; only by in-cluding both aspects may you compose a poem." That is, the goal is to pursue boundless imagination with limited vocabulary and construct a poetic imagery which corresponds to logic thinking.

Tu [13] suggests that poetry is a world of beauty in imagination which a poet uses words to create based on language and experience. In recent days, poetry is considered an expression of spiritual vigor. The process of reading a poem is not only to be in-toxicated regarding the content and the spiritual vigor of the poet, but to speculate, explore and appreciate the content and the spiritual vigor of the poet. Poetry must be an art of creation. Creation in metaphysics is a process where something spiritual is created out of nothing, while for physical techniques it means an innovative combina-tion of material or concepts for creating new relationships, new feelings, new understanding and new realms. It could also be an original technique for expression which results in new forms, new semantics, etc. A reader would be influenced by the process of "Associative Thinking Impact" during reading when the electro-magnetic fields of the brain waves are first altered so as to generate new sequences and produce a fresh sensation, a moving inspiration. In sum, poetry is produced with imagination, creates imagery, contains internal meaning and innovative techniques for expression, and is meant to inspire readers through a touching emotion.

In recent years, the creative industry has been actively seeking to restart interdisciplinary integration and development from various industries and levels and has thus created designs with a fresh new look. The new interpretation of traditional culture, classical literature and art are the exact sources of inspiration for the culture creative industry. The following are examples of current poetry employments in different fields. Tsai [12] has presented some case studies in transforming classical literature. For instance, Yu, Kuang-Chung's poem *Kua Fu* adopted and modified the traditional mythology "Kua Fu, in Pursuits of the Sun" to create an innovative imagery with new ideas. Also, Chang, Man-Chuan's modern "The River Merchant's Wife" converts the well-known poem initially written by Lee, Po into a new imagery.

There are also application cases for art performances. The internationally renowned Cloud Gate Dance Theatre extracted culture creative elements from the classical literature *Chu Ci*, *The Dream of the Red Mansion*, and Chinese calligraphy. The first example is the play "Moon Water" which originates from the quote, "Flower reflection in the mirror and moon reflection in the water are nothing but illusions" With illusionary scenes such as the water-flowing stage together with the dancer's reflection in the vertical mirror and in the water, poetic imagery is created for expressing how all beautiful things result in "emptiness". A second example derives from Tsao, Hsueh-Chin's *The Dream of the Red Mansion*. The performance began with the stone, originally located under the Qing Geng Peak in the heavenly world, coming down to earth and ended with the main character, Pao-Yu, becoming a monk and severing all links to the human world. The plot conveys the impermanence of life with the quote; "When we see fake as real, real becomes fake; when we take nihility as existence, the actual existence becomes nihility".

Poetry could also be employed for product design. The work "Shui Tiao Ke Tou" produced by the company Titton extracted the essence from the well-known poem of the Sung dynasty poet, Su, Shih; "Just as the moon waxes and wanes, so do people experience sorrow and joy." The round form of the product symbolizes the moon, while the crack on the right angle signifies the constant changes in life. Regardless of the changes, however, the relationship between two people will remain solid as the two mutually supporting poles signify. The above cases illustrate how poetry could be employed in related fields. The unique imagery creation and high popularity of these cases definitely suggests that the employment of poetry for the field of culture creative design is certainly worth exploration.

## 3    Applying "Polyphonic Pattern" as the Theoretical Basis for Creative Design

Yu [18] once said, "Creativity is a traceable psychological process. With a series of effective training, many people may experience the status of endless energy of creation." Converting classical poetry provides a platform for creative ideas not only to bloom but also to be able to be put into practice. Therefore, this study has integrated Traditional Chinese Painting Aesthetic, Poetics, and *The Literary Mind and the Carving of Dragons* as the theoretical foundation for the creative conversion of classical poetry.

### 3.1    Following Traditional Chinese Painting Aesthetics

Chinese poetry has always been the medium to convey the emotions of poets. Therefore it could also serve as the medium for designers' creative expressions. Research (Yeh, 2010) [16], *Applying Chinese Poetry's Form and Spirit in Culture Creativity*, has indicated that "The conversion process of transforming poetry into design is similar to that of painting.   Take Cheng, Pan Chiao's (1693~1765) experience in painting bamboo for example. The painting process went from 'Generating Concept' to 'Employing Brush Strokes'; the similarity between converting emotions into painting and converting poetic emotions into product design can correspond." Also presents, in Figure 1, is "the conversion process of transforming paintings and poetry into design and culture creative experience", from a further theoretical combination of Painting Aesthetics, Concept of Form and Spirit, and Chinese-Western Comparative Aesthetics. The first phase of this process shows the procedure of Chinese painting. The second phase is the corresponding procedure of converting poetry into design, illustrating how a designer can read a poem (the poetic meaning), stimulating the creative thinking in one's mind (state of mind), then converting the poet's emotions into the process of design (scenario). The last phase is the culture creative design hands-on experience. From the left, it introduces how consumers see the product with their "eyes", indulging themselves in the beautiful scenario of the poetic culture, leading to reflections drawn by the sentimental feelings, and eventually using it in reality. The ultimate goal for converting poetry into design is thus reached.

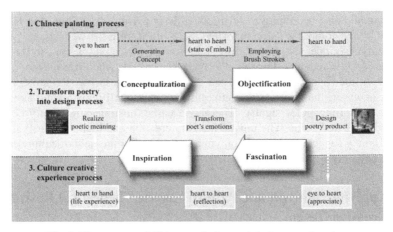

**Fig. 1.** The process of Chinese painting and design transforming

## 3.2    The Employment of "Six -Viewpoints" for Creative Design

*The Literary Mind and the Carving of Dragons* [17] as the integration of the domains of metaphysics and physical phenomena, such as cosmic ontology, cosmos attributes and the formation of the boundless universe, activity phenomenon, function utility, which are all-encompassed by this book. Rated as the macroscopic view of the philosophers, this master piece corresponds to the connections between literature and cosmic ontology, universal world, political society and meanings of life. To establish an objective text evaluation method, *The Literary Mind and the Carving of Dragons – Proper Evaluation* raised the concept of "Six-Viewpoints": "To understand the sentiments of text, you must observe the six aspects: first view position, second view writing, third view variation, fourth view means, fifth view allusion, sixth view syllable. If evaluations proceed this way, good work may reveal itself". In general, "Position" is to see the appropriate arrangements between sentimental sense and literary form; "Writing" is the measurement of whether the literary form suits the proper aesthetic norm; "Variation" is to observe the success of the text's inherited convention and innovation; "Means" is the adequate strategy of different writing appearances; "Allusion" is to succeed the correct use of allusion meanings; "Syllable" is to manage the most appropriate syllable for the text. Through the methodology of "Six Viewpoints", we may explore the six aspects to objectively evaluate the written work. Hence, this research employs this method to measure the most suitable Chinese poetry and devise selecting criteria for product design.

Furthermore, to make a guideline for employing the "six-viewpoints" principle into design more comprehensive, this research also takes Teresa M. Amabile (1983)(consensus assessment technique，CAT) as another reference so as to present all of the design attributes derived from the 'Six-Viewpoints' principle with three descriptive indicators, as the eighteen indicators shown in Figure 2. For "position", there are form, state analysis and time-space structure. For "writing", symbolic expression, phrasal interrelationship and semantic attributes are considered. Design principles, representation, and neatness are indicators for "variation". For "means", emotional expression, aesthetic performance and creative expression are included. "Allusion", the fifth viewpoint, includes color employment, material application and texture application. Finally, dynamic performance, situation and rhythmical variety are considered for "syllable". In this paper, View Writing is the main application principle.

## 3.3    "Polyphonic Pattern" as the Framework for Converting in Creative Design

The guideline for conversion—the polyphonic pattern—originated from the significant Ingarden Phenomenology, which is highly prominent in the western aesthetic field as You[17] mentioned. Ingarden[7] indicated in the N*ew Cognition of the Literary Work of Art* that the existence of literary art creation still continues after the termination of the author's intended expression because the physical existence of the creation makes it possible for aesthetes in various time and space to reconstruct the author's imagery. In addition, the inner structure hierarchy of literary art is analyzed into four independent levels yet each interconnects with one and another, penetrating deeper by each level.

There are the level of words, the second level of phrases, and the third and fourth levels of sentence groups. Such a literary discourse system establishes a reciprocal relationship with You's[17] literature analysis system as the quote describes; "The affection of viewing the objects seems an endowment to the object, the aroused inspiration by the object were as if rewards to the viewer."

Further, the relation between the two systems has been compared and contrasted in Yu's book[17] *New philosophical aspects for The Literary Mind and the Carving of Dragons*. For example, "Word Deliberation", "Tonal Pattern" can be compared to the first level (Figure 3) of the tones of words and words, while "Dual Phrase", "Section/Fragment", "Resemble/Imply", "Euphuistic", "Reference" can depict the second level of meaning in the sentence group. These two levels, which constitute the words and phrases, are the most fundamental and predetermined formation in not only expressing inner significance but also presenting the external foundation of phonological beauty. The third and fourth levels concern the deep structure of the literature work, providing readers an outline or a schematic drawing of the formation to which they need apply imagination while viewing so as to represent the imagery. The chapters of "Structure", "Sentiments", "Content/Form", "Nature Influence", "Style", "Integration", and "Profound" in *The Literary Mind and the Carving of Dragons* compare closely to these two levels.

These levels agree with Eco's[3] suggestion that a poem is the full integration of various discourses following different linguistic rules and operating on distinct meaningful levels. The purpose of the statement is mainly to examine themes on art imagination, configuration of the structure layers, the Gestalt effect in art, and the metaphysics regarding art creation. This concept also corresponds to Yu's[18] comprehensive statements on the structural framework of "Half-translucent viewing layers" and "All historical masterworks employ such structure so while ordinary readers accept the surface-layer presentation, and highest-level interpreters are able to dig into the deepest layer of the composition, transitional readers roam with wonder between the two layers, accessing a pathway to an aesthetical life." All the above presents what is most significant for poetic conversion and application.

The four hierarchy levels of the inner structure in Ingarden's theory gradually penetrates; first comes the level of words, which then composes into the second level of phrases, then the third and fourth levels of sentence groups (Figure 3), similar to the operational structure of time. Viewed vertically time-wise, an art piece possesses different sections which fall on the same time and all layers expand sequentially at the same time. From the horizontal point of chronicle time, the hierarchies of literary art, such as "Pronunciation", "Word and Phrase", "Sentence Group", "Section", and "Chapter", gradually accelerate the development of the levels in temporal progressions. A valuable piece of literary art must present diverse, sequential, and harmonious polyphonic artistic value. Such quality is similar to the musical texture of Polyphonic music in which a minimum of two choirs proceed at once. It is also parallel to the concept in visual arts that texture contains both the tactility itself as well as visual representation. Similarly, poetry possesses the attribute of calling for aesthetic harmony in its internal spirit and organic rhythm for its exterior structure. Therefore, this study will take up the "Polyphonic Pattern" structure as the guideline for converting poetry into design.

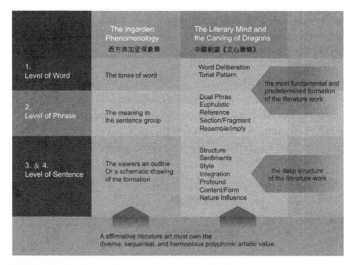

**Fig. 2.** "Polyphonic Pattern" as the Framework for Converting in Creative Design

## 4    Developmental Model of "Polyphonic Pattern" Design and Implementation Examples

In this section, an actual implementation example is presented for illustrating the development of an application model of "Polyphonic Pattern" design employing poetry. Kao[8] has suggested that insisting on applying western syntax for analyzing Chinese poetry could be fruitless. He indicated that Chinese parsing should not be limited by subject-predicate analysis from the west; "topic-comment" analysis could be adopted to allow various structural combinations and greater possibilities of unrestricted development. As Hsieh[6] stated, linguistic research methodology has turned to a dynamic study of language development and comprehension, shifting towards the development of Interdisciplinary Linguistics, an Applied Science. This study has thus synthesized related theories of the western Ingarden Phenomenology from *Cognition of the Literary Work of Art* and the Chinese construction from *The Literary Mind and the Carving of Dragons*, adopting the structure of "Polyphonic Pattern", and developed a significant model for converting poetry culture into design, with the organic formation concept of "Level of keyword", "Level of Phrase", and "Level of Sentence". The illustration presented here is the Ching Ping Melody, written by Tang dynasty poet Lee, Po, "the clouds want to become the garment of the royal beauty and flowers would like to become her beautiful face". The original meaning of the poem states, "Royal Lady Young is a fair lady, people associate her garments with colorful clouds and her delicate face with flowers." By applying the affection association process and recombining the organic composition of words, poetic rhythm and comprehensive imagery in the mind of the viewer could be displayed.

The first step is to extract the main keyword meaning, here in this poem we will take "think" (want to/would like to) as an example, as in Figure 3. Wu and Wiu[15] has explored near-synonyms and has discovered five basic modules in depicting an event--process, state, stage, punctuality and boundary--which are referenced by time tense and provide sample linguistic information.

**"Think"**

1. Miss, yearn . Example: Miss you.
2. Ponder, deliberate. Example: Thinking of solutions.
3. Dream, Desire, intend, hope. Example: Want to get married
4. Consider, feel. Examples: What do you think of this?
5. Speculate, surmise. Examples: Expect, reckon, guess.

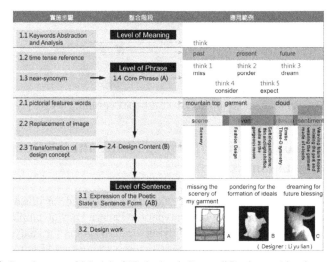

**Fig. 3.** Developmental Model of "Polyphonic Pattern" Design and implementation

Considering the meaning of the poem with the timeline features, we choose "past-present-future" as the reference point--"Think 1" is the major meaning of the verb "Think", "Think 2" signifies intention and hope, often resembles things which have not happened. By repeating this process, various near-synonym phrases will be generated, and the appropriate "Core Phrase" can be selected, as seen in Figure 4.

The second step is to retrieve the "pictorial features" in the word definitions, taking, for instance, the words in the figure "cloud", "garment", "mountain top", and "fence". Replace them within the image domains of "Sentiment/Reason/Scene/Event", convert them to a design concept and then the relevant "Design Content" can emerge. Via "Sentiment", the word "cloud" could symbolize "Weaving future hopes, missing the past and wearing the garment made of clouds". Via "Reason", it is analyzed as "Erratic", which then is interpreted as "three-dimensional asymmetry". Within the domain of "event", it can be manifested as "Soft elegant texture, thin and light chiffon, white as the gorgeous moon". The word "garment", via "Event", can be seen as "Fashion Design". "Mountain top" and "fence", via "Scene", are grouped as "Scenery".

The third step is to continue converting the "Core Phrase" and "Design Content", which are extended from "Keyword Definition" and "Pictorial Features" in word level, into an expressive Sentence Form of the Poetic State. For instance, "Missing the scenery of my garment" combines 2-dimensional garment and scenery to become item A; "pondering for the formation of ideals" converts into item B with the idealistic three-dimensional asymmetrical tailoring; "dreaming for future blessing" turns into item C forming a white-chiffon cloud-like garment. The model framework for the conversion into a substantial design series is completed as presented in Figure 3.

## 5　Conclusion

Poets and artists both possess the ability of "thoughtfulness" and "observation". As a result, readers will enter the poet's heart and enjoy in person their life and affection while reading a poem. Since art is about creation, creative imagination is required; creation does not reveal itself out of thin air, however, it is an innovative recombination of existing imageries. The inspiration for art creation is identical to that for design; it is never creating something out of nothing. Thus, to represent poetic imagery through design, a designer must first convert the original emotional experience of the poet, analyze the content of the poem next, and then employ the 'polyphonic' pattern for analyses of the organic formation of word meaning, phrases and sentences to develop a concrete process for converting poetry into creative design. There is no doubt that the process of a poet's converting his feelings into a poem is artistic creation. Creative design with poetry is just as well a re-creation of creation. Applying poetry for creative design also requires inventiveness, poetic sensitivity, and superior techniques from a designer, as poetry does from poets. Creative ability and sensitivity enable a designer to fully appreciate the "poetic meaning" of the original poem, while superior techniques make the recreation of "poetic imagery" possible for providing consumers with opportunities for experiencing the expressions of "poetry" through design products and verifying the emotional experience of "poetry" from the new generation. Along the long lasting history, we sincerely hope that classical Chinese poetry will rise and shine with a new glamour with the dialogue between the present and the past.

## References

1. Chu, K.C.: Literary psychology. Gin Feng, Taipei (1988)
2. Chu, K.C.: On aesthetics. Morningstar, Taipei (2003)
3. Eco, U.: A Theory of Semiotics. Indiana University Press, Bloomington (1979)
4. Fang, S.: Painting theory from Shan Jing Ji. Yi Wun Publishing, Taipei (1971)
5. Hegel, G.W.F.: Aesthetics: lectures on fine art (i) Knox, T. M (trans.). Oxford University Press, NY (1975)
6. Hsieh, C.H.: A Cognitive Linguistic Account of Conventional Metonymies in Contemporary Mandarin Chinese in Taiwan. Journal of Humanities and Social Sciences 4(1), 55–67 (2008)
7. Ingarden, R.: Cognition of the Literary work of Art. Chen, Y. K., Hsiao W. (trans.). Shang Ting Publishing, Taipei (1991)
8. Kao, Y.K.: Chinese Aesthetical Codes and literary research. Taiwan University press, Taipei (2004)

9. Langer, S.K.: Feeling and form: A theory of art developed from philosophy in a new key. Charles Scribner's Sons, NY (1953)

10. Li, Y.Y.: Culture and cultivation. Youth Culture, Taipei (1996)

11. Lin, R.T.: Cultural creativity added design value. Journal of Art Appreciation 1(7), 26–32 (2005)

12. Ts'ai, L.W.: Teaching Creative Conversion of Classical Poetry. Humanity and Social Science Research Papers 45(1), 59–82 (2010)

13. Tu, K.C.: Defining Poetry and Critiquing Poetry. Taiwan University Press, Taipei (2010)

14. Worringer, W.: Abstraction and empathy: A contribution to the psychology of style. Ivan R. Dee, Chicago (2007)

15. Wu, I.C., Liu, M.C.: Linguistic Differentiation and Message Communication of Psychological Verbs of "think, suppose, assume, and feel": an Analysis Using Corpora. In: Proceeding of the 14th Computational Linguistics Symposium. National Chang-Kung University, Tainan (2001)

16. Yeh, M.L., Lin, P.S., Hsu, C.S.: Applying Poetic Techniques of Shape- Spirit Transformation in Cultural Creative Design. Journal of Design 16(4), 91–106 (2011)

17. You, Y.Z.: New philosophical aspects for The Literary Mind and the Carving of Dragons. Student Publishing, Taipei (2010)

18. Yü, C.Y.: On Artistic Creation. Commonwealth Publishing Co., Taipei (2006)

# Part III

# International Usability Evaluation

# The Influence of the Nature of Need for Touch, Handcraft Material and Material Color on the Motivation for Touch

Si-Jing Chen[1], Chih-Long Lin[2], and Chiu-Wei Chien[1]

[1] Graduate School of Creative Industry Design, National Taiwan University of Arts,
Ban Ciao City, Taipei County 22058, Taiwan
[2] Crafts and Design Department, National Taiwan University of Arts,
Ban Ciao City, Taipei County 22058, Taiwan
{Jing0503,Chiewei}@gmail.com, CL.Lin@ntua.edu.tw

**Abstract.** The main purpose of this research is to investigate the effect of user characteristic – the need for touch (NFT), handcraft materials and material colors on motivation of touch and preference. A total of 70 subjects were recruited in the study. In addition to the NFT level (high score group and low score group) was evaluated, handcraft materials (wood, glass, pottery, plastic and metal) and material colors (red and yellow) were studied in the experiment. The dependent variables including the willingness of touch, preference and 16 pairs of opposite adjectives for sense of sight were measured by questionnaire interview. The study results showed that the effect of NFT affect significantly willingness of touch ($p<0.001$), preference ($p<0.01$) and the sense of warm-cold ($p<0.05$). All measures were affected significantly by handcraft material effect ($p<0.05$). On the other hand, 11 pairs of opposite adjectives are affected significantly by material color factor. The results of regression equations showed that the willingness of touch was mainly affected by subjective preference. Moreover, the subjective preference was mainly affected by the rating of beauty for product. Therefore, the subjective preference increased for a product was followed the rating of beauty and then the willing of touch was increased. The findings of this study can give an insight into the motivation of touch, and further provide some guidelines and recommendations about the product design and selling method to increase the competitive advantage of product.

**Keywords:** motivation of touch, need for touch, sense of vision, preference.

## 1 Introduction

In recent years, the rising of online, TV and catalog shopping is due to convenient. The visual or hearing information of product is presented with image or sound on media. However, it is difficult to show the haptic information like texture, softness, weight of product on screen or catalog. An inability to physically examine products would decrease consumers' confidence before purchase. Holbrook [1] pointed out it is difficult to evaluate some product especially for sweaters by picture, because subjects

P.L.P. Rau (Ed.): CCD/HCII 2013, Part I, LNCS 8023, pp. 281–287, 2013.
© Springer-Verlag Berlin Heidelberg 2013

strongly depend on tactile feedback. Thus, more and more studies about marketing and product design areas pay attention to haptic experience influence on consumers' behavior and purchase decision.

The product properties including texture, softness, weight, and temperature would affect haptic experience [2, 3]. The touch behavior is different for different product. The more product property is needed to evaluate, the more motive is acted to touch the product before purchase. For example, towels differ from texture and weight will cause touch more prior to purchase than cans or bottles, which material attributes are similar. Peck and Childers [7] videotaped the hand motions of subjects while they verbalize during product evaluations at the same time. The study results showed that the behavior and oral report was correspondence. Moreover, the touch time was longest for sweater or tennis racket evaluating which product properties varied most, followed by calculator or cell phone evaluating which product properties varied somewhat, and the touch time was shortest for cereal or toothpaste which didn't need to evaluate product properties. Further, haptic experience could be compensated even touch is unavailable. McCabe et al. [4] indicated that the differences in preference between the environment where allow physical examine and the environment where touch is not feasible were reduced when the product properties were verbally described. Peck and Childers [6] also concluded that a written description about product properties on brochure could compensate for lack of touch.

In addition, there is an individual difference in the preference for haptic experience. A Need for Touch (NFT) concept brought up by Peck and Childers [6] is defined as consumer's preference and motivation for the obtainment and utilization of information through touch. Then a 12-item scale which including two dimensions, an instrumental and an autotelic dimension was developed to reveal the different goal-directed touch behavior between purchase-directed and enjoyment-directed. Peck and Childers [6] found that confidence of consumers higher in NFT before purchase was less while physical examine is unavailable during product evaluation. On the contrary, the confidence in evaluation was not affected for low NFT consumers only there was an obvious image of the product. In a related study on compensation of untouchable situation, Peck and Childers [5] found that for high NFT subjects, a written description could compensate functional tactile information, like heaviness, but not compensate pleasant sensory property, like softness. On the other hand, for Low NFT subjects, they could extract information through visual cue instead of actual haptic exploration. Furthermore, subjects high in autotelic NFT made more impulse buying than low autotelic NFT subjects while tryout activities were offered in a grocery store [8].

Most early researches used functional or useful product as stimuli to evaluate the effect of subjects' NFT or material property on touch behavior and purchasing attitude. However, the result of using beautiful yet functionless things as stimuli is less discuss. Moreover, it is also worth to find out what kind of sense play an important role to active touch motivation. Therefore, the main purpose of this research is to investigate the effect of user characteristic – the nature of need for touch, handcraft materials and material colors on subject's motivation of touch and preference.

## 2    Methods

### 2.1    Subjects

Twenty-one men and forty-nine women participated in the experiment as paid volunteers. All participants were Taiwanese and free from any known musculoskeletal disorders. The mean age was 20.8 (sd=1.08) years.

### 2.2    Experiment Design

This study employed a nested factorial design. The independent variables included the degree of nature of need for touch (NFT) (high score group and low score group), handcraft materials (wood, glass, pottery, plastic and metal) and material colors (red and yellow). The subject was a random factor. There were a total of ten experiment conditions for each subject. Ten sample items, as illustrated in Fig. 1, were evaluated. The size of each sample was 10*10*10 cm cube. The degree of NFT was measured using the 12-item scale [5]. Scale item descriptors ranged from -3 (strong disagree) to +3 (strong agree) with the entire range represented in the sample. Higher and lower NFT were determined by a median split, with subjects scoring at or above the median (a score of 14 in the study) classified as high NFT (thirty-five subjects) and those scoring below the median classified as low NFT (thirty-five subjects). Due to the limitation of material itself, the color of each sample was made as similar as possible.

Three different kind dependent variables were measured in the study. They were willingness of touch (5-point scale, with 1 for "I really don't want to touch it", 3 for "normal feeling", 5 for "I really want to touch it"), preference(5-point scale, with 1 for "I really don't like it", 3 for "normal feeling", 5 for "I like it very much") and 16 semantic scales, defined by polar-opposite adjectives for sense of sight were measured by questionnaire interview. A 7-point Likert scale was applied on these opposite adjectives. A higher score indicates a more sense of ugly, sensibility, plain, ancient, boring, cold, popular, inelegant, wild, heavy, artificial, hard, male, peace, dark, and reserve. A lower score indicates a more sense of beautiful, sense, gorgeous, modern, interesting, warm, individuation, elegant, mild, light, nature, soft, female, excited, bright, and extroverted.

### 2.3    Experiment Procedure

Experiment was conducted under normal day light illumination. Before the experiment, the researcher explained the purpose and procedure to the subjects. After that, one sample was placed in front of subjects at a time. They watched the sample item 10 seconds and then were asked to assess subjective willingness of touch, preference and 16 pairs of opposite adjectives questionnaire based on its visual appearance without tactile interaction. The 10 treatment combinations were randomized for each subject and completed within 30 minutes.

**Fig. 1.** The sample items were used in this study. The upper row samples are red color and lower row are yellow color samples. The sample materials from left to right are wood, glass, pottery, plastic (acrylic) and metal (copper).

### 2.4    Data Analysis

Analysis of variance (ANOVA) was preformed to analyze the NFT group, handcraft materials and material colors effect on willingness of touch, preference and sense of sight.  Post hoc testing with the Duncan multiple range test (alpha=0.05) was then performed to identify significant differences within handcraft materials factor. Moreover, regression analysis with a forward stepwise procedure was conducted to construct two prediction models for willingness of touch and preference with independent factors including: gender, NFT group, handcraft materials, material colors, preference and adjectives of sense of sight. The significance level was set alpha=0.05.

## 3    Results

### 3.1    ANOVA Results

Analysis of variance (ANOVA) was performed to evaluate the need for touch, material colors and handcraft materials effects. The need for touch effect was only significant on the Willingness of touch ($F1,68=31.98$; $p< .001$), Subjective preference ($F1,68=11.82$; $p< .001$) and the sense of Warm-Cold ($F1,68=4.55$; $p< .05$). Moreover, the material color factor showed significant effect on eleven opposite adjectives questions. The handcraft material effect was significant on all measures. For two-way interactions, the handcraft materials and material colors interaction effect was significant on nine of the eighteen response measures which were Willingness of touch, Subjective preference, Sense–Sensibility, Gorgeous–Plain, Modern–Ancient, Mild–Wild, Light–Heavy, Nature–Artificial, Bright–Dark.

Tables 1 present the mean values of measures for the independent variables. The Willingness of touch for high NFT score group (3.46 scores) was significantly greater than that for low NFT group (3.02 scores). Similarly, the Subjective preference was also greater for high NFT score group (3.35 scores) than low group (3.10 scores).

There was only one of the 16 bipolar adjectives (warm-cold) were rated as significantly different; the subject high NFT has warmer feeling than who low NFT. The NFT developed by Peck and Childers includes two dimensions, an instrumental and an autotelic dimension. The instrumental dimension means that touch behavior is purchase goal-directed and the autotelic dimension is enjoyment goal-directed (Peck and Childers 2003b). The average score of autotelic dimension for high NFT group is 8.86 and greater than low NFT group (6.29 score). It could be the reason the motivation of touch for high NFT group is still stronger than that for low NFT group, even the experiment sample is functionless.

Both of the measurements of Willingness of touch and Subjective preference were not significantly affected by material color effect. However, the subjects' feel were partial to gorgeous, modern, boring, individuation, elegant, wild, heavy, artificial, female, dark, and reserve while watching red color samples. For yellow samples, the sense were partial to plain, ancient, interesting, popular, inelegant, mild, light, nature, male, bright and extroverted.

The Duncan grouping results indicate that the Willingness of touch for the handcraft material can be classified into three groups. The first group, with the highest willingness was for wood and pottery material, followed by plastic, metal and glass. While watching wood and pottery samples, the subjects rated about 1.5 score higher Willingness of touch than watching glass sample. Besides, the subjective preference can be classified into two groups. The higher preference group included wood and pottery samples. While watching wood and pottery samples, the feeling of beautiful, sensibility, plain, ancient, warm, popular, elegant, nature, female, peace, and reserve were higher than watching other materials. .On the contrary, the sense of sign under plastic or glass samples watching were partial to ugly, sense, gorgeous, modern, cold, artificial, excited, bright, extroverted etc.

## 3.2    Regression Analysis

This study obtains two regression models using a forward stepwise searching procedure (Table 2). Results show these models to be statistically significant ($p < .001$) with the coefficient of determination ($R^2$) 0.47 for predicting Willingness of touch and 0.52 for predicting subjective preference. Moreover, the standardized partial regression coefficient of the subjective preference is 0.45, greater than that of the sense of Beautiful–Ugly (0.25), the sense of Mild–Wild (0.11), and the sense of Light–Heavy (0.08). Subjective preference influence seems greater than other factors regardless of the handcraft material or color factor. Increase in subjective preference, the sense of beauty, the sense of mild, and the sense of heavy followed by an increase in the Willingness of touch. On the other hand, the subjective preference was mainly affected by the senses of beauty, individuation, peace and warm for a product. Therefore, the subjective preference increased was followed the rating of beauty and then the willing of touch was increased.

**Table 1.** Measurements under affect levels of each independent variable

| | Need for touch | | Material color | | Handcraft material | | | | |
|---|---|---|---|---|---|---|---|---|---|
| | Low | High | Red | Yellow | Wood | Pottery | Metal | Plastic | Glass |
| Willingness and preference | | | | | | | | | |
| Willingness of touch | **3.02** | **3.46** | 3.28 | 3.21 | $3.52^a$ | $3.54^a$ | $3.16^b$ | $3.01^b$ | $2.99^c$ |
| Subjective preference | **3.10** | **3.35** | 3.27 | 3.18 | $3.40^a$ | $3.47^a$ | $3.14^b$ | $3.11^b$ | $2.99^b$ |
| Opposite adjectives (1 point – 7point) | | | | | | | | | |
| Beautiful – Ugly | 3.79 | 3.65 | 3.66 | 3.78 | $3.51^b$ | $3.27^b$ | $3.88^a$ | $3.99^a$ | $3.96^a$ |
| Sense – Sensibility | 4.11 | 4.03 | 4.10 | 4.04 | $3.94^b$ | $4.78^a$ | $3.60^c$ | $3.96^b$ | $4.06^b$ |
| Gorgeous – Plain | 4.20 | 4.25 | **4.07** | **4.38** | $5.41^a$ | $4.87^b$ | $3.75^c$ | $3.45^c$ | $3.64^c$ |
| Modern – Ancient | 4.28 | 4.51 | **4.31** | **4.49** | $5.53^a$ | $4.75^b$ | $4.44^c$ | $3.44^e$ | $3.83^d$ |
| Interesting – Boring | 4.24 | 4.27 | **4.45** | **4.06** | $4.62^a$ | $3.84^c$ | $4.79^a$ | $3.92^b$ | $4.11^b$ |
| Warm – Cold | **4.13** | **3.83** | 3.94 | 4.01 | $3.31^d$ | $3.61^c$ | $5.16^a$ | $3.69^c$ | $4.10^b$ |
| Individuation – Popular | 3.94 | 3.79 | **3.68** | **4.05** | $4.14^a$ | $4.09^a$ | $3.52^b$ | $3.86^{ab}$ | $3.71^b$ |
| Elegant – Inelegant | 3.80 | 3.71 | **3.64** | **3.87** | $3.72^b$ | $3.24^c$ | $4.21^a$ | $3.84^b$ | $3.76^b$ |
| Mild – Wild | 4.42 | 4.65 | **4.80** | **4.27** | $5.01^a$ | $4.18^b$ | $5.17^a$ | $4.13^b$ | $4.16^b$ |
| Light – Heavy | 4.26 | 4.21 | **4.38** | **4.08** | $3.89^c$ | $3.14^c$ | $4.84^a$ | $4.81^a$ | $4.48^b$ |
| Nature – Artificial | 4.17 | 4.27 | **4.31** | **4.13** | $3.29^c$ | $3.10^c$ | $5.60^a$ | $4.52^b$ | $4.57^b$ |
| Soft – Hard | 4.61 | 4.82 | 4.76 | 4.67 | $4.44^c$ | $3.99^c$ | $5.76^a$ | $4.68^b$ | $4.73^b$ |
| Female – Male | 3.88 | 3.89 | **3.74** | **4.04** | $3.91^b$ | $3.45^d$ | $4.64^a$ | $3.64^{cd}$ | $3.80^{bc}$ |
| Excited – Peace | 4.06 | 4.29 | 4.15 | 4.20 | $4.95^a$ | $4.54^b$ | $4.55^b$ | $3.01^d$ | $3.84^c$ |
| Bright – Dark | 3.82 | 3.71 | **4.07** | **3.47** | $4.47^a$ | $3.55^b$ | $4.31^a$ | $2.79^c$ | $3.72^b$ |
| Extroverted – Reserve | 4.14 | 4.23 | **4.37** | **4.00** | $5.02^a$ | $4.48^b$ | $4.66^b$ | $2.89^d$ | $3.88^c$ |

a, b, c: Duncan grouping code; Bold indicates significant differences between levels of a factor for that measure.

**Table 2.** Regression equations for Willingness of touch (WT) and Subjective preference (SP)

| Equation | $R^2$ | Significance |
|---|---|---|
| WT=1.73+ 0.45SP-0.25(Beautiful–Ugly)-0.11(Mild–Wild) +0.08(Light–Heavy) | 0.47 | $p < .001$ |
| SP= 3.09- 0.60(Beautiful–Ugly)-0.14(Individuation–Popular) +0.13(Excited–Peace)-0.13(Warm–Cold) | 0.52 | $p < .001$ |

# 4    Conclusion

The objective of study is to investigate the effect of the degree of need for touch, material colors and handcraft materials on subject's motivation of touch, subjective preference and polar-opposite adjectives for sense of sight. The main findings are that both of the motivation of touch and subjective preference were significantly affected by need for touch and handcraft materials. Increase in subjective preference, the sense of beauty, the sense of mild, and the sense of heavy followed by an increase in the Willingness of touch. The findings of this study can give an insight into the motivation of touch, and further provide some guidelines and recommendations about the product design and selling method to increase the competitive advantage of product.

**Acknowledgement.** The authors would like to thank the National Science Council, Taiwan, R.O.C. for financially supporting this research under Contract No. <99-2218-E-144-002->.

# References

1.  Holbrook, M.B.: On the importance of using real products in research on marketing strategy. Journal of Retailing 59(1), 4–23 (1983)
2.  Klatzky, R., Lederman, S.: Stages of manual exploration in haptic object identification. Attention, Perception, & Psychophysics 52(6), 661–670 (1992)
3.  Klatzky, R., Lederman, S.: Toward a computational model of constraint-driven exploration and haptic object identification. Perception 22, 597–621 (1993)
4.  Mccabe, D.B., Nowlis, S.M.: The effect of examining actual products or product descriptions on consumer preference. Journal of Consumer Psychology 13(4), 431–439 (2003)
5.  Peck, J., Childers, T.L.: Individual differences in haptic information processing: The "need for touch" scale. Journal of Consumer Research 30(3), 430–442 (2003a)
6.  Peck, J., Childers, T.L.: To have and to hold: The influence of haptic information on product judgments. The Journal of Marketing 67(2), 35–48 (2003b)
7.  Peck, J., Childers, T.L.: Self-report and behavioral measures in product evaluation and haptic information: Is what I say how I feel? Advances in Consumer Research 32(1), 247 (2005)
8.  Peck, J., Childers, T.L.: If I touch it I have to have it: Individual and environmental influences on impulse purchasing. Journal of Business Research 59(6), 765–769 (2006)

# Evaluation of Human-System Interfaces with Different Information Organization Using an Eye Tracker

Kejin Chen and Zhizhong Li[*]

Department of Industrial Engineering, Tsinghua University, Beijing, 100084, P.R. China
zzli@mail.tsinghua.edu.cn

**Abstract.** The increasing use of digitalized displays in the instrumentation & control systems of nuclear power plants has brought new issues related to human-computer interaction, especially under emergency circumstances that are known to be very stressful. This paper studies how interfaces with different information organization (functional layout vs. process layout) influence human-computer interaction behaviors as emergency occurs in terms of search efficiency, difficulty of information abstraction, and workload by using the eye tracking technique on a simulated platform. The result shows that the average blink rate and average blink numbers at the two levels of information organization were different significantly. This may indicate that the functional design was superior to the process design in user workload. The results did not prove the superiority of the functional interface design to the process one in search efficiency and difficulty of information abstraction, since no significant difference was found in the number of fixations and fixations duration mean values.

**Keywords:** Functional based task analysis, Information organization, Eye tracking.

## 1 Introduction

The Fukushima Daiichi nuclear power plant (NPP) Accident in 2011 raised again great public concern about the nuclear safety, after 2 decades since Chernobyl Accident. Tsunami and earthquake which directly resulted in Fukushima Daiichi nuclear accident is far beyond human's ability, while most accidents in safety-critical industries so far are caused by human errors. More than 90% accidents in NPPs, 80% ones in the chemical and petro-chemical industries, and over 70% of aviation accidents were caused by human errors (Adihikari et al., 2008).

It is therefore reasonable to focus on operators and their behaviors. In a NPP, the main control room (MCR), as a core part of the system, is expected to provide appropriate information and human-machine interface to facilitate operators' behaviors. The past decades have witnessed remarkable upgrades in MCRs, including its layout, devices and design concepts.

Conventional buttons, switches, and other analog equipment are gradually replaced, which is a prime improvement in MCRs. In NPPs of new generation like AP 1000, digital displays are extensively used. Such transform on the one hand caters to

---

[*] Corresponding author.

P.L.P. Rau (Ed.): CCD/HCII 2013, Part I, LNCS 8023, pp. 288–295, 2013.
© Springer-Verlag Berlin Heidelberg 2013

the trend of technology advance, improving the safety and reliability of the systems; on the other hand, it brings high information burden, tedious interface management tasks, and other new problems (Kim & Seong, 2009). For this reason, designing a good digital interface in MCRs, which meets the task demand and the physical and psychological characteristics of operators, is of necessity. Several design philosophies have been put forward, for example, ecological interface design (EID) and 'User-centered design'. EID is based on two conceptual tools: the abstraction hierarchy and the skills, rules, and knowledge (SRK) taxonomy (Rasmussen, 1985). Review by Vicente (2002) can be referred to for specific instruction of EID. In the user-centered approach, task analysis is a key tool used widely to analyze user needs. What distinguishes EID from the user-centered approach lies mainly in the difference between abstraction hierarchy and task analysis.

The Function-Based Task Analysis (FBTA) proprietary to AP 1000 NPPs is one kind of task analysis. It breaks down goals in different levels according to their corresponding functions, providing which task information should be presented in the NPP interfaces. Wu et al.(2012) introduced FBTA in detail. Besides, in Wu's (2012) study, the functional display based on FBTA seemed better help understand system's operating status, ease the workload, while process displays helped the participants understand NPP's structure and working principles better. However, Wu's functional displays differ from the process displays principally in three aspects: information organization, information presentation and component representation. No research so far demonstrates which aspect influences the interaction and that to what extent the influence can be. This study aims to explore how interfaces with different information organization could influence human-computer interaction behaviors in terms of search efficiency, difficulty of information abstraction, and workload.

When users interact with an interface for a specific goal, they observe the interface, and articulate the desired task goal into input language. Since the observation and articulation are both cognitive behaviors, performance in the two processes is hardly measured directly. This study used eye tracking techniques to evaluate search efficiency, difficulty of information abstraction, and workload, which are supposed to reflect human cognition behaviors (Richardson & Spivey, 2004).

It is hypothesized in this study that the functional design is superior to the process design. Specifically, the functional design is supposed to possess higher search efficiency, less difficulty of information extraction, and less workload than the process one.

In the rest of this paper, Section 2 introduces the methodology of study, and Section 3 presents the results. Discussion and conclusions are presented separately in Sections 4 and 5.

## 2 Methodology

### 2.1 Independent Variables

The independent variable, information organization, has two levels: functional interface and process interface. Figure 1 illustrates the functional interface based on FBTA, and Figure 2 illustrates the process interface.

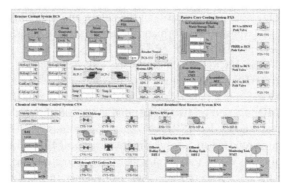

**Fig. 1.** Illustration of the functional interface

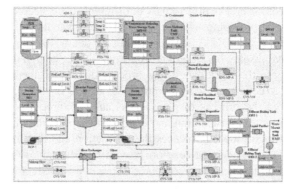

**Fig. 2.** Illustration of the process interface

There are two display screens. The left one is the main display for monitoring system status using the interfaces showed in Figures 1 and 2. The right one shows the computerized procedure for the participants to perform the emergency operations, as Figure 3 shows. The participants monitored the display on the left side, and took actions once the accident signal came up following the emergency operation procedure (EOP) presented on the right screen. The experiment was designed as within-subjects. When the participants finished the task with the functional (or process) interface, they took a short rest, and then began the task with process (or functional) interface. The order to show the interfaces was randomly arranged to reduce the learning effect. For each interface, the participants performed the EOP task 16 times. There were eight procedure routes in total and the participants should go through each route twice with every interface. The order of the routes was also randomly arranged by presenting the corresponding system status values (accident scenarios). Under such a circumstance, the participants had to carefully check system parameters from the presented interface to determine the selection of routes in the EOP. In this experiment, the initiative event was the High Pressurizer Level.

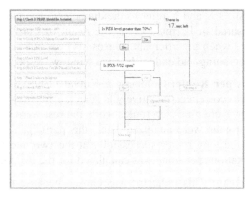

**Fig. 3.** Illustration of interface of the emergency operating procedure

## 2.2    Dependent Variables

When executing the tested EOP, the participants needed to observe the interface, collected information from it, and then followed branches of the EOP flow chart (as illustrated in Figure 3) in accordance with the current system status. Search efficiency and difficulty of information abstraction were the two aspects to evaluate whether the participants observed and collected information quickly or not. Number of fixations (Goldberg & Kotval, 1998) and fixation duration mean (Goldberg & Kotval, 1998) were measured for evaluating the two aspects. For each route in the EOP, the workload was assessed by blink rate and pupillary response to study whether the two interfaces required distinct cognitive effort.

All eye tracking measures in this study were recorded by the head-mounted eye tracker iView X from SMI© Company, with 50Hz sampling frequency.

**Blink Rate:** It refers to average number of blinking per minute. Brookling, Wilson and Swan (1996) reported that blink rate is more sensitive to workload than many other eye tracking measures. In this study, average blink rate for each interface was calculated.

**Average Percentage Change of Pupil Size (APCPS):** The participants were asked to relax their eyes before the experiment task was started, and their pupil sizes at the relaxed condition were recorded as the baseline. In this study, **APCPS** was calculated by formula (1), (2) and (3) (Iqbal et al., 2004).

$$Pupil\ size = \frac{Avg.\ Pupil\ Size\ X \times Avg.\ Pupil\ Size\ Y \times \pi}{4} \tag{1}$$

$$PCPS = \frac{PS\ Measured\ -\ PS\ Baseline}{PS\ Baseline} \tag{2}$$

$$APCPS = \frac{\int_{t_1}^{t_2} PCPS(t)dt}{t_2 - t_1} \tag{3}$$

where average pupil sizes X and Y refer to the diameters of a pupil on X and Y axis, respectively, PS measured in Formula (2) is the result of Formula (1), PS baseline refers to the pupil size when a participant relaxes his eyes before the experiment, and $t_1$ and $t_2$ refer to the beginning and end of the time window, respectively.

**Number of Fixations per Route:** Goldberg & Kotval (1998) demonstrated that the number of fixations was correlated negatively to search efficiency. Among the eight 8 routes in the EOP, four were nine-step routes while the rest were shorter routes. Since only successful long routes were analyzed later, the participants might accomplish different numbers of the long routes successfully at the two interface levels. Therefore, the number of fixations per route was calculated for the two interfaces.

**Fixation Duration Mean:** This indicator was chosen because the fixation duration mean was reported to be correlated positively to difficulty of information abstraction in Goldberg & Kotval (1998).

### 2.3    Participants

Web advertisements were used to recruit participants. There were 18 male students aged from 19 to 28 (mean= 21.9, SD = 5.8) studying engineering programs at Tsinghua University were recruited as participants.

The participants were required to have normal vision or to wear no more than 3 diopters glasses. Contact lenses were not allowed, due to the use of an eye tracker. They were informed about the details of the experiment protocol and voluntarily signed the informed consent form before the experiment proceeded.

### 2.4    Apparatus

The experiment scenario was showed in Figure 4. The headband-mounted eye tracker in this experiment comprised with eye- and scene camera assembly which was less than 80 grams. When a participant wore the eye tracker, the position (left or right) of eye- and scene camera in the front of the hat was adjusted according to the dominant eye of the participant. The eye tracker was lightweight so that it was low invasive relatively. Besides, a notebook PC specifically connected to the eye tracker was used for data collection and analysis via a piece of dedicated software.

**Fig. 4.** Illustration of experiment apparatus

## 2.5    Training and Pilot Study

To obtain stable operation data, the participants were trained for 2~3 hours to be familiar with the system operation. In the formal test session, all participants were asked to execute the same emergency operating procedure using the two interfaces separately. The eye tracker and its accompanied software collected data of pupil sizes, fixation numbers, fixation durations, blink numbers, and so on.

As a key parameter for data processing, fixation threshold is highly dependent on specific tasks. Therefore, a pilot study was conducted among 5 participants to separate fixation from scanning. The fixation threshold was set at 200 ms consequently.

## 2.6    Data Analysis

Among the 18 participants, 2 participants adjusted the head-mounted eye tracker arbitrarily and so the calibration was not accurate, thus their data was eliminated. The data of successful long routes of the rest 16 participants were selected for further analysis. All the data of blink number per route, fixation number per route, percentage change of pupil size passed the test of normality. Data for blink rate per minute and fixation duration mean did not pass the normality test. However, for two interface levels, their difference passed the test of normality. Therefore paired t-test with a significance level of 0.05 was adopted for analysis.

# 3    Results

The results of paired-samples test of the five variables are given in Table 1.

**Table 1.** Paired Samples Test Results

| Variables | Mean | SD | t | Sig. (2-tailed) |
|---|---|---|---|---|
| Blink number per route | 3.2 | 3.94 | 3.265 | 0.005 |
| Blink rate per min | 3.26 | 4.333 | 3.012 | 0.009 |
| Fixation number per route | 1.8 | 11.09 | 0.650 | 0.525 |
| Fixation duration mean | 0.0005 | 0.0379 | 0.049 | 0.962 |
| Percentage change of pupil size | -0.004 | 0.067 | -0.228 | 0.823 |

It can be seen from Table 1 that significant difference existed in blink number per route ($t=3.265$, $p=0.005$) and blink rate per minute ($t=3.012$, $p=0.009$) between the two interfaces. However, no significant difference was found in fixation number per route, fixation duration mean and percentage change of pupil size.

# 4    Discussion

When the participants performed the experimental task, the blink rate when using the functional interface was significantly lower than that when using the process interface. It indicates that functional interface based on FBTA led to lower workload significantly than the process interface. For the variable APCPS which was supposed to measure workload as well, however, there was no significant difference between the two interfaces. Wang (2011) points out that APCPS may interact with fatigue, nervousness, and other factors, and suggests that APCPS should not be used exclusively.

Number of fixations per route and fixations duration mean showed no significant difference between the two interfaces. This may reveal that the functional interface could not provide higher search efficiency and less difficulty of information abstraction than the process interface. Such non-significance can be explained by several reasons.

First, the experiment task may limit the superiority of functional interface in search efficiency. Components with similar functions were organized together in the functional interface, while similar components may be distributed in the process interface. If a task require a participant to locate a component, the participant can easily locate the region of the component, but then has to carefully check it out of other components with similar functions in the functional interface, while they may spend more time in locating the rough position of the component, but then need to spend little time in finding its exact position in the process interface. Therefore, the difference of the overall search efficiency when using the two interfaces may be not significant. Second, the performance difference between the two interfaces in terms of search efficiency and difficulty of information abstraction may be lessened after the participants were adequately trained. In this study, the participants were trained for 2~3 hours. The significance of performance difference may become too small to be detected with the limited sample size.

## 5     Conclusion

The influence of interfaces with different information organization on human performance in a simulated EOP task was studied. The findings from this study revealed the importance of designing an appropriate interface for EOP and similar tasks.

The experiment results show that the functional interface based on FBTA was superior significantly to the process interface in user workload. This advantage is of importance. In main control room of nuclear power plants, especially when executing emergency operations, operators are subjected to high pressure. The functional design can reduce workload and may thus further reduce human errors. The results did not prove the superiority of the functional interface to the process one in search efficiency and difficulty of information abstraction, since no significant differences were found in the number of fixations per route and fixations duration mean values.

There were some limitations in this study. (1) that the use of student participants may limit the generalization of the conclusions from this study. (2) The sample size was relatively small.

**Acknowledgement.** This study was supported by the National Natural Science Foundation of China (Project No. 70931003).

# References

1. Adihikari, S., Bayley, C., Bedford, T., Busby, J., Cliffe, A., Geeta, D., Eid, M., French, S., Keshvala, R., Pollard, S., Soane, E., Tracy, D., Wu, S.: Human Reliability Analysis: A review & critique. Manchester Business School Working Paper No. 589 (2009)
2. Brookings, J.B., Wilson, G.F., Swain, C.R.: Psychophysiological responses to changes in workload during simulated air traffic control. Biological Psychology 42, 361–377 (1996)
3. Goldberg, J.H., Kotval, X.P.: Eye movement-based evaluation of the computer interface. In: Kumar, S.K. (ed.) Advances in Occupational Ergonomics and Safety, pp. 529–532. ISO Press, Amsterdam (1998)
4. Iqbal, S.T., Zheng, X.S., Bailey, B.P.: Task-evoked pupillary response to mental workload in human-computer interaction. In: Proceeding of CHI 2004 Extended Abstracts on Human Factors in Computing Systems, pp. 1477–1480 (2004)
5. Kim, J.H., Seong, P.H.: Human Factors Engineering in Large-scale Digital Control Systems. In: Seong, P.H. (ed.) Reliability and Risk Issues in Large Scale Safety-critical Digital Control Systems, p. 163. Springer, London (2009)
6. Rasmussen, J.: The role of hierachical knowledge representation in decision making and system management. IEEE Transactions on System, Man, and Cybermetics SMC-15, 234–243 (1985)
7. Vincent, K.J.: Ecological Interface Design: Progress and Challenges. Human Factors 44, 62–78 (2002)
8. Wu, X.J., Gao, Q., Song, F., Dong, X.L., Li, Z.Z.: Display Design for AP1000 Nuclear Power Plant: FBTA Method vs. Traditional Method. In: The 11th International Conference on Probabilistic Safety Assessment and Management & Annual European Safety and Reliability Conference 2012 (PSAM 2011 & ESREL 2012), Helsinki, Finland, June 25-29 (2012)
9. Wang, Y.: Real-time empirical mental workload measurement in digitalized main control room of nuclear power plant. Bachelors' thesis. Tsinghua University, Beijing (2011)

# The Effects of Emotion on Judgments
# of Effectiveness and Good-Design

Hui Yueh Hsieh

Department of Visual Communication Design, Ming Chi University of Technology
84 Gungjuan Rd., Taishan, New Taipei City, Taiwan
tsauk@mail.mcut.edu.tw

**Abstract.** This study investigated participants' judgements of effectiveness and good-design with regard to visual messages of risks, as well as the relationships between their judgements and emotional responses. It examined whether fear-appeals influence emotional responses and judgements. The findings suggested that emotions appeared to be strong predictors of judgements of effectiveness and good-design. In general, for both the designers and users, the more emotionally salient (high arousal, high dominance and either high pleasure or high displeasure) stimuli were perceived, the more effective and the better the design they were judged. In addition, strong fear appeals were perceived as more effective and better designed.

**Keywords:** emotion, judgement, fear-appeals.

## 1 Introduction

A growing number of researchers in the design field have become aware that the emotional response to a visual artefact is vital to the message's success in communicating information to users. These researchers, often by examination of the visual aspect of a design, have endeavoured to understand how it can be affected by emotions. Cameron and Chan [1] pointed out that much of the research on risk communication has centred on cognitive mechanisms and rationality, but relatively little has been done to delineate the influence of emotion and imagery on health behaviour. Previous studies sought to understand the relationship between emotion and risk perception found that fear appeals can affect risk perceptions; there is, however, considerable debate as to whether fear appeals can affect attitudes, decision-making or behaviour.

Although visual messages designed to communicate risk are not always effective [2], sometimes even misleading, little empirical research has been carried out to investigate the use of visual display for risk communication. Most of these studies on visual communication of risks focuses on specific risk (e.g. HIV/AIDS), or specific precautionary behaviours [e.g. breast cancer screening in3]. In addition, research in the areas of psychophysics, and human factors has not examined risk communication fully. Studies on visual representation to communicate risk are often atheoretical [4, 5]. In the area of visual communication, although a great deal of attention has been

P.L.P. Rau (Ed.): CCD/HCII 2013, Part I, LNCS 8023, pp. 296–305, 2013.
© Springer-Verlag Berlin Heidelberg 2013

paid to visual health campaigns, especially campaigns in third world countries, these publications are largely advocacy-based and aesthetic judgements rather than empirical research.

This study investigated the possibility of differences in emotional responses and the judgements of effectiveness and good-design among the users and the designers. It sought to answer three questions: 1. Do participants' judgment of effectiveness correlate with their judgments of good design? 2. Do participants' emotional responses correlate with their judgements? 3. Whether fear-appeals influence emotional responses and judgements?

## 1.1    Emotional Design: A Visual Communication Perspective

More marketers and product designers recognise emotion as a vital factor in successful selling products [6] and that emotion-engendering products generate higher customer-perceived value [7]. Givechi and Velázquez said that better design can provoke positive emotions from people such as a feeling of achievement, inspiration and joy [8]. Noble and Kumar [9] suggested, positive emotions are strongly associated with marketing-based outcomes such as attachment, loyalty, commitment and passion. In the book "Designing Pleasurable Product", Jordan [10] proposed a three-level hierarchy model (Level 1: Functionality; Level 2: Usability; Level 3: Pleasure). When the functionality and usability are fulfilled, people will want something more - products that bring pleasure. He described three aspects which are associated with pleasurable products: emotional and hedonic and practical benefits. Similarly, psychologist Donald Norman published one of the most highly cited books in design: "Emotional Design: Why We Love (or Hate) Everyday Things", which emphasizes emotion plays an important role in product design; human-centred and attractive designs (products) work better [11]. A considerable research effort has been devoted to this area, for instance, Jordan [10] formulated a questionnaire for assessing 'product pleasurability' for Philips Corporate Design [as cited in 10]; Khalid and Helander [12] presented a framework for evaluation of affective design, and "the goal is to achieve a pleasurable and satisfying product" [12].

## 1.2    Fear Appeals

Previous studies have demonstrated a correlation between emotion and perceived risk. For example, when participants were asked to identify the first thought or image they associated with nuclear waste repository, most of the images that aroused people were emotionally negative, for example, dangerous/toxic, death/sickness [13, 14]. Many theorists believe that, arouse visceral emotion of fear in individuals will increase their perceived severity of the health risk. "Fear appeals are persuasive messages that emphasize the harmful physical or social consequences of failing to comply with message recommendations"[15]. Fear appeals evoke not only fear but a variety of emotions, such as anxiety and disgust, and each arousal emotion has separate and unique effects on persuasion [16, 17]. According to Cauberghe et al. [18] the term 'fear appeals' is incorrectly used when referring to 'threat appeals'. Nevertheless, because it is a prevailing usage in the literature, the term 'fear appeals' is used here.

**Dilemma of Fear Appeals.** Health promotional campaigns have been confronted with dilemmas involving whether to incite people's negative emotions, often using an imagery of grotesque body, to take up precautionary measure. Having reviewed the literature on fear appeals, Strahan and colleagues stressed that fear appeals can be effective in influencing health behaviour [19]. For example, in research which examined whether fear appeal messages related to skin cancer can promote skin protective behaviour, the results showed that participants who received highly threatening fear appeal messages (with pictures of people with skin cancer) expressed more willingness to take preventive measures to protect their skin than those who only received text messages alone [20]. Hammond and colleagues [21] found that smokers who had greater negative emotions in response to the graphic warning labels were more likely to have quit, attempted to quit, or reduced smoking. Studies on the web-based avian influenza (bird flu) education program found that the fear appeal program was more effective than the humour-based program in improving risk perception and educating the students about healthy behaviour [22]. Research has also demonstrated the effectiveness of both positive and negative emotional health messages in influencing relevant behaviour [23].

Although the above studies stressed the role of emotion in the effectiveness of health risk communication, there has been controversy over the use of fear appeals. Critics of this approach have opposed the use of fear appeal, contending that it is ineffective [1, 24]. It has also been suggested that using fear arousal as a persuasion tactic is unethical. Hastings and colleagues [25] pointed out that there may be consequential collateral damage. As fear appeal messages in mass media reach far larger audiences, and inevitably reach unintended audiences such as untargeted children.

### 1.3    The PAD Emotion Scales

The dimensional approaches of measuring emotions- the PAD Emotion Scales [26] were employed for this study. The PAD devised by Mehrabian and Russell is one of the most critically acclaimed emotional assessment instruments. Mehrabian and Russell [27] proposed a three-dimensional model of emotion, stating that all human emotions can be adequately described by three continuous, bipolar, and nearly orthogonal dimensions, pleasure (P), arousal (A) and dominance (D). One of the strengths of the PAD is that it permits calculation of the average emotional response of a group to any stimulus, and that it is designed to capture the entire domain of emotional experiences rather than to measure specific emotions.

The validity and reliability of the PAD is well established [28-30], and it has also been employed and gained recognition in various fields for assessing emotional responses, such as in consumer research [31, 32] and in design [33]. Havlena and Holbrook [28] assessed comparative reliabilities and validities of Mehrabian and Russell's PAD Emotion Scales and Plutchik's Emotion Profile Index (basic emotion approach), and posited that the PAD scheme allows one to describe an emotional experience in terms of specific emotions as well as the dimensions underlying the emotion states. They concluded that the PAD paradigm outperforms Plutchik's emotional categories.

Behavioural studies have shown that emotions are multidimensional [34]. How these multiple dimensions are processed in the brain is still not understood. Evidence from a recent fMRI study demonstrated that a three-dimensional approach is a more robust emotional assessment method than the discrete approach. Morris and associates identified different functional regions of the brain that correspond to both the pleasure and the arousal dimensions of the PAD Emotion Scales and found that there was a high correlation between the self–report PAD measurement and the fMRI data [35].

## 2    Method

### 2.1    Participants

A total of 324 Taiwanese participated in this study. The effective sample size was 289 (mean age 22.18, SD 6.08, range 18-63; 196 women: mean age 21.74, SD 5.30, range 18-45); 113 men: mean age 22.88, SD 7.10, range 18-63) after discarding invalid samples. Some data were eliminated from further analyses because of omitting items or a suspicion of careless responding, i.e. lack of variability and extremity bias [36]. Among the participants there were 180 from a visual communication design background and 109 from a non-design related background (such as engineering). The design students participating in the study were recruited from three universities in Taiwan.

### 2.2    Materials

The stimuli consisted of visuals representing different emotional dimensions and particularly whether fear or non-fear appeals. Mehrabian [37] believed that discrete emotion are better described as a three-dimensional PAD space, and single emotions always confound two or more of the PAD dimensions. It was found, "Fear = (- .64*P, +.60*A, -.43*D)", that fear is represented by low degrees of pleasure (-P), high arousal (+A), and involved low dominance (-D) [27]. The six stimuli that had the highest mean pleasure-displeasure scores (low pleasure) and the lowest mean arousal/non-arousal scores (high arousal) were selected for the fear-appeal group, and the four stimuli that had the lowest mean pleasure-displeasure scores (high pleasure) and highest mean arousal/non-arousal scores (low arousal) were selected for the non-fear group.

**PAD Scales.** The Chinese-language PAD Emotion Scales[38] were used to assess participants' emotional responses (see Table 1).

**Table 1.** 12 items PAD Emotion Scales

| Pleasure (P) | Arousal (A) | Dominance (D) |
| --- | --- | --- |
| P1: Happy-Unhappy | A3: Frenzied-Sluggish | D1: Controlling-Controlled |
| P2: Pleased- Annoyed | A4: Jittery-Dull | D2: Dominant –Submissive |
| P3: Satisfied-Unsatisfied | A5: Wide awake-Sleepy | D3: Influential-Influenced |
| P5: Hopeful –Despairing | A6: Aroused- Unaroused | D6: In control-Cared for |

## 2.3    Procedure

Using the 12-item Chinese version of the PAD Emotion Scales, participants viewed 15 visual stimuli and rated how each stimulus made them feel according to three dimensions of emotional response. They ticked one of seven spaces between two bipolar adjectives to show their evaluation. Two additional questions were asked with each stimulus to assess participants' opinions. The first question was "Do you think this visual artefact is effective?" and secondly "Do you think this is a good design?" Participants were requested to rate both questions on a 7-point-scale, from 'strongly disagree' to 'strongly agree'. The experiment took an average of 30 to 50 minutes to complete.

# 3    Results

Pearson correlation coefficients were calculated to reveal possible relationships between participant's judgement of effectiveness (E) and their judgement of good-design (G). The results showed that the overall Person correlation between E and G based on all participants was 0.65, $p < 0.01$. Further analyses confirmed that, irrespective of stimuli categories (i.e. fear or non-fear), high correlations between the ratings of effectiveness and ratings of good-design were observed for both designers and users (all at $p < 0.01$).

In order to determine whether emotional responses predict judgements of effectiveness and good-design, regressions were performed on the ratings of effectiveness and good-design using three PAD scales as the predictors. The multiple regression analysis revealed that, in response to non-fear appeals the same patterns were found for designers and users (Fig. 1 and 2). The ratings of effectiveness of both the designers and users were negatively correlated with arousal (all at $p < 0.01$), and the ratings of good-design were negatively correlated with pleasure and arousal (designers: all at $p < 0.01$; users: $p < 0.05$ for pleasure and $p < 0.01$ for arousal). These results imply that when the induced arousal was greater they evaluated the non-fear appeal stimuli as more effective, and when they perceived greater pleasure and arousal they rated the non-fear appeals as better designed.

In regard to fear appeals, different patterns were found for designers and users (Fig. 3 and 4). Designers' pleasure and arousal responses predicted their ratings of effectiveness and good-design. Pleasure was positively correlated with effectiveness ($p < 0.05$) but negatively correlated with good-design ($p < 0.01$); arousal was negatively correlated with both effectiveness and good-design (both at $p < 0.01$). These results indicate that when the designers perceived a greater displeasure and arousal they evaluated the fear appeal stimuli as more effective; however, greater pleasure and arousal were associated with better-designed. Users' arousal responses predicted their effectiveness ratings, and arousal and dominance responses predicted their ratings of good-design (all at $p < 0.01$), indicating that the users evaluated the fear appeal stimuli as more effective when they perceived a greater arousal, and when the perceived arousal and submissiveness were greater they rated the fear appeals as better designed.

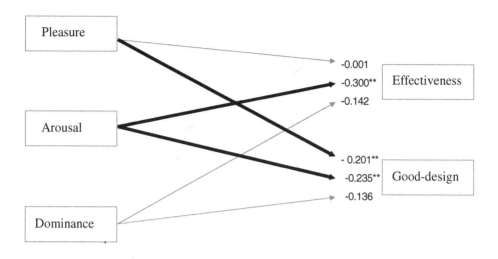

**Fig. 1.** Output diagram of emotion predicting ratings of effectiveness and good-design on non-fear appeals by designers

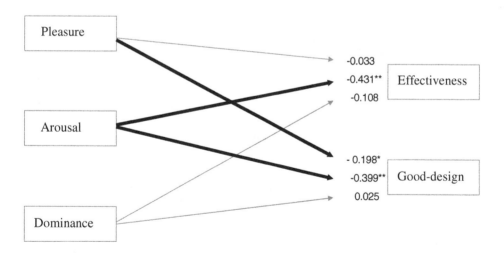

**Fig. 2.** Output diagram of emotion predicting ratings of effectiveness and good-design on non-fear appeals by users

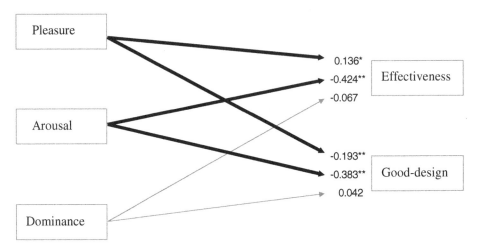

**Fig. 3.** Output diagram of emotion predicting ratings of effectiveness and good-design on fear appeals by designers

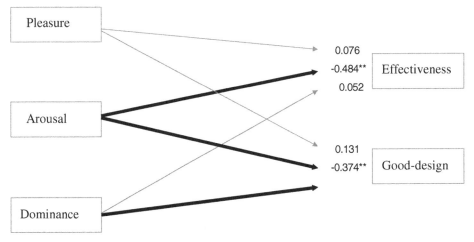

**Fig. 4.** Output diagram of emotion predicting ratings of effectiveness and good-design on fear appeals by users

## 4    Discussion

This study investigated participants' judgements of effectiveness and good-design, and whether emotional responses predict the judgements. For both designers and users and irrespective of stimuli categories, it was found that the ratings of effectiveness and ratings of good-design exhibited extremely high correlations, which indicates that they might be measuring similar concepts. The multiple regression analyses revealed a high degree of association between participants' ratings of effectiveness and good-design with three PAD scales.

Although the two questions, effectiveness and good-design, addressed somewhat different content, the Pearson correlations between the two were reasonably high. This indicates positive associations between the two questions; when the rating of effectiveness was high, the rating of good-design was high in both designers and users. Designer Milton Glaser recalled that 'good' used to refer to a quality of honest and truthful in the early fifties, but today, "good simply means effective" [39]. The current findings indicate that the concepts of good design and effective design might be similar for both participating designers and users, although the correlations between the two measures were marginally higher for users. An effective design may not be a good design; a good design requires a balanced combination of aesthetics, usability, ethics and effectiveness. The concepts of good design and effective design are not synonymous.

There is a high degree of association between judgements of effectiveness and judgements of good-design with three PAD scales. In general, for both the designers and users, the more emotionally salient (high arousal, high dominance and either high pleasure or high displeasure) stimuli were perceived, the more effective and the better the design they were judged. It also indicates that strong fear appeals were perceived as more effective and better designed.

The results of the regression analyses revealed that emotions were strong predictors of judgements of effectiveness and good-design. Pleasure and arousal accounted for most of the significant relations. Arousal stood out as the strongest predictor of the judgements of effectiveness and good-design; the higher the arousal, the more effective and the better the design for both the designers and users. In regard to fear appeals, different patterns were observed for designers and users. Pleasure and arousal predicted the judgements of effectiveness and good-design of designers, although pleasure appeared to exert opposite effects between their ratings of effectiveness and good-design. On the other hand, pleasure did not predict users' ratings of effectiveness and good-design, but dominance significantly correlated with users' judgements of good-design. These findings fit well with the observation that addresses the powerful influence of emotion on judgement, and reinforce the need for a better understanding of the emotional dimensions in visual communication of risks.

# References

1. Cameron, L.D., Chan, C.K.Y.: Designing Health Communications: Harnessing the Power of Affect, Imagery, and Self-Regulation. Social and Personality Psychology Compass 2, 262–282 (2008)
2. Stone, E.R., Sieck, W.R., Bull, B.E., Yates, F.J., Parks, S.C., Rush, C.J.: Foreground: Background Salience: Explaining the Effects of Graphical Displays on Risk Avoidance. Organizational Behavior and Human Decision Processes 90, 19–36 (2003)
3. Schapira, M.M., Nattinger, A.B., McAuliffe, T.L.: The Influence of Graphic Format on Breast Cancer Risk Communication. Journal of Health Communication 11, 569–582 (2006)

4.  Ancker, J.S., Senathirajah, Y., Kukafka, R., Starren, J.B.: Design Features of Graphs in Health Risk Communication: A Systematic Review. Journal of the American Medical Informatics Association 13, 608–618 (2006)
5.  Lipkus, I.M., Hollands, J.G.: The Visual Communication of Risk. Journal of the National Cancer Institute Monographs 25, 149–163 (1999)
6.  Seva, R.R., Duh, H.B.-L., Helander, M.G.: The Marketing Implications of Affective Product Design. Applied Ergonomics 38, 723–731 (2007)
7.  Boatwright, P., Cagan, J.: Built to Love: Creating Products That Captivate Customers. Berrett-Koehler, San Francisco (2010)
8.  Givechi, R., Velázquez, V.L.: Positive Space. In: McDonagh, D., Hekkert, P., Erp, J.V. (eds.) Design and Emotion: The Experience of Everyday Things, pp. 43–47. Taylor & Francis, London (2004)
9.  Noble, C., Kumar, M.: Using Product Design Strategically to Create Deeper Consumer Connections. Business Horizons 51, 441–450 (2008)
10. Jordan, P.W.: Designing Pleasurable Products: An Introduction to the New Human Factors. Taylor & Francis, London (2002)
11. Norman, D.A.: Emotional Design: Why We Love (or Hate) Everyday Things. Basic Books, New York (2004)
12. Khalid, H.M., Helander, M.G.: Customer Emotional Needs in Product Design. Concurrent Engineering 14, 197–206 (2006)
13. Slovic, P.: Perceived Risk, Trust, and the Politics of Nuclear Waste. Science 254, 1603–1607 (1991)
14. Slovic, P.: Trust, Emotion, Sex, Politics, and Science: Surveying the Risk-Assessment Battlefield. Risk Analysis 19, 689–701 (1999)
15. Hale, J.L., Dillard, J.P.: Fear Appeals in Health Promotion Campaigns: Too Much, Too Little, or Just Right. In: Maibach, E., Parrott, R.L. (eds.) Designing Health Messages: Approaches from Communication Theory and Public Health Practice, pp. 65–80. Sage, London (1995)
16. Dillard, J.P., Plotnick, C.A., Godbold, L.C., Freimuth, V.S., Edgar, T.: The Multiple Affective Outcomes of AIDS PSAs: Fear Appeals Do More Than Scare People. Communication Research 23, 44–72 (1996)
17. Kohn, P.M., Goodstadt, M.S., Cook, G.M., Sheppard, M., Chan, G.: Ineffectiveness of Threat Appeals About Drinking and Driving. Accident Analysis & Prevention 14, 457–464 (1982)
18. Cauberghe, V., De Pelsmacker, P., Janssens, W., Dens, N.: Fear, Threat and Efficacy in Threat Appeals: Message Involvement as a Key Mediator to Message Acceptance. Accident Analysis & Prevention 41, 276–285 (2009)
19. Strahan, E.J., White, K., Fong, G.T., Fabrigar, L.R., Zanna, M.P., Cameron, R.: Enhancing the Effectiveness of Tobacco Package Warning Labels: A Social Psychological Perspective. British Medical Journal 11, 183 (2002)
20. Stephenson, M.T., Witte, K.: Fear, Threat, and Perceptions of Efficacy from Frightening Skin Cancer Messages. Public Health Reviews 26, 147–174 (1998)
21. Hammond, D., Fong, G.T., McDonald, P.W., Brown, K.S., Cameron, R.: Graphic Canadian Cigarette Warning Labels and Adverse Outcomes: Evidence from Canadian Smokers. American Journal of Public Health 94, 1442–1445 (2004)
22. Kim, P., Sorcar, P., Um, S., Chung, H., Lee, Y.S.: Effects of Episodic Variations in Web-Based Avian Influenza Education: Influence of Fear and Humor on Perception, Comprehension, Retention and Behavior. Health Education Research (2008)

23. Lewis, I.M., Watson, B., White, K.M., Tay, R.: Promoting Public Health Messages: Should We Move Beyond Fear-Evoking Appeals in Road Safety? Qualitative Health 17, 61–74 (2007)
24. Ruiter, R.A.C., Abraham, C., Kok, G.: Scary Warnings and Rational Precautions: A Review of the Psychology of Fear Appeals. Psychology and Health 16, 613–630 (2001)
25. Hastings, G., Stead, M., Webb, J.: Fear Appeals in Social Marketing: Strategic and Ethical Reasons for Concern. Psychology and Marketing 21, 961–986 (2004)
26. General Tests of Emotion or Affect for Evaluating Consumer Reactions to Products and Services, Including User Interface, http://www.kaaj.com/psych/scales/emotion.html (accessed, May 2007)
27. Russell, J.A., Mehrabian, A.: Evidence for a Three-Factor Theory of Emotions. Journal of Research in Personality 11, 273–294 (1977)
28. Havlena, W.J., Holbrook, M.B.: The Varieties of Consumption Experience: Comparing Two Typologies of Emotion in Consumer Behavior. Journal of Consumer Research 13, 394–404 (1986)
29. Mehrabian, A.: Framework for a Comprehensive Description and Measurement of Emotional States. Genetic, Social and General Psychology Monographs 121, 339–361 (1995)
30. Brengman, M.: The Impact of Colour in the Store Environment - an Environmental Psychology Approach, Universiteit Gent (2002)
31. Petermans, A., Van Cleempoel, K., Nuyts, E., Vanrie, J.: Measuring Emotions in Customer Experiences in Retail Store Environments. International Journal of Retail & Distribution Management, 2257–2265 (2009)
32. Spangenberg, E., Grohmann, B., Sprott, D.: It's Beginning to Smell (and Sound) a Lot Like Christmas: The Interactive Effects of Ambient Scent and Music in a Retail Setting. Journal of Business Research 58, 1583–1589 (2005)
33. Tsai, T., Chang, T., Chuang, M., Wang, D.: Exploration in Emotion and Visual Information Uncertainty of Websites in Culture Relations. International Journal of Design 2, 55–66 (2008)
34. Rolls, E.T.: Emotion Explained. Oxford University Press (2005)
35. Morris, J.D., Klahr, N.J., Shen, F., Villegas, J., Wright, P., He, G., Liu, Y.: Mapping a Multidimensional Emotion in Response to Television Commercials. Human Brain Mapping 30, 789–796 (2009)
36. Paulhus, D.L.: Measurement and Control of Response Bias. In: Robinson, J.P., Shaver, P.R., Wrightsman, L.S. (eds.) Measures of Personality and Social Psychological Attitudes, pp. 17–59. Academic Press, London (1991)
37. Mehrabian, A.: Comparison of the PAD and PANAS as Models for Describing Emotions and for Differentiating Anxiety from Depression. Journal of Psychopathology and Behavioral Assessment 19, 331–357 (1997)
38. Hsieh, H.Y.: Taiwanese Version of the PAD Emotion Scales, pp. 21–26. Kaohsiung (2011) (in Chinese)
39. Holland, D.K.: Design Issues: How Graphic Design Informs Society. Allworth Press, New York (2001)

# Identifying Usability Problems
# in a Smart TV Music Service

Sheau-Farn Max Liang, Yi-Chung Kuo, and Shu-Chin Chen

National Taipei University of Technology, Taipei, Taiwan
maxliang@ntut.edu.tw

**Abstract.** Thirty-one usability problems for a smart TV music service system have been identified by different user groups through the cooperative evaluation method. Design solutions can be provided based on the priority of the identified usability problems, the classifications between functionality and quality issues, or between display and control issues, and the foci on specific user groups.

**Keywords:** Smart Interactive Television, Usability, Music Service.

## 1    Introduction

After the surge of smart phones and tablets in the market, information communication technology industry now aims at the next promising market: smart televisions (TVs). There are several relevant terms, such as the Internet Protocol TVs (IPTVs), Connected TVs, and Internet TVs to emphasize the capability of connecting with the Internet; the digital TVs to highlight digital information contents; and the interactive TVs (iTVs) to indicate the nature of interactivity. In this paper, we use "smart TVs" as the term to represent the TVs that can connect to the Internet and provide digital contents to people through their interactions with the TVs.

Various applications and services have been launched on the platform of smart TVs. However, application designers and service providers are still exploring the ways of understanding this new context of use and its associated user requirements. Cesar and Chorianopoulos [1] predicted that the traditional production-distribution-consumption model will be replaced by the new creation-share-control model. This new model could be achieve through the user interface design to enable the capabilities for TV viewers to act as directors for participating content authoring [2].

Compared to the context of using desktop computers, the interaction with smart TV is more entertainment-oriented and home-based rather than work-oriented and office-based. Families with different generations are usually the use groups of smart TVs. An ethnographic study in Austria about TV viewing experience reported that older households were more interested in receiving information from TVs compared to younger households who were used to receiving information from computers [3]. A telephone survey in Taiwan pointed out that the younger generation was more willing to adopt smart TV services than the older generation at home [4].

P.L.P. Rau (Ed.): CCD/HCII 2013, Part I, LNCS 8023, pp. 306–312, 2013.
© Springer-Verlag Berlin Heidelberg 2013

The design of interactions between users and smart TVs is a key to the success of smart TVs since people now not only passively watch smart TVs but also proactively use and interact with them. Conventional remote controls are still the major input appliances. A usability test revealed that users pushed arrow buttons more than the color buttons, and still had difficulty in text-inputs with conventional remote controls [5]. Therefore, new technologies and methods of smart TV control have been proposed, such as the second screen to use smart phones or tablets as the remote controls [6], automatic viewer detection technology [7], and control by gestures or voices [8].

This paper presents a usability analysis of a smart TV music service. The service has not met provider's expectation in terms of subscription rate, and the manager would like to know what might go wrong with the service. However, little literature has been published on smart TV music service. Previous research about the mobile music services has found out that the sound quality and content variety of the service were important to consumer adoption, whereas the personalization and usability of the service were the most desired features [9]. A design for home music appliances which focused on visual information seeking and screen displays has also been proposed [10].

Similar to its personal computer version, the home page of the studied music service system was clean and simple at the first glimpse. As shown in Figure 1, six rounded rectangle buttons were listed at the bottom of the screen from left to right. They represented six main functions of (1) billboard list, (2) random play, (3) new albums list, (4) song search, (5) my favorites list, and (6) my account management. A conventional TV remote control was the device to interact with the music service system. A preliminary expert review was conducted and found many potential usability problems related to system performance, display content and format, navigation, and control. To confirm our findings of usability problems, we decided to recruit prospective users to try out the system by applying the cooperative evaluation method [11].

**Fig. 1.** Schematic screen layout

## 2     Method

Cooperative evaluation was introduced by Monk and his colleagues [11]. It was an effective method for obtaining data about critical usability problems with the minimum of effort. The four main steps of this approach were: (1) recruit users, (2) prepare tasks, (3) interact and record, and (4) debrief [11].

### 2.1     Participants

Due to the time constraint, only five participants were recruited to represent three groups of users. Among the five participants, three were female and two were male. Two females were office workers in their early thirties, whereas the third female was a sixty-year-old stay-at-home mom. Two males were college students in their mid-twenties.

### 2.2     Apparatus

A room was set up to mimic a living room with a couch, a coffee table, an LCD TV connected with a set-up box, and a conventional remote control. A voice recorder was put on the coffee table for recording what participants said during the session.

### 2.3     Procedures

Each participant spent about two hours individually in trying out the music service system with the presence of the authors. Participants were asked to perform following tasks:

— Log in the account
— Find a specific song
— Find some songs and put them into my favorites list
— Go to random play and put the song heard into my favorites list
— Go to my favorites list and delete a specific song

During the session, participants were encouraged to speak out their opinions and feelings about the system, and to explore different functions as many as possible. Usability problems were then identified based on data about what participants said and what we observed during each session.

When the participant completed the tasks, an interview was conducted to understand participants' music listening habits, preferences on service functionality, and ideas for system improvement.

## 3     Results and Discussion

Total thirty-one usability problems have been pointed out by participants. Among these problems, ten have been identified by all five participants, four have been identified by four participants, seven have been identified by three participants, four have been identified by two participants, and six problems have been identified by only one participant. Table 1 lists the usability problems and the corresponding number of participants who identified them.

**Table 1.** Identified usability problems

|  | Usability Problem | # |
|---|---|---|
| 1 | System response lag | 5 |
| 2 | Difficulty in finding a song | 5 |
| 3 | Invalid songs in the playlist | 5 |
| 4 | Difficulty in using the remote control | 5 |
| 5 | Excessive results from the song search | 5 |
| 6 | Confusion with the music catelogs | 5 |
| 7 | No play control in the random play mode | 5 |
| 8 | No add-to-my-favorite function in the random play mode | 5 |
| 9 | No turn-a-page function and indication for the playlist | 5 |
| 10 | No back-to-the-first-page function on the last page of the playlist | 5 |
| 11 | Possibility to exit the system by accident | 4 |
| 12 | Duplicate songs in the playlist | 4 |
| 13 | Ambiguous organization of song search results | 4 |
| 14 | No playlist display function in the random play mode | 4 |
| 15 | No move-to-the-next-song function except in the karaoke mode | 3 |
| 16 | Unexpected addition of the song played into the playlist | 3 |
| 17 | No delete-multiple-songs function in the playlist | 3 |
| 18 | Incomplete display of song serach results | 3 |
| 19 | Response lag of the return-to-main-menu function | 3 |
| 20 | No back-to-main-menu function in the palylist | 3 |
| 21 | No lyrics display fuction in the karaoke mode | 3 |
| 22 | No standard English-to-Chinese traslation of artists' names | 2 |
| 23 | No partial modification function for type-ins | 2 |
| 24 | Incompatible layout between virtual keyboard and remote control | 2 |
| 25 | No find-movie-soundtracks function under the movie catelog | 2 |
| 26 | Possibility to delete all songs in the playlist by accident | 1 |
| 27 | No select-a-song-by-remote-number-buttons function in the albums list | 1 |
| 28 | No replay function in the playlist | 1 |
| 29 | Foreign language (English) for logging in the account | 1 |
| 30 | No log-in window displayed on the home page | 1 |
| 31 | No record of list for songs played in the random play mode | 1 |

Note: #: The number of participants identified the problem

There was not much different in the numbers of usability problems identified per participant (ranged from 17 to 24). Thirteen out of the 31 usability problems (No. 1-10, 11, 13, and 19 in Table 1) have been identified by the three groups (young female workers, young male students, and old stay-at-home mom). Nine usability problems (No. 12, 14-18, and 21-23 in Table 1) have been identified by both the groups of young female worker(s) and male student(s) but not by the old stay-at-home mom.

Two usability problems (No. 20 and 24 in Table 1) have been identified by both the young male student(s) and old stay-at-home mom but not by the young female worker(s). Four usability problems (No. 25, 28, and 30-31 in Table 1) have been identified by only the young male student. One (No. 26 in Table 1) usability problem has been identified only by the young female worker, and two (No. 27 and 29) usability problems have been identified only by the stay-at-home mom. Figure 2 presents the percentages of identified usability problems from different combinations of the three user groups. It indicates that while every group identified their own usability problems, about 80% of the usability problems have been identified by at least two of the three user groups.

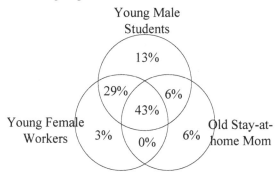

**Fig. 2.** Percentages of identified usability problems among the three user groups

The identified usability problems can be categorized into the problems related to functionality issues and quality issues. While functionality issues are about what the system is expected to have, quality issues are about how good to perform a function. Table 2 shows the corresponding usability problems and percentages of these two categories.

**Table 2.** Usability problems: fuctionality versus quality

| Category | Corresponding Usability Problems | Percentage |
|---|---|---|
| Functionality | 7-10, 14, 15, 17, 20, 21, 25, 27, 28, 31 | 42% |
| Quality | 1-6, 11-13, 16, 18, 19, 22-24, 26, 29, 30 | 58% |

As shown in Table 2, the studied music service system had significant usability problems in both functionality and quality issues.

These usability problems can also be classified as display issues and control issues. Table 3 shows the corresponding usability problems and percentages of these two categories.

**Table 3.** Usability problems: display versus control

| Category | Corresponding Usability Problems | Percentage |
|---|---|---|
| Dispaly | 3, 5, 6, 12, 13, 18, 24, 30 | 26% |
| Control | 1, 2, 4, 7-11, 14-17, 19-23, 25-29, 31 | 74% |

As shown in Table 3, the studied music service system had more significant usability problems in control than in display.

# 4    Conclusion

Results of the usability analysis were consistent with the findings from the preliminary expert review. The cooperative evaluation method applied in this study could identify usability problems with an effective and efficient manner. The findings of this research support the idea that the design suggestions therefore can be provided with various aspects: the priority of solving the usability problems can be based on the order listed in Table 1. While functionality and quality design issues can refer to Table 2, display and control design issues can refer to Table 3. Based on the findings, the service provider can also find better solutions for the (re)design of applications and services of smart TVs music service with the foci on specific user groups. A limitation of this study is that the numbers of participants were relatively small. It would be interesting to examine if any new usability problem will be identified with more participants to represent their user groups. Further research can also extend the results to the study of user experience on smart TV music services.

**Acknowledgement.** This research is funded by the Industrial Technology Research Institute (ITRI) of Taiwan. Thanks to Chao-Yin Chi of the ITRI for her coordination of the project.

# References

1. Cesar, P., Chorianopoulos, K.: The evolution of TV systems, content, and users toward interactivity. Foundations and Trends in Human-Computer Interaction 2(4), 279–373 (2008)
2. Chorianopoulos, K.: User interface design principles for interactive television applications. International Journal of Human-Computer Interaction 24(6), 556–573 (2008)
3. Obrist, M., Bernhaupt, R., Tscheligi, M.: Interactive TV for the home: An ethnographic study on users' requirements and experiences. Interactional Journal of Human-Computer Interaction 24(2), 174–196 (2008)
4. Li, S.-C.S.: Exploring the factors influencing the adoption of interactive cable television services in Taiwan. Journal of Broadcasting & Electronic Media 48(3), 466–483 (2004)
5. Bernhaupt, R., Obrist, M., Tscheligi, M.: Usability and usage of iTV services: Lessons learned in an Austrian field trial. ACM Computers in Entertainment 5(2), Article 6, 14 pages (2007)
6. Cruichshank, L., Tsekleves, E., Whitham, R., Hill, A. Kondo, K.: Making interactive TV easier to use: Interface design for a second screen approach. The Design Journal 10(3), ID 774, 14 pages (2007)
7. Silva, T., de Abreu, J.F., Pacheco, O., Almeida, P.: User identification: A key factor for elderly viewers to benefit from interactive television services. In: Cruz-Cunha, M.M., Varajão, J., Powell, P., Martinho, R. (eds.) CENTERIS 2011, Part III. CCIS, vol. 221, pp. 40–48. Springer, Heidelberg (2011)

8. Cooper, W.: The interactive television user experience so far. In: uxTV 2008, Silicon Valley, CA, USA, October 22-24, pp. 133–142 (2008)
9. Vlachos, P., Vrechopoulos, A.P., Doukidis, G.: Exploring consumer attitudes towards mobile music services. Int. J. Media Mgmt. 5(2), 138–148 (2003)
10. Rose, M.: Music in the home: Interfaces for music appliances. Pers. Tech. 4, 45–53 (2000)
11. Monk, A., Wright, P., Haber, J., Davenport, L.: Improving Your Human-Computer Interface: A Practical Technique. Prentice-Hall, New York (1993)

# A Human Factors Evaluation of the Spatial Gesture Interface for In-Vehicle Information Systems

Yishuo Liu, Zhihao Lu, and Pilsung Choe

Department of Industrial Engineering, Tsinghua University, Beijing, China
liuys@yahoo.cn, joeluk@163.com, pchoe@tsinghua.edu.cn

**Abstract.** The spatial gesture control system is an integrated control system, and a new hope for In-Vehicle Information Systems (IVISs). It needs lots of further research for practical use of the working systems in reality. Concept designs and evaluation standards can be investigated at the initial stage of the research. In this study, we established a usability evaluation model for the spatial gesture control system, and determinants for user satisfaction in driving have been investigated. Finally, some gesture interfaces were evaluated with a human factors experiment.

**Keywords:** spatial gesture control, IVISs, usability.

## 1 Introduction

Considering the complex computerized interior system of cars, driving is an integrated human-computer-interaction activity almost everyone gets involved every day. While driving a vehicle, the driver is performing varied tasks. These tasks can be classified into two main categories – the primary tasks and the secondary tasks.

While finishing the primary tasks depends largely on the hardware of a vehicle, the performance in finishing the secondary tasks leaves a lot work on the interface design. As the development of modern technology and entertainment, drivers have been gradually exposed to rows of buttons, knobs and touch-screens in order to control radios, CD players, GPS devices, lights, air conditioners, and even TV sets and Internet connections. All of these fancy features are joyful in using on one hand, while on the other hand, are stressful to use properly for drivers. Designers in the auto industry have been working on integrating many secondary controls into a single menu-based interactive system [1], with only the most frequent and important controls left as hard switches. The gesture control on capacitive screens has been proven a genuine success in the cell phone and tablet PC market, seems to be a revolutionary solution of the IVISs. However, it cannot be ignored that the touch-screen requires a certain level of visual attention and it might has negative impact on safety. Besides, a relative accurate position and movement of the finger(s) is often not easy in a bumpy context. Considering the requirements of visibility and reachability, a compromised position of the touch-screen may mean that the drivers must be held outstretched during operation, which might cause some level of muscle fatigue, and at the mean time, the position of the arm and fingers may obscure part of the screen [2]. Other solutions

P.L.P. Rau (Ed.): CCD/HCII 2013, Part I, LNCS 8023, pp. 313–322, 2013.
© Springer-Verlag Berlin Heidelberg 2013

such as voice recognition and steering wheel-mounted controls are often used to supplement IVISs [3], but they have "inherent limitations without significant safety benefits" [1].

The development of depth-sense camera technology in the recent years, however, shows a new possible solution by offering the detection of location and movements in 3D-form. Spatial gestures, or the 3D-form gestures, differ from conventional notion of gestures limited on a 2D interface. And we are able to develop interfaces marked with the spatial gesture control system to interact with the systems by using hand and body gestures in 3D-form.

In this study, as an exploration to this field, we built the evaluation model of the usability of this kind of system, and conducted a small-scale test on a subset of the parameters. Along with the experiments, we also aimed to collect some intuitive spatial gestures via interviewing the subjects.

## 2    Determinants of User Satisfaction in Driving

To assist the design and evaluation process of the system, we need to acquire a tool to predict the performance of the specific solution under real conditions of use. That requires a modeling process and technical standards for the definition of the performance. Card, Moran, and Newell proposed a model concerning the interaction between the task, user, and computer (represents for any interactive system) would enable designers to predict system performance [4]:

Model(Task, User, Computer)  →  System Performance

Since usability of a system is a part, or a kind, of the system performance, we specified the model for our study as:

Model(Task, User, Computer)  →  System Usability

According to this model, before predicting the system usability, the essence of the specific tasks, the users' requirements, and the features of the computer, need to be further understood.

**The Task**
Driving is a complex, multitasking activity [5], consisting of interactions between the driver, the car, and the environment [6]. As concluded in former sections, driving task includes two major categories – primary and secondary. Hedlund, Simpson, and Mayhew listed steering, accelerating, braking, speed choice, lane choice, maneuvering in traffic, navigation to destination, and scanning for hazards as the primary driving tasks [7]. Hedlund et al. also defined the secondary tasks as all other tasks performed by the driver that are not directly related to driving [7]. Secondary tasks are not essential to successful driving, but to enhance the driving experience while addressing the driver's needs [8]. Harvey et al. further concluded that the secondary tasks are to provide information, entertainment, and a means of communication, and enhance comfort to the driver [3].

**The User**

There are abundant technologies, software and hardware, supporting the in-vehicle interactions. Though the advance of technology itself boosts the driving experience, it cannot be neglected that the capabilities and fitness of the human operator, as a participant of the entire system, is a source of constraint. In some literatures, the focus has transited from technology, solely, to consideration of how to integrate the technology with the human element of the interaction [9]. And in the same literature, Walker et al. identified three main driver needs: safety, efficiency and enjoyment, which are considered important by automotive manufactures related to the information and communication technologies in vehicles [9].

The user safety is defined as the capacity to avoid risk or damage to the user in operation [10]. Based on a previous test, Klauer et al. estimated that distraction caused by secondary task interaction contributed to more than 22% of all crashes and near crashes, and the distraction caused by the interaction should also be noticed and considered during the design process [11]. The distraction of an IVIS should be measured. Efficiency is defined here as the capacity of reaching the destination in an acceptable time with acceptable expense. The efficiency of IVISs is defined by the degree of whose ability of presenting clear and useful information, successful and efficient input, and monitoring of the state, thus it is determined by the design of the system and its interface [3]. As transporting is not the only requirement for driving for many people, the enjoyment of driving can be a key issue in elevating the driving experience. Enjoyment comes from comfort and satisfaction, and can be measured subjectively by evaluating user's preferences [3]. Although enjoyment doesn't affect finishing the primary driving tasks directly, it does help the process by relieving the boredom and maintaining the driver's alertness [12].

**The System**

Automotive manufactures have attempted to integrate secondary driving controls into a single interactive, screen-based IVIS: touch screen as the direct way, and rotary controller as the indirect way [3]. Both solutions need screens to give the feedbacks and display the statuses of the systems. The major difference is the translation between the input from the user and the reaction of the device [13]. The indirect devices have this kind of translation, while the direct devices do not. Although touch screen has a significant advantage of direct devices - easy to learn, the inherent disadvantages caused by the position of the screen remain constraint of the user's experience. The spatial gesture control interface is a brand new realization of IVISs. By applying the spatial gesture control, it is hopeful to acquire the advantages of both solutions: easy to learn, and ergonomically optimal position of the screen.

And as a kind of information systems, van der Heijden stated that the nature of information systems could be classified into utilitarian and hedonic [14]. The former category provide external value via the interaction, and the latter one is to provide self-fulfilling and the internal satisfaction, rather than instrumental value to the user [15]. Other than the difference of the two categories, previous studies also found a significant relationship between perceived enjoyment and behavioral intention to use information systems [14]. In other words, the hedonic character of an information system may help increase the users' intention to perceive the external value by using it. This would be an advantage for the spatial gesture control system, if it were generally conceived that it is more fun than conditional control.

**Predicting the System Usability**

Six factors have been concluded in a previous review of literature relating to IVISs on how to measure and improve the usability of these devices: dual task environment, environmental conditions, range of users, training provision, frequency of use, and uptake [3]. Combined with features of the spatial gesture control system, the independent factors of the system usability are concluded and defined as bellow:

— Dual task environment: One of the most important factors relating to the usability of IVISs was that the interaction with this system was not the driver's main task [16], and most of the time is spent performing the primary driving tasks in vehicles [17,18].

— Environmental conditions: Unlike other information devices, the IVISs are designed to use in a variety of environmental conditions. Thus the impact of the environmental factors such as light levels, sound levels, road conditions, weather, and other road users, emergency levels (e.g., rushing to a hospital for severely injured passenger), need to be considered, tested, and measured.

— Range of users: The population of potential IVISs users is very diverse in physical, intellectual, and perceptual characteristics, thus requires special consideration in the design and evaluation [3]. Two of the most important and widely studied user characteristics are age and experience. Elder drivers and novice drivers are considered as the most vulnerable group in terms of balancing the dual task environment [19,20,21].

— Uptake: This factor describes how easy to learn and to use the system by initial users. The issue of uptake is strongly related to the user's subjective experience of the system, as this will determined whether the IVIS is with usability in driving [3].

— Weighs of functions: based on the original term "frequency of use" as listed by Harvey et al. [3], the weights of functions considered both the frequency of use and the perceived importance of each functions controlled by the system.

— Perceived controllability: As resembles the physical gaming devices, the spatial gesture control interface uses user's physical movement as input. Considering the motion-sense is the foundation of this system, the perceived controllability is proposed to represent the extent to which the user perceives the system is under his or her spatial gesture control.

— Perceived enjoyment: Since enjoyment is a key user requirement of the feature of the system, the perceived enjoyment is proposed representing the extent to which the user enjoys using the system. The possible muscle fatigue and any other impact of the body movement are to be considered in this issue.

— Perceived comfort: The spatial gesture interface requires the user controlling the system via physical movement in a defined pattern. Thus the characters of the movement, such as, the range, the direction and the trajectory of the movement will have impact on the physical and mental comfort the user perceived during the process.

All of the eight factors are intermediate points for further analysis. The analysis could work as an instructive segmentation of finding qualitative measurable independent variables of the system usability.

# 3    Case Study: An Experiment

Lehto, Mark, and Jim Buck defined that system usability includes three aspects: efficiency, effectiveness, and satisfaction [22]. As a subset of usability, the satisfaction was our primary focus in this study. To evaluate the satisfaction via an indoor test, we arbitrarily selected three of the eight factors we mentioned above to design the experiment: perceived controllability, perceived enjoyment, and perceived comfort. The following experiment was designed to reveal the relationship between these three factors and the gesture.

### Subjects
We invited 9 subjects for the test, aged from 21 to 53, and consisted of 6 male and 3 female. All of the subjects have driving license. Their driving frequency and experience are varied.

### Variables: Independent and Dependent Variables
Perceived controllability, perceived enjoyment and perceived comfort were chosen as the dependent variables. Since this test was to study the relationship of the spatial gestures and users' satisfaction, the independent variables should be able to define the gestures. Thus, three factors were defined as the independent variables:

— Gesture Direction: The trajectory of a spatial gesture can be a curve, a spatial quadrilateral, etc. While a straight line is the simplest one, thus the direction of "drawing" the line might have impact in to the dependent variables. The variable had two levels (horizontal, vertical) in the experiment.
— Gesture Part: The body movement appears in various scale. To make an action to the system, the user may move fingers, wrist, elbow and shoulder. Thus the movement can be scaled by the largest joint it takes, such as, wrist-scale, and elbow-scale. We choose two levels (wrist, elbow) in our experiment.
— Task: The functions of IVIS can be sorted into several classes, while there are two basic types: the control of ON/OFF, and of UP/DOWN. The first class is to change between two statuses; the second one is to adjust among several discrete statuses (i.e. switching radio) or to control a continuous variable (i.e. the volume of the radio). In this test, we choose the control of the doom light and of the radio volume as two levels of this factor.

Therefore, the test was designed to study the impact of the three independent variables to the three dependent variables.

**Experimental Design: $2^3$.** Full-Factorial, Within Subject Design
Each of the independent variables were given two status. The 2x2x2 factorial design was used for the experiment as shown in Fig. 1. In addition, a within-subject design was used for better comparisons with the eight treatments. That is, each subject tried all of 8 treatments. The trial order was randomized to minimize learning effects.

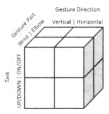

**Fig. 1.** The $2^3$ Full-Factorial Design

**Apparatus**

*Wizard of Oz Approach.* As an integrated IVIS, it requires immediate feedback from the system and the specific design and development remain variable in several aspects, thus making it difficult and inefficient to use functional prototype in a real vehicle. For this reason, we decided to conduct the experiment with a Wizard of OZ (WOz) approach, which was first used by Gould et al. [23]. We replaced the central computer with a human operator, observed the users and controlled the related functions and feedbacks in the prototype with a computer.

The Wizard of Oz method has been used for a variety of intentions in HCI literature. Dahlbäck et al. used this method to design and collect language corpora in speech-based systems [24]. Höysniemi et al. further developed the idea of using WOz method in collecting corpora, but based on the children's body language – their intuitive gestures in an interactive physical video game [25].

Although the Wizard of Oz approach is widely reported in HCI literature, the papers contain little ethical discussion related to the method [25]. We decided to specify our reasons for the application of the WOz method as follow,

— As to summarize an instruction to the further development of the final system, we need to use a prototype that can present the features, and at the same time feasible for rapid improvement. The key point is the ability to change the functions without laborious and time-consuming coding and debugging during the study.

— Using a wizard, combined with adequate training prior to the test to ensure the experience matching our design. The responsiveness and the successful recognition rate were important for this system.

— The method, in the process, can also help us gather valuable information on the natural and intuitive body language in the specific context. There is no existing research on the body language users prefer in a vehicular context, focusing on finishing the secondary tasks on IVISs.

Previous researches applying WOz also showed other benefits. As to the possible latency brings by a human operator, Höysniemi et al. stated in their paper that they were "surprised how well the wizard was able to adapt to the children's movements and rapid gesture changes" [25] because the wizard was able to anticipate.

*Experiment Setup.* The experiment was held in a lab with LCD to display instructions and simulated scene, as shown in Fig. 2.

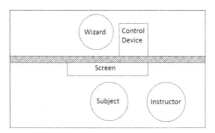

**Fig. 2.** Experiment Setup

Our experiment, following the WOz approach, involved a wizard, a subject, and an instructor. The wizard simulated as an integrated program, controlled the devices via a computer, observed the user's command, reacted to the user's actions, and took notes during the interviews. The instructor introduced the tasks, guided the testing and interviewed the user during and after the tests.

The experiment was conducted in two stages. After a brief introduction of the experiment, each subject was first given two tasks in the first stage: turn on and off the doom light, and turn up and down the volume of in-vehicle radio player. The subjects were required to finish each task without any instruction in order to record the natural and intuitive gestures. After a short interview and a break, came the second stage: Eight tasks were shown successively with their instructions of the specific spatial gesture we defined. After each task, the subject scored (1 to 7) the treatment and was interviewed after.

## 4     Results and Analysis

Eight treatments was applied to nine subjects, thus we had 72 data points. A summary of the algebra average is shown in Table 1.

After using ANOVA to analyze the interaction of the three factors, several conclusions were drawn as below.

First, for the interaction of reaction part and direction, treatments with wrist-scale movements and in the vertical direction had high score in all of the three criteria, while the combination of elbow-scale and horizontal gesture got the lowest score. Second, for the interaction of reaction direction and task, we found that there existed a preference of controlling the doom light with vertical movement and a horizontal one for the volume adjusting. Third, for the interaction of reaction part and task, all of the combinations got medium or high scores in all of the three criteria, except for the combination of controlling volume with arm, which was scored low in all the three.

**Table 1.** Average Score of each Treatment

| Treatment | Perceived Enjoyment | Perceived Controllability | Perceived Comfort | Sum |
|---|---|---|---|---|
| 1 | 4.78 | 5.22 | 5.22 | 15.22 |
| 2 | 5.11 | 5.33 | 5.44 | 15.89 |
| 3 | 4.89 | 5.33 | 5.33 | 15.56 |
| 4 | 4.89 | 5.44 | 5.56 | 15.89 |
| 5 | 5.33 | 5.67 | 5.67 | 16.67 |
| 6 | 5.22 | 5.11 | 4.78 | 15.11 |
| 7 | 5.78 | 6.11 | 5.89 | 17.78 |
| 8 | 5.78 | 6.00 | 6.00 | 17.78 |

Other than the pair interaction, we analyzed the means and variance of each treatment's impact on the three factors as shown in Fig. 3.

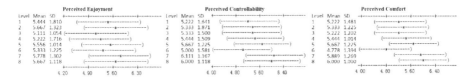

**Fig. 3.** Mean and Variance of the three Factors

The difference was not significant in perceived enjoyment. All of the nine subjects expressed their preference of the spatial gesture interface to the existing buttons and knobs. But treatment 6 (adjusting the volume with arm waving up/down) was significantly inferior to others in aspects of perceived controllability and perceived comfort. Subjects complained that this treatment was against their intuition in a degree, and the range of this function was too large considering the frequency. The difference among other treatments were not significant enough. But the situation might change for on-road test, concerning the frequency of use and the dual task environment.

Combined with the interview, we found that there were other preferences of performing a spatial gesture:

— Near the object: users preferred performing near to the object they were controlling, i.e. perform a gesture near the doom light to turn it on or off, near the radio to adjust the volume.
— Resemble the existing movement: during the first stage of the test and the interview after, subjects presented significant intention of using gestures that resemble the current movement. For example, some subjects preferred to adjust the volume by turning their hand clockwise/anti-clockwise as controlling with an invisible knob.
— Smaller the better: there is a strong preference of smaller scale gesture, especially for frequent functions, such as adjusting volume and choosing songs.

These preferences are important instructions in designing the standard set of controlling gestures in the future.

# 5    Discussion and Conclusions

In this study, we modeled the evaluation of the spatial gesture control interface, revealed the relationship of the gesture and user satisfaction via an experiment, and collected the intuitive gestures of two in-vehicle functions in the interview. However, there were several limitations of our study. First, we listed eight intermediate points for the evaluation of the spatial gesture interface, and three measurable independent variables of a subset of user satisfaction, but the entire group of quantitative measurable variables needs to be further defined and specified, as well as the interaction of the variables and the eight points. Second, we used a WOz approach in this study, but we believe a full-scale functional prototype would be better for further evaluation of this interface, considering the factors such as, dual task environment and environmental conditions. Third, a set of standard spatial gestures needs to be defined to make the interface fully-functional, and thus larger scale interview and experiments are in need. Although there still remains a lot for further research, the spatial gesture interface is a promising advance in the intersection of HCI and automobile research, as well as the future of IVIS.

# References

1. Pickering, C.A., Burnham, K.J., Richardson, M.J.: A review of automotive human machine interface technologies and techniques to reduce driver distraction. In: 2007 2nd Institution of Engineering and Technology International Conference on System Safety, IET (2007)
2. Taveira, A.D., Choi, S.D.: Review study of computer input devices and older users. Intl. Journal of Human–Computer Interaction 25(5), 455–474 (2009)
3. Harvey, C., et al.: In-Vehicle Information System to Meet the Needs of Drivers (2011)
4. Card, S.K., Moran, T.P., Newell, A. (eds.): The psychology of human-computer interaction. CRC (1986)
5. Lee, J.D., Young, K.L., Regan, M.A.: Defining driver distraction (2009)
6. Rakotonirainy, A., Tay, R.: In-vehicle ambient intelligent transport systems (i-vaits): Towards an integrated research. In: Proceedings of the 7th International IEEE Conference on Intelligent Transportation Systems, pp. 648–651. IEEE (2004)
7. Hedlund, J., Simpson, H., Mayhew, D.: Summary of proceedings and recommendations. In: International Conference of Distracted Driving (2006)
8. Engström, J., et al.: Meeting the challenges of future automotive HMI design: an overview of the AIDE integrated project. In: 4th European Congress on Intelligent Transportation Systems and Services, Budapest, Hungary (2004)
9. Walker, G.H., Stanton, N.A., Young, M.S.: Hierarchical task analysis of driving: A new research tool. Contemporary Ergonomics, 435–440 (2001)
10. Alonso-Ríos, D., et al.: Usability: a critical analysis and a taxonomy. International Journal of Human-Computer Interaction 26(1), 53–74 (2009)
11. Klauer, S.G., Dingus, T.A., Neale, V.L., Sudweeks, J., Ramsey, D.J.: The impact of driver inattention on near-crash/crash risk: An analysis using the 100-car naturalistic driving study data. No. HS-810 594 (2006)

12. Bayly, M., Young, K.L., Regan, M.A.: 12 Sources of Distraction inside the Vehicle and Their Effects on Driving Performance. Driver Distraction: Theory, Effects, and Mitigation 191 (2008)

13. Dul, J., Weerdmeester, B.: Ergonomics for beginners: a quick reference guide. CRC (2008)

14. Van der Heijden, H.: User acceptance of hedonic information systems. MIS Quarterly, 695–704 (2004)

15. Lin, H.-H., Wang, Y.-S., Chou, C.-H.: Hedonic and utilitarian motivations for physical game systems use behavior. International Journal of Human-Computer Interaction 28(7), 445–455 (2012)

16. Fastrez, P., Haué, J.-B.: Designing and evaluating driver support systems with the user in mind. International Journal of Human-Computer Studies 66(3), 125–131 (2008)

17. Ji, Y.G., Jin, B.S.: Development of the conceptual prototype for haptic interface on the telematics system. International Journal of Human-Computer Interaction 26(1), 22–52 (2009)

18. Stanton, N.A., Young, M.S.: Vehicle automation and driving performance. Ergonomics 41(7), 1014–1028 (1998)

19. Baldwin, C.L.: Designing in-vehicle technologies for older drivers: Application of sensory-cognitive interaction theory. Theoretical Issues in Ergonomics Science 3(4), 307–329 (2002)

20. Herriotts, P.: Identification of vehicle design requirements for older drivers. Applied Ergonomics 36(3), 255–262 (2005)

21. Stevens, A., et al.: Design guidelines for safety of in-vehicle information systems. TRL Limited (2002)

22. Lehto, M.R., Buck, J.: Introduction to human factors and ergonomics for engineers. CRC (2007)

23. Gould, J.D., Conti, J., Hovanyecz, T.: Composing letters with a simulated listening typewriter. Communications of the ACM 26(4), 295–308 (1983)

24. Dahlbäck, N., Jönsson, A., Ahrenberg, L.: Wizard of Oz studies—why and how. Knowledge-based Systems 6(4), 258–266 (1993)

25. Hoysniemi, J., Hamalainen, P., Turkki, L.: Wizard of Oz prototyping of computer vision based action games for children. In: Interaction Design And Children: Proceeding of the 2004 Conference on Interaction Design and Children: Building a Community, vol. 1(03) (2004)

26. Harvey, C., et al.: Context of use as a factor in determining the usability of in-vehicle devices. Theoretical Issues in Ergonomics Science 12(4), 318–338 (2011)

# Characteristics of UI English:
# From Non-native's Viewpoint

Ryutaro Nishino and Kayoko Nohara

Tokyo Institute of Technology, Tokyo, Japan
ryutaro@nishinos.com

**Abstract.** Multicultural aspects of user interfaces (UIs) have been studied for years. However, the characteristics of UI English from the viewpoint of non-native speakers of English have not been discussed widely. This study compares a UI English corpus with general English corpora using the word list coverage method and the lexical diversity method. It finds that UI English contains more words that are above introductory level but that it is less diverse than general English. Therefore, for non-natives to use software smoothly, they need to learn a relatively limited number of words that frequently appear in UIs.

**Keywords:** English, non-native, user interface, UI.

## 1 Introduction

Many software products have been developed by US-based companies and their user interfaces (UIs) are usually written in English. The Business Software Alliance says, "An estimated 65% of the PC software units in service worldwide in 2008 were from US-based companies." [1] More recently, distributing software globally through the Internet, such as web or smartphone applications, is becoming easier and easier.

English UIs are often translated and localized for global use. The importance of localization has been pointed out for years to market software products globally [2, 3]. Although some software applications are translated into users' languages, others are not due to cost or time constraints. As a result, many non-natives have a chance to use UIs written in English.

The first objective of this study is to clarify the characteristics of English currently used in UIs, from the viewpoint of how difficult the English is for non-natives. We see the difficulty from two points in this paper: 1) the coverage of a text by English word lists for learners and 2) the lexical or vocabulary diversity in a text. Clarifying the characteristics of UI English will eventually lead to better UIs, especially for non-natives. The second objective is to find characteristic words used in UIs. By learning these words, non-natives will be able to use software more comfortably. The second objective is rather a preliminary study for future work.

P.L.P. Rau (Ed.): CCD/HCII 2013, Part I, LNCS 8023, pp. 323–332, 2013.
© Springer-Verlag Berlin Heidelberg 2013

## 2     Related Research

### 2.1     Studies of UI from Multicultural and Non-natives Perspectives

UIs have been studied from the multicultural perspective for years by different researchers [4-6]. However, UIs have not been discussed widely from the perspective of non-native speakers of English, while some researchers pointed out the importance in remarks such as "The user interface must be designed and written so that it is understandable by a user who speaks English as a second language." [7]

Because large software companies now recognize the importance of writing English that is understandable for non-native users [8-10], scientific studies need to be done to better understand the characteristics of UI English from the viewpoint of non-native speakers of English, in addition to the multicultural perspective.

### 2.2     English Word Lists for Learners

One of the methods to describe the characteristics of the vocabulary in an English text is to compare it with word lists used by learners of English. By measuring how many percentage of a vocabulary is covered by word lists, one can guess how difficult the text is for learners. Note, however, that this method checks the vocabulary knowledge only, and other kinds of abilities such as listening or speaking will not evaluated.

Examples of the frequently used word lists are General Service List (GSL) [11] and Academic Word List (AWL) [12]. The GSL was developed from a corpus largely based on the basis of frequency [13]. It includes a total of 2,000 word families[1] with two different levels, 1,000 for each. The AWL includes 570 word families that are not in the GSL and that are frequently used in academic texts. The GSL and AWL have been used in combination to see the coverage of text in fields such as business [14] or public health [15]. Another example of word lists is the list developed by Paul Nation from the British National Corpus (BNC) [16]. This BNC list is in the order of frequency and has 14 levels, 1,000 word families for each.

Although not being a word list like ones explained above, the English Vocabulary Profile (EVP) is a vocabulary database with six proficiency levels based on the Common European Framework of Reference [17]. The levels are Basic User (A1 and A2), Independent User (B1 and B2), and Proficient User (C1 and C2).

### 2.3     Lexical Diversity

To find the characteristics of a text, a measure called lexical diversity is often used. Lexical diversity shows how many different words are used in an entire text.

---

[1]  A word family is a set of related words. For example, the headword "accept" has "acceptability," "acceptable," "unacceptable," "acceptance," "accepted," "accepting," and "accepts" as family members.

The oldest and most frequently used measure is type-token[2] ratio (TTR) [18]. The higher the TTR is, the more different words are used in a text. The problem in TTR is the dependence on text length [19]. As a text becomes longer, its TTR decreases because the same types are used repeatedly. To overcome this problem, other methods, such as Guiraud's index [20] or Herdan's index [21], have been proposed. However, such measures in practice depend on their text length [19], too. As a result, no index can reliably measure the lexical diversity between texts with different sizes. As a practical solution, Baayen [22] proposes to compare the number of types across texts with the same text sizes. In a recent study, different kinds of measures (TTR, Guiraud, Herdan, Uber, Maas, vocd-D, HD-D) are used in combination [18].

### 2.4    Keyword Extraction

There are several methods to extract terms specially used in a certain corpus. In recent years, comparing the numbers of appearance between a target corpus and a reference corpus is often used. In comparing corpora, different statistics are used to determine whether a certain word is specially used in a certain field.

There have been discussions of which statistic is valid or effective [23, 24]. Chujo and Utiyama [25] compare nine statistics for extracting keywords in the applied science field and claim that different statistics are effective to extract terms for learners with different proficiency levels. For example, the log-likelihood ratio (LLR) is effective for intermediate-level.

## 3    Methods

### 3.1    Preparing Corpora

**Target Corpus.** The target corpus is compiled from English used in UIs such as buttons or messages. We collected text from different genres of software that are well known and have many users so that the corpus represents the English actually seen and read by users. The genres of software are mobile, productivity, communication, and entertainment. We do not adjust the text size of each genre. Table 2 details the genre, name, and size. The text of Android applications is from Android Git repository [26] and the other text is from the Microsoft Language Portal [27].

Software text includes characters that should be removed or modified, such as HTML tags or variable placeholders. Because the types of such characters differ from software to software, we cleaned the files according to the basic policy: "Retain characters that are actually shown to users." Table 1 shows examples of what we did for the cleanup.

---

[2]    Tokens are the total number of words in a text. Types are the number of unique words. In the sentence "I ate an apple that I bought yesterday", for instance, tokens are eight and types are seven (because "I" appears twice). The TTR in this case is $7/8 = 0.875$ (87.5%).

**Table 1.** Modification of special characters in software

| Type of character | Example | Modification |
|---|---|---|
| Variable placeholder | %d,      %s1, {0} | Replaced with <variablehere> to indicate that something is displayed at runtime. |
| Metacharacter | /u2026,  ¥n | Removed, or replaced with the character it represents. |
| HTML tag | <b></b>, <br/> | Removed, or replaced with the character it represents. |
| Keyboard shortcut | Hi&de | Removed unneeded character ("&" is removed in the example). |
| Words without space | %sAuthor | Added a space to make them an individual word ("%s Author" in the example). |

We separately counted the tags that represent variable placeholders (i.e., <varablehere>) into the total number of words because we do not know if the word or sentence put here is known or unknown to the user until the software is actually executed. The final numbers of words after removal or replacement are in Table 2.

**Table 2.** Software in the UI corpus

| Genre | Application name | Size (number of words) |
|---|---|---|
| Mobile | Android applications[3] | 23,552 |
| Productivity | Microsoft Word 2007 SP2 | 80,304 |
| Productivity | Microsoft Excel 2007 SP2 | 109,821 |
| Communication | Internet Explorer 8 | 147,814 |
| Communication | Hotmail | 27,266 |
| Entertainment | Windows Media Player 10 | 18,762 |
| | | 407,519 |

**Reference Corpus.** We used the Brown Corpus, the Manually Annotated Sub-Corpus (MASC) of Open American National Corpus (OANC), and the CNN Tech news corpus as reference corpora. The Brown Corpus is an American English corpus with about 1 million words from the prose printed in the U.S. during the year 1961 [28]. The MASC is a balanced subset of 500,000 words of written and spoken text from OANC [29]. The CNN Tech news corpus was compiled by the authors from the CNN news articles published in 2011 and categorized under "Tech" [30]. The CNN Tech

---

[3]  Android applications: AccountsAndSyncSettings, AlarmClock, BasicSmsReceiver, Bluetooth, Browser, Calculator, Calendar, Camera, CellBroadcastReceiver, CertInstaller, Contacts, DeskClock, Email, Exchange, Gallery, Gallery2, Gallery3D, GlobalSearch, GoogleSearch, HTMLViewer, IM, KeyChain, Launcher, Launcher2, LegacyCamera, Mms, Music, MusicFX, Nfc, PackageInstaller, Phone, Protips, QuickSearchBox, Settings, SoundRecorder, SpareParts, SpeechRecorder, Stk, Tag, VideoEditor, VoiceDialer.

corpus has over 600,000 words, and many of the articles are IT-related topics including video games or consumer electronics, but excluding energy, environment, or space technologies. The reason why we use this corpus is to see whether or not IT-related terms, which are very often found in the UI corpus, affect the characteristics of the text. Thus, the first two corpora, Brown and MASC, are general American English corpus, and the last one, CNN Tech, is a corpus of a specific field.

## 3.2    Determining the Difficulty by Two Criteria

As stated in the introduction section, we see the difficulty for non-natives from two points: 1) the coverage by word lists and 2) the lexical diversity.

**Coverage by Word Lists.** We adopted the GSL+AWL and the BNC list by Nation to measure how much of a text is covered by the lists to estimate the vocabulary level. The GSL has two levels (Level 1 and 2) and the AWL is the extension of GSL (i.e., Level 3). The BNC list has 14 levels. We used these lists to check how much percentage of tokens in a corpus is covered by the lists. One can guess that the lower the coverage is, the more difficult the text is for non-natives because they need remember more words. We applied this method to different kinds of corpora to compare the relative levels of texts. The important assumption here is that non-natives learn vocabulary in the order of frequency (frequently-used words are learned first). To calculate the coverage, we used a software tool called AntWordProfiler [31].

**Lexical Diversity.** Because there is not a measure with established reputation, we here use the Guiraud's index (R) and the Herdan's index (C):

$$R = \frac{Types}{\sqrt{Tokens}} \tag{1}$$

$$C = \frac{\log_e Types}{\log_e Tokens} \tag{2}$$

We need to be careful that these indices depend on the text length (i.e., tokens). In addition to this, we compare texts after adjusting their sizes, as Baayen suggested [22]. We adjust the text sizes to the shortest one. The approximate sizes of the corpora we use are: the UI corpus: 400k, Brown: 1million, MASC: 500k, and CNN Tech: 630k. So, we cut the sizes to that of the UI corpus. First, we divide all corpora into the groups of 50k words. For instance, the UI corpus is divided into 8 groups (400k / 50k = 8). The reminder is simply discarded. Likewise, Brown is divided into 20 groups, MASC 10 groups, and CNN Tech 12 groups. And then, we randomly choose 8 groups from each of them to make corpora with 400k tokens.

We apply three methods (Guiraud, Herdan, and same-size comparison) to four corpora to compare their lexical diversity. The R software [32] and its package languageR [33] are used to count types and tokens. Before counting, we erased punctuation marks in the corpora. This is to avoid a word followed by such marks (e.g., "corpora.") to be recognized as one word. The following marks are replaced with a space:

.    ,    "    '    ?    !    (    )    [    ]    --

### 3.3    Finding Characteristic Words

We use the log-likelihood ratio (LLR) statistic to identify characteristic words used in the UI corpus. For a reference corpus, we combine the Brown and MASC corpora, which are general American English corpora, to make them an approximately 1.5 million-word corpus. The AntConc version 3.3.5 [34] is used to calculate LLR. Default settings are used, but a lemma list created by Yasumasa Someya (available from the AntConc website) is used with some modifications by the authors such as adding new words (e.g., app, email, etc.). No part-of-speech (POS) information is used.

After extracting words based on the LLR statistic, we manually pick up action-related words (mainly verbs) and create a list of top 10 words (due to the limitation of pages of this paper). The reason why we focus on action-related words here is that they describe human-computer interactions and are valuable compared to nouns that include many technology terms, which would disappear when new technologies appear. And then, we identify the proficiency levels for each word by using the GSL/AWL, the BNC list, and the English Vocabulary Profile (EVP).

## 4    Results

### 4.1    Coverage by Word Lists

Table 3 shows the coverage of the corpora by the GSL 1, GSL 2, AWL, variables (such as "%d" or "{0}"), and their total in percentage.

**Table 3.** Coverage by GSL+AWL (%)

|  | GSL 1 | GSL 2 | AWL | Variables | Total |
|---|---|---|---|---|---|
| UI corpus | **61.1** | 6.5 | **13.6** | 1.4 | 82.7 |
| Brown | 76.5 | 5.7 | 4.7 | - | 86.9 |
| MASC | 74.4 | 5.4 | 4.8 | - | 84.6 |
| CNN Tech | 72.5 | 5.5 | 6.0 | - | 84.0 |

Table 4 shows the coverage of the corpora by the different levels of the BNC list, variables, and their total in percentage. Each level has 1,000 word families.

**Table 4.** Coverage by BNC list (%)

|  | BNC 1 | BNC 2 | BNC 3 | BNC 4 | BNC 5 | BNC 6-14 | Variables | Total |
|---|---|---|---|---|---|---|---|---|
| UI corpus | **67.5** | **12.0** | **5.0** | **3.8** | 1.0 | 3.9 | 1.4 | 94.6 |
| Brown | 77.0 | 8.3 | 3.2 | 2.4 | 1.4 | 3.5 | - | 95.7 |
| MASC | 76.0 | 7.7 | 2.6 | 2.3 | 1.2 | 3.4 | - | 93.3 |
| CNN Tech | 75.3 | 8.6 | 2.8 | 2.6 | 0.9 | 3.2 | - | 93.3 |

## 4.2    Lexical Diversity

Table 5 shows the lexical diversity of the corpora using Guiraud and Herdan indices.

**Table 5.** Lexical diversity using Guiraud and Herdan indices

|            | Types   | Tokens      | Guiraud | Herdan |
|------------|---------|-------------|---------|--------|
| UI corpus  | 11,651  | 409,826[4]  | **18.20** | **0.72** |
| Brown      | 47,059  | 1,025,536   | 46.47   | 0.78   |
| MASC       | 35,537  | 500,227     | 50.25   | 0.80   |
| CNN Tech   | 28,904  | 635,315     | 36.26   | 0.77   |

Table 6 shows the lexical diversity of the corpora with the same text size.

**Table 6.** Lexical diversity using fixed text sizes

|            | Types   | Tokens   | Type-token ratio (%) |
|------------|---------|----------|----------------------|
| UI corpus  | 11,395  | 400,000  | **2.85**             |
| Brown      | 28,737  | 400,000  | 7.18                 |
| MASC       | 30,916  | 400,000  | 7.73                 |
| CNN Tech   | 22,932  | 400,000  | 5.73                 |

## 4.3    Characteristic Words

Table 7 lists the top 10 action-related words that are characteristic in the UI corpus compared with the general English corpus (Brown+MASC). The words are listed alphabetically with the proficiency levels on the word lists, and the LLR statistic.

**Table 7.** Top 10 characteristic action-related words

|           | GSL/AWL | BNC  | EVP       | LLR    |
|-----------|---------|------|-----------|--------|
| add       | 1       | 1    | A2        | 3409.8 |
| allow     | 1       | 1    | B1 or C1  | 3059.1 |
| change    | 1       | 1    | A2        | 3291.6 |
| click     | none    | 3    | A2        | 4939.9 |
| configure | none    | 8    | none      | 3180.9 |
| disable   | none    | none | none      | 4695.2 |
| enable    | 3       | 2    | B2        | 4263.2 |
| select    | 3       | 2    | B1        | 5072.1 |
| set       | 1       | 1    | B1 or B2  | 7339.2 |
| use       | 1       | 1    | A1        | 4508.1 |

---

[4]  The total number is slightly different from the one in Table 2 because different tools are used. Here we used languageR, which counts numbers such as "15.8" or "8000."

## 5     Discussion

As Table 3 shows, the coverage of the UI corpus by the GSL 1 (level 1) is as low as 61.1%, while other corpora are all above 70%. This means that non-natives with introductory vocabulary knowledge would have difficulty in reading UIs written in English compared with other types of English. The coverage by the GSL 2 (level 2) is almost at the same level, but the coverage by the AWL (level 3) is higher with a wide difference. In short, the UI corpus tends to use higher-level words. The overall coverage (GSL+AWL) either including or excluding variables is close. In Table 4, like the result of GSL+AWL, the coverage of BNC level 1 for the UI corpus is less than 70%, which is lower than other corpora. However, the coverage of level 2 to 4 is higher than others. This tells that the UI corpus includes less introductory level words and more intermediate level words. The overall coverage does not differ much.

As listed in Table 5, the UI corpus shows the least number in both Guiraud and Herdan indices compared with other corpora. This means that the UI corpus has the least diversity. Table 6 illustrates that the lexical diversity of the UI corpus is the least even after adjusting the corpus sizes. Therefore, in all three measures, the UI corpus has the least lexical diversity.

We included the CNN Tech corpus to see if IT-related words affect the results. The coverage and diversity results indicate that the CNN Tech is closer to general English than to UI English, and IT-related words do not affect the characteristic of the text.

When we see Table 7, we successfully pick up characteristic words in the UI corpus. Some words are closely related to software operations (click, configure, etc.), and other words look rather general (add, allow, change, etc.) but are used more frequently in UI English than in general English. We would like to further this study in the future by adding POS information or by extending to top 100, for instance.

## 6     Conclusion

From the results of the coverage by word lists and the lexical diversity, we conclude that UI English contains more words that are above introductory level but that it is less diverse than general English. Therefore, for non-natives to use software smoothly, they need to learn a relatively limited number of words that frequently appear in UIs, like the ones shown in the result of characteristic words. However, frequently appearing words include advanced level words such as "configure." For non-natives to use software comfortably, developers may avoid using these words in UIs, but at the same time, such words should be taught in English education because a natural language or existing UIs do not change easily in a short period of time.

**Acknowledgements.** This research report has made use of the English Vocabulary Profile. This resource is based on extensive research using the Cambridge Learner Corpus and is part of the English Profile program which aims to provide evidence about language use that helps to produce better language teaching materials. See http://www.englishprofile.org for more information.

# References

1. The Business Software Alliance: Free & Fair Trade, `http://www.bsa.org/country/PublicPolicy/global-trade/fair-trade.aspx` (accessed on February 11, 2013)
2. del Galdo, E.: Culture and Design. In: del Galdo, E., Nielsen, J. (eds.) International User Interfaces, pp. 74–87. Wiley Computer Publishing, John Wiley & Sons (1996)
3. Esselink, B.: A Practical Guide to Localization. Benjamins, John Publishing Company (2000)
4. Russo, P., Boor, S.: How Fluent is Your Interface?: Designing for International Users. In: Proceedings of the SIGCHI Conference on Human Factors in Computing Systems - CHI 1993, pp. 342–347. ACM Press, New York (1993)
5. Barber, W., Badre, A.: Culturability: The merging of culture and usability. In: Proceedings of the 4th Conference on Human Factors and the Web, pp. 1–14 (1998)
6. Marcus, A., Gould, E.W.: Crosscurrents: cultural dimensions and global Web user-interface design. Interactions 7, 32–46 (2000)
7. Nielsen, J., del Galdo, E., Sprung, R., Sukaviriya, P.: Designing for international use (panel). In: Nielsen, J. (ed.) Proceedings of the SIGCHI Conference on Human Factors in Computing Systems, pp. 291–294. ACM, New York (1990)
8. Apple Inc.: Apple Publications Style Guide, `https://developer.apple.com/library/mac/documentation/UserExperience/Conceptual/APStyleGuide/APSG_2009.pdf` (accessed on February 24, 2013)
9. Microsoft Corporation: Microsoft Manual of Style 4th edn. Microsoft Press, Redmond (2012)
10. DeRespinis, F., Hayward, P., Jenkins, J., Laird, A., McDonald, L., Radziski, E.: The IBM Style Guide: Conventions for Writers and Editors. IBM Press, Upper Saddle River (2011)
11. West, M.: A general service list of English words, with semantic frequencies and a supplementary word-list for the writing of popular science and technology. Longman, London (1953)
12. Coxhead, A.: A New Academic Word List. TESOL Quarterly 34, 213–238 (2000)
13. Nation, P.: A study of the most frequent word families in the British National Corpus. In: Bogaards, P., Laufer, B. (eds.) Vocabulary in a Second Language: Selection, Acquisition, and Testing, pp. 3–13. John Benjamins Publishing Company, Amsterdam (2004)
14. Konstantakis, N.: Creating a business word list for teaching Business English. Elia 7, 79–102 (2007)
15. Millar, N., Budgell, B.S.: The language of public health—a corpus-based analysis. Journal of Public Health 16, 369–374 (2008)
16. Nation, P.: How Large a Vocabulary is Needed For Reading and Listening? Canadian Modern Language Review 63, 59–82 (2006)
17. English Profile, `http://www.englishprofile.org/`
18. Šišková, Z.: Lexical Richness in EFL Students' Narratives. Language Studies Working Papers 4, 26–36 (2012)
19. Tweedie, F., Baayen, R.H.: How Variable a Constant be? Measures of Lexical Richness in Perspective. Computers and the Humanities 32, 323–352 (1998)
20. Guiraud, P.: Les caractères statistiques du vocabulaire: essai de méthodologie. Presses Universitaires de France, Paris (1954)
21. Herdan, G.: Type-token mathematics: a textbook of mathematical linguistics. Mouton & Co., The Hague (1960)

22. Baayen, R.H.: Analyzing Linguistic Data: A Practical Introduction to Statistics using R. Cambridge University Press (2008)
23. Dunning, T.: Accurate methods for the statistics of surprise and coincidence. Computational Linguistics 19, 61–74 (1993)
24. Kilgarriff, A.: Comparing corpora. International Journal of Corpus Linguistics 6, 97–133 (2001)
25. Chujo, K., Utiyama, M.: Selecting level-specific BNC applied science vocabulary using statistical measures. In: Selected Papers from the Fourteenth International Symposium on English Teaching, pp. 195–202 (2005)
26. Android Git repositories, https://android.googlesource.com/ (accessed on July 31, 2012)
27. Microsoft Language Portal, http://www.microsoft.com/Language/en-US/Translations.aspx (accessed on August 01, 2012).
28. Francis, W.N., Kučera, H.: Manual of Information to Accompany A Standard Corpus of Present-Day Edited American English, for use with Digital Computers (1979), http://icame.uib.no/brown/bcm.html (accessed on January 14, 2013)
29. Ide, N., Fellbaum, C., Baker, C., Passonneau, R.: The manually annotated sub-corpus: a community resource for and by the people. In: Proceedings of the ACL 2010 Conference Short Papers, pp. 68–73. Association for Computational Linguistics, Stroudsburg (2010)
30. Tech category of CNN.com, http://edition.cnn.com/TECH/ (accessed on February 24, 2013)
31. Anthony, L.: AntWordProfiler (Version 1.3.1) (Computer Software) (2012), http://www.antlab.sci.waseda.ac.jp/
32. The R Project for Statistical Computing, http://www.r-project.org/
33. Baayen, R.H.: languageR (Computer Program) (2011), http://cran.r-project.org/web/packages/languageR/
34. Anthony, L.: AntConc (Version 3.3.5) (Computer Software) (2012), http://www.antlab.sci.waseda.ac.jp/

# The Effects of Age, Viewing Distance
# and Font Type on the Legibility of Chinese Characters

Linghua Ran[1,*], Xin Zhang[1], Xiaoyuan Ren[2], and Huimin Hu[1]

[1] China National Institute of Standardization, Zhichun Road, 4,
Haidian District, Beijing 100088, China
[2] Shandong Normal University, Wenhua East Road, Jinan, Shan
Dong Province, 250014, China
ranlh@cnis.gov.cn

**Abstract.** This study evaluated the effects of age (30s and 55s), viewing distance (50 cm, 80 cm), font type (Lanting in simple, Lanting in complex, Yahei in simple, Yahei in complex) on the legibility of Chinese characters by using the two legibility measures (minimum character size for 100% correctness and minimum character size for the least comfort). Twenty subjects in each age group read the 12 word groups (two characters in each word group, character size varied from 4.5 pt to 18 pt) presented on a paper. Subjects subjectively rated the reading legibility of the word groups on a 3-point scale (1- indistinct, 2- distinct but need cost a little attention, 3- very distinct). According to the ANOVA procedure, age and viewing distance significantly affected the two dependent variables ($p < 0.05$). The younger group could see character sizes smaller than the old group could and the viewing distance of 50 cm showed character about 1pt smaller than those at a 80 cm viewing distance. There are no significant differences in font types. From a comparison of the results for correctness and comfort, people generally preferred larger character sizes to those that they could read. The findings of this study may provide basic data and guidelines for setting of character size and font type to improve the legibility of characters written in Chinese.

**Keywords:** age, viewing distance, font type, Chinese character.

## 1    Introduction

The legibility and readability of characters are important to our daily activities and tasks. If the sizes of the characters are too small or poorly designed, people may not obtain the correct information. The main factors which affect legibility are font size, type of font, thickness of font, space between fonts, contrast of colors, distance of sight, illumination and so on. Many researchers have studied the effects of font size, font type, viewing distance, age and contrast to the legibility of characters.

In a study of font sizes, Wang Jian et al. found the complexity of Chinese characters influence the Chinese character threshold [1].Zhou Aibao et al. explored processing

---

* Corresponding author.

P.L.P. Rau (Ed.): CCD/HCII 2013, Part I, LNCS 8023, pp. 333–339, 2013.
© Springer-Verlag Berlin Heidelberg 2013

speed influenced by the font, size, and characteristics of Chinese character [2]. The results show that among seven kinds of fonts, processing speed of Sungti, Zhengkai and Heiti is faster than that of Xingkai, Lishu, Weibei, and Caiyun. Japanese researchers have provided a standard for the various font sizes of Japanese characters in visual displays to make them legible to older and visually impaired people [3]. The US also has a standard on character sizes for the labeling of medical supplies [4].

Font type is also a significant factor for the legibility of words in hard copy. Wang You et al. measured the character recognition threshold or acuity of Chinese characters [5]. The results show that four types of Chinese character fonts (Songti, Heiti, Kaiti and Fangsong ) have different acuities: Heiti being the smallest, Kaiti larger, and Songti and Fangsong the largest. The Gothic fonts were smaller than the Ming fonts in Korean users' visual performance which tested two age groups (20s and 60s) for different font types of Korean letters and numbers at 50 cm and 200 cm viewing distances respectively [6]. An experiment was conducted to compare with recognition accuracy of four fonts, of Chinese characters under three various back illumination [7]. The results show the Song font and Black font were better than imitative Song font and Long Song font, and Long Song font was worse than imitative Song.

Age and viewing distances are main factors to affect the legibility of characters, but most studies of the effect factors for Chinese character are focus on the font, size, stroke and structure. Therefore, this study investigated the effects of age and viewing distance on the legibility (correctness) and subjective preference (comfort) of Chinese characters associated with different age groups. The objectives of this study were to: (1) provide guidelines for the minimum Chinese character size for 100% correctness; (2) suggest guidelines for comfortable Chinese character size on the basis of the age of the person.

## 2    Methods

### 2.1    Subjects

In all, 40 participants, comprising 20 young people (in their 30s) and 20 elderly people (in their 55s) were recruited, respectively, to investigate legibility in relation to age. The mean age and mean visual acuity of the young participants were 32.85 ($\pm 6.05$) years and 0.84 ($\pm 0.15$) respectively, whereas the mean age and mean visual acuity of the elderly groups were 56.90 ($\pm 4.15$) years and 0.36 ($\pm 0.15$), respectively. All subjects were tested and selected by a Landholt acuity test with a 30 cm distance measure. All participants were native Chinese speakers. None was color blind or had eye defects.

### 2.2    Procedure

Before the experiments, the personal data of the participants was asked. Then all participants were provided with a brief description of the goals and procedures of this study. The illuminance level was measured and recorded and to confirm it was in an appropriate range at the surface on which the test charts will be placed. And each participant's visual acuity was tested.

After the visual acuity test, each participant was asked to try to read characters presented on papers and determine the reading legibility of the word groups. And the participants rated the legibility by using a 3-point scale (1- indistinct, 2- distinct but need cost a little attention, 3- very distinct). The numbers of correct/wrong answers as well as the subjective reading legibility ratings of each character group were recorded. If a participant provided all wrong answers for the two characters twice consecutively, the experimental trial was stopped. After a trail, participant needed to report the least comfort character group depending on character size.

The measurement of the dependent variables were as follows: (1) 'minimum character size for 100% correctness', which was defined as the smallest font size among character sizes at which the participant correctly read all two characters in each group on papers; (2) 'minimum character size for the least comfort', which was defined as the smallest font size among character sizes at which the participant reported that the characters caused comfort while reading; The '100%' was employed to determine the minimum character size associated with age groups in this study.

## 2.3    Apparatus

A room was constructed specifically for this study and the environment was comfortable for participants. Two light sources which can control the intensity of illumination were located on the ceiling of the room. To test the legibility of the characters for paper, the surface illumination level was 50 lx in this study.

Each participant was instructed to read 12 sets of characters (two-syllable Chinese characters) shown on papers at viewing distances of 50 cm and 80 cm. Unmeaningful words were employed for two-syllable Chinese characters in this study(Fig. 1 shows an example). Altogether, 12 character sizes, ranging in size from 4.5 pt to 18 pt, were tested in this study. The spatial complexity of the stimuli was also described by stroke frequency [8]. In this study, characters that contain 10 or more than 10 strokes were described as "complex" characters; and characters that contain 1 to 9 strokes as "simple" characters. Lanting is similar to Yahei, however, there are still difference between them.

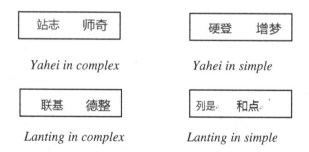

Yahei in complex          Yahei in simple

Lanting in complex          Lanting in simple

**Fig. 1.** An example of two-syllable Chinese characters

## 2.4    Experimental Design

The independent variables were age, viewing distance and font type. Levels for the independent variables are described in Table 1. Each participant performed 8 trials and all treatment combinations were performed in a random order.

This study investigated the effects of these independent variables on the following dependent variables. For measurement of the dependent variables: (1) 'minimum character size for 100% correctness'; (2) 'minimum character size for the least comfort'. To evaluate the effects of various independent variables [age (30s, 55s), viewing distance (50 cm, 80 cm), font type (Lanting in simple, Lanting in complex, Yahei in simple, Yahei in complex], on the two dependent variables, an ANOVA was employed.

**Table 1.** Description of the independent variables

| Independent variables | Levels |
| --- | --- |
| Age | 30s, 55s |
| Viewing distance | 50 cm, 80 cm |
| Font type | Lanting in simple, Lanting in complex, Yahei in simple, Yahei in complex |

# 3      Results

## 3.1      Analysis of Minimum Character Size for 100% Correctness

The effects of age and viewing distance on the minimum character size for 100% correctness were found to be statistically significant (all p-values < 0.05). There is no significant difference in font types.

In Figure 2, the 'minimum character size for 100% correctness' for people in their 30s was smaller (6.3 pt) compared to the people in their 55s (8.8 pt). Put more simply, young participants were able to correctly read character sizes smaller than those elderly participants with the same level of accuracy. The effect of viewing distance on the 'minimum character size for 100% correctness' was also evidently significant. Font sizes of 6.8 pt and 8.2 pt were reported as the 'minimum character sizes for 100% correctness' at a 50 cm viewing distance and at a 80 cm viewing distance, respectively. Though not significantly, the results of the 'minimum character size for 100% correctness' associated with the font type indicated that Yahei in simple (7.3 pt) and Yahei in complex (8.0 pt) allowed for smaller character sizes than Lantinghei in simple (7.6 pt) and Lantinghei in complex (8.4 pt) respectively.

## 3.2      Analysis of Subjective Minimum Character Size for the Least Comfort

Statistical analysis showed that age and viewing distance were significant factors for the 'minimum character size for the least comfort' (all p-values < 50.05). 'Minimum character size for the least comfort' means that the smallest font size among character sizes was such that a participant rated the character(s) as causing comfort while reading. There is no significant difference in font types.

Figure 3, showing the results of the main effects of 'minimum character size for the least comfort', indicates that the younger group described characters up to 8.8 pt in size as causing no discomfort to read, whereas the elderly group required a character size of at least 11.0 pt to read characters without discomfort. As expected, the effect of viewing distance was significant. The 'minimum character sizes for the least comfort' were 9.3 pt and 11.5 pt for 50 cm and 80 cm viewing distances, respectively. Though not significantly, the 'minimum character sizes for the least comfort' associated with the font type indicated that Yahei in simple (9.5 pt) and Yahei in complex (9.9 pt) allowed for smaller character sizes than Lantinghei in simple (10.3 pt) and Lantinghei in complex (10.5 pt) respectively.

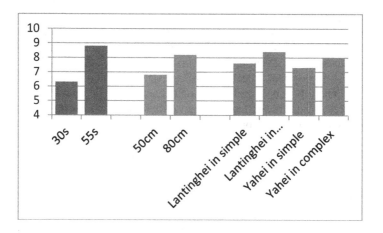

**Fig. 2.** The results of the main effects of 'minimum character size for 100% correctness'

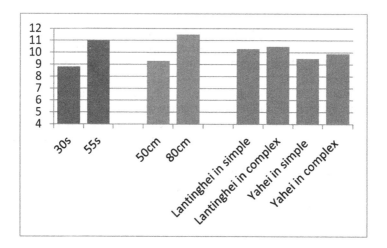

**Fig. 3.** The results of the main effects of' minimum character size for the least comfort'

## 4     Discussion

The present study investigated the effects of age, viewing distance and font type on two dependent variables: (1) 'minimum character size for 100% correctness'; (2) 'minimum character size for the least comfort'.

With regard to age, the young groups showed better legibility than elderly groups. The average character sizes for the two dependent variables of the group of subjects in their 55s were larger than those of the group of subjects in their 30s.That is, the average character sizes for subjects in their 55s were 6.3 pt and 8.8pt for the 'minimum character size for 100% correctness' and 'minimum character size for the least comfort', respectively, whereas those of subjects in their 30s were 8.8 pt and 11.0 pt, respectively. These findings might be explained by a reduction of light on the retina as well as the increasing of age.

According to the comparison analyses for correctness and comfort, the 'minimum character sizes for the least comfort' were larger than the 'minimum character sizes for 100% correctness'. This means that the character sizes that caused the least discomfort were significantly different from the character sizes at which people read with 100% correctness. Generally people preferred larger characters than the sizes at which people can nevertheless read with perfect accuracy. Therefore, performance as well as subjective preference should be considered when recommending character sizes for Chinese words to improve legibility, because even if the recommended character sizes ensure that they can be read correctly, people might still feel discomfort when reading.

## 5    Conclusions

This study examined the effects of age, viewing distance and font type on two dependent variables to evaluate the legibility of Chinese characters. A summary of the main findings is as follows:

Age: The young group (6.3 pt) could read character sizes smaller than those of the elderly group (8.8 pt) for the 'minimum character size for 100% correctness', respectively. In addition, the young group (8.8 pt) could read significantly smaller character sizes than those of the elderly group (11.0 pt) for the 'minimum character size for the least comfort', respectively.

Viewing distance: 50 cm (6.8 pt) allowed for character sizes about2pt smaller than those at 80 cm (8.2 pt) for the 'minimum character size for 100% correctness', respectively. In addition, 50 cm (9.3 pt) allowed for character sizes about 2pt smaller than those required at 80 cm (11.5 pt) for the 'minimum character size for the least comfort', respectively.

This study might be helpful in that they provide basic information with which to determine the legibility of Chinese characters.

## References

1. Wang, J., Shao, Z.F.: Size Threshold of Chinese Characters and Appropriate Character space in Electronic Map. Chinese Journal of Applied Psychology 114(1), 060–065 (2008)
2. Zhou, A., Zhang, X., Shu, H., He, L.G.: Cognitive Processes Based on the Font, Size and Characteristics in Chinese Two-Character. Psychological Science 32(1), 134–136 (2009)
3. Guidelines for the elderly and people with disabilities – visual signs and displays – estimation of minimum legible size for a Japanese single character. Japanese Industrial Standard, JIS S 0032:2003 (2003)

4. Guidance for industry: Labeling OTC human drug products questions and answers. Washington, DC: Food and Drug Administration. US Department of Health and Human Services (2005)
5. Wang, Y., Shao, Z.: Stroke Frequency and Font Effects on Chinese Character Recognition Threshold. Psychological Science 32(1), 134–136 (2009)
6. Kong, Y.-K., Lee, I., Jung, M.-C., Song, Y.-W.: The effects of age, viewing distance, display type, font type, colour contrast and number of syllables on the legibility of Korean characters. Ergonomics 54(5), 453–465 (2011)
7. Jin, W., Zhu, Z., Shen, M.: The effect of fonts of characters on recognition. Chinese Journal of Applied Psychology 7(2) (1992)
8. Zhang, J.Y., Zhang, T., Xue, F., Liu, L., Yu, C.: Legibility variations of Chinese characters and implications for visual acuity measurement in Chinese reading population. Investigative Ophthalmology & Visual Science 48(5), 2383–2390 (2007)

# A Study of a Human Interface Device Controlled by Formant Frequencies for the Disabled

Norihiro Uemi

Department of Architecture and Mechatronics, Faculty of Engineering, Oita University, Japan
uemi@oita-u.ac.jp

**Abstract.** We propose a human interface device using a formant frequency. It does not require complicated signal processing. The formant frequency means vocal tract resonance frequency which characterizes the phonemes. By using a microphone, we think it is possible to estimate the position of tongue and the opening of mouth. We investigated the relationship of formant frequencies and the manner of articulation. At first, we clarified the range of the formant frequencies by moving the mouth and the tongue freely. Next, we set the horizontal and vertical axes which correspond to the second- and first-formant frequencies respectively on a computer display screen. Subjects were asked to fit a mouse pointer controlled by their formant frequencies to a target appeared on a display. It is concluded that subject can be relatively easy to control the pointer within the range enclosed by five Japanese vowels formant points.

**Keywords:** Human Interface Device, Formant, Speech, the Disabled.

## 1 Introduction

A voice recognition system is one of the useful methods of human interface devices for the disabled. But it requires complicated signal processing and it is difficult to recognize the voice of the person who has articulation disorder.1,2,3

We propose a human interface device using a formant frequency that is one of the voice characteristic values. It does not require complicated signal processing. The formant frequency means vocal tract resonance frequency which characterizes the phonemes. It is known that fronting or backing of the tongue causes chiefly a raising or lowering of second formant frequency (F2) and closing or opening of the mouth causes a lowering or raising of first formant frequency (F1).[4]

By using a microphone, we think it is possible to estimate the position of tongue and the opening of mouth from formant frequencies. And the disabled might be able to utilize the function that was not used effectively before for a human interface device.

In this paper, we investigated the relationship of formant frequencies and the manner of articulation.

In the first experiment, we clarified the range of the formant frequencies by moving the mouth and the tongue freely.

P.L.P. Rau (Ed.): CCD/HCII 2013, Part I, LNCS 8023, pp. 340–345, 2013.
© Springer-Verlag Berlin Heidelberg 2013

In the next experiment, we set the horizontal and vertical axes which corresponded to the second- and first-formant frequencies respectively on a computer display screen. Subjects were asked to fit a mouse pointer controlled by their formant frequencies to a target appeared on a computer display screen.

## 2    The Range of the Formant Frequencies by Moving the Mouth and the Tongue Freely

In this paper, we propose a human interface device using the first and second formant frequency. It is necessary to check the range of the formant frequencies, because the range differs according to person.

In particular, if we use them as an input device for the disabled, it is necessary that the disabled can generate the formant frequencies easily. We investigated a range and an individual difference of the formant frequencies by moving a mouth and a tongue freely.

### 2.1    Experimental Method

In this experiment, an electrolarynx was used as a sound source. An electrolarynx is one of the artificial larynges. In the electrolarynx, an electromechanical vibrator is attached to the neck to put a sound source into oral cavity.5 It has a big burden on subject for a long time to continue vibrating the vocal cords to measure the formants. Therefore we think that using an outside sound source is practical. We input the sound that is uttered using the electrolarynx on a computer. The sound is performed linear predictive coding and the formants are extracted. The program to analyze the formants was written using LabVIEW programming software (National-Instruments). It analyzed the first peak frequency (F1: first formant frequency) of the spectrum of the sound and following peak (F2: second formant frequency). We can apply this analysis method to an artificial voice that is generally used in the formant analysis of the vowel.6

Analysis condition

— Vibrating frequency of an electrolarynx..........66Hz
— Sampling frequency .............................8000Hz
— Analyzing points ...............................512 points
— Window weighting..................Hamming window
— Analyzing order......................................12th

At first the subject practiced the electrolarynx. He was asked to move his mouth and tongue freely without overdoing it. The sound was recorded for two minutes. And this recording was repeated three times. The formant frequencies were analyzed afterwards. Five male healthy subjects participated in this experiment.

## 2.2    Experimental Results  and Discussion

Fig. 1 shows the F2-F1 chart of the five subjects. In this chart, the vertical axis shows the first formant frequency and horizontal axis shows a second formant frequency. The point on the F2-F1 chart shows the second and the first formant of the sound from the mouth. In this paper, we call this point 'formant point'. The F2-F1 chart is related to the position of the tongue and the shape of the mouth. For example, a formant point rises when the mouth is closed, and it falls when the mouth is opened. The formant point moves to the right when the tongue moves backward, and it moves to the left when the tongue moves forward. The white line on the chart is connecting the formant points of the vowels which a subject uttered using the electrolarynx. The existing area of the formant points is different depending on the subjects. The area where the formant points gather is near the formant point of each vowel. It is easy to generate the formant points between /a/ and /o/ and near the vowel position in Fig.1. The area with a few formant points is between/a/ and /e/, between /i/ and /u/, and a center of the area enclosed by the white lines. We do not use this area by everyday utterance. We think that it is difficult to generate a formant point in this area freely.

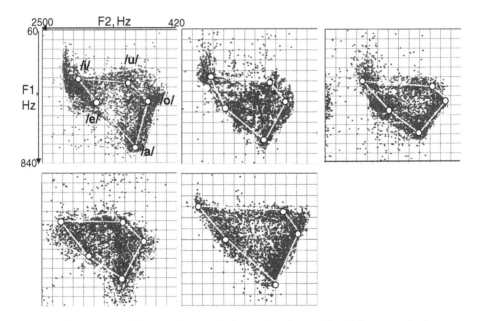

**Fig. 1.** The range of formant frequencies by moving the mouth and the tongue freely

# 3    The Range of Formant Frequencies When Subject Was Asked to Fit a Mouse Pointer Controlled by the Formant Frequencies to a Target Appeared on a Computer Display Screen

In the next experiment, we set the horizontal and vertical axes which correspond to the second- and first-formant frequencies respectively on a computer display screen. The plane on the screen is called "F2-F1 plane" and the point represented by first- and second-formant frequency on the F2-F1 plane is called "formant point" in this paper. As mentioned before, Subject can be relatively easy to control the pointer within the area enclosed by five Japanese vowels (/a/,/i/,/u/,/e/,/o/) formant points. But we thought that it was hard to generate the formant point at the center in this area because a few formant points existed at the center. Therefore we presented a target on the F2-F1 plane and asked subject to adjust a formant point to it. And we investigated the position that was easy to adjust the formant point and the position that was hard to adjust it in detail.

## 3.1    Experimental Method

Subjects were asked to fit a mouse pointer controlled by their formant frequencies to a target appeared on a computer display screen. Fig.2 shows the target position on the computer display screen. In this experiment, we investigated the formant point on the F2- F1 plane which could be controlled consciously.

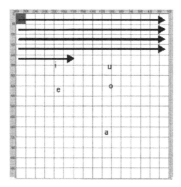

**Fig. 2.** Target position on the computer display screen

We set the horizontal and vertical axes which correspond to the second- and first-formant frequencies respectively on a computer display screen. We call the plane on the screen 'F2-F1 plane'. We prepared the target which moved on the F2-F1 plane in the display screen and asked the subject to fit a mouse pointer to the target. The target started from left-top position and moved to the right automatically every two seconds. When a target came to the right-side end, it moved to left-second position. The target was moved until right-bottom position. If a mouse pointer was fitted to the target and a switch was pushed, this target position was recorded. We performed this ten times and added up the number of times every position. Five male healthy subjects participated in this experiment.

## 3.2    Experimental Results and Discussion

Fig.3 is the experimental result. Target position where subject can fit a mouse pointer to a target many times is painted dark color. In Fig.3, we display the line connected the outline of the range of the formant points in Fig.1 and the line connected the position of the vowel. The area where the subject could generate the formant points expanded compared to the area in Fig.1. The target position chosen more than seven times were near the position of the vowel formant. In addition, the target positions chosen many times tended to be between /a/ and /o/. These positions were relatively easy to generate formants. The subject who could not choose the center area in Fig.1 could choose this area in Fig.3.

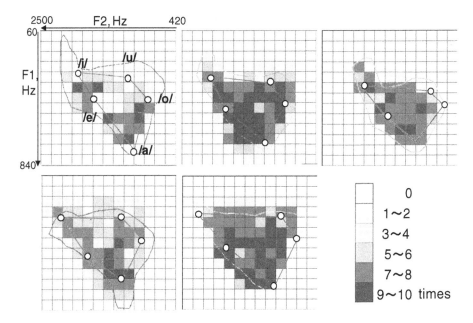

**Fig. 3.** Target position where subjects can fit a mouse pointer controlled by their formant frequencies to a target appeared on a computer display screen

Because subjects were able to choose the range near the center in the area enclosed by vowels, formants of these positions may be available for an input device. All subjects were able to choose the formant of the range near the vowel /a/. From this, it is easy to move a mouth and a tongue in the area that is close to the formant point of /a/. The area that was easy to produce a formant point differed with different  persons. When we use formant for an input device, coordinating a function is necessary.

# 4    Conclusion

We propose a human interface device using a formant frequency that is one of the voice characteristic values. In this paper, we investigated the relationship of formant frequencies and the manner of articulation.

In the first experiment, we clarified the range of the formant frequencies by moving the mouth and the tongue freely. The Existing area of the formant points is different depending on the subjects. The area where the formant points gather is near the formant point of each vowel. It is easy to generate the formant points between /a/ and /o/ and near the vowel position. The area with a few formant points is between /a/ and /e/, between /i/ and /u/, and a center of the area enclosed by the formants of vowels.

In the next experiment, we set the horizontal and vertical axes which corresponded to the second- and first-formant frequencies respectively on a computer display screen. Subjects were asked to put a mouse pointer controlled by their formant frequencies over a target appeared on a computer display screen. In this experiment, we investigated the formant point on the F2- F1 plane which could be controlled consciously. The target positions chosen many times tended to be between /a/ and /o/. These positions were easy to generate formants relatively. Because subjects were able to choose the range near the center in the area enclosed by vowels, formants of these positions may be available for an input device.

The area that was easy to produce a formant point differed with different persons. When we use formant for an input device, coordinating a function is necessary.

# References

1.  Noyes, J., Frankish, C.: Speech recognition technology for individuals with disabilities. Augmentative and Alternative Communication 8(4), 297–303 (1992)
2.  Kojima, H., et al.: Inarticulate speech recognition for the control of wheelchairs by the severely disabled. In: 29th Annual RESNA conference (2006)
3.  Simpson, T., Gauthier, M., Prochazka, A.: Evaluation of Tooth-Click Triggering and Speech Recognition in Assistive Technology for Computer Access. Neurorehabilitation and Neural Repair   24(2), 188–194 (2010)
4.  Fant, G.: Ericsson Technics 15(1), 21–23 (1959)
5.  Uemi, N., Ifukube, T., Takahashi, M., Matsushima, J.: Design of a New Electrolarynx having a Pitch Control Function. In: IEEE International Workshop on Robot and Human Communication, pp. 198–203 (1994)
6.  Markel, J.D., Gray, A.H.: Linear Prediction of Speech. Springer, New York (1976)

# Secondary Task Method for Workload Measurement in Alarm Monitoring and Identification Tasks

Xiaojun Wu and Zhizhong Li[*]

Department of Industrial Engineering, Tsinghua University, Beijing, 100084, China
zzli@tsinghua.edu.cn

**Abstract.** The operators who perform alarm monitoring and identification tasks in complex industrial systems, such as nuclear power plants, often suffer from heavy mental workload. Among the many existing mental workload measurements, secondary task method was chosen and examined for that it is sensitive to operator capacity, provides a common metric for different tasks, and easy to carry out, etc. In this study, a paper-based arithmetic secondary task was adopted to measure mental workload of the participants when they were performing alarm monitoring and identification tasks. A two-factor, two-level lab experiment was conducted to examine whether this secondary task method can discriminate different levels of mental workload, and whether it interferes with the primary task. The results showed that though the secondary task chosen in this experiment had good discriminability, its influence on the primary task performance and its interaction with scenario complexity were significant.

**Keywords:** Mental workload, secondary task, alarm monitoring, alarm identification.

## 1 Introduction

Modern industrial systems, such as nuclear power plant (NPP) and air flight control systems, are becoming more and more complex, and can often bring heavy mental workload to their operators (Hwang, et al, 2008). Therefore, it is very important to find out how high is the level of operators' mental workload when they are performing tasks such as alarm monitoring and identification.

Mental workload is characterized as a mental construct that reflects the mental strain which is resulted from performing a task under specific environmental and operational conditions, coupled with the capability of the operator to respond to those demands (Cain, 2007). Though there is no universally acceptable definition of mental workload, it has been generally defined as the amount of resource difference between task demands and capacity provision by an individual (Sanders and McCormick, 1987).

Hwang et al. (2008) divided the existing methods to measure mental workload into three categories: subjective ratings, performance measures, and physiological measures.

---

[*] Corresponding author.

P.L.P. Rau (Ed.): CCD/HCII 2013, Part I, LNCS 8023, pp. 346–354, 2013.
© Springer-Verlag Berlin Heidelberg 2013

For measuring the mental workload in alarm monitoring and identification tasks in the main control room (MCR) of a NPP, the pros and cons of these three different categories are summarized as follows.

It is widely claimed that the subjective measures have advantages such as inexpensive, unobtrusive, easily administered, widely transferable, and having high face validity (Casali and Wierwille, 1983; Wickens, 1984). However, it has shortcomings such as potential confounding of mental and physical workload, dissociation of subjective ratings and task performance, and raters' different interpretation of scale words, etc. (O'Donnell and Eggemeier, 1986; Meshkati et al., 1990). For alarm monitoring tasks which might experience fluctuations during a time period, the dependence of subjective measures on short-term memory might distort the workload rating for that period (O'Donnell and Eggemeier, 1986).

There are two categories of performance measures, including primary task performance measures and secondary performance measures. Primary task performance measures provide direct indications for interested task performance. However, they are not very sensitive to changes of workload, especially when operators have spare capability to increase their effort level. In this sense, primary task performance measures are not appropriate to be used in NPP MCRs. Secondary task method is one of the mostly widely used methods to measure workload, for that it provides a sensitive measure of operator capacity, a sensitive index of task impairment due to stress, and a common metric for comparison of different tasks (Gawron, 2008). However, it has one major disadvantage: the possible intrusion on the performance of the primary task (Willigs and Wierwille, 1979). As for the alarm monitoring and identification tasks, if we can find a secondary task that has little intrusion on the performance of the primary task, then it might provide us with continuous, objective, and direct measure of mental workload.

Physiological measures use the known features sensitive to operator loadings indicators to measure mental workload (Wierwille, 1979). The main advantage of physiological measures is that they can provide continuous and objective data of the operator's state. Usually, physiological measures mainly focus on the cardiovascular system, respiratory system, nervous system and biochemistry, with heart rate variability being probability the mostly widely used one (Hancock, 1988). As physiological measures have to explain the effect of workload through the psychological process happening on the body, they are indirect. Thus, it would provide a more complete understanding of the workload when combined with other workload assessment techniques. Besides, some physiological measures are invasive and will affect the performance of primary tasks (such as the respiratory system), while some of them require participants to stay still for reliable data collection (such as the nervous system), which is not appropriate to be used in NPP MCRs.

Currently, secondary task methods have been used to measure mental workload in aviation and vehicle driving domains (Wierwille et al, 1977; Williges and Wierwille, 1979; Casali, and Wierwille, 1983; Blanco et al., 2006). However, there are few studies which use secondary task methods to measure operators' mental workload in control rooms where monitoring and identification tasks are performed. Previous studies have showed that properly designed secondary tasks can be used to estimate the workload of primary task (Wierwille, 1977), while there existed some evidences that secondary tasks differ in the degree to which they interfere with the primary task, and they may also interact with the primary tasks, with the greatest interference and interaction occurring when the primary and secondary tasks involve similar processes or rely on similar brain regions (Troyer, 1999).

This study attempts to use the paper-based arithmetic secondary-task method for workload assessment of alarm monitoring and identification tasks in NPP MCRs. When operators are performing alarm monitoring and identification tasks, they should periodically look up the operating procedures to check whether the current parameter value exceeds its normal range or they should periodically put down some critical process parameters on paper for future filing. The arithmetic secondary task introduced in this study is different from the tasks that operators perform in the real situation. We want to examine whether this kind of secondary task can discriminate the different levels of operators' mental workload under different cases, and whether the secondary task we introduced will interfere with the performance of the primary task.

There were two hypotheses in this study. (1) The paper-based arithmetic secondary task method can discriminate the simple scenarios from the complex scenarios, with more correctly answered arithmetic calculations in simple scenarios than in complex scenarios. (2) The arithmetic secondary task does not interfere with the primary tasks, nor does it interact with the primary tasks. A two-factor, two-level within-subjects experiment design was adopted to test the above two hypotheses.

The methodology used in this study is described in Section 2. Section 3 reports the experiment results. Section 4 presents some discussion on the results. Conclusions from this study are given in Section 5.

## 2    Methodology

### 2.1    Participants

In total, 15 paid male students of engineering background from Tsinghua University participated in the experiment. Only male students were recruited to keep the gender consistency as that in NPP MCRs. The participants aged from 20 to 24 (Mean=21.73, SD=1.39), all had more than 5 years' experience with computers and were thus familiar with computer operations, but had very limited knowledge about nuclear power plants.

### 2.2    Independent Variables and Experiment Design

A two-factor within-subjects design was adopted in this study. The first factor was the secondary task. Each participant performed half of the task scenarios with the secondary task, and the other half of the task scenarios without the secondary task. The sequence of the two halves was randomized to minimize the learning effect. The second factor was complexity of task scenarios, which had two levels: simple scenarios with six alarms in two minutes, and complex scenarios with twelve alarms in two minutes. There were six simple task scenarios and six complex task scenarios. The order of the simple and complex scenarios were randomized and in an alternate manner.

## 2.3     Experiment Task

When an alarm was triggered, a participant pressed the button named 'Alarm Discovered' to report that he noticed the alarm and to press the button of the alarm that has been triggered to suppress the alarm. Then the participant made judgment about to which system component that the alarm was associated with and how severe it was. Both the correctness of alarm detection, and errors made when making alarm judgments were recorded for further analysis.

Each participant carried out the alarm monitoring and identification tasks for 12 scenarios in total. A paper-based arithmetic secondary task was introduced in half of the scenarios (six in total) during the experiment to measure the mental workload of the participants. The secondary task required the participants to perform two digits addition calculation. The secondary tasks were performed on paper, while both the alarm monitoring and identification task was performed on the computer. The participants were asked to do the secondary tasks as many as they could while trying their best not to affect the performance of the primary tasks.

## 2.4     Dependent Variables

Objective performance measurements were collected for hypothesis testing, including correctness of alarm detection (the ratio between the number of alarms correctly perceived and the total number of alarms presented), time to detect an alarm (the time interval between the moment when the alarm was triggered and the moment when participant pressed the button 'Alarm Discovered'), error rate of alarm identification (the ratio between the number of errors made in alarm identification and the total number of alarms triggered), time to   identify an alarm (the time interval between the time when a participant suppressed the alarm and the time when the participant made an identification of the alarm), and performance of the secondary task which indicates mental workload (the number of correctly answered arithmetic operations).

## 2.5     Experiment Platform and Experiment Procedure

The experiment was conducted on a personal computer with two screens. The program was coded with Visual Basic 2010, and the scenario data was contracted from the PCtran ™ simulation software, which can simulate different working conditions of a pressurized water reactor (PWR) NPP.

Fig. 1 illustrates one of the experimental displays. The alarms were divided into three severity levels. The Level 1 alarms indicate the plant wide, most severe ones, and were indicated with the red color to attract the attention of the participants. Level 2 alarms were system wide functional failures, which should be timely dealt with, and were indicated with the hotpink color. Level 3 alarms were parameter level malfunctions, the lower than normal range alarms were indicated with blue bars, which grew to the left side of the neutral position as a parameter value was decreasing, while the higher than normal range alarms were indicated with yellow bars, which grew to the right of the neutral position as a parameter value was increasing. All alarms kept flashing until they were suppressed by a participant.

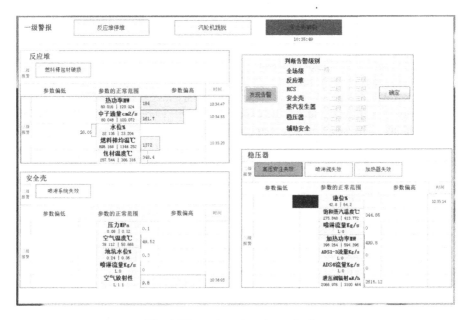

**Fig. 1.** Illustration of an alarm display

The experiment task lasted about 90 minutes for each participant. Before a participant began the experiment, his demographic information was collected and an informed consent was signed voluntarily. At the beginning, the participant was given a 30-minute training session about the NPP working principals and the usage of the alarm system. Then, the participant took a session of 20-minute practice to get familiar with the alarm system. Finally, the formal test in 12 scenarios was performed, lasting about 40 minutes.

# 3    Results

## 3.1    Mental Workload Measurement

The results listed in Table 1 show that the introduced arithmetic secondary task can discriminate the simple cases from the complex ones (*sig.* = 0.000 < 0.05) in the number of correctly answered arithmetic calculations, but not in the error rate of arithmetic calculations (*sig.* = 0.256 > 0.05). This means that when using the secondary task method, the number of correctly answered arithmetic calculations could be considered as a suitable secondary task performance criterion to reflect the workload of participants.

**Table 1.** Comparison of performance of the secondary task between simple and complex cases

| Performance of secondary task | Simple cases | | Complex cases | | Sig. |
|---|---|---|---|---|---|
| | Mean | SD | Mean | SD | |
| No. of correctly answered arithmetic calculations | 19.022 | 10.644 | 6.667 | 5.382 | 0.000* |
| Error rate of arithmetic calculations | 0.0109 | 0.0112 | 0.0193 | 0.0285 | 0.256 |

*: The difference is significant, with *sig.* < 0.05.

## 3.2     Interference with Primary Task Performance

The effect of the secondary task on the performance of the primary tasks was analyzed. The results are summarized in Table 2. It turns out that the introduction of the secondary task significantly reduced the correctness of alarm detection (sig. = 0.000 < 0.05), prolonged the time to detect an alarm (sig. = 0.017 < 0.05), and shortened the time to identify an alarm (sig. = 0.000 < 0.05). As for the error rate of alarm identification, no significant effect was found.

**Table 2.** Influence of secondary task on primary task performance

| Task | Performance criteria | Without secondary task | | With secondary task | | Sig. of secondary task | Sig. of complexity | Sig. of Interaction |
|---|---|---|---|---|---|---|---|---|
| | | Mean | SD | Mean | SD | | | |
| Alarm Monitoring | Correctness of alarm detection | 0.995 | 0.018 | 0.958 | 0.000 | 0.000* | 0.095 | 0.001* |
| | Time to detect an alarm | 3010 | 1299 | 3559 | 1225 | 0.017* | 0.000* | 0.005* |
| Alarm identification | Error rate of alarm identification | 0.023 | 0.027 | 0.022 | 0.034 | 0.948 | 0.952 | 0.163 |
| | Time to identify alarm | 2989 | 483.2 | 2711 | 506.6 | 0.000* | 0.019* | 0.788 |

*: The difference is significant, with *sig.* < 0.05.

The complexity of scenarios had significant effects on both the time to detect an alarm (sig. = 0.000 < 0.05) and the time to identify an alarm (sig. = 0.019 < 0.05), but had no significant influence on correctness of both alarm monitoring and identification.

There existed a significant secondary task * complexity interaction in alarm monitoring performance criteria, as Fig. 2 shows, but no significant interaction in alarm identification performance criteria. The introduction of the secondary task led to decreased correctness of alarm detection in both simple and complex cases, but the impairment in simple cases was much more severe than that in the complex cases (sig. = 0.001 < 0.05). As for the time to detect an alarm, it increased slightly in complex cases, while increased dramatically in simple cases (sig. = 0.005 < 0.05), because of the introduction of the secondary task. This means that the negative effects by the secondary task on performance of the primary tasks in simple cases was more significant than that in complex cases.

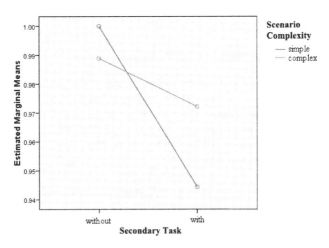

(1)    Correctness of alarm detection

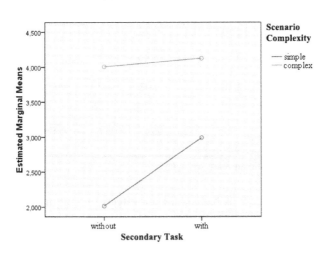

(2) Time to detect alarm

**Fig. 2.** Interaction effects of secondary task and scenario complexity

# 4    Discussion

From the results, it may be concluded that the introduced paper-based arithmetic secondary task can quantitatively discriminate different levels of mental workload.

However, by comparing the primary task performance with and without the secondary task, it is found that the introduction of the secondary task significantly affected the primary task performance. The alarm detection behavior was distorted in lower correctness and longer time of alarm detection, while the alarm identification behavior was distorted in shorter time to identify an alarm. As the participants had to allocate their attention and effort between the introduced secondary task and the primary task, the promptness and correctness of alarm detection might thus be negatively affected. Once an alarm was noticed, because of the existence of secondary task, the participants rushed their alarm identification process, causing the shorter time used to identify the system component that the alarm belonged to and how severe it was.

The interaction between secondary task and scenario complexity indicates that the introduction of the secondary task had more severe negative effect on simple cases than on complex cases. Very possibly the participants adopted a different strategy in the allocation of their attention and effort between the primary and secondary tasks under the two scenario complexity levels. When the scenario was complex, the participants focused on the primary tasks, while when the scenario is simple, they switched their emphasis to the performance of the secondary task.

Though the paper-based arithmetic secondary task seemed be able to discriminate different levels of mental workload, because of its negative effect on primary task performance and its interaction with scenario complexity, it may not be suitable for the measurement of mental workload in alarm detection and identification tasks. The ideal secondary task should not introduce negative effects on the primary task performance, nor should it interact with both the primary task and other factors in a study (Troyer, 1999).

# 5    Conclusions

In this experimental study, the effect of the paper-based arithmetic secondary task on alarm monitoring and identification task was examined. It was found that the arithmetic secondary task could provide objective, continuous and direct data about mental workload, but it interfered with the primary task, and interacted with scenario complexity.

The findings from this study are interesting. Although the arithmetic secondary task has been widely adopted for mental workload measurement in domains such as driving and aviation, it might not be appropriate for the domain of alarm monitoring and identification. This would encourage us to look for more appropriate methods for the measurement of mental workload in alarm processing tasks.

**Acknowledgement.** This study was supported by the National Natural Science Foundation of China (Project No. 70931003).

# References

1. Blanco, M., Biever, W.J., Gallagher, J.P., Dingus, T.A.: The impact of secondary task cognitive processing demand on driving performance. Accident Analysis & Prevention 38(5), 895–906 (2006)
2. Cain, B.: A review of the mental workload literature. Defence Research and Development Toronto, Canada (2007)
3. Casali, J.G., Wierwille, W.W.: A comparison of rating scale, secondary task, physiological and primary-task workload estimation techniques in a simulated flight task emphasizing communications load. Human Factors 25, 623–642 (1983)
4. Gawron, V.J.: Human performance, workload and situation awareness measures handbook, 2nd edn. CRC Press, Boca Raton (2008)
5. Hancock, P.A., Meshkati, N. (eds.): Human mental workload, vol. 52. North-Holland (1988)
6. Hwang, S.L., Yau, Y.J., Lin, Y.T., Chen, J.H., Huang, T.H., Yenn, T.C., Hsu, C.C.: Predicting work performance in nuclear power plants. Safety Science 46(7), 1115–1124 (2008)
7. Meshkati, N., Hancock, P.A., Rahimi, M., Dawes, S.M.: Techniques in mental workload assessment. In: Wilson, J.R., Corlett, E.N. (eds.) Evaluation of Human Work: A Practical Ergonomics Methodology, 2nd edn. Taylor & Francis, Philadelphia (1995)
8. O'donnell, R.D., Eggemeier, F.T.: Workload assessment methodology. Measurement Technique 42, 5 (1986)
9. Sanders, M.S., McCormick, E.J.: Human factors in engineering and design. McGRAW-HILL book company (1987)
10. Troyer, A.K., Winocur, G., Craik, F.I., Moscovitch, M.: Source memory and divided attention: Reciprocal costs to primary and secondary tasks. Neuropsychology 13(4), 467 (1999)
11. Wickens, C.D.: Engineering psychology and human performance. Charles E. Merril., Columbus (1984)
12. Wierwille, W.W., Gutmann, J.C., Hicks, T.G., Muto, W.H.: Secondary task measurement of workload as a function of simulated vehicle dynamics and driving conditions. Human Factors: The Journal of the Human Factors and Ergonomics Society 19(6), 557–565 (1977)
13. Wierwille, W.W.: Physiological measures of aircrew mental workload. Human Factors: The Journal of the Human Factors and Ergonomics Society 21(5), 575–593 (1979)
14. Williges, R.C., Wierwille, W.W.: Behavioral measures of aircrew mental workload. Human Factors 21, 549–574 (1979)

# Part IV

# Case Studies in Cross-Cultural Design

# A Cross-Cultural Comparison of UI Components Preference between Chinese and Czech Users

Jan Brejcha[1], Gong Hong Yin[2], Han Li[2], and Zhengjie Liu[2]

[1] Information Science and Librarianship, Charles University, Prague, Czech Republic
jan@brejcha.name
[2] Sino-European Usability Center (SEUC), Dalian Maritime University,
Dalian, 116026 P.R. China
gonghy_coin@qq.com, hherosoul@163.com, liuzhj@dlmu.edu.cn

**Abstract.** Thanks to the intensification of globalization through communication technology, we are faced more and more with UIs coming from different cultural backgrounds. In order to fit the user's cultural expectations as closely as possible, designers need to combine usability knowledge with cultural insights. By defining a usable set of UI design guidelines for a target culture, designers could market their products with lower costs than with cross-cultural testing. To promote this line of research, we carried a pilot study targeted at the habits, mental models and UI preferences of Chinese and Czech users. Our findings show there is a strong influence of globalization on the cultural markers mainly through the use of common software platforms. However, we found many important culture-specific differences as well in both groups. We present our results as guidelines that could be used to enhance the user's acceptance of the UI in a specific culture.

**Keywords:** Cross-cultural research, Cultural markers, Methodology, Design, Guidelines, User-interface, HCI, Semiotics.

## 1 Introduction

Thanks to the intensification of globalization through communication technology, we are faced more and more with UIs coming from different cultural backgrounds. There is also a growing need to design UIs that are usable and well accepted in a targeted culture. In order to match the user's cultural expectations as closely as possible, designers need to combine usability knowledge with cultural insights. Cross-cultural testing of UIs is the most comprehensive way to meet this goal, but it is also the most financially demanding. Therefore, by defining a usable set of UI design guidelines for a target culture, designers could market their products with lower costs and with better acceptance. In the field of cross-cultural comparison [3], we can build upon a body of previous research [7, 10, 11]. In our view, however, only limited work has been done in creating usable guidelines for cross-cultural UI design.

To promote this line of research and, to acquire the necessary insights, we carried a pilot study targeted at the habits, mental models and UI preferences of Chinese and

P.L.P. Rau (Ed.): CCD/HCII 2013, Part I, LNCS 8023, pp. 357–365, 2013.
© Springer-Verlag Berlin Heidelberg 2013

Czech users. For this purpose, we chose to work from the semiotic perspective which helps us uncover the sense-making processes of the users. We used semiotic methods to build a common framework to gather and analyze cross-cultural data. From our perspective, the UI is an example of complex language. Consequently, in our research we focused on different components of the UI language such as: discrete elements, interaction sentences, narration, rhetorical tropes, and patterns. [2] Discrete elements are the smallest elements to have a meaning. The interaction sentence is a meaningful unit describing a task in the user's interaction. The narrative in UI is made both by the designer's meta-communication and the temporal and/or sequential aspects of perceiving UI elements. Rhetorical tropes are devices of persuasion and emphasis, such as metaphors. Patterns are typical configurations of UI language components in different settings. Focusing on these UI language components allowed us to focus the scope of our research.

## 2     Research Methods

In order to find the prevalent and preferred UI components or cultural markers [1], we focused our study on the five following areas: personal information (demographics, exposure to other cultures and technologies), layout (discrete elements, patterns, interaction sentences and narration), color (discrete elements, rhetorical tropes), symbol (rhetorical tropes) and look and feel (interaction sentences, narration, patterns, and rhetorical tropes). There were few overlaps due to the broad scope we focused on in this pilot study.

For the pilot study, we gathered 45 hypotheses about the specifics of Chinese users. The hypotheses were drawn from the conclusions of previous research in usability testing, psychological studies, visual semiotics and linguistics. For the information value of UI components's spatial organization we worked with the oppositions of Given/New, Ideal/Real, and Center/Margin proposed by Kress and van Leeuwen [5]. In this context Given is a taken-for-granted information and New information is being introduced only after. Similarly, Ideal presents what might be, and Real what is, e.g., a specific or practical information. All of these oppositions can be combined with Center, a nucleus of information (or the most important information), and Margin, containing other dependent information.

Some of the conclusions were directly included in the hypotheses (e.g., favorite colors for the background: blue, purple, cyan, gray), some were modified according to our assumptions (e.g., because Given information in the West is expected on the left of a screen, we expected the information to work better on the right in China), some were constructed from our direct experience with the Chinese culture (e.g., red color with yellow text is used for special occasions), while some tested our more general assumptions (e.g., there is a close similarity between the sequential information structure in language and the horizontal structure in visual composition).

Our qualitative method was based on one-to-one and one-to-many interviews supported by note taking and filling in questionnaires. In order to test the different hypotheses, we created at least one question for each hypothesis. The questions were clustered according their areas, i.e., personal information, layout, color, symbol and look & feel. When appropriate, we used closed questions. However, because we carried an exploratory pilot study, we did not want to constrain our respondents and offered mostly open questions. The questionnaire was supported by examples of UI components.

To get data as reliable as possible, we wanted to limit the respondent's adaptation to a foreign culture. For that reason, we worked with students who were enrolled at a local university (Dalian Maritime University in China and Charles University in Prague, the Czech Republic) and were born and lived in the target cultures of our study. Also, the moderator of the interviews was a native speaker at both the locations. For each of the interviewed groups we chose a sample consisting of 20 respondents, evenly split between females and males. The Chinese respondents had a mean age of 23 years, while the Czechs had a mean age of 26 years. For this kind and depth of research, 20 respondents make for an adequate saturated sample size [4, 6, 8]. The results were analyzed both qualitatively and quantitatively with regard to the threshold of significance. The threshold of significance was set to 10 %. Only results of more than 10 % from one another were taken as different. This level is based on Sauro [9], where there is an 8 % margin of error for results from 20 respondents. We took into account only results greater than or equal to 60 %. The open questions were then analyzed with content analysis and contextual analysis across multiple questions where appropriate.

## 3   Results

Our findings show there is a strong influence of globalization on the cultural markers, mainly through the use of common software platforms. In spite of that, we found still many important culture-specific differences in both groups which are related to: spatial organization of information [5], shapes, direction of reading, motion, color, color combinations, semantic organization of content, use of icons and metaphors, user's preferences for different types of media, preference for culture-specific content and for cartoon imagery, trustworthiness of the content, navigation tools, visible and interaction grammar of menus and commands. Almost half (22) of our hypotheses were fully supported by the results from individual questions, 17 were partly supported (e.g. the result came second with a small difference in percentage after the first answer). 14 hypotheses were not supported, although useful information could be extracted. 2 hypotheses were impossible to verify due to lack of data. In the following sub-sections, we provide a summary of the hypotheses that were supported by the data, those that were not, as well as other interesting insights and comments. The summary is divided by the main themes of our research.

### 3.1   Layout

For testing the UI composition we used a matrix with 3 rows and 3 columns. The hypotheses that were supported in relation to the spatial organization of the UI, shapes, direction of reading and motion are:

- Given information is expected on the right of the screen.
- A central composition is regarded more aesthetically pleasing than triptych composition.

- An even number of elements is more preferred than odd number. Ideal is 8.
- Images placed symmetrically in the middle look better than on the left/right of the screen.
- Free-flow layout is easier to use than grid-based layout.
- Users tend to read from top-left towards the center of the screen.
- Left-to-right lines of text are easier to read than top-to-bottom and right-to-left.
- There is a close similarity between the sequential information structure in language and the horizontal structure in visual composition.
- Curves stand for softness (and would be better perceived), while straight lines for hardness.
- Rounded corners (curvilinear patterns) are better perceived than square corners (geometrical patterns).
- Copied UI elements are better perceived than original elements. This applies both on computer icons and design patterns.
- Icons presenting objects with a description are more understandable than those without a description.

The unsupported hypotheses, on the other hand, disclosed interesting details:

- Real information is expected on the bottom of the screen. The majority of Chinese respondents put real information in the middle level of the screen (middle row in the matrix), overlaying it thus partly on the new and ideal information.
- A square and double-square layout would be more preferred because it is widely used in Asia (a symbol of Earth, Japanese buildings, *etc.*). Instead, respondents preferred a golden-section layout, such as 16:9 or 4:3.

### 3.2    Color

For testing colors we used a 16 color palette [12]. The supported hypotheses regarding colors and color combinations were:

- Users would prefer lighter (pastel) colors and a white background.
- Personal websites would use a wider color palette than websites for other purposes.

Unsupported hypotheses were the following:

- UIs with the white and yellow colors in the foreground tend to be regarded as more aesthetic.
- Background color is more important than foreground color. Interestingly, the Czech sample results supported our hypothesis and valued the background very high.
- UIs with the following background/foreground color combination are most appealing: white on blue, white on gray blue, white on purple. The background color preference was shared among the groups, except for lime, which was chosen by the Chinese. For foreground, blue was a favorite for the Chinese, while red and silver for the Czechs. From the shared color combinations, black on white stood for clearness and naturalness for the Chinese, while for the Czechs it was for contrast and simplicity.

Moreover, some interesting insights into the perception of colors emerged:

- Black: The largest group of semantic items pertained to night and death, followed by solemn and elegant, and ink and information device.
- Navy: The largest shared groups contained painting and writing, sky, navy and sea.
- Green: The largest shared groups were related to grass and plants, spring and summer and a commonality was also found in environmental activism.
- Teal: The Chinese respondents connected this color to ink and paint, whereas the Czech respondents with water and swimming as well as relaxation. No shared meaning was found.
- Silver: Metal and machine was the most common shared group of items, followed by fashion and luxury. The Chinese respondents mentioned also cold and rain, while the Czech respondents Christmas decorations and snow.
- Blue: The most common shared meaning was related to the sky and ocean, followed by happy and fun. The Chinese group mentioned clean and relaxing while the Czech group regarded blue as neutral and cold.
- Lime: Spring, life, and vigor was the largest and single shared meaning of this color. For the Chinese, it was also a color of comfort and relaxation while for the Czechs it was connected with food and eating.
- Aqua: Sky and water was the most common meaning shared between the two groups, the second was positive and energy. For the Chinese group, it was a bright color while for the Czech respondents it was connected with angels and innocence.
- Maroon: Passion and blood was the commonest shared meaning. The Chinese respondents also answer hair and chestnuts, while the Czech respondents said women's apparel.
- Purple: Dress, luxury, and attractiveness was the largest and single shared meaning. For the Chinese group, the color was connected also with flowers while the Czech group named sweets and candy floss.
- Olive: No directly shared meaning was found. The Chinese respondents regarded the color as military or soil while the Czech respondents connected with it wood, food, and dirt.
- Gray: The single shared meaning was gloomy and unpleasant, mostly cited by the Chinese respondents. For them, it was also connected with rain and dust while for the Czech group the color pertained to neutral, city, and office.
- Red: Together with maroon, the largest shared group revolved around passion, blood, and energy. Alarm and warning came second, followed by happiness and fun. For the Chinese respondents, it was a color of the national flag, warmth, and lipstick while for the Czech group it was connected with berries and flowers.
- Fuchsia: The single largest shared group was connected with girlish fashion and apparel. For the Chinese group, it was also a color of flowers and beauty.
- Yellow: The single largest shared group orbited around brightness, warmth, good mood and activity. For the Czech respondents, it was a color of attention and highlighting while for the Chinese group it was for childhood and freshness.
- White: The largest shared group was related to cleanness, followed by hospitals. For the Czech group, it was connected with neutrality, potential and contemplation. The Chinese related the color to simplicity and holiness, snow, but also weddings (together with red).

### 3.3    Symbol

For testing symbols we used various examples of computer icons found in different applications, or we created the examples by ourselves. The supported hypotheses regarding user's preferences for different types of media, preference for culture-specific content and trustworthiness of the content were:

- Icons presenting situations are more intuitive than those containing objects. The Czech sample preferred image icons to those presenting situations, in contrast with the Chinese results.
- There is a close similarity between sequential information structure in language and the horizontal structure in visual composition. Verb (a pointer index) and adverb (a "+" sign) would mimic their position in sentence (*i.e.*, the verb comes before the adverb).
- Users can recognize visual patterns occurring in the UI.
- Copied UI elements are better perceived than original elements. This applies both on computer icons and design patterns.
- The sequence of input in a faceted search follows the sequence of natural language. The Subject comes first (relating to the user's gender, or size), followed by an implied Verb and adverb (purpose) and finally the Object (price, color, rating *etc.*). In contrast to the Chinese results, the Czech respondents would put size after gender (instead of purpose), purpose instead of price and price as the last, thus omitting color and rating.
- The use of Chinese calligraphy is very praised by the users.

The unsupported hypotheses:

- Icons presenting images are more intelligible than those containing characters
- There is a close similarity between sequential information structure in language and horizontal structure in visual composition. Noun (folder) and adjective (star attribute) would mimic their position in sentence (*i.e.*, the attribute precedes the subject).
- Long textual pages are considered more useful than texts on more screens because the former contain all the information in one place (show more context)
- Icons with symbols coming from users' own cultural background are better perceived and understood than those from a foreign culture.
- Given that most of the websites contain mostly text, text would be regarded the most useful media. In the Chinese sample, pictorial media (images, videos) had the highest acceptance and credibility. In contrast, the Czech respondents preferred images and texts to videos and sound, both in terms of the efficiency of information transmission and trustworthiness.
- A localized UI would be better accepted than non-localized UI. The respondents were used to use foreign, non-localized applications, so localization was their least concern. On the other hand, speed and usability was the major concern among users. Also, originality and aesthetics was highly praised. The Czech results, on the whole, and in contrast to the Chinese results, showed a preference for features instead of color.

### 3.4   Look and Feel

For testing the look and feel we used various examples found in different applications, or we created the examples by ourselves. The supported hypotheses in this section regarding user's preference for cartoon imagery, navigation tools, visible and interaction grammar of menus and commands were:

- Menus starting with a verb are considered more natural than those starting with nouns. Although a noun and verb menu was regarded as easy to understand, a verb-driven menu was preferred in that it showed a clear purpose to the user. In contrast, the Czech sample expressed a strong preference towards nouns as these were the most intelligible.
- Cartoon imagery (*e.g.* little animals) plays an important role in communication. The cartoons improve users' mood and help recall different applications better than characters.

Unsupported hypotheses were:

- Menus progressively disclosing a narrative (*e.g.* starting with "I want to…") are considered more natural.
- Theme-driven menus (*e.g.* starting with "I want to…") or role-driven menus (*e.g.* starting with "I am…") are more logical than menus driven by attributes or concepts.
- The proposed interaction is best understood when starting from a concrete situation (a use-case, *e.g.* "I want to…") rather than user-role (*e.g.* "I am…").

## 4     Proposed Guidelines for Chinese UI Design

To help cross-cultural UI designers utilize our findings, we present our results in the form of guidelines that could also be used to enhance the user's acceptation of the UI in a specific culture:

1. Important information should appear in the top-left corner or in the middle-center of the screen.
2. New (or problematic) information should appear in the middle-center or top-center of the screen.
3. Given (or familiar) information should appear in the bottom-right or middle-right of the screen.
4. Ideal (or general) information should appear in the middle-left or top-left of the screen.
5. Real (or detailed) information should appear in the middle-center or middle-left of the screen.
6. Images should be placed in the middle-left or top-right corner of the screen.
7. Put information meant to be easily noticed in the middle-center or top-left corner of the screen.
8. Carefully choose the images: they start the visual narration on the screen, followed by titles.

9. The layout should allow for a central composition (1-column, 3-column, central layout).
10. The layout should follow the golden ratio (4: 3, or 16: 9).
11. Design the layout to be read from left to right. New information should come from the right.
12. Layout dividers should be straight, windows should have rounded corners and icons should be rounded.
13. UIs should use common patterns so that users can transfer their knowledge from other UIs.
14. Use blue, purple, aqua (cyan), and gray (silver) for background color.
15. Use light pastel colors on a white background.
16. Use black, blue, and lime for foreground color.
17. Put more important information on the foreground.
18. For commercial websites, use the combination of white, silver and black. For personal websites white, blue, black and aqua. Lime and fuchsia would also be well received. For educational websites use white, blue and black. For governmental websites use white, red and black.
19. Do not put yellow text on red background.
20. Use silver on black, blue on lime, black on white.
21. Use icons containing characters and images.
22. Place icon attributes on the right from the icon.
23. Create shorter pages with fewer contexts.
24. Search facets should follow the order of the natural language (Subject, verb, object).
25. For the highest acceptance and credibility, use pictorial media (images, videos).
26. Above all, the UI should be fast (responsive) and usable as well as aesthetic.
27. When suitable, use Chinese calligraphy elements (readable is better).
28. Form menus from verbs, submenus from nouns. Alternatively, use a combination of verbs and nouns.
29. To improve users' mood and recall use, cartoon imagery in the UI.

## 5    Discussion

In our paper we tried to show what interesting and workable differences between user groups, if any, we can gather from cross-cultural research. Both the groups were exposed to similar computing environments which lead to similar preferences for the UI structure in general. However, we found a few cultural markers that were different and were related mostly to layout and color. The impact of the native language grammar on the spatial and logical UI organization was not so profound as we expected. More differences came from habits and cultural background.

Given the large scope of the initial research focus, we were not able to run more tests on topics where the results did not support previous research results or were not clear enough or promised more interesting data. In a future study, we would like to focus more on those questions.

We hope our results and proposed design guidelines will help the international HCI design community and they will contribute to a discussion on how to improve cross-cultural research.

**Acknowledgements.** The authors wish to thank for the assistance of the SEUC, namely of Sun Wenxin, Ma Yin, Zhou Yongjie, Xiao Sheng, Xiang Yong, and of Aaron Marcus, Principal Designer of AM+A, Inc.

# References

1. Barber, Badre: Culturability: The merging of culture and usability. In: Proceedings of the 4th Conference on Human Factors and the Web (1998)
2. Brejcha, Marcus: Semiotics of Interaction: Towards a UI Alphabet. In: HCII 2013 Conference Proceedings, Las Vegas (2013)
3. Dong, Lee: A cross-cultural comparative study of users' perceptions of a webpage: With a focus on the cognitive styles of Chinese, Koreans and Americans. International Journal of Design 2(2), 19–30 (2008)
4. Guest, et al.: How Many Interviews Are Enough?: An Experiment with Data Saturation and Variability. Field Methods 18(1), 59–82 (2006)
5. Kress, Van Leeuwen: Reading Images: The Grammar Of Visual Design. Routledge (2006)
6. Nielsen, Landauer: A mathematical model of the finding of usability problems. In: Proceedings of the INTERACT 1993 and CHI 1993 Conference on Human Factors in Computing Systems, pp. 206–213 (1993)
7. Marcus, Gould: Crosscurrents: cultural dimensions and global Web user-interface design. Interactions (2000)
8. Mason: Sample size and saturation in: PhD studies using qualitative interviews 11(3) (2010)
9. Sauro: Confidence Interval Calculator for a Completion Rate. Measuring Usability (2005), http://www.measuringusability.com/wald.htm (last accessed October 19, 2012)
10. Sheridan: Cross-cultural website design. MultiLingual Computing & Technology 12(7), 1–5 (2001)
11. Smith, et al.: A process model for developing usable cross-cultural websites. Interacting with Computers 16(1), 63–91 (2004)
12. Wikipedia. Web colors. (Chinese version), http://zh.wikipedia.org/wiki/网页颜色模式#HTML.E5.90.8D.E7.A7.B0 (last accessed September 9, 2009)

# Use Second Screen to Enhance TV Viewing Experiences

Yu-Ling Chuang, Chia-Wei Liao, Wen-Shiuan Chen, Wen-Tsung Chang,
Shao-Hua Cheng, Yi-Chong Zeng, and Kai-Hsuan Chan

Institute for Information Industry
1F., No. 133, Sec. 4, Minsheng E. Rd., Taipei City, Taiwan, R.O.C.
{ilmachuang,cliao,clairechen,wtchang,briancheng,
yichongzeng,kaihsuanchan}@iii.org.tw

**Abstract.** In this paper, we propose a second-screen interactive TV viewing scenario, and build an Android-based prototype to verify our concept and design. The demo app detects the TV program that a user is watching, and then dynamically pushes additional information through the second screen to the user. In this prototype, we apply audio fingerprinting technology to detect TV programs, and users do not have to manually surf hundreds of channels. In addition, face recognition and tennis event detection technologies have been employed to extract critical elements from the TV contents. With these content analysis tools, we can obtain video metadata more easily and need not rely on content providers. A usability test with 20 participants has been conducted. Our test shows participants are interested in our second screen app, and they would like more features and information from the app. Next, we plan to further refine the app's design to enhance user experience.

**Keywords:** Second Screen, User Experience, Video Content Analysis, Audio Fingerprinting.

## 1    Introduction

The survey of Red Bee Media shows that 52% of the respondents would like to search for additional information about the programs they have seen [1]. Unfortunately, most of the information on the Internet is fragmented. As the mobile device gets more popular, people use it as a second screen while watching TV. In Nielsen's 2011 report, 42% of tablet owners and 40% of smartphone owners use their devices in the TV viewing context [2]. For now, there is no direct link between TV and the second screen which are otherwise tightly coupled. Mobile devices such as smart phones and pads, as second screens, meet the increasing viewers' demand for information. We synchronize TV viewers' mobile devices with the TV, and push related real-time information to their devices (such as details of the products placed in the show, introduction of the cast). Although interactive TV comes with similar capability, interactive applications on the TV screen has been proved interruptive [3]. Using mobile devices as second screens of TV, our approach enhances the TV viewing experiences without much distraction to viewers. Moreover, second screen approach

P.L.P. Rau (Ed.): CCD/HCII 2013, Part I, LNCS 8023, pp. 366–374, 2013.
© Springer-Verlag Berlin Heidelberg 2013

offers a far richer interaction mechanism than conventional remote control devices coming with interactive TV [4].

Since product placement is restricted in certain areas (such as Taiwan), second screen concept provides another channel for TV marketing. We have built a prototype based on this concept to demonstrate and validate this second-screen approach with several pre-defined scenarios.

Our prototype is an Android application. It detects the TV program being watched, and pushes real-time information accordingly. To make sure that our design satisfies users' needs while watching different shows, we include a variety of genres in the prototype. Considering the needs of viewers and the capability of technology, we push primarily the brief information like introduction, summaries, and additional contents about the program. We collect the above information and timestamp manually unless they can be obtained from the content owner. However, to be more independent of content providers in the future, automatic video tagging and annotation based on, say, face recognition and sport event detection technologies have been developed to analyze TV programs and events in tennis games. Tags and annotations are, in our case, the metadata, and will later be pushed to viewer's second screen. To automatically synchronize the mobile devices with TV, we have also developed audio fingerprint detection and matching techniques to automatically identify the TV program.

There are 20 participants in our experiment to test the prototype, and each participant uses a second screen while watching TV in our simulation. During the experiment, they need to finish some assigned tasks and then give their feedback. This is to know participants' preferences when using a second screen and the information they would like most.

## 2    Related Work

Fallahkhair et al [5~6] combined interactive TV and mobile phones to facilitate informal language learning. Whoever wants to study a foreign language can learn from TV shows in that language. The researchers tried to extend this approach from TV to mobile devices. Viewers activate TAMALLE, running on interactive TV and mobile phones, to get instant information of exotic culture or help with language items before, during, or after watching the show. Language items can be saved for future use. Mobile phones also provide an alternative way of learning on the move.

In 2011, Basapur et al [7] proposed a dual device TV viewing experience. They built a browser-based web application, which updated time-synchronized feeds of the program. In their prototype, a browser tab shows content related post, comments from social network, and related multimedia. Another one shows episode and show details, and actor bios. Users need to click on a specific post to open its original source website in a new tab. In this prototype, researchers manually created the feeds within 24 hours after the program airs on the TV. A year later, they built another prototype [8] where the feeds came from the viewers' social circles instead of experts, so they could interact with the prototype during a live TV show. Thus these information feeds should be more personal and more relevant to program contents. However, no automatic synchronization mechanism has been deployed in these two prototypes. Viewers have to manually perform synchronization between devices.

Nowadays, more and more second screen apps are available on the market, such as IntoNow [9], GetGlue [10], Miso [11], and Zeebox [12]. They mostly deal with show details and social features, including TV program check-in, on-line chatting, and Facebook integration. IntoNow and Zeebox provide some kind of content related information, but they have no instant message and highly rely on specific content providers. RendezVous [13] aims to provide TV viewers interactivity and additional information about the program as well. It gathers and aggregates content related information from channel partners or their semi-editorial system. It is similar to our research. The main difference is we focus on automatic video and audio content analysis and event detection.

## 3    Design

In our prototype, 18 programs of various genres are selected, ranging from drama, variety show, talk show, sports, travel show, to movies. According to Goodman's research, people (i.e. website visitors) are particular interested in fan-based features and show annotations [14]. To better understand the audience of programs, we have interviewed potential viewers. Hundreds of ideas have been floated. Considering the limitations of time and resources, viewers' needs, innovation, and our technology capability, these ideas are boiled down to 6 categories (i.e. highlight, introduction, dynamic information, products, event, and statistics for sports only) of information that will be pushed to the second screen. Moreover, social features such as check-in, discussion forum and chatting are included in our prototype, too.

Fig.1 illustrates GUI samples of our prototype application. The "detection" button identifies the program currently playing on the TV, and then shows its highlight to present a brief introduction of the program to the viewers. In addition, viewers can easily access additional information through a feature menu as shown below.

|     (a)     |     (b)     |     (c)     |

**Fig. 1.** Second screen app UI: (a) main page (b) program highlight (c) dynamic information

1. Introduction. The section gives a brief introduction of the show such as the cast and summary. Viewers interested can further get more detailed information from related Wikipedia or Facebook via hyperlinks in this section. For certain genus (e.g. drama), a relation diagram among all characters is provided to help the audience follow the show more easily. For sports, the history and statistics of the players (or teams) is presented to the audience.

2. Dynamic Information. While the program is showing, the second screen app constantly and instantly shows the summary and updates the contents that range from plots, conversations, events, to products. This way, the viewers can well follow the program even if they have no time to watch the full show. In some countries (e.g. Taiwan), showing product placement is restricted though sometimes the audience would like to know about it. The second screen offers an alternative where the product's information can be pushed and displayed. Holmes [15] indicates that the second screen garners considerable visual attention, about 30% of the total viewing session. To minimize distraction to viewers, new-coming messages are placed at the top and old ones will be scrolled down and still kept on the UI. Information will be fed to the second screen during commercials to keep viewers glued.

3. Product. Items in the product placement are listed here. With a single click, TV viewers can mark whatever products they like as favorites, or even place an order. They can share the information of the product on Facebook. It serves as another way of promotion.

4. Event. The second screen can show instant messages about certain campaigns. Viewers can choose to participate and share the campaign information on Facebook.

5. Statistics. The statistics of a live Sports show is constantly and instantly updated, and made available to the viewers.

6. Check-in. Users share the information and comments of the program they are currently watching using Facebook. This very program will be further exposed to current viewers' social circles and promoted.

7. Discussion Forum/ Chatting Room. TV viewers communicate with one another using Discussion Forum for topic-independent messages and Chatting Room for free talk.

# 4    Prototype Implementation

A prototype based on the above design has been implemented. An Electronic Program Guide (EPG) containing 6 channels is used in our test, each representing a certain aforementioned genre. Three 5-minute long videos play repeatedly on each channel. A streaming server streams these programs, according to the EPG, and delivers related information to users as well. A push server is also installed.

## 4.1    Metadata Information Extraction

In our application scenario, we need to push additional information such as actors/actresses, products, location and events to the second screen. To effectively manage such information, the associated metadata from content owner is required, either generated manually or automatically. However, obtaining complete or sufficient metadata from TV companies is difficult, in practice. Hence we also develop content analysis technologies to automatically extract metadata from audio and video features. Initially, we focus on face recognition and tennis event detection.

With face recognition, we can identify the characters appearing in the show, and the relationship among them. Tennis event detection helps to detect events from a lengthy tennis game, and summarize it.

**Face Recognition.** Facial information is crucial that we can extract and manage/browse specific person in video contents. Nowadays accurate face recognition still poses a big challenge, although automatic face detection is mature and robust. To achieve robust face recognition, manual collection of faces as an identification basis is required. Our face recognition system consists of three steps which are face detection, face clustering, and recognition process.

First, a video is divided into scenes using frame-change detection. Lin and Liu's method [16] is used to detect human faces in each frame. Their detector is capable of detecting faces of different orientations. In a clip, close-by faces are clustered into a group. At the end, we apply face recognition to faces in each group.

After face recognition, the intervals of time when a character appears in the video are there. Generally speaking, the leading characters appear longer and more frequently in a video. Based on this assumption, we can compute the "importance" of each character, as shown in Fig. 2(a). The overlaps of the time intervals of two characters represent their correlation and degree of interaction. An interaction graph of characters can be constructed as shown in Fig. 2(b). Fig. 2(c) shows the interaction frames of the two selected characters based on the overlaps.

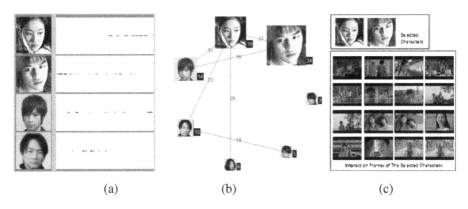

(a)                    (b)                    (c)

**Fig. 2.** Three applications based on human faces: (a) time-points of characters; (b) interaction graph of characters; and (c) interaction frames of the two selected characters

**Tennis Event Detection.** There are numerous video types, and oftentimes the video type classification is subjective. Each video type could need a content analyzer of its own, and each analyzer, itself, poses a big challenge to researchers and developers. We have implemented a content analyzer for tennis video event detection.

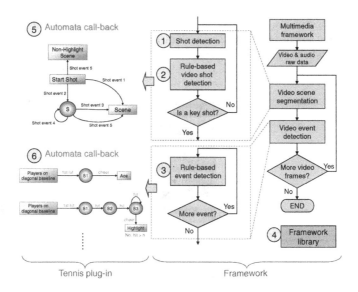

**Fig. 3.** Tennis video content analysis data flow

Below is brief explanation of the data flow Fig. 3. First, the content analyzer detects the shots, uninterrupted clips recorded by a single camera, by using a common video processing method. Then, rules are defined for scene segmentation and scene event detection. A scene is a collection of semantically related and temporally adjacent shots, depicting and conveying a high-level concept. In the scene event detection, some detectors compute the positions of the tennis court and the players. Please refer to [17] [18] for the details of the algorithm. We also have detectors to spot the sounds of hit and cheer. Most events occur during the rally between players, and are followed by cheers [17], if there are great shots. Audio plays an even more important role in event detection than video here. Audio features are cheaper to detect (than the video ones) and help significantly reduce the cost of the video processing (e.g. court and player tracking). Detected events will be exported in XML and pushed to viewer's second screen accordingly.

## 4.2    Audio Fingerprinting

Automatic synchronization between TV and second screen is a desirable feature for some TV viewers. The associated audio fingerprints are employed to detect the current TV program. We apply audio, over video, for easier management and computation. Moreover, recording audio is easier than recording video for most of the viewers. Push the "detect" button, and then app records the TV sound and instantly determines the program playing on TV.

An acoustic fingerprint is a condensed digital digest that deterministically computed from an audio signal. By comparing it with audio samples in an audio database [19], we can quickly find matched items. In our real time audio recognition system, the critical band analysis method from Kaller et al [20] is adopted to extract and match fingerprints. A server computes the fingerprint of (1) an audio clip recorded by the client app and (2) a stream immediately after it is received from a channel, and updates the audio database.

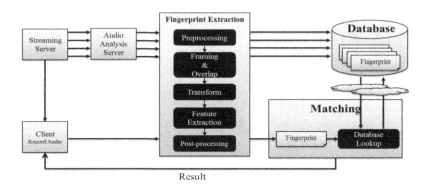

**Fig. 4.** Audio analysis system flow chart

## 5     Evaluation

We have conducted a usability test on our prototype. We have 20 participants from Taiwan (10 males and 10 females) of ages ranging from 22 to 40. Some of them are students, and others are our colleagues. None of them has ever participated in this project. They watch TV more than 1 hour per day on average, and use their mobile devices while watching TV at least once a week. From their feedback, we hope to better understand users' preferences and behaviors.

Since the second screen concept and apps are not popular in Taiwan yet, only 1 participant has ever used similar apps or services. However, 17 of them often search for additional information about TV on Google.

During the test, participants are asked to perform certain tasks in a simulated living room environment, which include (1) synchronizing TV with mobile device, (2) looking for additional information about a movie and the actress in the movie, (3) checking movie/ game status, and (4) purchasing a product. At the end, they each need to fill out a 5 Likert-based satisfaction questionnaire, and give comments on our prototype and second screen scenarios.

Overall, participants are positive about our prototype. They like the automatic program detection feature, and find it useful. Three of them would like our app to automatically detect channel change as well. The detection button on the app does not seem clear enough, and five participants suggest making it more eye-catching. They also show the concern about the reliability in a noisy environment. The information we provide in our app is appealing to participants. They particularly like the program introduction, dynamic information, products, and statistics. All participants would like to use this app in the future if it is free. If they have to pay, then more incentives are needed.

As for the usability of our prototype, participants are able to complete all assigned tasks, except for reviewing missing TV contents. Based on our test scenario, participants turn on TV to watch the movies that have already been playing for some time. To follow the movie, they are asked to check the content of the part they miss. Thirteen participants mistakenly click "introduction" instead of "dynamic information". They assume that TV content summaries should be placed in the program introduction session. Moreover, four participants click "introduction" to check personal statistics in a game. From their behaviors, we conclude that people tend to click "introduction" when they are lost. Therefore, the wording of the menu needs to be clearer and more intuitive. Ten participants click the wrong icon when synchronizing second screen with TV program. It is because the "Detect program" icon is too small to be distinguished from its logo.

When asked about the wish list for new features, six would like program recommendation, and four would like to control their TV directly with the app. TV schedule and more program related information (such as movie review, behind the scenes, game strategy) are desirable.

## 6    Conclusions and Future Work

In this paper, we propose second screen scenarios, which focus on the real-time delivery of additional program information. Our goal is to enhance the TV viewing experience with a second screen, and such information delivery should not interfere with users' normal TV viewing behavior, and additionally provide new business opportunities. An Android-based prototype app has been implemented. This app automatically detects TV program, and instantly pushes related information, such as program introduction, dynamic information, product, and statistics. Audio fingerprinting, face recognition, and tennis event detection technologies are employed in this app.

To verify our development work, an experiment involving 20 participants shows that people adopt the second screen quickly, and like it especially when this application is free. However, participants would like more diverse features and richer information on the second screen.

In the future, we plan to expand the scalability of our prototype to support more concurrent connections. To enrich our contents, we will continue developing new media analysis techniques. For example, live audio/video keyword detection and spotting is on the drawing board. We will iteratively revise the design of our system according to the feedback from users, and hope to release our product to the market as soon as possible.

## References

1. Red Bee Reports. Broadcast industry not capitalising on rise of the second screen: New research reveals that majority of TV viewers now dual screen but industry's take up of synchronous apps remains slow (2012), http://www.redbeemedia.com/sites/all/files/downloads/second_screen_research.pdf
2. Nielsen Consumer Reports. State of media: consumer usage report (2011), http://blog.nielsen.com/nielsenwire/mediauniverse/

3. Tsekleves, E., Whitham, R., Kondo, K., Hill, A.: Investigating media use and the television user experience in the home. Entertainment Computing 2(3), 151–161 (2011)
4. Cruickshank, L., Tsekleves, E., Whitham, R.: HILL, A, and Kondo, K. Making interactive TV easier to use: interface design for a second screen approach. The Design Journal 10(3) (2007)
5. Fallahkhair, S., Pemberton, L., Masthoff, J.: A dual device scenario for informal language learning: interactive television meets the mobile phone. In: Proceedings of the IEEE International Conference on Advanced Learning Technologies, pp. 16–20 (2004)
6. Fallahkhair, S., Pemberton, L., Griffiths, R.: Dual device user interface design for ubiquitous language learning: mobile phone and interactive television (iTV). In: Proceedings of the IEEE International Workshop on Wireless and Mobile Technologies in Education (WMTE 2005), pp. 85–92 (2005)
7. Basapur, S., Harboe, G., Mandalia, H., Novak, A., Vuong, V., Metcalf, C.: Field trial of a dual device user experience for iTV. In: Proceedings of the 9th International Interactive Conference on Interactive Television, pp. 127–136 (2011)
8. Basapur, S., Mandalia, H., Chaysinh, S., Lee, Y., Venkitaraman, N., Metcalf, C.: Proceedings of the 10th European Conference on Interactive TV and Video, pp. 87–96 (2012)
9. IntoNow Application, http://www.intonow.com/ci
10. GetGlue Application, http://getglue.com/
11. MISO Application, http://gomiso.com/
12. Zeebox Application, http://zeebox.com/tv/home
13. Poivre, S.R.: An editorial ruled based contextual TV information system. In: Adjunct Proceedings of the EUROITV 2011, p. 96 (2012)
14. Goodman, J.M.: Enhanced TV features on national broadcast and cable program web sites: An exploratory analysis of what features are present and how viewers respond to them. Master's Thesis, Scripps College of Communications of Ohio University (2009)
15. Holmes, M.E., Josephson, S., Carney, R.E.: Visual attention to television programs with a second-screen application. In: Proceedings of the Symposium on Eye Tracking Research and Applications, pp. 397–400 (2012)
16. Lin, Y.Y., Liu, T.L.: Robust Face Detection with Multi-class Boosting. In: Proceedings of the IEEE Computer Society Conference on Computer Vision and Pattern Recognition, vol. 1, pp. 680–687 (2005)
17. Chu, W.T., Tien, M.C., Wang, Y.T., Chou, C.W., Hsieh, K.Y., Wu, J.L.: Event detection in tennis matches based on real-world audiovisual cues. In: Proceedings of the 20th IPPR Conference on Computer Vision, Graphics, and Image Processing, pp. 541–548 (2007)
18. Tien, M.C., Wang, Y.T., Chou, C.W., Hsieh, K.Y., Chu, W.T., Wu, J.L.: Event detection in tennis matches based on video data mining. In: Proceedings of IEEE International Conference on Multimedia & Expo, pp. 1477–1480 (2008)
19. Acoustic fingerprint – Wikipedia, the free encyclopedia, http://en.wikipedia.org/wiki/Acoustic_fingerprint#cite_note-1
20. Haitsma, J., Kalker, T.: A Highly Robust Audio Fingerprinting System. In: Proceedings of the 3rd International Conference on Music Information Retrieval, pp. 107–115 (2002)

# A Study about the Culture Service Process and Tools Design

Chen-hao Fan[1], I-Hsin Fan[2], Chun Chieh Weng[3],
Jia-Haur Liang[4], and Huang-Tsun Lu[5]

[1] National Taiwan University of Arts/Taiwan Design Center, Taiwan
[2] National Union University, Taiwan
[3] The One Style Co., Ltd., Taiwan
[4] National Taiwan University of Arts, Taiwan
[5] Taiwan Design Center, Taiwan
Edward_Fan@tdc.org.tw, magfan@nuu.edu.tw,
eason.won@theonestyle.com, liang@ntua.edu.tw,
harveylu@tdc.org.tw

**Abstract.** Through the cultural accumulation of knowledge with the SECI model to bring out the re-integration of the design factors from the elements of Oriental design imagery metaphor by the experience exchange from different expertise. Transformation of the changes is from observation to interaction till stimulated the creativity that fertile the fundation of knowledge. The practice process is the result of the deconstruction of the elements to transforming the accumulation of knowledge till the implementation of construction of the actual production and final the validation is complete.

**Keywords:** Cultural and creative industries, bamboo, tea, qualia, SECI model.

## 1 Introduction

Culture and Creative Industries is a new trend of the world's industry. Not only can it create a phenomenal economy grow, but also has become the hottest industry to compete to other countries. Taiwan also needs to participate in this new trend. Taiwan's tea and bamboo can't fight only based on the quality but have to create a new story itself. In order to do so, Kansei is the way how writer interprets the new story.

Kansei experience is the core of this research. Taiwan's bamboo and tea were respectively as the appearance and content of the design, appliances and material. The bamboo is the material for the construction and tea as the connotation of function. The tea ceremony is inspired by five senses of Kansei. By go through the Evoked Metaphor and SECI model to prove that it is important for a design process to go by interdisciplinary discuss and integrate. After the integration, it still needs to workable, by then can we say the design has got the "perceptual field, moved experience and Quality goods" ability and called Qualia design.

P.L.P. Rau (Ed.): CCD/HCII 2013, Part I, LNCS 8023, pp. 375–383, 2013.
© Springer-Verlag Berlin Heidelberg 2013

Use "Case Study" to investigate tea restaurant and conclude with four elements how urban people experience created: space, experience, goods and narrative. And use them as the design's elements, undergo the SECI model, and integrate with Evoked Metaphor and Kansei design, then create a new design of carbonized bamboo tea set. To verify the marketing and possibility of commercialization with a tea ceremony of a complete experience designed the space by five senses.

Through the cultural accumulation of knowledge with the SECI model to bring out the re-integration of the design factors from the elements of Oriental design imagery metaphor by the experience exchange from different areas of expertise. Transformation of the changes is to observe the surrounding environment from the potential cultivation of knowledge in a particular field, to interact with the outside world, whether it is narrated of the text language or images shock, stimulate creative thinking, and fertile the next stage of accumulation of knowledge foundation. The practice of the process is the result of the deconstruction of the first element, transforming the accumulation of knowledge, the implementation of construction of the actual production, the validation is complete. Presented a people in cultural knowledge, co-innovation, and the corresponding DNA run in the industry.

## 2    The Study

A term of modern philosophy, "qualia" can be regarded as the entirety of what one perceives: it is the sum of "feelings" that one experiences when the mind interacts with the world; it is the very first "impact" that one senses from something without any dissimulation. Such an experience directly touches one's heart and is therefore a key factor to sympathy and sensation. Used in design, "qualia" may add an intense sensational trait to the simple utility of a product and transform it into an exceptionally adorable item. Among the various examples of successful qualia creations, we are especially intrigued by that of the Japanese *chado* (tea ceremony), a combination of oriental simplicity, serenity and solemnity with which the ceremony is imbued. Such is a sort of artistic beauty deeply rooted in the oriental culture. If one could integrate a bit of this beauty in utensil design, users would be able to constantly refresh themselves with a similar sensation at any given time or place. The current study is especially interested in the way of expressing the artistic simplicity of *chado* in design: not only will its unique qualia serve as the focus of design, but we will also test the positioning of conceived products in the market by comparing them to their counterparts in the modern experience of tea tasting.

Meanwhile, as Taiwan's cultural and creative industry evolves with that of the world, one may reconsider the role of bamboo, one of Taiwan's signature produces. In the following parts of the study, we will present the uniqueness of Taiwanese bamboo and its prospect of development as an important, environmentally friendly material that is becoming increasingly well-received in the world.

The current study seeks to investigate how Taiwan may transform its traditional material into modern products by introducing appealing design in indigenous bamboo.

It is hoped that the study may inspire other designers to reconsider the versatile and plastic nature of bamboo and to create even more ingenious designs. In this study we expect to achieve the following objectives:

1. To investigate in the literature review the applicability of bamboo as one of the world's new favorite materials as well as the conceptualization of qualia in design.
2. To identify the trend of development of bamboo material in the international market by studying existing literature and international exhibitions; to find the process of and essential elements of tea tasting in modern society by means of case study; to introduce the SECI Model by means of Evoked Metaphor (EM).
3. To classify and answer the questions encountered in the course of introducing the SECI Model so that future designers interested in conducting similar studies may use the answers as references.
4. To propose an integral example of innovative utility design by demonstrating in the EM and the SECI Model how knowledge is acquired and exchanged in the interaction of theories, from the original idea to the end product; to show how a dialogue between modern design and traditional craft may serve as an example of successful cultural and creative industry development.

With "qualia" as its theme, the study incorporates Taiwanese bamboo and Taiwanese tea as the body and soul of the designed products, which shall be made of bamboo, serve as teawares, and invigorate prospective users through their five senses. An Evoked Metaphor and a process of organizational knowledge creation (SECI Model) will exemplify the steps of a complete process of product development from conceptualizing interdisciplinary theories in design to testing the effect of such design with users. Such a process is epitomized as "sensitive field, impressive experience, qualia product."

Based on the case study, "field," "experience," "commodity" and "story" are identified as components of product design. Findings of a research method integrating SECI Model and Evoked Metaphor yielded innovative bamboo charcoal teawares as "commodity" and tea party as "field" in which users may "experience" through their five senses a created "story" whereas designers may test the market acceptance of their work and the possibility of commodification.

The SECI Model shows how certain metaphors found in Oriental design may fuse and then split into new design elements through interdisciplinary exchanges as designers' knowledge about culture evolves. Such fusion and fission are fueled by the interaction between internal knowledge and external environment in a given field. An inspiration, no matter occurring verbally or visually, stimulates creativity and is later internalized to complement or enrich existing knowledge. The process of product development presented in this study can be summarized as: deconstructing preexisting design elements in a sensational experience, transforming historical knowledge, reconstructing the design elements in a product, and testing the product. The process exemplifies how a collective innovation in knowledge and culture may be achieved by individuals of different times and spaces.

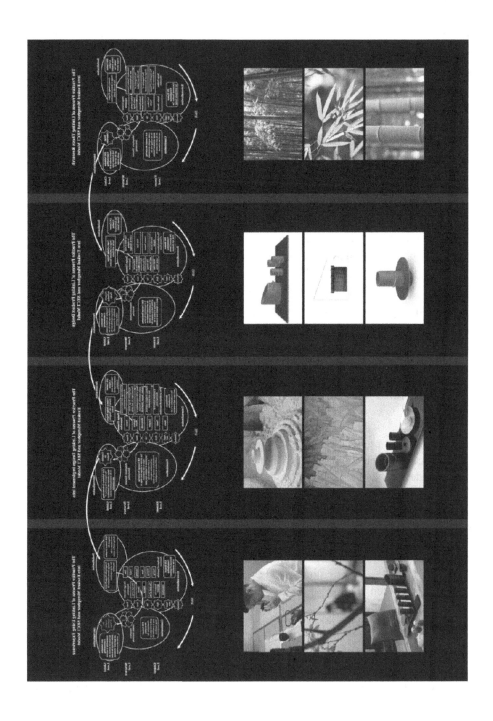

## Structure of the Study

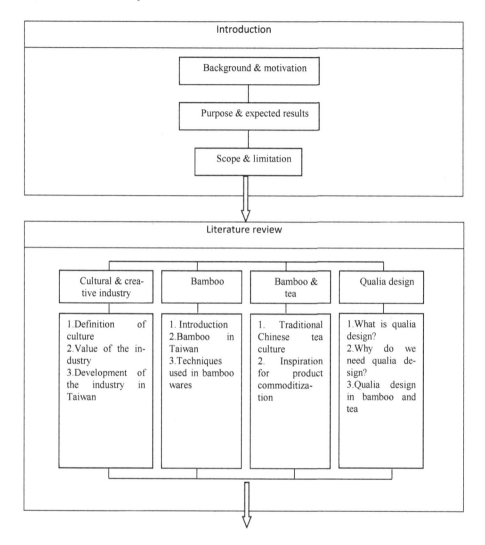

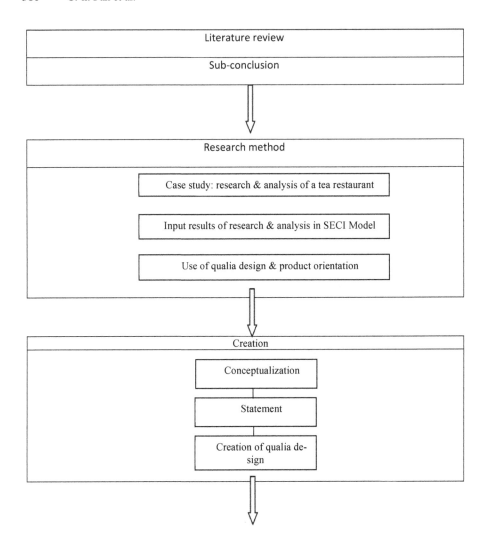

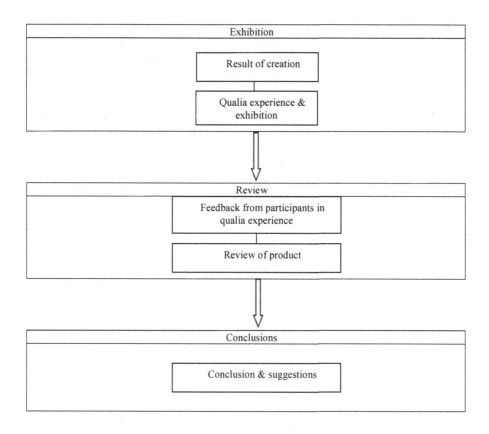

## 3    Conclusions

The two subjects of the current study, bamboo and tea, both important produces of Taiwan, are not only important metaphors in Oriental cultures but also representations of Taiwanese traditions. Having decided on the "body," or material, of the design product, we seek to find a "soul," or theme, with which the modern society can identify. Through field research in a tea restaurant, we were able to elicit a "qualia tea tasting ceremony" of urban residents in which field, experience, commodity and story are all indispensable components of a qualia design. Up to this point, we were clear about the "body" and "soul" of our qualia and were only left with the task of concretizing the practice. We therefore employed EM and SECI Model to theorize and concretize the practice so that we could propose a specific process as reference for future replication or improvement. The method should allow craftspeople from different disciplines and professions to exchange their know-how from designer's perspective in order to reach new heights in design. As these experts all have different skills, it is only through this method that they can come together with their expertise and contribute to an interdisciplinary qualia design. The study proposes the following conclusions:

1. Qualia should be the core of each design, because impressive qualia can not only touch people's heart but also promote the value of a design product. However, qualia cannot be achieved by the product alone; it takes all the four elements, namely field, experience, commodity and story, to construct a really impressive qualia. It is for this reason that we chose to test the design product in a tea party, where we constructed a field in which users were able to experience a story. This practice was accomplished by means of an EM interdisciplinary communication that involved craftspeople from different professions and with different knowledge and techniques. On the other hand, the SECI Model, which conceptualizes the cycle of knowledge dissemination and renewal, indicates that a qualia experience may be illustrated, referred to and replicated in other situations. The study shows how one may put related academic theories into practice.

2. The study may serve as an example of real practice in Taiwan's cultural and creative industry, which can be seen a value-added version of traditional manufacturing industry or emerging service industry. The two themes of this study (tea and bamboo) are in reality mature industries in Taiwan; however, the marriage of these two traditions brought about the innovation in material and medium use of bamboo charcoal teawares. EM and SECI Model taught us that successful design is in fact more than an occasional inspiration: not only does it have logical components, but it can also be forged through constantly fusing and splitting elements of various knowledge bases without changing the leitmotif of the design. And it is through this process that design reaches constantly newer heights.

3. The involvement of the SECI Model of organizational knowledge creation distinguishes EM from traditional design methods. In the new practice, the design elements are thoroughly communicated and understood by all actors in the design process; this allows us to avoid the problem of incompatibility between designers and executers without having to change the leitmotif of the design. Different from the traditional unilateral design method, EM proposes a process cycle that can be constantly refreshed to achieve the optimal result. In the study, this cycle allowed us to find out that only by extending the traditional thinking of craftspeople could we bring innovation to craftsmanship; only by grasping the properties of new materials could we integrate all of them in a set of teawares; only by reconsidering the dependent relations between design elements could we bring out the leitmotif in the products; only by recognizing user's needs could we craft artistic commodities that had a potential to sell.

4. Through the theoretical framework of EM and SECI Model, the study proposes a module of four phases: study, design, completion and experience, among which the phases of "study" and "experience" especially set the current practice apart from traditional design methods. On one hand, during the first phase, designers' past experience and new interdisciplinary knowledge interact to generate new design elements that split and fuse to form an orientation that guides the product design. On the other hand, during the last phase, designers ponder about such questions as "Will the end product be accepted by the market?" "What can we do to improve the process of commodification?" To properly test market acceptance, it is necessary to create an appropriate field of experience (i.e. one that facilitate the five senses) and to draft effective marketing strategies (story) so that designers may

gather sufficient information (experience of prospective consumers) about future marketing of the product.

5. The study presents a real practice in which a design product involved designers' perspective, craftspeople's professional know-how, and cross-border collaboration. In this practice, products of traditional industries were given a new life and a new story thanks to an exceptional collaboration between innovators, practitioners and academics. It is hardly possible to find in one person designers' knowledge about commercial value and modern creativity, craftspeople's excellent skills and researchers' expertise in theories. Nonetheless, through communication and dialogue, it is possible to achieve a cultural and creative product which not only is artistically conceived and skillfully made but also addresses users' needs. In this optic, a cultural and creative product can also be an art work. The current study is but an example of such collaboration; the feasibility of such a method is yet to be replicated by other designers in the future.

In sum, qualia is a key factor to the connection between cultural and creative industry and consumers because it is how one perceives the world and how the world touches one's heart. As qualia is powerful but elusive, one needs to conceptualize it through a specific process if he wishes to know what it takes to use qualia in cultural and creative design. To better demonstrate how qualia can inspire design, the current study exposes a theoretical framework as well as an actual practice. As qualia cannot be described in words, its most important part lies in users' experience with it. And it is exactly in users' sensational experience that one sees the connection between consumer and design product: it is in the exceptional qualia that one sees the real value of cultural and creative products.

# References

1. Dennett, D.C.: Quining qualia. In: Marcel, A., Bisiach, E. (eds.) Consciousness in Contemporary Science. Oxford University Press (1988)
2. Wright, E.: The Case of Qualia. MIT Press, Cambridge (2008)
3. Lowe, E.J.: Illusions and Hallucinations as Evidence for Sence Data. In: The Case of Qualia. MIT Press, Cambridge (2008)
4. Jackson, F.: Epiphenomenal qualia. Philosophical Quarterly (1982)
5. Nonaka, I.: The Knowledge-Creating Company. Oxford University Press, New York (1995)
6. Lévy, P., Lee, S., Yamanaka, T.: On kansei and kansei design a description of Japanese design approach. In: IASDR. University of Tsukuba, Japan (2007)
7. Caves, R.: Creative Industries: Contracts Between Art and Commerce (2003) 台北，典藏藝術家庭。
8. Howell, R.J.: Subjective Physcialism. In: The Case of Qualia. MIT Press, Cambridge (2008)
9. Robinson, W.S.: Experience and Representation. In: The Case of Qualia. MIT Press, Cambridge (2008)

# User Experience with Chinese Handwriting
# Input on Touch-Screen Mobile Phones

Qin Gao[1], Bin Zhu[1], Pei-Luen Patrick Rau[1], Shilpa Vyas[2], Cuiling Chen[1], and Hui Li[1]

[1] Department of Industrial Engineering, Tsinghua University, Beijing, 100084, China
{trishagao,binzhuw,plprau,cathychencl,hli.sunshine}@gmail.com
[2] Research in Motion UK Limited, Centrum House, 36 Station Road, Egham, Surrey, England
Shvyas@rim.com

**Abstract.** The fast development of mobile services in China and the recent trend of touch-screen handheld devices precipitate researchers to understand user experience with mobile Chinese handwriting input (HWI). This research attempts to provide an integrated picture of user experience with Chinese HWI on touch-screen mobile phones. Five usability experts were invited to inspect usability problems of seven handwriting-enabled mobile phones, which varied in type of screens, writing tools and interaction approaches, operation systems, and handwriting recognizers. In a following usability evaluation with five novice users, we collected both quantitative data and qualitative data to give an overall performance assessment to the seven mobile phones and furthermore to analyze the usability issues with HWI. As a result, we identified 16 usability issues related with handwriting recognizers, input interfaces, and devices/users respectively.

**Keywords:** Usability evaluation, heuristic evaluation, mobile phone, user interface, Chinese, handwriting input.

## 1    Introduction

The popularity of mobile data services in China (e.g. web surfing, IM, emailing, etc.) highlights the importance of mobile Chinese input methods. Recently the trend of touch-screen handheld devices in China, such as iPhone, triggered a new round of enthusiasm on handwriting input (HWI), which is considered as a superior solution for languages using a large and complicated character set such as Chinese (Mackenzie & Soukorff, 2002). Theoretically anyone who can write Chinese is able to input with HWI, including people with little computer experience, such as older people. Different from the popular Pinyin-based method on keypad-equipped phones, HWI is independent of the dialect spoken by the user. Furthermore, the "naturalness" brought by the pen-and-paper metaphor upon which HWI is based (Frankish, Morgan, &Noes, 1994) is very appealing, especially for novice users.

As Chinese HWI becomes more and more popular, people are raising their expectation about its ease of use. Currently there has been a few studies on the usability of mobile HWI of alphanumeric text (Bouteruche, Deconde, Anquetil, &Jamet, 2005;

P.L.P. Rau (Ed.): CCD/HCII 2013, Part I, LNCS 8023, pp. 384–392, 2013.
© Springer-Verlag Berlin Heidelberg 2013

Frankish, Morgan, &Noes, 1994; Frankish, Hull, &Morgan, 1995; MacKenzie & Zhang, 1997; Ren & Mizobuchi, 2005). None of these studies, however, have tried to provide a comprehensive understanding of issues influencing user experience throughout the entire inputting session, which involves interaction with the handheld device, the back-end handwriting recognizer, and the front-end input interface as a whole. Tasks in these studies were often constrained to inputting alphabet-numerical characters. In real use, users often need to carry out text input together with interface management operations (e.g., pointing, selecting), and often input characters from different vocabulary sets (e.g., insert an email address and a phone number in a message written in Chinese). Furthermore, the popularity of capacitive screen put forwards problems related to writing with fingers.

The current study aims to specify usability issues that influence user experience throughout the whole inputting session. In order to accomplish this goal, we started with a thorough review of existing usability studies on mobile HWI with particular focus on Chinese input. Then we invited five experts to identify usability problems on seven touch-screen phones that differ in brands, type of screens, writing tools, operation systems and handwriting recognizers. Following that, we compared user performance among the seven phones by usability testing with five novice users.

## 2    Related Work

There are mainly two alternative solutions for inputting text with touch-screen mobile phone: HWI and virtual keyboard (VKB). An early study by Lewis (1999) compared input rates for VKB and a simulated HWI. With the assumption of 100% recognition accuracy, HWI input speed averaged 23.6 words per minute (wpm) for sentences, which outperformed VKB (17.0 wpm). Liu, Ding, and Liu (2009) studied mobile Chinese input rate against novice users, and found that there was no significant difference in input rate between HWI and standard VKB, but users made more errors with HWI than with VKB. The result that even novice Chinese users can achieve a fairly good input rate may be explained by the fact that Chinese uses pictographic characters, and the complex forms and structures of Chinese character may provide more cues to handwriting recognizers (Dai, Liu, &Xiao, 2007), and consequently less selection operations. However, except for Lewis (1999) study that assumed a perfect HWI recognition accuracy, the error rate of HWI is found higher than that of VKB for both alphanumeric and Chinese input.

Error rate with HWI is closely related to the recognition accuracy of the recognizer. LaLomia (1994) found a HWI recognition accuracy of 97% or higher is generally acceptable. We did not find any study reporting such statistics with Chinese HWI, but results from a Japanese HWI study (Ren & Zhou, 2009) can be taken as a reference: the recognition accuracy for Chinese characters mixed with Kana characters was around 90% to 93%. Recognition accuracy is not only related with algorithm design of the recognizer, but also with users' writing style (Lumsden & Gammell, 2004) and the type and amount of training they received (MacKenzie & Zhang, 1997). Frankish (Frankish, Morgan, &Noyes, 1994) suggested recognition accuracy can be improved by putting limitations on the writing place (e.g., discrete cells for letters), the writing style (e.g., prohibiting cursive writing), the size of vocabulary (e.g., alphabetic letter only). But each of these measures may detract from the appeal of "naturally writing".

The importance of input interface quality has been recognized by a number of researches. Bouteruche et al. (2005) proposed a set of design guidelines based on the idea of maximizing spatial contiguity and minimizing attention switching from the writing task. These guidelines were implemented in their interface design of a HWI editor called DIGIME. For HWI using writing boxes, proper geometry and dimensions of the box are required to maximize the inputting speed and minimize the error rate. Ren and Zhou's (2009) study showed that the optimal writing area for inputting Chinese mixed with Kana characters is square box with a dimension of 14*14mm.

The physical aspect of handheld devices and writing tools may also influence usability of mobile HWI, as reflected by user comments in Lewis study (1999). However, we did not find many scholarly researches in this vein, except for Ren and Mizobuchi's study (Ren & Mizobuchi, 2005) on the optimal dimensions of stylus for Japanese people. Through two experiments they found the most suitable dimensions was: pen-length 11 cm, pen-tip width 0.5 cm, and pen width 7mm. To be noted is that participants of the experiment were Japanese, and the results should be generalized with cautious due to anthropometric difference among countries.

Previous studies imply that when a user input with mobile HWI, his/her experience is influenced not only by the handwriting recognizer, but also the input interface and the physical device. Though the impact of some specific features on usability has been studied, a purposeful examination is needed to obtain a big picture of usability issues that influence user experience with mobile Chinese HWI.

# 3    Methodology

To establish a comprehensive understanding of possible usability issues of mobile Chinese HWI, a wide examination of the state-of-art mobile HWI solutions on touch-screen phones    was needed. We selected seven mobile phones covering a wide range of brands (Apple, Nokia, Samsung, LG, HTC, Dopod, and a local brand) and operation systems (iOS, Android, Windows Mobile, Symbian, and model built-in systems), as shown in Table 1. We ran two studies to specify usability issues that influence user experience with mobile Chinese HWI. In the first study, five usability experts inspected usability problems of the seven phones through self-reporting questionnaire, think-aloud tests, and a focus group discussion. The results of study 1 also informed the design of the following usability testing with five novice users (study 2).

**Table 1.** The seven mobile phones in the expert review and user testing

| Mobile Phone | Operating System | Touch Screen | Writing Tool | Handwriting Software | HWI support |
|---|---|---|---|---|---|
| iPhone 3GS | iPhone OS 3.0 | Capacitive | Finger | OS Built-in | Chinese only |
| HTC Magic | Android 1.5 | Capacitive | Finger | OS Built-in | All (support mixed input) |
| Dopod T5399 | Win Mobile 6.5 | Resistive | Stylus | Malanhua | All (no mixed input) |
| Nokia N97 mini | Symbian S60 | Resistive | Finger | OS Built-in | All (support mixed input) |
| LG KP500 | Unspecified | Resistive | Stylus | OS Built-in | All (no mixed input) |
| Samsung S800 | Touch Wiz 2.0 | Resistive | Stylus | OS Built-in | All (no mixed input) |
| K-Touch N77 | Unspecified | Resistive | Stylus | OS Built-in | All (support mixed input) |

## 3.1    Study 1: Expert Review

**Participants.** Five usability experts with abundant touch-screen product experience were invited. Two were faculty majoring in usability engineering and human-computer interaction (HCI), one was a usability researcher who had led and worked in mutiple usability projects, and two were PhD students who had been trained for more than 4 years in the HCI program and also had adequate experience with usability evaluations.

**Procedure.** Each expert first tried out all the seven models separately in their working place and at their own pace. With each of the seven phones they were asked to complete the following tasks: creating and editing a contact, creating and sending short messages, sending and receiving emails, searching and browsing web contents, using mobile social networking services. For each task, the expert was asked to identify usability issues related to handwriting recognizer, input user interface issues, and general issues. Data were collected with a review form which experts filled in and returned to us at the end of their testing period of a phone. The seven phones were circulated between experts with coordination and a time slot of two hours for each phone with each expert was ensured.

Then each expert was invited to our usability laboratory for a think-aloud test. Two types of tasks were used in the think-aloud test: contact editing and messaging. Based on feedback from experts, the tasks were slightly revised and used in study 2, which were introduced in detail later. When performing tasks, experts were encouraged to speak aloud what they were looking at, thinking, and doing, and these were captured by video and audio recording. The testing sequence of the seven phones was randomized for each expert. Each session took about 3 to 4 hours.

Finally, we held a focus-group discussion with all five experts for discussing issues they found and generating further insights on usability of mobile Chinese HWI.

## 3.2    Study 2: User Testing

**Participants.** Five novice user testing sessions were held in our laboratory. All participants, including 3 females and 2 males, were graduate students from different department of Tsinghua University, aging from 23 to 27. They were all experienced mobile phone users, but none of them had ever own a touch-screen phone. It is interesting to find when being asked whether they want HWI feature, only one participant give positive answer. Concerns participants raised included: (1) keyboard (especially physical keyboard) input method is faster compared with HWI; (2) handwriting recognition has a relatively low accuracy rate; (3) a matter of habit and more accustomed to keyboard input mode; (4) the operation of handwriting sometimes needs both hands, thus not very convenient.

**Tasks.** The participants were required to complete five tasks with different length and content on each of the seven phones. Task design was guided by the goal to be representative of those users would encounter in real use. Task one and two involved creating new contacts by entering name, phone numbers, and email address in the contact manager of each phone. Task one involved a mixture of Chinese characters, English letters, while in task two, no Chinese characters were input. Task three to five involved sending messages to others. Task three was a greeting sentence in English; task four mixed a short English sentence, a Chinese sentence encouraging the recipient, and a phone number; task five was a Chinese ragged verse ended with an emoticon.

**Measurement.** 1) *Input rate* (characters per minute, cpm) was measured by the number of characters entered per minute. 2) *Error rate* (%) was measured by the ratio between the number of wrongly input characters and the number of total input characters (both correct and wrong). 3) *Correctness rate of the first character* (CRFC, %) was the ratio between the number of characters recognized by the first (default) alternative in the alternative list and the number of total input characters. It means the user does not need to extra selection action for the correct recognition. Compared with error rate, CRFC reflects more precisely the recognition accuracy of recognizer. 4) *Subjective satisfaction* was measured by the means of users' ratings on five satisfaction scales, asking about users' satisfaction with recognition accuracy, recognition speed, input interface, design of the contact/messaging function of the phone, and overall satisfaction with the HWI being used. Five-point Likert scales (1 for highly unsatisfied and 5 for highly satisfied) were employed in the questionnaire.

**Procedure.** Each user was tested individually in the usability laboratory of Tsinghua University. After being introduced the research, participants filled out a background questionnaire that collected demographic information and past experience with touch-screen phones. Before carrying out tasks, participants were allowed to experience each phone for a couple of minutes. Then, the participants completed the five tasks on each of the seven phones with HWI, except for iPhone, whose HWI recognized only Chinese characters and some simple punctuation but not others (this was no longer true for built-in HWI with latest iOS 4.3). The testing sequence of the seven mobile phones was randomized. Upon completion of tasks with a mobile phone, the participants then completed a satisfaction questionnaire for that phone. They were also shortly interviewed about usability problems they have found. Each session took about 2~3 hours.

# 4   Results Analysis

Quantitative analysis was first conducted to compare the performance of seven mobile phones. User performance and satisfaction from study 2 was reported in 4.1, and usability issues identified in both study 1 and 2 were synthesized and reported in 4.2.

## 4.1   User Performance and Satisfaction

**Error Rate and CRFC.** The means of error rate & CRFC for each mobile phone and task are demonstrated in Fig.1 (a) & (b). For Chinese input tasks, the performance of Nokia was the best (low error rate and high CRFC), while the performance of Dopod, LG, HTC, & Samsung was relatively worse. There were several factors influencing input accuracy of Chinese HWI. A major one is how the input method deals with mixed input of Chinese, English, and numbers. For example, Nokia supports mixed-input and also gives priority to the recognition of characters corresponding with the current mode. This setting can greatly decrease the errors, because users don't need to frequently switch recognition mode (e.g., Chinese mode, English mode), which is easily omitted by users. Dopod, Samsung and LG do not support mixed input.

Another key factor is the interference between screen operations and handwriting. The interference problem with Dopod was complained 8 times by participants during the studies. In addition, too few recognition alternatives also influence the accuracy a lot. For example, iPhone only provided 4 recognition alternatives, and it is more likely that no candidate is correct and users need to delete and re-write the character. Besides, the relatively low accuracy of LG was caused by its problematic writing area design. Its writing box looks like a 田, and participants easily regarded it as four independent sub-area, but in fact there is only two independent sub-area.

**Input Rate.** The average input rate for each mobile phone and task is demonstrated in Fig.1 (c). In terms of Chinese input tasks, Nokia got the highest input rate among the seven mobile phones, which was due to the mixed-input recognition feature of Nokia. The lowest input rate of K-Touch was mainly caused by the following reasons: 1) interference between screen operations and handwriting; 2) the slow reaction speed of back-end recognizer; 3) the difficulty with switching recognition mode. For English tasks, Dopod and iPhone were much faster than the other phones. In particular, Dopod supports continuous handwriting input recognition for English characters and numbers, while on iPhone participants used virtual keyboard for English letters and numbers.

**Satisfaction.** Satisfaction ratings with the seven mobile phones are shown in Fig.1 (d). Participants were most satisfied with iPhone and Nokia among the seven mobile phones. In particular they were most satisfied with the recognition accuracy of Nokia and the recognition speed/input interface of iPhone. From Fig.1 (d), we also found that in most cases the ratings of user interface were lower than the other items, which indicate that more attention should be paid to the interface design in the future.

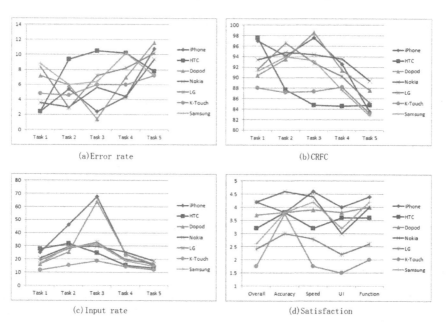

(a) Error rate

(b) CRFC

(c) Input rate

(d) Satisfaction

**Fig. 1.** The results of quantitative analysis

### 4.2    Usability Issues of Mobile Chinese HWI

Based upon the study 1 & 2, we compiled a list of usability issues, which were classified into three categories: input interface related issues, handwriting recognizer related issues, and device and users related issues.

- **Input Interface Related Issues**

1. *Visual style of stokes should resemble natural chirography in pen-and-paper writing.* The visual style of K-Touch was most appreciated in the experiment as it resembles the look of strokes in pen-and-paper writing. Participants complained that too thick (LG) or too thin (Dopod & Nokia) strokes were lack of a feeling of "natural writing".
2. *For writing area design, full-screen writing over the current window is preferred to full-screen writing in a new window; writing in a box tiled with the current window is preferred to writing in a box overlapping the current window.* For full-screen writing in a new window, users need to write in a totally new window after they activate the edit function, and return to the previous window after complete the writing. This way of jumping out and backward break the normal workflow of users. For overlapping writing box (e.g. the box mode of Nokia), when the box field overlaps the input field, users need to close the writing box and move the field and re-open the writing box again.
3. *Provide 5~7 recognition candidates.* Too few recognition candidates may reduce the possibility of "hitting" the correct target and also arouse anxiety from users. A number of 5~7 is recommended, though more scientific study is needed to prove its validity.
4. *Prediction characters should not be presented simultaneously with recognition candidates.* Predicting the next character based on available input is helpful for improving input rate and reducing user fatigue. But presenting predictive characters simultaneously with recognition candidates is very error-prone: users may click a predictive character but not a recognition candidate. It is better to present predictive characters after the user select a recognition candidate.
5. *Provide direct shortcuts to frequently used punctuation and other symbols on the input screen.* Displaying a list of frequently used punctuations and symbols on the interface is appreciated by users.
6. *Make correction operation easy to recognize and access.* The backspace key and the delete key are important correction tools, and should be designed visually prominent (e.g., bigger size, placing at the right corner) and physically easy to access.
7. *The icons on the handwriting input interface should be legible and easily recognized by user.* The icons should be simplified and could represent meanings clearly. The elements of icons (e.g. usage, appearance, borders) should be kept consistent.

- **Handwriting Recognizer Related Issues**

1. *User effort for switching between different modes should be minimized.* Repetitive and difficult switching among different modes was complained most. Possible approaches include: a) allowing mixed-input of frequently used symbols, numbers,

and English characters; b) making the switch operation easy and effective; c) the recognizer can adjust its mode to the input context automatically. For example, for form-filling tasks, such as editing contact information, the recognizer can switch its input mode according to current input field, such as digits or English letters.

2. *Users are more accustomed to timeout method instead of discrete writing box method for character segmentation.* The benefit of discrete writing box method is it allows users write in their own rhythm and prevent errors due to incomplete writing. However, we found neither experts nor novice users appreciate this benefit. Some novice users did not understand how this method works and still wrote as with a timeout method: they would not start writing a new character in the next box until the previous input character was correctly recognized.

3. *The timeout threshold should be defined according to the trade-off between speed and accuracy.* We found short timeout threshold leads to recognition errors due to incomplete writing, especially for complex characters with many strokes. According to Cui and Lantz (2005), optimal timeout options for fast, ordinary, and slow writers could be 350ms, 500ms, and 700ms respectively.

4. *It is best to provide continuous input recognition for English and number HWI.* The continuous input recognition can increase the input rate and accuracy greatly.

- **Device/User Related Issues**

1. *Ensure users have proper writing tool.* Writing with fingers or stylus is often decided by the type of screens. For **stylus input**, the size of stylus would influence the posture of pen-holding and writing. For **finger input**, it should not be assumed that all users have long-enough nails or similar size of fingers to produce efficient handwriting.

2. *The required force for writing on screen surface should allow users write for a long time without serious fatigue.* Participants found writing on K-Touch and LG KP500 very laborious since both requires high pressure on the screen. This usability issue relates to the design or selection of touch-screens. Further study should be conducted to find out how big the force should be.

3. *Tracking speed should be fast enough to allow continuous writing experience.* We found slow tracking speed not only lead to longer writing time, but also incurs errors. The recognizer sometimes misinterpreted this pause as a signal of accomplishment and started recognition, which will cause errors. Miller (1968) suggested 0.1 second as the limit of response time for a system response to be perceived as immediate and part of the mechanic action induced by the user.

### 4.3    Conclusion and Limitations

In this paper, we evaluated usability of mobile Chinese HWI applications of seven mobile phones. Based upon the results from expert inspection and usability testing, we finally identified 16 usability issues related to handwriting recognizers, input interfaces, and devices/users. We expect this list of usability issues give mobile HWI designers a more integrated view of usability requirements from users and provide a handy reference to inspecting usability problems of a certain solution.

The current study is in its nature exploratory, and is inadequate to give definite answers to the identified issues. More strictly controlled experiment research in the future are expected to provide elaborated and validated guidelines based on the framework of the current study. In particular, we found mobile HWI design guidelines for older people in great need due to the sheer volume of the Chinese grey population and potential digital gap resulted from inaccessible informational product design.

**Acknowledgements.** This study was supported by Research In Motion UK Limited.

# References

1. Bouteruche, F., Deconde, G., Anquetil, E., Jamet, E.: Design and Evaluation of Handwriting Input Interfaces for Small-size Mobile Devices. In: 1st Workshop on Improving and Assessing Pen-Based Input Techniques, pp. 49–56 (2005)
2. Cui, Y., Lantz, V.: Stroke Break Analysis: a Practical Method to Study Timeout Value for Handwriting Recognition Input. In: 7th International Conference on Human Computer Interaction with Mobile Devices & Services, pp. 263–266. ACM (2005)
3. Dai, R., Liu, C., Xiao, B.: Chinese Character Recognition: History, Status and Prospects. Frontiers of Computer Science in China 1(2), 126–136 (2007)
4. Frankish, C., Morgan, P., Noyes, J.: Pen Computing: Some Human Factors Issues. In: IEE Colloquium on Handwriting and Pen-Based Input, IET, pp. 5/1–5/3 (1994)
5. Frankish, C., Hull, R., Morgan, P.: Recognition Accuracy and User Acceptance of Pen Interfaces. In: SIGCHI Conference on Human Factors in Computing Systems, pp. 503–510. ACM Press/Addison-Wesley Publishing Co. (1995)
6. LaLomia, M.: User Acceptance of Handwritten Recognition Accuracy. In: Conference Companion on Human Factors in Computing Systems, pp. 107–108. ACM (1994)
7. Lewis, J.R.: Input Rates and User Preference for Three Small-Screen Input Methods: Standard Keyboard, Predictive Keyboard, and Handwriting. In: 43th Annual Meeting of Human Factors and Ergonomics Society, pp. 425–428 (1999)
8. Liu, Y., Ding, K., Liu, N.: Immediate User Performances with Touch Chinese Text entry Solutions on Handheld Devices. In: 11th International Conference on Human-Computer Interaction with Mobile Devices and Services, pp. 56:1–56:2. ACM (2009)
9. Lumsden, J., Gammell, A.: Mobile Note Taking: Investigating the Efficacy of Mobile Text Entry. In: Brewster, S., Dunlop, M. (eds.) Mobile HCI 2004. LNCS, vol. 3160, pp. 156–167. Springer, Heidelberg (2004)
10. MacKenzie, I.S., Zhang, S.X.: The Immediate Usability of Graffiti. In: The Conference on Graphics Interface 1997, pp. 129–137. Canadian Information Processing Society (1997)
11. Mackenzie, S., Soukoreff, W.: Text Entry for Mobile Computing: Models and Methods,Theory and Practice. Human-Computer Interaction 17(2&3), 147–198 (2002)
12. Miller, R.B.: Response Time in Man-computer Conversational Transactions. In: Fall Joint Computer Conference, Part I, pp. 267–277. ACM (1968)
13. Ren, X., Mizobuchi, S.: Investigating the Usability of the Stylus Pen on Handheld Devices. In: 4th Annual Workshop on HCI Research in MIS, pp. 30–34 (2005)
14. Ren, X., Zhou, X.: The Optimal Size of Handwriting Character Input Boxes on PDAs. International Journal of Human-Computer Interaction 25(8), 762–784 (2009)
15. Soukoreff, R.W., MacKenzie, I.S.: Recent Developments in Text-entry Error Rate Measurement. In: Extended Abstract of the ACM Conference on Human Factors in Computing Systems (CHI), pp. 1425–1428 (2004)

# Reception of Space: Inspiring Design without a Designer

Yihua Huang[1] and Kin Wai Michael Siu[1,2]

[1] School of Design, The Hong Kong Polytechnic University, Hong Kong
[2] Department of Architecture, Massachusetts Institute of Technology, USA
{yihua.wong,m.siu}@polyu.edu.hk, msiu@mit.edu

**Abstract.** Designers nowadays consider themselves as the only experts to have conceptualized the everyday practice of the ordinary. They deal with design at a fantastic pace, with the aim of satisfying "public interest" instead of designing for individual users. For instance, with the reclaimed area of Hong Kong, which has been transformed into a public space dedicated to facilitate the vibrant transformation of Hong Kong into a world city, the government constantly set up strategies assuming a standardized user practice in order to achieve legislative approval for the project. Actually, the processes of conceptualization and standardization may not sufficiently summarize the specifications of everyday life. In other words, current ways of design based on public interest do not always meet what users actually want and need, since these design methods tend to identify all users as "average people" within standard dimensions. Nevertheless, what we are given every day is an everyday life that is not "banal and meaningless." The acts of city users cannot be defined merely as mechanical or according to a stereotype. Although users' reactions or responses to their living environments have been changed gradually with the urban transformation, their behaviours are not simply passive reactions or responses to space, but a kind of active reception in the creative acts or art performed by city users in the space. This research mainly elaborates on the "reception of space" in order to inspire design generations without a designer, and bring designers, planners, administrators, and government a perspective of user-oriented design. It includes an empirical study with intensive observations and direct interviews in Wan Chai North and South to review the importance of considering everyday life in design, based on users' tactical and creative receptions of public living environments. The study then redefines the role of city users in the urban spaces in which they practice and exercise, and argues that users of urban space require that designs be more inclusive.

**Keywords:** City Users, Everyday Space, Reception, User-oriented Design.

## 1    Introduction

When reviewing the urban development of Hong Kong, it is easy to notice that the government does not usually take the time to conduct serious research on what each city user needs. In addition, government designers and planners seldom observe the everyday practices of ordinary people and the degree of fitness between city users'

P.L.P. Rau (Ed.): CCD/HCII 2013, Part I, LNCS 8023, pp. 393–402, 2013.
© Springer-Verlag Berlin Heidelberg 2013

needs and their living environments. In doing so, designers and planners dealing with "public interest" urban projects that are obviously based on economic-oriented design principles with profit in mind tend to carry out massive urban redevelopment strategies that may swallow up or frustrate the everyday practice of ordinary people. Moreover, as "a land hungry place," Hong Kong strongly relies on land reclamation approaches to provide inhabitable city space for people and maintain the city's status as a world city in Asia. Unfortunately, the approaches to reclamation follow the planning principles of administrators who "accompany the deliberate forms of operational rationalism, and tend to neglect the human factor" (Lefebvre, 1996, p. 83). Rational planning emphasizes that the city should be developed under a comprehensive master plan that integrates scientific technology and quantitative analysis. On the face of it, urban diversity has been diminished by rational planners who identify all city users as "average people" in order to easily manage and control city spaces. Public spaces with restrictive standards cannot really fulfil the needs and preferences of the users. Obviously, urban planning design is completely different from product design for individual uses. When conducting urban projects, it is difficult to test the response of public space users in advance, and the users cannot simply select those products that they like and then dismiss the rest (Siu, 2003). Hence, urban design must define users' responses to their everyday space so that designs and plans can be more inclusive and fitted.

By adopting empirical studies related to the tactical living of users, this paper attempts to argue that the creative acts or art of city users activates the self-motivation driven by their own needs and preferences for a better life and living environment. In other words, the sociology of everyday life gives us a new perspective to contemplate city users' ways of operating and reveals that city users tactically fix unfit designs without using a designer. Actually, those who create designs for public users are not aware of the degree to which small, everyday practices can inspire design or innovation. Hence, this paper aims to verify that city users are also competent to create self-sufficient designs, and that the government should shift the passive role of city users to motivate design thinking during the design process.

## 2    Reception of Space

Most of the literature focuses on undertaking urban studies from a macroscopic point of view; studies seldom elaborate detailed research on the everyday lives of ordinary people. However, some sociologists and philosophers, including Michel de Certeau, Henri Lefebvre, and Michel Maffesoli, generally seek to excavate tactical living by looking at users' everyday practices. They aim to prove that people do not strictly follow the orders imposed by the authorities when it comes to fulfilling the process of production in their lives. Also, according to Lefebvre (1991), everyday life should be "a work of art and the joy that man gives to himself". Therefore, all individuals are living artists who understand "what is willed to them and what holds them intimately from the inside" (Leuilliot, 1977). Given this, the ways in which city users operate cannot be defined merely as unchanged customs and traditions. Their behaviours represent subjective emotional responses and individual interpretations of the space; thus, they exhibit active participation in the text of life rather than a passive reaction.

In *The Practice of Everyday Life* (1984), Michel de Certeau begins by studying city users. He substitutes the word "reception" for response, and describes reception as an "art". This is similar to Cuddon (1998), who regards city users as "receptors," meaning: "the person (or group of persons) experiencing a work of art" (p. 733). By borrowing the ideas of user reception, urban design theory considers space as a vessel that reflects many innovative acts that are not completely restricted by the city's form. In short, users' "reception of space" are the artistic activities and tactical living practices derived from the physical demands of life, rather than the rules of a space.

Unlike widespread perception, which defines city users as passive recipients of space, the concept that they have a reception of space gives us a new perspective on city users' creativity. This perspective must inspire further design generations in order to ensure that urban spaces are usable. Most of the time, the users play an active role by adopting designs to their own purposes, and attempt to change the design's original function and purpose in order to fulfil their "individual interest". Therefore, to understand users' "reception of space" requires us to base design on our observations and analyses of the "creative acts" or "art" of city users under current living environments and urban policies (de Certeau, 1984, p. 37; Hsia, 1993, p. 329).

# 3    Methods of Study

In order to better understand city users' "reception of space", the most practical method would be to see, listen, smell, touch, and sense the everyday life of city users without putting any obstructive change in their living environments (Siu 2009). Hence, field work will be carried out on selected case study sites in order to conduct an in-depth exploration of the objectives of the research.

## 3.1    The Case of Wan Chai

As a strategy of design research, a case study is effective for investigating different outcomes in the ambiguous urban space. As Merriam (1988) states, a "case study is an ideal design for understanding and interpreting observations of social phenomena" (p. 2) and "Case study is a design particularly suited to situations where it is impossible to separate the phenomenon's variables from their context[s]" (p. 10). In order to get "real-life context," this research has adopted unobtrusive observation to gain understanding of the ways in which city users interact with public urban space. This method can "cover events in real time and cover the context of an event" (Yin 1994, pp. 13, 18).

In order to form an in-depth understanding of "reception of space" in terms of urban design and policy, this study selected Wan Chai as a case. Wan Chai is an ever-transforming urban area located in Hong Kong Island. Its particularity stems from urban reclamations and multimodal living spaces that have resulted in a hybrid urbanism for this area and a clear demarcation between Wan Chai North (newer area) and South (older area) by a major road (Gloucester Road). This study is based on comparing Wan Chai North to Wan Chai South, as different kinds of people interact with different types of public spaces in these areas. Such spaces include traditional market streets, main arterial roads, pedestrian bridges, and waterfront promenades. Meanwhile, the comparative works also provide a view to prove that city users' "reception of space" can generate extensive feedbacks to benefit urban design and sustainable development.

**Fig. 1.** Wan Chai with its north-south demarcation. The area north of Gloucester Road is often called Wan Chai North, and it is one of the busiest commercial areas in Hong Kong. It comprises business towers, hotels, spectacular buildings, and landmarks. The spaces in Wan Chai South are mixed-use, mostly involving ground floor retail shops and restaurants with residential, office, and other uses above.

### 3.2    Observations and Interviews

Observation is a good approach "of looking at action between people and their environment" (Sanoff, 1992, p. 33), conducive to discovering "what goes on in the subculture or organizations being studied" and gaining "insight into their operation (especially hidden aspects not easily recognized) and how they function" (Berger, 1998, p. 105). Nevertheless, field observations should focus on appropriate methods and objects of observation, in order to be effective (Rutledge, 1985). Sanoff (1992) further points out that "Observing unobtrusively allows the study of people's behavior without their realizing that their activities are important" (p. 33). Thus, "unobtrusive direct observations" have been adopted in the studies to illustrate how city users interact with their living environments and deal with public spaces and products. This study has produced a new set of methods for observing public spaces, which includes fixed-point continuous photo capture techniques within longitudinal studies. In addition, the direct interviews have been used to clarify the data collected in observations, in order to assess not only "What have people done?" but also "Why have people done it?" (Berger, 1998, pp. 55–62). Thereby, the observation and interviews conducted in this study can acquire a more genuine picture of users' reception of public spaces.

# 4    A New Perspective to See City Users' Everyday Practices

In this section, the arguments offer us valuable insight into how city users deal with public spaces and products, and indicate the disparity of users' receptions of urban development and public use space in Wan Chai North and South. According to the empirical field studies, the authorities tend to attain a higher level of social order in the northern (newer) area of Wan Chai than in the southern (older) area. Thus, the government seeks authority through legislation to manage city spaces, and confine unwanted behaviours to Wan Chai South. Rational planning such as this leads to less participation of the individual user in public spaces, which also makes designs or products meaningless. In Wan Chai South, there is a high-degree of urban diversity that manifests how the city users exercise their living environment, although the constructed environment and urban facilities look old and timeworn. The people prefer to engage with the space without any restrictions, which on the other hand can give design its meaning, and can help researchers to discover design issues in a space by assessing the everyday practice of city users in that space. The nature of life motivates tactical behaviours that we never even dream of in design; this kind of user participation and tactics can be called an act of production. These acts can help us rethink what the public spaces provide people and thereby design products that fit users' needs.

## 4.1    Reception of Space in Wan Chai North

Wan Chai North has a markedly mono-functional design of space compared to the southern area. The functions of its various spaces are clearly zoned and controlled by authorities and planners. For example, the areas between Convention Avenue and Gloucester Road are only zoned for office and commercial users. Thus, the area was composed of a number of free-standing single buildings. Each individual building was rationally and logically located in the area, with clear and conspicuous demarcations. Furthermore, open spaces have been designated in the form of playgrounds, parks, and gardens. However, the government and private owners impose different rules and restrictions on use of the space in order to prevent unacceptable behaviours and to maintain social order.

Different types of people and activities are segregated in mono-functional zones. For example, the Golden Bauhinia Square (in proximity to Wan Chai Waterfront Promenade) only attracts tourists, and only permitted hawkers are allowed to do business there. Furthermore, the trading areas and types of commodities have also been controlled by the administration: only paintings and photographs are approved to be sold. In addition, the administration is likely to more stringently impose regulations and take enforcement action to secure the "ideal" social order. Another example is that, in order to construct a world city and provide inhabitable city spaces for people, the Hong Kong government has built many neat public spaces in Wan Chai North. However, people do not use these spaces because there are too many restrictions on their use. Some public facilities have merely been seen as public displays. As the administration emphasizes regulation and public order in this area, people only perform necessary activities, such as walking to another place, waiting for a bus, delivering mail, or smoking. Thus we see that designs with excessive controls and restrictions are at risk of being wasted spaces; they do not become functional spaces without user participation and practice.

**Table 1.** The public space with many restrictions

| Dealing with Space | Description | Reception of Space |
|---|---|---|
| | In the public space of Northern Wan Chai, ordinances and restrictions have been set up to secure ideal social order. | There are no more responses and reactions between the users and environment, which means the design is not given its proper meaning. |

**Table 2.** The public facilities with many constraints

| Dealing with Product | Description | Reception of Space |
|---|---|---|
| | The government has set up some constraints in order to eliminate the unwanted behaviours of sleeping or lying on benches. | The public facility has become a public display rather than a comfortable product for people's leisure. |

### 4.2     Reception of Space in Wan Chai South

In the Southern Wan Chai area, most of the spaces and buildings were developed and constructed in mixed-use patterns. Mixed-use developments contain a complementary conglomeration of space usage, such as residential, retail, commercial, employment, civic, and entertainment spaces, in close proximity—sometimes in the same building. This leads to a high degree of pedestrian diversity and interaction.   Streets in Wan Chai South attract people mainly because of the diverse human activities that can be found there, rather than because they contain a "well-designed" landmark or sculpture.

For instant, Cross Street and Tai Yuen Street, located between Queen's Road East and Johnston Road, are typical open-air bazaars. They are not simply places where one can buy daily necessities, but also a favourite place for people to meet, gather, stroll, rest, and window-shop. In fact, both street markets have become a kind of ur-ban facility that people engage with every day. As a facilitator and designer of the space, the stall owner provides the necessities of the urban facility, such as a chair for rest, a table for the storage of goods, and a handcart for carrying items, in order to make people more comfortable in the space.

A high degree of pedestrian diversity can be found on these streets. Mixed-use spaces that attract a diverse cross-section of the population (for example, locals and tourists; women, children, and the elderly; students, workers, and businessmen) are more likely to be liveable and exciting. Due to the variety of functions possible in the space, public spaces are redefined sometimes as chatting places by older people, as activity places by performers, as demonstration places by protestors, and so on. For example, a public space near Johnston Road was designed originally for smoking and circulation. However, the city users produced another meaning and function of this space, which they exercised on Christmas Eve. At that time, a group of performers wearing Christmas caps converted the space into a theatre and sang Christmas carols to attract people for enjoyment.

The use of Hennessy Road is another good example of how the city user's "recep-tion of space" is not always what the designer had planned. Originally, this street was used for vehicle traffic. In order to facilitate social democracy, the city users are al-lowed to tactically deploy some slogans and facilities—that is, to protest. The use of this space for demonstrations thus redefined the functions of the street. Tolerance for diverse social activities in the southern Wan Chai area is higher than in the northern Wan Chai area. Hence, the city users may be seen as spatial producers, who aim to make up for the deficiencies of design and product when using spaces in Wan Chai South.

As shown below, public facilities and products present all kinds of design mean-ings and functions for people's everyday lives. In short, innovation and generation of design should derive from the everyday practice of individual users in order for de-signs to fit the users; users should play an active role in design to enhance the space's meaning and function.

**Table 3.** Public Spaces in Another Function and Meaning

| Deal with Space | Description | Reception of Space |
|---|---|---|
| | In general, the street market provides some necessities for everyday life. However, it can be a public facility sometimes, as well, where old people can sit and rest. | The stall owner, as a true spatial producer, understands the needs of users and has filled in design gaps and functional defects. |
| | The public space is actually designed for meeting and smoking. On Christmas Eve, this place became a theatre for singing Christmas carols. | The city users present a strong sense of self-motivation driven by the needs of everyday life. |
| | Normally, this street is a major road for circulation. When it was time for the procession, the street was transformed into a place of demonstration. | The creative acts and art of city users are able to redefine design meaning, which can be called an act of production. |

**Table 4.** Public Facilities in Another Function and Meaning

| Deal with Product | Description | Reception of Space |
|---|---|---|
| | At this bus stop in Wan Chai, many older people sit on the fire hydrant to have a rest while they wait for the bus. | Different types of users compose urban diversity and behavioural hybridity. The city users in Wan Chai South are good at creating living tactics to make public spaces and facilities fulfil their preferences and needs. Furthermore, the city users are not as banal as they are identified in northern Wan Chai. They have created some unexpected acts of creation and transformation that designers and planners never considered. |
| | In Wan Chai South, railings are intended as a measure of safety, but people also sit and lie upon them. | |
| | Originally, the traffic cone was placed on the road to temporarily redirect traffic in a safe manner. However, the old man usually stores something in a traffic cone. | |

## 5    Conclusion

City users still play a passive role in the design process, since designers and planners are deemed to be the people who have the expertise to provide good city space and products for people. However, blindly relying on designers' knowledge and responsibility ignores the city user's paramount role in the process of design interaction and communication. Therefore, I wonder whether designs could be improved without the expertise of designers. This paper suggests that we have to shift our attention from the designer and design to the individual user. This shift of attention aims to explore and understand the small practices of everyday life in order to inspire designers, planners, professionals, administrators, and governments to create more usable space. For example, much of the designs mentioned above were redefined by the tactical behaviours of city users; given this, it makes sense that the users should be active participants in the design process, as their life experiences and daily use of the space will inform gaps in the designer's "expertise".

Urban transformation has also become a process that places city users in a passive role. The studies of this research illustrate that rational planning was used as an active force to segregate people and streets. The government set up many constraints and restrictions to control the city space. For instance, the authorities have imposed some organized public spaces in Wan Chai North with different limitations and ordinances in order to maintain social order. As a result, the design becomes a display, and loses its functional meaning for the everyday lives of potential users. Thus we see that designs with excessive controls will create a negative "reception of space", which can result in the generation of a soulless city.

This paper provides us a user-oriented perspective. By perusing users' reception of design in their everyday lives, the designer should respect and recognize the diversity of users' needs and lifestyles in order to create more inclusive, usable designs.

**Acknowledgements.** This research was fully supported by Hong Kong Research Grants Council's General Research Grant (Ref: 548310) and School of Design of The Hong Kong Polytechnic University. The authors would also like to acknowledge the support of MIT for the final stage of analysis and preparation of this paper.

# References

1. Berger, A.A.: Media Research Techniques. Sage, London (1998)
2. Cuddon, J.A.: A Dictionary of Literary Terms and Literary Theory. Blackwell, Malden (1998)
3. de Certeau, M.: The Practice of Everyday Life. University of California Press, Berkeley (1984)
4. Hsia, C.J.: Space, History and Society. Taiwan Social Research Studies-03, Taipei (1993)
5. Lefebvre, H.: Critique of Everyday Life: Volume I. Moore, J. (trans.) Verso, New York (1991)
6. Lefebvre, H.: Writings on Cities. Kofman, E., Lebas, E. (trans. & eds.). Blackwell, Cambridge (1996)
7. Leuilliot, P.: Preface to Guy Thuillier. In: Pour Une Histoire Du Quotidien Au XIX Siecle En Nivernais, xi–xii, Paris. The Hague, Mouton (1977)
8. Merriam, S.B.: Case Study Research: A Qualitative Approach. Jossey-Bass, San Francisco (1988)
9. Rutledge, A.J.: A Visual Approach to Park Design. John Wiley and Sons, New York (1985)
10. Sanoff, H.: Integrating Programming, Evaluation and Participation in Design: A Theory Z Approach. Ashgate, Hants (1992)
11. Siu, K.W.M.: Users' Creative Responses and Designers' Roles. Design Issues 19(2), 64–74 (2003)
12. Siu, K.W.M.: Reader Response and Reception Theories: User Oriented Design. In: Siu, K.W.M. (ed.) New Era of Product Design: Theory and Practice. Beijing Institute of Technology Press, Beijing (2009)
13. Yin, R.K.: Case Study Research: Design and Methods. Sage, London (1994)

# The Influence of Design Training and Spatial Solution Strategies on Spatial Ability Performance

Hanyu Lin

Industrial Design Department, National Kaohsiung Normal University
No.62, Shenjhong Rd., Yanchao, Kaohsiung, Taiwan
hanyu@nknu.edu.tw

**Abstract.** This study investigates the following two issues: (1) whether spatial ability is enhanced following design training; and (2) whether differing solution strategies are applied or generated following design training. Based on these issues, we considered design and non-design groups to be independent variables, and spatial tests and solution strategies to be dependent variables. The study findings indicated that the spatial ability factors of spatial visualization and relation were influenced by design training, although the perceptual speed factor was not. In addition, the solution strategy analysis results showed that the holistic solution strategies of the design group were applied more significantly than those of the non-design group, whereas the analytical solution strategies of the non-design group were employed more significantly than those of the design group. In other words, the participants in design group tended to employ holistic solution strategies, whereas those in non-design group tended to adopt analytical strategies.

**Keywords:** spatial ability, design training, solution strategies.

## 1    Introduction

Spatial ability is crucial in the field of design. Roth [1] asserted that in the design process, creative thinking, problem solving, and concept generation relate to spatial ability. In this context, numerous issues warrant attention within the body of research on spatial ability, such as whether training can enhance spatial ability, whether solution strategies differ with varying spatial abilities, whether gender differences occur regarding spatial ability, how to effectively evaluate spatial ability, the influence that aging has on spatial ability, and whether the transfer effect exists in spatial ability. Among these varied topics, the effects of training have been extensively discussed, yet investigations of solution strategies are lacking. Thus, this study explored the influences that design training and solution strategies have on spatial ability.

### 1.1    Spatial Ability and Training

Numerous studies have asserted that spatial ability can be enhanced following training. For example, Lord   [2]   used a paper folding test to measure participants' spatial visualization ability. People with low spatial abilities were selected and split into

P.L.P. Rau (Ed.): CCD/HCII 2013, Part I, LNCS 8023, pp. 403–409, 2013.
© Springer-Verlag Berlin Heidelberg 2013

two groups. One group of participants underwent spatial visualization training and testing for 12 weeks, and the other group did not. The results indicated that the group that completed the spatial visualization training showed greater achievements on their spatial tests compared to the group that did not participate. Thus, Lord contended that spatial visualization abilities can be enhanced through training. However, although training enhances spatial ability, whether this training influences trainees' professional performance remains to be determined. Wanzel, Hamstra, Anastakis, Matsumoto, and Cusimano [3] investigated the relationship between surgical procedures and visual-spatial ability. Their results indicated that mental rotations tests (MRTs) were related to learning spatially complex surgical procedures. Resident physicians with high mental rotation abilities exhibited superior machine operation performance scores. Nevertheless, the test scores of physicians with low rotation abilities significantly improved following mental rotation training and feedback, and no differences were observed compared to the physicians in the high mental rotation group when performing a two-flap Z-plasty surgery. Wanzel et al. further asserted that surgeons who achieve high spatial scores through training or practice can transfer their spatial abilities to new tasks after training. They believed that spatial abilities have transferable effects following training. This effect refers to acquired spatial abilities that can be converted into task performance related to spatial topics.

Cherney [4] found that computer game training enhances spatial abilities. The participants in that study were split into two training groups (massed and distributed) to complete controlled computer game training. The overall training time was identical for all participants. The study results showed that the participants' scores for the Vandenberg and Kuse Mental Rotation Test (VMRT) and Card Rotation Test (CRT) differed before and after training; specifically, the participants' mental rotation performance significantly improved following training. Further investigations indicated that the degree of mental rotation testing improvement in the massed training group was superior to that of the distributed training group. In other words, massed training methods were more effective for improving spatial ability.

Although many studies have reported that spatial ability is enhanced by training, a number of studies do not support this notion. For example, in studies relating to apparel design, no training programs or curricula have been proved to improve performance on spatial visualization tests. Workman, Caldwell, and Kallal [5] investigated the relationship between spatial ability and apparel design. In their experiment, they considered training to be the independent variable, and the Apparel Spatial Visualization Test (ASVT) and Differential Aptitude Test-Space Relations (DATSR) scores to be the dependent variables. The experiment results indicated that the ASVT scores of the training program or curriculum participants significantly exceed those of the participants with no training, although no differences were observed between the DATSR scores of the trained and non-trained participants. These findings suggested that although training influences professional performance, professional training does not influence spatial ability performance. In addition, the researchers found that DATSR and ASVT were unrelated, which indicates that spatial ability tests cannot predict the professional performance of apparel design.

A consensus regarding spatial ability and training has yet to be reached in relevant studies. Some studies have asserted that training enhances spatial abilities, although others have not achieved the same results. Therefore, further discussion of whether design training enhances spatial abilities is necessary.

## 1.2    Spatial Abilities and Solution Strategies

Solution strategies influence spatial test scores. Different people use different solution strategies to solve the same problem [6]. Studies of solution strategies are scarce, mainly because solution strategies are difficult to assess or estimate. Currently, numerous methods are used to assess participants' solution strategies; the most commonly employed is the introspective method. This method involves the participants describing their conscious experiences. These descriptions are then used to determine the psychological processes participants undergo during spatial testing. Other methods used to explore solution strategies include response times and eye movement tracking and analysis.

Snow [7] collected introspective reports from numerous people who completed a paper folding test. Snow found that the first action performed by the participants was item or topic analysis, which included analyzing the contours, angles, symmetry and other characteristics of the patterns or figures. The participants reported that they extracted pattern characteristics, used matching or pairing strategies, or employed elimination strategies to disregard incorrect options. Finally, some participants stated that elimination was an alternative strategy when no solutions were produced after applying matching or pairing strategies.

In the context of research on spatial strategy applications, Workman and Lee [8] investigated whether changes, as well as the cultural differences in these changes, existed between spatial and professional abilities before and after apparel design lessons or classes. They conducted retrospective interviews and instructed the participants to recall the strategies they applied when answering questions. Their findings indicated that the participants' spatial and professional abilities after attending lessons for one semester were significantly superior to their previous abilities. Additionally, their results did not show cultural differences. The participants applied seven strategies, that is, stimulus analysis, extraction of a landmark, matching, elimination, checking, relying on expectations based on prior knowledge, and guessing.

Meanwhile, other studies have divided solution strategies for spatial testing into holistic and analytical strategies [9]. Tzurial and Egozi [10] further investigated the relationship between holistic and analytical strategies and mental rotation abilities. Their results indicated that children with high mental rotation abilities tended to apply holistic strategies. They also found that boys and girls applied different strategies. Most boys used holistic strategies, whereas most girls employed analytical strategies. Tzurial and Egozi contended that holistic strategies were comparatively more effective for solving mental rotation tasks compared to analytical strategies. This implies that the use of different strategies may be one reason for the spatial ability differences between boys and girls.

However, whether these strategies can be generalized for other tests, that is, whether the strategies employed for spatial tests are used in other tests, remains to be determined. Janssen and Geiser [11] investigated the relationship between strategies and two spatial tests. Their findings indicated that participants who tended to apply analytical strategies to Test A also applied the same strategies to Test B. Thus, we can infer that strategies can be generalized to other spatial tests. In addition, findings have shown that more women apply analytical strategies to MRTs compared to men, and that the solution efficiency of men exceeds or is more rapid than that of women.

## 2    Methodology

Numerous studies have found that spatial abilities are improved through training, and the majority of these studies have adopted mental rotation as their spatial ability test. However, mental rotation is only one aspect of spatial ability. Therefore, it is necessary to more comprehensively measure spatial ability, so as to determine which aspects or factors of spatial ability are improved through training. Moreover, solution strategies are among the key factors that generate spatial ability differences. Whether design training changes the application of strategies remains to be determined. Consequently, this study established the following two objectives: (1) to analyze whether spatial ability differences exist between design and non-design groups, and to identify the spatial factors in which differences occur if they do exist; and (2) to analyze whether solution strategy application differences exist between the design and non-design groups using a retrospective questionnaire survey.

### 2.1    Participants

A total of 72 participants were recruited and evenly allocated to a design group and a non-design group. The design department participants were students from the Department of Industrial Design at National Kaohsiung Normal University. The non-design department students were students from the Department of Education, Department of Optoelectronics and Communication Engineering, and the Industrial Technology Education Department. The participants ranged between 18 and 25 years of age.

### 2.2    Material

Regarding spatial tests and based on the perspectives of Carroll [12] and Miyake, Friedman, Rettinger, Shah, and Hegarty [13], three spatial ability factors and the tests commonly employed for these factors, were selected. These factors comprised spatial visualization, spatial relation, and perceptual speed. For spatial visualization, the VMRT and cube comparison test (CCT) were adopted; for spatial relation, the CRT was employed; and for perceptual speed, the hidden pattern test (HPT) was applied.

The spatial solution strategies were based on those proposed by Moè, Meneghetti, and Cadinu [14]. Following the completion of the MRT, the participants were instructed to complete a strategy-item questionnaire survey. The questionnaire comprised four holistic and two analytical items. The participants completed the questionnaire according to the strategies used for the MRT, with a score of 1 representing the weakest use of a strategy and 7 representing the strongest use of a strategy.

## 2.3     Procedures

The participants completed the spatial tests in a quiet environment in small groups of three to eight people. The tests were conducted in a paper format, and before each test began, two examples were provided for practice. Formal testing was employed following the confirmation of participants' understanding of how to complete the test. The solution strategy questionnaires were provided to the participants after the spatial tests. The participants completed the questionnaires based on the solution methods used for the MRT.

# 3     Results

The descriptive statistics for participant performance on the four spatial ability tests are tabulated in Table 1. To further assess whether design training influenced spatial ability performance, and to identify the spatial ability factors that were influenced, independent sample t tests were conducted to compare performance differences on the four spatial tests between the design and non-design groups.

**Table 1.** Descriptive statistics for the four spatial tests

|        | Range   | Mean   | SD    |
|--------|---------|--------|-------|
| MRT    | 1-13    | 6.94   | 2.41  |
| CCT    | 6-20    | 12.83  | 2.96  |
| CRT    | 36-147  | 86.73  | 22.67 |
| HPT    | 32-182  | 130.93 | 24.92 |

Regarding mental rotation, the t test results indicated that t (70) = 4.82, p < .01. Based on calculations of the mean, the design group scored 8.13 and the non-design group scored 5.75. This suggests that the MRT performance of the design group was significantly superior to that of the non-design group. Regarding cube comparison, the t test results indicated that t (70) = 5.35, p < .01. The mean score for the design group was 14.41, and 11.25 for the non-design group. This suggests that the CCT performance of the design group was significantly superior to that of the non-design group. For card rotation, the t test results indicated that t (70) = 2.41, p < .05. According to mean calculations, the design group scored 92.97 and the non-design group scored 80.50. This demonstrates that the CRT performance of the design group was significantly superior to that of the non-design group. Finally, regarding hidden patterns, the t test results indicated that t (70) = 1.86, p = .07. These results did not achieve significance. This indicates that the HPT performance of the design and non-design groups were similar.

For solution strategies, t tests were also conducted to compare the holistic and analytical item scores of the design and non-design groups. Regarding the holistic items, the scores for the four items were summed and divided by four to obtain an overall holistic item score. Subsequently, the differences between the scores for the design and non-design groups were compared. The t test results indicated that t (70) = 7.97, p < .01. The design group mean score was 3.80 and that for the non-design group was 2.86. This suggests that participants in the design group applied holistic strategies at a higher rate during spatial testing compared to those in the non-design group. Regarding the analytical items, the scores for the two items were summed and divided by two to obtain the overall analytical score. Subsequently, t tests were conducted to determine whether differences existed between the analytical strategies employed by the design and non-design groups. The results indicated that t (70) = -6.14, p < .01. Based on calculations of the mean, the design group scored 2.62 and the non-design group scored 3.78. This suggests that participants in the non-design group applied analytical strategies at a higher rate during spatial testing compared to those in the design group.

Based on the Pearson product-moment correlation test results, mental rotation abilities were positively correlated to the holistic items (r = .40) and negatively correlated to the analytical items (r = -.37). This suggests that higher mental rotation scores were obtained with higher holistic item scores. Conversely, lower mental rotation scores were obtained with higher analytical item scores.

## 4    Conclusion

In this study, we investigated whether spatial abilities increased following design training, whether different solution strategies are applied after design training, and explored the relationship between holistic and analytical strategies and spatial test performance. Thus, we considered the design and non-design groups independent variables, and considered the four spatial tests and solution strategies dependent variables. The results indicated that the design group's mental rotation, cube comparison, and card rotation performances significantly exceed those of the non-design group. The MRT and CCT corresponded to the spatial visualization factor, and the CRT corresponded to the spatial relation factor. Consequently, the spatial ability factors of spatial visualization and relation are influenced by design training, although perceptual speed is not affected. In addition, we found that the design group tended to apply holistic strategies, whereas the non-design group tended to apply analytical strategies. Further investigation of the relationship between holistic and analytical strategies and mental rotation scores showed that the MRT was positively correlated to holistic strategies and negatively correlated to analytical strategies. In other words, solution strategies influence spatial test performance.

**Acknowledgment.** This research was supported by the National Science Council of Taiwan under grant NSC100-2221-E-17-14.

## References

1. Roth, S.: Visualization in Science and the Arts. Presented at the In Art, Science and Visual Literacy: Selected readings from the Annual Conference of the International Visual Literacy Association, pp. 81–85 (1993)

2. Lord, T.: Spatial Teaching. Science Teacher 54, 32–34 (1987)
3. Wanzel, K.R., Hamstra, S.J., Anastakis, D.J., Matsumoto, E.D., Cusimano, M.D.: Effect of Visual-Spatial Ability on Learning of Spatially-Complex Surgical Skills. The Lancet 359, 230–231 (2002)
4. Cherney, I.: Mom, Let Me Play More Computer Games: They Improve My Mental Rotation Skills. Sex Roles 59, 776–786 (2008)
5. Workman, J., Caldwell, L., Kallal, M.: Development of a Test to Measure Spatial Abilities Associated with Apparel Design and Product Development. Clothing and Textiles Research Journal 17, 128–133 (1999)
6. Lohman, D.F., Kyllonen, P.C.: Individual Differences in Solution Strategy of Spatial Tasks. In: Dillon, R.F., Schmeck, R.R. (eds.) Individual Differences in Cognition, pp. 105–135. Academic, New York (1983)
7. Snow, R.: Aptitude Processes. In: Snow, R., Federico, P., Montague, W. (eds.) Cognitive Process Analyses of Aptitude, pp. 27–64. Erlbaum Associates, Hillsdale (1980)
8. Workman, J., Lee, S.: A Cross-Cultural Comparison of the Apparel Spatial Visualization Test and Paper Folding Test. Clothing and Textiles Research Journal 22, 22–30 (2004)
9. Linn, M., Petersen, A.: Emergence and Characterization of Sex Differences in Spatial Ability: A Meta-Analysis. Child Development 56, 1479–1498 (1985)
10. Tzuriel, D., Egozi, G.: Gender Differences in Spatial Ability of Young Children: the Effects of Training and Processing Strategies. Child Development 81, 1417–1430 (2010)
11. Janssen, A.B., Geiser, C.: On the Relationship Between Solution Strategies in two Mental Rotation Tasks. Learning and Individual Differences 20, 473–478 (2010)
12. Carroll, J.: Human Cognitive Abilities: A Survey of Factor-Analytic Studies. Cambridge University Press, New York (1993)
13. Miyake, A., Friedman, N., Rettinger, D., Shah, P., Hegarty, M.: How Are Visuospatial Working Memory, Executive Functioning, and Spatial Abilities Related? A Latent-Variable Analysis. Journal of Experimental Psychology General 130, 621–640 (2001)
14. Moè, A., Meneghetti, C., Cadinu, M.: Women and Mental Rotation: Incremental Theory and Spatial Strategy Use Enhance Performance. Personality and Individual Differences 46, 187–191 (2009)

# Service Based Design Solutions –
# A Case of Migrant Workers' Affective Links
# with Their Families in Rural Areas of China

Jikun Liu[1], Qing Liu[2], and Chenyu Zhao[1]

[1] Academy of Arts & Design, Tsinghua University,
Haidian District, Beijing 100084, China
[2] College of Technology & Innovation, Arizona State University,
Tempe, Arizona, USA
`ljk@tsinghua.edu.cn, Qing.Liu.7@asu.edu,`
`z_dian_dian@163.com`

**Abstract.** The outgoing of migrant workers from China rural areas brings many negative impacts upon their stay-at-home children, most of which are relevant to lack of family love and emotional connections. This joint project of Tsinghua University Design & Human Factors Lab and Nokia Research Center Beijing aims at investigating the daily lives of and interactions between the migrant workers in cities and their children staying at rural homes, and inventing some conceptual solutions to help them to treat this sort of problems. "DreamSeed", "WeMoment" and "LinkBoard" are just three conceptual solutions generated in this joint project, which attempt to contribute to promoting the emotional connections of migrant workers with their families, especially their children at rural home.

**Keywords:** migrant workers, stay-at-home children, emotional connection, user research, service design.

## 1    Introduction

According to National Bureau of Statistics of China, by 2011, there are around 252.78 million migrant workers in China, and 158.63 million of them work far away from their homes and families. [1] This results in 58 million stay-at-home children in their rural homes, and around 40 million of whom are schoolers under 14 years old. [2]

The outgoing of parent migrant workers brings their stay-at-home children many negative impacts on study and lives, and most of which are related to kinship indifference and shortage of affective connections with their parents. This can be illustrated from some previous research, such as Fang Fan, Xiaoyan Shen, Cen Wu, Helong Zhang, Jingzhong Ye and Yunsheng Lao etc. [3, 4, 5]

In the view of above questions, the Lab of Design & Human Factors at Academy of Arts & Design, Tsinghua University and Nokia Research Center Beijing had set up a joint project in 2011, to mainly research into needs of outgoing migrant workers'

P.L.P. Rau (Ed.): CCD/HCII 2013, Part I, LNCS 8023, pp. 410–419, 2013.
© Springer-Verlag Berlin Heidelberg 2013

emotional connections with their stay-at-home family members, especially their children, and design opportunities, and then generate some concept solutions, in order to promote a better affective communication between migrant workers and their stay-at-home children. (Fig. 1)

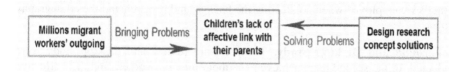

**Fig. 1.** The back ground of the project

## 2    Process, Methods and Results

### 2.1    Overall Process

The overall approach and process of this project is shown as below in Fig. 2. In the initial stage, our research team did the desktop study and literature review, or the background research, then conducted field investigation. From the results of the desktop study and field observations, we concluded key findings, the starting points to lead to solution ideas.

After that, we conducted brainstorming sessions to transfer some key findings into trigger ideas that may stimulate further concepts in the workshop conducted in the Nokia Research Center Beijing. The workshop participated by both our research team members in Tsinghua University and diversified research staff from Nokia Research Center worked out some candidate concepts that might solve the problems or respond to the insights we had concluded and combined from the desktop study and the field research.

And finally, we reviewed candidate concepts by street interceptive interview of both city migrant workers and their children who shortly stayed with them. We concluded the final concept solutions by adapting the candidate concepts with the result of the street interception.

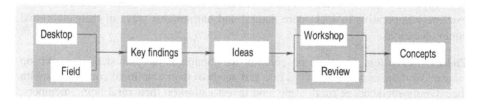

**Fig. 2.** The overall methodology of the project [6]

## 2.2     Research Methods

In the early stage of this project, we followed Human-Centered Design principles and User Value Innovation Theory [7, 8]. We assembled a multidiscipline research team of nine members, including a professor, a lab staff member, two graduate students, and five undergraduate students. The following are general descriptions about the methods we employed when conducting the background research and the ethnography studies.

**Background and Desktop Study.** The literature review and desktop study were conducted for the second hand achievement about migrant workers and their affective links with their family member at home (especially their stay-at-home children). From the review, we found out that the phone calls are the major communication means for their connections, only a quarter stay-at-home children call their parents working at cities once a week, and sixty percent of them call once a month; a half of them talk less than 3 minutes per call, and only twenty percent of them talk longer than 5 minutes. The contents of their talking are just children's learning, diet, health, safety, following the guardian's words, following teachers' words and some daily lives in the order of frequency priority. Generally, what the parents most care are learning performance and safety of their children, as well as whether they obey their guardian, but the children most care their parents' health status. [8] The effect of emotional communication between the parents and their stay-at-home children is not satisfying, and reasons are concluded below: [9]

(1) Migrant workers could not understand stay-at-home children due to spending too little time with them;
(2) Communication between stay-at-home children and their outgoing parents deviates a normal life situation;
(3) Phone call could not fully express their feelings, not only because the time of calling is too short, but the talking contents are repetitive as well;
(4) Migrant workers and their children also lack communicative skills to exchange their feelings only though a phone call;
(5) Migrant workers care too much about their children's learning performance, which easily triggers tension relationship between them.

From the literature review, it is obvious that children staying at rural home only depend on phone calls to communicate with their parents working in cities, which are both expensive and difficult to reach the effect of emotional exchange. Thus, it is extremely imperative to seek more natural and harmonious ways of their emotional communications.

**Field Observation.** The field observation we conducted has two steps: research on migrant workers in cities for status quo and needs of their emotional connections with their family members at rural home, and investigation on their rural home members, especially their say-at-home children, to understand their daily lives, the status quo and potential needs of their emotional connections with their migrant parents working far away their homes. Based on the findings from this two aspects investigations above, we concluded the design opportunities.

*Sample Users.* The samples for these two steps are different. In the first step, we interviewed and observed 9 migrant workers (6 males and 3 females with ages from 20 to 40) working in Beijing with their children staying at rural homes. And their stay-at-home children in rural areas age from 1 to 15 years old. The occupations of the migrant workers investigated in the first step are cooks, public security staff members, assembling workers, gatehouse watchers, cleaning attendants and practitioners in food processing industry.

In the second step, our researchers went to the rural homes of the migrant workers investigated in the first step to talk to their family members, and especially their stay-at-home children. We totally visited 7 left-behind families distributed different places of Hebei province in the north of China, and Hunan province in the middle south of China. Most of the families we visited are consist of wives and children left-behind, and in some families have only grandparents with the children. The children's ages of these families are from 5 months to 16 years old.

*Research Methods.* We employed user research methods including user in-depth interviewing, field video ethnography, and street intercept interviewing. In the first step, we interviewed 9 migrant workers in city of Beijing, and recorded the interviews and their working and living environments. We also shadowed, observed and videotaped their daily lives and working periods. The first research step totally lasted three weeks. Six research team members were divided into three groups with two members in each. The purposes of the investigation we proposed are consist of three parts: for understanding the basic lives of city migrant workers, for understanding their basic communication status, and for understanding their emotional connections with their family members in rural homes.

In the second step, we still used the in-depth interview and field observation methods, but what we interviewed and tour are the rural homes and family members of the migrant workers who were working in the city. We observed and videotaped the left-behind home environments and their daily lives. The purposes of the second step is to find the left-behind families', particularly stay-at-home children's status quo and needs in their emotional connections with their migrant worker parents. In this step, we also divided our six team members into 3 groups and assigned them to visit 7 families distributed at Yiyang in Hunan province and Rongcheng county and Baoding city in Hebei province respectively. The visits and observations lasted two weeks. The contents of investigation are similar to the first step, about basic daily lives and basic communication status quo, as well as their emotional connections with their outgoing parents.

## 2.3     Research Results

After these two kinds of researches above, desktop study and field observation, each group had conducted comprehensive analysis respectively, then each group briefed and presented researches and observation to get empathy of whole team members. And finally the whole team members discussed together and concluded 11 key findings below (Table 1).

**Table 1.** Key findings with migrant workers and their families

| | |
|---|---|
| *Basic life style of migrant workers and their family members* | *(A) Migrant workers and their families prefer face to face communication.*<br>*(B) Migrant workers most concern their stay-at-home children's education issues.*<br>*(C) Most migrant workers and their families use mobile phone as fixed-line, some family members share one mobile phone and/or the same SIM card.* |
| *Affective needs of outgoing migrant workers and their stay-at-home family members* | **(D) Migrant workers have a strong emotional reliance on their family members, their most mobile phone wallpapers are photos of their family members, some elderly extremely appreciate paper photos of their children outgoing.**<br>**(E) Stay-at-home children feel strongly solitary, though most with their grandparents or relatives.**<br>**(F) Migrant workers hope to timely know the current situation of their family members at rural country.** |
| *Communication needs of migrant workers and their stay-at-home family members* | *(G) Migrant workers and their families have emergent need of video calls.*<br>*(H) Migrant workers and their families are extremely sensitive to communication expenses.*<br>**( I ) Stay-at-home elderly and children have obstacles with complicated functions and features of the communication devices.**<br>*(J) Migrant workers and their families care much about the brands of communication devices.*<br>*(K) Most migrant workers do not actively seek new application services for mobile phones.* |

## 2.4    Workshop

According to the 11 key findings above, our research team brainstormed some seed concept ideas, which would be as triggers for brainstorming session of the workshop conducted in the Nokia Research Center in Beijing.

Totally more than 28 people participated in the workshop, 8 our research team members, 8 from another parallel research team of Tsinghua University Academy of Arts & Design, and 12 from the GUE (Growth market User Experience) and other groups, including technique departments, of Nokia Research Center Beijing.

In this multidiscipline participated workshop, our research team presented user research process and research results, as well as the trigger ideas. Then, we divided the participants into 7 groups to evaluate and improve the seed ideas and brainstorm new ideas after a coffee break. Finally, each group presented the new ideas generated during the brainstorming session.

## 2.5     Concept Review

Our project team polished the concept ideas generated in the workshop. Then we conducted return interviewing with the migrant workers and street interception interviewing with stay-at-home children. The research team was still divided into three groups, and each group was consist of two researchers.

We firstly interviewed the migrant workers working in city of Beijing who had been interviewed in the early stage. One researcher presented the interviewees the printed scenario of each concept ideas, and the other researcher asked questions with interviewing outline.

For the interview with stay-at-home children, we used street interception method, as it was too hard to return to the families of migrant workers who accepted our early stage interview, and we would like to try some fresh air as well. So we let each group to go to some villages in City of Beijing, the migrant workers lived in, and interview each child they met, who fortunately paid a very short visit to their parents from their rural home during the summer vacation.

Both the interviews with migrant workers and visiting stay-at-home children provided us very positive responses, though they suggested some small improvements as well. The next section will present the improved concept solutions with some discussions for each of them.

## 3     Concepts and Discussions

After the workshop and street interception concept review, we got the final concept solutions: "DreamSeed", "WeMoment" and "LinkBoard". In the following text, we will present and discuss each of them.

**DreamSeed.** DeamSeed is a concept with a smart phone app for outgoing migrant worker parents and a device for their stay-at-home children, which will promote them to communicate in daily lives through planting a virtual tree together.

When the migrant workers who work far away from their homes purchase a smart phone, they also get free a device called DreamSeed for their children staying at rural homes. With DreamSeed terminal and app software, the stay-at-home children and their migrant worker parents can plant and cultivate a virtual tree together. The stay-at-home children need to take care of the tree every day, otherwise the tree will be becoming withered and declined. The parents can watch the growth situations of the tree their children take care of, deliver directions for their children how to cultivate the tree, and even help grow the tree if the weather keeps bad in their rural homes the children live in. (Fig. 3)

The children love to take care of the tree, because it is the one their parents give them. Generally, the time the tree grows up and bares fruits is the same time as their parents come back home, and they can get extra gifts from their parents for their efforts to take good care of the tree. (Fig. 4)

The water and sunshine are natural resources provided according to the weather situation of the places the children live in. However, the fertilizer and other substance such as pesticide have to be bought by the children using point coins, which need to be earned through good learning performance, some daily life chores, performance of obeying grandparents or other guardians, and so on.

**Fig. 3.** The child and the mother taking care of the tree respectively

**Fig. 4.** The time tree grow up is the same time as parents return home

At early stage, we found from literature review that spending little time together, relying only on very short call communication, lacking communicative skills, are the reasons to cause the emotional indifference of the stay-at-home children. The migrant workers' too caring about the children's learning in the short phone call is easily trigger tensional relationship between them.

DeamSeed could solve the above problems of stay-at-home children in primary school to some extent. And it could also reduce the outgoing parents' concerns about their children's learning (key finding B), and their children's strong solitary at rural homes (key finding E).

The concept of DreamSeed can be adapted in actual applications. The app in the parents' smart phones may fixed into the hardware for reducing phone cost, though nowadays the price of smart phone is getting decreased. Also the device for the children may be integrated into their electronic learning tools in the future.

**WeMoment.** WeMoment is a concept of system which integrate a terminal device with TV set at rural home and cell phone with outgoing migrant workers.

WeMoment terminals are also free for outgoing migrant workers when they buy cell phones from special stores. The terminal is consist of two parts: body and base. The terminal body can be carried-on by stay-at-home children for sound recording and photo taking. The terminal base with SIM card built-in can send and receive files of sound and image, and can be connected to TV set. On the base there is a quickcall key for the children to talk to their migrant worker parents easily. (Fig. 5)

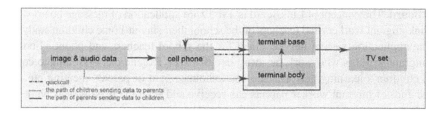

**Fig. 5.** The working model of WeMoment

The stay-at-home children can take the body around and record their daily lives or anything they may think to need to share with their parents. Later, they can connected the body to the base and send the recording to their parents' cell phone. On the other hand, the outgoing parents of migrant workers can send their photos and sound to the base, and their children and other family members such as grandparents can share them on TV set. (Fig. 6)

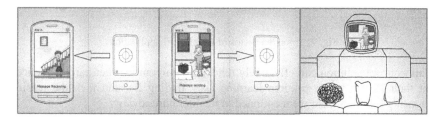

**Fig. 6.** The scenarios of WeMoment application

Therefore, this solution of WeMoment can help migrant workers and their stay-at-home families, especially the children, share some "significant moments" far away from the following points:

(a) It can meet the migrant workers' emotional dependence to their families at rural area, and let them know status quo of their family members in time. (key finding D)

(b) It allows the stay-at-home children easily communicating with their far away parents, which will much relieve their intense feeling of loneliness. (key finding E)

(c) It allows outgoing migrant workers timely know family members' especially stay-at-home children's living conditions, to meet their need of knowing lives of their families. (key finding F)

(d) The features of the terminal devices are simple and concise, the interfaces will be very clean and easy to operate, in order to avoid the operating barriers of the children and the elderly. (key finding I)

Furthermore, WeMoment may help migrant workers' families to adjust family atmosphere, optimize their spiritual lives, and improve the quality of their lives.

**LinkBoard.** The concept of LinkBoard is a software application of message board which can link migrant workers and teachers of the school their stay-at-home children study in.

The application system has PC client for the school teachers and phone client for the migrant workers who work far away in cities. The PC end can disseminate course plan, children's learning performance and announcement of parents meeting etc. The phone ends of migrant worker parents can receive and send the messages as well. The parents can use the app to interact with school teachers if necessary, such as check and sign their children's performance, and some important notices. (Fig. 7)

**Fig. 7.** Some Scenarios of LinkBoard application

This concept solution can effectively relieve the migrant worker parents' concerns about their stay-at-home children learning (key finding B), and then the tensional relationship between them we mentioned in the literature review.

## 4    Conclusion

This joint research project between Tsinghua University and Nokia Research Center Beijing aims at revealing the needs, desires and problems of outgoing migrant workers and their stay-at-home children in their emotional communications, and then putting forward relevant concept solutions to lay a foundation for further product and service development. In the early stage, we employed the research methods of in-depth interviewing, field observation, video ethnography and street interception. The interview outline had been used to ensure the validation of data. Videotaping and photography had been conducted for the significant events, home environments and typical daily life situations. The street interception interviewing was just for testing the concept solutions in the later stage, and its purpose was to avoid deviation and invalidation of the data in the return interviewing due to the researchers' being acquainted with the interviewees interviewed by the researchers in the early stage.

The development of information technology, maturity of three-in-one network and decrease of communication charges will be much more increasing our concepts feasibility. For example, three-in-one network will much more simplify the operating procedure of the concepts, using cost deduction will let migrant workers and their families can afford more video files transmission, and so on. In the near future, these concept solutions can be expended and used for other target user groups as well.

**Acknowledgments.** The project of research into urban migrant workers' affective link with their families is sponsored by Nokia Research Center Beijing, China. We appreciate the direction of Ying Liu and Xiantao Chen, the principal researcher and researcher of the Center's GUE Group, who guided project from Nokia side.

We would like to thank other team members and participants: Yutong Gu, Ying Shao, Xuanbai Li, Hao Li and Mengyuan Tu. We would also like to thank Ms. Changzhi Wang, the technical staff at Design & Human Factors Lab of Tsinghua University Academy of Arts & Design.

# References

1. National Bureau of Statistics of China: Investigation and Survey Report of China Migrant Workers in 2011 (2011), http://www.stats.gov.cn/tjfx/fxbg/index.htm
2. Stay-at-home Children, http://baike.baidu.com/view/109106.htm
3. Wan, M., Mao, R.: Many Issues For Present "Stay-at-home Children" Study in China. J. Academic Journal of Northwest Normal University (Social Science Edition), vol. 1 (2010)
4. Hou, Y., Xu, Z.: Aloneness and inferiority complex of stay-at-home children in countryside. J. Children's Mental Health 8 (2008)
5. Ye, J., Wang, Y., Zhang, K., Lu, J.: The Impact of Outgoing of Migrant Workers on Stay-at-home Children's emotional Lives. J. Issues of Agricultural Economics 4 (2006)
6. Zhao, C., Liu, Q., Liu, J.: WeMoment: A Conceptual Solution For Migrant Workers' Emotional Link With Their Families. In: Liu, J., Cai, J. (eds.) Proceedings of 2011Tsinghua-DMI International Design Management Symposium, pp. 124–130. Beijing Institute of Technology Press, Beijing (2011)
7. Liu, J.: From Value Analysis to Value Innovation: A Theoretical Framework of Value Innovation in Industrial Design. Ph.D. dissertation. Tsinghua University, Beijing (2007)
8. Liu, J., Liu, X.: User Value Based Product Adaptation: A Case of Mobile Products for Chinese Urban Elderly People. In: Kurosu, M. (ed.) HCD 2009. LNCS, vol. 5619, pp. 492–500. Springer, Heidelberg (2009)
9. Ye, J., Wang, Y., Lu, J.: How outgoing work of parents effects emotional lives of stay-at-home children. J. Rural Area Economic Issues 4 (2006)
10. Liao, Y., Song, S., Chen, B.: Study on problems of rural stay-at-home children's emotional communication with parents working far away of their homes 8 (2009)
11. Nokia Research Center GUE Team: Chinese Rural Field Study in Shannxi. Nokia Research Center, Beijing (2008)
12. Liu, X., Jikun, L.: User Study on Migrant Workers, Tsinghua-Nokia Joint Project (2007)
13. NRC ESSEX Project: User Experience Study on Chinese Internal Migration. Nokia Research Center, Beijing (2006)

# Affective Fusion of PAD Model-Based Tactile Sense: A Case Study of Teacups

Jui-Ping Ma, Mei-Ting Lin, and Rungtai Lin

Graduate School of Creative Industry Design, National Taiwan University of Arts
New Taipei City 22058, Taiwan
rupm08@gmail.com, gua_gua@mail2000.com.tw, rtlin@ntua.edu.tw

**Abstract.** This study explores on emotion and perception of teacups in subject teams of sighted people and blind people through the tactile sense. Two subject teams are arranged individually to touch the teacups one by one separated by curtains in a room. After observing and investigating, PAD emotion scale will be applied to evaluate emotion of participants. The researcher explores whether haptic sense effect is produced from participants' tactual behavior with one set teacup. The finding is shown that: (1). The emotional effects of the blind subjects are more extreme than the sighted subjects in pleasure and arousal dimensions; (2). A teacup with oblique relief texture can make the unsighted subjects more pleasure emotions; (3). A straight line makes the blind subjects more uncertainty feelings and result in a negative emotional state; (4). Compare to the unsighted subjects, there is only a little difference between positive and negative emotion in the pleasure state of sighted subjects.

**Keywords:** Haptic, PAD scale, Emotion.

## 1    Introduction    .

Human being received most of 80% information and messages through sight [5]. That is the reason why researchers have taken much more time and energy devoting to the study of picture perception in vision than in touch [15]. However, affective expression of people is naturally communicated by multiple body sense organs [6]. Differently, the blind must contact everything from tactile and hearing sense. Recently, some researchers have represented that distinct emotions such as anger, fear, happiness, sympathy, love, and gratitude can be formed by touching communicating [9]. Moreover, the emotions communicated by haptic is commensurate to facial and vocal displays of emotion [10]. It is known that the blind will be more sensitive than sighted people caused by their impaired vision that resulting in penetrative tactile of hands. That is, to survey the tactile actions of blind people seems to infer their state of emotion and perception.

In this paper, we engaged in participant-observation to observe and record behaviors of subjects on touching with the teacups. Then we measure emotion and perception of the tactile sense by using PAD model, validate PAD theory's correctness and applicability in haptic area and verify its feasibility.

P.L.P. Rau (Ed.): CCD/HCII 2013, Part I, LNCS 8023, pp. 420–429, 2013.
© Springer-Verlag Berlin Heidelberg 2013

The experiment is designed to collect mainly PAD data following the guidance of original M-R (Mehrabia-Russell, 1974) model [16], traditional Chinese version [11]. Then, we also divide tactile emotion into eight spaces (+/-pleasure, +/-arousal, +/-dominance) based on Mehrabia's model [8] and built a PAD data set.

The object of this paper is trying (1) to explore the emotional difference between the unsighted and sighted people through touch "Persona Teacup"; (2) to compare the difference of affective fusion between the unsighted and sighted people with PAD scale. The paper is organized as follows. Section 2 reviews the related literatures on haptic sense, the blind, and PAD model. Section 3 describes the case study of tactile experiment. Section 4 presents experimental results, and Section 5 concludes the paper.

# 2     Literature Survey

This section first reviews related literatures of haptic sense of the blind, then, introduces the features of PAD model that may be applied to questionnaire design, then; the tools of PAD scale are applied to evaluate the tactile experiment of two subject teams. Finally, statistical analysis will do with the experimental data and be discussed.

## 2.1     Haptic Sense of the Blind

Previous many approaches have been explored to discuss the tactile sense of the blind, for instance, whether subjects touch graph in single hand then draw down graph or express the name of the graph after touching, acquired unsighted people is better than innate unsighted people[1]. Moreover, graphic experience of innate unsighted people shaped from haptic experience. When congenital unsighted people want to form specific graph experience, they must realize absolutely the size and range to the object, while the object which is touched should be similar to real entity [7].

An important research of human factor named "two-point threshold" show that the near fingers' tip is, the smaller the value of two-point threshold is, it means that the sensitivities of fingertips are more intense than other parts of hands [20]. For correct relationship of tactile exploring strategy and shape matching, another early study from [12] concluded five exploring strategy including： (1) thoroughness; (2) tracing; (3) feature comparison; (4) congruent perimeter comparison; (5) mirror-image perimeter tracing. Another study pointed out three limitations of the tactile cognition and recognition of the blind: (1) experience and style; (2) haptic modes; (3) influence of the environment each other [2].

In an experiment on observation named sensitive about index fingers, the visually impaired subjects and sighted subjects but are blindfolded can be noticed that all of them touch the surface on an object by the tip of fingers [15]. The visually impaired subjects usually catch enough information more effectively to construct a mind map by a pair of hands. Nevertheless, sighted subjects used to touch icon or relief by one hand or a finger resulted from aid of memory in mind, even if they are blindfolded [18].

## 2.2    PAD Model

PAD emotional model was established by Albert Mehrabian and James A. Russell in 1974, and then some studies took it to be a measurable tool for peoples' emotion. The PAD emotional model was regarded as more effective in evaluating emotional responses of subjects than others [8].

To conduct the PAD model approach, some researchers can measure emotional tendencies and affective states along three dimensions: pleasure vs. displeasure, arousal vs. non-arousal and dominance vs. submissiveness. According to three dimensions of PAD scale, Lang [13] developed "SAM" (Self-Assessment Manikin) scale uses emotional keywords of PAD are replaced by five icons within SAM. The evaluation method is that after subjects watch every stimulant material, then, to choose an icon which is matched subjects' emotion. Based on SAM, Desmet [4] built another dynamic icon system to supersede still icons named "PrEmo" scale. In "PrEmo" scale, seven negative mood icons at the left, while seven positive mood icons at right and stimulant on the corner of left.

Li [14] announced the simple Chinese version of PAD (SCP) emotional scale, which is composed of adjectives of 12 couples, decreased from 18. However, Hsieh [11] argued that there was no satisfactory on reliability and validity when PAD scale was transferred to SCP. The SCP with well reliability and validity in "pleasure" and suitable reliability and validity in "arousal", whereas without enough value in "Dominance".

# 3    Research Design

This section represents the methods that adopted in this case study. The sixteen subjects touch the teacups individually one by one in order. The experimental data are collected and analyzed by an applied statistics.

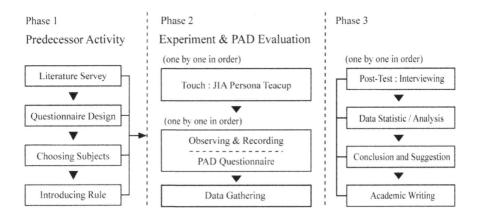

**Fig. 1.** Research Flowchart

## 3.1    Research Flowchart

The main goal of this study is to explore the emotion and cognition of tactile sense generated through the blind and non-blind participants' touching with two sets of teacups. We do with the PAD questionnaire interviews of participants. They are asked individually to describe and explain how they feel as detailed as possible. Finally, researchers integrate data to run statistical program and analyze the result to summarize the study. The research flowchart is shown by Figure 1.

## 3.2    Stimuli and Design

Four teacups of one set named "Persona Teacups" (in Chinese:異同杯) are selected from brand JIA to be our stimuli materials. Although "Persona Teacups" whole set is all made by porcelains and same compendium in shape, they are quite out of divergence in decorative design with different low relief textures on their bodies. Therefore, we call the teacups basing on their textures to be: A-Circle Dot; B-Straight Line; C-Square Dot; D- Oblique Line. To handle experiment smoothly and avoid the visual interference, we separate four teacups to put in independent boxes and cover top only retain front transparent for taking pictures. The "Persona Teacups" and their relief textures are shown by Figure 2.

A-Circle Dot    B-Straight    C-Square    D- Oblique

**Fig. 2.**  "Persona Teacups" and Their Relief Textures

## 3.3    Subject Teams

Sixteen subjects (eight blind people) volunteered to take part in the experiment. Age ranged from 20 to 24 years. All subjects we choose from one organization at random. Due to experimental necessity, the unsighted subjects can be selected only congenital blind people not acquired blind people. All subjects are asked to confirm that they have no experience in touching "Persona Teacup". All of subjects: (1) age without big difference; (2) boy and girl are same; (3) half sighted people and half blind people. The information of two subject teams is listed by Table 1.

Table 1. The Information List of Subject Teams

| No. | Blind(B) / Sighted (S) | Age | Gender | Code Name |
|---|---|---|---|---|
| 1 | B | 21 | Male | 01BM21 |
| 2 | B | 22 | Female | 02BF20 |
| 3 | B | 20 | Male | 03BM19 |
| 4 | B | 20 | Female | 04BF20 |
| 5 | B | 22 | Male | 05BM22 |
| 6 | B | 21 | Female | 06BF21 |
| 7 | B | 23 | Male | 07BM20 |
| 8 | B | 24 | Female | 08BF20 |
| 9 | S | 20 | Male | 09SM20 |
| 10 | S | 22 | Female | 10SF22 |
| 11 | S | 21 | Male | 11SM21 |
| 12 | S | 20 | Female | 12SF22 |
| 13 | S | 24 | Male | 13SM23 |
| 14 | S | 21 | Female | 14SF24 |
| 15 | S | 21 | Male | 15SM21 |
| 16 | S | 22 | Female | 16SF22 |
| Total | B:8 / S:8 | F:21.5 (mean) / M:21.5(mean) | F:8 / M:8 | 16 |

## 3.4 Evaluative Tool

Due to language translation and difference of meaning, we take traditional Chinese version of PAD scale and refer to English version as evaluative tool. The 18 pairs of keywords are shown by Table 2.

## 3.5 Experimental Procedure

Before beginning of experiment, the researcher told the subjects the aim, answering rules of the study and explained that there were no absolute correct answers, no limited time, just relied on their own emotion state. The experiment was conducted in a room individually; one subject felt free to put his (her) one or two hands into a test box to touch a teacup and next step finish the questionnaire at once. This procedure was repeated until four tests had been finished. We use a Likert scale with the typical 5-level item to ask the subjects writing down (sighted subjects) or answering (the blind subjects) the PAD scale questionnaire. Although many psychometricians support to use seven or nine levels, however, a recent study argued that there was very little difference between the scale formats like 5-, 7- or 9- point in terms of variation about the mean, skewness or kurtosis [3].

**Table 2.** The 18 Pairs of Keywords in PAD Scale

| Dimension | "+"Positive Mood | "—" Negative Mood |
|---|---|---|
| **P(Pleasure)** | Happy (快樂) | Unhappy (不快樂) |
| | Pleased (愉悅) | Annoyed (惱怒) |
| | Satisfied (滿意) | Unsatisfied (不滿意的) |
| | Contented(滿足) | Melancholic (沮喪) |
| | Hopeful (希望) | Despairing (絕望) |
| | Surprised (驚奇) | Bored (無聊) |
| **A(Arousal)** | Stimulated (刺激) | Relaxed (放鬆) |
| | Excited (興奮) | Calm (平靜) |
| | Frenzied (瘋狂) | Sluggish (懶散) |
| | Jittery(緊張) | Dull(枯燥) |
| | Awake (清醒) | Sleepy (睏倦) |
| | Aroused (喚起) | Unaroused (未被喚起) |
| **D(Dominance)** | Controlling (控制) | Controlled (被控制) |
| | Influential (有影響力) | Influenced (被影響) |
| | Uncrowned(不擁擠) | Crowded (擁擠) |
| | Important(重要) | Awed (不重要) |
| | Dominant (支配) | Submissive (服從) |
| | Free (自由) | Restricted (被限制) |

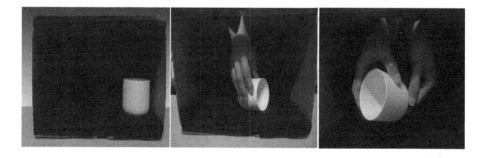

F.3-1 A teacup in Test Box     F.3-2 Test (Sighted Subject)     F.3-3 Test (Blind Subject)

**Fig. 3.** Three Pictures of the Experiment

After whole haptic experiment was finished, researchers interviewed every subject independently at one time. Finally, all data will be evaluated and integrated. The experimental procedure was shown by Figure 3. In F.3-1, we set black cloth and a teacup on it within a test box. The sighted subjects used one hand to touch texture of a teacup (F.3-2), however, all of blind subjects adopt two palms to feel the texture of a teacup (F.3-3).

# 4     Results

## 4.1     Data Gathering

The scores on the questionnaire by five-level Likert's item, can be: 2-strongly agree/1-agree/0-neither agree nor disagree/-1-disAgree/-2-strongly disagree. The emotional attribution can be identify as "+": it means positive emotional mood of subjects; "-": it means negative emotional mood. All scores are shown by Table 3.

**Table 3.** The Summated Rating of PAD Data from Subjects

|   |   | A | | B | | C | | D | |
|---|---|---|---|---|---|---|---|---|---|
|   |   | B | S | B | S | B | S | B | S |
| **P** | Happy — Unhappy | +10/-0 | +1/-5 | +0/-2 | +3/-0 | +0/-4 | +0/-8 | +7/-0 | +6/-4 |
|  | Pleased — Annoyed | +10/-0 | +2/-1 | +4/-1 | +4/-0 | +0/-4 | +2/-1 | +8/-0 | +4/-4 |
|  | Satisfied — Unsatisfied | +5/-0 | +2/-2 | +0/-6 | +0/-6 | +12/-0 | +1/-0 | +3/-2 | +3/-2 |
|  | Contented — Melancholic | +3/-0 | +2/-4 | +0/-5 | +0/-6 | +6/-0 | +2/-0 | +4/-1 | +0/-4 |
|  | Hopeful — Despairing | +6/-0 | +2/-0 | +0/-4 | +3/-1 | +2/-0 | +6/-0 | +3/-4 | +2/-4 |
|  | Surprised — Bored | +10/-0 | +6/-1 | +0/-4 | +0/-6 | +12/-0 | +11/-0 | +10/-0 | +5/-3 |
| **A** | Stimulated — Relaxed | +4/-3 | +6/-2 | +0/-9 | +0/-7 | +6/-0 | +9/-0 | +4/-2 | +0/-7 |
|  | Excited — Calm | +0/-2 | +0/-1 | +0/-12 | +0/-2 | +0/-13 | +1/-7 | +0/-4 | +2/-5 |
|  | Frenzied —Sluggish | +0/-13 | +0/-9 | +0/-2 | +0/-0 | +0/-13 | +0/-2 | +0/-2 | +0/-0 |
|  | Jittery — Dull | +0/-6 | +0/-3 | +0/-3 | +0/-12 | +0/-7 | +0/-6 | +3/-3 | +4/-5 |
|  | Awake — Sleepy | +5/-0 | +11/-0 | +6/-0 | +0/-3 | +10/-0 | +8/-0 | +6/-0 | +0/-3 |
|  | Aroused — Unaroused | +8/-0 | +7/-0 | +0/-13 | +0/-4 | +7/-0 | +3/-2 | +3/-2 | +6/-0 |
| **D** | Controlling — Controlled | +0/-9 | +0/-9 | +0/-13 | +0/-6 | +0/-7 | +0/-6 | +9/-0 | +5/-3 |
|  | Influential — Influenced | +6/-2 | +3/-5 | +0/-8 | +0/-5 | +7/-6 | +2/-8 | +9/-0 | +7/-1 |
|  | Uncrowded — Crowded | +0/-10 | +0/-11 | +0/-13 | +0/-5 | +0/-12 | +0/-14 | +8/-0 | +1/-4 |
|  | Important — Awed | +0/-6 | +0/-0 | +9/-0 | +2/-2 | +4/-0 | +6/-1 | +7/-0 | +7/-0 |
|  | Dominant — Submissive | +0/-11 | +0/-6 | +0/-11 | +0/-2 | +0/-3 | +0/-3 | +0/-11 | +0/2 |
|  | Free — Restricted | +0/-10 | +0/-12 | +0/-14 | +0/-2 | +0/-3 | +0/-14 | +0/-10 | +0/-5 |

*B:Blind Subjects  S:Sighted Subjects

To represent further, we amount to each PAD dimension of the questionnaire items individually and integrate to positive and negative sections of scores. The integrated scores listed are shown by Table 4.

**Table 4.** The Integrated Scores of Each PAD Dimension

| | A | | B | | C | | D | |
| | B | S | B | S | B | S | B | S |
|---|---|---|---|---|---|---|---|---|
| **P** | +44*/-0 | +15/-13 | +4/-22* | +10/-19 | +32/-8 | +22/-9 | +35/-7 | +20/-21 |
| **A** | +17/-24 | +24*/-15 | +6/-48* | +0/-19 | +23/-33 | +21/-17 | +16/-13 | +12/-20 |
| **D** | +3/-39 | +6/-34 | +9/-59* | +2/-22 | +11/-31 | +8/-46 | +33*/-21 | +20/-15 |

B:Blind Subjects  S:Sighted Subjects  " * " : highest score

In general, SD (Standard Deviation) can be illustrated how much variation or "dispersion" exists from the mean; from the above table 4, we integrate values of positive and negative emotions to calculate three-dimensional scores of PAD by arithmetic mean (AM) and standard deviation (SD) individually. The data are shown by Table 5.

**Table 5.** The Standard Deviation & Arithmetic Mean values of Each PAD Dimension

| | P | | | | A | | | | D | | | |
| | B | | S | | B | | S | | B | | S | |
| | + | − | + | − | + | − | + | − | + | − | + | − |
|---|---|---|---|---|---|---|---|---|---|---|---|---|
| **AM** | 28.8* | 9.3 | 16.8 | 15.5 | 15.5 | 29.5* | 14.3 | 17.8 | 14 | 37.5* | 9 | 29.3 |
| **SD** | 14.96 | 7.98 | 4.66 | 4.77 | 6.10 | 12.82 | 9.34 | 1.92 | 11.36 | 13.96 | 6.71 | 11.82 |

AM：Arithmetic Mean; SD：Standard Deviation
" * " : highest score  +": positive emotion; "-": negative emotion

## 5    Conclusion

Although this is a pilot study, and we adopt small samples in this experiment, the finding is shown as followed:

1. In this case study, "A" teacup can give rise to pleasure emotion state of the blind subjects significantly.
2. "B" teacup result in a more negative emotional state in terms of other teacups, especially in the blind subjects. The three-dimensional values of PAD tested by the blind subjects achieve to be higher level than the sighted subjects. To interview the blind subjects, they state that the texture of straight line makes them more uncertainty feelings.
3. In PAD scale, "Pleasure" means to measure how pleasant an emotion may be, in case of comparing two subject teams, complex texture especially oblique pattern

like teacups "A", "D" can bring more pleasurable feeling to the blind subjects, however, the sighted subjects prefer neat texture to more variational, oblique pattern, hence, for sighted subjects, "C" teacup is pleasurable.

4. In PAD scale, "Arousal" means to measure the intensity of the emotion, "C" teacup seems to stimulate the sighted subjects more positive response than others, and "A" and "D" teacups for the blind subjects, too.

5. In SD values, "Pleasure" SD of the sighted subjects shows an equal value nearly. However, there is an extreme gap between positive and negative emotions of the blind subjects by "Pleasure" SD and "Arousal" SD.

**Acknowledgement.** The authors would like to thank Association For the Blind of Taiwan (AFBT) for their helps on our experiments. We also thanks our students from National Taiwan University of Arts for their participating to experiment.

# References

1. Satō, Y.: Shì jiào zhàng hài xué rù mén, Gakugei Tosho, Tokyo (1991) (in Japanese)
2. Lowenfeld, B.: The visually handicapped child in school. John Day Books in Special Education, 359–368 (1973)
3. Dawes, J.: Do Data Characteristics Change According to the number of scale points used? An experiment using 5-point, 7-point and 10-point scales. International Journal of Market Research 50(1), 61–77 (2008)
4. Desmet, P.: Designing emotions. Published doctoral dissertation. Delft University of Technology, Netherlands (2002)
5. Geruschat, D., Smith, A.: Low vision and mobility. In: Blasch, B., Wiener, W., Welsh, R. (eds.) Foundations of Orientation and Mobility. American Foundation for the Blind, New York (1997)
6. Gilroy, S.W., Cavazza, M., Niiranen, M., Andre, E., Vogt, T., Urbain, J., Benayoun, M., Seichter, H., Billinghurst, M.: PAD-based Multimodal Affective Fusion. In: ACII 2009, pp. 1–8 (2009)
7. Karlsson, G.: The experience of spatiality for congenitally blind people: A phenomenological-psychological study. Human Studies 19(3), 303–330 (1996)
8. Havlena, W.J., Holbrook, M.B.: The varieties of consumption experience: Comparing two typologies of emotion in consumer behavior. Journal of Consumer Research 13(3), 394–404 (1986)
9. Hertenstein, M.J., Keltner, D., App, B., Bulleit, B., Jaskolka, A.: Touch communicates distinct emotions. Emotion 6, 528–533 (2006)
10. Hertenstein, M.J., Verkamp, J., Kerestes, A., Holmes, R.: The communicative functions of touch in humans, non-human primates and rats: A review and synthesis of the empirical research. Genetic, Social, and General Psychology Monographs 132, 5–94 (2006)
11. Hsieh, H.Y.: Taiwanese Version of the PAD Emotion Scales. In: KEER Conference (2011) (in Chinese)
12. Kleinman, M.J.: Developmental changes in haptic exploration and matching accuracy. Developmental Psychology 15(4), 480–481 (1979)
13. Lang, P.J.: Behavioural treatment and bio-behavioural assessment: Computer applications. In: Sidowski, J.B., Johnson, J.H., Williams, T.A. (eds.) Technology in Mental Health Care Delivery Systems, pp. 119–137. Ablex, Norwood (1980)

14. Li, X., Zhou, H., Song, S., Ran, T., Fu, X.: The reliability and validity of the chinese version of abbreviated pad emotion scales. In: Tao, J., Tan, T., Picard, R. (eds.) ACII 2005. LNCS, vol. 3784, pp. 513–518. Springer, Heidelberg (2005)
15. Heller, M.A., McCarthy, M., Clark, A.: Pattern Perception and Pictures for the Blind. Psicologica 26, 161–171 (2005)
16. Mehrabian, A.: Pleasure-Arousal-Dominance: a general framework for Describing and measuring individual differences in temperament. Current Psychology: Developmental, Learning, Personality, Social 14(4), 261–292 (1996)
17. Wijntjes, M.W., Kappers, A.M.: Angle discrimination in raised line drawings. Perception 36, 865–879 (2007)
18. Symmons, M., Green, B.: Raised line drawings are spontaneously explored with a single finger. Perception 29(5), 621–626 (2000)
19. Gilroy, S.W., et al.: Pad-based multimodal affective fusion. In: Proc. ACII Workshops, pp. 1–8 (2009)
20. Vallbo, A.B., Johansson, R.S.: The tactile sensory innervation of the glabrous skin of the human hand. In: Gordon, G. (ed.) Active touch: The mechanism of Recognition of Objects by Manipulation: A Multidisciplinary Approach, pp. 29–54. Pergamon, Oxford (1978)

# What's Your Point?

## How Chinese and Americans Achieve
## Their Conversational Aims in Cross-Cultural
## and Gender Interactions in CMC

Nancy Marksbury and Qiping Zhang

Palmer School of Library and Information Studies
LONG ISLAND UNIVERSITY, POST CAMPUS
720 Northern Boulevard, Brookville, NY 11548, USA
{nancy.marksbury,qiping.zhang}@liu.edu

**Abstract.** In this study of computer-mediated communication (CMC), Chinese and American students were paired cross-culturally and within same- and mixed-gender dyads. IM transcripts were analyzed for linguistic indicators of conversational management and interactional style. Our results revealed interesting interaction effect of culture and gender pairings. Females used more indicators of interaction style and males used a conversational management strategy for achieving their conversational aims. However, both Chinese males and females were more linguistically active when paired with an American of the opposite gender, while American females displayed more cultural acceptance when paired with a Chinese female than a Chinese male. American males talked more when paired with a Chinese male than when paired with a Chinese female. These findings have implications for working in global virtual teams and system design for cross-cultural collaborations.

**Keywords:** IM, gender, culture, computer-mediated communication, linguistics.

## 1    Introduction

Technology extends human capacity, allowing people to interact and exchange ideas across multiple boundaries – boundaries of time and space, as well as boundaries imposed by various stereotypes of social or cultural differences. In communications, dissimilar cultural and social orientations can introduce ill-timed interruptions, misunderstood silence, or ambiguous phraseology that adds confusion. Particularly for internationally diverse members communicating in a lean media channel like instant messaging (IM), misunderstandings and miscommunications may be avoided by understanding how cross-cultural and mixed gender interactions in IM are conducted.

Prior work in the effects of cultural differences in communication report the ways culture and media-type influence behavior. In an earlier study, Chinese and American intra-cultural behaviors were compared [1]. Zhang and Marksbury report that Chinese participants spent more time in discussions than did the Americans, and performed the

P.L.P. Rau (Ed.): CCD/HCII 2013, Part I, LNCS 8023, pp. 430–439, 2013.
© Springer-Verlag Berlin Heidelberg 2013

task more efficiently. If prior relational interaction promotes task effectiveness, an analysis of the structure and content of task-related discussions are important to observe. Our objective is to investigate how cultural differences manifest in CMC. To aid cooperation among individuals involved in remote collaborations, and to add to what is understood about the interaction of gender and culture in CMC, the aim of this paper is to report the results of conversational interactions of cross-culturally, diverse gender pairings.

## 2    Related Work

### 2.1    Gendered Talk

Gender-related styles of communicating have long been studied. In studies of face-to-face and written language, results are framed in theoretical viewpoints that certain drivers influence linguistic behavior. One explanation stems from the theory of gendered social roles assigning women as nurturing caretakers and men as action-oriented agents [2]. Social role theory predicts that females are socialized to be more collaborative and males more instrumental. This theory has been used to explain gender-related conversational differences, exemplified by females' cooperative and accommodating language and males using more assertive and active language [3].

**Partner Influence.** McMillan, et al [4] advocate that to understand the interactional elements between males and females, it is necessary to distinguish with whom the speaker is paired. Female friendships with other females are characterized with intimacy and emotional expressiveness, while the emphasis of males' friendships with other males is placed on shared activity [5]. Females tend to use more grammatically correct language and make requests using more words than males, while males in mixed gender conversations respond to these supportive interactions by talking more [6]. When paired with a female, males talked longer than when paired with another male, or than when females were paired [7]. Males also interrupted more when in face-to-face conversations with females than when speaking with other males [8].

**Gender in IM.** IM conversations are found to exhibit gendered conversation similar to patterns in spoken language. Previous studies of CMC have found that women in conversations with other women are more likely to talk longer [9], use more emoticons and more extensive openings and closings in their discussions [10]. Females in conversation with other males used more emoticons [9] and more words [11]. Ellipses, emoticons and acronyms become IM's nonverbal cues [9, 12] that provide emphases for meaning interpretation. The act of encouraging interaction is also seen in using multiturn sets (MTS). Particular for chatting channels, multiturn sets or "utterance chunks" [13] are the sequentially related messages a speaker uses to communicate several messages across several turns.

## 2.2 Cultural Influences

Another driver of linguistic behaviors is explained by an effect of culture. Stylistic differences between American and Chinese cultures align with the individualist-collectivist dimension [14, 15], a framework to account for nationalistic differences. Cross-cultural CMC research frequently employs models of cultural dimensions to interpret aggregate measures of culturally based behaviors. While second-language communicators using English complicates interpretation, English remains a language common to many global industries, academics, and the *"lingua franca* of professional communication"* [16, 339]. Cultural orientation, even when analyzed by linguistic indicators in a common language, should not be overlooked.

**Culture in IM.** Cultural influences in CMC include channel preferences, feature utilization, as well as communicative behaviors. Asians report preferences for lean media, stemming from concerns of language fluency [17], time in interpreting and responding [18], as well as higher ratings of emoticon importance [19]. North Americans are more likely to prefer direct communication, punctuated by debate and confrontation, while Asians may use time delays and other ambiguities that provide more time to digest message content and compose responses. Language-based indicators among Asian participants include more politeness and greater message production when compared to US participants, suggesting a more involved interactional style [20]. Despite this important work, the sociolinguistic analysis of IM remains relatively under-explored.

**Cross-cultural Partner Influences.** Other sociolinguistic analyses attempt to isolate media richness and task-type. In text-dominant media, collectivist cultural tendencies features conversational measures made richer by prolonged discussions with deeper interactions [21]. Conversational context is an important consideration, and nationalistic differences may be reduced or amplified in cross-cultural interactions.

## 2.3 Conversational Aims

In this study, conversational aims describe the goals each participant wishes to achieve in their communications. Reviewing related studies suggests that females will naturally seek out interaction by encouraging others' involvement, and males will be task-oriented and more directive in their communications. Culturally, members of a collectivist culture will strive for relational knowledge by encouraging interaction. Members of an individualistic culture, like the US, are likely to also be more efficient, task-focused and less effusive.

In order to help us think about the kinds of verbal indicators associated with the conversational aims, we divide the frequencies of indicators into two broad categories: conversational management and interaction style.

**Conversational Management.** Adapted from an extensive analysis of verbal behavior [22], conversational management is defined by the elements used to achieve participants' communication goal. These elements include the number of turns, the number of multiturn sets (MTS), and the length of turns, measured in words. Conversational management represents the characteristics of posting and is used in this analysis to quantify how individuals negotiate turn-taking and message conveyance to ensure the conversational aim is achieved. From a structural viewpoint, taking the floor and directing the conversation are ways to control communicational flow. These indicators are measured by turn and word production.

**Interactional Style.** Interactional style describes modifiers of language used in IM to encourage communication and are measured by indicators that suggest a collaborative intent. This conversational aim is achieved by imbuing one's conversation with additional cues to provide explicit meaning and personality. Three measures were used in this study to reflect interactional style: emoticons, unusual punctuation, and words in establishing presence. Emoticons are the ASCII text usually displayed sideways to indicate an emotional state, as in ": )". Unusual punctuation includes added punctuation (!!!) and abbreviations (LOL, IDK). Using humor, emoticons and unusual punctuation are ways to add emphasis for meaning interpretation, help clarify one's meaning and signal communicative encouragement. Word frequency in the introductory phase communication is an indicator of interactional style for establishing presence. By indicating interest in a person's name, their day or mood, the message sender uses more words and more turns at the initial stage of the conversation to establish a relationship.

### 2.4   Research Hypotheses

We are interested in how computer-mediated communication channels influence people from China and the US. While the body of previous work includes many studies examining CMC and culture, the present study investigates the interaction of gender pairing and culture by analyzing linguistic indicators in CMC. We explore how women and men interact cross-culturally in a negotiation task. Linguistically, males tend to be more active and assertive [3, 8] and talk longer in conversations with females [7]. Females paired with males will use more emoticons [9], will talk more [11], and produce more talk when establishing presence. Therefore, we predict:

> *H1a: Males will evidence more conversational management indicators.*
> *H1b: Females will demonstrate more indictors of an emphatic interactional style.*

Cross-culturally, conversation management especially measured by multi-turn (MTS) may indicate two possible linguistic aims. On the one hand, frequent usage of MTS by non-native speakers may slow down the conversation slow of the native speakers. On the other hand, a frequent usage of MTS can also be considered as a politeness by sending out frequent short messages rather than requesting the partner to wait for a long message. Given this, we predict that:

> *H2: Chinese will use more MTS than Americans in their communication.*

## 3    Method

*Participants:* Eighty-one students at a US university participated in this study: 41 Chinese (born and raised in mainland China or Taiwan, and residing the in the US for no more than 4 years) and 40 American students (born and raised in the US). All participants were paired cross-culturally with 4 confederates (Chinese male, Chinese female, US male and US female). Gender pairing (female-female, female-male, male-female, and male-male) was counter balanced. All participants conversed in English.

*Task:* An investment game, *Daytrader* [23] based on a prisoner's dilemma was used in the study. Participants were instructed to make as many points as possible, and after every 7 rounds entered an IM discussion through GChat (Google Chat). The game lasted a total of 21 rounds, allowing for 3 discussions. Participants were advised to discuss their investment performance of previous rounds or possible strategies for investing in future rounds.

*Procedure:* Upon arrival, participants responded to items on a background survey. Game instructions were explained and practice rounds were played in the presence of the researcher. After the task, participants were debriefed with the experimenter to share their experiences and comments.

## 4    Results

Linguistic indicators of conversational management and interactional style were analyzed from the transcripts of GChat conversations. Analyses of Variance (ANOVA) were performed to regress frequencies of linguistic categories by culture (China or US) and by gender pairings (female-female, female-male, male-female, and male-male).

### 4.1    Conversational Management Indicators

**Turns.** Analyzing frequencies of turns used overall, by culture and gender pairing revealed approaching significance of a main effect of culture, with Chinese using more turns ($F$ (1,78) = 3.04, $p < .09$), and an interaction effect of culture and gender pairing ($F$ (3,78) = 2.27, $p < .09$). A post hoc $t$-test of the interaction effect revealed two significant comparisons: First, cross-culturally, Chinese males (CM) used more turns than American males (AM) in a mixed gender pairing ($t$ (18) = 2.07, $p < .05$). Second, CM used more turns in a mixed gender pairing than in an all-male pairing ($t$ (18) = 2.09, $p < .05$). The peak of Chinese males' turns overall is seen in figure 1.

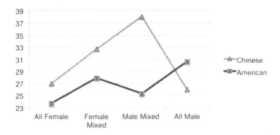

**Fig. 1.** Turns Overall

**Multiturn Sets.** Analyzing frequencies of MTS' used overall, by culture and gender pairing reveal a main effect of culture with Chinese using more MTS' than Americans ($F$ (1,78) = 5.52, $p$ < .02). Additional ANOVA for turns used within MTS' were also significant for a cultural effect. Across all discussions, Chinese used more turns within MTS' ($t$ (77) = 2.38, $p$ < .02). There was no difference between cultures for the frequency of words within MTS' (F (1,78) = 32.95, p = .93).

**Word Total.** Analyzing total of words by culture and gender pairing revealed a significant main effect of culture with Americans using more words than Chinese ($F$ (1,78) = 4.34, $p$ < .05), and a significant interaction effect of culture and gender pairing ($F$ (3,78) = 3.15, $p$ < .03. The post hoc analyses of the interaction effect showed two significant comparisons: American males used significantly more words than Chinese males in all-male pairings ($t$ (17) = 3.64, $p$ < .005); American males also used significantly more words when paired with a Chinese male (all-male) than when paired with a Chinese female (male-mixed) ($t$ (17) = 2.90; $p$ < .01). The peak of American males' word total is seen in figure 2.

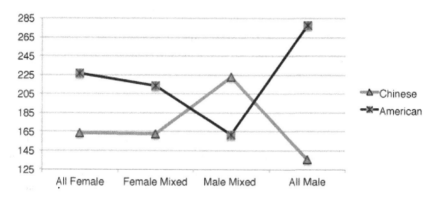

**Fig. 2.** Words Overall

## 4.2   Interaction Style Indicators

**Emoticons.** Analyzing frequencies of emoticons used overall, by culture and gender pairing was significant for culture with Chinese using more emoticons than Americans ($F$ (1,78) = 5.62, $p$ < .02), gender pairings ($F$ (3,78) = 4.59, $p$ < .01), and for an interaction of culture and gender pairing ($F$ (3,78) = 5.49, $p$ < .01). For Chinese comparisons, CF in both all-female and female mixed pairings used more emoticons than CM in both male mixed ($t$ (19) = 2.41, $p$ < .03) and all-male pairings ($t$ (16) = 2.73, $p$ < .02). For American comparisons, AF when paired with CF (all-female) used more emoticons than with CM (female mixed) ($t$ (17) = 3.35, $p$ < .01), and more than AM with CM (all-male) ($t$ (17) = 2.63, $p$ < .02). Cross-culturally, CF used more emoticons than AF in female mixed pairings. The peak of emoticon usage by Chinese female and American female (in all-female) is shown in figure 3.

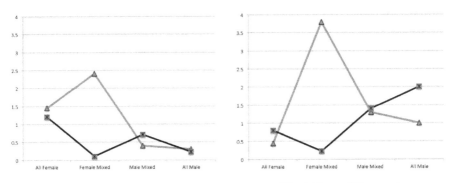

**Fig. 3.** Emoticons                    **Fig. 4.** Unusual Punctuation

**Unusual Punctuation.** Analyzing frequencies of unusual punctuation used overall, by culture and gender pairing showed an interaction effect of culture and gender pairing ($F$ (7,78) = 2.14, $p < .05$). For gender pairing comparisons, Chinese female (CF) when paired with AM (female mixed) used more unusual punctuation than when paired with AF (all female) ($t$ (19) = 2.54, $p < .02$), and more than when CM paired with AM (all male) ($t$ (18) = 1.94, $p < .07$). For cross-cultural comparisons, CF used significantly more unusual punctuation than AF in female mixed pairing ($t$ (17) = 2.45, $p < .03$). The peak of unusual punctuation indicators by Chinese female is demonstrated in figure 4.

**Words in Establishing Presence.** The first discussion is used to establish common ground in learning how the game works. Total word count in this period is used as a measure of establishing presence. Analyzing frequencies of words used in establishing presence, by culture and gender pairing showed an interaction effect approaching significance of culture and gender pairs ($F$ (3,78) = 2.28, $p < .09$). The gender pairing comparison revealed two areas of significance: AF used significantly more words in establishing presence in all female (paired with CF) than in female mixed (paired with CM) ($t$ (17) = 2.52, $p < .02$); CM in male mixed (paired with AF) used more words in establishing presence than in all male (paired with AM) ($t$ (11) = 2.18, $p < .05$). Cross-culturally, CM used more words in establishing presence than AM in male mixed pairings ($t$ (18) = 2.25, $p < .04$). Chinese males' show no difference from American females' peak for word frequency in establishing presence, as in figure 5.

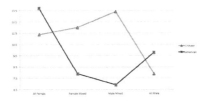

**Fig. 5.** Word Total in Establishing Presence

## 5    Discussion

The objective of this study was to investigate how gender and culture interacted in computer-mediated communication, especially in instant messaging (IM). Linguistic indicators were analyzed to explore the conversation management and interactional styles in cross-cultural Chinese and American communications.

H1a predicted males would demonstrate more conversational management indicators than females. Our results support it. In order to gain the floor, Chinese males favored more turns (Fig. 1), while American males favored more words (Fig. 2). However opposite to previously-cited work that males talked longer in conversations with females [7], American males in our study actually used more words when paired with a Chinese male than with a Chinese female. It is likely that when interacting cross-culturally, American males used more words with a male from a minority culture to assert their dominance than they did with a female from a minority culture.

H1b predicted that females would evidence more interaction. Our results support it. Chinese females used more emoticons than Chinese males in all gender pairings. Chinese females also dominated in their use of unusual punctuation. American females used the highest frequency of words in the introductory period of establishing presence, but only when paired with a Chinese female. American females used more emoticons and more introductory words when paired with a Chinese female but not when paired with a Chinese male. This suggested that American females displayed more cultural acceptance when paired with a Chinese female than a Chinese male.

H2 predicted that Chinese would use more multi-turn sets (MTS) than Americans as a conversation management strategy to achieve their conversation aim. Our results confirmed it. Furthermore, there were no cultural differences in word count within MTS, but Chinese still used more turns within MTS than Americans. In other words, both cultures demonstrated similar word production within MTS, but Chinese used more turns in gaining the floor. Chinese turn frequency within MTS may be used to slow down the conversation, and show their politeness by communicating in short, easy-to-read messages.

While males and females in this study provided evidence of high frequencies aligning with predicted conversational aims, distinct gender pairing differences in cultural interactions are noted. Chinese integration with members of the American university cultures exemplifies their attempt to acculturate and yet both genders appear to prefer interaction with members of the opposite gender. Chinese males used the most turns, particularly when paired with an American female, and perhaps as a way to control the fast flow of English. Chinese females used the highest frequency of emoticons and unusual punctuation, particularly when paired with an American male, and perhaps to provide additional cues absent from IM for meaning interpretation. Americans demonstrated an opposite response. US females displayed more additional cues in their discussions, but more so when paired with a Chinese female, while US males used words as a way to dominate their discussions, particularly when paired with a Chinese male.

## 6    Conclusion

Results from this study suggest that cross-cultural and diverse gender pairing impacts communicational behavior in online discussions. Explanations might be found by considering challenges inherent to a culturally immersive environment.

Considering conversational aims in CMC helps us understand the goals others seek, and might provide insight to individuals for communicating more effectively. Implications of these findings are valuable for analyzing preliminary conversations in global virtual teams. Particularly when assigned to work with people who are strangers, individuals must manage their pre-conceived notions about another's culture and gender. Limitations to generalizing these findings to other situations are noted in both the size and context of this subject pool. Students may not be fully representational of professionals employed in multinational enterprises. Students in this study may in fact be overly sensitive to mixed gender pairings, given the contextual impact of attending college in one's early adulthood. Future work should explore these dynamics in naturalistic professional environments. The ways in which we communicate with one another and the points we make, impact the success of information exchange, knowledge transfer and meaning interpretation. Conversational behavior in work groups is important for increasing efficiency and productivity of teams united in a task, both distant and co-located.

**Acknowledgements.** The authors gratefully acknowledge support from a grant sponsored by the National Science Foundation (#IIS-0803225) that made this research possible.

## References

1. Zhang, Q., Marksbury, N.: Once Broken, Never Fixed? The Impact of Culture and Medium on Repairing Trust in CMC. In: Rau, P.L.P. (ed.) IDGD 2011. LNCS, vol. 6775, pp. 341–350. Springer, Heidelberg (2011)
2. Eagly, A.: Sex Differences in Social Behavior: a Social-Role Interpretation. Erlbaum (1987)
3. Kapidzic, S., Herring, S.C.: "Gender, Communication, and Self-presentation in Teen Chatrooms Revisited: Have Patterns Changed? Journal of Computer-Mediated Communication 17, 1083–6101 (2011), doi:10.1111/j.1083-6101.2011.01561.x
4. McMillan, J.R., Clifton, A., et al.: Women's Language: Uncertainty or Interpersonal Sensitivity and Emotionality? Sex Roles 3(6), 14 (1977)
5. Carli, L.L.: Gender, Language, and Influence. Journal of Personality and Social Psychology 59(5) (1990), doi:10.1037/0022-3514.59.5.941
6. Ridgeway, C.L., Smith-Lovin, L.: Gender and Interaction. In: Saltzman Chafetz, J. (ed.) Handbook of the Sociology of Gender, pp. 247–274. Kluwer / Plenum Publishers (1999)
7. Mulac, A.: "Men's and Women's Talk in Same-Gender and Mixed-Gender Dyads: Power or Polemic?". Journal of Language and Social Psychology 8(23) (1989)
8. Hopper, R. (ed.): Gendering Talk. Michigan State University Press, East Lansing (2003)

9. Baron, N.S.: See You Online: Gender Issues in College Student Use of Instant Messaging. Journal of Language and Social Psychology 23, 397–423 (2004)

10. Sun, X., Wiedenbeck, S., et al.: The Effect of Gender on Trust Perception and Performance in Computer-Mediated Virtual Environments. Proceedings of the American Society for Information Science and Technology 44, 1–14 (2008), doi:10.1002/meet.1450440211

11. Ling, R., Baron, N.S.: Text Messaging and IM: Linguistic Comparison of American College Data. Journal of Language and Social Psychology 26(8) (2007)

12. Hancock, J.T., Dunham, P.J.: Impression Formation in CMC Revisited. Communication Research 28(3) (2001), doi:10.1177/00936501028003004

13. Baron, N.S.: Discourse Structures in Instant Messaging: The Case of Utterance Breaks. Language@internet 7 (2010), http://www.languageatinternet.org/articles/2010/2651

14. Hofstede, G.: Cultures and Organizations: Software of the Mind. McGraw-Hill, UK (1991)

15. Triandis, H.C.: Individualism and Collectivism. Westview, Boulder (1995)

16. Androutsopoulos, J.: Introduction: Sociolinguistics and CMC. Journal of Sociolinguistics 10(4), 1467–9841 (2006), doi:10.1111/j.1467-9841.2006.00286.x

17. Setlock, L.D., Fussell, S.R.: "What's It Worth to You?: The Costs and Affordances of CMC Tools to Asian and American Users." In: Proceedings of the Computer Supported Cooperative Work, pp. 341–350 (2010), doi:10.1145/1718918.1718979

18. Massey, A., Hung, Y.C., et al.: "When Culture and Style Aren't About Clothes: Perceptions of Task-Technology "Fit" in Global Virtual Teams.". In: Proceedings of the Conference on Supporting Group Work (2001), doi:10.1145/500286.500318

19. Kayan, S., Fussell, S.R., et al.: Cultural Differences in the Use of Instant Messaging in Asia and North America. In: Proceedings of 2006 CSCW (2006), doi:10.1145/1180875.1180956

20. Wang, H.-C., Fussell, S.R.: Cultural Difference and Adaptation of Conversational Style in Intercultural Computer-Mediated Group Brainstorming. In: Proceedings, Human Factors in Computing Systems, pp. 669–678 (2009), doi:10.1145/1499224.1499286

21. Setlock, L.D., Quinones, P., et al.: Does Culture Interact with Media Richness? The Effects of Audio vs. Video Conferencing on Chinese and American Dyads. In: Proceedings, Hawaii International Conference on System Sciences, vol. 13 (2007), doi:10.1109/HICSS.2007.182

22. Mulac, A., Wiemann, J.M., et al.: Male/Female Language Differences and Effects in Same-Sex and Mixed-Sex Dyads: The Gender-Linked Language Effect. Communication Monographs 55(4), 21 (1988)

23. Bos, N., Olson, J.S., et al.: Effects of Four CMC Channels on Trust Development. In: Proceedings of Human Factors in Computing Systems, pp. 135–140 (2002), doi:10.1145/503376.503401

# Improving the User Interface for Reading News Articles through Smartphones in Persian Language

Sanaz Motamedi[1,*], Mahdi Hasheminezhad[2], and Pilsung Choe[1]

[1] Industrial Engineering Department, Tsinghua University, Beijing, China
[2] Engineering and Technology Department, Tarbiat Modares University, Tehran, Iran
Motamedis10@mails.tsinghua.edu.cn, mehdi@hasheminezhad.com,
pchoe@tsinghua.edu.cn

**Abstract.** Space limitation in small devices such as smartphones which are able to access the Internet is an important issue in regard to increasing usage of these devices. Moreover, a browser is a one of tools for transition of a website which is designed for a big screen like the display of a desktop computer. This paper experimentally evaluated user-interface alternatives based on three tasks (finding, re-finding, reading, and browsing) and two display orientations (horizontal, vertical). In addition, the survey results showed the methods (Pop out, Full screen, and Auto zooming) and the orientations affect actual usage.

**Keywords:** Localization, Website layout adaptation, Smartphone interface, News reading on smartphones.

## 1 Introduction

Checking news is a popular action that each person does during a day. In recent years, the trend of using small devices such as cell phones, tablet computers smartphones and PDAs (Personal Digital Assistants) to access the Internet is increasing [1]. People use these devices to check news because of convenient access and their versatile functions. However, these devices significantly differ from powerful desktop computers in many ways. In particular, the screen size of small devices put constraints on properly representing Web contents that are originally designed for the display of desktop computers. To meet the constraints mentioned above, websites need to adapt their contents to the small screens of these devices.

Although there are various forms of publications about website adaptations for small devices such as applications and browsers, many users do not rely on these tools and check news in smartphones because of the following reasons:

- The way that applications and browsers change the layout of news websites
- The unreadable font of articles in small devices, which users are forced to zoom-in and zoom-out frequently

---

* Corresponding author.

P.L.P. Rau (Ed.): CCD/HCII 2013, Part I, LNCS 8023, pp. 440–449, 2013.
© Springer-Verlag Berlin Heidelberg 2013

- Compounding or excluding of some part of original websites, which can be found in the display of desktop computers such as pictures and old news
- Lack of memory in small devices for installing applications

This paper aims to find some proper structures that can improve the user interaction with small devices for checking news. This article considers all these challenges in order to obtain a better transition of websites from the screen of desktop computers to small devices. Section 2 describes the literature review of page layout adaptation, and Section 3 explains user study. The results are given in Section 4, and discussion is presented in Section 5. Finally, Section 6 summarizes the conclusion.

# 2    Literature Review:    Page Layout Adaptation

Although the small size of displays is useful for carrying them everywhere, some limitations are also created because of this privilege. Recently, several research projects have initiated the investigation for solutions to the constraint of the limited screen size. These techniques are referred to as page layout adaptation [2]. In general, the adaptation layout can be categorized into three approaches.

## 2.1    Direct:

In this technique, users navigate through the original page. It is the simplest and popular method to transit websites from the screen of desktop computers to such small devices as smartphones. Nevertheless, users have to scroll all the time vertically and horizontally. Virpi et al. insist horizontal scrolling is much harder than vertical scrolling [3]. This paper suggests the narrow and tall layout that user just need vertical scrolling.

## 2.2    Manual:

Manual also refers to device specific authoring. The content provider, who is a typical professional in Web design, has customized the Web content for each individual device [4]. In the most part, this method provides the best user experiences for mobile device users. However, due to mass labor work manually involved, this technique can be only applied to small set of websites and it is limited in scalability [5].

## 2.3    Automatic:

The automatic method usually is based on a proxy like transcoders that render and filter useful contents and transforms them for browsing on devices with small displays. In general, this method requires minimum user intervention [4]. In addition, it can take arbitrary Web documents and generate adapted version on-the-fly [3]. Therefore, it has the most potential for widespread use.

There are many methods that transform original page to small devices' monitors automatically.

### 2.3.1 Format Conversion:

This method can split original pages into different small cards [6]. Therefore, each card can fit into one screen. Chen et al. have provided a guideline to split websites in logical part such as footer, header and etc. According to the guideline, each logical unit is designed to fit in the device screen [7]. Links are made between cards to enable browsing. This method seems useful but it has some disadvantages. Firstly, it does not allow retention of layout and presentation style of the original document. Thus, users are likely to be confused when accessing the same website on a desktop computer and a small device. Secondly, this method makes websites so deep. Hence, the number of clicks which an average user needs to perform is too high, which potentially discourages the users from browsing with small devices [4]. Designers need to sacrifice functionality to offset the reduced steps in all function of small devices [8].

### 2.3.2 Overview:

This method first provides the overall context. It then allows users to "zoom in" at any point for detail viewing. B. Mackay et al. proposed the method of "Gateway" [9]. Users navigate the Gateway by selecting individual sections, either by clicking or by rollovers, on the website that are expanded and superimposed over the overview. Moreover, users can make selections on the section, such as choosing a menu item or following a link, as they would be on the large websites. The key disadvantage of this method is that users need to go back and forth between the overview of the page and its individual blocks [4].

### 2.3.3 Summarization:

Text summarization techniques typically parse, analyze and record the text based on its semantic and certain psychological and statistical rules. Therefore, this method is also referred to semantic conversion in some publications [10], [11]. Text summarization seems to work perfectly when most of the content on a website is a pure text. However, the method will collapse when images are added onto the website, since this technique does not know how to "summarize" images [3].

### 2.3.4 Linear:

The layout of information from the main website is changed to a long linear list that fits within the width constraints of small devices [9]. These kinds of methods extract all hyperlinks of the original website. Meanwhile, it also extracts some non-link contents such as telephone numbers. A menu is generated, with all the extracted links and contents as the menu items. By doing this, websites effectively separates the navigation and the action, making navigation simply a matter of selecting a link to follow from a list. The action interface becomes much more powerful which users can apply various web-based services to any link now [5]. One of drawbacks of these methods is the new structure that happened which is confused the user who has experience about the website in desktop as well.

# 3      User study:

## 3.1      Methodology

Although there is a wide variety of actual usage measurements, in this study usability is counted as a primary factor in determining the acceptability and consequent success of any kind of adaptations. Users' satisfaction, time efficiency and effectiveness play the main role in usability based on ISO 9241. Furthermore, compatibility [12] and enjoyment [13] are other factors of using small devices.

The mentioned factors are used to evaluate the proposed methods of page layout adaptation to catch the best transition websites from the screen of desktop computers to small devices. Experiments and surveys in this paper are performed among 12 people (6 male and 6 female) in the range between 25 and 35 years old. The language of the news is chosen Persian due to couple of reasons such as special alphabets of this language that can have a noticeable effect on readability, and style of writing starting from right to left rather than left to right.

For each method (Pop out, Full screen, and Auto zooming), the potential impact on subsequent navigation of a website is examined with different data types performing tasks of finding, re-finding, reading and browsing in small screen and in two orientations.

Furthermore, the most important factor and main reason for this research is the small screen of hand-held screen devices such as smartphones. Due to different sizes of them, this research chooses one common small device, Galaxy Nexus Sprint Android Smartphone. The size of this smartphone is 4.88" * 2.48" * 0.44", and the main display's resolution is 800*480 pixels.

Moreover, there are many other factors as educational background, age, culture etc. Users are chosen randomly to avoid the effect of those factors which are considered in this research.

## 3.2      Hypothesis:

According to the factors which this study desires to measure, hypotheses are defined as following:

- H1: Methods affect compatibility.
- H2: Methods affect satisfaction.
- H3: Methods affect effectiveness.
- H4: Methods affect efficiency.
- H5: Methods affect enjoyment.
- H6: Orientations affect compatibility.
- H7: Orientations affect satisfaction.
- H8: Orientations affect effectiveness.
- H9: Orientations affect efficiency.
- H10: Orientations affect enjoyment.

This paper tries to whether prove or reject these hypotheses with the experiments and surveys which were explained in the Section 3.1.

## 3.3    Implemented Methods

In this paper three ways of migration from large to small screen in two orientations, which are totally automatic, are compared. As opposed to many screen adaptations from desktop computers to small devices, the methods avoid excluding or compounding of any part of websites. These methods do not replace or create a new layout for websites by considering the small size of monitors. Moreover, the mentioned methods decline zooming action during checking news.

In practical, every website consists of different elements, namely page structure (HTML file), styling definitions (CSS files) and page interactions (JavaScript files). This paper comes up with a set of JavaScript functions which can plug into the existing page structures. These JavaScript methods monitor and detect all clicks on the page. If any news title is clicked, the JavaScript methods fetch the target page in the background and display the page according to the predefined methods.

With prepared framework which can adapt to any kind of websites, these methods can be simulated on various mobile phones. Figure 1 illustrates the simulation of the BBC sports news website.

**Fig. 1.** The simulation of BBC website

**First Method: Pop out.** The Pop out method provides an exact reduced replica of the large screen website while maintaining a consistent distortion. Users navigate the Pop out by selecting individual sections by clicking on the website that is expanded and superimposed over the overview. In this method at first users have an overview as same as desktop computers, and then they can choose and click on their favorite part in order to read in a bigger font size. Figure 2 shows the example of the Pop out method.

**Fig. 2.** First Click with the First Method, Pop out

**Second Method: Full Screen.** This method splits a website in a few blocks. At first, users can see an overview of the website, and then users click on each part of page in which they can see full screen of that block. Figure 3 illustrates this method.

**Fig. 3.** First Click with the Second Method, Full Screen

**Third Method: Auto zooming.** This method is a scheme that positions the viewing window automatically based on the page layout information detected by the algorithm. Users can switch back and forth between the thumbnail and original website to provide the scrolling-by-block function. Auto zooming method is very similar to the page Full screen method. This method is depicted in figure 4.

**Fig. 4.** First Click with the Third Method, Auto-positioning

### 3.4     Study:

The experiment consists of seven parts. First, users became familiar with the large BBC website on the display of desktop computer by opening stories and using the menu items. Before the actual experiments, users performed the same manipulation check to ensure they have a minimum level of familiarity with the website. In the second part, finding task, users were asked to perform a task using desktop to find one specific headline in the website, and then users were asked to re-find the same headline in all methods (Pop out, Full screen, Auto zooming) in the smartphone and two orientations. Afterwards, users should do finding task. They were asked to find new specific headlines in each method and orientation. In fifth part, users read one story with all methods and orientations, and lastly they would have 30 seconds in each method and orientation to find as many headlines as they can among seven specific headlines.

These steps make users to do re-finding, finding, reading, and browsing. After these 6 steps, experienced study group were ready to answer the survey which asks about the rank of methods and orientations about all factors that were mentioned as measurement of actual usage in this paper.

It is noticeable that sequence of these modes of navigation is chosen randomly for each user to avoid learning curve.

## 4     Results:

### 4.1     Experiment:

Based on the two-way ANOVA using recorded data, orientation has effect on re-finding task. Furthermore, the average time of re-finding in vertical mode totally is well under horizontal one. This analysis does not show any significant effect on finding task, whereas methods have a significant effect on reading part. According to the observed result from method 2 (Full screen), users spent least time on reading task for one specific story. In case of browsing task, *p*-value of methods was less than α=0.05 by approximately 0.02 which shows a significant effect of this task as it can be seen in table 1. Due to the highest average of found headlines with method 1, Pop out can be counted as the best method of browsing. It should be mentioned that orientations do not have effect on reading and browsing tasks.

**Table 1.** ANOVA Analysis of Browsing Task

| Source of Variation | SS | df | MS | F | P-value | F crit |
|---|---|---|---|---|---|---|
| Sample | 0.888889 | 1 | 0.888889 | 0.820513 | 0.368325 | 3.986269 |
| Columns | 7.583333 | 2 | 3.791667 | 3.5 | 0.035917 | 3.135918 |
| Interaction | 0.027778 | 2 | 0.013889 | 0.012821 | 0.987264 | 3.135918 |
| Within | 71.5 | 66 | 1.083333 | | | |
| Total | 80 | 71 | | | | |

## 4.2    Survey:

The analysis of the survey, which asked directly about such measurement of actual usage in this paper as efficiency, effectiveness, satisfaction, enjoyment and compatibility, showed some significant effects of orientations and methods. For instance, methods have an effect on efficiency and compatibility. Also users prefer method 2, Full screen, in mentioned two factors. For orientations, participants gave higher rank to vertical mode of methods for satisfaction and enjoyment factors.

Overall, there is not any significant interaction effect on both surveys and experiments data. Table 1 summarizes the external variables (methods and orientations) which have a significant effect on the tasks and the factors. In all these ANOVA results, α is authentic for both 0.05 and 0.1.

**Table 2.** Summary of Results

| Mode | Tasks | | | | Factors | | | | |
|---|---|---|---|---|---|---|---|---|---|
| | Re-finding | Finding | Reading | Browsing | Efficiency | Effectiveness | satisfaction | compatibility | Enjoyment |
| Method1 | | | | * | | | | | |
| Method2 | * | | * | | * | | | * | |
| Method3 | | | | | | | | | |
| Vertical | * | | | | | | * | | * |
| Horizontal | | | | | | | | | |

# 5     Discussion

According to the observed results, horizontal mode as same as method 3 (Auto zooming) did not have a significant effect on any task and factor. Auto zooming method is the novel way of transition that users should try to learn.

Additionally, users get use to navigating with cell phone in vertical mode rather than horizontal one. As a result, users are more satisfied and enjoyed with the vertical display. The results show that orientations do not impact on compatibility, effectiveness, and efficiency which are related to H6, H8 and H9 respectively.

In contrast with Auto zooming, Full screen is the best way for re-finding and reading news as well as more efficiency and compatibility from users' perspective. As it was explained in the implemented part, method 2 provides full screen of news after one click on the specific headline in the small monitor of smartphones. This action cut zooming action and making news readable. Hence, users spend less time for reading with this method. Moreover, Full screen method is extremely similar to the way of checking news in desktop computers. Therefore, users do not need to learn any new skill which means Full screen method is compatible with checking news in laptop. Furthermore, users can re-find news more convenient and efficient.

It is worth noting that method 1, Pop out, is the best method of browsing due to providing overview during reading the news. Users can check specific news with the bigger font as same time as they have overview of whole page. Thus, this ability of Pop out method makes it the best method for browsing based on experiment. Finally, only effectiveness is independent in regarding to the influence of methods on factors. Therefore, H3 can be rejected.

# 6     Conclusion:

In this research, three automatic methods of page layout adaptation (Pop out, Full screen, and Auto zooming) from desktop computers to smartphones are compared. All these methods are prepared overview of websites which users can see in desktop computers as well. Based on the experiment and survey results, Full screen is the most popular method for such tasks as finding, re-finding, and reading while Pop out is better method for browsing only. In addition, using Full screen method in smartphones is more efficient and compatible with desktop computers compared to other two methods. Moreover, the results revealed that users are more satisfied and enjoyed with vertical mode rather than horizontal one.

This paper provides a chart to compare navigation for different migration techniques and web tasks. Not only the chart can be used to guide the information migration from the large screen to the small screen and optimize navigation for specific tasks, but also it can be significant results to customize Persian news websites.

In addition, this paper is limited by and accessibility to native speakers. Thus, only 12 users could be caught to participate in this study. In order to achieve more trustfulness results further studies can extend the number of participants.

# References:

1. Wu, J.-H., Wang, S.-C.: What drives mobile commerce? An empirical evaluation of the revised technology acceptance model. Information and Management 42 (2005)
2. Mohommed, A., Chin, J.C., De Lara, E.: Community Driven Adaptation: Automatic Content Adaptation in Pervasive Environment. In: Mohommed, A., Chin, J. (eds.) 6th IEEE Workshop on Mobile Computing Systems and Applications (WMCSA), English Lake District, UK (2004)
3. Roto, V., Kaikkonen, A.: Perception of Narrow Web Pages on a Mobile Phone. In: International Symposium on Human Factors in Telecommunication 2003 (2003)
4. Cai, J.: Page Layout Adaptation for Small Form Factor Devices, University of Toronto (2006)
5. Schilit, B.N., Trevor, J., Hilbert, D.M., Koh, T.K.: Web interaction using very small internet devices. In: Proc. of the 7th Annual Int'l. Conf. on Mobile Computing and Networking, Rome (2001)
6. Choi, J.H., Lee, H.-J.: Facets of simplicity for the smartphone interface: A structural model. International Journal of Human-Computer Studies (2011)
7. Chen, Y., Ma, W., Zhang, H.: Detecting Web Page Structure for Adaptive Viewing on Small Form Factor Devices. In: Proc. WWW 2012 Conference (2003)
8. MacKay, B., Watters, C., Duffy, J.: Web Page Transformation when Switching Devices. In: Brewster, S., Dunlop, M.D. (eds.) Mobile HCI 2004. LNCS, vol. 3160, pp. 228–239. Springer, Heidelberg (2004)
9. Choi, J.H., Lee, H.-J.: Facets of simplicity for the smartphone interface: A structural model. International Journal of Human-Computer Studies (2011)
10. Ahmadi, H., Kong, J.: Efficient Web Browsing on Small Screens. Advanced Visual Interfaces (2008)
11. Chen, Y., Ma, W.-Y., Zhang, H.-J.: Detecting Web Page Structure for Adaptive Viewing on Small Form Factor Devices. In: International Conference on World Wide Web (2003)
12. Sonnenwald, D.H., Maglaughlin, K.L., Whitton, M.C.: Using innovation diffusion theory to guide collaboration technology evaluation: work in progress. In: Proceedings of the IEEE 10th International Workshop on Enabling Technologies: Infrastructure for Collaborative Enterprises (WETICE 2001) (2003)
13. Davis, F.D., Bagozzi, R.P., Warshaw, P.: Extrinsic and intrinsic motivation to use computers in the workplace. Journal of Applied Social Psychology 22, 1111–1132 (1992)

# The Acceptance and Adoption of Smartphone Use among Chinese College Students

Dan Pan, Na Chen, and Pei-Luen Patrick Rau

Department of Industrial Engineering, Tsinghua University, Beijing 100084, P.R. China
pand10@mails.tsinghua.edu.cn, chenn4@gmail.com,
rpl@mail.tsinghua.edu.cn

**Abstract.** This study aims to develop a questionnaire to investigate the acceptance and adoption of smartphone among college students in China, and to find factors affecting the acceptance and adoption. A total of 402 valid questionnaires were received from Chinese college students. The internal reliability of the questionnaire was pretty high and acceptable (cronbach's $\alpha= 0.939$). Extended Technology Acceptance Model (TAM) is attempted to be utilized to explain users' Behavior Intention (BI) to smartphone use. Structural Equation Model was used to test the extended TAM, and the results demonstrated majority relationships of the extended TAM. The study also found that social influence, entertainment utility and compatibility of smartphone impact Chinese college students' perceived usefulness and attitude to use. That is very valuable implication for manufacturers to improve smartphone's interactive interface to win bigger market share.

**Keywords:** Smartphone, extended TAM, Social influence, Entertainment utility, Compatibility, Structural equation model.

## 1 Introduction

In the past decade, mobile phone experienced a tremendous growth. With the development and innovation of technology, smartphone arises at the historic moment. It was invented by Lee, Han, and Hwang in 2007 [10]. Its core functions are not only phone calls and text massages, but also include camera, wireless communication, and multimedia messaging and so on. It integrates mobile phone and many other technologies into one single device, which can be regarded as a handheld computer, like the Apple, Nokia N-series, Samsung, Motorola, HTC, MI, etc.

According to the investigation on 30,000 mobile phone users in Unite State by the market research institute comScore [14], the market share of smartphone in USA has been 51.9% by October 2012, which is higher 6% than that in July 2012. In China, smartphone has spread from high-end consumer group to mid- and low-end consumer groups. Young college student is main force of the mid-/low-end consumer groups. The population of college students has reached more than 20 million in 2010 [5]. They are young adults pursuing fashion and new technology products. That presents a sizeable market opportunity for smartphone, as well as a challenge to provide

P.L.P. Rau (Ed.): CCD/HCII 2013, Part I, LNCS 8023, pp. 450–458, 2013.
© Springer-Verlag Berlin Heidelberg 2013

appropriate smartphone products for this group. Therefore, understanding the fundamentals of what determines smartphone use among this group is worth being studied. It can lead to more effective and meaningful strategies for smartphone manufacturers and thus, allows them to remain competitive. However, few literatures about such studies have been found. Therefore, the purpose of this study is to investigate the acceptance and adoption of smartphones among Chinese college students and the factors affecting such acceptance behaviors, and to explore the critical external variables affecting users' attitude to use and perceived usefulness of smartphone.

## 2    Background Literature

The technology acceptance model (TAM) was proposed by Davis [6]. It was originated from the theory of reasoned action (TRA) which is used for explaining and predicting people's behavior. TAM was widely used to explain and analyze information technology usage behavior. Previous research has proven that it is a useful theoretical model in helping to understand and explain users' behavior in information system implementation [11].

Basic TAM has five components: Perceived Usefulness (PU), Perceived Ease of Use (PEOU), Attitude (AT), Behavior Intention (BI), and actual use. In the context of smartphone acceptance, mobile services can be available at any time and any place. PU is defined here as "the degree to which a user believes using a smartphone would enhance his or her life quality and could integrate into their daily activities" [9] and recognized as the most important variable to predict technology acceptance in several studies [1, 8]. However, if a product is too hard to use, even if potential users believe that it is useful, the acceptance could also be influenced. Thus, PEOU is also considered as an important variable to influence usage. PEOU here refers to the degree to which a user believes that using a smartphone would be free of effort.

Based on the structure of the model, five relationships are suggested among the five components: (1) PEOU affects PU; (2) PEOU affects AT; (3) PU affects AT; (4) AT affects BI; and (5) PU affects BI. Finally, the actual use is influenced by behavior intention (BI). Venkatesh et al. [17] and Wu et al. [20] suggested that PEOU and PU are the two most important factors in explaining technology use. Studies had empirically proved the relationships between factors in TAM based on smartphone use in healthcare [15] and delivery service [2, 3]. When PEOU increases, users' PU of a smartphone will also increase and this will influence their behavioral intentions to use. Both PU and PEOU would have a positive effect on users' attitude and this would influence their behavioral intentions to use.

Additionally, several researchers proposed that self-efficacy also influences users' acceptance of technology. Self-efficacy was defined as users' perception of their ability to use a product to accomplish a task [4]. Self-efficacy measures user's perception on how he/she is able to complete a task. Without skill, performance is not possible; without self-efficacy, performance may not be attempted. Users' self-efficacy and perceptions contribute to the causal relationship between acceptance of technology and user's cognitive factors [15]. Literature empirically proved that users' self-efficacy affected perceived ease of use (PEOU) and behavior intention to use [2, 3, 7, 15, 16]. From this literature, it is postulated that confident users in learning to use a smartphone are likely to perceive it as easier to use while those who are not confident in learning the smartphone use perceive it as harder to use. Therefore, self-efficacy was included in the extended TAM and the extended TAM is attempted to be utilized to explain users' behavior to smartphone use in this study.

Finally, which external variables contributing to the acceptance of smartphone is another important purpose of this study. Like the diffusion of innovation theory, persuasive social information such as peer influence, advertisement may increase people's perceived usefulness of a service or technology [16]. Social influence here was defined as "the degree to which individual has the impression that others believe they should use advanced mobile services" [18]. Social influences have been demonstrated to have an indirect impact, via PU, on people's behavior intention. Lu et al. [13] proved that social influences can affect a person's perceived usefulness of advanced wireless Internet. Therefore, social influence is considered as one of the main external variables.

# 3    Research Framework and Hypotheses

The purpose of this study was to examine the acceptance level of the smartphone technology and the factors that affect such an acceptance, and to explore the critical external variables affecting users' attitude to use and perceived usefulness of smartphone. Based on the discussion in the previous chapter, the conceptual model of research framework is proposed as shown in **Fig. 1**. It showed factors derived from extended TAM and external variables from literature and pilot study which may affect smartphone use. According to the research framework and the research purpose, hypotheses are proposed.

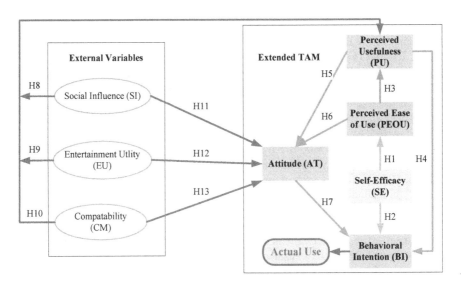

**Fig. 1.** Research Framework

**H1:** Users' self-efficacy to smartphone positively influences perceived ease of use.

**H2:** Users' self-efficacy to smartphone positively influences behavioral intention.

**H3:** Perceived smartphone ease of use positively affects perceived usefulness.

**H4:** Perceived smartphone usefulness positively affects behavioral intention.

**H5:** Perceived smartphone usefulness positively affects attitude.

**H6:** Perceived smartphone ease of use positively affects attitude.

**H7:** Users' attitude to use smartphone positively affects behavioral intention.

**H8-H10:** External variables significantly influence users' perceived usefulness of smartphone.

**H11-H13:** External variables significantly influence users' attitude to use smartphone.

## 4    Experiment

### 4.1  Pilot Study

**Research Instrument.** The research instrument was a questionnaire which contained two sections. The first section contained questions relating to demographic information (i.e., gender, age and education level). Using experience with smartphone, the manufacturer and model of user's current smartphone, the most commonly used functions, and suggestion for function improvement are also included.

The second section contained items used to measure factors from extended TAM and the external variable *social influence* (SI), which are mainly from the study of Park et al. [15], Liu et al. [12], Zhang et al. [22] and Wang et al. [19]. Multi-items were used to measure each. A five-point Likert-type scale was used in constructing the questionnaire. The scale ranged from 1 (strongly disagree) to 5 (strongly agree).

The questionnaire was constructed in English and was translated into Chinese by using the method of back-translation to make sure the translated Chinese does not violate the original meanings of the English questionnaire items. After back-translation, the questionnaire was reviewed by three classmates to ensure clarity and face validity.

**Sample.** A total of 188 valid questionnaires (130 males and 58 females) were received. Respondents averaged 23.4 years of age (SD=1.25 years). All respondents were Chinese college students which consisted of 170 graduate students (90.4%) and 18 undergraduate students (9.6%).

**Reliability.** As shown in **Table 1**, the cronbach's α of all variables were higher than 0.7 and the cronbach's α of the whole scale was 0.922, which mean the internal reliability of the questionnaire was pretty high and acceptable.

**Table 1.** Cronbach's α in pilot study

| Variable | Cronbach's α | Variable | Cronbach's α |
|---|---|---|---|
| Self-efficacy (SE) | 0.79 | Behavioral intention (BI) | 0.87 |
| Perceived ease of use (PEOU) | 0.80 | Attitude (AT) | 0.86 |
| Perceived usefulness (PU) | 0.86 | Social influence (SI) | 0.77 |
| **Whole Scale** | **0.922** | | |

**Results.** The investigation also found that except making phones, the top three of the most commonly used function were internet (66.2%), chat tools (43.8%) and mobile games (32.1%). The improvement suggestions from respondents mainly focused on smartphones' entertainment functions, compatibility and battery endurance ability.

Based on these results, the questionnaire was revised. Except social influence, entertainment utility and compatibility were also considered as important external variables that contributing to smartphone acceptance. Items of *entertainment utility* (EU) and *compatibility* (CM) in the revised questionnaire were created based on the results of pilot study.

### 4.2 Final Study

**Research Instrument.** The first section of the questionnaire was the same as that in pilot study. The second section of the revised questionnaire contained 40 items about factors from extended TAM (i.e., SE, PEOU, PU, AT & BI) and external variables (SI, EU & CM).

**Sample.** A total of 402 valid questionnaires (244 males and 158 females) remained for further analysis. Respondents averaged 21.4 years of age (SD=2.96 years). All respondents were Chinese college students which consisted of 138 graduate students (34.3%) and 264 undergraduate students (65.7%).

**Reliability.** See **Table 2** for cronbach's $\alpha$ in final experiment. Cronbach's $\alpha$ of the whole scale was 0.939, and except compatibility (cronbach's $\alpha$= 0.637), cronbach's $\alpha$ for other variables were higher than 0.70. Thus, it could be concluded that the internal reliability of the questionnaire was acceptable.

**Table 2.** Cronbach's $\alpha$ in final study

| Variable | Cronbach's $\alpha$ | Variable | Cronbach's $\alpha$ |
|---|---|---|---|
| Self-efficacy (SE) | 0.789 | Attitude to use (AT) | 0.860 |
| Perceived ease of use (PEOU) | 0.868 | Social influence (SI) | 0.706 |
| Perceived usefulness (PU) | 0.863 | Entertainment utility (EU) | 0.810 |
| Behavioral intention (BI) | 0.830 | Compatibility (CM) | 0.637 |
| **Whole Scale** | **0.939** | | |

**Descriptive Statistics.** There were 20 manufacturers represented in final study, and the six most popular manufacturers accounted for more than 80% of the samples: Apple (22.9%), Nokia (19.7%), Samsung (14.7%), HTC (12.2%), Motorola (5.5%), Huawei (4.5%) and Mi (2.7%).

Of respondents, as shown in **Fig. 2** for using experience, 5.0 percent indicated that total using experience of smartphone was 4 years and above; 7.2 percent between 3 years to 4 years; 17.2 percent between 2 years to 3 years; 25.4 percent between 1 year to 2 years; 21.9 percent between 0.5 year to 1 year; and 23.4 percent less than 0.5 year. From these results, we can draw that smartphone is more and more popular among Chinese college students.

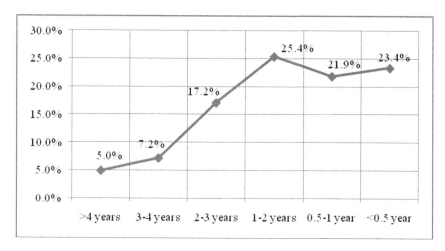

**Fig. 2.** Respondents' using experience of smartphone

## Hypotheses Testing.

*Extended TAM.* The extended TAM including self-efficacy (H1-H7) is analyzed through structural equation modeling using AMOS. The results were provided in **Fig. 3** and **Table 3**.

H1-H7 tested the causal relationships demonstrated in extended TAM. As shown in **Table 3**, except AGFI, other adapter indexes all met the adapter criteria, which mean that using the extended TAM to explain the acceptance of smartphone among Chinese college students was pretty well. From the results in **Fig. 3**, this study confirmed the majority relationships of the extended TAM.

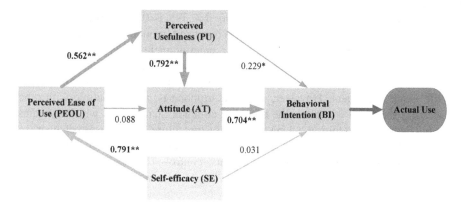

**Fig. 3.** Test results of extended TAM (*p<0.01, **p<0.001)

Table 3. Adapter index of extended TAM

| Absolute adapter index | Adapter criteria[21] | Value-added adapter index | Adapter criteria | Contracted adapter index | Adapter criteria |
|---|---|---|---|---|---|
| GFI: 0.914 | >0.90 | NFI: 0.92 | >0.90 | PGFI: 0.697 | >0.50 |
| AGFI: 0.887 | >0.90 | RFI: 0.903 | >0.90 | PNFI: 0.76 | >0.50 |
| RMR: 0.034 | <0.05 | IFI: 0.96 | >0.90 | CN: 401.94 | >200 |
| RMSEA: 0.048 | <0.05 | TLI: 0.951 | >0.90 | NC: 1.938 | 1<NC<3 |
| | | CFI: 0.959 | >0.90 | | |

Supporting H1, Self-efficacy was found to have a significant effect on PEOU ($\beta$=0.791, p<0.001). This implied that if college students felt confident about using smartphone they generally demonstrated a higher perceived ease of use. Supporting H3, PEOU had a significant positive impact on PU ($\beta$=0.562; p<0.001). Supporting H5 and H6, PU positively determined attitude to use smartphone ($\beta$=0.792; p<0.001) and had a positive impact on behavioral intention to use ($\beta$=0.229; p<0.01). Supporting H7, Chinese college students' behavioral intention to use was largely influenced attitude to use ($\beta$=0.704, p<0.001).

These results indicated that the attempt of extended TAM into the investigation of college students' behavioral intention to use smartphone was successfully demonstrated in this study.

*External variables.* H8-H13 examined the relationship between external variables and factors of extended TAM, especially, the influence of external variables on users' perceived usefulness of smartphone and attitude to use smartphone. Regression analysis was used to test this relationship. The results (see **Table 4**) indicated that social influence, entertainment utility, compatibility all had a significant positive impact on user's perceived usefulness of smartphone ($\beta$=0.398, $\beta$=0.410, $\beta$=0.580; p<0.0001) and user's attitude to use smartphone ($\beta$=0.406, $\beta$=0.395, $\beta$=0.617; p<0.0001).

These results were easy to understand. On one hand, mobile games are very popular among young people in nowadays, so the entertainment utility of smartphone is important to them. On the other hand, the initial purpose of smartphone invention was to give users a single solution for all personal communication needs and to make users life more convenient. However, if the smartphone is not compatible with other devices like laptop, it will make the life more complex than before, which is against its initial purpose. In addition, China is collectivism culture and Chinese behavior was easily affected by external factors. Especially, for Chinese college students, they are just free from high school and without parents' control. Their behaviors were quite easy to be affected by peer and society. Thus, social influence to their behaviors was understandable.

**Table 4.** Regression analysis for external variables

| Hypotheses | Relationship | $R^2$ | Standardized coefficients | Results |
|:---:|:---:|:---:|:---:|:---:|
| H8 | SI→PU | 0.159 | 0.398 | Supported (p<0.0001) |
| H9 | EU→PU | 0.168 | 0.410 | Supported (p<0.0001) |
| H10 | CM→PU | 0.337 | 0.580 | Supported (p<0.0001) |
| H11 | SI→AT | 0.165 | 0.406 | Supported (p<0.0001) |
| H12 | EU→AT | 0.156 | 0.395 | Supported (p<0.0001) |
| H13 | CM→AT | 0.381 | 0.617 | Supported (p<0.0001) |

**Notes:** PU – Perceived usefulness; AT – Attitude to use; SI – Social influence; EU – Entertainment utility; CM – Compatibility.

## 5    Conclusion

User's perceived acceptance under TAM and external attributes have been previously explored, this study extended prior research by providing research constructs for Chinese college students, especially found the external variables which affect acceptance of smartphone. Our findings confirmed the majority relationships of the extended TAM (SE→PEOU→PU→AT→BI→actual use). The results also showed that attitude to smartphone use among college students was found to be affected significantly not only by PEOU and PU, but also by social influence, entertainment utility and compatibility among college students.

These findings imply that the smartphone manufacture should pay attention to the entertainment utility when designing smartphone for college students. Meanwhile, compatibility of smartphone should be taken into serious consideration during designing the man-machine interactive interface for young people, especially college students. Besides, according to suggestions from respondents, the battery endurance ability, which was an essential problem for smartphone and hadn't been studied in this study, would be studied in the future study.

## References

1. Chau, P.Y.K.: An Empirical Assessment of a Modified Technology Acceptance Model. Journal of Management Information Systems 13(2), 185–204 (1996)
2. Chen, J.V., Yen, D.C., Chen, K.: The acceptance and diffusion of the innovative smartphone use: A case study of a delivery service company in logistics. Information & Management 46, 241–248 (2009)
3. Chen, K., Chen, J., Yen, D.: Dimensions of self-efficacy in the study of smartphone acceptance. Computer Standards & Interfaces 33, 422–431 (2011)
4. Compeau, D., Higgins, C.A.: Computer self-efficacy: development of a measure and initial test. MIS Quarterly, 189–211 (June 1995)
5. Data on Students in Higher Education. In: China Education Yearbook. China Academic Journal Electronic Publishing House (2010)

6.  Davis, F.D.: Perceived usefulness, perceived ease of use and user acceptance of information technology. MIS Quarterly 14, 319–340 (1989)
7.  Davis, F.D., Bagozzi, R.P., Warshaw, P.R.: User acceptance of computer technology: a comparison of two theoretical models. Management Science 35, 982–1003 (1989)
8.  Igbaria, M., Parasuraman, S., Baroudi, J.J.: A Motivational Model of Microcomputer Usage. Journal of Management Information Systems 13(1), 127–143 (1996)
9.  Kleijnen, M., Wetzels, M., de Ruyter, K.: Consumer acceptance of wireless finance. Journal of Financial Services Marketing 8(3), 206–217 (2004)
10. Lee, Y.J., Han, B.K., Hwang, C.H.: United States Design Patent of Smartphone. US D548, 713 S (August 14, 2007)
11. Legris, P., Ingham, J., Collerette, P.: Why do people use information technology? A critical review of the technology acceptance model. Information & Management 40, 191–204 (2003)
12. Liu, J., Liu, Y., Rau, P.L., Li, H., Wang, X., Li, D.: How socio-economic structure influences rural users' acceptance of mobile entertainment. In: CHI 2010, Atlanta, Georgia, USA, April 10-15 (2010)
13. Lu, J., Yao, J., Yu, C.: Personal innovativeness social influences and adoption of wireless Internet services via mobile technology. Journal of Strategic Information Systems 14, 245–268 (2005)
14. The survey of smartphone market share in Unite States, China E-business Research Center (2012), http://b2b.toocle.com/detail-6029270.html
15. Park, Y., Chen, J.V.: Acceptance and adoption of the innovative use of smartphone. Industrial Management & Data Systems 107(9), 1349–1365 (2007)
16. Venkatesh, V., Davis, F.D.: A theoretical extension of the technology acceptance model: four longitudinal field studies. Management Science 46(2), 186–204 (2000)
17. Venkatesh, V., Morris, M.G., Davis, G.B., Davis, F.D.: User acceptance of information technology: toward a unified view. MIS Quarterly 27(3), 425–478 (2003)
18. Verkasalo, H., Lopez-Nicolas, C., Molina-Castillo, F.J., Bouwman, H.: Analysis of users and non-users of smartphone applications. Telematics and Informatics 27, 242–255 (2010)
19. Wang, L., Rau, P.L., Salvendy, G.: Older adults' acceptance of information technology. Educational Gerontology 37(12), 1081–1099 (2011)
20. Wu, I.L., Wu, K.W.: A hybrid technology acceptance approach for exploring e-CRM adoption in organizations. Behavior & Information Technology 24(4), 303–316 (2005)
21. Wu, M.L.: Structural Equation Model: the operation and application of AMOS. Chongqing University Press, Chongqing (2010)
22. Zhang, T., Rau, P.L., Salvendy, G.: Exploring critical usability factors for handsets. Behavior & Information Technology 29(1), 45–55 (2010)

# Modeling of a Human Decision-Making Process with Prospect Theory

Dongmin Shin[1], Hokyoung Ryu[2], Namhun Kim[3], and Jieun Kim[4]

[1] Department of Information and Industrial Engineering, Hanyang University, Ansan, Korea
[2] Department of Industrial Engineering, Hanyang University, Seoul, Korea
[3] School of Design and Human Engineering,
Ulsan National Institute of Science and Technology, Ulsan, Republic of Korea
[4] Innovation Design Engineering, School of Design, Royal College of Art, England
{Dmshin,hryu}@hanyang.ac.kr,
nhkim@unist.ac.kr, jieun.kim@network.rca.ac.uk

**Abstract.** The aim of the present study is to examine what rationality conditions are ignored and why it happens when users have more than one dimension in conflict, such as *perceived security* and *usability* in the online banking use experience. In a controlled experiment, thirty subjects used two different online banking authentication interfaces: a fingerprint interface and a normal four-step interface, in a reverse order. The empirical findings revealed that a different combination of rationality conditions was employed based on a change from effortless interaction (e.g., the fingerprint) to effortful interaction (e.g., the four-step logon system) or vice versa. We also provided some design implications for HCI practitioners, and proposed a new approach to evaluate user experiences as there are benefits and drawbacks mixed in user interface design.

**Keywords:** Prospect theory, Decision making, Perceived security, rational ignorance, user experience.

## 1   Introduction

HCI practitioners and designers often encounter two or more design factors in conflict. For instance, the aesthetic aspect of design and its relationships to other design dimensions, such as usability and usefulness, have gained significant attention in the design community (e.g., [7]), in particular, when these two or three aspects cannot be in parallel. Recent, the relationship between usability and its privacy concern has also become a focus in social media design (e.g., Facebook). In a similar vein, the friction between user's security and usability in online banking system design has been much in the foreground (e.g., [3,6]). In certain cases, it is necessary, for the purpose of security, to include behavior that is complex. Conversely, it is also possible to weaken the security of a system by simplifying or automating certain elements, which usually improve usability. These mixed interpretations imply that a certain level of in-security (or "un-usability") in a system is inevitable for usability (or security). Online banking users seem to accept a certain level of insecure system for the sake of usability, and vice versa.

P.L.P. Rau (Ed.): CCD/HCII 2013, Part I, LNCS 8023, pp. 459–466, 2013.
© Springer-Verlag Berlin Heidelberg 2013

However, we do not respond blankly to in-secure or un-usable system. Every such decision involves balancing the uncertain rewards of actions against the potential losses. In particular, many private identity data for enhancing security, this propensity is influenced by the potential rewards of risk taking, and perceptions of the risk are influenced by one's own (or others) experience (or belief) of losses. Hence, unless there is no experience on this matter, people tend to have the propensity to take risks. Several empirical studies, surveys and anecdotal evidences supported this account, emphasizing an apparent dichotomy between perception on security and their actual behavior. In detail, many online banking users are willing to trade security for convenience or bargain the release of personal information in exchange for relatively small gain or benefit such as usability [1,6]. Herley [4] goes further on this, arguing that users rationally reject security advice, because the burden of complying with security procedures often outweighs any gain in protection, because it would be a future benefit rather than an instant reward. Marked interesting is a vast body of economic and psychological literature has already identified several forms of psychological deviations from rationality that affect such irrational decision-making [3,5]. However, HCI designers or practitioners have lacked for applying them to take account of user experience as yet.

A key to the present study is to see an online banking use experience from such psychological deviations that make offset users' rationality conditions, and how they might stand in assessing individual's user experience.

## 2     Kahneman and Tversky's Prospect Theory and Evaluating User Experience

When people make every judgment, it is virtually impossible to take all variables into account at once. They have certain cognitive limits, such as computational capacity, memory, incomplete information and so forth. This makes them quick decisions using various heuristics, e.g., "good enough" heuristic, which will serve as one of the reference points in the following comparison. In support of Kahneman and Tversky [5]'s prospect theory, many empirical studies have demonstrated an idiosyncrasy between losses and gains in uncertain circumstances.

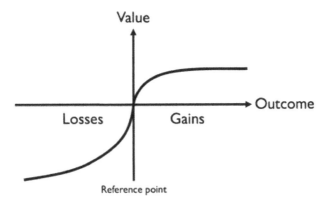

**Fig. 1.** The Value Function Proposed in Prospect Theory [5]

As depicted in Figure 1, Kahneman and Tversky [5] described the asymmetric valuation of gains and losses, concave for gains and convex for losses, where in general, losses are weighed heavier than gains of the same absolute value. Thus, people are prone to have loss aversion and there is relatively a diminishing sensitivity for higher absolute deviations in gains. One important consequence of loss aversion is the endowment effect and the status quo bias (ibid.). The endowment effect means people are less likely to give up the old benefit against a new one unless it is alarmingly acceptable. This implies that our innate bounded rationality limits our ability to acquire, memorize, perceive and process all relevant information, and it makes us rely on several very simplified mental models, approximate strategies and heuristics. These also suggest that HCI practitioners need to replace theoretical quantitative approaches with descriptive qualitative evaluations, to assess user experiences.

In this context, we carried out an empirical study of online banking system use, which inevitably have two conflicting rationality conditions (i.e., usability vs. security), in which people would assess the loss and gain with a contingent trade-off.

# 3     An Empirical Study: Online Banking System Design

The experimental setting in the present study deliberately involved two mixed rationality conditions to be used by the participants: security and usability. In so doing, two types of online banking authentication interface were developed: a fingerprint logon (single-step), and an authentication by entering four different personal identity data. It is assumed that each interface has a different level of usability and perceived security. The experiment was to examine changes in user's rationality conditions when they used both, but in a reverse order (i.e., one group used the fingerprint interface first and then the four-step logon, and the other used them in the other way round).

## 3.1     Method

**Participants.** Thirty students (15 males, 15 females) in a tertiary institution voluntarily participated in the study, all of whom had no prior experience with any fingerprint systems. We presented them with a simulated online banking system equipped the two ways of authentication (see Figure 2). Half of the participants first used the fingerprint logon system (Figure 2b), and then the four-step logon system (Figure 2a), which included id, password, date of birth, and email address registered by themselves before the experiment (hereafter this is called as Condition I). The other half used both too, but in the reverse order (Condition II).

**Apparatus/Procedure/Design.** Prior to the experiment, all participants needed to register their fingerprints. In the main experiment, they only needed to scan their index fingertip on the fingerprint reader, which virtually simulates a single-step logon process. Once they used each online banking authentication system and performed several transaction with the two interfaces, all of them rated the two statements on a five-point Likert scale, respectively: "It was easy for me to use the online banking system"; "I would feel totally secure to use the online banking system". At the end of the experiment, the participants were asked to choose one of them for their preference.

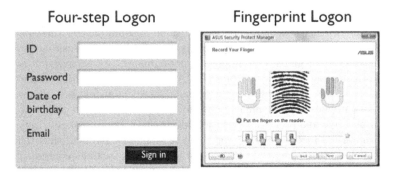

**Fig. 2.** The four-step (left) and fingerprint (right)

## 4    Results

Figure 3 showed the tally of preferences of the two interfaces. In Condition I, when participants used the fingerprint first, they seemed to show significant preference of the fingerprint logon interface over the four-step authentication (i.e., 12 of 15 chose fingerprint for their preference). By comparison, the participants in Condition II showed no difference in preference. A chi-square test of this contingency supported this interpretation (p-value ≈ 0.05).

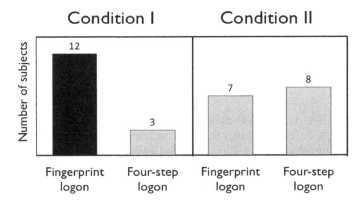

**Fig. 3.** Preference of the two interfaces

Table 1 detailed the changes in their rationality conditions (security and usability) for the two authentication systems. The subjects who used the fingerprint first (Condition I) seemed to positively rate the perceived security of the four-step logon system (mean 4.20 → 4.53, d'=+0.33), although they poorly rated its usability (mean 4.40 → 2.60, d'=−1.80). That is, the participants in Condition I highly ranked the benefits of the fingerprint interface in terms of the vivid usability dimension, which also implies the rational ignorance on perceived security (this is interesting that our participants did not see the smaller gain of the four-step interface in terms of security).

Table 1. Mean scale ratings (standard deviation)

| Condition/Order | | Security | Usability |
|---|---|---|---|
| **Condition I** | 1. Fingerprint | 4.20 (0.56) | 4.40 (0.74) |
| | 2. Four-step | 4.53 (0.52) | 2.60 (0.63) |
| | **d'** | **+0.33** | **−1.80** |
| **Condition II** | 1. Four-step | 4.27 (0.59) | 3.93(0.59) |
| | 2. Fingerprint | 4.60 (0.51) | 4.87 (0.35) |
| | **d'** | **+0.33** | **+0.94** |

Conversely, with the participants who first used the four-step logon system (Condition II), the fingerprint logon interface was perceived as being more secure (mean 4.27 → 4.60, d'=+0.33), positively shifting the ratings of security. Likewise, they rated the usability of the fingerprint highly (mean 3.93 → 4.87, d'=+0.94). Thus, the sample participants developed their rationality conditions of the fingerprint system in a mixed way based on both usability and security.

# 5    Discussion

Although statistical comparisons of the two conditions are inappropriate due largely to the order of the systems exposed to our sample population, this trial does demonstrate that the rationality conditions are quite different. We tried to interpret these phenomena according to the systematic psychological deviations from rationality that might affect individual decision-making, and how this understanding can help HCI practitioners to design novel user experiences.

## 5.1    Loss-Aversion and Rational Ignorance: Condition I

In Condition I, the conversion from the fingerprint logon (effortless interaction) to the four-step logon system (effortful interaction) would make our participants to perceive both gain and loss. From the perspective of gain, only minor increment (+0.33) was observed in security. However, the loss is much greater than the gain (-1.80) in terms of usability. Thanks to this inconsistent prospect, many users would take loss-aversion decision if there are no clear mental models of the gain given. That is the reason behind why the fingerprint interface was preferred by our participants (see Figure 3). The shaded area in Figure 4 confirmed that the motivation of loss has a greater impact than the motivation of gain does, in making a decision on their preference. In particular, even though the four-step interface seems to be more secure than the fingerprint interface, it can be seen that our subjects consider the gains in security negligible. It might be due to the fact that security is an abstract and future value, which might not be authentic, as people have no such mental models to highly weigh the gain. This consequently demonstrated 'rational ignorance' regarding security, which is in line with Herley's study [4].

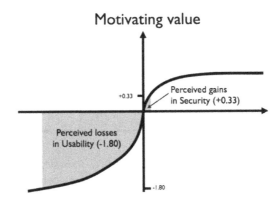

**Fig. 4.** A comparison of motivational value and the prospect theory of analysis of relationships between perceived security and its usability in Condition 1

### 5.2    Endowment Effect and Rational Ignorance: Condition II

Condition II can be rather distinctively interpreted. The fingerprint interface was positively rated than the four-step interface in both dimensions. There are extra gains in terms of both security (+0.33) and usability (+0.94) (See Figure 5). However, on the contrary to Condition I, only half of the participants preferred the fingerprint logon experience. This seems to be irrational, because even though the fingerprint use experience was highly rated in both dimensions, our participants did not show any preference to the interface. This interpretation is relevant to user experience change from effortless interaction (e.g., the fingerprint) to effortful interaction (e.g., the four-step logon).

Put it simply, when he or she needs to adopt a new interaction style, she needs to learn the new interaction with effort. Of course, because she is accustomed to the old system, she does not want to use further efforts to adopt the new interaction. Hence, when she needs to adopt the new interaction style, it is highly associated with the decision under risk. If the perceived risk is greater than gain expected, she would be reluctant to take the risk. Otherwise, she will take the new interaction style. That said, our participants in Condition II seem to show risk-aversion thanks to the gains (0.33 for security and 0.96 for usability) from the change negligible and do not mind the complicated logon procedure. This is much in line with endowment effect [3,5] which means that people tend to place a higher value on objects, concepts, and beliefs they already own (in Condition II, the four-step logon user experience) relative to new ones they do not (in Condition I, the fingerprint interface). This case also seems to demonstrate rational ignorance on the extra gains from both security and usability.

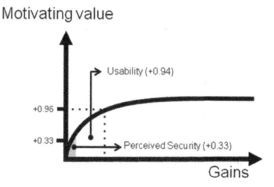

**Fig. 5.** A comparison of motivational value and the prospect theory of analysis of relationships between the perceived security and usability in condition II

## 6    Implications for User Experience Design

Experience design is getting tricky due to the fact that individual's decision-making varies depending on their prior experience that is also subjective. In addition, the systematic psychological deviations resulting from loss-aversion and endowment effect [3,5] would cause irrational or biased behaviors that might be quite different from what the designer has originally thought of. Behind this approach, it can be seen that the designer wrongly assumes that users do not possess a set of pre-defined preferences for every contingency of user experience. However, our experiment showed that it is more likely that user's preferences are constructed in the process of making a choice or judgment. That being said, the context and procedures involved in making choices or judgments influence the preferences or preferred experience that are implied by the elicited response. In practical terms, this means that behavior is likely to vary across situations that HCI practitioners might have considered as identical. An evaluation dimension, which is unequivocal in theory, might produce different outcomes if its exposing sequence (in our experimental scope) against other evaluation dimensions influences the evaluation outcome.

For instance, in Condition I, when there is a potential gain in security (even this is an abstract value) by the four-step logon system compared to the guaranteed loss of making the poor-usability decision (this is a concrete value), the twelve users (see Figure 3) would not be much inclined to take the risk (i.e., prefer the fingerprint interface to the four-step one). This means that these users might have status quo bias, and how this bias would be associated with experience design is in urgent need of further investigation by HCI designers. Similarly, in Condition II, the eight users who did not prefer the fingerprint interface, though they saw the gains of the interface, cannot be interpreted by conventional HCI evaluation methods. In this regard, the results imply that users might subjectively perceive both loss and gain although both of them are objectively measured, and their contingent trade-off is much susceptible to rational ignorance, consequently affects what would be shadowed. However, if a clear mental model of gain or loss is sufficiently given, the prospect of the risk can be re-calculated; then people would re-assess the loss and gain with more rational contingent trade-off. Hence, in experience design, it is first to determine what gains or losses of a design dimension might be rationally ignored by users.

## 7    Conclusions and Future Works

Based on theoretical principles and empirical findings above, we are currently working toward developing a framework for modeling rationality conditions of user experience. Our preliminary data showed that security and usability attitudes are complex but are also compatible with the explanation that loss aversion and the diminishing sensitivity of a higher absolute value (so that people have rational ignorance on the higher absolute value - status quo) could lead to underestimate security and overestimate usability. In conclusion, we do not support a linear model of user experience to describe individual preference, though we acknowledge that the current experimental setting is somewhat arbitrary and not perfect to pinpoint what user experience would be disclosed by the experimental setting. A further work on individual's biased behavior and the experimental validation are still needed.

**Acknowledgments.** This work was supported by the National Research Foundation of Korea (NRF, 2011-0028992) grant and Agency for Defense Development.

## References

1. Davinson, N., Sillence, E.: It won't happen to me: promoting secure behavior among Internet users. Computers in Human Behavior 26(6), 1739–1747 (2010)
2. Gilovich, T., Griffin, D.W., Kahneman, D.: Heuristics and Biases: The psychology of intuitive. Cambridge University Press (2002)
3. Gunson, N., Marshall, D., Morton, H., Jack, M.: User perceptions of security and usability of single-factor and two-factor authentication in automated telephone banking. Computers & Security 30(4), 208–220 (2011)
4. Herley, C.: So Long, And No Thanks for the Externalities: The Rational Rejection of Security Advice by Users. In: Proc. New Security Paradigms Workshop (2009)
5. Kahneman, D., Tversky, A.: Prospect theory: An analysis of decision under risk. Econometrica 47(2), 263–291 (1979)
6. Mannan, M., Oorschot, P.C.: Security and usability: the gap in real-world online banking. In: Proc. New Security Paradigms Workshop, pp. 1–14 (2007)
7. Tractinsky, N., Katz, A.S., Ikar, D.: What is beautiful is usable. Interacting with Computers 13, 127–145 (2000)

# Designing Government Funded Religious E-Readers by Adopting User Experience Methods

[1] Sheng Kai Tang, [2] Wen Kang Chen, [2] Chih Hao Tsai, and [1] Yi Ting Chen

[1] Mobile Communication Product Business Unit, ASUSTeK Computer Inc.,
15, Li-Te Rd., Peitou, Taipei 112, Taiwan
shengkait@gmail.com, florina_chen@asus.com
[2] AJA Creative Design, 10F.-1, No. 48, Sec. 1, Huanshan Rd., Neihu, Taipei 114, Taiwan
david@aja.com.tw, hao520@yahoo.com

**Abstract.** The design concept of user experience has been popularized and widely accepted in Taiwan. Many companies have successfully transformed from OEM into ODM, and even created their own brand by establishing their internal user experience design department. However, the current user experience research and design in Taiwan focusing too much on mainstream products is going to make the field become another red ocean. In order to prevent another outbreak of price war, the Taiwanese government has put in extensive resources to assist Taiwan's well-known brand companies in R&D, expecting to develop and establish a new product benchmark via the researches on special consumer groups. This research introduce an actual government funded project of ASUS focusing on developing an electronic platform for a special consumer group, Tzu Chi. By going through a series of user experience design and research process, we eventually retrieve some valuable points which could be beneficial to the design of future e-reader.

**Keywords:** E-Reader, User Experience Design, Contextual Inquiry.

## 1 Introduction

The design concept of user experience has been popularized and widely accepted in Taiwan. Many original equipment manufacturers (OEMs) engaged in consumer electronics have established their internal user experience design department and invested greatly on resource and manpower. Owing to the introduction of this concept, most companies have successfully transformed from OEM into ODM (original design manufacturer), and even created their own brand.

Such brand companies with user experience design capacity mainly undertake the development, design and manufacture of mainstream consumer electronic products, with the design experience mainly focused on office workers aged 20- 40 years old. A few years later, precious user experience data about these target users, such as cultural background, lifestyle, visual preference and mental model, have been obtained via systematic methods in not only Asia-Pacific areas but the whole world.

P.L.P. Rau (Ed.): CCD/HCII 2013, Part I, LNCS 8023, pp. 467–476, 2013.
© Springer-Verlag Berlin Heidelberg 2013

However, the redundant researches on the above-mentioned target group have resulted in the excessive concentration of popular products and are guiding Taiwan's consumer electronic industry to another red ocean which may drain the value of user experience design, outbreak another price war, and return to the old road of OEM. Being aware of such dilemmas and realizing the importance of developing new Blue Ocean Strategy, the Taiwanese government has put in extensive resources to assist Taiwan's well-known brand companies in R&D, expecting to develop and establish a new product benchmark via the user experience design and research of special groups.

Hence, by introducing an actual research and design case subsidized by the Technology Development Program of Taiwanese government, this study illustrates how a government supported project of a brand company (ASUS) focuses on the user experience design and research of special consumer groups (Tzu Chi) and what innovative ideas based on the findings in the research are proposed.

## 2    Case Background

### 2.1    Technology Development Program (TDP)

The full name of TDP is called Technology Development Grants Program [3], which is the economic development program administered by the Ministry of Economic Affairs, Taiwan. In this program, government provides funds to enterprises to share the risks, encourage the developments on risky technologies, cultivate professional talents and create opportunities for new innovative companies.

### 2.2    ASUSTek Computer

Established in 1990, ASUS originally focused on motherboard development and manufacture. The company became famous for its notebook PC in 2001 and created a wave of subnotebooks in 2007 with its Netbook EeePC. In recent years, it concentrated on tablet computers and made the tablet computer market become more diversified. The Asus Design Center [2] was established in 2001 focusing on the design and R&D of all ASUS products with its offices distributed in Taiwan, Shanghai and Singapore. Its User Experience Design Department was set in 2007.

### 2.3    Tzu Chi and Its Electronic Platform

Tzu Chi [4] is the largest Buddhist charity team founded in Hualien by Master Zen Yen in 1996, mainly undertaking the businesses of charity, education, medical service and culture, with more than one million volunteers all over the world. Since the members have to read the instructional talks by the Venerable Master and Buddhist scriptures, as well as learn the activity messages and donation fundraising projects, it authorized ASUS to develop an electronic platform for Tzu Chi. By 2011, a total of 5000 Tzu Chi electronic platform of Generation 1 have been manufactured and put into service for Tzi Chi members. After learning the joint development of an electronic platform between Asus and Tzu Chi, the Ministry of Economic Affairs encouraged them to apply for the Technology Development Program to start the improvement of Generation 2, so as to enhance the R&D investment in special groups. Furthermore, apart from deeply studying about user experiences in electronic platform of special groups, it also hopes to set another trend via the newly created electronic platform as well as ASUS' brand experiences.

## 3    Research Method

Entrusted by Asus, the user experience research and design team, AJA Creative Design [1], conducts the improvement researches on the first generation of Tzu Chi's electronic platform and puts forward the design concept for the second generation. Based on the user experience research methods, including interview, contextual inquiry and participatory observation, the team tries to figure out the potential design strategies and creates an interactive design prototype to conduct design communication and user testing. All the experiment processes of the three methods are recorded in videos and audio materials which are further analyzed by using method of protocol analysis.

### 3.1    Interview

Six Tsu Chi members who have been long-term users of the Generation 1 electronic platform were interviewed. Through the open interviews, the users' subjective opinions on using the platform were obtained. During the interviews, the users were requested to operate the platform to achieve the specified tasks, such as reading the instructional talks by the Venerable Masters, reading Buddhist scriptures, searching for activity messages, writing reading notes of book club and raising donations. The researchers asked further questions depending on the users' special operating behaviors (Fig. 1).

**Fig. 1.** The actual interview scenario

### 3.2    Contextual Inquiry

Another six Tzu Chi members were selected to undergo the contextual inquiry, which practically observes the operation of electronic platform by users in actual contexts, such as Tsu Chi Bodhimanda, fundraising aspect and their homes. During which, the researchers asked questions to deeply understand the various ways of using under different contexts. In addition to the set contexts, they also observed and recorded the users' related life contexts (when not using the electronic platform), expecting to dig out the users' potential demands.

### 3.3    Participatory Observation

Considering the regular reading group by Tsu Chi members every week, the study selects the co-reading contexts of a large size (100 persons) and a small size (ten persons) to conduct the participatory observation (Fig. 2). The researcher acted as one of the members to participate in the reading group and interact with the users, so as to observe and record dynamically.

**Fig. 2.** The small size reading group

### 3.4    Design Strategy

Through the above-mentioned research methods, the team conducts the protocol analysis of the 15 hour-long audio-video materials. The analysis encodes the materials based on the keyword definition and classification, so as to find out the specific repetitive activities and behaviors. Finally, the study summarizes the users' top five demands, whereby the design team further obtains five design strategies including providing up-to-date information, simplifying e-book classification, enabling intuitive sharing, increasing the speed of taking and searching notes, and linking related information. These strategies are further transferred into actual design solutions in the next stage.

### 3.5    Design Prototype

**Synchronizing with the Tsu Chi Information Center .** The instructional talks by the Venerable Masters are all uploaded to the website via the Tsu Chi Information Center to enable the members to access them immediately. However, the study finds out that the on-line information requires users' initiative in searching, while accessing the internet information is not easy for Tsu Chi members who intensively work outside or those middle-aged and elder. Consequently, the study proposes to add dynamic instructional talks and activity information on the portal of the electronic platform to push information to users actively (Fig. 3).

**Fig. 3.** The designed portal with dynamically pushing information

**Replacing Folders by Label Classifications .** Most of the electronic Tsu Chi scriptures have been digitalized already and can be downloaded into Tzu Chi electronic platform easily via internet. However, due to the large quantity of scriptures, it is not easy to search the one required, thus the willingness and frequency of users to read electronic scriptures are reduced. Accordingly, the study suggests displaying the frequently-read scriptures on the portal of the electronic platform and adding dynamic label classifications to replace the stable classification folders (Fig. 4).

**Table 1.** **Fig. 4.** Using tagging system for classifying a great amount of scriptures

**Synchronizing Multi-person Sharing Screen .** How to share the desired contents to the members in the reading group or achieve the sharing result is another demand that needs to be satisfied in this study, since both the Tzu Chi electronic platform and the existing e-readers on the market fail to provide such services currently. In this study, the researchers put forth that the participators of a reading club can be connected via internet and be visualized on the platform, so that their contents can be shared to everybody by clicking the specified participators. The sharing modes contain both whole screen sharing and individual selection (Fig. 5).

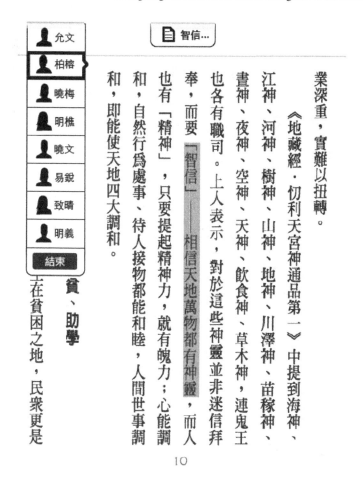

**Fig. 5.** Sharing content to group members by easily selecting and clicking

**Note Marking and Content Labeling .** It is a common behavior requirement of Tsu Chi members to write down important messages on papers or sticky notes anytime anywhere. Hence, the study presents that if the functions of easy-notes and easy-search are embedded into the electronic platform, a better user experience can be created. Users can just click the texts to be commented on and make notes in the pop-up noting-window; besides, a bookmark label will be shown on the side area of the platform screen to indicate the locations of the comments, so that they can be found quickly by clicking the labels (Fig. 6).

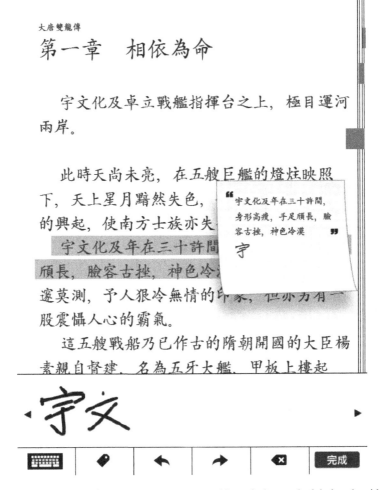

**Fig. 6.** Simply selecting texts pops up a note taking window and a label at the side

**Direct In-Time Searching by Selecting Texts .** Extended reading is a frequent required demand, when Tsu Chi members read scriptures. They often intensively switch from one scripture to another relevant one to look for quoted information. As a result, the automatic searching among different e-books is one of the primary functions that must be provided by the electronic platform. The study proposes to activate the searching in both online and electronic libraries when the users select specified texts, and then display search results dynamically to the users.

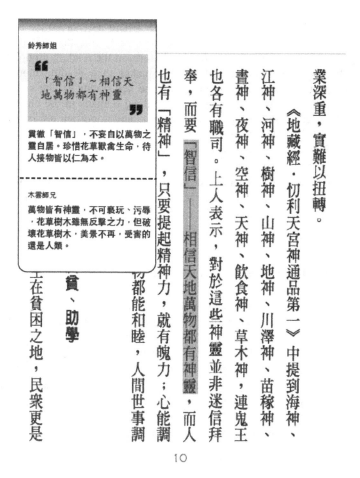

**Fig. 7.** Selecting a sentence triggers relevant content searching among e-books in both digital and online libraries.

### 3.6    User Testing

After implementing an interactive prototype, another six Tsu Chi members were invited to conduct the users testing. The testing adopts contextual inquiry, namely, operating designated tasks in specific contexts by users. Similarly, the whole process is recorded in videos and audios to conduct protocol analysis.

## 4    Analysis and Discussion

In the last user test period, we found several interesting and important points. First, the user thinks the dynamic information center on the portal is very useful, as they will not miss important activities in this way. In the past, most of the activity information was delivered by word of mouth, which often lacks timeliness. Second, with electronic scriptures categorized by tags, the Tzu Chi members who are mostly over forty years old don't have to memorize the folder where they saved the e-scriptures. Third, in the past, it was difficult for attendees to quickly find the content the sharer was talking about when using the electronic platform in the reading group. The function of synchronizing and sharing information makes their reading more efficient. Fourth, in the past, the user often wrote down the key points on the notepad while reading the scriptures. Now, the intuitive note taking realizes in the electronic platform so that the user doesn't need a notepad or miss any important information. Fifth, the function of in-time searching improves the quality of reading due to not being interrupted by the search for other scriptures.

Of course, there are also some problems that need to be improved. First, the character size must be enlarged to make it easier to read; secondly, the note labels should be large enough for users to find and click easily; and lastly, the handwriting area shall be expanded for convenience. However, all three points are main requirements of elder users, and researches on such visual capacities are relatively few in this study.

## 5     Conclusion and Future Research

The e-reader will become a trend in future development. Current products on the market pay more attention to the individual reading needs and the acquisition of reading content. But in this paper, it is found that the needs of group reading and the integration of the e-reader with the dynamic information platform are both needed by a special group like Tzu Chi. Though lacking in evidence, we believe that the findings and design of this study are very likely to be useful and successful when applying on ordinary users. A case in point is the co-reading mode. It is possible that the encouragement of e-reading through the integration of the co-reading function and its application to teaching will bring about another e-reader trend.

## References

1  AJA Creative Design, http://www.aja.com.tw/
1. Asus Design Center, http://www.asusdesign.com/
2. Technology Development Grants Program, http://www.moea.gov.tw/Mns/doit/content/Content.aspx?menu_id=5375
3. Tzu Chi, http://www.tzuchi.org.tw/

# Social Media's Impact on Teenagers

Rahul Vasanth[1] and Seema Swamy[2]

[1] University of Illinois, Urbana-Champaign
[2] CMR Insights
rvasant2@uiuc.edu, seemaswamy@cmrinsights.com

**Abstract.** McLuhan's "media is the message" has never been more relevant than in the age of the ubiquitous digital media. The social influences by the peer group and access to information of all kinds leaves the door open to influences that may or may not necessarily be positive. The access to communicate to large groups of people relatively easily and quickly has the impact of impacting social dynamics, by reducing social inhibitions, and redefining normative actions. More importantly there are potential short-term and long-term implications for these actions. This paper explores some of these influences and consequences as well as actions that adults can potentially take to sensitize and curb potentially damaging behaviors among teenagers.

**Keywords:** Social networking, digital media, Internet, mobile phones, chats, facebook, twitter, SMS, instant messenger, Tumblr, email.

## 1    Introduction

The wide proliferation of digital media with its versatile functionality that enables wide outreach to people is fundamentally changing the way teenagers communicate. With the proliferation of information, teenagers have access to a wealth of information that can enrich their academic lives and provide tools that promote collaboration and group work.

However, the negative unintended consequences of social media can be extremely severe. Fundamental social norms are being redefined. The socio-psychological impact of these actions can be extreme, leading to irreversible consequences in some cases. While change is inevitable, when it is rapid and disruptive, it raises questions about protecting the youth from itself.

Social media is redefining social norms of communication among teenagers and potentially increasing the impact of peer groups as a source of influence compared to that of authority figures such as parents, teachers, and other elders. This paper examines various factors that enhance or control the effect of social media, both positive and negative.

## 2    Methodology

Insights were derived from in-depth interviews of 10 teenagers, four women and six men between the ages of 13-19 years. Most of these interviews were conducted in the

P.L.P. Rau (Ed.): CCD/HCII 2013, Part I, LNCS 8023, pp. 477–485, 2013.
© Springer-Verlag Berlin Heidelberg 2013

homes of the participants. They were encouraged to demonstrate the use of social media through various devices. All the participants had access to a mobile phone and a laptop.

The criteria for the selection of these participants was that they should be teenagers with access to a Smart Phone and have the consent of their parent/guardian to participate in the study. The insights from the participants were extremely personal in nature in the case of some of the participants. These may potentially be attributed to a selection bias. Nevertheless, the insights are relevant for the situational contingencies.

# 3     Digital Experience

According to Pew Internet & American Life Project, fully 95% of all teens ages 12-17 are now online and 80% of those online teens are users of social media sites. 70% of these go to the Internet daily and about 46% visited multiple times a day in 2011 which was doubled since November 2004. About 80% of the teenagers go to social networking site such as Facebook and Twitter. Girls tend to use the Internet significantly more than boys and teens from families with less than $50,000 annual income tend to use the social media sites about 11% more than teens from families with more than $50,000 annual income (Lenhart, Madden, Smith, Purcel, Zickuhr, Rainie, 2011).

In this qualitative study, in the case of half of the participants, their household also had a desktop computer that they had access to but they used it rarely. The sample may be biased because they were from the San Francisco Bay area which is the hub of the Silicon Valley with significant adopters of technology with high use.

Participants demonstrated that they had a seamless digital experience across devices. Their digital lives took a significant proportion of their time.

# 4     Parental/Adult Control

The influence of the peer groups was significant even outside the school and within the home environment. Several teens checked their social networking sites including Facebook, Tumblr, Instagram, SMS, and email multiple times. There appears to be an addictive effect of the digital experience for some of the teens. For instance, one of the parents of a teenager who took part in the study imposed strict controls on access to the Internet through various devices including a Smart Phone. When the teenager was given access to the Smart Phone during the duration of the study when the researchers visited his home, he divided his attention between responding to the questions of the researchers and playing an interactive game with his friend. His explanation was that he needed to maximize all the time he could have with the device to play and win the game with his friend. He admitted that he often cheated and took the phone surreptitiously from his parent's hiding place to connect with his friends digitally despite having dedicated face time with his friends provided by his parents.

Another teenager reported that his parents had blocked access to the Internet on his phone over the weekdays when he was home and they required all the children to do their work in a common area to ensure transparency. He reported that he had hacked the password and often texted his friends without the knowledge of his parents. The desire to remain connected constantly appears to be a combination of a need for satisfaction experienced from social connectedness to the peer group as well as peer pressure of being able to communicate with his friends at all times. Often this connectedness did not translate into a higher quantity of participation. However, it appears to be important to some of the teens to be in the know as the communication unfolded. Most of the communication appears not to have much depth in thought. In some ways, this need for constant connectedness with one's peer group appears to come at the cost of the strength of relationship within one's family.

One of the teens explained that if he did not participate in real time to the *events* as he termed his friends' communication, then he would feel that he missed out from the experience. A few of the teens reported being adept at subterfuge where they appeared to be engaged in the academic work but were in fact multi-tasking by interacting with multiple groups.

Research has demonstrated that when individuals multitask, the quality of their work is deeply impacted negatively (Jacobsen & Forste, 2011). The disruptive influence of these facilitated social media appears to impact the amount of learning and the depth of understanding of academic material when their concentration is repeatedly interrupted by messages by the social group they belong to either through primary membership or secondary membership.

## 4.1  Parental Boundaries

The family structure and the strength of family ties also appeared to have a strong impact on the teenagers' academic performance. Teens from homes with strong parental involvement and controls tended to be high achievers compared to teens from families where parents were either extremely liberal in their parenting styles and allowed the teens the freedom to engage with digital media, did not have the time to monitor them, or had a dysfunctional relationship with each other.

Although this is a qualitative research, teens with lax parental controls tended to have relatively lower grades. Both the parents and teens from such household tended to have lower aspirations for advanced academic career compared to families where parents tended to provide more restrictions (whether completely successfully or not) on the time their children spent on the Internet in social media sites. Interestingly, this also seemed to correlate with the socio-economic status of the parents. When parents did not have a college education, they tended to be more relaxed about their children's media usage.

### Weak Parental Boundaries

In one of the families, the mother found the word monitoring her children's time as being offensive. She said that her children were good and did not require being monitored. She said that she aspired to be a friend to her children and wanted a trusting relationship and not one where she dictated how much time and when her children used the Internet or spent time on social media.

In the case of another teenager, one of the parents had abandoned the mother and the mother aspired to create a close bond between herself and her children. As a consequence, she not only provided them with all the digital devices they asked for, but did not set any firm responsibilities or schedules. She claimed that her children were her best friends and therefore her responsibility was to keep them safe, well-fed, and driven to school on time. Other than that, they were responsible individuals who should portion their time as they saw fit.

When parents had a dysfunctional relationship with each other, the influence of the peer group tended to be significantly higher. In the case of one of the teenage participants, she sided with one parent and blamed the other parent for the difficult relationship between her parents. As a consequence, she deliberately disregarded the controls placed on the amount of Internet time and openly flouted the rules of the parent she blamed. The other parent supported the disrespectful behavior of his child in the game of one-upmanship. This often resulted in significant and loud arguments between the parents. As a consequence, the teen relied more on the support and advice of his peer group (which consisted of other members of similar age group that lacked the maturity to provide sound advice). This over reliance on the peer group also became a substitute for peaceful productive interactions she lacked in her home environment.

In the case of one of the families, the young adult son tended to stay out at all hours of the night and came home whenever he felt like it to sleep. His education at a community college was interrupted because of his party schedule that he said was facilitated by the social media. His peer group texted each other and planned party events on social media sites. However, he demonstrated more concern for his teenage siblings than he did for himself. He did not want his brother and sister to follow his footsteps and tried to impose rules on them. The father on the other hand did not connect his young adult son's behaviors with his own lack of parental rules and appeared frustrated that despite his giving his son all the freedom to do the right thing, he was choosing the wrong path. He also did not set any rules for his younger children and instead expressed hope that they would demonstrate more sense compared to his elder son.

With most of these interactions with other teens happening in group chats or comments on social media sites such as Facebook, private situations often become public spectacles with a permanent record in the ether world. For instance, one of the participants reported that someone on his Facebook friends group used cuss words to describe her parents because they insisted on her completing her household chores. Although he felt it was an inappropriate forum, he was also understanding about her frustration. In another instance, students employed the social media as an acceptable venue to criticize the teaching skills of their teachers.

**Strong Parental Boundaries**

In the case of one of the families, although both the parents worked outside home, one of the parents was home by 6 in the evening. In the case of two other families, the mother was a stay at home parent. In one of the families, the mother worked part-time and was also studying towards a professional degree.

In the case of all these families, the dominant expectation was that the academic performance of the children should be strong. There was a spoken expectation of attending a four-year college and potentially obtaining a higher degree. The children were required to work in the common area to complete their homework and there was an expectation of transparency.

Although the children tended to be creative to cheat and visited social networking sites through their tablets or phones or in some cases openly went to these sites professedly for academic collaboration, they had to be surreptitious about the amount of time and degree of non-academic related interactions. They also tended to feel that they were missing out while their friends had relatively more freedom to interact with each other without as much parental interference. However, the academic grades of these children tended to be significantly higher and they also tended to participate and achieve distinction in an extra-curricular activity.

While the link between parental supervision and academic performance is well documented and not surprising, it is interesting to note that the teenagers from families with high supervision and expectations tended to feel left out (there was one exception).

Not all parents were equally strict. One of the parents in the strong parental control group allowed her daughter to use Chat for academic purposes but understood that the daughter did not use it strictly for that purpose. She however required her daughter to give her access to her account but did not realize that her daughter had created an alternative account for her exclusive use. All *these behaviors underscore the power of the social ties of the peer group that appear to be taking precedence or are at least more influential in the age of the digital media* than in earlier generations.

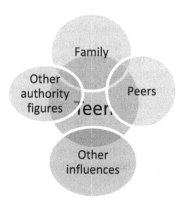

**Fig. 1.** Influence of Peers increasing pre Social Media (representation not statistical)

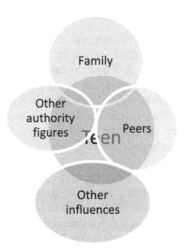

**Fig. 2.** Influence of Peers Post Social Media (representation not statistical)

# 5    Social Media and Health Implications

## 5.1    Cyber Bullying

The social media is a powerful tool to target and bully specific individuals. The social networking group of these individuals ranged from about 600 to 1350 connections. None of the participants had employed any controls over who could view their page or content. Therefore, any post could be viewed by all their contacts and therefore a powerful tool for bullies to intimidate victims.

Bullies have the ability to harness the power of the social group through social media tools to tag and besmirch the reputations of individuals. In extreme cases, such bullying has driven impressionable individuals to commit suicide as well (Kim, 2008). The power to inflict significant pain is magnified with social media. While our study did not find such extreme outcomes, there were two instances where individuals reported discussing a girl in a derogatory language because she was involved in a relationship and the couple had broken up with each other.

In the case of another instance, one of the classmates apparently had body odor. Instead of speaking to him directly, his classmates turned this into a discussion on the social media site thereby turning an embarrassing incident into a potentially mortifying one. The manifold impact of these discussions is potentially extremely painful psychologically for the targeted individuals (Sebastian et al., 2010). At the time when teenagers are crystallizing a sense of self, social isolation through ostracism can deeply impact how they view themselves at least in relation to others.

## 5.2    Sleep Deprivation

Multiple participants reported being active well into the night beyond their normal sleeping hours either actively participating or lurking in social media sites through mobile phones and computers (Rasmussen, 2012). Some of the participants were inseparable from a digital device at almost all times. Access to text message was almost constant for at least half of the participants. The parent of one of the participants could hear the pinging sound of messages received well into the night. Sometimes the teenage participants woke up in the middle of the night to check the text messages received through SMS. Prevalence of sleep interruption reported tended to be much more among older teenagers than among younger teenagers. Lack of sufficient sleep has been correlated with depression among teenagers.

## 5.3    Gaming

The amount of time spent on the Internet playing games online either through their mobile devices or the computer was significant. This had the impact of negatively affecting the amount of time they spent on academics resulting in lower quality of classwork and homework or delay in submissions of schoolwork.

## 5.4    Sexting

The prevalence of camera feature on computers as well as mobile phones and easy access to adult sites appears to correlate with the increase in sexting. In the MetroWest Adolescent Health Survey (2011), defined sexting as the act of "using the Internet, cell phones, or other electronic devices to send or forward nude, sexually suggestive, or explicit photos or videos of someone you know."

Two of the participants reported that their friends engaged extensively in sexting. This appears to be in line with the third person effect - it is generally easier to attribute non-normative behaviors to others rather than to oneself. The research on sexting is difficult as it is a challenging topic to discuss and generally requires long-term interaction with participants.

The potential for abusing the capability of sexted materials is immense where the recipients sometimes mass mail these materials to others either in a bid to increase their own social capital or to punish the sender when she or he breaks up with the recipient. This victimization of the senders of sexting material renders them vulnerable and violated. This has even led to the sender of sexting to commit suicide in some instances as reported by other sources (Celizic, 2009) although none of the participants in this study reported any drastic outcomes.

# 6    Social Media as Collaborative Tools

The power of the social media is not only dysfunctional disruptive, but it is also sometimes harnessed positively for significant and meaningful achievement. Some of the teenagers employed it to plan events and activities that had a positive impact both on an individual level as well as at a group and community level.

When there was a hate group that planned to come to the school and demonstrate loudly with their message, some of the teenagers in the in the community communicated a plan to blunt the impact. They planned to hold a solidarity bonding singing songs promoting peace as a way to disrupt the impact of the hate group.

This rapid response could not have been achieved without the ability to connect to large groups of people rapidly through social connectivity facilitated through the social media.

In another instance, one of the teenagers was an office holder of the Speech and Debate club in his high school and used the Chat and Facebook group to ensure that there was a meaningful exchange of ideas. He employed the social media tools to ensure those who could not meet physically to practice nevertheless shared the experience digitally.

Two of the articipants employed the social media to place a video of their choreography for the benefit of their group for a group dance performance.

Academic achievement is facilitated and enhanced when goal directed high achieving teenagers collaborate through social media. A meta analyses of 12 studies that examined various styles of learning concluded that cooperative learning that the social media enables, improves the learning of gifted and high achieving children (Neber, Finsterwald, & Urban, 2010). Almost all the teenagers employed the social media at one time or another to interact with their peer group to help or receive academic assistance and for positive learning experiences.

## 7    Conclusions and Future Directions

Clearly, social media have helped redefine social dynamics. While social media have tremendous power in affecting positive changes, they also appear to have a significant negative impact. These changes are more severe as they impact the fundamental normative behaviors in the impressionable minds of teenagers and young adults.

The social media sites have taken the flavor of a town crier and reduced the boundaries of inhibition. With their peer groups not judging inappropriate behaviors and comments harshly, the social rudeness tends to become more acceptable. More troubling is the addictive need for remaining connected with peer groups at all times which appears to also lessen the impact of parental and other authority figures' impact. In addition, it also has the tendency to affect both the physical and mental health of teenagers who use social media excessively.

Parents and pedagogues may have to explore venues such as employing security features to limit the amount of time teens interact on social media as well as monitor the quality and content of interaction when it transgresses social norms and legal rules.

When technology outpaces and dictates social change, the adults may have to explore ways of saving teenagers from themselves.

## References

1. Brennan, J.: Pew Internet: Teens (2012), http://pewinternet.org/Commentary/2012/April/Pew-Internet-Teens.aspx
2. Celizic, M.: Her teen committed suicide over 'sexting' (2009), http://student services.dadeschools.net/sexting/pdfs/Her_Teen_Committed_Suicide_Over_Sexting.pdf

3. Jacobsen, W.C., Forste, R.: The Wired Generation: Academic and Social Outcomes of Electronic Media Use Among University Students. Cyberpsychology, Behavior, and Social Networking 14(5), 275–280 (2011)
4. Kim, Y.S.: Bullying and suicide. A review. International Journal of Adolescent Medical Health 20(2), 133–154 (2008)
5. Lazarsfeld, P.F., Merton, R.K.: Mass Media, Popular Taste, and Organized Social Action. In: Byron, L. (ed.) The Communication of Ideas, pp. 95–118. Harper (1948)
6. Lenhart, A., Madden, M., Smith, A., Purcell, K., Zickuhr, K., Rainie, L.: Teens, kindness and cruelty on social networking sites (November 2011)
7. MetroWest Adolescent Health Survey (2011), http://www.wellesley.k12.ma.us/schoolcom/pdfs/MWAHSReportFall2011.pdf
8. Neber, H., Finsterwald, M., Urban, N.: Cooperative Learning with Gifted and High-achieving Students: A review and meta-analyses of 12 studies, pp. 199–214. Rouledge, Taylor & Francis Group (2010)
9. O'Keeffe, G.S., Clarke-Pearson, K.: The Impact of Social Media on Children, Adolescents, and Families. Pediatrics (65), 800–804 (2011)
10. Sebastian, C., Viding, E., Williams, K.D., Blakemore, S.J.: Social brain development and the affective consequences of ostracism in adolescence. In: S.J. Segalowitz (ed.) Brain and Cognition: A Journal of Experimental and Clinical Research, 134-145. Elsevier (2010)
11. Rasmussen, R.H.: Digital Media Causes Sleep Deprivation in Children. Kids and Media (March 2012), http://www.kidsandmedia.co.uk/digital-media-causes-sleep-deprivation-in-children/

# An Analysis of Microblogging Behavior on Sina Weibo: Personality, Network Size and Demographics

Lingyu Wang[1,2], Weina Qu[1], and Xianghong Sun[1]

[1] Institute of Psychology, Chinese Academy of Sciences, Beijing, China
quwn@psych.ac.cn
[2] University of Chinese Academy of Sciences, Beijing, China

**Abstract.** In China, Sina Weibo is one of the most popular microblogging services. The relationship between Weibo users' microblogging behavior and their personality as well as demographics was addressed in current study. 498 users completed the online survey and their social networking data was downloaded based on the Application Programming Interfaces. The results showed that: 1) Weibo users' personality was associated with some aspects of microblogging behavior, especially, Extraversion and Openness significantly positively correlated with some aspects of microblogging behavior, while neuroticism significantly negatively correlated with that; 2) There were associations between some demographical factors and some aspects of microblogging behavior, for instance, the time spent in microblogging related to the age, educational level and monthly discretionary money, respectively. 3) The effect of gender on Weibo social networking size was significant, that was the amount of male Weibo users' followers was significantly greater than that of female users'.

**Keywords:** Personality, Microblogging, Sina Weibo, Demographics.

## 1 Introduction

As a new way to build relationship, Social Networking Services (SNSs) are being almost the first choice for countless users all around the world. For example, in the US, Facebook and MySpace have more than 117 million US visitors in 2009, which continue to attack wider range of users throughout the world [1]. Among all the SNSs, microblog has emerged as a new and popular platform for short, frequent communication which differs from the most SNSs in that the relationship of follower and followee doesn't requires reciprocation [2]. One of the most popular microblog, Twitter, a microblogging service which established less than six years, has more than 510 million users in July 2012[3]. However, in China, where Facebook and Twitter were not available, one substitute for twitter is Weibo, a Twitter-like social networking service established in August 2009. At the very beginning, only 13.8percent of Internet users used Weibo in 2010[4]; in 2011, almost half the Chinese Internet population (48.7 percent) used the service—a total of 250 million users [5].

What motivates so many people to use this platform? A large amount of survey aimed at analyzing the motivations and usage of microblogging service. Most of the previous analyses involve two sorts of antecedents: 1) self-description, 2) demographical

P.L.P. Rau (Ed.): CCD/HCII 2013, Part I, LNCS 8023, pp. 486–492, 2013.
© Springer-Verlag Berlin Heidelberg 2013

factors [6]. Despite the increasing research on microblogging, the correlation between microblogging behavior and personality traits is not known very much. In the context of China, Sina Weibo is one of the most popular microblogging services. Based on this platform, we conducted this study to enhance the understanding of the relationship between microblogging behavior and personality traits as well as demographical factors.

## 2    Methods

### 2.1    Data Collection

In our study, we mainly focused on the general active users of Sina Weibo. In order to select the target group from the population, we conducted the screening process in two stages. At the first stage, we aimed at getting the Weibo users' ID as many as possible. Beginning with 100 users, we firstly downloaded the users' relationship network through breadth search by calling Sina Weibo's open application programming interface (APIs) in March 2012. Removing the repeated relationship, we got 15,767,158 users' IDs. Then we captured these users' profiles, including the amount of their updates, followees and followers. After preliminary analysis of these data, we found that the range of the amount of followers from 1000 to 3300 was very important. In this range, the amount of the users was relatively higher and the users' ID was less likely to belong to the same user. So we got 291,039 users' IDs of which the amount of followers fell in the range between 1000 and 3300.

At the second stage, we took the 291,039 users' IDs as the expanded seed for breadth search. We captured 1,116,408,085 users' IDs by following these users' relationship networking on April 12, 2012. After removing the repeated IDs, there were 96,497,290 users' IDs. Then we downloaded these users' profiles on April 18, 2012. On average, there were 136.65 updates (SD=788.87) per user in this dataset. We defined active users as people who posted at least 532(M+0.5SD, in this dataset) updates and we excluded the highest 5 percent data. So the interval of the active users' total updates was [532, 4194]. According to this criterion, we got 6,047,966 users. And we downloaded the detailed information of 5,919,087 users successfully on April 25, 2012.

Also there were many star users and advertisers. These people should be excluded from the target group because they were not the general active users. According to the following standards, we screened the target group: 1) the amount of updates was equal or more than 532; 2) the last microblog was posted after 2012; 3) the interval between the time of the last microblog released and the time of Weibo ID registered was more than one month; 4) the average amount of microblogging was not more than 100 every day. Then we got 5,807,999 users' IDs. On average, there were 2.84 updates per user in this dataset every day. Using 40 as the up boundary of the average daily amount of microblogging, we got the range between 2.84 and 40. Finally, we screened out 1,953,485 users who fell in this interval as our target group. We randomly divided these people into 20 parts (19 parts including 200 thousands, the remained as the last part). Then we randomly selected 30 thousands users from the first part to take part in our study. We used the "@" function of Weibo to invite these users to participant an online survey and 505 users responded. After further screening according to the data integrity, 498 copies of data were remained.

Participants completed the online questionnaire from May 1 through July 22 in 2012. The questionnaire contained 3 parts, as following: 1) Demographics information; 2) Big five personality measures; 3) Internet and Weibo use experience. And also we down-loaded these users' profiles, including the amount of updates, favorites, followees and followers, as well as the social networking size which referred to the total of the user's followees and followers.

## 2.2    Measures

**Demographics Information.** Personal information, including gender, age, education-al level (Edu.), occupation (Occu.), disposable money every month (Monthly Money), growth location, place of the current residence(Cur. residence) and time at current address(Time Add.), was collected in the first part.

**Big Five Personality Measures.** In the second part, we adopted the Big Five Inventory-44(BFI-44) to measure the users' personality. This is a self-report personality inventory which is designed to assess the Big Five Factors of personality: Extraversion, Agreeableness, Conscientiousness, Neuroticism, and Openness to Experience [7]. The BFI-44 has substantial internal consistency and retest reliability. For example, John et al stated that "in U.S. and Canadian samples, the alpha reliabilities of the BFI-44 typically range from .75 to .90 and average above .80; three-month test-retest reliabilities range from .80 to .90, with a mean of .85" [8].We translated all the questions into Chinese and all participants answered this inventory according to a 5-point Likert scale (from 1= "strongly disagree" to 5= "strongly agree").

**Internet and Weibo Use Experience.** In the third part, we measured the users' general use of the internet and Weibo by asking the following 8 questions which all adopted a 5-point scale except the last two. The first two questions were used to measure the users' experience of internet use: (a) How long have you started to use the internet (i.e. duration of starting to use Internet, Dur.Internet)? (1= less than 1 year, 2= 2-3 years, 3= 3-5 years, 4= 5-10 years, 5= more than 10 years) and (b) How often do you use the internet now (i.e. frequency of using internet, Fre.Internet)? (1= sometimes when necessary, 2= less than 2 hours a day, 3= 2-4 hours a day, 4= 4-8 hours a day, 5= more than 8 years a day).

The next two questions were about the users' general Weibo use experience: (c) How often do you use Sina Weibo now (i.e. daily frequency of using Weibo, Fre.Weibo)? (1= seldom, 2= sometimes, 3= several times a week, 4= several times a day, 5= always) and (d) How much time do you spend on Sina Weibo every day at present (i.e. daily duration of using Weibo, Dur.Weibo)? (1= less than 15 minutes, 2= 15-30 minutes, 3= 30 minutes to an hour, 4= 1-2 hours, 5= more than 2 hours).

Another four questions were adapted to measure the idiosyncratic features of Weibo: (e) How many people do you know and are familiar with among your followees on Weibo (i.e. number of acquaintance among followees, Num.Followee)? (1= 0-50, 2= 50-100, 3= 100-200, 4= 200-500, 5= more than 500). (f) How many people do you know and are familiar with among your followers on Weibo (i.e. number of acquaintance among followers, Num.Follower)? (1= 0-50, 2= 50-100, 3= 100-200, 4= 200-500, 5= more than 500). (g) About how many times do you vote on Weibo every week (i.e. times of voting weekly, Times.Voting)? (1= 0 time, 2= 1-3 times, 3= 4-6 times, 4= more than 7 times). (h) About how many times do you use the "@" function of Weibo to mention others a day (i.e. times of using "@" daily, Times. @)? (1= 0 time, 2= 1-3 times, 3= 4-9 times,

4= more than 10 times). The participants answered the last two questions according to a 4-point Likert scale.

All these questions mentioned above could be seen as the index of the users' microblogging behavior.

# 3     Results

## 3.1     Sample Distribution of Demographics

In our study, 498 participants finished the online survey. There were 189 males and 309 females (see Table1). And 14 percent of these users were under 18 years, 80 percent were 18-30 years and 6 percent were above 31. Among these users, 42.2 percent had a bachelor's degree, 22.1 percent had junior college degree, 30.5 percent had high school diploma and under. As for their occupation, 52.6 percent of the users were students. And 63.6 percent of these users were born in city and 84.2 percent now are living in the city.

**Table 1.** The sample distribution of the Weibo users' demographics (n=498)

| Demographics | Frequency | Percent | Demographics | Frequency | Percent |
|---|---|---|---|---|---|
| Gender | | | Growth Location | | |
| Male | 189 | 38.0 | Provincial level city | 135 | 27.1 |
| Female | 309 | 62.0 | Ordinary city | 182 | 36.5 |
| | | | Town | 104 | 20.9 |
| | | | Village | 77 | 15.5 |
| Age group | | | Occu. | | |
| Under18 | 70 | 14.0 | Worker | 5 | 1.0 |
| 18-20 | 136 | 27.3 | Civil servant | 12 | 2.4 |
| 21-25 | 190 | 38.2 | Medic & nurse | 10 | 2.0 |
| 26-30 | 72 | 14.5 | Office worker | 93 | 18.7 |
| 31-35 | 16 | 3.2 | Journalist | 14 | 2.8 |
| 36-40 | 5 | 1.0 | Student | 262 | 52.6 |
| 41-45 | 6 | 1.2 | Researcher & teacher | 16 | 3.2 |
| Above 46 | 3 | 0.6 | Independent operator | 18 | 3.6 |
| | | | Unemployed | 32 | 6.4 |
| | | | Else | 36 | 7.2 |
| Edu. | | | Cur. Residence | | |
| High school & Under | 152 | 30.5 | Provincial level city | 226 | 45.4 |
| Junior college | 110 | 22.1 | Ordinary city | 193 | 38.8 |
| Bachelor | 210 | 42.2 | Town | 67 | 13.5 |
| Master & Above | 26 | 5.2 | Village | 12 | 2.3 |
| Monthly Money | | | Time Add. | | |
| Less than 500 | 116 | 23.3 | 1 year & Less | 53 | 10.6 |
| 500-1000 | 115 | 23.1 | 1-3 years | 123 | 24.7 |
| 1000-2000 | 126 | 25.3 | 3-5years | 74 | 14.9 |
| 2000-5000 | 111 | 22.3 | 5-10year | 58 | 11.6 |
| More than 5000 | 30 | 6.0 | More than10 years | 190 | 38.2 |

## 3.2    Personality and Microblogging Behavior Correlations

Our results showed that Weibo users' microblogging behavior correlated with their personality traits. As table 2 showed, Extraversion positively correlated with the frequency of using Weibo, the number of acquaintance among followees and followers, the times of voting weekly as well as the daily times of using the "@" function. But Neuroticism negatively correlated with the number of acquaintance among followers. Conscientiousness was positively correlated with the times of voting weekly and Openness was positively correlated with the daily times of using the "@" function.

**Table 2.** The descriptive statistics of personality traits and Pearson correlation values between microblogging behavior and personality traits

|  | M | SD | Dur. Internet | Fre. Internet | Fre. Weibo | Dur. Weibo | Num. Followee | Num. Follower | Times. Voting | Times. @ |
|---|---|---|---|---|---|---|---|---|---|---|
| Extra. | 3.03 | 0.63 | .07 | .00 | .09* | .02 | .19** | .23** | .14** | .19** |
| Agree. | 3.61 | 0.57 | .12** | .03 | .05 | .03 | -.02 | .00 | -.01 | .05 |
| Cons. | 3.15 | 0.57 | .06 | -.03 | -.08 | -.08 | .06 | .04 | .09* | .05 |
| Neuro. | 3.06 | 0.64 | -.05 | .02 | .02 | .03 | -.05 | -.09* | -.09 | -.08 |
| Open. | 3.60 | 0.57 | .13** | -.03 | .02 | .02 | .09 | .06 | .05 | .10* |

*Note: * p<.05; **p<.01;***p<.001, the same as following tables.*

## 3.3    Relationship between Microblogging Behavior and Demographics

In table 3, the results showed that the users' microblogging behavior were not independent of the demographical valuables. For example, the frequency of using Weibo was different across the educational levels and occupation and the duration of using Weibo was different across the age, educational levels, as well as monthly disposable money. Also there was an association between the number of acquaintance among followees and age. And there was a significant difference in the times of voting weekly across the current residence. The daily times of using the "@" function related with gender, age and occupation too.

**Table 3.** Contingency table test for the users' microblogging behavior and demographics (Pearson Chi-Square values)

|  | Dur. Internet | Fre. Internet | Fre. Weibo | Dur. Weibo | Num. Followee | Num. Follower | Times. Voting | Times. @ |
|---|---|---|---|---|---|---|---|---|
| Gender | 1.63 | 1.04 | 7.81 | 7.37 | 9.06 | 5.48 | 7.01 | 9.15* |
| Age Group | 170.44*** | 104.50*** | 17.59 | 53.90** | 56.53*** | 27.95 | 22.06 | 33.54* |
| Edu. | 75.51*** | 41.17*** | 36.28*** | 32.84*** | 12.23 | 14.50 | 16.79 | 11.12 |
| Occu. | 110.63*** | 104.96*** | 60.65** | 48.17 | 45.06 | 47.98 | 28.60 | 53.15** |
| Monthly Money | 126.96*** | 77.83*** | 21.02 | 39.35*** | 25.21 | 13.62 | 15.61 | 15.99 |
| Growth. Location | 32.38*** | 8.86 | 11.88 | 11.74 | 8.86 | 9.16 | 14.96 | 14.70 |
| Cur. Residence | 55.51*** | 22.06* | 14.58 | 9.04 | 13.97 | 12.07 | 20.18* | 10.50 |
| Time Add. | 27.79* | 17.40 | 12.42 | 16.26 | 12.68 | 18.18 | 19.35 | 7.23 |

### 3.4    Differences in Demographics

The results in table 4 showed that the effect of gender and growth location on the amount of followers and Weibo social networking size was respectively significant. Specifically, the amount of followers and Weibo social networking size of the male users was significantly more than that of the female users. The users grown up in the town had significantly more followers and bigger social networking size than those grown up in the provincial level city, Ordinary city and Village.

**Table 4.** The significance test for the users' profiles under the demographics by independent sample T-test and ANOVA

|                        | Gender (t-value) | Age group | Edu. | Occu. | Monthly Money | Growth Location | Cur. Residence | Time Add. |
|------------------------|------------------|-----------|------|-------|---------------|-----------------|----------------|-----------|
| Amount of Followers    | 2.84**           | 0.34      | 0.38 | 0.40  | 0.41          | 3.13*           | 1.78           | 0.94      |
| Amount of Followees    | 1.29             | 1.81      | 3.23*| 1.59  | 1.81          | 1.98            | 0.47           | 1.30      |
| Amount of updates      | 0.56             | 0.46      | 1.84 | 1.84  | 0.91          | 0.27            | 0.07           | 1.50      |
| Amount of favorites    | 0.54             | 0.23      | 0.90 | 2.45* | 1.89          | 0.84            | 1.50           | 1.21      |
| Social networking size | 2.87***          | 0.38      | 0.54 | 0.40  | 0.47          | 3.07*           | 1.59           | 1.04      |

And also there was significant difference in the amount of favorites across the users' occupation. And specifically, the amount of favorites of the journalist users was the highest and significantly more than that of other users except for the worker users. And the amount of followees was significantly different across the users' educational levels. The results of Post Hoc Tests showed that the users having junior college diploma had significantly more followees than those having high school diploma and under, as well as master degree and above.

## 4    Conclusions

In this study, first we picked out the active users of Sina Weibo and downloaded their users' profiles information, and then we invited the active users to take part in our online survey. We measured their personality and microblogging behavior and collected their demographical information.

These data were analyzed and the results showed that the users' personality was correlated with some aspects of the microblogging behavior, such as Extraversion positively correlated with the frequency of using Weibo, the number of acquaintance among followees and followers, the times of voting weekly as well as the daily times of using the "@" function. And there was a relationship between some microblogging behavior and the demographics, for instance, the frequency of using Weibo was different across the educational levels and occupation. Besides, the effects of some demographical factors on the users' profiles were significant. For example, the amount of followers and Weibo social networking size of the male users was significantly more than that of the female users.

**Acknowledgements.** We would like to thank Professor Tingshao Zhu and Lin Li, Ang Li, and Bibo Hao for their help in collecting data. This work was supported by Chinese Academy of Sciences "Strategic Leading Science and Technology Special Program" (No. XDA06030800).

# References

1. Eldon, E.: ComScore, Quantcast, Compete, Nielsen show a strong December for Facebook traffic in the US (January 22, 2010), http://www.insidefacebook.com/2010/01/22/comscore-quantcast-compete-show-a-strong-december-forfacebook-traffic-in-the-us/ (accessed January 10, 2010)
2. Barnes, Böhringer: Continuance usage intention in microblogging services: the case of twitter. In: Proceedings of the 17th European Conference on Information Systems, Verona, Italy, June 8-10 (2009)
3. Semiocast: Geolocation analysis of Twitter accounts and tweets (2012), http://semiocast.com/publications/2012_07_30_Twitter_reaches_half_a_billion_accounts_140m_in_the_US
4. China Internet Network Information Center: The 27th statistical reports on the Internet development in China 37, (2011), http://www.cnnic.net.cn/hlwfzyj/hlwxzbg/201101/P020120709345289031187.pdf
5. China Internet Network Information Center: The 29th statistical reports on the Internet development in China 4-5 (2012), http://www.cnnic.net.cn/hlwfzyj/hlwxzbg/201201/P020120709345264469680.pdf
6. Yu, Y., Zhu,Y.: Follow Me: An Analysis of Self-traits, Motivation, Microblog Usage and Attractiveness of One's Microblog. In: Proceedings of the 2012 9th International Conference on Service Systems and Service Management, pp. 148–153 (2012)
7. John, O.P., Donahue, E.M., Kentle, R.L.: The Big Five Inventory–Versions 4a and 54. University of California Berkeley, Institute of Personality and Social Research, Berkeley, CA (1991)
8. John, O.P., Srivastava, S.: The Big-Five Trait Taxonomy: History, Measurement, and Theoretical Perspective. In: Pervin, L., John, O.P. (eds.) Handbook of Personality: Theory and Research, 2nd edn. Guilford, New York (1999) (in press)

# The Research on Cognition Design
# in Chinese Opera Mask

Tai-Jui Wang[1], Yu-Ju Lin[2], and Jun-Liang Chen[2]

[1] Department of Mass Communication, Chinese Culture University
Yang-Ming-Shan, Taipei 11114, Taiwan
[2] Graduate School of Creative Industry Design, National Taiwan University of Art
Ban-Ciao City, Taipei 22058, Taiwan
tyraywang@gmail.com

**Abstract.** Making up a facial symbolism is a very specific skill and makeup art in the Chinese opera. The performers use colorful paintings to paint variety of symbolism and line arts on their faces. These emphasize the characteristics, positions, ages, and the provenances of the characters. The method of this research applies the content analysis method to comprise a literature review of the painted-face of Jing role in the Chinese opera. The literature review has been handled and coded using the qualitative data analysis software NVivo 10. The results of this research found some indication by painted-face attribute values comparison, sources diversity reference, and nodes clustered by attribute value for indicating similarity or unusual from the original texts. In conclude the object of analysis in this research, the facial patterns which appear on the face of a Jing character, can be defined as "descriptive", "hereditary", "imitative", and "name-based" in generally. To the uninitiated audience, the face patterns and colors, which appear upon the stage, may rapidly become an indistinguishable blur. Fortunately in performer's position, one has to unravel the secrets of Chinese face painting is to learn to recognize the symbols and signs stamped upon each Chinese opera character's face.

**Keywords:** Chinese opera, Painted-face, Facial Symbolism, Content Analysis.

## 1 Introduction

For the ritual purposes in worldwide, masks and facial makeup are common in singing and dancing activities in different cultures. Throughout the human history, the masquerades in Europe and the facial makeup of American Indians both enjoy a long makeup experiences. But in Chinese society, mask and facial makeup were assimilated into traditional opera and developed along a unique and magnificence path. Scholars of Chinese opera are unable for certain to say where the tradition of painted-face of Chinese opera came about, but they seem surmise it began with the wearing of masks for the battle of war in Chinese ancient times. The earliest record of mask wearing dates to the Zhou Dynasty (1046-256 BC), during which masks were worn when stories about ghosts and gods were performed. Another historical story mentions King Lanling of the Northern Qi Dynasty (550-577). It seems King Lanling

P.L.P. Rau (Ed.): CCD/HCII 2013, Part I, LNCS 8023, pp. 493–502, 2013.
© Springer-Verlag Berlin Heidelberg 2013

was a brave warrior, but his facial appearance was quite feminine, and he found it difficult to be intimidating in a battle. He eventually took to wearing a horrify mask when riding on his horse showed in every combat after all. The legend of King Lanling somehow gave rise to a form of song and dance performance well known as "Big Face". During the Tang Dynasty (618-907), "Big Face" performances were popular, as they were believed to confer good fortune upon Tang soldiers to embark upon a military campaign. "Big Face" performers who used their teeth to keep the masks in place wore wooden masks [1]. Hampered by the necessity of using their mouths, mask-wearers could not sing. Later, Masks and makeup were universal for the zaju (a variety play consisting of a prelude, the main play in one or two scenes, and a musical epilogue) by the time of the Song (960-1279) and Jin (1115-1234) dynasties [2]. After the formation of northern zaju and southern drama, the techniques of masks and makeup were improved incessantly. The masks were abandoned in favor of face painting. It applied directly to the face as actors began to both sing and dance during the performances. From the very beginning of the face painting, there are only four colors of pace painting were used which are red, white, black and blue. Over time, the patterns and colors employed were stylized and standardized from generation to generation [3], and the transformations of Chinese opera painted-faces design were different during the Periods (see Fig. 1).

According to the above historical records, such progress from those masks made by wood, or to the practice of face paintings on a real human face, the painted-face of Chinese opera does transformed by some factors not only from the artist themselves but also the social aspect both in life styles of audience and artificial techniques. Thus, the purpose of this research is not going to discuss about the sociology of historical aspects but focus on analyzing the fundamental basis of cognition design about the painted-face of Chinese opera performances.

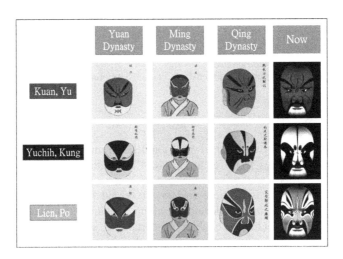

**Fig. 1.** The Transformation of Chinese Opera Painted-faces Design during different Periods

## 2    Literature Review

### 2.1    The Extraordinary Appearance of Chinese Opera Mask

To talk about traditional aesthetics of facial symbolism in Chinese opera, the colors of the facial symbolism especially stand for the personalities and the characteristics [1]. For examples, the red means the loyalty and righteousness, like Kuan, Yu had a red face (the martial god in Chinese society) in the time of Three Kingdoms period (220-280). The green face means the violent man. The blue face means fierce and insidious characteristics. The black face means straight-minded. The yellow face means slyness. The golden and silver color on the face means the characters are are the roles of Chinese fairy. The purple face means steadiness. The white face means very bogus and evil man like Tsao Tsao for example.

Making up a facial symbolism is a very specific skill and makeup art in the Chinese opera. The performers use colorful paintings to paint variety of symbolism and line arts on their faces. These emphasize the characteristics, positions, ages, and the provenances of the characters. This kind of characters is called "Jing" or "Hualian" (painted-face role) by Chinese opera professional. Each kind of painted-faces has its own specific way of makeup called "Facial Symbolism". Every facial symbolism of the paintings and the drawings of Jing characters have different styles. They will be painted on the parts of performers' face (forehead, the two sides of the nose, cheeks, eyebrows, and mouth). Generally speaking, there are four kinds of characteristics of the characters by the facial symbolism in the Chinese opera: the furious and raging people, the bad guys, ghosts and fairy figures and those who showed up in the histories and fictions. In general, the less colorful and complicated the painted-faces are, the higher positions the characters are, and the steadier personalities the characters are. On the contrary, the more colorful and complicated the painted-faces are, the lower positions the characters are, and the more violent characteristics the characters are.

In this research, we were not include all of the painted-faces from the texts that we found but choose only 48 painted-faces of characters [4], whom had with background story, out of a total 500 more (see Fig. 2).

**Fig. 2.** The Visual Sources of 48 Painted-faces in Nvivo10 Software

## 2.2    The Combinations of Facial Symbolism in Chinese Opera

Art historians have commented that Chinese artists traditionally seemed less interested in creating realistic depictions of the natural world, and more concerned with capturing the spirit or essence of an object [1]. As shown in table 1 and 2, we indicate categories of texts that the major colors, facial patterns, eyebrows, eyes, foreheads, nose, and mouth were represent different parts of facial painting in Chinese opera.

**Table 1.** The Attributes of Classification Comparison

| | |
|---|---|
| Colors | Black, Blue, Gold, Gray, Green, Light-green, Ocher, Oil-white, Pink, Purple, Red, Silver, White, Yellow |
| Facial Patterns | Fractured, Genie, Monk, Numeral Six, Numeral Ten, Ruined, Solid, Three-tile, Unique, Variegated, Villainous |
| Eyebrows | Basic Eyebrows, Bat Eyebrows, Buddhist Swastika Eyebrows, Butterfly Eyebrows, Cudgel Eyebrows, Dot Eyebrows, Downward-sloping Eyebrows, Duck's Egg Eyebrows, Elderly Eyebrows, Fire Eyebrows, Gourd Eyebrows, Ladle Eyebrows, Numeral One Eyebrows, Praying Mantis Pincher Eyebrows, Random Eyebrows, Reclining Silkworm Eyebrows, Saw-toothed Eyebrows, Sky-piercing Eyebrows, Sword Eyebrows, Tiger-hook Eyebrows, Triangular Eyebrows, Uneven Eyebrows, Villain Eyebrows, Willow-leaf Eyebrows, Wolf's Tooth Eyebrows |
| Eyes | Bird Eyes, Elderly Eyes, Kidney Eyes, Large Villain Eyes, Laughing Eyes, Phoenix Eyes, Ring Eyes, Straight Eyes, Villain Eyes |
| Foreheads | Bat Forehead, Blue-green Forehead, Eight Trigrams Forehead, Fire Forehead, Gold Coin Forehead, Golden Forehead, Good Fortune Forehead, Gourd Forehead, Long-life Forehead, Marred Forehead, Moon Forehead, Original Form Forehead, Peach Forehead, Random Forehead, Red Forehead, T'ai Chi Forehead, Tiger Forehead, True Nature Forehead |
| Nose | Basic Nose, Curled Nose, Full Nose, Hooked Nose, Laughing Nose, Long or Short Nose, Villain Nose |
| Mouth | Bird Mouth, Crooked Mouth, Disdainful Mouth, Fire Brazier Mouth, Gold Ingot Mouth, Tiger Mouth, Water Chestnut Mouth, Bearded |

## 2.3    The Processes of Painted-Face in Chinese Opera

A typical make-up kit contains brushes, water-based paints, powder and oil-based paints [1]. The facial patterns of a Jing character are most often painted on with a brush, but they can be applied by hand as well. Although the basic pattern for a particular character is standardized, the face-painter must take into account the individual shape and features of the face upon which he is working. Figure 3 shows the basic steps for the make-up of four main roles in Chinese opera performance. For the Jing role, Kao Teng, the make-up processes are: 1.) A base of white powder is applied, and black powder is applied around the eyes to prevent oil-based make-up from seeping into them during a performance; additional black powder is applied under the nose to prevent the beard slipping off from the actor's face. 2.) A brush dipped in white paint is used to draw the approximate position of the eyebrows, eyes, nose, and facial patterns. 3.) Black oil-based paint is applied to the unpainted areas. 4.) Another layer of white paint is added to set the facial pattern in place. 5.) Pink powder is dusted onto the cheeks over the white paint. 6.) A single line of oil-based red paint is applied to the forehead [4].

**Table 2.** The Facial Pattern Distribution of 48 Jing Roles

| Jing Roles | Colors | Eyebrows | Eyes | Facial Patterns | Forehead | Mouth | Nose |
|---|---|---|---|---|---|---|---|
| Chang, Fei | Black | Butterfly Eyebrows | Ring Eyes | Numeral Ten | Marred Forehead | Bearded | Laughing Nose |
| Chang, Yu-Chun | Purple | Sword Eyebrows | Straight Eyes | Three-tile | Good Fortune Forehead | Bearded | Basic Nose |
| Chao, Kuang-Yin | Red | Uneven Eyebrows | No specific classification | Solid | Marred Forehead | Bearded | No specific classification |
| Chiang, Chung | Black | No specific classification | No specific classification | Fractured | Long-life Forehead | Bearded | Long or Short Nose |
| Chiang, Wei | Red | Triangular Eyebrows | Straight Eyes | Three-tile | T'ai Chi Forehead | Bearded | Basic Nose |
| Chiao, Tsan | Black | Willow-leaf Eyebrows | Laughing Eyes | Variegated | Marred Forehead | Bearded | Hooked Nose |
| Chin Chien Pao | Gold | No specific classification | No specific classification | Genie | Original Form Forehead | Tiger Mouth | No specific classification |
| Chou, Tsang | Black | Numeral One Eyebrows | No specific classification | Variegated | Blue-green Forehead | Bearded | No specific classification |
| Chu, Ling | Black | Downward-sloping Eyebrows | No specific classification | Fractured | True Nature Forehead | Bearded | No specific classification |
| Fake-Li, Kuei | Black | Willow-leaf Eyebrows | No specific classification | Fractured | Marred Forehead | Bearded | Long or Short Nose |
| Hsishou, Yuan | Black | No specific classification | Laughing Eyes | Fractured | Long-life Forehead | Bearded | Hooked Nose |
| Hsiang, Yu | Black | Buddhist Swastika Eyebrows | No specific classification | Unique | Marred Forehead | Bearded | No specific classification |
| Hsieh, Hu | Blue | No specific classification | Straight Eyes | Three-tile | Peach Forehead | Disdainful Mouth | Basic Nose |
| Hsin, Wen-Li | Black | Wolf's Tooth Eyebrows | No specific classification | Fractured | Marred Forehead | Bearded | Long or Short Nose |
| Hsu, Chu | Black | Bat Eyebrows | No specific classification | Variegated | Bat Forehead | Bearded | Long or Short Nose |
| Hsu, Shih-Ying | Green | Wolf's Tooth Eyebrows | No specific classification | Fractured | Marred Forehead | Disdainful Mouth | Long or Short Nose |
| Hua, Te-Lei | Oil-white | Villain Eyebrows | Large Villain Eyes | Three-tile | Marred Forehead | Bearded | Villain Nose |
| Huang, Chao | Red | Numeral One Eyebrows | No specific classification | Unique | Gold Coin Forehead | Bearded | No specific classification |
| Huang, Kai | Red | Dot Eyebrows | No specific classification | Numeral Six | Marred Forehead | Bearded | No specific classification |
| Kao, Teng | Oil-white | Praying Mantis Pincher Eyebrows | Large Villain Eyes | Three-tile | Marred Forehead | Bearded | Villain Nose |
| Kuan, Ping | White | Sword Eyebrows | Straight Eyes | Three-tile | Marred Forehead | No specific classification | Curled Nose |
| Kuan, Yu | Red | Reclining Silkworm Eyebrows | Phoenix Eyes | Solid | Marred Forehead | Bearded | No specific classification |
| Li, Ching | Red | Triangular Eyebrows | Straight Eyes | Three-tile | Golden Forehead | Bearded | Basic Nose |
| Li, Kuei | Black | Willow-leaf Eyebrows | No specific classification | Fractured | Marred Forehead | Bearded | Long or Short Nose |
| Liao, Chi-Chung | Red | Triangular Eyebrows | Elderly Eyes | Three-tile | Marred Forehead | Bearded | Basic Nose |
| Lien, Po | Pink | Elderly Eyebrows | Elderly Eyes | Three-tile | Marred Forehead | Bearded | Basic Nose |
| Lu, Chih-Shen | White | Cudgel Eyebrows | Kidney Eyes | Monk | Marred Forehead | Bearded | Laughing Nose |
| Ma, Wu | Blue | Saw-toothed Eyebrows | No specific classification | Variegated | Marred Forehead | Bearded | Long or Short Nose |
| Meng, Liang | Red | Gourd Eyebrows | No specific classification | Variegated | Gourd Forehead | Bearded | Hooked Nose |
| Niu, Mao | Green | Bat Eyebrows | No specific classification | Fractured | Marred Forehead | Bearded | Long or Short Nose |
| Pao, Cheng | Black | Ladle Eyebrows | No specific classification | Solid | Moon Forehead | Bearded | No specific classification |
| Ssuma, Shih | Red | Bat Eyebrows | No specific classification | Variegated | Marred Forehead | Bearded | Hooked Nose |
| Sun, Wu-Kung | Red | No specific classification | No specific classification | Genie | No specific classification | No specific classification | No specific classification |
| Ti, Lung-Kang | Purple | Elderly Eyebrows | Elderly Eyes | Three-tile | Marred Forehead | Bearded | Basic Nose |
| Tien, Wei | Yellow | No specific classification | No specific classification | Fractured | Marred Forehead | Bearded | Long or Short Nose |
| Tou, Erh-Tun | Blue | Tiger-hook Eyebrows | Straight Eyes | Three-tile | Marred Forehead | Bearded | Long or Short Nose |
| Tsao, Jen | Red | Triangular Eyebrows | Straight Eyes | Three-tile | Marred Forehead | Bearded | Basic Nose |
| Tsao, Tsao | White | Basic Eyebrows | Villain Eyes | Villainous | Marred Forehead | Bearded | No specific classification |
| Wu, Cheng-Hei | Black | Villain Eyebrows | No specific classification | Fractured | Marred Forehead | Bearded | Long or Short Nose |
| Wu, Chu | Black | No specific classification | No specific classification | Fractured | Marred Forehead | Tiger Mouth | Long or Short Nose |
| Wu, Li-Hei | Black | Butterfly Eyebrows | No specific classification | Variegated | Marred Forehead | Bearded | Long or Short Nose |
| Yang, Kuang | Purple | Numeral One Eyebrows | No specific classification | Variegated | Original Form Forehead | Bearded | Long or Short Nose |
| Yang, Yen-Ssu | Black | Saw-toothed Eyebrows | No specific classification | Variegated | Tiger Forehead | Tiger Mouth | Long or Short Nose |
| Yao, Chi | Black | Elderly Eyebrows | Elderly Eyes | Numeral Ten | Marred Forehead | Bearded | Basic Nose |
| Yao, Kang | Black | Saw-toothed Eyebrows | No specific classification | Variegated | Marred Forehead | Tiger Mouth | Villain Nose |
| Yuchih, Kung | Black | Dot Eyebrows | Elderly Eyes | Numeral Six | Marred Forehead | Bearded | No specific classification |
| Yuchih, Pao-Lin | Black | Sky-piercing Eyebrows | No specific classification | Variegated | Marred Forehead | Tiger Mouth | No specific classification |
| Yuwen, Cheng-Tu | Yellow | Uneven Eyebrows | No specific classification | Three-tile | Marred Forehead | Bearded | Long or Short Nose |

Above categorized and listed painted-face sources were by Nvivo10 software

**Fig. 3.** The Make-up Steps of the Four Main Roles in Chinese Opera

# 3     Research Methods

Content analysis is one of the most direct methods of textual analysis which can be applied to a range of media and cultural artifacts. But the main weakness of content analysis to date has been that it is very laborious: coding hundreds of facial graphics and texts of Chinese opera can be very time-consuming [5]. So, this research comprises a literature review of the painted-face of Jing role in the Chinese opera. The literature review has been handled and coded using the qualitative data analysis software NVivo 10. It was easier with counting and classifying for the texts. In the first phase will be import 48 visual sources then processed the codes and nodes by selected texts of that in the software. Second will be query and analysis of literature exploring the necessity of researching on the Jing role in Chinese opera culture, the obligation of the research orientation to develop guidelines for this research, and the unique aspects of the painted-face that complicate the process of cognition design those mask painting methodology. The third phase will be find out some indication by attribute values comparison, sources diversity reference, and nodes clustered by attribute value for indicating similarity or unusual from the original texts.

# 4     Findings and Discussion

The facial patterns of Jing role are highly stylized and resemble not at all an actual person's face. This is the beauty of face painting in Chinese opera. By sacrificing realism, the artists of Chinese opera are able to capture the inner nature of a character in all its glory or ugliness. The object of analysis in this research, the facial patterns which appear on the face of a Jing character, can be defined as "descriptive", "hereditary", "imitative", and "name-based" in generally.

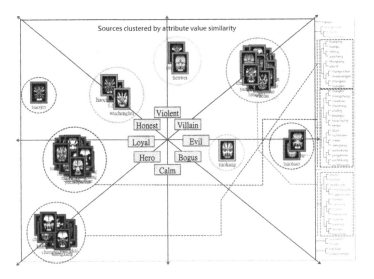

**Fig. 4.** The Clustered Comparison of Personality Types

### 4.1   Descriptive

The faces of most opera characters are designed to be illustrative of their personality. For example, villains have white faces to symbolize their cold-bloodedness. The character Hsiang, Yu, who were in the time of Chu Kingdom during the period of Warring States (1030-223 BC), is depicted with an iron trident inscribed upon his forehead to symbolize his great strength and proclivity towards violent action. The coding of personalities in this research are categorized as "hero", "villain", "violent", "calm", "loyal", "evil", "honest", and "bogus". The findings in this approach as shown in Figure 4, the clustered comparison of personality types are based on the attribute value similarities of painted-face in Chinese opera. It indicates that the character Tsio, Jen is a villain man but had a loyal personality. On the contrary, the character Yao, Kang is a hero but had bad inner personalities. The rest painted-faces of the results are indicated with each other to each group as by personality attributes.

### 4.2   Hereditary

Father and son characters feature similar facial patterns and colors to indicate a family resemblance. In such a case, a character's face may not be a true indicator of his personality. As shown in figure 5, both groups are in the relationship of father and son. But frankly, fewer items as shown in the facial pattern comparison of father and son are really not a true indicator of personality.

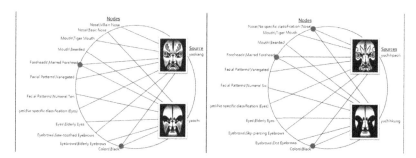

**Fig. 5.** The Facial Pattern Comparison of Father and Son

### 4.3   Imitative

When two characters are similar in personalities and behaviors, they may be made up to resemble one another. This is the case with the characters Li, Kuei and his imposter, Li, Kuei, as well as for the characters Chang, Fei and Chiao, Tsan. According to the texts, the latter two are so similar in personality that their painted-faces are identical with each other but the exception of that Chang, Fei has large eyes while Chiao, Tsan has small eyes [1]. As shown in table 3, we found out the first two characters mentioned above are all at same categories, but the second two characters are the same in the fewer items.

So, we used a model for indicating clearly the patterns of Chang, Fei and Chiao, Tsan as shown in figure 6. It shows these two characters' personalities are the same types. But in the facial pattern parts are not really at the same categories. So, we tried to dig in more by scientific way on the quantitative method, Pearson Correlation

Coefficient, in the Nvivo 10 software. The findings are shown in table 4 and figure 7 to evident more about this unusual issue that these two characters are not exactly the same in nowadays even they were same in the past.

**Table 3.** The Attributes of Classification Comparison

| Painted-face (All Attributes) | Colors | Facial Patterns | Eyebrows | Eyes | Forehead | Nose | Mouth |
|---|---|---|---|---|---|---|---|
| Chang, Fei | Black | Numeral Ten | Butterfly Eyebrows | Ring Eyes | Marred Forehead | Laughing Nose | Bearded |
| Chiao, Tsan | Black | Variegated | Willow-leaf Eyebrows | Laughing Eyes | Marred Forehead | Hooked Nose | Bearded |
| Li, Kuei | Black | Fractured | Willow-leaf Eyebrows | No specific | Fractured | Long or Short | Bearded |
| Li, Kuei (imposter) | Black | Fractured | Willow-leaf Eyebrows | No specific | Fractured | Long or Short | Bearded |

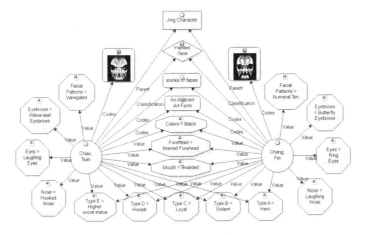

**Fig. 6.** The Face Design Comparison of Chang, Fei & Chiao, Tsan

**Table 4.** The Clustered Comparison of Chang, Fei and Chiao, Tsan

| Clustered Comparison | Pearson Correlation Coefficient |
|---|---|
| By Word Similarity | 0.5 |
| By coding Similarity | -0.769231 |
| By Attribute Value Similarity | 0.381513 |
| By Attribute Value Similarity (with Types A to E) | 0.626667 |

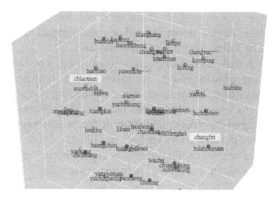

**Fig. 7.** The Clustered Comparison by Coding Similarity of Chang, Fei & Chiao, Tsan

## 4.4    Name-Based

According to the texts, often a character's name or nickname influences the look of the character's face in Chinese opera performance [1]. In a case that keeping with his nickname "Green-faced Tiger", the character Hsu Shih-ying is depicted with a green face as shown in figure 8, while coding stripes were analyzed in the Nvivo 10 software.

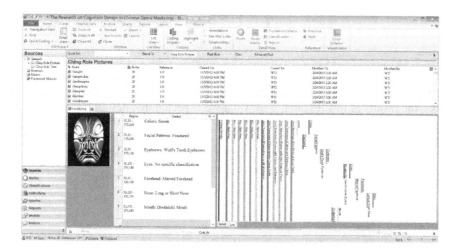

**Fig. 8.** Jing Role's coding stripes: "Green-faced Tiger" (Hsu, Shih-ying)

## 5    Conclusion

After the limitation of this content analysis research, firstly we could conclude to the uninitiated audience, the face patterns and colors, which appear upon the stage, may rapidly become an indistinguishable blur. Fortunately in performer's position, one has to unravel the secrets of Chinese face painting is to learn to recognize the symbols and signs stamped upon each Chinese opera character's face. Such makeup for characters in Chinese opera has been passed down in methods and formations from generation to generation and must be learned from specialist masters.

So, the skill in such makeup is extremely sophisticated: a person's face, even physique, can be radically transformed in accordance with dramatic needs to become handsome or ugly, fat or thin, tall or short. What makes Jing characters such a colorful and fascinating part of Chinese opera is the fact that the patterns painted upon their faces are very revealing of their personalities in different attribute value combinations (See Figure 9). Whether the characters are hero or villain, calm or violent, loyal or evil, honest or bogus, higher or lower social status, an experienced viewer of Chinese opera has only to glance upon the face of a Jing character to know his true nature only by two attributes, colors and facial patterns, are good enough.

**Fig. 9.** 48 Painted-faces Compared by Selected Attribute Value Combinations in Nvivo10

Thus, in terms of the relationships among cognitive design on those patterns of masks, the results of this research were what we expected that design factors could be of enormous value to a performer oneself. But both in the social and cognitive dimensions are essential issues for sure in nowadays. For the patterns design competence of Chinese opera painted-face is one thing, but for the naturalization and globalization will be another barrier to conquer in the mass culture society.

# References

1. Wang, S.Z.: The Face of Chinese Opera. Han Guang Culture Press, Taipei (1984)
2. Bao, C.J., Cao, J.: Culture of China: Fascinating Stage Arts. Foreign Languages Press, Beijing (2002)
3. Zhang, B.J.: Chinese Opera and Painted-Face. National Fu-Hsing Dramatic Arts Academy, Taipei (1981)
4. Official Website of Chinese Opera-Peking Opera, http://jinju.koo.org.tw
5. Stokes, J.: How to Do Media and Cultural Studies. SAGE Publications Ltd., London (2013)

# Feature Extraction of Individual Differences for Identification Recognition Based on Resting EEG

Rui Xu, Dong Ming[*], Yanru Bai, Jing Liu, Hongzhi Qi, Qiang Xu, Peng Zhou, Lixin Zhang, and Baikun Wan

Department of Biomedical Engineering,
College of Precision Instrument and Opto-electronics Engineering,
Tianjin University, Tianjin 300072, China
richardming@tju.edu.cn

**Abstract.** Biometric recognition based on individual difference was commonly used in many aspects in life. Compared with the traditional features used in person identification, EEG-based biometry is an emerging research topic with high security and uniqueness, and it may open new research applications in the future. However, little work has been done within this area. In this paper, four feature extraction techniques were employed to characterize the resting EEG signals: AR model, time-domain power spectrum, frequency-domain power spectrum and phase locking value. In our experiments using 20 healthy subjects, the classification accuracy by support vector machine reached 90.52% with AR model parameters, highest of the four kinds of features. The results show the potential applications of resting EEG signal in person identification.

**Keywords:** individual differences, person identification, resting EEG, AR model, support vector machine.

## 1 Introduction

In recent years, biometric recognition has received general concerns all over the world and played a key role in identification recognition applied to access control system, building gate control, digital multimedia access, transaction authentication or secure teleworking [1]. Each kind of biometric features needs to be evaluated in some aspects, such as universality, uniqueness, permanence and so on [2]. Common-used features including fingerprint, eye retinas and irises, and facial patterns, have achieved wide applications. But there exists limitations to the traditional biometric recognition methods to some extent. Therefore, it is necessary to come up with novel methods that could compensate these limitations.

Our attention is paid on the individual differences based on resting EEG signals which is a novel attempt in this field of biometric recognition. Genetically-specific features of EEG form the basis of a person identification method. Compared with other biometric features like fingerprint, this modality has several advantages: 1) it is

---

[*] Corresponding author.

P.L.P. Rau (Ed.): CCD/HCII 2013, Part I, LNCS 8023, pp. 503–509, 2013.
© Springer-Verlag Berlin Heidelberg 2013

confidential, 2) it is difficult to mimic, and 3) it is almost impossible to steal [1]. It has been shown in previous studies that the brain-wave pattern of every individual is unique and that electroencephalogram (EEG) can be used for biometric identification [3]. In 1999, the group of M. Poulos et al first made an attempt to experimentally investigate the connection between a person's EEG and generally-specific information using AR Modeling and achieved correct classification scores at the range of 72% to 84%, which showed the potential of EEG used for person identification [4]. Then Palaniappan et al extracted biometric features based on the spectral power of EEG signals for classification by a fuzzy Neural Network [5]. More recently, Isao Nakanishi et al adopted the concavity and convexity of spectral variance in the alpha band of EEG as the features with low computational load and obtained Equal Error Rate of 11% [6].

Autoregressive (AR) methods have been used in a number of studies to model EEG data by representing the signal at each channel as a linear combination of the signal at previous time points [7-10]. This method provides a compact, computationally efficient representation of EEG signals, and AR model parameters are invariant to scaling changes in the data that can arise from inter-subject variations, such as scalp and skull thickness [10]. Time-Domain and Frequency-Domain Power Spectrum are two methods to estimate the power distribution among different time and frequencies. Unlike these methods mentioned above, Phase Locking Values (PLV) was developed to quantify in a statistical sense the phase synchronization of such systems from experimental data and to characterize their coupling [11-13]. It was first proposed to estimate the instantaneous phase relationship between two neuroelectric or biomagnetic signals and to apply it to intracortically recorded signals in humans [14]. Support vector machine was adopted to classify these feature parameters.

The main purpose of this study is to highlight the individual differences in resting EEG by using four kinds of feature extraction techniques and apply this feature into biometric recognition on the basis of support vector machine. The reminder of this paper is organized as follows: Section 2 briefly describes the methods of feature extraction and classification. Section 3 summarizes the results. Finally, Section 4 concludes.

## 2    Methods

### 2.1    Subjects

Twenty healthy right-handed subjects (mean age: 23.20±1.28) participated in this present study. None of the subjects reported any neurological or chronic diseases. The written informed consents were given by all the subjects prior to the experiments.

### 2.2    EEG Recordings

Subjects were comfortably seated in an electrical shield room during the experiment. They were asked to keep their body still and eyes closed for two minutes during the EEG recording.

The resting EEG was collected using a Neuroscan Synamps apparatus with an electrode cap of 64 electrodes (referenced to channel Cz). The recording was undertaken with a sampling rate of 1000 Hz and a bandpass filter (0.05–100 Hz). As Cz was set as the reference, the EEG at Cz, CPz, Pz and other central channels was very weak and it was difficult to extract features from these channels. Then offline, we changed the reference from Cz to left and right mastoid, precisely the mean value of EEG at mastoids.

## 2.3    Feature Extraction

Four kinds of approaches, including AR Modeling, Power Spectrum in Time Domain and Frequency Domain and Phase-Locking Values, were adopted to extract the individual difference information from resting EEG.

**AR Modeling.** The AR model is described by a linear difference equation in the time domain as

$$x(k) = \sum_{i=1}^{P} a(i)x(k-i) + e(k) \tag{1}$$

where a current sample of the time series $x(k)$ is a linear function of previous samples plus an independent and identically distributed (i.i.d) white noise input $e(k)$ [15], and $P$ denotes the number of time points in the past that are used to model the current time point.

In our study, the model order was set to 4 according AIC. In detail, the first four parameters of AR Modeling of each channel of EEG were used as the features for identification, totally forming a feature vector with 64×4 dimensions per sample.

**Time-Domain Power Spectrum.** This spectrum feature is defined as

$$TPS(c) = \frac{1}{N} \sum_{n=1}^{N} [x_c(n)]^2 \tag{2}$$

where $x(n)$ is time series of EEG signals, $N$ is the number of points and $c = 1, \cdots, 64$ denotes the EEG channel.

In order to minimize the difference between EEG from different channels, a standardization method was employed:

$$TPS_S(c) = \frac{TPS(c)}{\sum_{k=1}^{64} TPS(k)} \tag{3}$$

The TPS feature $TPS_S$ of each subject was calculated to a vector of 64×1 dimensions.

**Frequency-Domain Power Spectrum.** The power spectrum in frequency domain reveals energy changes in different frequencies.

$$FPS(c) = \frac{1}{N} \sum_{n=1}^{N} [\tilde{x}(n)]^2 \qquad (4)$$

where $\tilde{x}(n)$ was the EEG amplitude in a given frequency range, and $N$ was the total number of frequency points in this frequency range. The standardization method was also used as:

$$FPS_S(c) = \frac{FPS(c)}{\sum_{k=1}^{64} FPS(k)} \qquad (5)$$

In our study, EEG signals were transferred into frequency domain using Fast Fourier Transform (FFT). The whole frequency range was divided into five parts. The FPS calculation was taken within each of these five frequency ranges, and thus the FPS feature of each subject was a vector of 64×5 dimensions.

**Phase-Locking Values.** In order to obtain the instantaneous phase, we adopted the Hilbert transformation to transfer the EEG $x(t)$ to a complex-valued signal.

$$\tilde{x}(t) = Hilbert(x(t)) \qquad (6)$$

The instantaneous phase $\varphi$ was obtained analytically:

$$\varphi(t) = \mathrm{Im}(\ln(x(t))) \qquad (7)$$

The phase difference between two channels of EEG signals $x_1(t)$ and $x_2(t)$ was calculated as $\Delta\varphi = \varphi_1 - \varphi_2$. So the PLV could be obtained by

$$PLV = \left| \left\langle e^{i\Delta\varphi} \right\rangle \right| \qquad (8)$$

where $\langle \cdot \rangle$ meant time average.

The computation of Phase-Locking Values was made between each of 676 pairs of EEG recorded from different channels, obtaining a feature vector with 676 dimensions per sample.

## 2.4    Classification

The features extracted by the above mentioned techniques were classified by support vector machine (SVM) to obtain the statistical classification accuracy of all samples. Simultaneously, $k$-fold cross validation was applied during the classification to make the accuracy reliable.

Support vector machine developed by V. Vapnik, was a modern computational learning method based on statistical learning theory. The central idea was to separate data $X$ into two classes by finding a weight vector $\omega \in R^d$ and an offset $b \in R$ of a hyper plane

$$H : R^d \rightarrow \{-1,1\}$$
$$x \mapsto sign(\omega \cdot x + b)$$

(9)

with the largest possible margin [16]. $x$ was the element of $X$ with the dimension of $d$. The purpose of SVM was to separate one class from the other. In order to recognize twenty classes or subjects, we used 190 classifiers to separate every two of these twenty classes. Finally, 10-fold cross validation was adopted to calculate the classification accuracy.

## 3     Results

The dimensions of above-mentioned feature vectors were displayed in Table 1. These vectors with different dimensions composed the inputs of classifiers.

**Table 1.** The EEG features to be classified

| Classes | Samples/Class | Feature Dimensions | | | |
| --- | --- | --- | --- | --- | --- |
| | | AR Model | TPS | FPS | PLV |
| 20 | 40 | 256 | 64 | 320 | 676 |

The results in this thesis showed that the best method of feature extraction for individual recognition was AR Modeling with the highest accuracy of 90.52%, followed by 82.63% with Time-domain Power Spectrum, 80.00% with Phase Locking Values and 67.37% with Frequency-domain Power Spectrum. The efficiency of AR Modeling was in accordance with what had been proposed in previous studies [17][18].

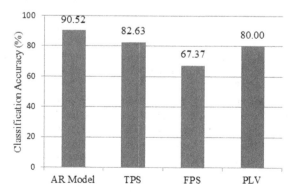

**Fig. 1.** The result of classification based on SVM for four kinds of features (AR model, TPS, FPS and PLV)

## 4     Conclusion

In this paper, a novel idea was provided for the individual differences analysis of resting EEG and for its practical design in the field of human-computer interaction especially for individual rehabilitation robots. In details, we investigated AR model, time-domain and frequency-domain power spectrum and phase locking value to extract the characteristic features of resting EEG among different subjects.

Our research proposed a feasible way for feature extraction in identification recognition, taking advantage of individual differences in EEG signals. Except for the frequency-domain power spectrum, the classification accuracies of these features were all above 80.00%, which verified the fact that EEG signals could be used as a kind of biometric feature. AR model parameters with the highest classification accuracy (90.52%) could represent individual differences in resting EEG well.

However, there may be more appropriate mental tasks for person identification than the resting EEG. In practice, different categories of EEG signals and channel optimization should be added in the following works, and EEG should be used with other biometric features to show complementary advantages in the future.

**Acknowledgments.** The authors would like to acknowledge all members of the Neural Engineering & Rehabilitation Lab of Tianjin University (TUNERL) for their valuable contributions to this research. This research was supported by National Natural Science Foundation of China (No. 30970875, 81171423, 61172008, 90920015), National Key Technology R&D Program of the Ministry of Science and Technology of China (No. 2012BAI34B02) and Program for New Century Excellent Talents in University of the Ministry of Education of China.

## References

1. Marcel, S., del R. Millán, J.: Person Authentication Using Brainwaves (EEG) and Maximum A Posteriori Model Adaptation. IEEE Transactions on Pattern Analysis and Machine Intelligence 29, 743–748 (2007)
2. Clarke, R.: Human Identification in Information Systems: Management Challenges and Public Policy Issues. Information Technology & People 7, 6–37 (1994)
3. Marcel, S., del R. Millán, J.: Person authentication using brainwaves (EEG) and maximum a posteriori model adaptation. IEEE Transactions on Pattern Analysis and Machine Intelligence 29(4), 743–748 (2007)
4. Poulos, M., Rangoussi, M., Chrissikopoulos, V., Evangelou, A.: Person identification based on parametric processing of the EEG. In: The 6th IEEE International Conference on Electronics, Circuits and Systems, vol. 1, pp. 283–286 (1999)
5. Palaniappan, R., Ravi, K.V.R.: A new method to identify individuals using signals from the brain. In: The Joint Conference of the 4th International Conference on Information, Communications and Signal Processing, vol. 3, pp. 1442–1445 (2003)
6. Nakanishi, I., Baba, S., Miyamoto, C.: EEG based biometric authentication using new spectral features. In: International Symposium on Intelligent Signal Processing and Communication Systems, pp. 651–654 (2009)

7. Paranjape, R.B., Mahovsky, J., Benedicenti, L., Koles, Z.: The electroencephalogram as a biometric. In: Electrical and Computer Engineering (2001)
8. Poulos, M., Rangoussi, M., Alexandris, N., Evangelou, A.: Person identification from the EEG using nonlinear signal classification. Methods of Information in Medicine 41(1), 64–75 (2002)
9. Palaniappan, R.: Electroencephalogram signals from imagined activities: a novel biometric identifier for a small population. In: Belli, F., Radermacher, F.J. (eds.) IEA/AIE 1992. LNCS, vol. 604, pp. 604–611. Springer, Heidelberg (1992)
10. Lawhern, V., David Hairston, W., McDowell, K., Westerfield, M., Robbins, K.: Detection and classification of subject-generated artifacts in EEG signals using autoregressive models. Journal of Neuroscience Methods 208, 181–189 (2012)
11. Rosenblum, M.G., Pikovsky, A.S., Kurths, J.: Phase synchronization of chaotic oscillators. Phys. Rev. Lett. 76, 1804–1807 (1996)
12. Rosenblum, M., Pikovsky, A., Kurths, J., Schafer, C., Tass, P.A.: Phase synchronization: from theory to data analysis. In: Moss, F., Gielen, S. (eds.) Handbook of Biological Physics, vol. 4, pp. 279–321
13. Sazonov, A.V., Ho, C.K., Bergmans, J.W.M., Arends, J.B.A.M., Griep, P.A.M., Verbitskiy, E.A., Cluitmans, P.J.M., Boon, P.A.J.M.: An investigation of the phase locking index for measuring of interdependency of cortical source signals recorded in the EEG. Biological Cybernetics 100, 129–146 (2009)
14. Lachaux, J.-P., Rodriguez, E., Martinerie, J., Varela, F.J.: Measuring phase synchrony in brain signals. Human Brain Mapping 8, 194–208 (1999)
15. Jain, S., Deshpande, G.: Parametric modeling of brain signals. In: Proceedings of Technology for Life: North Carolina Symposium on Biotechnology and Bioinformatics, pp. 85–91 (2004)
16. Lal, T.N., Schröder, M., Hinterberger, T., Weston, J., Bogdan, M., Birbaumer, N., Schölkopf, B.: Support vector channel selection in BCI. IEEE Transations on Biomedical Engineering 51(6), 1003–1010 (2004)
17. Übeylï, E.D.: Least squares support vector machine employing model-based methods coefficients for analysis of EEG signals. Expert System with Applications 37, 233–239 (2010)
18. Lawhern, V., David Hairston, W., McDowell, K., Westerfield, M., Robbins, K.: Detection and classification of subject-generated artifacts in EEG signals using autoregressive models. Journal of Neuroscience Methods 208, 181–189 (2012)

# Enhancing People's Television Experience by Capturing, Memoing, Sharing, and Mixing

Tun-Hao You, Yi-Jui Wu, Cheng-Liang Lin, and Yaliang Chuang

Industrial Technology Research Institute, Rm. 515, Bldg. 51, 195,
Sec. 4, Chung Hising Rd., Chutung, Hisnchu 31040, Taiwan
{michaeloil,yjwu,chengliang,yaliang}@itri.org.tw

**Abstract.** Television has long played an important role in providing rich information and delightful entertainment. However, the trend of applying smart technologies in the design of television has yielded complexities that reduce people's enjoyment in television watching. Contextual interview results from our study showed that the participants needed solutions for helping them save interesting content rather than using advanced functions. In line with the rapid development of mobile communications and social networking services, we created and implemented a CatchPo system that includes a CutX TV Memo app that can help viewers use their mobile phone to catch interesting content they are watching on television. Editing the memo and sharing it with friends is easy. Consequently, different cultural groups that consume different media can be connected. Together with the additional CutMix app that enables the viewer to create a collage with their photos and the TV show, the system enhances people's TV experience with useful technology.

**Keywords:** Social TV, Social Network Service, Media Consumsion, Contextual Interview.

## 1 Introduction

Since 1926 when the Scottish inventor John Logie Baird successfully demonstrated a working television system to members of the Royal Institution and to a newspaper reporter(http://en.wikipedia.org/wiki/History_of_television), television has become the most important entertainment and information source for most people. Combined with the development of related technologies, picture and sound quality has greatly improved. Viewers in the United States are currently able to watch various types of content on hundreds of channels. In the 1990s, Internet Protocol television (IPTV) was launched. The first show to broadcast over the Internet was ABC's World News Now [1]. Since then, numerous companies have attempted to enhance the Internet service experience for TV viewers. BBC launched the iPlayer in 2007 to allow viewers to access content that was broadcast 2 weeks prior. In 2010, the first Android based Google TV was released on the market. This innovative product was collaboratively developed by Google, Sony, Intel, and Logitech. The user can use it to watch traditional TV shows and to access over 100,000 on-demand shows, apps, and websites. It was considered the first popular SmartTV model on the market [2].

P.L.P. Rau (Ed.): CCD/HCII 2013, Part I, LNCS 8023, pp. 510–518, 2013.
© Springer-Verlag Berlin Heidelberg 2013

However, comparing available market products, the main SmartTV design is borrowed from the smartphone [3]. A user can download various applications from the App Store. Although certain apps are creative and useful, Park [4] found that because of unreliable computation and Internet connections, most of his study participants were not satisfied using the apps with their SmartTVs. Bächle-Gerstmann [5] also found that participants seldom used SmartTV apps. People simply enjoy watching shows on their TV.

Based on the Park and Bächle-Gerstmann's studies, we considered certain new possibilities for improving the viewer experiences. To understand people's behavior and experience in using their TVs, we chose a contextual interview method [6] for our investigation. Thirty-three participants (aged between 20-70, mean = 35.2) were recruited and interviewed in their homes. Unlike traditional methodologies, this contextual approach emphasizes interaction between the researcher and the participant and helps to observe people's behavior and their environment regarding latent information that is not easy to recall in other places. When the researcher has difficulty understanding a participant's description, the researcher can ask for immediate clarification. This helped us capture real problems and experiences as they existed in participant lives. Our contextual study yielded four interesting points:

1. Television is the main source of entertainment and information for most participants. All of the participants had missed some shows they planned to watch. To resolve such disappointments, 83% of the participants attempted to find the shows through the Internet. However, it is typically difficult to find a show on the Internet. Consequently, two of the participants even called the TV stations to ask them to broadcast the show again. One of the participants asked if it was possible to buy the DVD.
2. Twenty-six percent of the subjects participated in interactive games on Television shows. They tried to play a call-in game, accessed the website to answer questions, and joined the show's *Facebook* fan page. Unfortunately, none of the participants ever won the games or obtained rewards.
3. In addition, 61% of the participants took notes while watching television. One of the participants even had a memo book specifically for television. The information collected is diverse. For example, they recorded the receipt of meals from the cooking show, discount shopping information, and sightseeing places introduced on a travel show, and so forth. They liked to share these notes with friends. Certain participants even planned weekend family activities based on the memos.
4. Finally, 65% of the participants indicated they use other computing devices (e.g., laptop PC, tablet PC, mobile phone) while watching television. The main uses include playing online games, surfing websites, and chatting with friends through social media. They seldom checked information related to the show they were watching. Certain participants indicated that if they needed to focus on the show, they turned off other devices.

Numerous studies have focused on people's behaviors in using complementary secondary screens. In research of viewers in the United States, 40% of tablet and smartphone owners used their devices while watching TV [7]. Only 30% of the usage time was spent gathering information related to the current show being viewed. Similar results found in our cultural interviews reflect this finding. Based on our user study, a television memo concept has been created to develop a mobile App that can facilitate the television viewer in capturing interesting contents of shows he or she watches.

To realize the idea, we implemented a CatchPo system. CatchPo is a television program-capturing cloud service that enables television viewers to instantly capture images and video clips from the program they are watching and provides viewers with metadata on their captured images and clips, such as to location, actors, and product information. The CutX–television memo is the first application based on the CatchPo system that can be used with mobile devices. Since it was launched on December 23, 2012, CutX has been downloaded more than 15,000 times and more than 383,000 memos been created by users.

In the following sections, we review related works and then present the system structure of our service, the design and evaluation of the user interface, and the usage analysis of this service.

## 2    Related Works

New social television systems have been developed related to the convergence trend in media consumption and the growing applications of social networking services (SNS) [8, 9]. Some are focused on networks (such as neXtream), and some are devoted to social interaction between viewers (e.g., IntoNow and GetGlue). Certain systems (e.g., Teleda, developed by NHK in Japan) use online discussions as a mechanism to encourage viewers to watch shows they have not watched before.

### 2.1    NeXtream

NeXtream [9] takes advantage of the integrating capabilities of multiple devices, including smartphones, tablets, notebooks, desktop PCs, and television and restructures the traditional television network by using social networks. The system leverages user interests, communities, and peers to create customized channels specific to each user with contents from TV shows and online materials. A user can watch the streams on any of their devices and the other will act synchronously. Users can continue to watch a television show and use a phone to discuss the content with friends, share opinions, rate the show, and search related information.

This project creates an interface to explore television socially and connects a user with a community through the contents and provides varying levels of interactivity, from passively consuming a series, to actively crafting one's own television and social experience.

### 2.2    IntoNow and GetGlue

IntoNow (http://intonow.com) and GetGlue (http://getglue.com/) are two mobile applications available in the United States. The similarity of these two apps is that they use secondary screens to enhance people's entertainment with checking-in and sharing. They also provide viewers recommendations for shows based on their own or their friends' behavior. By integrating with Twitter and Facebook, viewers can see relevant discussions when watching their favorite television show and "check-in" with IntoNow or GetGlue. They can also comment or interact with others who are also checked-in. To help the user easily find the show to check-in, IntoNow is embedded with SoundPrint technology to detect what he or she is watching. Then, in approximately 5 seconds, the system provides relevant information and social connectedness that can help enrich his or her experience.

### 2.3     NHK's Teleda

With most broadcast media, the relationship between the content and the viewer is similar to a "vertical link." People tend to watch only their familiar shows and seldom try new ones. To encourage viewers to expand their considerations, the Teleda system was proposed by NHK, the public broadcasting organization in Japan [10].  Teleda is a platform that combines video-on-demand and social-networking-service to create "horizontal links" between viewers. By conducting a large-scale trial with 1,032 participants in three months, it was found that interaction between viewers greatly increase their motivations to discover and watch new shows. The system is able to broaden viewers' perspectives and lead them to important issues occurring in the community.

# 3     System Design

Beyond using social networking services, the CatchPo system presented in this paper further to facilitates viewers to capture interesting content and share it instantly with friends. The image or video clips are spread across social media (such as Facebook) and viewed by many people who did not see the traditional broadcast shows. This system connects people from different cultural groups based on their consumption behaviors.

We develop three main components in the CatchPo system in this study. First, a web service provides the contents and data. Second, an application (called CutX) operates on the users' mobile devices. Third, a monitor application enables the content providers to track and control the data captured and shared by viewers.

### 3.1     Usage Scenario

Figure 1 shows a CatchPo system user scenario. A viewer who watches a live basketball game on television can use CutX on a smartphone to capture exciting scenes and share the video clip on his or her personal page of a social networking service (such as Facebook). Alternatively, when another viewer finds a restaurant serving delicious food on a television show, he or she can use CutX to capture an image of the restaurant along with the embedded additional information (e.g., name, location, menu, etc.) provided by the CatchPo system.

Content providers can also benefit from CatchPo. They can use CatchPo to design interactive games and activities with viewers to promote television shows. They can insert a specific object into a television show and ask viewers to capture an image that includes the object to win a prize, or they can ask viewers to capture their favorite scenes, add comments, and post them on television show forums. CatchPo also provides a new television viewer rating method that is superior to traditional techniques.

When a user tries to capture a scene from a TV show, CatchPo records the timestamp and channel information of the request. CatchPo can use this information to analyze the trends of user interest for the TV show. In addition, content providers can recommend advertising related to captured scenes for different capture requests from users.

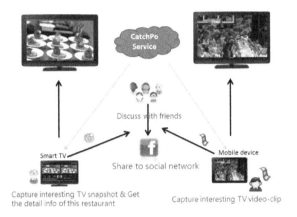

**Fig. 1.** Usage scenario for the CatchPo system

### 3.2  System Architecture

Figure 2 shows the three blocks that compose the system architecture: the content capturing system, a backend web service, and a metadata controlling system.

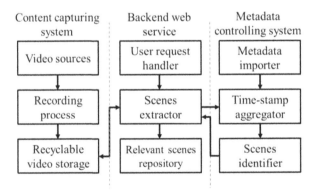

**Fig. 2.** Three function blocks of the CatchPo system

- The content-capturing system continuously records each TV channel (currently supports sources from DTV, cable, and IPTV) and extracts images and video clips according to viewer requests.
- The backend web service is the core of CatchPo and is responsible for handling capture requests from users, classifying scenes, and mapping relevant metadata to scenes. When a user picks a captured scene (an image or a video clip), the backend

web service requests metadata (e.g., purchasing information) that relates to the scene from the metadata control subsystem.

- The metadata controlling system extends the Television Object Promoting System (TOPS) [11] and prepares time-synchronized metadata on products and scenes. When a user requests an image capture or a video clip, the metadata controlling system analyzes the timestamp and TV channel of the request, identifies metadata relevant to the captured image or video, and provides it to the scene extractor.

### 3.3   User Interface Design of CutX

CutX is an application for mobile devices (available for Google's Android and Apple's iOS platforms). A viewer who sees interesting content on television can use CutX to capture the scene as a still image or as a video clip (see Figure 3a). He or she can then add tags or notes to it and save it as a memo in a proper category (see Figure 3b). In addition, if viewers miss a favorite show, they can use the recall function to see missed content of a show broadcasted during the previous 24 hours (see Figure 3c). This involves substantial design work to solve viewers' major problems discovered during our initial user study. Finally, Facebook is integrated with CutX. People can easily share memos with friends on their Facebook pages or send the memo link to friends in an e-mail or message (see Figure 3d).

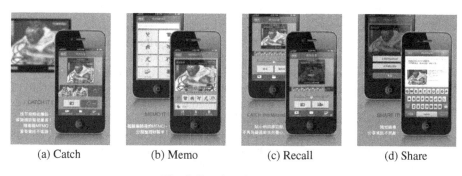

| (a) Catch | (b) Memo | (c) Recall | (d) Share |

**Fig. 3.** User interface of CutX

## 4   Evaluation of the User Interface Design

To evaluate the usability of the user interface, an experiment with 7 target users was conducted. They were asked to complete 33 tasks, including downloading and installing the app, capturing interesting content, editing memos, and sharing them with friends. The study was completed in the participant's environment. To understand users' thought processes and discover latent problems, think aloud methodology [12] was used in the study. It took approximately 50 minutes for each participant to complete the experiment. The major findings are summarized as follows:

1. To start, the participant needs time to experiment with the functions of the user interface. Although instructions have been shown on the user interface, they were obviously not seen by most of the participants. People's behavior when using mobile apps is

different from their behavior when using a personal computer. On a mobile device, they tend to explore by touching elements on the screen rather than reading the instructions. To improve user interaction, we tried to provide an image overlay on the interface (see Figure 4). When a user touches the screen, the image will automatically fade out and he or she will be able to operate the system normally.

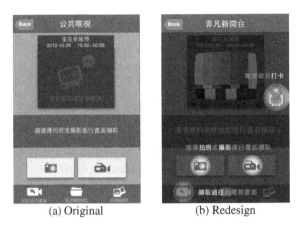

(a) Original                    (b) Redesign

**Fig. 4.** The design and redesign of instructions in the user interface

2. Typically, participants thought CutX was a useful app for enhancing their TV experience. In our country, about 90 channels are broadcast on the cable system. However, due to copyright issues, not all of them are available in our system. Currently we have agreements with nine content providers, and about a quarter (20) of cable channels are included. This means, of course, that some channels a viewer watches on TV are not found in CutX. This will likely lead to user disappointment. To simplify the process necessary for viewer to select a show from the list (as shown in Figure 5a), a category menu has been added (see Figure 5b). The users can easily see lists in a specific category and select a show.

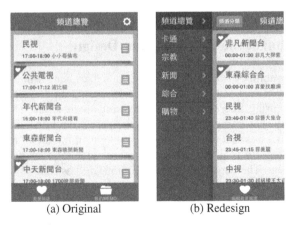

(a) Original                    (b) Redesign

**Fig. 5.** Design and redesign of the selection function

Through the evaluation study, several small problems were detected in the user interface design, problems such as the use of words, the meaning of an icon, the procedure for editing memos, and so forth. We then redesigned the user interface to improve the usability of the app.

## 5    Conclusion

In the context of trends in media consumption and social networking services (SNS), we present the development of the CatchPo system. Unlike other applications, our solution provides information related to a scene and enables viewers to capture interesting content and share the vivid image or a video clip with friends.

Since our system was officially launched on December 23, 2012, more than 15,000 viewers registered and captured content from TV shows. In two months, viewers have created 370,000 images and 17,000 video clips and saved them as memos in their smartphones. Captured images have been viewed more than 1.5 million times and captured video clips were been viewed more than 130 thousand times on social media, demonstrating the sharing power of social media. In line with the results of our user study and evaluation, the CatchPo system was thought to be an effective application to enhance people's experience in watching television shows.

We are currently developing several new apps to explore and improve viewer enjoyment, one of which is called CutMix. As the name indicates, a user can use this app to mix his or her photos with scenes captured from TV shows. This will help them create collages or funny jokes that can be easily shared with friends on SNS. We believe this will help create a positive user experience. The main user interface of CutMix is shown in Figure 6 and will be soon be available in app stores (for Google's Android and Apple's iOS platforms).

**Fig. 6.** Main user interface of CutMix

## References

1. TNN. What is IP television? Economic Times (November 27, 2006),
   http://articles.economictimes.indiatimes.com/2006-11-27/news
   /27425252_1_iptv-service-internet-protocol-television-boxes-
   with-broadband-internet

2. Tapp, P.: Is smart TV the most significant change in TV history? (December 23, 2010), http://scoop.intel.com/smart-tv-most-significant-change-tv-history/ (retrieved August 12, 2012)

3. Fan, W. J.: The game apps are the new competitive market for Samsung's and LG's smartTV. *Digitimes* (August 6, 2012), http://www.digitimes.com.tw/tw/dt/n/shwnws.asp?Cnlid=1&cat=20&cat1=10&id=0000296408_KZK3 ATHE1QQBH377LY32J&ct=a (retrieved August 15, 2012)

4. Park, C.: Slow connected TV interfaces inhibit App store exploration. Strategy Analytics, Boston (2012)

5. Bächle-Gerstmann, M.: Lean -back vs. lean -forward: Do television consumers really want to be increasingly in control? Paper Presented at the 10th European Interactive TV Conference, SeminarisCampus Hotel Berlin, Berlin, Germany (July 5, 2012)

6. Beyer, H., Holtzblatt, K.: Contextual design: Defining customer-centered systems. Morgan Kaufmann, San Francisco (1998)

7. Nelson: 40% of Tablet and Smartphone owners use them while watching TV (2011), http://blog.nielsen.com/nielsenwire/online_mobile/40-of-tablet-and-smartphone-owners-use-them-while-watching-tv/ (retrieved August 1, 2012)

8. Montpetit, M.J., Klym, N., Mirlacher, T.: The future of IPTV: Adding social networking and mobility. In: Proceedings of the 1st International Workshop on IPTV and Applications, pp. 405–409. IEEE Computer Society, Washington, DC (2009)

9. Martin, R., Santos, A.L., Shafran, M., Holtzman, H., Montpetit, M.J.: neXtream: A multi-device, social approach to video content consumption. In: Proceedings of the 7th IEEE Conference on Consumer Communications and Networking Conference, pp. 779–783. IEEE Press, Piscataway (2010)

10. Miyazaki, M., Hamaguchi, N., Fujisawa, H.: User behavior in the "teleda" social TV service– Achieving a public forum on the network. In: IEEE International Symposium on Multimedia, pp. 345–350. IEEE Computer Society, Washington, DC (2011)

11. You, T.H., Wu, Y.J., Yeh, Y.J.: TOPS: Television object promoting system. In: Proceedings of the 24th Annual ACM Symposium Adjunct on User Interface Software and Technology, pp. 55–56. ACM Press, New York (2011)

12. Hackos, J.T., Redish, J.C.: User and task analysis for interface design. Wiley, New York (1998)

# The Application of Consistent User Interface
# in Common Use Self Service (CUSS)

Horng-Yi Yu[1], T.K. Philip Hwang[2], Jisook Han[2], and Tsung-Hsian Wang[3]

[1] College of Design, National Taipei University of Technology, Taiwan
[2] Department of Industrial Design, National Taipei University of Technology, Taiwan
[3] Creative Design Department II, Wistron Corporation, Taiwan
1, Sec. 3, Chung-hsiao E. Rd., Taipei,10608,Taiwan, R.O.C.
phwang@ntut.edu.tw

**Abstract.** The Common-use self-service check-in kiosks (CUSS) allows passengers to access multiple airlines check-in from one machine efficiently, and avoid long queue at specific airline service counter. However, every single airline has different CUSS interface designs in page layout and operation sequences, which can confuse passengers. This study is intended to employ wizard user interface, interface consistency and Overview Plus Detail (OPD) to improve the usability of CUSS systems for divers passengers. The operation sequence, screens layout and option buttons, in CUSS among airlines are redesigned for two Taiwanese major airline's existing CUSS systems. The study remarked that users were able to easily identify the location of information, process of operation, and progress through interactively and deliberately designed page layout.

**Keywords:** CUSS, consistent user interface, wizard interface.

## 1    Introduction

In order to respond to the demand of increasing number of passengers, some major airports have executed Common Use Self-service Check-in Kiosk (CUSS) promoted by IATA. The effectiveness of CUSS is to integrate all airline systems in the same machine, which allows passengers to access multiple airlines check-in from one machine efficiently, and to avoid long queues at specific airline service counter. Las Vegas McCarran International Airport is the best known implementer of CUSS. Samuel Ingalls, Assistant Director of Aviation, Information Systems at McCarran, referred the kiosks have proved to be a clear triple win, for the airport, the airlines, and most importantly, for the passengers. Check-in Kiosk could greatly enhance passenger processing efficiency, taking the check-in process outside of traditional bounds to various terminal locations and even off-airport.[1]

---

[1] Howes, J.: Moving to Common Use Self-Service - On the Cusp of CUSS. Kiosk Europe , 14-18. (2006).

P.L.P. Rau (Ed.): CCD/HCII 2013, Part I, LNCS 8023, pp. 519–524, 2013.
© Springer-Verlag Berlin Heidelberg 2013

The kiosk is a computer-based information system with an intuitive interface for user input and output, located in a public area, used by an anonymous user who is standing, and required a relatively short time to use.[2] The Common-use self-service check-in kiosks (CUSS) allows passengers to access multiple airlines check-in from one machine efficiently, and avoid long queue at specific airline service counter. However, every single airline has different CUSS "wizard user interface" in their page layout and operation process, which confuse the passenger (as shown in Fig. 1). In additional, the operation sequence and screens layout of "wizard user interface" by different airlines are not consistent, and do not perfectly match to user's mental model (as shown in Fig. 2).

**Fig. 1.** The various operation sequence and screens layout of three existing CUSS systems frequently confused the passenger. (Top: China Airlines, middle: EVA Airways and bottom: KLM Royal Dutch Airlines.).

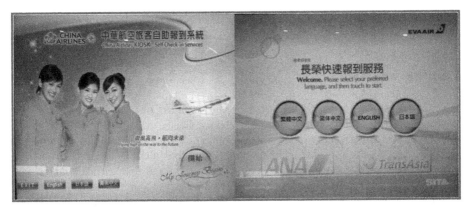

**Fig. 2.** Layout fundamentals such as shape, size and position of option buttons in CUSS among airlines need to be redesign employing the principle of interface consistency. (Left: China Airlines and right: EVA Airways.).

---

[2] Holfelder, W. and Hehmann, D.: A Networked Multimedia Retrieval Management System for Distributed Kiosk Applications. In Proc. Multimedia Computing and Systems, 342-351. (1994).

## 2    Literature Review

Although all existing CUSS have used wizard interface structure, the interface consistency among pages and airlines still need to be improved for better usability. In addition, the concept of Overview Plus Detail (OPD) needs to be emphasized for effective awareness of location of information, process of operation and progress for the user.

### 2.1    Wizard Interface

A wizard is an interactive computer program which attempts to guarantee success in using a feature by stepping the user through a series of dialog boxes by Microsoft, and they have rapidly gained popularity among programmers and user interface designers. Each of the wizard's dialogs asks users a question or two, and the user learns that he merely clicks the Next button on each screen without critically analyzing why. [3] For usability of software, the wizard interface fulfills the requirements of learnability and memorability. It provides first-time users with explicit guidance through the process of a specific task.

This study reviewed the consumer-oriented operating systems including wizard user interface. Relatively fewer literatures emphasized the importance of consistent display and consistent graphic design among wizard pages that improves easy discoverability of possible actions for first-time users. Through detail analysis of the requirement for affordance and mental model application, a set of layout patterns and entities attributes were defined for improving design of "wizard" pages. Consistent shape and graphic details of buttons were defined, while proper locations of buttons, options and text instructions were given.

### 2.2    Consistent Interface

In addition to wizard interface, consistent interface and Overview Plus Detail were also frequently used to help users prevent error operation. The internal consistency (e.g., layout, terminology, color, etc.) is a crucial issue in the usability of highly interactive computer programs (Shneiderman 1992; Reisner 1990; Nielsen 1989). [4] Nielsen referred that consistency leads to "improved user productivity by leading to higher throughput and fewer errors because the user can predict what the system will do in any given situation and can rely on a few rules to govern use of the system." He also pointed out "it is desired to have the system be consistent with users' expectations whether formed by other applications or by non-computer systems."

Consistent interface allows users to quickly understand the system, and help them build accurate mental models. Based on the existing system and UI design theory, this study defined the page layout of CUSS that contained main title, option buttons,

---

[3] Cooper, A., Reimann, R., & Cronin, D.: About face 3: the essentials of interaction design ([3rd ed.). Indianapolis, IN: Wiley Pub. (2007).

[4] Shneiderman, B.: Designing the User Interface: Strategies for Effective HumanComputer Interaction, second edition, Addison-Wesley, Reading, MA, (1992); Reisner, P.: "What is Inconsistency?" Proceedings of the IFIP Third International Conference on Human-Computer Interaction, Interact '90. Elsevier Science Publishers. B.V., North-Holland, 175-181. (1990); Nielsen, J.: Executive Summary: Coordinating User Interfaces for Consistency, in Nielsen, Jakob (editor), Coordinating User Interfaces for Consistency, Academic Press, San Diego, 1-7. (1989).

cancel option and feedback. Graphic details were also defined, including color, graphics, button shape and size. Consistent shape and graphic details of buttons were defined, while proper locations of buttons, options and text instructions were given.

### 2.3    Overview Plus Detail

The concept of Overview Plus Detail (OPD) was employed in the new design of CCUS. OPD is a way of dealing with complexity: present a high-level view of what's going on, and let the user 'drill down' from that view into the details as they need to, keeping both levels visible for quick iteration. Edward Tufte used the terms 'micro and macro readings' to describe a similar concept for maps, diagrams, and other static information graphics. The users have the large structure in front of them at all times, while being able to peer into the small details at will: 'the pace of visualization is condensed, slowed, and personalized'. Similarly, users of 'Overview Plus Detail' can page methodically through the content, jump around, compare, contrast, move quickly, move slowly, or even rearrange it. The overview can serve as a 'You are here' sign and users can tell at a glance where they are in the larger context. [5]

## 3    Discussion

Based on the existing guidelines of Wizard interface and context analysis of users' mental model, a set of layout patterns and entities attributes were defined for improving design of "wizard" pages. Consistent shape and graphic details of buttons were defined, while proper sizes and locations of buttons and text instructions were given (as shown in Fig. 3). Consequently, a prototype of CUSS was designed following above principles and then developed into two CUSS systems with various

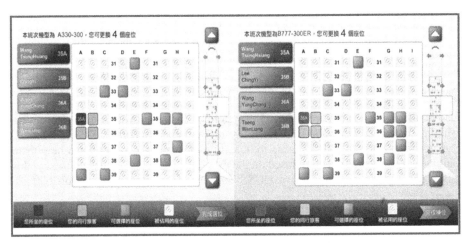

**Fig. 3.** The prototype of CUSS systems for China Airlines and EVA Airways have consistent layout

---

[5] Tufte, E. R.: Envisioning information. Cheshire, Conn. (P.O. Box 430, Cheshire 06410): Graphics Press. (1990).

company images which are of China Airlines and EVA Airways (as shown in Fig. 4). Finally, CUSS systems for two airlines were consulted by usability experts and airlines service staffs, and then modified. As a result, the application of consistent user interface of Common Use Self Service System not only benefits to usability of the wizard user interface, but also accommodates passengers to the operation of different airlines check-in system.

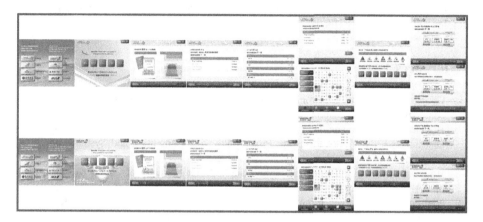

**Fig. 4.** The prototype of CUSS systems for China Airlines and EVA Airways have the same step and operating process

**Fig. 5.** User knows the step of operating process any time because the CUSS systems were integrated with the wizard user interface, consistent interface and OPD

## 4    Conclusion

The prototypes of CUSS for two major airlines were tested by thirty passengers. The result showed that the prototypes improved obviously, but several passengers didn't notice the existence of overview ribbon. The overview ribbon was then rearranged for visually noticeable display and size according to the user's experience. Color and graphic emphases for better operation sequence indication were also designed to implement the usability rule of Overview Plus Detail.

## References

1.  Cooper, A., Reimann, R., Cronin, D.: About face 3: the essentials of interaction design, 3rd edn. Wiley Pub., Indianapolis (2007)
2.  Holfelder, W., Hehmann, D.: A Networked Multimedia Retrieval Management System for Distributed Kiosk Applications. In: Proc. Multimedia Computing and Systems, pp. 342–351 (1994)
3.  Howes, J.: Moving to Common Use Self-Service - On the Cusp of CUSS, Kiosk Europe, pp. 14–18 (2006)
4.  Nielsen, J.: Executive Summary: Coordinating User Interfaces for Consistency. In: Nielsen, J. (ed.) Coordinating User Interfaces for Consistency, pp. 1–7. Academic Press, San Diego (1989)
5.  Reisner, P.: What is Inconsistency? In: Proceedings of the IFIP Third International Conference on Human-Computer Interaction, Interact 1990, pp. 175–181. Elsevier Science Publishers. B.V, North-Holland (1990)
6.  Shneiderman, B.: Designing the User Interface: Strategies for Effective HumanComputer Interaction, 2nd edn. Addison-Wesley, Reading (1992)
7.  Tufte, E. R.: Envisioning information. Graphics Press, Cheshire, Conn. (P.O. Box 430, Cheshire 06410) (1990)

# A Qualitative Study of Older Adults' Acceptance of New Functions on Smart Phones and Tablets

Jia Zhou, Pei-Luen Patrick Rau, and Gavriel Salvendy

Department of Industrial Engineering, Tsinghua University, Beijing 100084, China
zhou-jia07@mails.tsinghua.edu.cn, rpl@mail.tsinghua.edu.cn,
salvendy@purdue.edu

**Abstract.** This study examined why older adults accepted or rejected new functions and how they made their decision. 44 older adults were asked to use eight functions on two smart phones and two tablets. Then, they were interviewed about their acceptance of functions. They had the lowest acceptance of the mircroblog function. Finally, older adults reported reasons of accepting or rejecting functions. The result was a model to represent older adults' decision process, which was influenced by eight factors. This decision process generated four major findings. First, substitutes seemed to be a big obstacle to older adults' acceptance of new functions on smart phones and tablets. Second, openness influenced whether older adults stressed the usefulness of a new function. Third, contexts and lifestyles influenced older adults' judgment of usefulness. Fourth, older adults seemed to tolerate some complexity, but it should not be more than they could handle after learning.

**Keywords:** Older adults, Acceptance, New functions, Smart phones and tablets.

## 1 Introduction

Tremendous elderly-specific functions on smart phones and tablets provide significant utility, but most older adults are not using these functions. New functions (i.e., functions that older adults never used before) could be intimidating and overly complicated for older adults, because they had a cumbersome experience with feature phones. They had difficulties with the poor readability on small displays, typing on compressed buttons, and navigating in the hierarchical menu. As a result, most older adults only used core functions on feature phones (phone calls and short messages) and dared not to try new functions.

Luckily, many difficulties with feature phones could be solved by smart phones and tablets. Smart phones and tablets have large displays, support finger-based direct input, and no longer have hierarchical menus, thus they would provide a brand new experience for older adults. This might change older adults' perception of mobile phones based on their past experience. With this new perception, older adults might try new functions.

Functions on smart phones and tablets face the competition from substitutes. That is, a function on mobile phones could be replaced by the same function on desktop

P.L.P. Rau (Ed.): CCD/HCII 2013, Part I, LNCS 8023, pp. 525–534, 2013.
© Springer-Verlag Berlin Heidelberg 2013

computers (e.g. email and web browsing) or specialized products (e.g. GPS navigation devices, e-book readers, and digital frames). Besides, functions on smart phones and tablets also face the competition among themselves. Hundreds of thousands of functions are available on smart phones and tablets, and a new function has to stand out from the crowd to be liked by older adults.

This study aimed to extend older adults' mobile phone usage from core functions to new functions. First, older adults would have an experience of using new functions on smart phones and tablets. Then, this study examined why older adults accepted or rejected these functions and how they made their decision.

# 2    Literature Review

## 2.1    Older Adults' Acceptance of Mobile Phones

Two factors that influence people's acceptance of information technology are perceived ease of use and perceived usefulness [1]. However, older adults had lower perceived usefulness and lower perceived ease of use than younger adults [2].

New technology's usefulness and ease of use are not equally important for older adults. Some older adults perceived usefulness more important than ease of use. That is, they would accept a useful device even if it was difficult to use. Melenhorst and Rogers [3] found that benefits were more influential than costs (e.g. effort, lack of skills, expenses) on older adults' intention to use email. This could be explained older adults' decision process proposed by Fisk et al. [4]: older adults first judged the usefulness and then disadvantages of a new technology. Only when its usefulness outweighed disadvantages, older adults would accept it.

Apart from perceived ease of use and perceived usefulness, ease of learning also influences older adult's intention to use mobile phones. Older adults had difficulty in learning how to use mobile phones [5, 6], and they found mobile phones more difficult to learn than younger adults [7].

Previous studies investigated older adults' use of two functions which usually involved little text entry: route navigation and web browsing. As to the navigation function, Goodman et al. [8] investigated different modalities to present the information of landmarks on mobile phones. As to the web browsing function on mobile phones, new design of web pages was proposed for older adults [9].

Older adults made many errors during text entry on mobile phones, no matter they used typing [10] or handwriting [11]. These problems influenced the use of functions requiring text entry. One typical example is the medication adherence application. It turned out to be difficult to use because it needed older adults to enter the text of medication information [6, 12].

# 3    Methodology

The first phase of this study is actual use of smart phones and tablets for about 50 minutes. During this period, the instructor trained participants and then asked them to use functions independently. In the second phase, participants were interviewed about their acceptance of functions, and reasons for accepting or rejecting functions.

This study included actual use of functions for two reasons. First, actual use of mobile phones influenced older adults' perceived ease of use and perceived usefulness [2]. Second, many older adults' mental model of functions which was formed through their experience with feature phones may be out of date [13].

Four touch-screen smart phones and tablets were used (shown in Figure 1): Apple iPod Touch (3.5″, iOS), Dell Streak (5″, Android), Samsung Galaxy Tab (7″, Android), and Apple iPad (9.7″, iOS). The order to use four devices was counterbalanced. The brands on the four devices were covered with a masking tape. Two camcorders were used: one at the upper right side of participants and the other one directly above the display.

**Fig. 1.** Two smart phones and two tablets

Finger-based input usually involved four actions: tapping buttons, pinch zooming, tapping on-screen keyboards, and handwriting. The former two actions were used in study 1, and the latter two actions were used in study 2.

### 3.1    Study 1: Use of Functions without Text Entry

12 older adults (Mean age=66.4; SD=5.6; Range=59-77) participated in the first study. They were randomly divided into four groups. They used four functions on smart phones and tablets: photo album, document reader, Google map, and web browsing (shown in Figure 2). The photo album function and the Google map function are iOS's own and Android's own functions, and the other two functions are the document reader (Office Suite in Android, the default PDF reader in iOS), and the web browsing (Internet Explorer in Android, and Safari in iOS).

In order to make participants experience gesture input, the content on the photo/document/map/web page was set at a small size. Participants zoomed in to view the content. To check whether they read the content carefully, the cloze test was conducted. Participants wrote down answers on a piece of paper. Each participant used two ways of zooming in/out: pinch zooming and tapping the zooming in/out buttons.

- Task 1: Browse the album. Zoom in each photo and write down the predefined digit on the photo.
- Task 2: Read the document. Zoom in each page and write down the missing words.

- Task 3: Plan the route. Zoom in the map to find the destination and write down the route to the destination.
- Task 4: Browse web pages. Zoom in predefined web pages, read the content, and write down the missing words.

**Fig. 2.** Sample screen shots of four functions in study 1

### 3.2     Study 2: Use of Functions Requiring Text Entry

32 older adults (Mean age=67.2; SD=5.53; Range=60-79) participated in the second study. They were randomly divided into four groups. They used four functions: contacts, microblog, Google search, and email (shown in Figure 3). The contacts function and the email function are iOS's own and Android's own functions, and the other two functions are Sina Microblog (China's version of Twitter) and Google Search widget/application.

In order to make participants experience text entry, they were asked to enter a short sentence including Chinese characters, digits, and punctuations. Each participant either used handwriting or typing on the on-screen keyboard.

- Task 1: Create a new entry in the contact function.
- Task 2: Post a message in Sina Microblog
- Task 3: Search keywords in Google Search
- Task 4: Send an email to a predefined contact

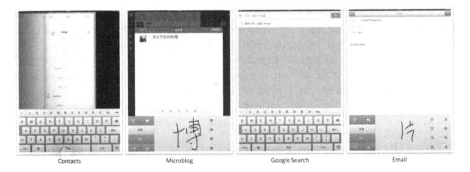

**Fig. 3.** Sample screen shots of four functions in study 2

# 4    Results and Discussion

## 4.1    Acceptance of Functions

Taking all the eight functions together, the photo album was participants' favourite function, as shown in Figure 4. This is supported by previous finding that older adults liked taking and viewing photos [14, 15].

Microblog was participants' least desirable function among eight functions. consistent with previous studies, older adults did not accept socializing through Internet, so their initial perception of social media was strongly negative [16]. Most participants did not like the microblog for four main reasons: (1) they did not want to expose themselves, (2) they preferred email, phone calls, or short messages rather than the microblog to keep in touch with friends, (3) they preferred to meet other people in person. (4) they did not want to make new friends. Instead, they wanted to keep in-depth communication with old friends. And they thought the constraints on the number of words made the microblog not suitable for in-depth communication.

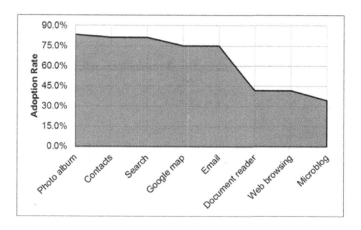

**Fig. 4.** Adoption rate of eight functions

## 4.2    Factors Influencing Older Adults' Acceptance of New Functions

Based on the results of the interview, a flow chart is proposed to represent older adults' decision process about accepting or rejecting a new function (shown in Figure 5). This process is influenced by eight factors, which are introduced one by one in the following section.

**Social Influence**
Participants tended to try a new function if their family or friends recommended it. They wanted to maintain ties to family and friends. Besides, family members bought mobile phones for participants and urged them to use certain functions. This is consistent with previous studies, which reported that older adults were under social pressure to adopt mobile phones [17]. Nine participants indicated that they would explore a new function under social influence. Apart from this, sometimes using new functions might be mandatory work requirements.

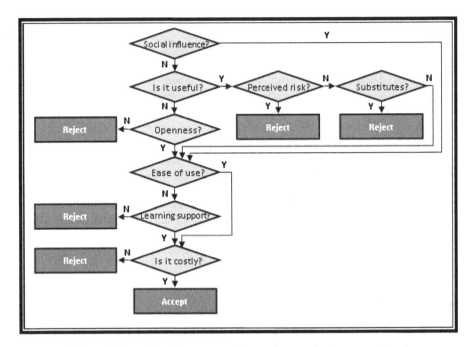

**Fig. 5.** Participants' decision process of accepting or rejecting a new function

**Perceived Usefulness**

Participants judged usefulness in different ways. Some participants held that a function was useful if it could help activities in the real world. Particularly, functions on mobile phones were perceived useful if they could help older adults out in emergency [5]. In contrast, other participants held that a useful function did not need to be practicable. Instead, it could just make people feel good. This is similar to the finding that older adults would accept enjoyable information technology [14].

Perceived usefulness was influenced by contexts and lifestyles. Different contexts blurred the line between acceptance and rejection. Participants rejected a function on smart phones and tablets for usage at home, but they accepted it when they went out or when an emergency happened. This influence of contexts was reported by ten participants. Besides, older adults' lifestyle influences their acceptance. Participants who often went out and traveled around seemed to be willing to use Google map, and those who did not have the habit of reading books and newspapers were reluctant to use the document reader function and the web browsing function.

**Perceived Risk**

After knowing the usefulness of a new function, participants evaluated its disadvantages. Participants were also afraid that they might break the devices or the devices might get lost or robbed. However, the major risk was about the invasion of privacy. Participants felt it not safe to expose themselves through Internet. This is not surprising, because older adults were cautious to give private information. Their privacy concern was so strong that it became the most important reason for rejecting social media [16]. Only when the usefulness outweighed privacy concern would older adults consider a new function.

## Substitutes

Many functions on smart phones faced the competition from substitutable devices and substitutable activities. 11 participants in this study rejected new functions because of substitutes. They would use the web browsing/search/email function on desktop computers rather than on smart phones and tablets, use digital cameras/camcorders rather than smart phones and tablets. Similarly, these participants also stuck to their routine activities. They preferred watching TV/reading books/newspapers rather than reading on smart phones and tablets, and preferred meeting people in person/calling people rather than contacting people through Internet. The influence of substitutes on older adults' acceptance is ignored by previous studies.

## Openness

Some participants would like to try a new function even if it was not useful. Their personality made them open to new things. They would decide to accept or reject a new function after they tried it. Three participants reported that they enjoyed exploration as long as there were new functions. This is backed up by previous studies. Korzaan & Boswell [18] also found that individuals who rated high on openness were also more willing to experience new technology.

## Ease of Use

Participants would like to consider functions which were easy to use. However, difficult-to-use functions were not necessarily rejected. Some participants reported that they were willing to learn to use difficult-to-use functions as long as functions were very helpful. The influence of ease of use was mentioned by 13 participants.

Participants usually judged ease of use from three aspects. First, 10 participants perceived that large displays, big fonts, and sufficient contrast represented easy output. They did not want to carry around eye glasses to read too small text, and they also did not want to scroll to read too large text. They desired the size that is just right. Second, some participants perceived that a small number of functions represented ease of use. Older adults had great difficulties with the broad and deep hierarchical menu of feature phones, so less functions was believed to be the solution. However, limited functions may drop sales of mobile phones. When people choose from two devices at the same price, they usually buy the one with more functions [13]. Third, some participants perceived that handwriting and voice input represented easy input. It should be noted handwriting and voice input might also cause new problems [13].

## Learning Support

Ten participants stressed the importance of getting help from other people. They felt scared if nobody helped them with problems during learning. Most of them would like family members to teach them. However, some participants refused to ask help from younger people, because younger people did not express in the way understood by older adults. Previous studies reported that older adults learned mobile phones mainly from two sources: manuals and other people. Since manuals were difficult to understand [19], older adults usually turned to other people for help. The importance of support is also stressed by Wang et al. [14], who found that support availability influenced older adults' acceptance of information technology.

**Cost**
13 participants reported they would consider the cost of using a new function. Since many functions on smart phones and tablets needed Internet access, older adults cared about how much it would cost. Some participants rejected functions as long as there was Internet access fee, while other participants compared the fees between mobile phones with other substitutes and then chose the cheaper one. The influence of cost was not included in older adults' acceptance models.

# 5    Conclusion

This study analyzed older adults' decision process of accepting or rejecting new functions on smart phones and tablets. New acceptance factors (i.e. substitutes and openness) were discovered, and the understanding of well-documented acceptance factors was enriched. Results of this study could not only help improve the quality of life for older adults, but also help practitioners promote new functions to increase public acceptance and market share.

There was a big gap in participants' acceptance of functions on smart phones and tablets. Participants had high acceptance of functions that were needed in frequent activities (e.g. photo album, contacts, and email) or in infrequent but emergent activities (e.g. Google search and Google map). However, most participants were reluctant to read small text on smart phones and tablets, and they were not ready to socialize through Internet and preferred traditional social ways (e.g. meeting in person, calling, SMS).

The difference in participants' acceptance could be explained by their decision process, which was influenced by eight factors: social influence, perceived usefulness, perceived risk, substitutes, openness, perceived ease of use, learning support, and cost. This decision process generates four major findings. Accordingly, implications for improving acceptance of new functions on smart phones and tablets are identified.

First, substitutes seemed to be a big obstacle to older adults' acceptance of new functions on smart phones and tablets. This implies that knowing what a new function can do is not enough for older adults. Instead, knowing what smart phones and tablets can do but substitutes cannot do may be more important.

Second, openness influenced whether or not older adults stressed the usefulness of a new function. This implies that persuading different older adults to use new functions needs different strategies: stressing enjoyment for open-minded older adults while stressing usefulness for others.

Third, contexts and lifestyles influenced older adults' judgment of usefulness. This implies that a deep understanding of older adults' daily life is needed. Based on that, dividing older adults into groups of individuals would help practitioners find out what is really useful for a group of older adults.

Fourth, older adults seemed to tolerate some complexity, but it should not be more than they could handle after learning. This implies that if a new function is not easy to use, practitioners should first stress its usefulness to trigger older adults' learning motivation and then provide learning support.

Three limitations should be noted when generalizing the results. First, the sample in this study was a sample of convenience, which may not well represent the older population. Second, text in study 2 was Chinese characters, so the results might be not applicable to other languages. Third, participants had short-time exposure (50 minutes) to new functions.

**Acknowledgement.** The authors would like to acknowledge the support from National Natural Science Foundation in China (70971074) and National Science Fund for Distinguished Young Scholars (71188001).

# References

1. Davis, F.D.: A technology acceptance model for empirically testing new end-user information systems: Theory and results (Unpublished doctoral dissertation). MIT Sloan School of Management, Cambridge, MA (1986)
2. Arning, K., Ziefle, M.: Understanding age differences in PDA acceptance and performance. Computers in Human Behavior 23, 2904–2927 (2007)
3. Melenhorst, A.-S., Rogers, W.A.: Older adults' motivated choice for technological innovation: Evidence for benefit-driven selectivity. Psychology and Aging 21, 190–195 (2006)
4. Fisk, A.D., Rogers, W.A., Charness, N., Czaja, S.J., Sharit, J.: Designing accommodations for aging-in-place. Designing for older adults: Principles and creative human factors approaches, 2nd edn. CRC Press, Boca Raton (2009)
5. Kurniawan, S.: Older people and mobile phones: A multi-method investigation. International Journal of Human-Computer Studies 66(12), 889–901 (2008)
6. Sterns, A.A.: Curriculum design and program to train older adults to use personal digital assistants. Gerontologist 45(6), 828–834 (2005)
7. Mayhorn, C.B., Lanzolla, V.R., Wogalter, M.S., Watson, A.M.: Personal digital assistants (PDAs) as medication reminding tools: Exploring age differences in usability. Gerontechnology 4, 128–140 (2005)
8. Goodman, J., Brewster, S., Gray, P.: How can we best use landmarks to support older people in navigation? Behaviour & Information Technology 24, 3–20 (2005)
9. Sayago, S.: Some aspects of ICT accessibility, usability and design methods with the young elderly (2006), http://www.nttdocomo.com/press/publications/mobility/archives.html (retrieved)
10. Wright, P., Bartram, C., Rogers, N., Emslie, H., Evans, J., Wilson, B., Belt, S.: Text entry on handheld computers by older users. Ergonomics 43, 702–716 (2000)
11. Lee, C.-F., Kuo, C.-C.: Difficulties on small-touch-screens for various ages. Paper Presented at Universal Access in Human–Computer Interaction, Coping with Diversity, Beijing, China, July 22-27, pp. 968–974 (200)
12. Sterns, A.A., Collins, S.C.: Transforming the personal digital assistant into a health-enhancing technology. Generations-Journal of the American Society on Aging 28(4), 54–56 (2004)
13. Zhou, J., Rau, P.L.P., Salvendy, G.: Use and design of handheld computers for older adults: A review and appraisal. International Journal of Human-Computer Interaction 28(12), 799–826 (2012)
14. Wang, L., Rau, P.-L.P., Salvendy, G.: Older adults' acceptance of information technology. Educational Gerontology 37(12), 1081–1099 (2011)

15. Zhou, J., Rau, P.L.P., Salvendy, G.: Older Adults' use of smart phones: An investigation of the factors influencing the acceptance of new functions. Behaviour & Information Technology (in press)
16. Xie, B., Watkins, I., Golbeck, J., Huang, M.: Understanding and changing older adults' perceptions and learning of social media. Educational Gerontology 38(4), 282–296 (2012)
17. van Biljon, J., Renaud, K.: A qualitative study of the applicability of technology acceptance models to senior mobile phone users. In: Song, I.-Y., Piattini, M., Chen, Y.-P.P., Hartmann, S., Grandi, F., Trujillo, J., Opdahl, A.L., Ferri, F., Grifoni, P., Caschera, M.C., Rolland, C., Woo, C., Salinesi, C., Zimányi, E., Claramunt, C., Frasincar, F., Houben, G.-J., Thiran, P. (eds.) ER Workshops 2008. LNCS, vol. 5232, pp. 228–237. Springer, Heidelberg (2008)
18. Korzaan, M.L., Boswell, K.T.: The influence of personality traits and information privacy concerns on behavioral intentions. Journal of Computer Information Systems 48(4), 15–24 (2008)
19. Bruder, C., Wandke, H., Blessing, L.: Improving mobile phone instruction manuals for seniors. Gerontechnology 5, 51–55 (2006)

# On Class Design Using Multi-Mouse Quiz by Elementary Schoolteachers

Juan Zhou[1], Mikihiko Mori[2], and Hajime Kita[2]

[1] Graduate School of Informatics Kyoto University,
Yoshida Nihonmatsu-cho, sakyo-ku, Kyoto 606-8501, Japan
zhou.juan.27s@st.kyoto-u.ac.jp
[2] Academic Center for Computing and Media Studies Kyoto University,
Yoshida Nihonmatsu-cho, sakyo-ku, Kyoto 606-8501, Japan
{miki,kita}@media.kyoto-u.ac.jp

**Abstract.** Multi-Mouse Quiz System consisting of Multi Mouse Quiz (MMQ) and MMQEditor is an application set to treat quizzes in a classroom. The MMQ is an application of Single Display Groupware (SDG) which enables multiple users to answer quizzes by connecting several mice to an ordinary personal computer (PC). The MMQEditor is a PC application designed to edit quizzes for MMQ. The authors have asked several elementary schoolteachers to use the MMQ system and observe the class activities. The class practices show that the schoolteachers designed various class activities and quiz content along with the context of their school and class. This paper reports these practices from viewpoints of class design, their effectiveness and problems. We also discuss importance of collaboration among schoolteachers who design and practice class, and researchers who develop the system and analyze the class activities learnt through this study.

**Keywords:** Face-to-face collaborative learning, Quiz, Single Display Groupware, Elementary school, class design.

## 1 Introduction

Elementary education, as the formative education in the compulsory education, has special roles in teaching rudimentary knowledge and developing good study habits. Children in this period have characteristics that they prefer to pay attention only to what they are interested in. There are several studies designing practices of attracting children's attention through the collaborative learning or quiz study[1]. Many teachers also encourage children's motivation using Information and Communication Technology (ICT) environments. Nowadays, in Japan, the number of computers introduced to elementary schools has reached at one computer per 6.6 children, and 72.5% elementary school has at least one electronic blackboard (large LCD display) in the every classroom[2].

The authors focus on the collaborative learning using ICT environment, and Single Display Groupware (SDG) proposed by Stewart[3] as a candidate technology to support collaborative learning in classroom. SDG is a CSCW/CSCL

P.L.P. Rau (Ed.): CCD/HCII 2013, Part I, LNCS 8023, pp. 535–544, 2013.
© Springer-Verlag Berlin Heidelberg 2013

environment in which multiple users have control of a computer by using multiple input devices such as mice sharing information on a single display. Since SDG shows all of the mouse cursors on the screen, the users can see the others' behavior. This feature encourages communication among users[4]. Further, SDG can be implemented on an ordinary PC only with software and several mice connected to it. It is a big advantage in practical use in elementary schools because their budget and human resources for ICT are quite limited.

As a concreted application of SDG, the authors have developed Multi-Mouse Quiz (MMQ), a quiz software that can ask quizzes to several users simultaneously. We asked several elementary school in Kyoto, Japan to use the MMQ in their classes, discussed class design with schoolteachers, and observed the class practices. In these practices, the schoolteachers designed various class activities and quiz content along with the course subjects and other context of their school and class. In this paper, these class practices are reported and discusses them from a viewpoint of class design, their effectiveness and problems. We also discuss importance of collaboration among schoolteachers who design and practice class, and researchers who develop the system and analyze the class activities learnt through this study.

This paper is organized as follows: After introduction of this section, Section 2 gives overview of related work. Multi-Mouse Quiz System is explained in Section 3. Class practices in several elementary schools are stated in Section 4. In Section 5, these class practices are discussed from a viewpoint of class design. Section 6 gives conclusion of this paper.

## 2 Related Work

The Single Display Groupware (SDG) model[3] proposed by Stewart refers to systems with which each of collocating users uses an input device such as mouse sharing information shown in a display. It is shown that SDG encourage communication among collocating users[5]. The SDGtoolkit is a middle ware for Windows that provides multi-user interaction environment through multiple mice and keyboards handled independently[6]. Similar middle ware is also provided by Microsoft as Mouse Mischief based on the research for education in developing country[7]. The authors interested in SDG as tool to support collaborative learning in classroom, and studied it by developing several applications[8],[9]. Multi-Mouse Quiz (MMQ) is one of such applications.

In this paper, we report two practices of using MMQ for teaching arithmetic. There are many practices that studying mathematics through game playing on computer[10][11]. Hennessy pointed that it is helpful to children's learning objectives when teachers were developing and trialing new strategies specifically for mediating ICT supported learning[12]. Also study with quizzes provides students an opportunity to self-assess their current level of knowledge. It also provides feedback, helping students determine how to adjust their behavior to ensure acquisition of the missing knowledge. Study by quiz was wildly used with a variety of methods, such as amuse children to maintain the attention as well as to encourage the enthusiasm to learn. Pollard, J.K. used a Web-based Quiz to let student to reflect their studies[13]. Recently, mainly in university, Clickers are often used to pose quiz in classes which encourage students' engagement.

## 3   Multi-Mouse Quiz System

The Multi-Mouse Quiz system is an application for treating quizzes in a class-room or other learning environment. The system consists of the Multi Mouse Quiz (MMQ), a quiz application of SDG and MMQEditor, an ordinary PC application for editing quizzes for MMQ. Figure. 1 and Figure. 2 show the screenshots of MMQ and MMQEditor.

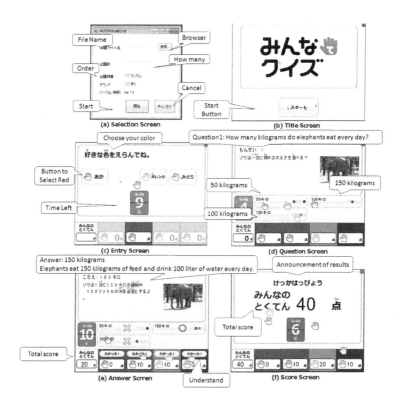

**Fig. 1.** Interface of MMQ[14]

MMQ is implemented with the SDG Toolkit[6] and can be used on a Windows PC by connecting several mice to it. Currently, up to four players can answer quizzes simultaneously. In screen (a) of Figure.1, the teacher can choose the question file and other options such as number and asking order of quizzes to show, and on-off of sound. In (b), any user can start quiz by clicking the start button. In (c), users choose their own color to make registration of quiz session.

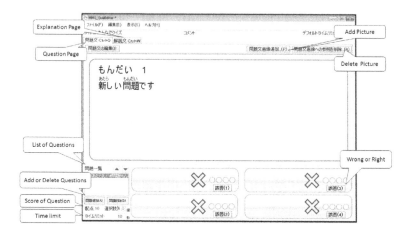

**Fig. 2.** Interface of MMQEditor[14]

**Table 1.** Class Practices using MMQ System

| No. | School | Grade | Subject | Class Size |
|---|---|---|---|---|
| 1 | H | $5^{th}$ | Social Study | 28 |
| 2 | S | $6^{th}$ | Social Study | 32 |
| 3 | F | $6^{th}$ | General Study | 25, 27 (two classes) |
| 4 | T | $6^{th}$ | Arithmetic | 27 |
| 5 | N | $4^{th}$ | Arithmetic | 4 |

Screen (d) is a screen of asking quiz where users answer the quiz by clicking an alternative within a prescribed time limit. Screen (e) shows the correct answer and commentary of the asked quiz. After answering all of the quizzes, the total score for all users is shown in (f), and the system goes back to screen (a).

MMQEditor is a quiz editor for MMQ. With this editor, users can edit quiz questions, choices, explanation and other options for MMQ. To make operation easy to understand, we designed the user interface of MMQEditor as close to MMQ as possible.

## 4   Studies of Using MMQ System

With assistance of the Kyoto Municipal Board of Education, we carried out five practices using MMQ System in public elementary schools in Kyoto, Japan. Table. 1 shows the list of practices. Class subjects were social studies (such as geography and history), arithmetic, and Sogo-Gakushu (general learning), and they were held in four to six grade classes.

We have reported practices No.1[15], No.2[16], No.3[17] and brief summary of them are given below. As for practices No.4 and No.5, we explain more in detail. In this paper, there are two class design with social studies, two class design with mathematics studies, and one class design with 'Sogo- Gakushu'(general learning).

### 4.1   Practice in H Elementary School

In H elementary school, MMQ was used for a $5^{th}$ grade class of 28 children in 'social studies'. Since two electronic blackboards were available, we used two sets of MMQ totally having 8 mice for the class. Three or four children shared one mouse as a group.

The teacher designed the class activity using MMQ aiming at enhancement of children's writing ability through discussion in group. Quiz content were created by the teacher. In the beginning, rather easy quizzes were posed so as to make children have confidence in answering, and gradually more difficult quizzes were asked. Finally children had to answer quizzes that require common sense as well as knowledge explicitly learned in classes. He also asked a quiz without choice. Then he handed worksheets to children and ask to have discussion and write descriptive answer. In this practice, children did not only remember the knowledge asked in the quizzes, but they also could write the descriptive answer. The teacher said quality of writing were better than usual.

### 4.2   Practice in S Elementary School

In S elementary school, MMQ was used for a $6^{th}$ grade class of 32 children in 'social studies'. One MMQ set was used, and a mouse was shared by a group of 8 children. The teacher tried class management that makes children feel class was fun. Along with this policy and so as to raise concentration of children that share mice in rather larger group, he tried to ask children to make quizzes by themselves. First, after experience of answering quizzes with MMQ, the children were asked to design quizzes and write them on paper. Then the teacher collected and reviewed them before entering them into the MMQ system. Finally the children answered the quizzes made by them with MMQ. In answering quizzes they made, the children were more concentrated on the contents of quizzes keeping high motivation compared with answering quizzes made by the teacher.

### 4.3   Practice in F Elementary School

In F elementary school, MMQ was used for two classes of $6^{th}$ grade having 25 and 27 children, in 'Sogo-Gakushu' (general learning). In this course, children studies historic places of learnt materials such as books, and later they visit the actual places. The activities were held in a computer room of the school. MMQ was used to show what they learnt to other children. Each class spent three class time of 45 minutes. First, they created quizzes personally with MMQEditor, and combined quizzes into one files in group of 3 or 4 children. Then, use MMQ they tried to answer quizzes created by other groups.

In this practice, children successfully created quiz questions with MMQEditor without special assistance of the researchers. Even children of low scholastic ability could make at least one question. In the activity of answering quizzes with MMQ, we observed that the children not only answered the quizzes but also carefully read the explanation.

## 4.4    Practice in T Elementary School

In T elementary school, MMQ was used for a $6^{th}$ grade class of 27 children in arithmetic. We used two MMQ sets of 8 mice in total, and children learnt in 8 group of 3 or 4 children. This class aimed at to solve difficult arithmetic problems through discussion in group as course unit of "Attempt to challenge a variety of issues". The following are examples of the asked questions:

Question 1: How many kinds of possibility to choose 3 people from 6?
Choices:        A:   20        B:   60        C:   120        D:   18

The activity was held in one class period of 45 minutes. Eight quizzes were asked in the class. For each quiz, first the teacher showed the quiz written in a large sheet of paper on the blackboard, and let one child read it. The each group was asked to discuss how to solve in. Ideas proposed by the group members were written on a white board given to each group. Then, the question screen of MMQ was shown and the groups answered their solutions. After explanation screen was shown on MMQ, the teacher paused the MMQ and let children explain their choice using whiteboard to the whole class.

The teacher evaluated that this was a good practice, and felt the MMQ more affect to the children who didn't like arithmetic. He said that if this lesson was held in a traditional way with printed hand out, children of higher scholastic ability might achieve more, but children of lower scholastic ability children might feel difficult, and give up to work. This class was shown to other teachers in the school, one of the teachers said that he was impressed that children could concentrate in these difficult arithmetic quizzes, and all of the children didn't give up until the time limit.

## 4.5    Practice in N Elementary School

In N elementary school, the MMQ was used for a $4^{th}$ grade class of four children in arithmetic. This school area is small, hence the class of the four grade has only a few children. The course unit was "What is the original number?", it aims to understand the concept of relationship diagram to find the value of a variable from the given condition. An example question is as following:

Question1:  I bought six notebooks of a same price. Then I also bought a bottle of juice, it cost me 100 yen. I spent 940 yen in total. So how much is the price of one notebook.

Figure 3 is a sample of the used diagram (translated in English). It shows the relationship of forward and inverse calculation to assist children to decide the asked value. This class held in connected 2 periods of 45 minutes each without break. In the first period, the teacher explained the arithmetic rules to calculate of question 1 as showing above using the relationship diagram. She gave one page

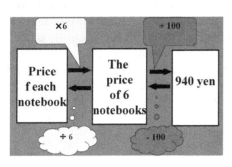

**Fig. 3.** Diagram

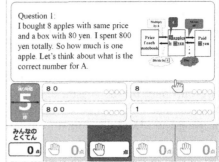

**Fig. 4.** Quiz on MMQ

handout to each child on which a similar question, say question 2 is printed, and give them a few minutes to let them think about how to calculate. In the 2nd period, the children wrote down the relationship diagram, arithmetic formula, and the solution of question 2. Then, the teacher started up the MMQ let every child has a mouse when they finished writing. The teacher made 5 quizzes about the relationship diagram and one quiz for arithmetic formula which treat question 2 in step-by-step manner. Figure 4 is a translated example of the question on MMQ. As well as asking children to answer in MMQ, the teacher paused the MMQ, not only let children explain the reason of their choice, but she also asked children to explain the reason of the choice they did not chose.

The teacher evaluated operation of MMQEditor was not difficult, and they used MMQ to support their pedagogical research in Arithmetic. She said that the children used the MMQ with the high motivation, because they designed this practice with two class periods, she worried about the engagement of a less able child having difficult moods in the class, but he could concentrate in this practices. Different from other practices of MMQ, we observed each child choose different choices along with their idea, while in other practices, children often follow others choices. On it, the teachers opinion was that the class size was so small, hence children might not be afraid of making mistakes in front of their classmates.

## 5   Discussion

In this section, we discuss the class activities from "engagement and usability", "class subjects", "cobination of activities", "quiz content", "facilitation using pause", and "collaboration among schoolteachers and researchers" various viewpoints relating design of classes.

### 5.1   Engagement and Usability

In all of the practices, the teachers evaluated effectiveness of the MMQ in encouraging children's motivation to study in class. One of the teacher mentioned that all of the children seemed to feel happy to use the computer. Teachers and children could use MMQ without particular difficulty. As for MMQEditor, it also could be used by the teachers not difficulty. Further in F elementary school, 6 grade children could use the MMQEditor by themselves without difficulty. It is also important issue that using MMQ encourage participation of children of lower scholastic ability. Both usage of the computer for interaction and study in group may be the reason of such involvement. It also should be noted that oral communication is encouraged in these practices. This might also the effect of using the MMQ developed as an application of SDG.

## 5.2   Class Subjects

The teachers used the MMQ for class subjects of the social studies, arithmetic, and periods of general studies. Due to the social studies requires to remember many facts and concepts, it fits to use quiz. In the both practices for arithmetic, the teachers wanted to children could comprehend difficult contents through discussion in a group and encouraging participation using the MMQ. In F elementary school, MMQ is used for the general studies where children learn more actively along with the theme set by the teachers. The children created quiz questions with MMQEditor, and appreciate them mutually with the MMQ.

## 5.3   Combination of Activities

In the above practices, various activity were combined with answering quizzes with the MMQ. That is, the following activities were combined with the MMQ along with the class subject and teaching aims:

- Group discussion (all the schools)
- Oral explanation of children's ideas (H and N schools)
- Writing descriptive answer (H school)
- Quiz Creation and Mutual Appreciation (S and F schools)

It should also be noted that the teachers select media that fit for the activities. Both the teachers and children use paper as well as the computer. In these activities, quiz creation is interesting because children engaged in learning both in quiz creation phase and quiz appreciation phase. Even in answering quizzes, children concentrate more because the questions were made by their classmates.

## 5.4   Quiz Content

We found a common strategy from the content created by schoolteachers, that is teachers arrayed the quizzes considering difficulty level from easy ones to difficult ones in the H, N, T school. The teacher designed the quizzes in this order so as to gave children confidence in answering the questions, and gradually attack difficult ones through discussion in group.

### 5.5 Facilitation Using Pause

The pause function of MMQ were often used by the teachers aiming at control of the progress, giving hints, and combining other activities such as discussion in group, oral answering, and writing on paper or whiteboard.

### 5.6 Collaboration among Schoolteachers and Researchers

All of these practices, class plans were designed mainly by the teachers. Then, the researchers discussed with the teachers to confirm implementation of their plans, and necessary support in carrying out the classes. Then, if needed we revise the MMQ such as introducing pause function and improvement of stability of the system on computers in the schools. Further, the researchers also recorded the data of these practices using questionnaires, interview, voice, and video. And made analysis of them. We think such continuous interaction and collaboration among schoolteachers and researchers are important for both school teaching and academic research.

## 6 Conclusion and Future Work

We studied several class practices with the MMQ System to support collaborative learning in multiple elementary schools in Kyoto, Japan. This paper mainly focused on the class design by the teachers in these practices. These practices showed that schoolteachers could use MMQ System without difficulty, and they designed independently along with their educational aims with the MMQ System. Furthermore, the schoolteachers also felt advantages of this system in their classes. For successful use, the researchers took roles of technical support and system revision along with the teachers' class design, and recording and analysis of class practice for evaluation of their design. As a future work, the authors are planning the following:

- To encourage community of schoolteachers by gathering and sharing the cases of class design with the MMQ and quizzes for MMQ.
- To develop other applications of SDG, by exchanging opinions with schoolteachers.

**Acknowledgement.** The authors would like to thank to the children and the teachers in the studied elementary schools, and Kyoto Municipal Board of Education for their cooperation.

## References

1. Cortright, R.N., Collins, H.L., Dicarlo, S.E.: Peer instruction enhanced meaningful learning: ability to solve novel problems. Advances in Physiology Education 29(2), 107–111 (2005)

2. Japan Government Statistics Portal (e-Stat).: The situation of computer and the realities of the internet connection status by prefecture (2012), http://www.e-stat.go.jp/SG1/estat/List.do?bid=000001041083&cycode=0 (retrieved December 17, 2012)

3. Stewart, J., Bederson, B.B., Druin, A.: Single Display Goupware: A Model for Co-present Collaboration. In: CHI 1999, pp. 286–293 (1999)

4. Scott, S.D., Mandryk, R.L., Inkepen, K.M.: Understanding children's collaborative interactions in shared environments. Journal of Computer Assisted Learning 19, 220–228 (2003)

5. Scott, S.D., Mandryk, R.L., Inkpen, K.M.: Understanding Children's Collaborative Interactions in Shared Environments. Journal of Computer Assisted Learning 19, 220–228 (2003)

6. Tse, E., Saul, G.: Rapidly prototyping Single Display Groupware through the SDG-Tookkit. In: AUIC 2004 Proceeding of the Fifth Conference on Australasian User Interface, vol. 28, pp. 101–110 (2004)

7. Moraveji, N., Inkpen, K., Cutrell, E., Balakrishnan, R.A.: Mischief of Mice: Examining Children's Performance in Single Display Groupware Systems with 1 to 32 Mice. In: Proceedings of the 27th Annual Chi Conference on Human Factors in Computing Systems, vol. 2009(1-4), pp. 2157–2166 (2009)

8. Hagiwara, G., Ikeda, K., Mori, M., Uehara, T., Kita, H.: On Socialization of Personal Computing. In: Creating Connecting and Collaborating through Computing 2007, pp. 71–75 (2007)

9. Mori, M., Kita, H., Zhou, J.: Development of an Information Organizing Tool with a Shared Display for Face-to-Face Collaboration. In: Creating Connecting and Collaborating through Computing 2012, pp. 53–59 (2012)

10. Ke, F.F.: Computer-game-based tutoring of mathematics. Computers & Education 60(1), 448–457 (2013)

11. Brom, C., Sisler, V., Slavik, R.: Implementing digital game-based learning in schools: augmented learning environment of 'Europe 2045'. Multimedia System 16(2010), 23–41 (2010)

12. Hennessy, S., Ruthven, K., Brindley, S.: Teacher perspectives on integrating ICT into subject teaching: commitment, constraints, caution, and change. Journal of Curriculum Studies 37(2), 155–192 (2005)

13. Pollard, J.K.: Student reflection using a Web-based Quiz. In: Information Technology Based Higher Education and Training 2006, pp. 871–874 (2006)

14. Zhou, J., Mori, M., Ueda, H., Kita, H.: Quiz Making Activities using the Multi-Mouse Quiz System in an Elementary School. International Journal of Distance Education Technologies (proposal process)

15. Zhou, J., Mori, M., Uehara, T., Kita, H.: Practice using Multi Mouse Quiz in elementary school social studies. JSE 11(1), 305–312 (2011) (in Japanese)

16. Zhou J., Mori M., Uehara T., Kita H.: Evaluation of Classes using Multi-Mouse Quiz in Elementary Schools. SSS, 73–80 (2011) (in Japanese)

17. Zhou, J., Mori, M., Kita, H.: Using the Muliti-Mouse Quiz System for Quiz Making Activities in an Elementary School. In: IIAI international Conference on Advanced Applied Informatics, pp. 63–66 (2012)

# Author Index